About Philosophy

About Philosophy

Seventh Edition

Robert Paul Wolff
Professor of Afro-American
Studies and Philosophy
University of Massachusetts, Amherst

Prentice Hall
Upper Saddle River, NJ 07458

Library of Congress Cataloging-in-Publication Data

Wolff, Robert Paul.
    About philosophy / Robert Paul Wolff. —7th ed.
        p. cm.
    Includes bibliographical references and index.
    ISBN 0-13-744251-3
    1. Philosophy—Introductions.   I. Title.
    BD21.W64   1998
    100—dc21   97-6114
                                                           CIP

Editorial Director: Charlyce Jones Owen
Acquisitions Editor: Angie Stone
Director of Production and Manufacturing: Barbara Kittle
Project Manager: Jean Lapidus
Manufacturing Manager: Nick Sklitsis
Prepress and Manufacturing Buyer: Tricia Kenny
Creative Design Director: Leslie Osher
Interior and Cover Designer: Maria Lange
Cover Art: "Simple Cuisine" by Celia Johnson. GERALD &
        CULLEN RAPP, INC.
Photo Research: Rona Tuccillo
Indexer: Richard Genova
Copy Editor: Maria Caruso
Editorial Assistant: Elizabeth Del Colliano

This book was set in 10/12.5 x 28 Sabon by The Clarinda Company
and was printed and bound by RR Donnelley & Sons Company.
The cover was printed by Phoenix Color Corp.

Printed in the United States of America
10 9 8 7 6 5 4 3 2

ISBN 0-13-744251-3

Prentice-Hall International (UK) Limited, London
Prentice-Hall of Australia Pty. Limited, Sydney
Prentice-Hall Canada Inc., Toronto
Prentice-Hall Hispanoamericana, S.A., Mexico
Prentice-Hall of India Private Limited, New Delhi
Prentice-Hall of Japan, Inc., Tokyo
Simon & Schuster Asia Pte. Ltd., Singapore
Editora Prentice-Hall do Brasil, Ltda., Rio de Janeiro

◆

To Susie, whose courage in the face of adversity is the manifestation of a true philosophic spirit

◆

CONTENTS

PREFACE

With this seventh edition of *About Philosophy*, I have continued the strengthening of the theme of applied philosophy that has marked the text from its first appearance twenty years ago. The most important change is the introduction of an extended section on Biomedical Ethics in Chapter 2, Ethical Theory. The development of Biomedical Ethics, occasioned by the extraordinary advances in medical technology, has brought the most abstract considerations of ethical theory into direct relation to some of the most painful and pressing decisions facing lay people and medical professionals today. For many editions now each chapter has been concluded with a "Contemporary Application," so that students can see the implications for daily life of the philosophical arguments they have been studying. However, Biomedical Ethics is so important an "Application" that it deserves a place in the body of the text.

I have also made a number of other changes, principally in response to the helpful comments from teachers of Philosophy who are actually using the book in their classrooms. The material that has for many editions taken up two chapters, on social and political philosophy, is now combined into a single chapter. The material on Black Philosophy that was isolated in a concluding chapter in the last edition is now distributed throughout the book, so that it is integrated into the flow of the exposition. And a number of other changes have been made that will, I hope, keep the material challenging and current.

Two decades is a long time in the life of a book, and in the life of its author as well, but it is, of course, the mere blink of an eye in the life of Philosophy. It remains true today, as it was when I was a young student, that the *Dialogues* of Plato, the *Meditations* of Descartes, and the *Critique* of Kant, are the best possible introduction to the eternal questions of the philosophical adventure. In all the lengthenings, shortenings, additions, and subtractions that have shaped this book over seven editions, I have tried to be true to the subject that won my heart as a young man, and has held me with its fascination ever since.

I would like to thank the reviewers: Robert A. Dyal, Southwest Texas State University; Bernard Boxill, University of North Carolina, Chapel Hill; Dr. John-Christian Smith, Youngstown State University; and William C. Gentry, Henderson State University. Finally, I should like to offer a special word of gratitude to Ms. Lucinda Ealy, a gifted young women who helped me greatly with the preparation of this edition. I hope she will soon be joining our doctoral program in Afro-American Studies.

Robert Paul Wolff
Pelham, Massachusetts

❧ ABC News/PH Video Library for
About Philosophy

Video is the most dynamic of all supplements you can use to enhance your class. But the quality of the video material and how well it relates to your course can still make all the difference. For these reasons, Prentice Hall and ABC News have decided to work together to bring you the best and most comprehensive video ancillaries available in the college market.

Through its wide variety of award-winning programs—*Nightline, Business World, On Business, This Week with David Brinkley, World News Tonight,* and *The Health Show*—ABC offers a resource for feature and documentary-style videos related to text concepts and applications. The programs have extremely high production quality, present substantial content, and are hosted by well-versed, well-known anchors. Prentice Hall, its authors, and its editors provide the benefit of having selected videos on topics that will work well with this course and text and give the instructor teaching notes on how to use them in the classroom.

"The ABC News/PH Video Library for *About Philosophy*" offers video material for almost every chapter in the text. An excellent video guide is included in the Instructor's Manual and carefully and completely integrates the videos into your lecture.

❧ New York Times Supplement

The New York Times and Prentice Hall are sponsoring *Themes of the Times:* a program designed to enhance student access to current information of relevance in the classroom.

Through this program, the core subject matter provided in the text is supplemented by a collection of time-sensitive articles from one of the world's most distinguished newspapers, *The New York Times*. These articles demonstrate the vital, ongoing connection between what is learned in the classroom and what is happening in the world around us.

To enjoy the wealth of information of *The New York Times* daily, a reduced subscription rate is available. For information, call toll-free: 1-800-631-1222.

Prentice Hall and *The New York Times* are proud to co-sponsor *Themes of the Times*. We hope it will make the reading of both textbooks and newspapers a more dynamic, involving process.

ABOUT THE AUTHOR

Robert Paul Wolff was born in New York City in 1933. He was educated at Harvard, where he was awarded the doctorate in Philosophy in 1957. He has taught at Harvard, the University of Chicago, and Columbia University, and since 1971 at the University of Massachusetts, Amherst. Wolff is the author or editor of twenty books on the philosophy of Immanuel Kant, social and political philosophy, the philosophy of education, the philosophy of law, the philosophy of David Hume, and the economic theories of Karl Marx. He has taught political science at Chicago, Boston University, and Yale, and microeconomics at the University of Massachusetts. Wolff's books have been translated into more than a dozen languages, and have sold more than three-quarters of a million copies. They have been assigned as required reading for the Moral Tripos at Cambridge University, and have been read by students in Soweto, South Africa.

In 1990, Wolff founded University Scholarships for South African Students, Inc. which he runs as a volunteer charitable organization. USSAS currently supports 110 Black students at universities in South Africa.

In 1992, Wolff was invited to join the W. E. B. DuBois Department of Afro-American Studies at the University of Massachusetts. He is currently professor of Afro-American Studies and Philosophy, and serves as Director of Graduate Studies in the doctoral program in Afro-American Studies.

Robert Paul Wolff is married to his childhood sweetheart, Susan, and has two sons, Patrick, 29, and Tobias, 27. Asked to describe himself succinctly, he said, "In religion, I am an atheist; in politics, I am an anarchist; in economics, I am a Marxist." A former editor, Ted Bolen, suggested he not go around saying things like that.

SOCRATES

Socrates (469?–399 B.C.) *was tried by the Athenians on charges of "impiety" and "corrupting the young of Athens," but it seems clear that his real offense was opposition to, or even lack of sufficient support for, the leaders of the newly restored democratic regime. Socrates had associated with the aristocratic families that overthrew the first democracy, and his disciple, Plato, was a member of one of the powerful families that ruled Athens for a while before the restoration. Since an amnesty had been declared, it was legally impossible for the rulers to prosecute Socrates for political offenses, so they trumped up the religious accusations and enlisted a religious fanatic, Meletus, to bring charges against the seventy-year-old philosopher.*

Socrates could have fled from Athens before the trial, conviction in which could carry a death sentence. Even after his conviction, he could have proposed banishment as an alternative to death, and the Athenian jury of 501 citizens would almost certainly have accepted such a compromise. But Socrates was convinced that he had done Athens no harm by his philosophical questioning. Indeed, he insisted that he had, by his activities, been a benefactor of his native city, and so, as an alternative to the death penalty demanded by the prosecution, he proposed that Athens pension him off as a respected citizen. The Athenian rulers, trapped by Socrates' uncompromising integrity, were forced to carry out the sentence of death, though they would probably have been all too happy to allow their prisoner to escape before the execution. One month after the trial, following a long night of philosophical discussion with his friends, Socrates drank the poison hemlock prepared for him by his jailers and died.

What Is Philosophy?

- ✦ **What Do Philosophers Do? The Study of Human Nature**

- ✦ **What Do Philosophers Do? The Study of the Universe**

- ✦ **What Do Philosophers Do? Human Nature and the Universe**

- ✦ **The Limitations of the Western Philosophical Tradition**

What Do Philosophers Do? The Study of Human Nature

When I was a student, one of my professors told us about the conversations he would strike up in the club car on the train from Boston to New York. A group of men would gather around the bar, and each in turn would introduce himself, saying a few words about the line of work he was in. One would announce himself as a lawyer, a second as a traveling salesman, a third as an engineer. When it was my professor's turn, he would say, "I am a philosopher." That, he told us, would always bring the conversation to a dead halt. No one knew quite what to say to a man who described himself as a philosopher. The others were too polite to ask, "What does a philosopher do?" But the announcement always cast a pall over the gathering. Eventually, he took to saying, "I am a teacher." That went over all right, and so long as no one asked what he taught, they could get on to more congenial topics, such as the prospects for the Red Sox, or the weather.

What *do* philosophers do? Oddly enough, that is a question philosophers have been asking for as long as there has been a discipline called *philosophy*. Indeed, "What do philosophers do?" is probably the most common philosophical question! But all this sounds like double talk, which is just what makes people nervous about philosophy in the first place. You all know what a doctor does; you know what physicists, historians, composers, and sanitation engineers do. Most of you probably even have some sort of idea of what microbiologists do. But philosophers are something else again. Philosophers ask questions—odd questions, such as "What right does the government—any government—have to tell me what to do?"

The best way to find out what philosophers do is to take a look at one of them, and on anyone's list, the natural first choice must be the most famous philosopher of all times, *Socrates*. Socrates was born in 469 B.C. to a stonemason and a midwife in the Greek city-state of Athens. As far as we know, he spent his entire life in and about Athens, serving his time in the army at one point, taking his turn in the government at another. He was a rather homely man in a society that prized manly beauty, and though he was hardly poor, he seems to have managed on much less money than his friends and disciples had. Athens itself was a city of 130,000, busy and prosperous by the standards of the time but small enough so that everyone who was anyone knew everyone else. In his youth, Socrates studied the scientific theories a number of original thinkers had developed in the preceding several centuries, but he soon became convinced that the most important and puzzling subject was the human condition itself. He developed the practice of going into the public squares and meeting places of Athens to cajole, goad, or draw his fellow townsmen into discussions about how men ought to live their lives. (In the Athens of

Socrates' day, it was taken for granted that women would play no role in these discussions, or indeed in any other public business.) Socrates was quick-witted, clever, and tenacious. He had a knack for asking hard or embarrassing questions that forced others to think a good deal more than they really wanted to. Because some of the people he quizzed were important politicians and famous teachers, it was fun to watch him trip them up—as long as you weren't one of those made to look foolish. So a number of wealthy young men gathered around Socrates as a band of disciples and as a sort of permanent audience. Sometimes he talked with them, quizzing them in the same way and forcing them to examine their own lives; sometimes they watched as he took on a local bigwig or visiting personage.

If this practice of asking questions were all there was to Socrates' life, we would never have heard of him 2,400 years later, and we certainly wouldn't think of him as a great philosopher. But three things transformed Socrates

The school or Academy of Athens, founded c. 387 B.C. by Plato as a center of philosophical, mathematical, and scientific research. The Academy continued to operate uninterruptedly for 900 years, until it was closed by the Roman Emperor Justinian in 529 A.D. There is an Academy in Athens today that claims to be the descendant of Plato's school. (North Wind Picture Archives.)

from a local curiosity and general pain in the neck into the patron saint of philosophy and one of the great figures of Western civilization.

The first thing was an accident. Among those who followed Socrates was a brilliantly gifted, wealthy young man named Plato. Plato was only twenty-eight years old when his teacher died, but he was deeply, permanently affected by his relationship with the aging Socrates, and many years later he began to write Dialogues, playlets in which the style and personality of Socrates were captured, transformed, and elevated into works of great art. Most of what we believe about Socrates comes to us from these Dialogues, including, most importantly, our conception of Socrates' techniques of questioning. Scholars still debate how much in the Dialogues is Plato's artistic invention and how much is accurate historical portrayal. But there can be no question that the essential style belonged to Socrates himself.

The second thing that happened was not really an accident, though it may seem so at first glance. The rulers of Athens decided that Socrates was more than an annoyance; he was becoming a threat to their political security. So they trumped up some charges against him and put him on trial. Socrates could have plea-bargained, in effect, and gotten off with a punishment of exile, which would have put him safely out of Athens without making him a martyr. However, he chose instead to defend himself and his life without excuses or apologies. He had done nothing wrong, he insisted, and now that he was seventy, Athens should be thinking of giving him a pension rather than threatening to put him to death. In the end, Socrates forced the government's hand, and a sentence of death was handed down. Even then, he probably could have escaped from jail with the help of his friends, but he stayed and took the poison his jailers gave him. And so he became the first martyr to philosophy. It is easy to second-guess the Athenian rulers and conclude that they could have spared themselves a lot of trouble by handling the case a bit more skillfully. But Socrates' persistent questioning of established doctrines and received opinions really was a threat, not only to the government, but also the lifestyle of the families who ruled Athens. In a way, the accident is not that Socrates was put to death at the age of seventy, but rather that he had been permitted to go on for so long before those in power landed on him.

Philosophy Literally, love of wisdom, Philosophy is the systematic, critical examination of the way in which we judge, evaluate, and act, with the aim of making ourselves wiser, more self-reflective, and therefore better men and women.

The third and most important reason for Socrates' immortality is no accident at all, but the very essence of his life and calling. Witty though he was, irreverent though he could be, annoying though he certainly became, Socrates was deadly serious about his questioning. His death only confirmed what his life had already proved—that for him, the relentless examination of every human action and belief was more important than survival itself. As Socrates said at his trial, "The unexamined life is not worth living," and by drinking the poison, he showed that he would rather die honorably in the cause of that principle than flee in dishonor to some foreign refuge.

Each of us makes countless decisions that affect our lives and the lives of those around us to some degree. Many of the decisions are of very little importance, such as whether or not to go to the movies, where to have dinner, or what to wear. A few of the decisions are truly momentous—whom to marry, what career to pursue; and for some of us, caught up in a war or facing personal tragedy, our decisions may literally determine life and death. Socrates believed in his own time (and I think he would still believe if he were alive today) that these decisions must be questioned, examined, and criticized if we are to live truly good and happy lives. Most of us make even the most important decisions without really asking ourselves what principles we are basing our choices on, and whether those principles are worthy of our respect and commitment. When war comes, young men and women go off to fight and die with hardly more than a passing thought about whether it is morally right to kill another person. A student spends ten years of his or her life working to become a doctor, simply because Mom and Dad have always wanted it. A man and a woman drift into marriage, have children, buy a house and settle down, and only twenty years later does one of them ask, "What am I doing here?"

Socrates had a theory about how each of us ought to examine his or her life, subjecting it to critical analysis and questioning. He never set this theory down anywhere, of course (he never set *anything* down, actually), but from what Plato has reported, we can reconstruct what Socrates had in mind. This theory, on which he based the special style of teaching and philosophizing that has come to bear his name, rested on four basic principles:

1. The unexamined life is not worth living. In other words, it is undignified, not really honorable, simply to live from day to day without ever asking oneself, "What am I doing here? Why am I living as I am?" To be truly and completely human, Socrates thought, each man and woman must subject his or her life and convictions to the test of critical self-examination. What is more, by means of this process of self-examination, one can achieve genuine happiness.

2. There really are valid principles of thought and action which must be followed if we are to live good lives—if we are to be, at the same time, genuinely happy and genuinely good. These principles are objective—they are true for all men and women, whenever and wherever they may live. Some people are unjust, self-indulgent, obsessed with worthless goals, estranged from their fellow men and women, confused and blind about what is truly important. These people do not know that certain things are beneath notice, unimportant. They are terrified of shadows, incapable of living or of dying with grace. Such people need to find the truth and live in accordance with it.

3. The truth lies within each of us, not in the stars, or in tradition, or in religious books, or in the opinions of the masses. Each of us has within, however hidden, the true principles of right thinking and acting. In the end, therefore, no one can teach anyone else the truth about life. If that truth were not within you, you would never find it; but it is within you, and only relentless critical self-examination will reveal it to you.

4. Although no one can teach anyone else about the fundamental principles of right action and clear thinking, some people—call them teachers, philosophers, gadflies—can ask questions that prod men and women to begin the task of self-examination. These teachers may also be able to guide the process, at least in its early stages, because they have been over the same ground themselves and know where the pitfalls are.

From these four principles, it follows that philosophy consists of a process of question and answer, a **dialogue** between two people, one of whom is seeking rational insight and understanding, the other of whom has already achieved some measure of self-knowledge and wishes to help the novice. The dialogue begins with whatever beliefs the student brings to the quest. If she thoughtlessly repeats the traditional moral sayings of her society, then the philosopher will try to force her to question those sayings; if she takes up the position that everything is relative, that nothing is true or valid for all persons (a stance many students adopt at about the time they leave home or cut loose from their parents), then the philosopher will try a different line of questioning. The end point of the journey is always the same: wisdom, rational insight into the principles of thought and action, and thus a happier, more integrated, more worthwhile life. But the starting points are as many as the students who make the journey.

Socrates discovered that each journey to wisdom has an enormous obstacle blocking the road. Modern psychoanalysts call the roadblock "resistance," but a simpler way of putting it is that no one wants to admit that he or she needs to learn. Certainly, the politicians and public figures with whom Socrates talked didn't think of themselves as in need of further wisdom. They were quite convinced they already knew how to run the state and how to order their own lives. Socrates had to discover a trick for getting inside their defenses so that he could make them see—really see—that they were not yet truly wise. What he did was to invent a verbal form of judo. The basic trick of judo is to let your opponent's force and momentum work for you. Instead of launching a frontal attack, you let him swing or grab, and then you roll with his motion so that, in effect, he throws himself on the mat. Socrates achieved the same effect in his debates by means of a literary device called "irony." Although this is a book about philosophy, not literature, it might be worth taking a few moments to explain how irony works, so that we can see what Socrates was trying to accomplish.

Irony is a kind of speech or communication that assumes a *double audience*. When a speaker makes an ironic statement, she seems to be directing it at one group of people. This group is called the first, or superficial, audience. But in reality, she is directing her remarks at a second audience, called the real audience. Her statement has a double meaning, and the trick of the irony is that while the first audience understands only the superficial or apparent meaning, the second audience understands *both* meanings. This second audience knows that the first audience has misunderstood, so the irony becomes a private joke between the speaker and the second audience—a joke at the expense of the first audience, which never suspects a thing.

For example, suppose a stranger drives up to the general store in a small town to ask directions. "You there!" he says to a farmer seated on the front porch of the store. "Can you tell me the fastest way to get to the state capital? Be quick about it! I have a very important meeting with the governor." "Yes," replies the farmer, with just the slightest wink to his friends on the porch. "I *can* tell you the fastest way." He then proceeds to give the stranger totally wrong directions that will take him hours out of his way.

The farmer is speaking ironically. The stranger is the superficial audience, and the other people on the porch are the real audience. The apparent meaning, as understood by the stranger, is that this country bumpkin, who has been properly impressed with the stranger's importance, can tell him the fastest way and has done so. The real, secret, ironic meaning is of course that the farmer can tell this pompous ass the fastest way but has no intention of doing so because he has been so rude. The reply is a private joke between the farmer and his friends at the stranger's expense.

When Socrates strikes up a conversation with a self-important, self-confident, but really rather ignorant man, he does not try a frontal attack, arguing directly against his opponent's false beliefs. That would simply lead to an impasse, in which each participant would be asserting his own convictions and neither would engage in critical self-examination. Instead, Socrates says, with a deceptively modest air, "Of course, I don't know anything at all, and you seem to be very wise indeed, so perhaps you would be

Cartoon: "General Store." The farmer is speaking ironically. (Drawn for Robert Paul Wolff by Prentice Hall.)

so good as to enlighten me." His opponent, thinking Socrates means literally what he says, gets all puffed up with his own importance and pontificates on goodness or justice or truth or beauty or piety. Then Socrates goes to work on him, pretending to be puzzled, asking politely for clarification, poking away at just those places in his opponent's position that are most vulnerable. After a while, the poor man is thoroughly deflated. Embarrassed by his inability to give coherent, defensible answers to Socrates' apparently humble questions, he finally reaches the rather painful conclusion that he doesn't know what he thought he knew. Now, and only now, can Socrates help him to set out on the path to wisdom, for as Socrates so often insists, the first act of true wisdom is to admit that you are ignorant.

When Socrates says that he himself is ignorant, he is speaking ironically. In fact, he is uttering what students of literature call a "double irony." In the first place, he is having a private joke with his followers, at the expense of the man with whom he is debating. His opponent thinks Socrates is really being deferential, that Socrates actually wants to sit at the great man's feet and learn great truths. But of course Socrates means that he is "ignorant" of those great "truths" just because they are false, confused, and not worth knowing. We have all met someone who thinks he is an expert on some subject when in fact he doesn't know beans about it. "Tell me more!" we say, and sure enough he does, not realizing that we are kidding him.

At a deeper level, which Socrates' own followers sometimes don't really understand, Socrates genuinely means that he is ignorant, in the sense that *he* doesn't have a truth to teach any more than his puffed-up opponent does. The disciples think that Socrates knows what truth, beauty, justice, goodness, and wisdom really are, and they expect that just as soon as he has deflated his opponent, he will teach them. But Socrates believes that every man must find the truth for himself, and so his followers cannot shortcut their journey by learning the truth from Socrates any more than they could by observing the mistakes and confusions of Socrates' opponents. In this deeper double irony, we, the readers of Plato's Dialogue, are the real audience, and both Socrates' opponents *and* his disciples are superficial or apparent audiences.

The process of questions and answers by which we gradually, step by step, reach a deeper and deeper insight into the principles of truth and goodness, has come to be called the **Socratic Method.** It is a very powerful technique of argument, of course, and Socrates clearly used it because it gave him an edge on those with whom he argued. But it also serves an independent theoretical purpose—a philosophical purpose, we might say. This next point is a bit tricky, but it is worth paying attention to, because it gives us a real insight into what Plato (or Socrates) is doing.

According to Socrates, things are not always what they seem. We all know that there may be a difference between the way things look on the surface, or at first, and how they really are. A stick half in water and half out looks bent, even though it is straight. The sun looks larger when it is low on the horizon than when it is high in the sky, although it hasn't changed its size. The magician looks as though she is pulling that coin out of your ear, but really it is coming out of her hand, and so forth.

Socrates took this old, familiar distinction between the way things seem to be and the way they really are and ran with it. He extended the distinction into areas where we might not be so used to encountering it. He pointed out

> ⌒ **Socratic Method** A technique of probing questions, developed by Socrates, for the purpose of prodding, pushing, and provoking unreflective persons into realizing their lack of rational understanding of their own principles of thought and action, so that they can set out on the path to philosophical wisdom. As used by Socrates, this method was a powerful weapon for deflating inflated egos.

that sometimes an experience *seems* bad for us, but is really good (the dentist is a familiar example). Frequently, the opinions of our friends, our family, or our society *seem* correct, but are really wrong. And so forth.

Socrates thought that in every part of our lives, we must try as hard as we can to get behind the misleading surface appearances and grasp the true, underlying reality. Indeed, a large part of Socrates' wisdom consisted precisely in being able to tell appearance from reality, whether in politics, in ethics, or in daily life.

Now, the superficial meaning of an ironic statement is like the surface appearance, behind which the reality lies. Just as the world of the senses is merely an appearance of the true reality grasped by reason, so too the superficial meaning of an ironic statement is the apparent meaning that hides the deeper, real meaning intended for the real audience. Thus, the structure of language mirrors the structure of reality.

This idea—that there is a parallel between language and the world—comes up again and again in philosophy. It is a very important notion, and for 2,000 years philosophers have been turning it this way and that, extracting interesting conclusions from it. Socrates is the philosopher who first developed the idea and used it in his own philosophy.

We have talked enough about Socrates and his debating tricks. It is time to see him in action. The following passage comes from the most famous of Plato's Dialogues, the *Republic.* Socrates and some friends have been having a discussion about the nature of *justice,* by which they mean the fundamental principles of right and wrong. Several suggestions have been made, which Socrates has disposed of without much trouble, and now a young, very excitable, and very bright member of the party named Thrasymachus jumps into the debate. He has been listening to the others impatiently, barely able to control himself.

What is the matter with you two, Socrates? Why do you go on in this imbecile way, politely deferring to each other's nonsense? If you really want to know what justice means, stop asking questions and scoring off the answers you get. You know very well it is easier to ask questions than to answer them. Answer yourself, and tell us what you think justice means. I won't have you telling us it is the same as what is obligatory or useful or advantageous or profitable or expedient; I want a clear and precise statement; I won't put up with that sort of verbiage.

This is a shrewd attack on Thrasymachus' part, for if he can get Socrates to advance a definition, then perhaps he can turn the table on the master. But his own uncontrolled impetuosity gets the better of him. When Socrates turns aside the attack with a few mock-humble words, Thrasymachus cannot resist the temptation to teach the teacher. And that, as we

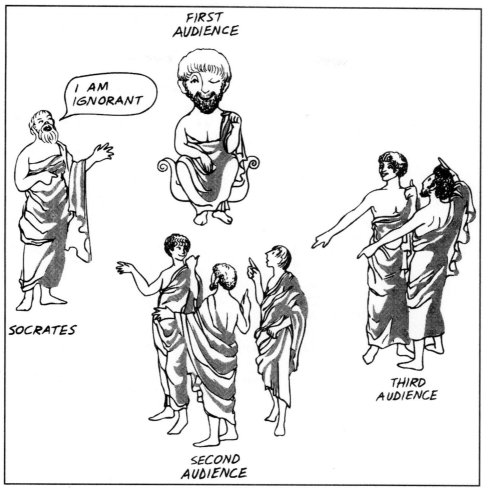

Cartoon: "First audience." First, or superficial, audience thinks Socrates is humbly confessing inferiority to him. Second audience (Socrates' followers), realizing Socrates is making fun of first audience, laughs at first audience. Third audience (the reader) laughs at first audience, smiles at second. Third audience realizes *both* that Socrates is making fun of first audience *and* that Socrates' own followers don't realize the true meaning of his statement. (Drawn for Robert Paul Wolff by Prentice Hall.)

shall see, is his downfall. Thrasymachus is no pushover for Socrates, and in a sense their debate ends in a deadlock. In this passage, however, we can see how Socrates used Thrasymachus' own self-confidence to trip him up, just like a judo master who allows his opponent to rush at him headlong and then with a flip of the hip tosses him on his back. Notice the ironic modesty with which Socrates turns aside Thrasymachus' blunt attacks, each time gently showing him that he has not yet thought clearly or deeply enough. The contrast between Socrates' inner quiet and Thrasymachus' tempestuousness is also intended by Plato to teach us a lesson, for he, like Socrates, believed that the truly wise possess a tranquility which the ignorant cannot achieve.

PLATO,
Republic

The Nature of Justice

Listen then, Thrasymachus began. What I say is that "just" or "right" means nothing but what is to the interest of the stronger party. Well, where is your applause? You don't mean to give it to me.

I will, as soon as I understand, I said. [This is Socrates talking.] I don't see yet what you mean by right being the interest of the stronger party. For instance, Polydamas, the athlete, is stronger than we are, and it is to his interest to eat beef for the sake of his muscles; but surely you don't mean that the same diet would be good for weaker men and therefore be right for us?

You are trying to be funny, Socrates. It's a low trick to take my words in the sense you think will be most damaging.

No, no, I protested; but you must explain.

Don't you know, then, that a state may be ruled by a despot, or a democracy, or an aristocracy?

Of course.

And that the ruling element is always the strongest?

Yes.

Well, then, in every case the laws are made by the ruling party in its own interest; a democracy makes democratic laws; a despot, autocratic ones; and so on. By making these laws they define as "right" for their subjects whatever is for their own interest, and they call anyone who breaks them a "wrongdoer" and punish him accordingly. That is what I mean; in all states alike "right" has the same meaning, namely what is for the interest of the party established in power, and that is the strongest. So the sound conclusion is that what is "right" is the same everywhere: the interest of the stronger party.

Now I see what you mean, said I; whether it is true or not, I must try to make out. When you define right in terms of interest, you are yourself giving one of those answers you forbade to me; though, to be sure, you add "to the stronger party."

An insignificant addition, perhaps!

Its importance is not clear yet; what is clear is that we must find out whether your definition is true. I agree myself that right is in a sense a matter of interest; but when you add "to the stronger party," I don't know about that. I must consider.

Go ahead, then.

I will. Tell me this. No doubt you also think it is right to obey the men in power?

I do.

Are they infallible in every type of state, or can they sometimes make a mistake?

Of course they can make a mistake.

In framing laws, then, they may do their work well or badly? No doubt.

Well, that is to say, when the laws they make are to their own interest; badly, when they are not?

Yes.

But the subjects are to obey any law they lay down, and they will then be doing right?

Of course.

If so, by your account, it will be right to do what is not to the interest of the stronger party, as well as what is so.

What's that you are saying?

Just what you said, I believe; but let us look again. Haven't you admitted that the rulers, when they enjoin certain acts on their subjects, sometimes mistake their own best interest, and at the same time that it is right for the subjects to obey, whatever they may enjoin?

Yes, I suppose so.

Well, that amounts to admitting that it is right to do what is not to the interest of the rulers or the stronger party. They may unwittingly enjoin what is to their own disadvantage; and you say it is right for the others to do as they are told. In that case, their duty must be the opposite of what you said, because the weaker will have been ordered to do what is against the interest of the stronger. You with your intelligence must see how that follows. . . . Now, Thrasymachus, tell me, was that what you intended to say—that right means what the stronger thinks is to his interest, whether it really is so or not?

Most certainly not, he replied. Do you suppose I should speak of a man as "stronger" or "superior" at the very moment when he is making a mistake?

I did think you said as much when you admitted that rulers are not always infallible.

That is because you are a quibbler, Socrates. Would you say a man deserves to be called a physician at the moment when he makes a mistake in treating his patient and just in respect of that mistake; or a mathematician, when he does a sum wrong and just insofar as he gets a wrong result? Of course we do commonly speak of a physician or a mathematician or a scholar having made a mistake; but really none of these, I should say, is ever mistaken, insofar as he is worthy of the name we give him. So strictly speaking—and you are all for being precise—no one who practices a craft makes mistakes. A man is mistaken when his knowledge fails him; and at the moment he is no craftsman. And what is true of craftsmanship or any sort of skill is true of the ruler: he is never mistaken so long as he is acting as a ruler; though anyone might speak of a ruler making a mistake, just as he might of a physician. You must understand that I was talking in that loose way when I answered your question just now; but the precise statement is this. The ruler, insofar as he is acting as a ruler, makes no mistakes and consequently enjoins what is best for himself; and that is what the subject is to do. So, as I said at first, "right" means doing what is to the interest of the stronger.

Very well, Thrasymachus, said I. So you think I am quibbling?

I am sure you are.

You believe my questions were maliciously designed to damage your position?

I know it. But you will gain nothing by that. You cannot outwit me by cunning, and you are not the man to crush me in the open.

Bless your soul, I answered, I should not think of trying. But, to prevent any more misunderstanding, when you speak of that ruler or stronger party whose interest the weaker ought to serve, please make it clear whether you are using the words in the ordinary way or in that strict sense you have just defined.

I mean a ruler in the strictest possible sense. Now quibble away and be as malicious as you can. I want no mercy. But you are no match for me.

Do you think me mad enough to beard a lion or try to outwit a Thrasymachus?

You did try just now, he retorted, but it wasn't a success.

Although it may not be obvious on first reading, the crucial turning point in this exchange is the point at which Socrates gets Thrasymachus to admit that the people should obey their superior rulers *only* when the rulers are issuing commands that really are in their own interest. If the strong, through ignorance or error, accidentally issue commands that work to the benefit of the weak, then the weak are not to obey!

This may not look like much of an admission, but it is actually fatal to Thrasymachus' position. The reason is that it introduces into the discussion the idea that rulers have a right to be obeyed only when they are, in some way or other, using their intellectual abilities to rule well. At this point, of course, "ruling well" simply means "ruling in such a way as to advance their own interests," but once Thrasymachus has agreed that standards are to be applied to the performance of the rulers, he has started down a slippery slope. Now Socrates has an opening in which to start talking about good and bad rulers, and that permits him to raise all sorts of issues that Thrasymachus has no desire to all to let into the debate.

Needless to say, Socrates foresees all of this when he asks the first innocent-looking question, just as a chess master foresees the next ten moves when he makes his first simple move. That is part of the skill of philosophical argument.

What Do Philosophers Do? The Study of the Universe

I told you that Socrates spent some time when he was young studying the theories about the nature of the universe which had been developed by other Greek thinkers during the 200 years before his own time. The Greek word for world or universe is *kosmos,* so we call the study of the nature of the world **cosmology.** The study of the human condition and the study of the cosmos are the two great branches of philosophy, and there is no division more fundamental in philosophy than that between philosophers who study the human experience and the philosophers who speculate about the order of the entire universe. (Later on, we shall see that some philosophers have tried to unite the two in a single theoretical framework, but that is getting ahead of our story.)

The Greeks, like all people, had their religious myths about the creation of the world and the origins of their civilization, but some time roughly 600 years before the birth of Christ, a number of men began to search for a more rational, more factually well-grounded theory of the composition, order, and origin of the world. Some of these early scientists—for that is what they were—flourished in a city-state named Miletus on the coast of what is now Turkey, in the eastern Mediterranean. They are known as Milesians, after their hometown, and they appear to have been the very first philosophers in what we are calling the cosmological tradition. For various reasons, only bits and pieces of what they wrote still survive, and most of what we know about them must be learned indirectly from what other ancient writers say about them. They are little more than names to us today, but perhaps it is worth telling you their names, for we owe them an intellectual debt almost too great to calculate. There was *Thales,* usually spoken

Cosmology Literally, the study of the order of the world. Now used to refer to the branch of astronomy that investigates the organization and structure of the entire physical universe, including its origins. In philosophy, cosmology is a part of the subfield called metaphysics, or the study of first principles.

of as the very first philosopher of all. Thales was what we today would call an astronomer; the story is told that while walking one evening with his eyes turned to the stars, he fell into a well and thereby created the myth of the absentminded professor. But it is also said of him that by using his superior knowledge of the weather, acquired by his astronomical studies, he managed to corner the market in olive oil and make a fortune. Following Thales were the Milesians *Anaximander* and *Anaximenes,* who expanded and developed speculative theories about the basic components of nature and their order. Their names are strange, and we have long since lost almost all of what they wrote and said, but as you study your physics, chemistry, or astronomy, or watch a rocket lift off for yet another space probe, you might just give them a thought, for they started Western civilization on its scientific journey.

The theories of the ancient cosmologists seem odd to modern readers. When we look behind the surface detail, however, we can see some surprisingly modern ideas. The fundamental problem of the Milesians was to determine the basic stuff or component matter from which all the variety of things in the world were composed. The four categories into which they divided all things were earth, water, air, and fire. Thales claimed that at base everything in the universe was water; earth, air, and fire were simply forms of water, or water in other guises. Anaximenes, by contrast, said that everything was air. Now all of this sounds quaint and very peculiar, but suppose that we say solid instead of earth, liquid instead of water, gas instead of air, and energy instead of fire. Then we have the theory that everything in the universe is solid, liquid, gaseous, or some form of energy, and that isn't a bad guess at all! What is more, the search for some underlying element that simply *appears* in one or another of these forms has a distinctly modern ring to it. The nineteenth-century theory of the atom, for example, told us that ninety and more elements found in nature could really be reduced to differing arrangements of three basic building blocks: neutrons, protons, and electrons. The theory of subatomic particles has become much more complicated since that simple model of the atom was proposed, but the Milesian search goes on today for the building blocks of the universe.

The second great theme of the Milesians and their successors was that natural events were to be understood by appeal to natural forces, not by appeal to the actions of the gods or the interventions of some non-natural forces. The keynote of these early philosopher-scientists was that nature is natural, and in their speculations and observations, they showed remarkable shrewdness and good sense. For example, water seems to turn to ice (a solid) when it is very cold, and into steam (a gas) when it is very hot. Solid things (such as iron) which are very solid indeed actually melt when made hot enough. All of this suggests that there is some underlying stuff which takes on different forms under different conditions.

Map of spheres according to Ptolomaeus, with the earth in the center of a globe of the world. There are seven heavenly bodies orbiting about the earth: the sun, the moon, Mercury, Venus, Mars, Jupiter, and Saturn. Note that the representation on the earth of Africa and the Orient is pretty accurate. (From Dutch Atlas by Gerard Valck, 17th century. Corbis–Bettmann.)

Here is a short passage from a philosopher who lived very much later in the ancient world, but whose attention to the evidence of his senses is typical of the cosmological frame of mind. Lucretius was a Roman philosopher and poet who lived in the first century before Christ, nearly five centuries after the Milesians. He defended a cosmological theory called atomism, according to which everything in the universe, including even the human soul, is composed of little bits of matter called atoms, which are so small that they cannot be seen by the naked eye (another surprisingly modern doctrine!). As you can see, Lucretius uses a variety of familiar observations to prove that despite appearances to the contrary, all things are com-

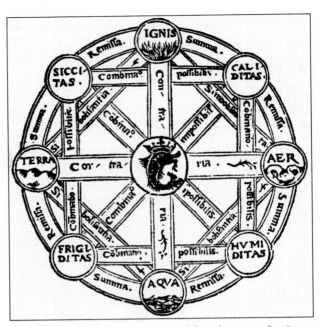

In this schematic representation of the elements, fire is at the top, air on the right, water at the bottom, and earth to the left. The fifth substance, or "quintessence," is in the center. Fire is a mixture of dryness and heat, air is a mixture of heat and humidity, water is a mixture of humidity and coldness, and earth is a mixture of coldness and dryness. (From PH College Archives.)

posed of tiny, indestructible atoms which themselves have no parts and are absolutely solid.

LUCRETIUS,
On the Nature of Things

Now mark me: since I have taught that things cannot be born from nothing, cannot when begotten be brought back to nothing, that you may not haply yet begin in any shape to mistrust my words, because the first-beginnings of things cannot be seen by the eyes, take moreover this list of bodies which you must yourself admit are in the number of things and cannot be seen. First of all the force of the wind when aroused beats on the harbours and whelms huge ships and scatters clouds; sometimes in swift whirling eddy it scours the plains and strews them with large trees and scourges the mountain summits with forest-rending blasts: so fiercely does the wind rave with a shrill howling and rage with threatening roar. Winds therefore sure enough are unseen bodies which sweep the seas, the lands, ay and the clouds of heaven, tormenting them and catching them up in sudden whirls. . . . Then again we perceive the different smells of things, yet never see them coming to our nostrils; nor do we behold heats nor can we observe cold with the eyes nor are we used to see voices. Yet all these things must consist of a bodily nature, since they are able to move the senses; for nothing but body can touch and be touched. Again clothes hung up on a shore which waves break upon become moist, and then get dry if spread out in the sun. Yet it has not been seen in what way the moisture of water has sunk into them nor again in what way this has been dispelled by heat. The moisture therefore is dispersed into small particles which the eyes are quite unable to see. Again after the revolution of many of the sun's years a ring on the finger is thinned on the under side by wearing, the dripping from the eaves hollows a stone, the bent ploughshare of iron imperceptibly decreases in the fields, and we behold the stone-paved streets worn down by the feet of the multitude; the brass statues too at the gates show their right hands to be wasted by the touch of the numerous passers by who greet them. These things then we see are lessened, since they have been thus worn down; but what bodies depart at any given time the nature of vision has jealously shut out our seeing. . . . Nature therefore works by unseen bodies.

Cosmological speculation goes on today, as it did 2,500 years ago. From the earliest times, philosophers have been actively involved in the experimental and theoretical advances of what today we call science. Indeed, it is difficult to say just where hard science leaves off and speculative, philosophical cosmology begins. Thales himself, for example, was said to have discovered a method for measuring the height of the Egyptian pyramids, by waiting until the precise hour of the day when a body's shadow was equal to its height. Anaximander devised an instrument known as a gnomon, a rod whose shadow permits us to calculate the direction and height of the sun. The great fourth-century B.C. philosopher Aristotle, pupil and follower of Plato, virtually invented the science of formal logic and made significant contributions to what we would today call taxonomy. Plato's school of followers, the Academy, did important work in the branch of mathematics known as solid geometry. Two thousand years later, René Descartes, the French philosopher and scientist, invented analytic geometry (which we still study in school today) as a tool for analyzing and giving expression to his theory of the nature of the material universe. His successor, Gottfried Leibniz, invented a version of the differential calculus as part of his dispute with Descartes about the nature of matter. In our own century, the logicians and philosophers Bertrand Russell and Alfred North Whitehead established the modern discipline of mathematical logic with their monumental *Principia Mathematica*. Throughout the entire course of Western civilization, philosophical speculation, scientific experiment, and pure logical and mathematical theorizing have advanced together, often in the writings of the same thinkers, sometimes in the very same works. The philosophical enterprise begun by the ancient Milesians has borne splendid fruit, both in an expanded scientific understanding of nature and in a refined conceptual sophistication about those original questions of the nature and order of the cosmos.

One final point before we move on. Thales, Anaximander, and the rest are called "philosophers" in the dictionaries of biography or histories of Western thought. But the people who investigate these questions today are usually classified as "scientists," not as "philosophers." Why is it that cosmological questions are investigated by scientists today, although they were investigated by the philosophers 2,000 years ago? Is this just what labor unions call a "jurisdictional dispute" or has some important theoretical change taken place here?

The most common answer to this question is that "philosophy" used to include just about everything that men and women did by way of systematic, reasoned investigation of the heavens, the earth, or the human condition. In the writings of Plato, Aristotle, and the other ancients, we find discussions which today would be labeled physics, mathematics, astronomy, biology, psychology, economics, political science, sociology, anthropology, theology, and even engineering. Over the past two millennia, one after another of these branches of human knowledge has pulled itself together, broken off from "philosophy," and established itself as an independent discipline with its own rules of inquiry, objects of investigation, and theoretical framework. Philosophy today, according to this way of looking at things, is what remains after all the intellectual children have left home. Roughly speaking, that reduces philosophy to conceptual analysis plus some armchair speculation on whatever the other sciences haven't laid claim to yet.

There is another view, however, which seems to me to be a good deal closer to the truth. Philosophy, it holds, is the systematic reflection of the mind on the criteria of right thought and right action which it employs in all of its activities. On this view, there is a "philosophical" component to virtually everything we do. Political scientists (and politicians too), scientists, artists, economists, and astronomers all need to reflect on the nature of their enterprises, and the people officially called philosophers are simply those among us who concentrate their attention on this self-critical or reflective side of our intellectual undertakings.

What Do Philosophers Do? Human Nature and the Universe

Although the study of the human condition and the study of the cosmos are the two great themes of Western philosophy, it must not be supposed that they developed in an unconnected way. Philosophers are, above all else, seekers after unity. Where human experience presents a manyness, they seek the underlying oneness. In the long history of Western thought, philosophers have tried two basically different strategies for bringing the two branches of philosophy into some interconnected whole.

The first strategy was tried by some of the earliest philosophers, among whom were a group known as **Stoics**. The Stoics claimed that the natural world exhibits a rational order which can be explained by appeal to the existence and operations of a power of reason, which they called *logos*. (We get our word logic from this term, and also the word ending -ology, meaning "study of.") In the cosmos, this logos was often identified with what we today would call God, but it could also be identified with the power of reason in each human being. Therein lies the principle that bridges the gap between the study of human nature and the study of physical nature, for the very same fundamental logos or rational order which makes itself known in the order of the planets, the succession of the seasons, and the regular behavior of natural bodies in space and time also exhibits itself in our capacity for logical reasoning, in our ability to control our passions by the power of our understanding, and in the proper order and arrangement of men and women in a stable, just, and rationally ordered society. Our power of reason was said to be a "spark" or fragment of the divine Logos which informs and governs the universe. Eventually, this ancient Greek doctrine was taken up into the theology of the Christian, Jewish, and Muslim religions and became the basis for much of the religious theology that flourished in the Middle Ages.

After studying cosmology as a youth, Socrates turned away from it, convinced that the proper study for us is our own nature. But if the Stoics were correct, then a philosopher could study human nature and physical nature together, for the same principles that explained the arrangement of the heavenly bodies would, properly understood, also explain how we should live our lives within a well-ordered set of social arrangements.

The unifying doctrine of the Stoics gave rise to one of the most important philosophical ideas in Western thought—the idea of **natural law.** God, or the power of Reason, created the universe in accordance with a rational idea of the proper form and order of its organization. On the cosmic level, this conception determines the existence, nature, and relative positions of the stars, the sun, the moon, and the earth. At the social level, this same idea determines the appropriate hierarchy of classes and statuses from the king or emperor down to the lowliest serf. Within each individual human being, the same idea determines the relative order and importance of the rational, passional, and appetitive elements of the soul. Human beings are unique in the natural order by virtue of their possession of a spark of that logos or reason, for it permits them at one and the same time to understand the grand plan and also to live their own lives freely and responsibly in conformity with it.

Fifteenth–century French illuminated manuscript depicting the sack of Rome by Alaric and the Goths in A.D. 410. In the upper left corner of the painting, St. Augustine is shown offering his book "The City of God" to the Pope. It was the sack of Rome by the Goths that prompted Augustine to write this famous work. (Bibliotheque Nationale.)

Among the greatest of the ancient Stoics was a Roman emperor who ruled from A.D. 161 to 180. Marcus Aurelius combined great skill as a general and ruler with a contemplative nature. His reflections on the universe and our brief stay in it have come down to us in the form of a series of meditations. Following are a few selections that convey the themes and something of the flavor of his thought.

MARCUS AURELIUS, *Meditations*

Constantly regard the universe as one living being, having one substance and one soul; and observe how all things have reference to one perception, the perception of this one living being; and how all things act with one movement; and how all things are the co-operating causes of all things which exist; observe too the continuous spinning of the thread and the contexture of the web.

The intelligence of the universe is social. Accordingly it has made the inferior things for the sake of the superior, and it has fitted the superior to one another. Thou seest how it has subordinated, co-ordinated and assigned to everything its proper portion, and has brought together into concord with one another the things which are the best.

All things are implicated with one another, and the bond is holy; and there is hardly anything unconnected with any other thing. For things have been co-ordinated, and they combine to form the same universe (order). For there is one universe made up of all things, and one God who pervades all things, and one substance, and one law, one common reason in all intelligent animals, and one truth; if indeed there is also one perfection for all animals which are the same stock and participated in the same reason.

To the rational animal the same act is according to nature and according to reason.

So, the first strategy devised by philosophers for uniting the study of human nature with the study of physical nature was the Stoic doctrine of natural law. The second strategy was worked out 2,000 years later by a brilliant group of seventeenth- and eighteenth-century philosophers in the British Isles and on the continent of Europe. We shall be taking a close look at some of their theories in Chapter 6 when we talk about the branch of philosophy known as the "theory of knowledge." In this introductory look at the nature of philosophy in general, we ought nevertheless to try to form some preliminary idea of what they were doing, for their ideas and their writings have been among the most influential in the entire literature of Western thought.

The key to the new strategy is a very simple, very powerful idea: the universe is vast, and ten thousand generations would be too short a time to say everything that can be learned about it; but every single fact, every theory, every insight, guess, hypothesis, or deduction is *an idea in the human mind*. So instead of turning our eyes outward to the universe, let us turn our eyes inward to the nature of the human mind itself. Let us study *the way in which* we know, rather than *what* we know. The universe may be infinite, but the mind is finite. What is more (these philosophers thought), though the universe is infinitely varied, the human mind is everywhere and always exactly the same. Instead of writing many books on cosmology, physics, psychology, politics, morals, and religion, we need to write just one book on the powers, capacities, forms, and limits of the human mind. So during the seventeenth and eighteenth centuries, we find titles like the following cropping up in the philosophical literature: *An Essay Concerning Human Understanding,* by the Englishman John Locke; *Principles of Human Knowledge,* by the Irishman George Berkeley; *A Treatise of Human Nature,* by the Scotsman David Hume; and the greatest of them all, *Critique of Pure Reason,* by the Prussian Immanuel Kant.

Now it might look at first glance as though these philosophers had simply taken Socrates' advice to forget about the study of physical nature and seek instead a knowledge of human nature. But that would be a mistake, for the British empiricists (as Locke, Berkeley, Hume, and their lesser

MARCUS AURELIUS

Marcus Aurelis (A.D. 121–180) was one of the most remarkable men to hold the exalted position of Roman emperor. For almost five centuries, Rome ruled a vast empire stretching from Great Britain through what is now Western Europe, entirely around the shores of the Mediterranean Sea, and deep into northern Africa and the Middle East. Marcus was both a gifted and successful general, winning many battles against the barbarian tribes who repeatedly attacked Rome's border provinces; and also a wise and thoughtful philosopher, learned in the writings of the Greeks and his Roman predecessors, and without illusions about the fleetingness of the power and glory that were his as emperor. During the second century after the birth of Christ, the empire persecuted the followers of that Eastern prophet, and Marcus, despite (or perhaps even because of) his commitment to Stoicism, carried forward these persecutions. It was not until more than a century later, with the conversion of the Emperor Constantine, that Christianity ceased to be the object of official attack and became instead the established religion of the Roman Empire.

compatriots are called) and the Continental rationalists (Descartes, Leibniz, Kant and their fellow philosophers) had got their hands on a wholly different way of doing philosophy. Socrates never imagined that we could learn something about the natural sciences by studying ourselves. He simply thought that the search for the just and happy life was more important than speculation about the elements of the universe or the origin of the order of the heavenly bodies. The British empiricists and Continental rationalists, by contrast, thought they had found a device for combining the study of human nature and the study of the universe in one single philosophical enterprise. If they could learn *how* we know—whether it is by looking with our eyes, touching with our hands, and listening with our ears; or whether it is by reasoning with our minds and ignoring the evidence of our senses; or perhaps whether it is by some combining of what the senses tell us with what reason tells us—if philosophy could study the process of knowledge rather than getting all tangled up in the details of particular bits of knowledge of this and that, then maybe philosophy could give us some very general answers to such questions as, Can we know anything at all? How much can we know? Can we know about things that happened before we were born, or somewhere else in space? Can we know that things *must* happen the way they do, or can we simply say, "This happens, and then this . . ." and let it go at that? Can we know about things we can't see or feel, like atoms, or the unconscious, or even God? Can one person know for sure that there are other persons in the world, and not just bodies that look like persons? Can I, myself, be sure that the whole world isn't simply my dream? All these questions, and many more besides, might be answered by a systematic study of the human mind itself. In this way, the study of physical nature would be combined with the study of human nature, not through a theory of universal logos or intelligence, as the Stoics thought, but through a theory of how we know.

One of the best statements of the new strategy is to be found in the introduction to David Hume's great work, *A Treatise of Human Nature.* Hume was a Scotsman, born in 1711. The *Treatise,* in three volumes, was published in 1739 and 1740, when Hume was not yet thirty years old! There are three important points to notice in the following passage from Hume's *Treatise.* First, as we have already remarked, the basic idea of Hume's strategy is to turn the multiplicity of sciences and fields of study into a unified examination of human nature and the mind's power of knowing. Second, Hume thinks that he shall have to study "the nature of the ideas we employ," for it is from those ideas that we form whatever judgments we wish to make in physics, religion, politics, or morals. And finally, Hume says, he shall have to examine "the operations we perform in our reasonings." In Chapter 6, we shall see that this distinction between the nature of our ideas, on the one hand, and the nature of our reasonings with our ideas, on the other, is an important weapon in the strategy of the new theorists of knowledge.

Reading selections from the works of the great philosophers is a bit like watching videotaped replays of the moves of great football stars. Since

☞ **Empiricism/Rationalism** Empiricism and rationalism are the two leading epistemological theories of the past four centuries. Empiricism is the theory that all human knowledge comes from the evidence of our five senses, and therefore that we can never know more, or know with greater certainty, than our senses will allow. Rationalism is the theory that at least some human knowledge comes from reason, unaided by the senses, and therefore that we can know about things that the senses do not reveal to us and can know with greater certainty than the senses will allow.

D A V I D   H U M E

David Hume (1711–1776) was one of those precocious philosophers whose greatest work was done early in life. Born and reared near Edinburgh in Scotland, Hume attended Edinburgh University, where he studied the new physics of Isaac Newton and the new philosophy of John Locke. When still a teenager, Hume conceived the idea of developing a full-scale theory of human nature along the lines of Newton's revolutionary theory of physical nature. After what seems to have been some sort of mental breakdown, Hume went to France to rest and recover, and while there he wrote his first and greatest book, the monumental *A Treatise of Human Nature.*

Hume went on to become an extremely popular and successful essayist and man of letters. His six-volume *History of England* established his reputation as the first major modern historian. Nevertheless, his skeptical doubts about religion and his attacks on the metaphysical doctrines of his Continental and British predecessors earned him many enemies. One of his most brilliant works, twelve *Dialogues Concerning Natural Religion,* was published only after his death. His friends, including the economist Adam Smith, persuaded him that the book was too controversial and might permanently damage his reputation.

As you can see from the portrait of Hume, the lightness and quickness of his mind was entirely hidden by the lumpishness of his appearance. Nature often plays such tricks on us!

we know who made it to stardom, it is easy for us to spot their greatness from the very first. But let us have a little pity on the poor book reviewer who was handed an anonymous work entitled *A Treatise of Human Nature* and told to write a brief review of it in a few weeks. Here is what one nameless unfortunate had to say about Hume's *Treatise,* in a literary journal rather imposingly called *A History of the Works of the Learned.*

> . . . A Man, who has never had the pleasure of reading Mr. Locke's incomparable Essay, will peruse our author with much less Disgust, than those can who have been used to the irresistible Reasoning and wonderful Perspicuity of that admirable Writer.

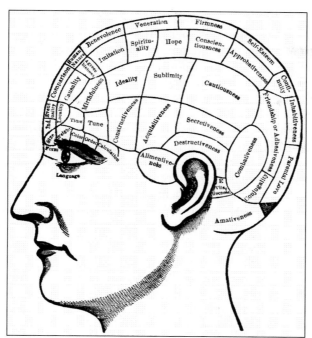

Model head illustrating phrenology. The British and Continental philosophy of the seventeenth and eighteenth centuries sought to determine the limits of human knowledge by a study of the powers and capacities of the mind itself. (Corbis–Bettmann.)

Poor Hume was so upset by the negative reviews of the *Treatise* that later in life he disowned it, saying it was merely a first effort of his youth. How many of us, I wonder, would recognize the greatness of a new book of philosophy within months of its publication? Here is a passage from the introduction to the *Treatise*.

It is evident, that all the sciences have a relation, greater or less, to human nature; and that, however wide any of them may seem to run from it, they still return back by one passage or another. Even *Mathematics, Natural Philosophy,* and *Natural Religion,* are in some measure dependent on the science of MAN; since they lie under the cognisance of men, and are judged of by their powers and faculties. It is impossible to tell what changes and improvements we might make in these sciences were we thoroughly acquainted with the extent and force of human understanding, and could explain the nature of the ideas we employ, and of the oper-

DAVID HUME,
*A Treatise of
Human Nature*

ations we perform in our reasonings. And these improvements are the more to be hoped for in natural religion, as it is not content with instructing us in the nature of superior powers, but carries its views further, to their disposition towards us, and our duties towards them; and consequently, we ourselves are not only the beings that reason, but also one of the objects concerning which we reason.

If, therefore, the sciences of mathematics, natural philosophy, and natural religion, have such a dependence on the knowledge of man, what may be expected in the other sciences, whose connection with human nature is more close and intimate? The sole end of logic is to explain the principles and operations of our reasoning faculty, and the nature of our ideas; morals and criticism regard our tastes and sentiments; and politics consider men as united in society, and dependent on each other. In these four sciences of *Logic, Morals, Criticism,* and *Politics,* is comprehended almost everything which it can anyway import us to be acquainted with, or which can tend either to the improvement or ornament of the human mind.

Here then is the only expedient, from which we can hope for success in our philosophical researches, to leave the tedious lingering method, which we have hitherto followed, and, instead of taking now and then a castle or village on the frontier, to march up directly to the capital or center of these sciences, to human nature itself; which being once master of, we may everywhere else hope for an easy victory. From this station we may extend our conquests over all those sciences, which more intimately concern human life, and may afterwards proceed at leisure, to discover more fully those which are the objects of pure curiosity. There is no question of importance, whose decision is not comprised in the science of man; and there is none, which can be decided with any certainty, before we become acquainted with that science. In pretending, therefore, to explain the principles of human nature, we in effect propose a complete system of the sciences, built on a foundation almost entirely new, and the only one upon which they can stand with any security.

The new study of the mind's capacity for knowing came to be called epistemology, from the Greek for the study or science (-ology) of knowledge *(episteme)*. It was not to be merely descriptive, like psychology, however. Its purpose was to settle some ancient philosophical disputes by finding out what we can legitimately claim to know, and what we cannot claim to know because our claims carry us beyond the limits of the powers of the mind. This *critical* dimension of the new strategy extended across the entire spectrum of philosophical investigations, as the passage from Hume's *Treatise* indicates. In

> **Epistemology**   Literally, the study of knowledge. Epistemology is the study of how we come to know things, what the limits are of our knowledge, and what sort of certainty or uncertainty attaches to our knowledge. Psychology also studies how we come to know, but epistemology is concerned less with the mechanics of knowing than with the possibility of defending, proving, or justifying what we think we know. Since the early seventeenth century, epistemology has been the most important branch of philosophy.

a brief excerpt from Immanuel Kant's *Critique of Pure Reason,* you can get some sense of what a dramatic challenge the new critical epistemology was to the established ways of thinking.

We often hear complaints of shallowness of thought in our age and of the consequent decline of sound science. But I do not see that the sciences which rest upon a secure foundation, such as mathematics, physics, etc., in the least deserve this reproach. On the contrary, they merit their old reputation for solidity, and, in the case of physics, even surpass it. The same spirit would have become active in other kinds of knowledge, if only attention had first been directed to the determination of their principles. Till this is done, indifference, doubt, and, in the final issue, severe criticism, are themselves proof of a profound habit of thought. Our age is, in especial degree, the age of criticism, and to criticism everything must submit. Religion through its sanctity, and law-giving through its majesty, may seek to exempt themselves from it. But they then awaken just suspicion, and cannot claim the sincere respect which reason accords only to that which has been able to sustain the test of free and open examination.

IMMANUEL KANT, *Critique of Pure Reason*

The Limitations of the Western Philosophical Tradition

Thus far, we have been sketching in very broad strokes the major themes and authors of an intellectual tradition that we usually call "Western Philosophy." As we have seen, the tradition has its beginning in the eastern Mediterranean in the sixth century B.C., in the cosmological speculations of a number of thoughtful and observant residents of what are now Greece and Turkey. Although commonly associated with Western Europe, the tradition actually draws heavily on the religious and scientific thought of Egyptian culture. During its 2,500-year history, the tradition has encompassed the religious doc-

trines of the Near East [Judaism and Christianity], the metaphysical speculations of the Arabic philosophers of North Africa, Arabia, and the Middle
East, and in recent times, the writings of thinkers in North America, Australia, New Zealand, and South Africa.

Nevertheless, this ancient and very broad tradition of thought and literature is strikingly limited in certain ways. Despite the fact that it is largely the
product of "dead white males"—to use a phrase that has achieved a certain
popularity lately—this tradition presents itself as the philosophical tradition
of Western Civilization. And yet, in this tradition, the voices of women and
persons of color are scarcely ever heard. What is more, the major thinkers in
the tradition present their doctrines as universally true—true for all human
beings, or even, in the case of Kant, for example, true for all rational beings,
whether human or not.

There is a great deal to be learned from the Western philosophical tradition, as I hope I shall convince you in the pages of this book. But as we proceed to study this tradition, we must ask, in the familiar words of Shakespeare's character Hamlet, whether "there are more things in heaven and
earth than are dreamt of in [this] philosophy." In particular, we as Americans
must ask whether the experiences, insights, and self-understandings of the
substantial groups in our population who are not white males require us to
amend, or even to call into question, the received truths of the established tradition of philosophy.

As we move from one part of Philosophy to another, we shall come
back to this question again and again—in the Chapter on Ethical Theory, in
the Chapter on Social and Political Philosophy, and elsewhere as well. In this
final section of the Introductory Chapter, let me begin the process by considering how we might broaden our understanding by including the perspective
of African-American thinkers.

We could begin, of course, by canvassing the writings of the major figures we shall encounter in this book. Since they are among the most profound, thoughtful, and rigorous thinkers ever to put pen to paper—or stylus
to tablet—we might expect them to have something helpful to say about the
experiences and insights of persons different from themselves. However, were
we to follow this suggestion, we would come across some rather surprising
and troubling passages.

Consider, for example, several of the major thinkers associated with
what we call The Enlightenment—that period during the eighteenth and
early nineteenth centuries when the orthodoxies of religion, science, and politics were called into question, and the authority of tradition was replaced
by the claims of reason. Because these writers speak so movingly about the
virtues of reason and the dangers of superstition, we might hope to find a
clear-eyed recognition of the variety and richness of the human experience in
their writings.

In some of them, no doubt, we do, but all too often we are disappointed. Here, as just one example, is David Hume, in an essay entitled *Of National Characters*. Speaking of the effect of climate on human cultural and intellectual achievements [a favorite topic for eighteenth century writers], he remarks that "there is some reason to think, that all the nations which live beyond the polar circles or between the tropics, are inferior to the rest of the species, and are incapable of all the higher attainments of the human mind." Then, in a footnote that has become justly infamous, he continues:

I am apt to suspect the Negroes to be naturally inferior to the Whites. There scarcely ever was a civilized nation of that complexion, nor even any individual eminent either in action or speculation. No ingenious manufactures amongst them, no arts, no sciences. On the other hand, the most rude and barbarous of the Whites, such as the ancient Germans, the present Tartars, have still something eminent about them, in their valour, form of government, or some other particular. Such a uniform and constant difference could not happen, in so many countries and ages, if nature had not made an original distinction between these breeds of men. Not to mention our colonies, there are Negro slaves dispersed all over Europe, of whom none ever discovered any symptoms of ingenuity; though low people, without education, will start up amongst us, and distinguish themselves in every profession. In Jamaica, indeed, they talk of one Negro as a man of parts and learning; but it is likely he is admired for slender accomplishments, like a parrot who speaks a few words plainly.

DAVID HUME,
of National Characters

Hume's contemptuous view of Africans was challenged by James Beattie, another British philosopher. Beattie wrote a book called *Essay on the Nature and Immutability of the Truth,* in which he mounted a vigorous attack on Hume's most famous book, *A Treatise of Human Nature.* In the course of his attack, Beattie took on Hume's views about people of color. He pointed out that Hume's sweeping condemnations were completely unsupported by observation or evidence. That was a telling blow to Hume, who made so much of the importance of observation elsewhere in his writings.

Immanuel Kant had read Hume's remarks, and cited them approvingly in his important early essay, *Observations on the Feeling of the Beautiful and Sublime.* He had also read Beattie, by the way, but he doesn't seem to have been much impressed by Beattie's arguments.

Kant actually added a story of his own, in an attempt to reinforce Hume's dismissive views of Africans. Kant cited a story by a Dominican missionary, Father Labat, concerning a Negro carpenter. Labat criticized the carpenter for his haughty treatment of his wives, Kant tells us. The carpenter replied with what certainly sounds like a rather shrewd dig: "You whites are indeed fools, for first you make great concessions to your wives, and afterward you complain when they drive you mad."

Kant then adds a comment that I personally consider the single most appalling sentence ever written by a great thinker: "And it might be that there were something in this which perhaps deserved to be considered; but in short, this fellow was quite black from head to foot, a clear proof that what he said was stupid." Even the great Kant could not trust himself to evaluate the merits of a statement when it came from the mouth of a Black man, but instead judged its truth by the color of the skin of its author.

These casually dismissive remarks about persons of color, turning up in the pages of even the greatest thinkers of the eighteenth century, were given a world-historical justification by the most important figure of nineteenth-century thought, the German philosopher Georg Hegel. In his most influential book, *Lectures on the Philosophy of History,* Hegel attempted nothing less than a systematic survey of all of human experience and history. He devoted seven or eight pages in his lengthy Introduction to the continent of Africa, describing the inhabitants of that vast continent as child-like creatures whose minds had not developed sufficiently to permit anything interesting to be said about them.

After repeating, as though they were true, a number of fantastic tales about cannibal tribes with gory practices, Hegel draws the comforting conclusion that for these savages, slavery is actually a step *up* the scale of human development from their previous existence, and hence should be removed only very gradually. Hegel concludes grandly in this fashion: "At this point, we leave Africa, not to mention it again. For it is no historical part of the world. . . . What we properly understand by Africa, is the Unhistorical, Undeveloped Spirit, still involved in the conditions of mere nature, and which had to be presented here only as on the threshold of the World's History."

Not all the great minds of the western philosophical tradition view persons of color, whether in Europe, in Africa, or in the Americas, as beneath contempt and devoid of any intellectual capacities. Nor do they all justify the institution of slavery, by any means. But by now it should be obvious to us that if we want to know what philosophical insights we can gain from persons of color, we should stop rummaging about in the writings of Hume or Kant or Hegel, and instead look at what persons of color have themselves written.

Once we have made this decision, we can turn either to the philosophical literature now being written by philosophers living in Africa, or to the writings of those of African descent whose parents or grandparents were brought as slaves to other parts of the world. By way of introduction, I have chosen to start with the writings of one of the most interesting philosophers of any color ever to live and write in this country: William Edward Burghardt Du Bois.

Du Bois was born in 1868, just five years after Abraham Lincoln signed the Emancipation Proclamation freeing most of the American men and women who were held in slavery. Brought up in western Massachusetts, in the town of Great Barrington, Du Bois attended Fisk University in Nashville, Tennessee and then took a doctorate at Harvard University—the first African American to do so.

Du Bois spent the first part of his long life studying the condition of Black people in both the North and the South. In addition to scholarly research, he engaged all during his life in political activity aimed at securing some measure of political and economic equality for former slaves and their descendants. He published ground-breaking books on the period of Reconstruction following the end of the Civil War, and on the large Black community in Philadelphia. During the same period, from the late 1800s to the early 1900s, he played a central role in founding the National Association for the Advancement of Colored People—the NAACP—and for many years edited its magazine, *The Crisis*.

Du Bois traveled throughout the world, studying in Germany and participating in the first Pan-African Congresses ever organized. For more than half a century, he was the strongest progressive voice in the United States for the interests and aspirations of Black people. In 1961, Du Bois gave up his American citizenship and emigrated to Ghana in West Africa, where he died two years later.

W. E. B. Du Bois lived to be ninety-five, his life spanning the century from the end of the Civil War to the beginning of the modern civil rights movement. Three decades after his death, he remains the dominant figure in Afro-American Studies. His name graces many organizations, academic chairs, and departments, including the W. E. B. Du Bois Department of Afro-American Studies at the University of Massachusetts, of which I am now a member.

These are the opening words of the *Forethought* to Du Bois' masterpiece, *The Souls of Black Folk*, published in 1903:

> Herein lie buried many things which if read with patience may show the strange meanings of being black here at the dawning of the Twentieth Century; for the problem of the Twentieth Century is the problem of the color line.

The problem of the twentieth century is the problem of the color line

The founder of psychoanalysis, Sigmund Freud, once remarked that if there was any subject, however trivial, that a patient would not allow to be discussed in the course of a psychoanalytic therapy, sooner or later the entire

therapy would come to be about that subject. In a way, America's unwillingness to confront openly and honestly the problem of the color line, the line
separating blacks from whites, has resulted in the public discourse of this
country being everywhere and always a concealed debate about race. As we
approach the end of the twentieth century, it appears that Du Bois' diagnosis
will apply as well to the twenty-first.

Du Bois, who was himself descended both from former slaves and
from Dutch and French immigrants, thought deeply about the experience
of being "black" in a country that consigned nonwhites to second-class citizenship. In a famous passage at the beginning of the first chapter of *Souls,*
he invoked two biblical images to describe the experience: the image of a
veil shutting him off from the white world, and the image of a double consciousness, born of the fact that he saw himself both as he was to himself,
inwardly, and also as he was perceived to be by the white world that
looked at him from the outside. Here is the way he describes this distinctive self-awareness:

DU BOIS,
The Souls
of Black Folk

Between me and the other world there is ever an unasked question:
unasked by some through feelings of delicacy; by others through the
difficulty of rightly framing it. All, nevertheless, flutter round it.
They approach me in a half-hesitant sort of way, eye me curiously
or compassionately, and then, instead of saying directly, How does
it feel to be a problem? they say, I know an excellent colored man
in my town; or, I fought at Mechanicsville; or, Do not these Southern outrages make your blood boil? At these I smile, or am interested, or reduce the boiling to a simmer, as the occasion may
require. To the real question, How does it feel to be a problem? I
answer seldom a word.

And yet, being a problem is a strange experience—peculiar
even for one who has never been anything else, save perhaps in
babyhood and in Europe. It is in the early days of rollicking boy-
hood that the revelation first bursts upon one, all in a day, as it
were. I remember well when the shadow swept across me. I was a
little thing, away up in the hills of New England, where the dark
Housatonic winds beween Hoosac and Taghkanic to the sea. In a
wee wooden schoolhouse, something put it into the boys' and girls'
heads to buy gorgeous visiting-cards—ten cents a package—and
exchange. The exchange was merry, till one girl, a tall newcomer,
refused my card,—refused it peremptorily, with a glance. Then it
dawned upon me with a certain suddenness that I was different
from the others; or like, mayhap, in heart and life and longing, but
shut out from their world by a vast veil. I had thereafter no desire
to tear down that veil, to creep through; I held all beyond it in
common contempt, and lived above it in a region of blue sky and

great wandering shadows. That sky was bluest when I could beat my mates at examination-time, or beat them at a foot-race, or even beat their stringy heads. Alas, with the years all this fine contempt began to fade; for the worlds I longed for, and all their dazzling opportunities, were theirs, not mine. But they should not keep these prizes, I said, some, all, I would wrest from them. Just how I would do it I could never decide: by reading law, by healing the sick, by telling the wonderful tales that swam in my head,—some way. With other black boys the strife was not so fiercely sunny: their youth shrunk into tasteless sycophancy, or into silent hatred of the pale world about them and mocking distrust of everything white; or wasted itself in a bitter cry, Why did God make me an outcast and a stranger in mine own house? The shades of the prison-house closed round about us all: walls strait and stubborn to the whitest, but relentlessly narrow, tall, and unscalable to sons of night who must plod darkly on in resignation, or beat unavailing palms against the stone, or steadily, half hopelessly, watch the streak of blue above.

After the Egyptian and Indian, the Greek and Roman, the Teuton and Mongolian, the Negro is a sort of seventh son, born with a veil, and gifted with second-sight in this American world— a world which yields him no true self-consciousness, but only lets him see himself through the revelation of the other world. It is a peculiar sensation, this double-consciousness, this sense of always looking at one's self through the eyes of others, of measuring one's soul by the tape of a world that looks on in amused contempt and pity. One ever feels his twoness,—an American, a Negro; two souls, two thoughts, two unreconciled strivings; two warring ideals in one dark body, whose dogged strength alone keeps it from being torn asunder.

There is a great deal in this brief passage. Let us begin with the theme of double consciousness. To be black in this country, Du Bois is telling us, is always to be de-centered, to be both inside oneself, as all persons are, but also outside oneself, seeing oneself as others see one—experiencing oneself in stereotypical ways, not as W. E. B. Du Bois, but as *a black man*. Those of you reading this book who are black or Latin-American or Asian-American will understand immediately what Du Bois means. Those of you who are white must try, by an act of imagination, to understand what it is like to be divided in this way.

This de-centering, thrust upon people of color by a dominant white society, has intellectual consequences that reach far beyond the psyches and personal lives of those immediately affected. As African-American thinkers like Du Bois have reflected on this curious condition, struggling to understand it and thereby to make sense of their lives, they have been led to a much broader critque of the history, politics, social customs, culture, religion, and public myths of white American society. Indeed, it is not too much to say that the reflective self-understandings of black intellectuals constitute the most sustained critique of American society ever attempted.

Is there such a thing as an *African-American philosophy?* What would such a philosophy be? Well, there are now a number of African Americans writing philosophy, most of them teaching in colleges and universities. But a collection of their writings would not constitute an authentic African-American philosophy, any more than a collection of the writings of female professors of philosophy would constitute a feminist philosophy.

There is also a growing literature devoted to the question of the possibility of an authentic African philosophy, most but not all of it written by professors at sub-Saharan African universities, but that also does not constitute a distinctively African-American philosophy.

I should like, rather tentatively, to suggest that a true African-American philosophy must be a literature devoted to an exploration of the philosophical implications of the African-American experience. That exploration, I believe, must focus on what Du Bois labels the "second sight" into the American world yielded by the "double consciousness" thrust upon African Americans by the "color line." Such a literature already exists, as the brief passages from Du Bois' work show. But there is much more to be done, for the double consciousness produced by the color line shifts our perception of every aspect of American life and society.

Consider something as simple as the story of immigration to the American colonies and then to the United States. As that story is told, in school books and scholarly historical treatises, it is a story of English, Scots, Irish, Polish, German, Italian, and Scandinavian immigrants. But in fact, for the first 200 years of the history of immigration, many more men and women arrived [as slaves] from Africa than came from Europe. Not until the middle of the nineteenth century, after the slave trade was ended, did the flow of white immigrants exceed the flow of black immigrants.

Even the most fundamental philosophical categories, such as time and space, can come to have racial meanings encoded in them. When I was young, students in American schools learned to think of Africa as "the dark continent." This phrase, which some of you have probably heard, echoes Hegel's description of Africa as a "land of childhood . . . enveloped in the dark mantle of night." Now, I have been to Africa many times, and I can report that it isn't dark at all! To many Europeans and Americans, Africa may be mysterious, dark, unknown, a blank space on the world map. But to the millions of men and women who live in Africa, it is home—as familiar, natural, and sun-lit as Kansas or Michigan or Florida.

Nor is Africa "lost in time." Popular writers often talk about Africa as a world in which the prehistoric past lives today. They talk as though when Americans travel to Africa, they are going "back in time" to an earlier period of human development. But the men and women who live in Africa today live in the late twentieth century, as do the men and women who live in Europe, North America, or Asia. African communities have histories that reach as far into the past as communities elsewhere in the world.

When you read books, or see television programs, in which Africa is portrayed as a dark continent, somehow outside the time and space of the modern world, your philosophical understanding is being fundamentally distorted and warped by the racial encoding attached to people of color. All of this, and more, is what Du Bois is trying to show us when he talks of the "double consciousness" created by the *color line*.

What would it be like, philosophically, to overcome this double consciousness? How must we change the way we think about ourselves and the world, if we are to erase the color line? If you are black, the first step, I believe, is to reflect on your own understanding of the world, in order to identify ways in which you have developed a double consciousness. Then *use* that double consciousness, that reflective self-awareness, as a tool with which to criticize the way the majority white society talks about themselves and about you. If you are white, then you must develop the imagination to put yourselves in the shoes of a person of color, and try to understand, from the inside, what it would be like to grow up with a double consciousness.

The result of this process, whether you are a person of color or not, will be a much more complicated understanding of American society. The statements of politicians, teachers, business leaders, religious leaders, and your own friends and acquaintances will take on a new meaning. Then you may be able to achieve what W. E. B. Du Bois calls "second sight." You may be able to penetrate the "veil," and see the world as it truly is. That, as Socrates would certainly agree, is the beginning of wisdom.

Now that you are launched into the study of philosophy, it might help you to know what is coming up in the chapters ahead. You will start with a group of four chapters devoted to philosophical investigations of various aspects of the human condition, including theoretical and applied ethics (Chapter 2), social and political philosophy (Chapter 3), the philosophy of art (Chapter 4), and the philosophy of religion (Chapter 5). They are followed by three chapters dealing, in one way or another, with our knowledge of ourselves and the cosmos, and our knowledge of knowledge itself, starting with epistemology (Chapter 6), and then going on to the philosophy of science (Chapter 7). We conclude with a look at Metaphysics and Philosophy of Mind (Chapter 8). That is more than enough for one semester or quarter, and should give you a pretty good idea of what my old Professor meant when he told his traveling companions that he was a "philosopher."

At the end of each chapter, a special section contains a modern discussion of some immediate practical problem to which the philosophy of the chapter can contribute. In this way, you will learn how today's thinkers—both philosophers and nonphilosophers—try to bring the wisdom of philosophy to bear on our current concerns. Perhaps by the time you have finished reading this book, you will find new ways to make philosophy relevant to modern life.

The Main Points in Chapter One

1. The first great philosopher, Socrates, thought of philosophy as a process of critical self-examination, the purpose of which is to arrive at correct principles of judging, choosing, and acting.

2. The Socratic Method of question-and-answer uses *irony* to penetrate the defenses of those who do not wish to face the fact that they are ignorant or confused.

3. The two major traditions of philosophy are (a) the study of human nature and (b) the study of nature. The ancient philosophers who studied nature came up with very modern-sounding theories of atoms and their combinations.

4. In the seventeenth and eighteenth centuries, philosophers combined the two traditions of philosophy in order to discover the limits of our knowledge of nature. This new technique began with Descartes and was brought to its height by Kant.

Questions for Discussion and Review

1. These days, astronomers study the stars, physicists study subatomic particles, psychiatrists study the nature of the healthy personality, and neurophysiological psychologists study the relation between the physical and psychological aspects of personality. What is left for philosophers to do? Is philosophy an activity that has, over the past several centuries, put itself out of business?

2. The first great philosopher to make a living as a professor of philosophy was Immanuel Kant in the eighteenth century. These days, it seems, everyone who is considered a philosopher earns a living as a professor. Is there something odd, or inappropriate, about a philosopher being paid money

to teach philosophy? If Socrates is right that no one can teach anyone else wisdom, what is it that philosophers teach?

3. The great seventeenth- and eighteenth-century philosophers all thought that a study of human nature could reveal the limits and foundation of our knowledge of nature. How would they have responded to the possibility that there are rational, nonhuman forms of life in the universe that have knowledge, but not a human nature?

4. It is pretty clear what you hope to get out of studying French, or physics, or history, or business administration. What can you hope to get out of studying philosophy? How can you tell whether you are getting out of philosophy what you hope to get? Is your grade in this course a good indicator? Why? Why not?

IMMANUEL KANT

Immanuel Kant (1724–1804) was born, lived out his life, and died in the provincial city of Königsberg in Prussia. Kant's early studies were concentrated in the areas of natural science, mathematics, and philosophy. At the University of Königsberg, he learned the philosophical theories of Leibniz, as interpreted by a widely read German philosopher, Christian Wolff. After graduating from the university, Kant took a number of jobs as a tutor to children in the houses of Prussian aristocrats. Finally, he returned to the university to become what was called a privatdozent. *This meant that he was licensed by the university to offer lectures, which the students could attend. But he was not paid by the university; instead, he had to collect fees from the students. The more popular he was, the more money he made! For more than a dozen years, Kant lectured as much as twenty-one hours a week on virtually every subject imaginable, from mathematics and logic to geography and history. Finally, in 1770, he was appointed to the position of Professor of Logic and Metaphysics.*

Kant was already well known throughout Germany for his writings on physics, astronomy, and metaphysics, but his important work was still far in the future. For eleven years, from 1770 until 1781, he published virtually nothing. All that time, he was struggling with fundamental problems of human knowledge. Finally, in 1781, there appeared the book that was to revolutionize all philosophy: his Critique of Pure Reason. *During the next ten years, book after book flowed from his pen. After the* Critique, *Kant published* Prolegomena to Any Future Metaphysics *(1783),* The Groundwork of the Metaphysic of Morals *(1785),* Metaphysical Foundations of Natural Science *(1786),* Critique of Practical Reason *(1788), and* Critique of Judgment *(1790).*

Kant continued writing and revising his theories until finally, at the age of eighty, shortly after the start of the new century, he died. Though he had never left his native Königsberg, his mind had spanned all time and all space, and he had left an indelible mark on the thought of his civilization.

Ethical Theory

THE VARIETIES OF ETHICAL THEORY

✦ Kant and the Commands of Duty

✦ Three Reasons to Think About Ethics

✦ Ethical Disagreement and the Categorical Imperative

✦ Utilitarianism and the Calculation of Pleasures and Pains

✦ The Theory of the Healthy Personality

✦ The Feminist Critique of Ethical Theory

✦ *Contemporary Application: Same-Sex Marriage*

THE ETHICAL DIMENSIONS OF MEDICINE

✦ The Ethical Dimensions of Medical Decisions

✦ Withholding Food and Water

✦ The Buying and Selling of Human Organs

✦ What Should the Doctor Tell the Patient?

✦ *Contemporary Application: Assisted Suicide*

THE VARIETIES OF ETHICAL THEORY

⚘ Kant and the Commands of Duty

Irwin Edman, a well-known early-twentieth-century Columbia University professor of philosophy is said to have stopped a student on the street one day. "Excuse me," Edman said. "Can you tell me whether I am walking north or south?" The startled student replied, "You are walking south, Professor." "Ah, good," Edman replied. "Then I have already eaten lunch."

Well, it isn't much of a joke, and it has been told of half the professors in America, but it does capture the popular impression of philosophy professors as rather unworldly characters, out of touch with the real world—people, as American businesspeople are fond of saying, who have "never met a payroll."

Immanuel Kant is the greatest philosopher to live and write since the ancient times of Plato and Aristotle: he is the first great philosopher in modern times (after the end of the Middle Ages) to make his living as what we would call a professor of philosophy; and he is also about as close as any great philosopher has ever come to the standard caricature of the professor. Kant is said to have lived so regular and retiring a life that the townspeople of Königsberg, his lifelong home, could set their clocks by him as he went on his daily walk. One would expect a professorial type like Kant to make contributions to such abstruse technical fields as cosmology, metaphysics, or the theory of knowledge, and so he did. But it is rather surprising to discover that Kant also wrote profound, powerful, and deeply moving books on the problems of morality. Despite the uneventful regularity of his own private life, Kant was able to confront and grapple with the great issues of duty, right, justice, and virtue which have troubled the human soul since the ancient times recorded in the Old Testament. The contrast between Kant's outer life and his inner thoughts serves as a reminder to us that the greatness of a philosopher's insights cannot readily be measured by the external excitements of his or her life or times.

Kant was born on April 22, 1724, to a north Prussian family of modest means in the port city of Königsberg on the North Sea. Two centuries earlier, Luther had turned Central Europe upside down with his Reformation of the Catholic Church, and out of Luther's challenge to the institution of the papacy and to the rituals of medieval Christianity had sprung a number of Protestant sects. Kant's family belonged to the sect known as Pietism, an extremely individualistic form of Protestant Christianity which rejected the mystery, ritual, and ceremony that the Catholic Church had interposed between the ordinary Christian and his God. Pietism emphasized the direct, inner relationship of the individual worshiper to God. It placed a strong inner conscience and a stern self-control at the center of its religious doctrine. Kant's mother was particularly devout, and it was universally said of him that he owed both his religious faith and his overpowering sense of moral duty to her influence.

Although he was a believing Christian, Kant rejected the notion that religious doctrine could provide a foundation for morality. Quite to the contrary, he insisted that our moral principles must be established on purely rational grounds, open to criticism and capable of a defense as solid as that which philosophers offered for the principles of pure logic itself.

For Kant, the central question of morality was not, What should I do? This he firmly believed was perfectly well-known to every decent man and woman, whether a peasant or a professor. As he remarked at one point in his moral writings, the truths of **ethics** had been known for thousands of years, so a moral philosopher could hardly expect to discover something *new* in ethics. Rather, Kant saw the real moral problem in the way that most Puritans and other individualistic Protestants did, as the constant struggle to do what we know is right in the face of temptations and distractions. The soldier who knows that his duty requires him to stand fast even as his fear tempts him to run; the merchant who knows that she should give honest measure for honest measure in the marketplace, but nevertheless secretly wishes to tilt the scales in her own favor; the good husband who knows that his marriage vow is absolutely binding but feels the temptation of adultery—these and others like them are the men and women Kant has in mind when he writes on moral questions.

Kant was a student of the new science of Newton as well as a deeply committed Pietist. He saw a fundamental conflict between the scientific explanation of natural events, which emphasized their subordination to causal laws, and the moral assumption that we are free to choose our actions and hence are morally responsible for what we do. How can we demand that a person resist temptation and hold to the moral law if every action is merely another causally determined event in the universal natural order? How can we conceive of persons as free, responsible beings and yet also acknowledge their place in the system of events and objects studied by science?

⌒ Ethics   In philosophy, the systematic study of how we ought to act, both toward ourselves and to others; and also the study of what things, character traits, or types of persons are good, estimable, admirable, and what kinds are bad, reprehensible, worthy of being condemned. Ethics deals both with general rules or principles and also with particular cases.

Equally important to Kant, how can we prove, absolutely and without the slightest room for doubt or uncertainty, that the fundamental moral beliefs shared by all right-thinking persons are true, and not merely public opinion? As we saw in the first chapter, Kant insisted that even religion and morality submit to the spirit of *criticism*. The simple peasants and proud professors of north Prussia might believe that they knew the truth about ethics, but until they could produce a valid proof of their beliefs, they would have no argument to offer against the skeptic, the relativist, the doubter who said that all opinions are equally good or even that there is no truth about ethics to be known at all.

Kant had some ideas about how to handle these two problems. He thought that he could work out a philosophical truce between ethics and science that would give each its rightful place in the totality of human knowledge; at the same time, he hoped to provide a proof of the fundamental principles of ethics. In this way, he would bring all the parts of his own life and work into harmony with one another. In his philosophical system, there would be a place for the devout faith imparted to him by his mother, a proof of the moral maxims he had grown up with and which to his death he never doubted, and a conceptual framework for the great new achievements of science and mathematics which so dominated the intellectual world of his day and to which he devoted so much of his own life and work.

Kant's struggle to achieve a harmonious accommodation among his scientific interests, his moral convictions, and his religious faith was a model for many later struggles by other philosophers. Today more than ever, science seems to encroach upon religion and morality. New developments in behavioral psychology threaten our age-old belief in moral freedom. Though many philosophers have challenged Kant's solution, few would deny that he saw deeply into the problem and forced the rest of us to confront it as philosophers.

❧ Three Reasons to Think About Ethics

Having read this far into a chapter on ethics, some of you may have the feeling that you don't quite recognize the subject as one that you can relate to. Perhaps Kant knew perfectly well what was right, but many of *us* are filled with doubts. Furthermore, you may want to say, his single-minded emphasis on duty, on conscience, on doing the *right* thing, misses the real flavor of much of our thinking about how to live our lives. The fact is that although this book contains only one chapter titled Ethics, there are many quite different sorts of problems that have been discussed under that name since the time of the ancient Greeks. There is hardly enough room in a single book, let alone in one chapter, to talk about all these problems, but at least *three* are important enough to demand some extended examination.

Kant has already introduced us to the first reason that people worry about what is called ethics—namely, a desire to discover an absolutely certain, irrefutable proof of the moral principles which we are already convinced are true. This proof serves two purposes: first, it answers the skeptic, who denies that there are any moral truths at all; and second, it answers the relativist, who says, in effect, "Everyone's opinions are as good as everyone else's."

A second reason why people worry about ethics is that sometimes we get into situations in which we want to do the right thing but really don't know what it is. For example, a woman may find out that she is pregnant and feel that to have a baby will simply turn her life inside out. Perhaps she wants to continue her studies in order to prepare for a career; perhaps the pregnancy is the result of a casual affair with a man whom she does not love; perhaps she and her husband already have as many children as they want and feel they can care for. Should she have an abortion? Part of her says that abortion is morally wrong; another part tells her that to have the baby would be wrong. She wants to do what is right, but she just doesn't know what *is* right in the situation.

Or a young man wants to leave home and start a life of his own, despite his parents' pleas that he remain with them and care for them. On the one hand, he feels love for his parents and a debt of gratitude and loyalty for all the years they have given to him. On the other hand, he knows that this is his only life, and that it is wrong for him to sacrifice it to the needs or demands of his parents. Again, he wants to do what is right, but he does not know whether he really has an obligation to stay at home, and if he does, for how long.

In philosophy, cases such as these are sometimes called "hard cases." They are real-life moral dilemmas in which ordinary moral opinions are either hopelessly contradictory or else just confused. Many philosophers have sought some method or rule by which we could decide hard cases, either by a process of moral reasoning or even by a sort of calculation. Genuine confusion rather than temptation is the motivation here, and frequently the emphasis is less on an absolutely rock-solid *proof* of things we already believe than it is on some genuinely new insight into an otherwise unsolvable dilemma.

But the oldest tradition of ethical reflection in Western thought has nothing to do with rights and duties, temptations and their denial, hard cases and tortured choices. For Plato, for Marcus Aurelius, for the ancient Stoics, and for countless philosophers since their time, ethics has been concerned with the definition, analysis, search for, and achievement of the *good life*. Our stay on this earth is brief, the years pass faster and faster as we grow older, and all too soon we are forever dead. As we grow up and grow old, how shall we live our lives? What set of precepts, what style of inner feelings and outer relationships, what set of commitments will make us truly happy during the short passage of our lives? Should we strive to pile wealth upon wealth? fulfill our talents? aim for power and fame? retire to quiet contemplation? taste every experience, pleasurable or not, before death comes? Can reason and philosophy even help us in this choice? Or is the life of the mind itself just one path among many, and not the happiest at that?

Sometimes when we say that someone lived a "good life," we mean that he or she experienced a great deal of pleasure—ate, drank, made merry. As it is said in Italian, such a person lived *la dolce vita,* the "sweet life." But just as often, we mean that the life was one of virtue, of service, of honor and dignity, that it was a life in which there was goodness. Many philosophers deliberately preserve this ambiguity because they believe that a truly happy life must also be a virtuous life, a life of goodness. Plato is perhaps the philosopher most often associated with this claim, and we shall read something by him on the subject later on in this chapter. But many other philosophers have, in one way or another, made the same claim, among whom are such unlikely bedfellows as Confucius and Karl Marx.

Here, then, are three reasons for thinking about ethics—or better, three searches which are usually grouped under the heading "ethics": the search for absolutely certain, universally valid first principles of conduct that can stand against the challenges of the skeptic and the relativist; the search for a method or process of reasoning to help us in deciding hard cases and other real-world moral choices; and the search for the good life, the life that combines virtue and happiness in true human fulfillment. Most of the remainder of the first half of this chapter will be devoted to a deeper examination of these three approaches to the subject of ethics.

Ethical Disagreement and the Categorical Imperative

When we are very little, our parents stop us from doing things we shouldn't—hitting baby brother, eating paint, touching a wall plug—by physically pulling us away and saying "No!" in a loud, firm voice. You can't have a philosophical discussion with a two-year-old, as I was forced very quickly to recognize with my own two sons. As we grow older, we internalize those "No's" in the form of some set of rules, or norms, some conception of what is right and wrong. For a very long time, we simply accept these rules as given, a part of the world just as trees and tables or our parents and friends are part of the world. Pretty early on, of course, we discover that not everyone abides all the time by the rules that our parents have taught us, but we can handle that fact, conceptually, by means of the category "bad." "Why can't I hit my brother? Tommy does." "Because it is wrong. Tommy is a bad boy, and I don't want you to be a bad boy like him."

So we grow older, with a more or less coherent moral code as part of our mental equipment. There are bad guys, naughty children, villains, criminals, but they are the "others," the ones who aren't nice, the sort of people we don't want to be like.

Then, one day, somewhere, there comes the great shock. It may be when we are still children, or when we go away to college, or when we move from a tight little homogeneous neighborhood to a big, heterogeneous city. It may simply be something we see on television. But all of a sudden, we encounter a whole group of people who seem to be good, decent, respectable, law-abiding, and upright, except that they call good what we call bad! We think it is good to fight for our country, and they think it is wicked. We think homosexuality is a perfectly acceptable lifestyle, and they think it is evil. They think abortion is a sensible technique for rational family planning and population control, and we call it murder.

This discovery, in whatever form it comes, is a genuine shock. The problem doesn't lie in the realization that some people do bad things. Ever since we saw Tommy hit his brother, we have known that. The real problem is that these people doing "bad" things and living by the "wrong" rules are *good* people. They are responsible; they are respected by their friends and neighbors. They may even be held up to children as models of virtue. And yet they do bad things! A man comes home from a war in which he gunned down two hundred defenseless women and children in a village, and he is paraded along Main Street as a hero. A mother and father refuse to allow their baby to receive medical treatment, the baby dies, and they are praised in their church as pillars of rectitude. A governor calls out the National Guard to shoot striking prison inmates, and he is immortalized in marble in front of the state capital.

If it is unsettling to encounter men and women within our own society whose moral codes differ markedly from our own, think how much more unsettling it is to discover whole cultures or civilizations in which what we call virtue is despised as vice and what we condemn as wicked is celebrated as noble! Even a study of the history of the literate civilizations of the East and West provides countless examples of this sort of variation in moral beliefs. When the anthropologists' experiences with nonliterate cultures are added to our stock of information, it begins to appear that there isn't a single rule, precept, or moral belief that has been accepted by decent men and women everywhere. War? Torture? Child murder? Adultery? Suicide? Theft? Lying? Every single one has been condemned by some cultures and accepted, approved, or even praised by others.

There are basically three ways in which a philosopher can deal with the troublesome problem of the variation in moral codes from person to person, group to group, and culture to culture. The first way is to deny that the variation exists, despite appearances to the contrary. The second way is to admit that the variation exists and conclude that there are therefore no universally valid moral norms applicable to all persons in all places at all times. The third way is to acknowledge the variation but insist nonetheless that some moral principles are true and other supposed principles are false, no matter how many people believe them. Those who take this last route then do their best to provide some sort of proof for the principles they believe to be valid.

How can philosophers possibly maintain that there is no real disagreement about norms and moral principles, when the evidence of personal and cultural variation is all around them? Essentially, their tactic is to argue that when two people or two cultures seem to disagree about what is right or good, they are *really* only disagreeing about some of the facts of the case. If they could settle that disagreement, then it would turn out that they actually make the same moral judgments. For example, the Christian Scientist, like the nonbeliever, wants what is best for his sick child. But he firmly believes that the body is not real and that salvation depends upon holding firm to that belief. So for him to consent to an operation for his child would be as irresponsible (on his assessment of the facts) as for another parent to give a diabetic child all the candy she wants. To take another example, the culture that condemns abortion may believe that the fetus is already a person; the culture that approves abortion does not think the fetus is a person until after it is born. Both condemn murder, defined as the willful killing of a person, but they disagree on the factual question of whether the fetus is a person.

A number of philosophers have taken this line, including the Scotsman David Hume whom you encountered in Chapter 1. Anthropologists have actually carried out cross-country surveys of norms in an effort to discover any constants. Although it does appear that the ban or taboo on incest is widespread, the effort has essentially been a failure. There aren't any broad moral principles of justice, charity, equity, or benevolence which can be discovered in the moral systems of all cultures. (There is a much deeper question which we have not touched on yet. Even if there *were* universally accepted norms, what would that fact prove? Does everybody believing something make it right? Don't we need some justification for our moral convictions which goes beyond saying, "Everybody agrees with me?" This problem troubled Kant a great deal, and a bit later in this chapter, we shall see how he tried to deal with it.)

The second response to moral disagreement—the denial of objective, universal moral norms—has actually been relatively rare in the history of Western ethical theory, but it has had its defenders from the time of the ancient Greeks to the present day. There are two forms of this position: *ethical skepticism* and *ethical relativism*. Ethical skepticism denies that we can have the slightest certainty about questions of the right and the good. Sometimes the ethical skeptic says that words like "right," "good," "ought," and "duty" just don't have any meaning; sentences containing them are a bit like incantations or cheers of approval or perhaps just plain gibberish. Because the very words we use to make moral judgments have no meaning, our moral judgments can hardly be called true or false, valid or invalid. At other times, the ethical skeptic merely points out that no valid argument can be found for any particular moral principle. If I doubt that murder is wrong, you cannot find an argument that will prove to me that it is. If I can't see why I should help another person in distress, there is no way it can be demonstrated to me that I should. Philosophers who take either of these lines frequently think that science and scientific language are the models on

> 👁 **Ethical Relativism**   The theory that whether an act is right or wrong depends on—is relative to—the society in which one lives. Sometimes ethical relativists merely claim that we must take social contexts and rules into account, but sometimes they assert that one and the same act is right for men and women in one society and wrong for men and women in another. Frequently confused with *Ethical Skepticism*, which doubts that any acts are right or wrong, and *Ethical Nihilism*, which denies that any acts are either right or wrong.

which we should base all of our knowledge. They point to the nondescriptive character of moral statements (they don't tell us how things are; they claim to tell us how things ought to be). They contrast the orderly experimentation and examination of data in the sciences with the haphazard, intuitive, unfactual character of moral disputes. Sometimes they suggest that moral arguments really come down to disagreements over matter of taste, and as the old saying has it, *de gustibus non disputandem est* (there is no disputing in matters of taste).

The *ethical skeptic* is sometimes joined in the fight against objective moral principles by the ethical relativist. How often, in a bull session, have we heard someone say, "Oh well, it's all relative!" Sometimes that means "Everyone *has* her own opinion." Sometimes it means, "Everyone is *entitled* to her own opinion." But sometimes it means "Everyone's opinion is true to her, even though it may not be true for someone else." As a student said to me once in class when I asked whether he thought that Hitler had been wrong to kill millions of people in death camps, "Well, it wouldn't be right for me, but I guess it was right for him."

In the following passage, the American anthropologist Ruth Benedict draws on her wide knowledge of the varieties of human culture to argue for the fundamental relativity of moral judgments. There is something very unsettling about the fact that a scientist who has seen so much of human culture and society in all its forms should come to a relativist position.

No one civilization can possibly utilize in its mores the whole potential range of human behavior. . . .

Every society, beginning with some inclination in one direction or another, carries its preference farther and farther, integrating itself more and more completely upon its chosen basis, and discarding those types of behaviors that are uncongenial. Most of those organizations of personality that seem to us more incontrovertibly abnormal have been used by different civilizations in the very foundations of their institutional life. Conversely the most valued traits of our normal individuals have been looked on in differently orga-

RUTH BENEDICT, *Anthropology and the Abnormal*

Varieties of human culture. Crowd scene. (Joel Gordon Photography.)

nized cultures as aberrant. Normality, in short, within a very wide range, is culturally defined. . . . The very eyes with which we see the problem are conditioned by the long traditional habits of our own society.

It is a point that has been made more often in relation to ethics than in relation to psychiatry. We do not any longer make the mistake of deriving the morality of our own locality and decade directly from the inevitable constitution of human nature. We do not elevate it to the dignity of a first principle. We recognize that morality differs in every society, and is a convenient term for socially approved habits. Mankind has always preferred to say, "It is morally good," rather than "It is habitual," and the fact of this preference is matter enough for a critical science of ethics. But historically the two phrases are synonymous.

Immanuel Kant is the strongest opponent of the ethical relativist position. A major aim of Kant's philosophical efforts was to provide an absolutely solid, totally universal proof of the validity of that moral principle which he considered the foundation of all ethics, the principle which he called the Categorical Imperative. Kant was well aware that there were serious ethical disagreements among philosophers on particular questions of moral judgment, though he was not so impressed as Hume had been by the systematic cultural differences which appeared to divide "cultivated" peoples. But Kant was extremely concerned about the lack of solid foundations for even those ethical beliefs which are more or less broadly agreed upon. In a number of profound and very difficult treatises on ethics. Kant undertook to lay those foundations.

[A cautionary word: Kant tried to think in a totally universal way about ethics, and yet, as we have seen, he gave voice to some vicious racist prejudices that were commonplace in his day. It might make us wonder what views we hold now, unthinkingly, that later generations will find appalling.]

Saying just a few words about Kant's philosophy is like saying just a few words about quantum mechanics or the theory of relativity! Nevertheless, some of the key notions of Kant's moral philosophy can be understood pretty well without plunging into the depth of his argument, and in the remainder of this section, I shall introduce you to those notions through a combination of my exposition and Kant's own words.

Kant first set out his moral philosophy in a little book called *Groundwork of the Metaphysic of Morals* (a rather imposing title). He intended the book to be just an introduction to his theory, and shortly thereafter he published another, longer work called *Critique of Practical Reason*. But as often happens, the short "introductory" book took on a life of its own, and today it is widely viewed as the finest statement of Kant's position.

The aim of the *Groundwork* is to discover, analyze, and defend the fundamental principle of morality. As you know, Kant didn't think he had discovered a *new* principle, and he liked to say that his Categorical Imperative was nothing more than a philosophically more precise statement of

---

 ⌒ **Categorical Imperative**   A term invented by Immanuel Kant to refer to a command that orders us to do something unconditionally—that is, regardless of what we want or what our aims and purposes are. According to Kant, we experience the principles of morality as Categorical Imperatives. The term is also used, by Kant and those following him, to refer to one particular moral principle, which Kant calls The Highest Moral Law.

the old Golden Rule: Do unto others as you would have others do unto you. Here is the way in which Kant revised and restated that rule:

The Categorical ‖ Act only on that maxim through which you can at the same time will
Imperative that it should be a universal law.

That doesn't *look* much like the Golden Rule, but Kant thought it contained the same basic notion, which is that we ought to put aside our own private interests and act instead on the basis of rules that would be equally reasonable for all moral agents to adopt as their own. "Do unto others as you would have others do unto you" doesn't mean "Go ahead and steal from your neighbor so long as you don't squawk when he steals from you." It means something more like "Treat other people with the same respect and dignity that you expect to be treated with." As we shall see, the idea of human dignity plays a central role in Kant's moral philosophy.

Moses coming down from Mount Sinai. Kant believed that the Golden Rule, "Do unto others as you would have others do unto you," is a summary statement of the Ten Commandments, and that his Categorical Imperative is simply a philosophical re-statement of the Golden Rule. (Woodcut by Gustave Dore. Corbis–Bettmann.)

There are three ideas that lie at the heart of Kant's ethics. If we can understand something about each of them, we can form at least a preliminary notion of his theory. The ideas are, first, that persons are rational creatures, capable of thinking about the choices they face and selecting among them on the basis of reasons; second, that persons have an infinite worth or dignity which sets them above all merely conditionally valuable things in this world, that they are what Kant calls ends-in-themselves; and, third, that persons, as rational ends-in-themselves, are the *authors* of the moral law, so that their obedience to duty is not an act of slavish submission but an act of dignified *autonomy.* Persons as rational agents, as ends-in-themselves, and as autonomous—these are the basic building blocks out of which Kant constructs his proof of the Categorical Imperative.

When Kant asserts that persons are rational agents, he means more than merely that they are capable of making judgments about the nature of the world, or inferences from one set of propositions to another. A rational agent is a person who is capable of *moving himself or herself to act* by reason. David Hume, like many other philosophers, had thought that reason was incapable of moving us to action. Hume argued that *desire* moves us to act; reason merely points out the most efficient path to the goal that desire chooses. So Hume said, in a much-quoted passage, that "reason is, and ought only to be the slave of the passions, and can never pretend to any other office than to serve and obey them" (*A Treatise of Human Nature,* Book III). Kant replied that if we are to make any sense at all of our condition as creatures capable of choice and deliberation, we must acknowledge that we can be moved by *reasons,* not merely by *desires.*

If Kant is right that we can be moved by reason, then it makes sense to ask whether we have acted wisely or foolishly, whether we have reasoned consistently in our choice of ends and means. It makes sense, also, to ask whether in our reasoning we have taken special account of our own particular wishes and interests, or instead have limited ourselves only to reasons which would be compelling reasons for any person in the same circumstances. In short, it makes sense to ask whether we have acted *rationally.*

This notion of "reasons good for all rational agents" is a difficult one to grasp. Perhaps one way to get some idea of Kant's meaning is to compare a moral agent to a mathematician doing a geometry problem. Suppose the mathematician is trying to show that the square of the hypotenuse of a right triangle is equal to the sum of the squares of the other two sides (the so-called Pythagorean theorem that some of you studied in high school). Now, the first thing she does in developing the proof is to draw a triangle, and because every triangle has to be some size and shape or other, the particular triangle the mathematician draws will be some particular size (maybe $4\frac{1}{2}$ inches by 6 inches by $7\frac{1}{2}$ inches), and it will also be some particular color (depending on the color of the paper she draws it on), and so forth. But of course she isn't supposed to pay any attention to the actual size and color of the triangle.

They are there, all right, but she is supposed to ignore them. The only thing she is allowed to count in her proof is the fact that the triangle has a right angle in it. If our imaginary mathematician constructs her proof by using only the fact that her triangle is a right triangle, then her conclusions, when she gets them, will apply to *all* right triangles, not just to the one she actually drew.

In the same way, Kant claims that moral agents, when they reason about what they ought to do, should ignore all the particular facts about their own interests, special desires, individual circumstances, and so on, and concentrate just on those facts which hold for *all* rational agents as such. If they do that, he says, then the conclusions they come to will be valid for all rational agents, not just for themselves. In short, their conclusions will be universal laws, not just personal rules. Kant uses the word "maxim" to mean a personal rule on which we actually base our decisions. (In the following selection, he also uses the term "subjective principle" with this meaning.) So he is telling us that when we make our decisions, we, like the mathematician, should restrict ourselves to rules, or maxims, that could just as well serve any rational agent. In other words, he tells us to restrict ourselves to maxims that could serve as universal laws. That is what he is trying to say in the Categorical Imperative: Act only on that maxim through which you can at the same time will that it should become a universal law.

If we do succeed in acting in a genuinely rational way, Kant says, we show ourselves to possess a dignity that sets us above everything else in the world. Indeed, the statement that moral agents, as persons, have an infinite worth or dignity is, according to Kant, just another way of saying what has already been said in the Categorical Imperative. Here is the famous passage in which Kant develops the notion that persons are ends-in-themselves. Difficult as Kant's argument is, I think you will be able to see in it something of the grandeur and profundity that has so impressed generations of readers:

IMMANUEL KANT,
Groundwork of the Metaphysic of Morals

Now I say that man, and in general every rational being, *exists* as an end in himself, *not merely as a means* for arbitrary use by this or that will: he must in all his actions, whether they are directed to himself or to other rational beings, always be viewed *at the same time as an end*. All the objects of inclination have only a conditioned value; for if there were not these inclinations and the needs grounded on them, their object would be valueless. Inclinations themselves, as sources of needs, are so far from having an absolute value to make them desirable for their own sake that it must rather be the universal wish of every rational being to be wholly free from them. Thus the value of all objects that can *be produced* by our action is always conditioned. Beings whose existence depends, not on our will, but on nature, have none the less, if they are nonrational beings, only a relative value as means and are consequently called *things*. Rational beings, on the other hand, are called *persons* because their nature already marks them out as ends in themselves and consequently imposes to that extent a limit on all arbitrary treatment of them (and is an object of reverence). Persons, therefore, are not merely subjective ends whose existence as an object of our actions has a value for *us:* they are *objective ends*—that is, things whose existence is in itself an end, and indeed an end such that in its place we can put no other end to which they should serve *simply* as means; for unless this is so, nothing at all of absolute value would be found anywhere. But if all value were conditioned then no supreme principle could be found for reason at all.

If then there is to be a supreme practical principle and a categorical imperative, it must be such that from the idea of something which is necessarily an end for every one because it is an *end in itself* it forms an *objective* principle of the will and consequently can serve as a practical law. The ground of this principle is: *Rational nature exists as an end in itself.* This is the way in which a man necessarily conceives his own existence: it is therefore so far a *subjective* principle of human actions. But it is also the way in which every other rational being conceives his existence on the same rational ground which is valid also for me; hence it is at the same time an *objective* principle, from which, as a supreme practical ground, it must be possible to derive all laws for the will. The practical imperative will therefore be as follows: *Act in such a way that you always treat humanity, whether in your own person or in the person of any other, never simply as a means, but always at the same time as an end.*

Hume had described reason as the "slave" of the passions, subservient to their direction. If my reason is the slave of my passions, then I forfeit the dignity that I possess in virtue of being an end-in-myself. There is no honor in subservience to passion, any more than in subservience to a king or emperor. In the inner life of each man and woman, as in the public life of the state, honor is to be found only in submission to self-made laws. The citizen of a republic, who makes the laws to which he bows his head, loses no dignity by his obedience, for he is obeying only himself when he abides by the law. His obedience is an act of responsibility rather than of servitude.

The same principle, Kant thought, holds true within the individual soul. When reason bows to passion, it forfeits its claim to honor and dignity. But if reason can itself legislate the laws to which it submits, if reason can itself write the Categorical Imperative that binds it, then it will preserve its freedom in the very act of submission. To give laws to oneself is, following the Greek, to be *auto-nomos*—giver of law to oneself—in short: autonomous. The principle of the autonomy of reason is, Kant says, yet another version of the Categorical Imperative.

Having set forth three key principles—(1) the rationality of the will, (2) the infinite worth of persons as ends-in-themselves, and (3) the self-legislating, or autonomous, character of reason—Kant now pulls them all together in the notion of a society of moral agents, all of whom govern their actions by reason, all of whom are ends-in-themselves, and all of whom are autonomous. He calls this society a *kingdom of ends,* and we can imagine it as an ideal community of upright, responsible, rational men and women who base their actions on universally valid laws which they autonomously lay down for themselves. It is a community that lives according to the Categorical Imperative. In our last passage from Kant, we see all of these themes united:

IMMANUEL KANT,
Groundwork of the Metaphysic of Morals

In the kingdom of ends everything has either a *price* or a *dignity.* If it has a price, something else can be put in its place as an equivalent; if it is exalted above all price and so admits of no equivalent, then it has a dignity.

What is relative to universal human inclinations and needs has a *market price;* what, even without presupposing a need, accords with a certain taste has a *fancy price (Affektionspreis);* but that which constitutes the sole condition under which anything can be an end in itself has not merely a relative value but has an intrinsic value—that is, *dignity.*

Now morality is the only condition under which a rational being can be an end in himself; for only through this is it possible to be a lawmaking member in a kingdom of ends. Therefore morality, and humanity so far as it is capable of morality, is the only thing which has dignity. Skill and diligence in work have a market price; wit, lively imagination, and humour have a fancy price; but fidelity to promises and kindness based on principle (not on instinct) have an intrinsic worth. In default of these, nature and art alike contain nothing to put in their place; for their worth consists, not in the effects which result from them, not in the advantage or profit they produce, but in the attitudes of mind which are ready in this way to manifest themselves in action even if they are not favoured by success. Such actions too need no recommendations from any subjective disposition or taste in order to meet with immediate favour and approval; they need no immediate propensity or feeling for themselves; they exhibit the will which performs them as an object of immediate reverence; nor is anything other than reason required to *impose* them upon the will, nor to *coax* them from the will—which last would anyhow be a contradiction in the case of duties. This assessment reveals as dignity the value of such a mental attitude and puts it infinitely above all price, with which it cannot be brought into reckoning or comparison without, as it were, a profanation of its sanctity.

What is it then that entitles a morally good attitude of mind to make claims so high? It is nothing less than the *share* which it affords to a rational being in the *making of universal law,* and which therefore fits him to be a member in a possible kingdom of ends. For this he was already marked out in virtue of his own proper nature as an end in himself and consequently as a maker of laws in the kingdom of ends—as free in respect of all laws of nature, obeying only those laws which he makes himself and in virtue of which his maxims can have their part in the making of universal law (to which he at the same time subjects himself). For nothing can have a value other than that determined for it by the law. But the law-making which determines all value must for this reason have a dignity for the appreciation of which, as necessarily given by a rational being, the word *"reverence"* is the only becoming expression. *Autonomy* is therefore the ground of the dignity of human nature and of every rational nature.

Utilitarianism and the Calculation of Pleasures and Pains

How shall we deal with those terrible situations in which we want very much to do the right thing but simply cannot figure out what it is? Sometimes, there are two different and conflicting things, both of which seem right in the situation. Sometimes the situation is such a tangle that we are just at a loss. The source of our uncertainty is not temptation, or skepticism, or relativism, but the genuine moral difficulty of the case itself. One of the most ancient attempts to deal with such hard cases, and also to lay down a rule for action which will always tell us what we ought to do, is the moral philosophy which these days goes under the name of **utilitarianism.** In this section, we are going to take a look at several varieties of utilitarianism, see what the theory says and how it works, and also consider some serious objections to it.

Utilitarianism is simply the rule that we should always try to make as many people as possible as happy as possible. Indeed, it is sometimes called The Greatest Happiness Principle for this reason. The cosmologist Lucretius was a utilitarian, and so was the man whose teachings he followed, Epicurus. In the modern world, the most famous utilitarian, generally credited with establishing the doctrine as a serious contender in moral philosophy, was the eighteenth-century Englishman Jeremy Bentham.

Bentham argues that however people may appear to use the words "good" and "evil," they really just mean "pleasant" or "painful": "Pleasant" when they say "good" and "painful" when they say "evil." More good is better than less, which is to say that more pleasure is better than less. And, of course, less pain is better than more. The only good reason for doing anything is to increase the amount of pleasure that human beings experience, or at least to reduce the amount of pain. What is more, pleasures and pains can, in a manner of speaking, be added to and subtracted from one another. I can ask myself, Which gave me more pleasure: the good movie I saw last week or the mediocre movie I saw last night plus the really good pizza I had afterward? I can also ask myself, Which will be more painful: three dentist's visits now, complete with drillings, or a toothache followed by an extraction followed by the annoyance of a missing tooth later? If the mediocre movie plus the pizza gave me more pleasure, then the next time I have to choose between a good movie and no pizza or a mediocre movie and pizza, I ought to take the mediocre movie plus pizza. And, more seriously, if the dentist's visits, bad as they are, add up to less pain than the rotting of my tooth, then I ought to go to the dentist even though I don't want to, because the only rational thing to do is to minimize the total amount of pain in my life.

Bentham announced the doctrine now known as utilitarianism in a book entitled *An Introduction to the Principles of Morals and Legislation,* first printed in 1780 and formally published in 1789. Here is a selection from the opening chapter. Notice the complete identification of pleasure with good and pain with evil. This is the heart and soul of Bentham's utilitarian doctrine.

JEREMY
BENTHAM,
*An Introduction
to the Principles
of Morals
and Legislation*

Nature has placed mankind under the governance of two sovereign masters, *pain* and *pleasure*. It is for them alone to point out what we ought to do, as well as to determine what we shall do. On the one hand the standard of right and wrong, on the other the chain of causes and effects, are fastened to their throne. They govern us in all we do, in all we say, in all we think: every effort we can make to throw off our subjection, will serve but to demonstrate and confirm it. In words a man may pretend to abjure their empire: but in reality he will remain subject to it all the while. The *principle of utility* recognizes this subjection, and assumes it for the foundation of that system, the object of which is to rear the fabric of felicity by the hands of reason and law. Systems which attempt to question it, deal in sounds instead of sense, in caprice instead of reason, in darkness instead of light.

But enough of metaphor and declamation: it is not by such means that moral science is to be improved.

The principle of utility is the foundation of the present work: it will be proper therefore at the outset to give an explicit and determinate account of what is meant by it. By the principle of utility is meant that principle which approves or disapproves of every action whatsoever, according to the tendency which it appears to have to augment or diminish the happiness of the party whose interest is in question: or, what is the same thing in other words, to promote or to oppose that happiness. I say of every action whatsoever; and therefore not only of every action of a private individual, but of every measure of government.

By utility is meant that property in any object, whereby it tends to produce benefit, advantage, pleasure, good, or happiness (all this in the present case comes to the same thing) or (what comes again to the same thing) to prevent the happening of mischief, pain, evil or unhappiness to the party whose interest is considered: if that party be the community in general, then the happiness of the community; if a particular individual, then the happiness of that individual.

The interest of the community is one of the most general expressions that can occur in the phraseology of morals: no wonder that the meaning of it is often lost. When it has a meaning, it is this. The community is a fictitious *body*, composed of the individual persons who are considered as constituting as it were its *members*. The interest of the community then is, what?—the sum of the interests of the several members who compose it.

It is in vain to talk of the interest of the community, without understanding what is the interest of the individual. A thing is said to promote the interest, or to be *for* the interest, of an individual, when it tends to add to the sum total of his pleasures: or what comes to the same thing, to diminish the sum total of his pains.

An action then may be said to be conformable to the principle of utility, or, for shortness sake, to utility (meaning with respect to the community at large) when the tendency it has to augment the happiness of the community is greater than any it has to diminish it.

A measure of government (which is but a particular kind of action, performed by a particular person or persons) may be said to be conformable to or dictated by the principle of utility, when in like manner the tendency which it has to augment the happiness of the community is greater than any which it has to diminish it.

The crucial step in Bentham's argument is his move from the total pleasure and pain experienced by one person to the total pleasure or pain experienced by all the members of the community taken together. This is the device which permits Bentham to extract a moral principle from his theory. The point is that whenever I do anything at all, my action has effects which impinge on the lives of other people. Sometimes I cause them pleasure, sometimes I cause them pain, and sometimes of course I cause some of them pleasure and others pain. For example, if the young man we mentioned earlier decides to stay at home with his parents rather than leave and set out on his own, he will probably cause himself pain and his mother and father pleasure. That is just why he doesn't know what to do! If his staying at home caused his parents pain too (they, after all, might want to live their own lives), then the decision would be an easy one for him.

CHAPTER 2

JEREMY BENTHAM

Jeremy Bentham (1748–1832) was the founder of the ethical doctrine now known as utilitarianism. He began his long life during the reign of King George II and died in the year of the Reform Bill that extended the franchise to virtually all of middle-class England. He lived through the American Revolution, the French Revolution, the Napoleonic wars, and the rise of parliamentary government in England, and he nearly survived into the reign of Queen Victoria. He was the godfather of John Stuart Mill, son of his friend and colleague James Mill. John Stuart Mill was, in his own turn, the godfather of Bertrand Russell, the great English philosopher who near the end of his own long and distinguished life led the British campaign for nuclear disarmament in the 1960s. So in three generations of great English philosophers, we move from the mid-eighteenth-century world of wigs, carriages, and kings, to the mid-twentieth-century world of jets, nuclear weapons, and popular democracy.

Bentham's primary concern as a philosopher was with legal and social reform. The law in the eighteenth century was a crazy quilt of precedents, quibbles, hanging offenses, and rank injustices. Several of Bentham's books were devoted to the attempt to sort things out and find some rational system of principles to put in place of the tangle that had grown up over so many centuries. He hoped that his simple, intuitively appealing principle of utility—the Greatest Happiness of the Greatest Number—would serve as the basis for a thoroughgoing reform of the law.

Whenever we face hard choices, Bentham tells us, we can translate an impossible moral dilemma into a problem of addition and subtraction. For the young man, the choice is between staying home with his parents and leaving. He adds up all the pleasure and pain (negative values for pain, of course) that anybody in the situation will experience as the result of his staying and compares it with the total pleasure and pain that everyone will experience as a result of his leaving home. He then chooses the alternative with the highest positive total (or, if it is one of those "least of evils" situations, the alternative with the smallest negative total). For example, suppose that the young man desperately wants to leave home. Then we can assume that he will suffer great pain if he must stay, and he will gain great pleasure if he goes. Let us also assume that his parents would like him to stay at home, but they are not dead set on it. They will manage all right if he leaves. Now we have great pain plus moderate pleasure on the side of staying and great pleasure plus moderate pain on the side of going. Obviously, this adds up to a decision to go.

A great many objections can be raised to utilitarianism, and I am about to raise several of the more serious ones. But before we start chopping this theory down, it is worth taking a few moments to look at its very considerable strengths. In the first place, utilitarianism assumes that everyone wants to be happy, and it is hard to argue with that. But even more important, utilitarianism explains happiness in terms that everyone can understand. It doesn't say that happiness is oneness with the infinite, or self-fulfillment, or the integration of adult roles with childhood ego formation, or what have you. It says that happiness is pleasure, unhappiness is pain, and the more pleasure or the less pain the better.

Nor does utilitarianism demand strange, painful sacrifices from its believers. Kant believed, for example, that we should keep our promises and tell the truth no matter who gets hurt. That is a dark saying, fraught with potentiality for terrible choices where lives are lost or hideous pain inflicted simply because someone will not violate an absolute moral rule. But Bentham says nothing of that sort. By all means lie, he says, if the total pain produced by the truth is greater than that produced by the lie. Make sure to add in the side effects of the lie, such as the likelihood that the next time you tell the truth it won't be believed. But when all those long-term, short-term, direct, and indirect effects have been calculated, then just choose the course promising the greatest happiness for the greatest number of people.

The most impressive strength of utilitarianism is its ability to transform seemingly impossible problems of moral deliberation into manageable empirical problems of investigation and addition. To see what that means, imagine that we lived a long time ago in an agricultural society which had not yet discovered geometry. Each year, as the flood waters from the river

To Leave Home or Not to Leave Home: A Utilitarian Calculation

If I Leave	Units of Pleasure	If I Don't Leave	Units of Pleasure
1. Independence	+1000	1. Lack of independence	−1000
2. Loneliness	− 200	2. Parents' happiness	+2000
3. Parents' unhappiness	−1000	3. No personal growth	− 600
4. New experiences	+ 350	4. Family wrangling	− 250
5. Setting a good example for younger sister	+ 400	5. Financial burden on parents	− 400
The utility of leaving	+ 550	The utility of staying	− 250
+550 IS GREATER THAN −250. THEREFORE, I LEAVE.			

According to Bentham, the rational person will choose the alternative that offers the greatest total of pleasure. Does anyone ever make an important decision this way? Would you?

receded, it would become necessary to divide up the land again for the spring planting. The plots all must be triangular (owing to some religious belief, we may suppose). The high priest would stake out each family's land, and then the arguing would begin over whose plot was bigger, and who had been slighted in the dividing up. The wise men would gather, great deliberations would ensue, with much prayer and meditation, and in the end no one would really be satisfied with the high priest's decisions. Now just think what it would mean, in such a society, for someone to discover the simple geometric theorem that the area of a triangle is equal to one-half the base times the height. All those moral and religious disputes would be dissolved in an instant into a process of calculation. The royal surveyor would just measure the bases of the family plots, multiply by their heights (the plots', not the families'), and then make adjustments until each family had the same area. It would put the royal moral philosopher and the royal priest out of business.

Well, Bentham had hopes that his Greatest Happiness Principle would do the same for the modern wizards who in his own society did the job of the ancient priests and moral philosophers—namely, the judges and lawyers. He believed that rational legislators, with the principle of utility to guide them, could replace the hideous tangle of laws and punishments of the English common law with a single reasonable schedule of punishments designed to produce the greatest happiness for the greatest number. Where the legislators

Egypt: Surveying. Measuring of fields by royal supervisor and his staff. Cords are being used as measure units. The ancient Egyptians were forced to re-survey their fields each year after the Nile River overflowed its banks. This practical problem led them to make important advances in mathematics. (Undated fresco. Corbis–Bettmann.)

lacked enough facts to make a sensible decision, instead of digging around in their law books for precedents and corollary cases, they could go out and collect some facts to settle the matter.

Utilitarianism has probably had more words written about it than all the other moral theories put together. It is a clear, simple, natural-sounding moral philosophy, and it has a thousand things wrong with it as a theory! That is a perfect formula for a philosophical argument. Two sorts of objections turn up over and over again in philosophical discussions. First, critics say that although utilitarianism looks clear and simple, it is actually so confused that we can't tell exactly what it says. And, second, these same critics argue that even after we have decided what utilitarianism says, we find that it tells us to do things that most of us would consider deeply immoral. Let us take a look at both of these objections.

What does utilitarianism say? Very simple: maximize happiness. But what exactly does that mean? The most natural answer is, add up all the pleasure experienced by all the people in the world, subtract all the pain they suffer, and that is the total. Then anything that increases the total is good, anything that decreases it is bad, and if two actions promise to increase the total, the one that offers a bigger increase is just that much better. What could be clearer?

Ah well. A little philosophy teaches us that a trap very often lurks in even the simplest-looking statement. If *total* happiness is all that counts, then a world with a *billion* slightly happy people will be morally better than a world with a *million* extremely happy people. The point is that if the very happy people are only five hundred times happier than the marginally happy people, then one billion times the small happiness in the first world will be a bigger total than one million times the tremendous happiness in the second world. Something is obviously wrong with that conclusion. In an already overcrowded world, it makes no sense to go on increasing the population as

☞ **Act Utilitarianism/Rule Utilitarianism** Utilitarianism is the moral theory that holds that everyone—private individuals or lawmaking governments—should always seek to produce the greatest happiness for the greatest number of people. *Act Utilitarianism* asserts that each of us should use this rule in choosing every single act that we perform, regardless of whether we are private citizens or legislators making general laws for a whole society. *Rule Utilitarianism* says that governments should use this rule in choosing the general laws they enact, but then should simply treat individuals fairly according to the existing rules, with like cases handled in a like manner.

long as each additional person can be said to experience a slight balance of pleasure over pain. Surely Bentham wasn't merely arguing for a population explosion.

So maybe what he really meant was to maximize the *average* happiness experienced by the people already on this earth. That makes a good deal more sense. A world of a million very happy people is obviously preferable to a world of a billion marginally happy people, because in the first world, the *level* of happiness—in other words, the average—is higher. And it is the level of happiness we are really interested in.

But once again, serious problems arise. Suppose we can make some people very happy indeed by making other people miserable. That isn't an implausible hypothesis at all. Slavery is a social system which lays the burden of work and suffering on one group—the slaves—so that another group—the

Scene at an 18th century trial. Bentham hoped to correct the abuses of the English legal system. (Undated illustration. Corbis–Bettmann.)

masters—can lead easy, comfortable lives. (So is capitalism, but we shall get to that later.) Is Bentham really in favor of slavery?

Bentham has an answer, of sorts. His principle, he claims, calls for "the greatest happiness of all those whose interest is in question." Because everyone (even a slave) is someone whose interest is in question, it follows that utilitarianism calls for the greatest possible happiness for everyone, not just the greatest happiness for the slave-owners, or the capitalists, or the rulers. Now the trouble with this interpretation of the Principle of Utility is that on closer examination, it turns out not to be any sort of rule at all.

Sometimes, life offers me a way to make everybody happier at the same time, and obviously when a chance like that comes along, I take it. Too often, life offers me a way to make everybody unhappier at the same time, and if I have any sense at all, I stay away from chances like that. But most of the time, what I do will make some people happier and other people unhappier. Remember the young man trying to decide whether to leave his parents? His first choice, to stay home, makes his parents happier and him unhappier. His second choice, to leave, makes him happier and his parents unhappier. There just isn't any way to make all of them happier at the same time. That is precisely why it is a hard case. Now, we don't need Bentham to tell us what to do on those rare occasions when we can make everyone happier simultaneously. But utilitarianism is supposed to give us a rule, a method, for handling just the hard-to-decide cases in which one person's happiness has to be balanced off against another person's unhappiness. Plausible as "the greatest happiness for the greatest number" sounds, it doesn't work out in practice to be a rule that is going to settle any hard cases for us.

Suppose we go back therefore to the notion of the greatest average happiness. (Notice, by the way, that if you keep the population stable, working for the greatest average happiness amounts to the same thing as working for the greatest total happiness, so that is probably what Bentham had in mind.) How does that stand up as a rule for deciding what to do? At least it is unambiguous; if we have enough information to predict the outcomes of our actions, then we can add up the pleasures, subtract the pains, divide by the total population, and get some sort of average. But now we run into the second sort of objection to utilitarianism—namely, that it tells us to do things that seem immoral.

Once again, the problem is making some people suffer so that others may be happy. Let me sketch out a bizarre example that will help to make this point. Suppose that Americans, like the ancient Romans, positively enjoyed watching people being tortured. (Naturally, such an assumption is totally contrary to the real facts, because American taste in movies, television shows, and novels shows that we are all kindly, peace-loving, sympathetic creatures who hate the sight of violence!) Now Bentham will obviously believe that torture is an evil to the person who suffers it, for torture is painful, and pain is evil. But the pleasure that a group of sadists gets from watching the torture is good, for pleasure, says Bentham, is good. So for a utilitarian, torture can be justified when the total pleasure produced outweighs the total pain produced, including side effects, long-run effects, and so forth. What is more, if torture produces, in total and on balance, greater happiness than any other alternative open to us, then it is the positively right thing to do, according to utilitarianism.

We shall therefore institute a new TV show called "Torture of the Week." This is a live show in which real victims really do get tortured. (Sadists get little or no pleasure from watching simulated torture.) The victims are simply snatched off the street by force (no one except a masochist is going to offer himself as a victim, and real sadists don't enjoy watching masochists undergo torture). According to utilitarianism, if there are enough viewers who are ecstatic at the sight of this torture, then their pleasure must outweigh the pain suffered by the victim. And if no other show on television has anything resembling its high ratings, then we can assume that putting on the torture show is not only justified, but positively morally obligatory!

Just to handle an obvious objection, let us also assume that a board of social psychologists concludes that the torture show does not increase the probability of violent crime in the society. Indeed, it may even decrease such crime, by offering an outlet for sadistic desires. In short, assume that from any point of view, this torture show meets the criterion of the Principle of Utility.

What is wrong with this proposal? Don't tell me that there aren't enough people around who would enjoy the show. The point of the example was to show that according to utilitarianism the show *would* be right if there *were* such people in America. Besides, we could always increase the pleasure product by beaming the show overseas so that sadists all over the world could watch it. And don't tell me that the pain of the victim's suffering outweighs the pleasure of millions of sadistic viewers. That is implausible, and what is more, I can always adjust the torture inflicted on the victim downward until the pleasure of the viewers outweighs it.

No, what really convinces me that my proposal is immoral (and I suspect many of you feel the same way) is that society has *no right* to make one man or woman suffer for the mere amusement of others. This is one of those cases, something inside me says, where adding up pleasures and pains is the wrong way to find out what we ought to do. If America's sadists have to suffer the pain and frustration of losing their favorite show, then so much the worse for them!

We have opened up a very large and complicated subject with this appeal to the notion of *rights,* and a few words can only begin to indicate some of its ins and outs. Nevertheless, let's explore if for a bit, just to see what makes Bentham's pleasure-pain calculus seem such an inadequate expression of our moral convictions. To begin with, we must not go overboard and say that society *never* has the right to derive benefits from the suffering of one of its members. Leaving aside obvious but controversial cases like wars, we can simply recall that every time a major bridge or tunnel is built, several workers lose their lives. It may seem callous when we put it into words, but all of us employ a rough utilitarian calculation in judging the social desirability of large-scale public works. We try hard to minimize the loss of life in heavy construction, but we refuse to bring building to a dead halt simply because we know that men and women lose their lives on the job. If a project is going to cost hundreds of lives, we will probably veto it. If only a few are likely to be killed, we will give it the go-ahead. Aren't we weighing one person's life against the convenience of the motorists who will use the bridge? How does that differ from weighing the pain of the victim against the pleasure of the sadistic viewers?

Well, one answer is that the construction workers choose voluntarily to work on the bridge, knowing that it is a risky job, whereas the torture victim is forced into his or her role. That certainly is part of the difference, for I imagine we would take a *somewhat* different view of the show if we knew that the victims were volunteers.

But there still seem to be other differences. The motorist benefits from the work of the construction worker, to be sure. And the worker is injured (suffers) while performing that work. But that suffering isn't the *object* of the motorist's pleasure. The sadist, on the other hand, takes pleasure in the victim's pain. Now, it seems to me that there are some pleasures that are evil in and of themselves. They are bad pleasures, pleasures which people should not have; and pleasure taken in the pain of another person is one of those evil pleasures. So the torture example suggests, at least to me, that Bentham's original assumption was wrong. Not all pleasures are equal, save for quantity or intensity. And "good" does not simply mean "pleasant." So when we perform Bentham's social arithmetic, adding up pleasures and pains in order to evaluate a social policy, we most certainly ought not to put the sadist's pleasure on the plus side. He or she doesn't have a right to that pleasure, and if it is to be weighed at all, it ought to be put on the negative side with the pains. (Needless to say, there may be some pains which ought to go on the positive side. As you can see, this subject gets more and more complicated the deeper into it you go.)

It may even be, as Immanuel Kant thought, that there are some considerations more important than pleasure and pain—considerations of justice and freedom. Kant would argue that the torture show degrades both the victim and the viewers, that it treats them—in his famous phrase—as means merely and not at as ends-in-themselves.

But when all is said and done, when examples like the torture show have been brought forward to refute utilitarianism, when the unclarities in the very meaning of the principle have been exposed to view, there still remains a natural appeal of Bentham's theory that will not go away. In

Chapter 3, when we meet John Stuart Mill, Bentham's most famous follower, we shall try once again to discover the kernel of truth that seems to lie inside the moral philosophy of utilitarianism.

❧ The Theory of the Healthy Personality

The Greeks spoke of the search for the principles of the good life. The Romans had a phrase, *mens sana in corpore sano*—a sound mind in a sound body. Karl Marx wrote of "alienation" and a future of "unalienated labor." Psychoanalysts today talk about an integrated ego. The idea is essentially the same in each case, even though the emphasis, the underlying theory, or the viewpoint differs. For ages, men and women have been seeking a style of life and spirit that achieves a wholeness, an integration, an authenticity of mind and body, of reason, passion, and desire. These days, the search is left to psychologists and the religious—at least in England and America—but in the tradition of Western thought, it is philosophers who have given the most sustained and thoughtful attention to the search for the good life.

Everyone who has reflected for even a short while on the problem of achieving an integrated, fulfilled, virtuous life agrees that the key to a solution lies in the discovery of the proper internal order of the self itself (what the Greeks call the "soul" or *psyche*). And, needless to say, there are almost as many theories about the precise nature of that desirable inner order as there are writers on the subject. But on one fundamental issue, the philosophers of the good life divide into two distinct camps. One group, which includes Stoics like Marcus Aurelius, claims that inner peace and harmony can be achieved regardless of the character of the society in which we live, regardless of the external circumstances of peace or war, tyranny or justice, health or disease. The other group emphasizes the interplay between the individual personality and the larger society, claiming that not even a wise man or woman can be truly happy save in a truly just and virtuous society. In this latter category we find Plato, Aristotle, Karl Marx, and such modern psychological theorists as Eric Fromm and Erik Erikson. You have already had an opportunity to read a bit of what Marcus Aurelius wrote about the good life. In this section, we shall explore the view of Plato and others that the inner harmony of the self must be integrated with a proper order of society before a truly good life can be achieved.

In philosophy, we return to the same great books again and again. In Chapter 1, you read a selection from an early section of Plato's immortal Dialogue, the *Republic*. Now we shall jump ahead more than a hundred pages to the point at which Plato pulls together the long argument he has been developing. The official subject of the *Republic* is a search for a definition of "justice," a word to which Plato gives a broader meaning than we do today. Plato suggests two analogies or comparisons as aids in discovering the nature of justice, or true morality. The first analogy is between the soul (that is, the personality) and the body. He argues that we can speak of a healthy body and also of a healthy soul, of a diseased body and also of a diseased soul. Health of the body rests on a proper harmony or order of the bodily elements, and health of the soul in like manner consists of the correct ordering of the psychic elements. In this Dialogue, Plato distinguishes three functional parts of the soul. (I say "in this Dialogue" because Plato didn't have a fully worked out theory of psychology, and in other Dialogues he divided the human personality up in other ways. Don't just memorize "the parts of the soul in Plato"—try to see what he is driving at, and put his thought into your own words if you can.) The three elements are (1) reason, or the power to deliberate, compare alternatives, suppress unwise impulses, and make sensible choices; (2) the "spirited element," or the aggressive, warlike, willful part of one's personality; and (3) appetite or desire. Each of these elements has a role to play in the healthy, virtuous soul, but each must learn its proper function and perform it willingly and in harmony with the other elements. Reason must rule, governing the spirited element and directing its aggression in wise, nondestructive ways. The healthy, necessary appetites must be regulated by reason and satisfied in the proper proportion and to the appropriate degree. Too much indulgence of one or many desires may produce superficial and short-lived pleasure but in the end causes inner conflict and unhappiness. A well-integrated soul is a smoothly functioning whole in which each element performs its proper function and all together maintain balance, health, and true happiness.

Aristotle and his pupil, Alexander. (Undated engraving. Corbis–Bettmann.)

The second of Plato's analogies is between the individual soul and the society as a whole. Just as there are several elements in the soul with special functions and a just order of subordination to one another, so there are several classes of citizens in the society with special functions and a proper social relationship to one another. The wisest citizens must rule in society, as reason does in the soul, for they possess at one and the same time the knowledge of what is truly good for the society and the rational self-control to resist the temptation of harmful desires.

In this passage from the *Republic,* Socrates is summarizing his argument. Thrasymachus and most of the others have dropped out of the conversation, and there remain only two young men, Glaucon and Adeimantus (in real life, Plato's older brothers). Socrates speaks first.

The Rule of Reason

And so, after a stormy passage, we have reached the land. We are fairly agreed that the same three elements exist alike in the state and in the individual soul.

That is so.

Does it not follow at once that state and individual will be wise or brave by virtue of the same element in each and in the same way? Both will possess in the same manner any quality that makes for excellence.

That must be true.

Then it applies to justice: we shall conclude that a man is just in the same way that a state was just. And we have surely not forgotten that justice in the state meant that each of the three orders in it was doing its own proper work. So we may henceforth bear in mind that each one of us likewise will be a just person, fulfilling his proper function, only if the several parts of our nature fulfill theirs.

Certainly.

And it will be the business of reason to rule with wisdom and forethought on behalf of the entire soul; while the spirited element ought to act as its subordinate and ally. The two will be brought into accord, as we said earlier, by that combination of mental and bodily training which will tune up one string of the instrument and relax the other, nourishing the reasoning part on the study of noble literature and allaying the other's wildness by harmony and rhythm. When both have been thus nurtured and trained to know their own functions, they must be set in command over the appetites, which form the greater part of each man's soul and are by nature insatiably covetous. They must keep watch lest this part, by battening on the pleasures that are called bodily, should grow so great and powerful that it will no longer keep to its own work but will try to enslave the others and usurp a dominion to which it has no right, thus turning the whole of life upside down. At the same time, those two together will be the best of guardians for the entire soul and for the body against

all enemies from without: the one will take counsel, while the other
will do battle, following its ruler's commands and by its own bravery
giving effect to the ruler's designs.

Yes, that is all true.

And so we call an individual brave in virtue of this spirited
part of his nature, when, in spite of pain or pleasure, it holds fast
to the injunctions of reason about what he ought or ought not to be
afraid of.

True.

And wise in virtue of that small part which rules and issues
these injunctions, possessing as it does the knowledge of what is good
for each of the three elements and for all of them in common.

Certainly.

And, again, temperate by reason of the unanimity and concord of
all three, when there is no internal conflict between the ruling element
and its two subjects, but all are agreed that reason should be ruler.

Yes, that is an exact account of temperance, whether in the
state or in the individual.

Finally, a man will be just by observing the principles we have
so often stated.

Necessarily.

Now is there any indistinctness in our vision of justice, that
might make it seem somehow different from what we found it to be
in the state?

I don't think so.

Because, if we have any lingering doubt, we might make sure by
comparing it with some commonplace notions. Suppose, for instance,
that a sum of money were entrusted to our state or to an individual
of corresponding character and training, would anyone imagine that
such a person would be specially likely to embezzle it?

No.

And would he not be incapable of sacrilege and theft, or of
treachery to friend or country; never false to an oath or any other
compact; the last to be guilty of adultery or of neglecting parents or
the due service of the gods?

Yes.

And the reason for all this is that each part of his nature is exercising its proper function, of ruling or of being ruled.

Yes, exactly.

Are you satisfied, then, that justice is the power which produces
states or individuals of whom that is true, or must we look further?

There is no need; I am quite satisfied.

And so our dream has come true—I mean the inkling we had
that, by some happy chance, we had lighted upon a rudimentary
form of justice from the very moment when we set about founding

our commonwealth. Our principle that the born shoemaker or carpenter had better stick to his trade turns out to have been an adumbration of justice; and that is why it has helped us. But in reality justice, though evidently analogous to this principle, is not a matter of external behavior, but of the inward self and of attending to all that is, in the fullest sense, a man's proper concern. The just man does not allow the several elements in his soul to usurp one another's functions; he is indeed one who sets his house in order, by self-mastery and discipline coming to be at peace with himself, and bringing into tune those three parts, like the terms in proportion of a musical scale, the highest and lowest notes and the mean between them, with all the intermediate intervals. Only when he has linked these parts together in well-tempered harmony and has made himself one man instead of many, will he be ready to go about whatever he may have to do, whether it be making money and satisfying bodily wants, or business transactions, or the affairs of state. In all these fields when he speaks of just and honorable conduct, he will mean the behavior that helps to produce and to preserve this habit of mind; and by wisdom he will mean the knowledge which presides over such conduct. Any action which tends to break down this habit will be for him unjust; and the notions governing it he will call ignorance and folly.

That is perfectly true, Socrates.

Good, said I. I believe we should not be thought altogether mistaken, if we claimed to have discovered the just man and the just state, and wherein their justice consists.

Indeed we should not.

Shall we make that claim, then?

Yes, we will.

So be it, said I. Next, I suppose, we have to consider injustice.

Evidently.

This must surely be a sort of civil strife among the three elements, whereby they usurp and encroach upon one another's functions and some part of the soul rises up in rebellion against the whole, claiming a supremacy to which it has no right because its nature fits it only to be the servant of the ruling principle. Such turmoil and aberration we shall, I think, identify with injustice, intemperance, cowardice, ignorance, and in a word with all wickedness.

Exactly.

And now that we know the nature of justice and injustice, we can be equally clear about what is meant by acting justly and again by unjust action and wrongdoing.

How do you mean?

Plainly, they are exactly analogous to those wholesome and unwholesome activities which respectively produce a healthy or unhealthy condition in the body; in the same way just and unjust conduct produce a just or unjust character. Justice is produced in the soul, like health in the body, by establishing the elements concerned in their natural relations of control and subordination, whereas injustice is like disease and means that this natural order is inverted.

Quite so.

It appears, then that virtue is as it were the health and comeliness and well-being of the soul, as wickedness is disease, deformity, and weakness.

True.

And also that virtue and wickedness are brought about by one's way of life, honorable or disgraceful.

That follows.

So now it only remains to consider which is the more profitable course; to do right and live honourably and be just, whether or not anyone knows what manner of man you are, or to do wrong and be unjust, provided that you can escape the chastisement which might make you a better man.

But really, Socrates, it seems to me ridiculous to ask that question now that the nature of justice and injustice has been brought to light. People think that all the luxury and wealth and power in the world cannot make life worth living when the bodily constitution is going to rack and ruin; and are we to believe that, when the very principle whereby we live is deranged and corrupted, life will be worth living so long as a man can do as he will, and wills to do anything rather than to free himself from vice and wrongdoing and to win justice and virtue?

Yes, I replied, it is a ridiculous question.

For the first two millennia of Western philosophy, the wise understanding of the human condition was the province of philosophers and poets. In the past century, however, their intuitive insight has been supplemented, though not supplanted, by the systematic scientific investigations of countless theorists of human personality. Plato's brilliant recognition of the analogy between the health of the body and the health of the mind has been embodied in a branch of medicine called psychiatry, whose practitioners study the forms, causes, symptoms, and cures for what we now routinely call "mental illness." With psychiatrists, as with philosophers, there is a fundamental split between those who examine the individual psyche in separation from its social setting and those who study the connections between individual mental health or illness and the network of social and institutional relationships which surround the patient.

Sigmund Freud (1856–1939), the founder of modern psychoanalytic theory and practice, tended toward the first method of investigation. Although he wrote several provocative essays on the psychic roots of social phenomena, his

> **Identity Crisis** A term invented by the psychoanalyst Erik Erikson
> to refer to the period of instability, uncertainty, and personality formation
> through which teenagers pass in societies like ours. Erikson intended to
> suggest, by the term, that the period is one of genuine flux and indeter-
> minacy, with the outcome—a healthy, coherent adult personality—hang-
> ing in the balance.

primary interest was in the inner dynamics of the psyche itself. Among all those
who have followed Freud's lead in developing a science of psychiatry, perhaps
no figure comes closer to Plato both in spirit and fineness of sensibility than the
psychoanalyst, historian, author, and philosopher Erik H. Erikson (1902–
1994). Erikson sought to build on Freud's investigation of the infantile stages
of personality development by analyzing the later stages through which each of
us passes in coming either well or badly to maturity and old age. It was Erikson who actually coined the now familiar phrase *identity crisis* in an essay on
the emotional upheaval that so many young men and women go through in
late adolescence and early adulthood. But Erikson was also interested in the
continuing development of personality later in life. He discovered from his
clinical practice with patients of all ages that as an individual grows through
infancy, childhood, adolescence, young adulthood, mature adulthood, and old
age, he or she faces a series of turning points, or crises. At each stage, the individual may resolve the crisis successfully and grow into a stronger, more fulfilled person, or fail to handle the crisis well and bear ever after the scars of that
failure. In old age, those who have lived the cycle of childhood, adulthood, and
maturity well achieve thereby an inner harmony which Erikson calls "ego
integrity." It is very much like what Plato calls wisdom. This ego integrity gives
meaning to the life that has been lived and permits the individual to face
impending death with acceptance, dignity, and pride. Here is Erikson's description of this final stage of the life cycle.

ERIK H.
ERICKSON,
*Childhood
and Society*

Ego Integrity
Only in him who in some way has taken care of things and people and
has adapted himself to the triumphs and disappointments adherent to
being the originator of others or the generator of products and ideas—
only in him may gradually ripen the fruit of these seven stages. I know
no better word for it than ego integrity. Lacking a clear definition, I
shall point to a few constituents of this state of mind. It is the ego's
accrued assurance of its proclivity for order and meaning. It is a post-
narcissistic love of the human ego—not of the self—as an experience
which conveys some world order and spiritual sense, no matter how
dearly paid for. It is the acceptance of one's one and only life cycle as

something that had to be and that, by necessity, permitted of no substitutions; it thus means a new, a different love of one's parents. It is a comradeship with the ordering ways of distant times and different pursuits, as expressed in the simple products and sayings of such times and pursuits. Although aware of the relativity of all the various life styles which have given meaning to human striving, the possessor of integrity is ready to defend the dignity of his own life style against all physical and economic threats. For he knows that an individual life is the accidental coincidence of but one life cycle with but one segment of history; and that for him all human integrity stands or falls with the one style of integrity of which he partakes. The style of integrity developed by his culture or civilization thus becomes the "patrimony of his soul," the seal of his moral paternity of himself. . . . In such final consolidation, death loses its sting.

The lack or loss of this accrued ego integration is signified by fear of death; the one and only life cycle is not accepted as the ultimate of life. Despair expresses the feeling that the time is now short, too short for the attempt to start another life and to try out alternate roads to integrity. Disgust hides despair, if often only in the form of "a thousand little disgusts" which do not add up to one big remorse. . . .

Each individual, to become a mature adult, must to a sufficient degree develop all the ego qualities mentioned, so that a wise Indian, a true gentlemen, and mature peasant share and recognize in one another the final state of integrity. But each cultural entity, to develop the particular style of integrity suggested by its historical place, utilizes a particular combination of these conflicts, along with specific provocations and prohibitions of infantile sexuality. Infantile conflicts become creative only if sustained by the firm support of cultural institutions and of the special leader classes representing them. In order to approach or experience integrity, the individual must know how to be a follower of image bearers in religion and in politics, in the economic order and in technology, in aristocratic living and in the arts and sciences. Ego integrity, therefore, implies an emotional integration which permits participation by followership as well as acceptance of the responsibility of leadership.

Webster's Dictionary is kind enough to help us complete this outline in a circular fashion. Trust (the first of our ego values) is here defined as "the assured reliance on another's integrity," the last of our values. I suspect that Webster had business in mind rather than babies, credit rather than faith. But the formulation stands, and it seems possible to further paraphrase the relation of adult integrity and infantile trust by saying that healthy children will not fear life if their elders have integrity enough not to fear death.

❦ The Feminist Critique of Ethical Theory

Thus far, we have been looking at three different sorts of questions that philosophers have discussed under the general heading of "ethics" over the past 2,000 years. But different as these questions are, the discussions all have one thing in common: they are carried on by *men*. Indeed, as you will discover in the remaining chapters of this book, the Western philosophical tradition is almost exclusively a male tradition, a series of dialogues, treatises, essays, poems, and critiques written by men. Although there have been a handful of exceptions to this general rule over the centuries, it is really only during the present century, and more particularly during the last thirty or forty years, that the philosophical arguments and reflections of women have come to be an important part of the total philosophical scene.

Does this make a difference? Is the philosophy of the Western tradition not merely written principally by men but also significantly *masculine* in its tone, content, form of reasoning, aims, concerns, questions, and theoretical bent? If the answer is *yes,* then the entire tradition may turn out to be fatally one-sided, despite the enormous range of alternative views expressed within it. Are we in the position of a student of religion who looks at Catholicism, Methodism, Presbyterianism, Unitarianism, and Baptist Fundamentalism and thinks he has surveyed the entire spectrum of religious experience, not noticing that these are all variations of just one religious tradition, Christianity?

Clearly, an entire Introduction to Philosophy could be written to answer this question, for it arises in every branch of the subject. If we cannot do that, then at least we must take a look at one such challenge to the standard male-voiced tradition, in order to enable you to ask this question at each stage in your introductory survey of philosophy.

Needless to say, there is nothing resembling agreement among the many women who have written philosophical critiques of the Western tradition from the point of view of a woman viewing a predominantly male tradition. Some feminist philosophers argue that the experience of women is fundamentally different from that of men, because women are treated differently from men virtually from the moment they are born. Our society—indeed, it would appear most if not all societies—has quite different expectations for women, with regard both to their inborn natures and to the social roles they will fill. We give a little girl a doll for her birthday and a little boy a truck, without first looking to see which toy each is more likely actually to enjoy. We speak to little girls and little boys in different voices, we praise them for different sorts of behavior, we expect different responses from them, we encourage in them different expectations about their futures. Small wonder, then, many have argued, that women and men grow up experiencing the world in different ways, reacting to it in different ways, *even reasoning about it in different ways.*

So, those thinkers conclude, philosophical theories about how we perceive the world, how we should act in the world, how we can reason about the world, what we can and cannot know about the world, will be one-sided and incomplete if they are based solely on the experiences, insights, and reflections of men. It would be as foolish to think that men alone could understand the full spectrum of the human experience as it would be to suppose that slave-owners' accounts of slavery could tell the whole story, or that factory-owners' accounts of industrial organization exhausted the truth about what it is like to work on the assembly line.

A second group of feminist theorists—not necessarily disagreeing with the first, but definitely saying something different—tells us that women are innately different from men, over and above the way in which they are treated in any particular society, and hence they have ways of experiencing the world, ways of conceiving it and thinking about it, ways of relating to other persons which are *constitutionally* different from those of men. On this view, even if society were to start treating men and women in exactly similar ways (however unlikely that might be), women would *still* have access to experiences, insights, points of view that are closed of to men.

Let us first take a look at a programmatic statement by Alison Jaggar entitled "Feminist Ethics: Some Issues for the Nineties." In the opening pages of her essay, Jaggar offers three criteria or tests of whether an ethical theory should be considered "Feminist." Because, as she says, her characterization is "quite loose," it will help us to get clearer about what Feminist ethics is without prejudging any of the important issues that Feminist ethical theorists are currently debating.

Feminist approaches to ethics are distinguished by their explicit commitment to rethinking ethics with a view to correcting whatever forms of male bias it may contain. Feminist ethics, as these approaches are often called collectively, seeks to identify and challenge all those ways, overt but more often and more perniciously covert, in which western ethics has excluded women or rationalized their subordination. Its goal is to offer both practical guides to action and theoretical understandings of the nature of morality that do not, overtly or covertly, subordinate the interests of any woman or group of women to the interests of any other individual or group.

While those who practice feminist ethics are united by a shared project, they diverge widely in their views as to how this project may be accomplished. These divergences result from a variety of philosophical differences, including differing conceptions of feminism itself, a perennially contested concept. The inevitability of such disagreement means that feminist ethics cannot be identified in terms of a specific range of topics, methods or orthodoxies. For example, it is

ALISON M. JAGGAR,
Feminist Ethics: Some Issues for the Nineties

a mistake, though one to which even some feminists occasionally have succumbed, to identify feminist ethics with any of the following: putting women's interests first; focusing exclusively on so-called women's issues; accepting women (or feminists) as moral experts or authorities; substituting "female" (or "feminine") for "male" (or "masculine") values; or extrapolating directly from women's experience.

Even though my initial characterization of feminist ethics is quite loose, it does suggest certain minimum conditions of adequacy for any approach to ethics that purports to be feminist.

1. Within the present social context, in which women remain systematically subordinated, a feminist approach to ethics must offer a guide to actions that will tend to subvert rather than reinforce this subordination. Thus, such an approach must be practical, transitional and nonutopian, an extension of politics rather than a retreat from it. It must be sensitive, for instance, to the symbolic meanings as well as the practical consequences of any actions that we take as gendered subjects in a male dominated society, and it must also provide the conceptual resources for identifying and evaluating the varieties of resistance and struggle in which women, particularly, have tended to engage. It must recognize the often unnoticed ways in which women and other members of the underclass have refused cooperation and opposed domination, while acknowledging the inevitability of collusion and the impossibility of totally clean hands.

2. Since so much of women's struggle has been in the kitchen and the bedroom, as well as in the parliamentary chamber and on the factory floor, a second requirement for feminist ethics is that it should be equipped to handle moral issues in both the so-called public and private domains. It must be able to provide guidance on issues of intimate relations, such as affection and sexuality, which, until quite recently, were largely ignored by modern moral theory. In so doing, it cannot assume that moral concepts developed originally for application to the public realm, concepts such as impartiality or exploitation, are automatically applicable to the private realm. Similarly, an approach to ethics that is adequate for feminism must also provide appropriate guidance for activity in the public realm, for dealing with large numbers of people, including strangers.

3. Finally, feminist ethics must take the moral experience of all women seriously, though not, of course, uncritically. Though what is *feminist* will often turn out to be very different from

what is *feminine*, a basic respect for women's moral experience is necessary to acknowledging women's capacities as moralists and to countering traditional stereotypes of women as less than full moral agents, as childlike or "natural." Furthermore, as Okin, among others, has argued, empirical claims about differences in the moral experience of women and men make it impossible to assume that any approach to ethics will be unanimously accepted if it fails to consult the moral experience of women. Additionally, it seems plausible to suppose that women's distinctive social experience may make them especially perceptive regarding the implications of domination, especially gender domination, and especially well equipped to detect the male bias that has been shown to pervade so much of male-authored western moral theory.

On the surface, at least, these conditions of adequacy for feminist ethics are quite minimal—although I believe that fulfilling them would have radical consequences for ethics. I think most feminist, and perhaps even many nonfeminist philosophers would be likely to find the general statement of these conditions relatively uncontroversial, but that inevitably there will be sharp disagreement over when the conditions have been met. Even feminists are likely to differ over, for instance, just what are women's interests and when they have been neglected, what is resistance to domination and which aspects of which women's moral experience are worth developing and in which directions.*

All three of Jaggar's criteria deserve careful attention. Notice that for her, ethics is active, engaged, political. She wants those who think and write about ethics also to be willing to act in the world, to engage with life rather than to withdraw to an ivory tower of reflection. Note too that for Jaggar, Feminist ethics is engaged on the side of the oppressed, the left-out, the subordinated. Ethicists must not tell themselves that they are neutral, above the battle, professionals with no personal commitments.

Jaggar also makes it clear, under her third heading, that although she insists on taking the moral experience of *all* women seriously, she is also prepared to evaluate that experience in order to judge for herself what its significance is for ethical theory.

But all of this is rather general and programmatic. What would a serious Feminist discussion of ethical issues look like in practice? How do these criteria translate into real moral reflection and insight? The next selection will give us some idea of the answers to those questions. Mary Raugust's short essay on "Feminist Ethics and Workplace Values" very nicely illustrates

Journal of Social Philosophy 20, 1-2 (Spring/Fall 1989): 91-107.

Jaggar's three points. Notice that Raugust's reflections grow out of a practical experience, the Kennedy Aging Project that she directed.

MARY C.
RAUGUST,
*Feminist Ethics
and Workplace
Values*

A striking phenomenon in contemporary managerial and professional employment is the discontent of some notably talented and successful women employees. This discontent sometimes culminates in leaving a "good job" to search for a more satisfying career direction. The specific discontent at issue here arises from discomfort experienced in the values demonstrated in workplace arrangements.

Prevailing—and patriarchal—values of autonomy, rights, and individualistic justice are manifest in many or most workplace arrangements, in the ways that co-workers regard and relate to each other and in the ways that work products are measured and esteemed. In contrast, a feminist ethics based on cooperation, relationship, and interdependent nurturance may engender workplace arrangements that are more sustainable for women employees.

Three confluent streams lead to this discussion. Two streams arise within the field of ethics itself. The first is the growing tendency to impose an ethical analysis on "hard cases": commonly these are situations that appear to present mutually exclusive options, neither leading to a fully satisfactory outcome, the dilemma requiring resolution that will significantly affect individuals or groups. This tendency to search for and analyze ethical dilemmas reflects a growing acknowledgment that choices based on values surround and direct the course of our lives, and that ethical dilemmas are an inevitable characteristic of our choice-filled society.[1]

The second contemporary development that leads to this discussion is the elaboration of a "feminist" ethics, a formulation of ethical principles and process based on women's experience and on women's choices as demonstrated in behavioral and attitudinal study.[2] Feminist ethics, as it forms a basis for this consideration of workplace values, included these assumptions:

- Traditional androcentric ethics has failed to take account of women's lives.
- Adding women's experience to androcentric philosophical theories is not sufficient; an alternative way of knowing is demanded.
- Feminist ethical discourse attends to values of cooperation, relationship, and interdependent nurturance.
- A feminist ethical epistemology is rooted in practical, everyday realities.

The third stream that feeds this discussion is the aforementioned discontent, on the part of some women, with patriarchal workplace arrangements. The second wave of feminism dovetailed with worldwide economic shifts in the 1960s and 1970s to produce a cadre of well-educated women ready to step into positions of status and control in the paid workforce. Many women planned to accept roles of power commensurate with their accomplishments; some even hoped to "feminize" those worlds of power by force of their womanly experience and values.

In fact, significant numbers of talented, well-educated, and energetic women have entered paid employment, and some have made their way to positions of substantive power. But many are restless and dissatisfied, and some are leaving their jobs, or even their chosen areas of concentration. They voice complaints that range from perceived demands that they sustain the status quo and not rock any boats, to their exclusion from positions of real power, to the apparent likelihood that these worlds of power will continue to resist feminization.[3]

Many of those who are most discontent with their experience in paid employment remark that they are offended by the values and expectations embodied in the very fabric of the work environment. These workplace values are seen collectively as metaphor for broader assumptions about human nature, possible styles in relationships, and criteria for choices in behavior.

Workplace values, then, provide an illustrative frame of reference in which to examine the contemporary utility of ethical analyses, as well as the implications of competing ethical paradigms. This examination is speculative and meant to advance feminist assumptions about the intersections of ethics and everyday behavior.

It would be careless to oversimplify the reasons that talented, well-trained, and accomplished women resign from good jobs, abandon their professions, or leave the workforce altogether. Sexist discrimination is alive and well, and women walk away from jobs for a variety of reasons: inequities of pay and status, boredom and a lack of opportunity to learn new skills and to work at a variety of tasks, and myriad other discontents and desires. But here the focus is on that more narrowly defined group of women who find workplace environments to be so antithetic to their values that they come to believe that they must not continue to participate in the creation and maintenance of those environments.

The specific exemplars of this essay come from a three-year, foundation-funded demonstration project, the "Kennedy Aging Project,"[4] of which I was the (feminist) director. The project was charged with teaching health professionals about the problems and care of people who are both mentally retarded and old. All staff were selected by myself as director; as staffing proceeded, newly selected staff themselves collaborated in the ongoing selection process. Almost all staff members were harmonious in their philosophic and political outlooks, although there had been no explicitly feminist criteria utilized in the selection process.

The concept of "health" envisioned in the project was holistic; professional disciplines ranged from doctor to nurse to lawyer and social worker, to recreation therapist and spiritual counselor, among others. The project provided service as a first priority. Teaching was the second priority and research—the accumulation and analysis of data—was carried out only insofar as that work did not interfere with service or teaching.

The workplace arrangements of the project were chosen thoughtfully, deliberately, and cooperatively. Although our work with clients was imbued with ethical considerations from the beginning of the undertaking,[5] it was only toward the end of the three years of work that it became clear to us that our workplace itself could be seen as embodying certain ethical tenets, in fact, tenets of feminist ethics. This embodiment can be examined by pairing specific tenets of feminist ethics with certain domains of workplace values that appear to correspond, as an ethics-in-the-field.

The first tenet is that relationship with other beings, rather than the declaration, defense, and exercise of individual rights, is the central priority of ethical enactment. In the work described here, the participants, (professional and nonprofessional, faculty and students) chose to work in service to people who were not only mentally retarded but also old, people who are doubly disparaged and neglected by most of the professional community. Our charge was to teach health professionals about these people as clients; the interdisciplinary team chose to do that teaching in a context of direct, face-to-face service. And while most medical personnel focus on the curable (the transformative) transaction, the staff of the Kennedy Aging Project, in contrast, accepted profound levels of disability and handicap as givens, and worked to better the day-to-day context of lives that we came to see as triumphs of a survival spirit.

A second tenet of feminist ethics is that the giving and receiving of care, appropriate to specific persons and their situations, is a principal measure of outcome for ethically determined behavior. By contrast, the patriarchal system of ethical measure looks to the autonomy and/or liberty of the singular individual. In the Kennedy Aging Project the central force of our work was to take care of our clients—and their caregivers—and of each other. The office space was planned so that waiting clients and their caregivers would be amused and pleased. Waiting itself was kept to a minimum. Telephone contacts and opportunities of introduction were consciously courteous and welcoming. Our lunchtimes were deliberately social occasions, occasions for expression of a familial interest and concern. No effort was made to bolster a sense of the autonomy of individuals, except in our intent to respect the independent decision-making capacities of our clients. Work efforts of fellow workers were also respected, in the sense that each was an independent and self-regulating worker and no one was exclusively the waitperson for any other.

Third, feminist ethics emphasizes interdependence over individualism, and a mutuality of giving and receiving over entitlements to one-sided taking of nurture from others. The manifestation of these aspects of feminist ethics in a day-to-day work environment appears most consistently as a leveling of status. In the Kennedy Aging Project, every faculty person and administrator participated in direct, face-to-face contact with clients who were old and mentally retarded. Each was personally responsible for telephone calls to caregivers, contact agencies, and family members on behalf of clients, and for summary letters that described in detail the findings and recommendations of the interdisciplinary team. The interdisciplinary team itself played out the themes of interdependence and mutuality, as no one discipline was preeminent. Each representative of a distinct discipline (law, medicine, social work, ministry, nursing, psychology, rehabilitation medicine, and leisure) was responsible for teaching all other team members a rudimentary familiarity with their own special disciplinary language, concepts and processes.

A fourth tenet of feminist ethics requires focus on a distinct and particular "other," in contrast to patriarchal ethics, which speaks of the "other" as generalized, faceless, and impersonal. The staff of the Kennedy Aging Project steadfastly refused to reduce the clients that we worked with to a statistically blended "population." In fact, one special gift that each of us took from our work in the project was a compendium of interviews, home visits, and accounts of life histories of intensely memorable individuals. The power of this experience would be reduced if it were to be leveled into impersonal generalities, as in the common manner of research.

Fifth, feminist ethics also counters the process by which patriarchal ethics proposes formulaic, deductive decisions. Instead, decisions that are rooted in context and are responsive to the particularities of the individual case are sought. In the Kennedy Aging Project this preference was played out in meticulous examination of the life circumstances of each client, with detailed examination of every aspect not only of dysfunction, disability, and handicap but also of resource and capability. We were helped, of course, by the fact that each case came to us because there were dilemmas of care, and required thoughtful brainstorming to search out all possible avenues of solution for finding needed services.

Sixth, the characteristic processes of feminist ethics are described as being circular rather than linear, atemporal rather than time-bound, and accepting rather than transformative. These characteristics of feminist process were played out at the Kennedy Aging Project in the establishment of rituals, repeated acts of mutual help, and social exchanges based on storytelling. For instance, a potluck party was held every three months, with ritualized formalities of invitation, decoration, and food specialties. Every Monday morning two or three of us brought freshly baked bread as part of team meeting. We served as an interdisciplinary clipping service for each other, bringing items of interest not only in direct relation to our shared work but also in response to personal interests such as quilting, backpacking, and cooking. And we told and retold stories of our families, especially our children, and our own hobbies and avocations, so that we all became observers of each other enmeshed in the small everyday details of our individual lives.

Finally, it is a tenet of feminist ethics that virtue is seen as the highest good—an emphasis that takes precedence over justice—and that at every juncture exploitation and hurt are to be avoided by vigorous intent and effort. I believe that this perspective was embodied in the work of the Kennedy Aging Project by our devoted attention to provision of the best possible service to our clients, and the best possible education for our "students," both those with whom we worked directly and those with whom we communicated by written materials. By this firm attention to service and education—the *content* of our appointed work—we de-emphasized any focus on power relations within our project or as we were embedded in a larger agency. We wasted little energy firming our position in the agency, and we did not need to maneuver for power with each other within the project.

The Kennedy Aging Project can be seen as a model of a workplace environment that instantiates many of the values of feminist ethics. The project offered all of us who identified with these values an environment that felt welcoming, appreciative, and appropriate.

These examples of work at the Kennedy Aging Project are cited as embodiments of feminist ethics. A certain correspondence of theoretical tenets and workplace arrangements is alleged. This correspondence is put forward as a (partial) solution to the problem of the voluntary attrition of talented and successful women from positions of managerial and professional responsibility. Women who leave their work because they are ill-at-ease about the value climate of the workplace, and discontent with the apparent bases of decision-making, are entitled to an alternative experience of workplace arrangements. A recurrent query from these women is whether they can find places to work "within the system," or whether they must occupy their hearts, minds, and energies in a separatist and therefore economically fragile alternative system.

The time seems right for the application of ethical analyses to the everyday arrangements that determine our everyday experiences at the workplace. The perspective offered by feminist ethics provides an alternative way of analyzing and deciding according to our values that are harmonious with women's experience. Perhaps this insight into our need for a commensurate ethical framework will lead us to workplace values that can sustain our best efforts at meaningful work.

What might defenders of the tradition of ethical theory respond to the Feminist critique? Are Feminist theorists right when they say that the tradition is flawed by patriarchal thinking and oblivious to the experiences and insights of women? Do the ethical writings of Feminist philosophers introduce distinctively new themes and a genuine alternative to the tradition of Western ethical theorizing discussed in the earlier part of this chapter?

Obviously, this is not a question of fact, such as "What is the capital of South Dakota?" to which I can simply supply an answer. It is a question of judgment and interpretation, to which different philosophers will give different answers. Let me give my own view of the matter, and in your classroom discussions, you can develop other answers as well.

First of all, it seems to me that the primary target of Feminist ethical theorists is the Kantian tradition—an ethical theory of rules, rationality, autonomy, obligation, and individualism. This has undoubtedly been the dominant theme in Western ethical writings for the past two centuries or so, but it is by no means the dominant theme in Western ethical theory as a whole. If you read the works of Plato from cover to cover, you will find little or nothing about duty, obligation, rules, and universal reason—although you *will* find a great deal about *reason* in a wider, more inclusive sense. The Feminist emphasis on the integration of feeling and thought, on the importance of the particular context of action, on the special importance of relationships *between* people—all of that fits in rather comfortably with the ancient Greek approach to the moral dimension of life, even though Greek society severely restricted the lives of women and treated them, in a variety of ways, as inferior beings.

Even in recent philosophical history, when the Kantian point of view has been so widely accepted, we find many writers who think and write about personal relationships, and the role of feelings in the good life. Karl Marx writes that way, even though in his personal life he exploited the women closest to him (and, as it happens, the men as well). So does the great Russian novelist Tolstoy, the American philosopher John Dewey, the American social scientist and philosopher George Herbert Mead, and the French writer and philosopher Jean-Paul Sartre.

Indeed, to some extent what we have here is an old and very deep clash between two traditions of Christian doctrine, the Protestant and the Catholic. Kant, you will recall, was a member of the extremely individualistic Pietist Christian sect, whose point of view can be traced back at least to the writings of Paul in the New Testament. This is a religious tradition that emphasizes duty, autonomy, and individual's relation to God, the suppression of desire and the body, and the rigorous obedience to rules. But there is an equally ancient tradition, sometimes identified with the gospel according to St. John, that celebrates the body as well as the spirit, that speaks of love, redemption, forgiveness, community, and the emotionally supportive fellowship of the Church. Speaking only somewhat in jest, we might say that Feminist ethicists are reviving a Catholic tradition as against the recently dominant Protestant point of view. But of course both of these traditions, and the non-Christian tradition of Greek thought as well, consign women to a subordinate and secondary role both in society and in their ethical theories.

In my judgment, the Feminists are right that the *practice* of ethical theory, and of philosophy in general in the Western tradition, has reflected an ingrained and mostly unexamined bias against women. The very same criticism can justly be made of philosophy's treatment of the nonwhite portion of the human species. What must still be determined is whether correcting those biases requires a change in the fundamental *conception* of philosophy as well as in its *practice*.

Let me add a personal note here if I may. When I began the study of philosophy almost half a century ago, I accepted unthinkingly and unreflectively the unexamined assumption that the story of philosophy can be told entirely in the voices of the men whose works dominate this, or any other, philosophy text. I assumed as well that the insights and perspectives of the nonwhite majority of the world could safely be ignored. If anyone had asked me, I think I would have said, "Of course, we must listen to everyone's voice," but that is just the point: No one ever asked me, and I never thought to ask myself! Now, in Chapter One, we heard Socrates tell us that the unexamined life is not worth living. Well, as I am sure he would agree, it is also true that the unexamined assumption is not worth holding. What you see in this Seventh Edition of this book is my on-going effort to examine my own previously unexamined assumptions, and thereby, perhaps, to get just a little bit closer to the truth. If I live to be a hundred, and this book goes through twenty editions, I am sure there will still be questions I have not yet asked, and unexamined assumptions I have not yet subjected to criticism. Our philosophical understanding must always be a work in progress. If this book teaches you nothing else but that, it will be a success.

Main Points in Chapter Two, Part One

1. The eighteenth-century Prussian philosopher Immanuel Kant tried to find a way to make the science of Newton compatible with the strict moral beliefs of his Protestant upbringing and also to provide a rigorous logical proof of the fundamental principles of morality.

2. When philosophers talk about ethics, there are really three very different questions they ask, namely:

   a. How can I be certain that my moral beliefs are correct?
   b. How can I decide moral hard cases?
   c. How can I live a good life?

3. Kant put forward a moral principle called the Categorical Imperative as the absolutely right principle for all persons in any situation. Ethical relativists *and* ethical skeptics deny that there is any such universally valid principle.

4. To decide hard cases, defenders of utilitarianism, such as Jeremy Bentham and John Stuart Mill, offer the Principle of the Greatest Happiness for the Greatest Number. Utilitarianism is the most widely debated moral theory of modern-day philosophy.

5. Philosophers from Plato to Karl Marx have put forward theories of the health of the self or personality as the basis for a conception of the good life. The central idea of these philosophers is that the way to have a genuinely good life is to develop an inwardly well-ordered or healthy psyche. Today, these same ideas are explored by psychoanalysts as well as philosophers.

6. Feminist critics of the Western tradition of ethical theory have argued that the various main theories all embody a male or patriarchal point of view and fail to express the experiences and insight of women.

NOTES

1. P. Singer, *Practical Ethics* (New York: Cambridge University Press, 1979); S. Spicker, S. Ingram, and I. Lawson, eds., *Ethical Dimensions of Geriatric Care* (Boston: Reidel, 1987).

2. E. Kittay and D. Meyers, eds., *Women and Moral Theory* (Totowa, N.J.: Rowman and Littlefield, 1987); S. Benhabib and D. Cornell, eds., *Feminism as Critique* (Minneapolis: University of Minnesota Press, 1987); C. Gilligan, *In a Different Voice: Psychological Theory and Women's Development* (Cambridge, Mass.: Harvard University Press, 1982).

3. M. Campbell, *Why Would a Girl Go into Medicine? Medical Education in the United States: A Guide for Women,* 2d ed. (Old Westbury, N.Y.: The Feminist Press, 1979).

4. M. Howell, D. Gavin, G. Cabrera, and H. Beyer, eds., *Serving the Underserved: Caring for People Who Are Both Old and Mentally Retarded* (Boston: Exceptional Parent Press, 1989); M. Howell, T. Barbara and R. Pitch, *Death and Dying: A Guide for Staff Serving Developmentally Disabled Adults* (Boston: Exceptional Parent Press, 1989); M. Howell and R. Pitch, *Ethical Dilemmas: A Guide for Staff Serving Developmentally Disabled Adults* (Boston: Exceptional Parent Press, 1989).

5. Howell and Pitch.

CONTEMPORARY APPLICATIONS

Same-Sex Marriage

There are some subjects that seem to get people worked up out of all proportion to their larger importance in the overall scheme of things. Thirty odd years ago, when the Beatles burst onto the cultural scene, people were simply outraged by the fact that they wore their hair shoulder length, even though they also appeared neatly dressed in ties and jackets! Poverty, domestic violence, racial oppression, even war didn't get folks as totally worked up as the length of the hair on the heads of four popular musicians. The same frenzy is generated by even a little nudity, or some impolite language. It seems that what have come to be labeled "cultural values" and "family values" hit some of us with a force that can't easily be explained.

In the past year or two, absolutely nothing has stirred people up quite so much as the idea that two gay men or two lesbian women might go through a marriage ceremony and be considered by the state to be legally married. Nothing less than the downfall of Western Civilization [or of all civilization, for that matter] has confidently been predicted if such an event should ever take place. *Same-sex marriage,* as this issue has come to be called, clearly triggers the most powerful of feelings in scores of millions of Americans.

It is not hard to understand why gay and lesbian Americans want the right to enter into legal marriages. Aside from the emotional significance of such ceremonies, there are a great many legal and economic benefits of legal marriage that are now denied to homosexual partners. For example: In most health insurance plans, an employee can claim medical benefits for his or her spouse, but not for someone with whom there is no legal marital relationship. Child custody, home ownership, credit availability, tax exemptions, legal rights in trials, and countless other extremely important rights, benefits, and privileges are tied to marriage, and hence unavailable to gay and lesbian couples who are not permitted to enter into formal matrimony. One of the most painful and poignant problems is the attempt by the partners of dying AIDS sufferers to be with them at their bedside, a right that would automatically be granted a husband or wife but that is frequently denied the life partner of a gay or lesbian AIDS patient.

The issue of same-sex marriage burst onto the political stage when it first appeared that a state judge in Hawaii would rule in favor of a gay couple suing for the right to enter into a legal marriage. Although no such ruling has been handed down as these words are being written, the mere possibility of such a decision provoked a national debate and Congressional action. In

1996, the Congress passed, and President Clinton signed, a bill permitting states to withhold recognition from a same-sex marriage allowed by the courts of some other state. Even though legal scholars are virtually unanimous in their judgment that this law is unconstitutional, and will never survive a challenge in the Supreme Court, politicians rushed to enact the law, convinced that same-sex marriage, like Social Security, had the potential of becoming the "third rail" of American politics [i.e., "touch it and you die."]

Well, pretty clearly this issue raises all manner of ethical questions, the resolution of which requires us to think deeply about many of the theoretical themes discussed in the first part of this chapter, so I have chosen to make same-sex marriage the Contemporary Application for Part One of the chapter devoted to Ethical Theory. One word by way of total disclosure: I am not at all neutral on this issue. As the father of a fine young man who is gay, I look forward with great anticipation to attending his wedding to the man of his choice, and I resent bitterly the attempt by politicians to deny me that fatherly pleasure. However, as with all the controversial issues discussed in this book, it is in the end your considered opinion, and not mine, that matters.

꘎ ꘎ ꘎ ꘎ ꘎ ꘎ ꘎ ꘎ ꘎ ꘎ ꘎ ꘎ ꘎

LEAVE MARRIAGE ALONE
William Bennett

There are at least two key issues that divide proponents and opponents of same-sex marriage. The first is whether legally recognizing same-sex unions would strengthen or weaken the institution. The second has to do with the basic understanding of marriage itself.

The advocates of same-sex marriage say that they seek to strengthen and celebrate marriage. That may be what some intend. But I am certain that it will not be the reality. Consider: the legal union of same-sex couples would shatter the conventional definition of marriage, change the rules which govern behavior, endorse practices which are completely antithetical to the tenets of all of the world's major religions, send conflicting signals about marriage and sexuality, particularly to the young, and obscure marriage's enormously consequential function—procreation and child-rearing.

Broadening the definition of marriage to include same-sex unions would stretch it almost beyond recognition—and new attempts to expand the definition still further would surely follow. On what *principled* ground can Andrew Sullivan exclude others who most desperately want what he wants, legal recognition and social acceptance? Why on earth would Sullivan exclude from marriage a bisexual who wants to marry two other people? After all, exclusion would be a denial of that person's sexuality. The same holds true of a father and daughter who want to marry. Or two sisters. Or men who want (consensual) polygamous arrangements. Sullivan may think some of these arrangements are unwise. But having employed sexual relativism in his own defense, he has effectively lost the capacity to draw any lines and make moral distinctions.

Forsaking all others is an essential component of marriage. Obviously it is not always honored in practice. But it is the ideal to which we rightly aspire, and in most marriages the ideal is in fact the norm. Many advocates of same-sex marriage simply do not share this ideal; promiscuity among homosexual males is well known. Sullivan himself has written that gay male relationships are served by the "openness of the contract" and that homosexuals should resist allowing their "varied and complicated lives" to be flattened into a "single, moralistic model." But that "single, moralistic model" has served society exceedingly well. The burden of proof ought to be on those who propose untested arrangements for our most important institution.

A second key difference I have with Sullivan goes to the very heart of marriage itself. I believe that marriage is not an arbitrary construct which can be redefined simply by those who lay claim to it. It is an honorable estate, instituted of God and built on moral, religious, sexual and human realities. Marriage is based on a natural teleology, on the different, complementary nature of men and women—and how they refine, support, encour-

age and complete one another. It is the institution through which we propagate, nurture, educate and sustain our species.

That we have to engage in this debate at all is an indication of how steep our moral slide has been. Worse, those who defend the traditional understanding of marriage are routinely referred to (though not to my knowledge by Sullivan) as "homophobes," "gay-bashers," "intolerant" and "bigoted." Can one defend an honorable, 4,000-year-old tradition and not be called these names?

This is a large, tolerant, diverse country. In America people are free to do as they wish, within broad parameters. It is also a country in sore need of shoring up some of its most crucial institutions: marriage and the family, schools, neighborhoods, communities. But marriage and family are the greatest of these. That is why they are elevated and revered. We should keep them so.

Bennett, editor of "The Book of Virtues," is a codirector of Empower America. The author states: 'It is not an arbitrary construct which can be redefined simply by those who lay claim to it.'

੩ ੩ ੩ ੩ ੩ ੩ ੩ ੩ ੩ ੩ ੩ ੩ ੩

LET GAYS MARRY
Andrew Sullivan

A state cannot deem a class of persons a stranger to its laws," declared the Supreme Court last week. It was a monumental statement. Gay men and lesbians, the conservative court said, are no longer strangers in America. They are citizens, entitled, like everyone else, to equal protection—no special rights, but simple equality.

For the first time in Supreme Court history, gay men and women were seen not as some powerful lobby trying to subvert America, but as the people we truly are—the sons and daughters of countless mothers and fathers, with all the weaknesses and strengths and hopes of everybody else. And what we seek is not some special place in America but

merely to be a full and equal part of America, to give back to our society without being forced to lie or hide or live as second-class citizens.

That is why marriage is so central to our hopes. People ask us why we want the right to marry, but the answer is obvious. It's the same reason anyone wants the right to marry. At some point in our lives, some of us are lucky enough to meet the person we truly love. And we want to commit to that person in front of our family and country for the rest of our lives. It's the most simple, the most natural, the most human instinct in the world. How could anyone seek to oppose that?

Yes, at first blush, it seems like a radical proposal, but, when you think about it some more, it's actually the opposite. Throughout American history, to be sure, marriage has been between a man and a woman, and in many ways our society is built upon that institution. But none of that need change in the slightest. After all, no one is seeking to take away anybody's right to marry, and no one is seeking to force any church to change any doctrine in any way. Particular religious arguments against same-sex marriage are rightly debated within the churches and faiths themselves. That is not the issue here: there is a separation between church and state in this country. We are only asking that when the government gives out *civil* marriage licenses, those of us who are gay should be treated like anybody else.

Of course, some argue that marriage is *by definition* between a man and a woman. But for centuries, marriage was *by definition* a contract in which the wife was her husband's legal property. And we changed that. For centuries, marriage was *by definition* between two people of the same race. And we changed that. We changed these things because we recognized that human dignity is the same whether you are a man or a woman, black or white. And no one has any more of a choice to be gay than to be black or white or male or female.

Some say that marriage is only about raising children, but we let childless heterosexual couples be married (Bob and Elizabeth Dole, Pat and Shelley Buchanan, for instance). Why should gay couples be treated differently? Others fear that there is no logical difference between allowing same-sex marriage and sanctioning polygamy and other horrors. But the issue of whether to sanction multiple spouses (gay or straight) is completely separate from whether, in the existing institution between two unrelated adults, the government should discriminate between its citizens.

This is, in fact, if only Bill Bennett could see it, a deeply conservative cause. It seeks to change no one else's rights or marriages in any way. It seeks merely to promote monogamy, fidelity and the disciplines of family life among people who have long been cast to the margins of society. And what could be a more conservative project than that? Why indeed would any conservative seek to oppose those very family values for gay people that he or she supports for everybody else? Except, of course, to make gay men and lesbians strangers in their own country, to forbid them ever to come home.

Sullivan is a senior editor of The New Republic and the author of "Virtually Normal: An Argument about Homosexuality." The author states: 'It would promote monogamy and the disciplines of family life for those cast on the margins.'

ಚಿ ಚಿ ಚಿ ಚಿ ಚಿ ಚಿ ಚಿ ಚಿ ಚಿ ಚಿ ಚಿ ಚಿ

MARRIAGE'S TRUE ENDS*

There is every likelihood that Hawaii's Supreme Court will soon overturn that state's prohibition on same-sex marriage. The court's reasoning will be simple enough: Hawaii's constitution forbids discrimination on the basis of sex, and for the state to deny the benefits of marriage to same-sex couples without demonstrating a "compelling state interest" does precisely that. Should Hawaii license same-sex marriage, other

states may be bound to recognize those marriages under the Full Faith and Credit clause of the Constitution. The U.S. Supreme Court, it seems certain, will eventually be asked to rule on the constitutionality of the heterosexual exclusivity of marriage.

For the state to license same-sex unions will entail a fundamental reappraisal of the nature of marriage and the balance struck between rights of individual self-determination and the integrity of basic social institutions such as the family. American society has much to gain from a fair-minded debate about such questions, and much to lose if

Commonweal, May 17, 1996, pages 5–7.

we retreat further from reasoning together about the nature and aims of our common life.

Whether there are compelling enough reasons to preserve the heterosexual exclusivity of marriage is a question that arises in the wake of profound changes in how we think about sexual morality, procreation, and marriage. Historically, marriage forged a powerful connection between sexual love, procreation, and the care of children. However, contemporary understandings of marriage increasingly stress the primacy of individual self-fulfillment, not intergenerational attachments. Moreover, contraception and abortion have essentially severed any unwilled connection between sex and procreation. That connection has been further attenuated by technological advances allowing us to separate biological, gestational, and relational parenting at will. In this context, marriage's meaning seems anything but secure.

But is a further erosion of marriage's traditional linkage between sexual love and human procreation desirable? Advocates of same-sex marriage advance two arguments. First, denying same-sex couples the marriage rights enjoyed by heterosexual persons is discriminatory, an imposition of unjustified inequality. Second, same-sex marriage is presented as an embrace of, not an assault on, what is acknowledged to be a uniquely valuable social institution. If society wishes to promote the human goods of marriage—emotional fulfillment, lifelong commitment, the creation of families, and the care of children—marginalizing homosexuals by denying civil standing to their publicly committed relationships makes little sense, advocates argue.

In modern democratic societies wide latitude is given to individuals and groups pursuing often conflicting and incompatible conceptions of the good. Still, a broad tolerance and a high regard for individual autonomy cannot result in the equal embrace of every private interest or social arrangement. Economic freedom, for example, must be balanced against environmental concerns. Parents' rights to instill their own values in their children must accommodate the state's mandate to set educational standards for all children. The exclusive legal status of monogamous marriage, it is useful to remember, was once challenged by Mormon polygamy. But polygamy was judged inimical to the values of individual dignity and social comity that marriage uniquely promotes.

Now we must weigh the implicit individual and social benefits of heterosexual marriage against those of same-sex unions. In this light, advocates of same-sex marriage often argue that laws prohibiting it are analogous to miscegenation statutes. But the miscegenation analogy fails. Miscegenation laws were about racial separation, not about the nature of marriage. Legalizing same-sex unions will not remedy a self-evident injustice by broadening access to the traditional goods of marriage. Rather, same-sex marriage, like polygamy, would change the very nature and social architecture of marriage in ways that may empty it of any distinctive meaning.

Recent social history can guide us here. Proponents of no-fault divorce argued that the higher meaning of marriage, and even the health of children, would be better served in making marriage easier to dissolve. Yet the plight of today's divorced women and their children refutes such claims. In fact, the loosening of marital bonds and expectations has contributed to the devaluation and even the abandonment of the marriage ideal by many, while encouraging unrealistic expectations of marriage for many more. How society defines marriage has a profound effect on how individuals think and act. And how individuals fashion their most intimate relationships has an enormous impact on the quality of our common life. The dynamic involved is subtle, but real.

Should marriage be essentially a contractual arrangement between two individuals to be defined as they see fit? Or does marriage recognize and embody larger shared meanings that cannot be lightly divorced from history, society, and nature—shared meanings and social forms that create the conditions in which individuals can achieve their own fulfillment? Popular acceptance of premarital sex and cohabitation gives us some sense of the moral and social trajectory involved. Both developments were welcomed as expressions of greater honesty and even better preparations for marriage. Yet considerable evidence now suggests that these new-found "freedoms" have contributed to the instability and trivialization of marriage itself, and have not borne the promises once made for them of happier lives. Similarly, elevating same-sex unions to the same moral and legal status as marriage will further throw into doubt marriage's fundamental purposes and put at risk a social practice and moral ideal vital to all.

The heterosexual exclusivity of marriage can be defended in the same way social policy rightly shows a preference for the formation of intact two-parent families. In both cases, a normative definition of family life is indispensable to any coherent and effective public action. Certainly, mutual love and care are to be encouraged wherever possible. But the justification and rationale for marriage as a social institution cannot rest on the goods of companionship alone. Resisting such a reductionist understanding is not merely in the interests of heterosexuals. There are profound social goods at stake in holding together the biological, relational, and procreative dimensions of human love.

"There are countless ways to 'have' a child," writes theologian Gilbert Meilaender of the social consequences and human meaning of procreation (*Body, Soul, & Bioethics,* University of Notre Dame Press, 1996). "Not all of them amount to doing the same thing. Not all of them will teach us to discern the equal humanity of the child as one who is not our product but, rather, the natural development of shared love, like to us in dignity. . . . To conceive, bear, give birth to, and rear a child ought to be an affirmation and a recognition: affirmation of the good of life that we ourselves were given; recognition that this life bears its own creative power to which we should be faithful."

Is there really any doubt that in tying sexual attraction to love and love to children and the creation of families, marriage fundamentally shapes our ideas of human dignity and the nature of society? Same-sex marriage, whatever its virtues, would narrow that frame and foreshorten our perspective. Marriage, at its best, tutors us as no other experience can in the given nature of human life and the acceptance of responsibilities we have not willed or chosen. Indeed, it should tutor us in respect for the given nature of homosexuality and the dignity of homosexual persons. With this respect comes a recognition of difference—a difference with real consequences.

Still, it is frequently objected that if the state does not deny sterile or older heterosexual couples the right to marry, how can it deny that right to homosexual couples, many of whom are already rearing children?

Exceptions do not invalidate a norm or the necessity of norms. How some individuals make use of marriage, either volitionally or as the result of some incapacity, does not determine the purpose of that institution. In that context, heterosexual sterility does not contradict the meaning of marriage in the way same-sex unions would. If marriage as a social form is first a procreative bond . . ., then marriage necessarily presupposes sexual differentiation, for human procreation itself presupposes sexual differentiation. We are all the offspring of a man and a woman, and marriage is the necessary moral and social response to that natural human condition. Consequently, sexual differentiation, even in the absence of the capacity to procreate, conforms to marriage's larger design in a way same-sex unions cannot. For this reason sexual differentiation is marriage's defining boundary, for it is the precondition of marriage's true ends.

ꕔꕔꕔꕔꕔꕔꕔꕔꕔꕔꕔꕔꕔ

WHAT *IS* MARRIAGE?
E.J. Graff*

Congress is rushing to the cultural barricades with the Defense of Marriage Act, legally defining marriage as a union between one man and one woman. The president is planning to alienate two constituencies at once by signing the act with one hand while mopping his brow with the other as he bemoans the act as unnecessary gay-bashing.

From what, exactly, is Congress trying to defend marriage? Within two years, a case now winding through Hawaii's courts will almost certainly widen that state's marriage laws to include same-sex couples—and since states are the final arbiters on marriage, there will be no appeal. What's not clear is whether same-sex couples legally married in Hawaii would still be married—as most couples would—when they fly home to such places as Framingham and Nashua.

The act has sparked passionate debate. For many people, the idea of same-sex marriage sounds logically impossible, a disturbing contradiction in terms—something like Samuel Johnson's bemused comment that "a woman preaching is like a dog's walking on his hind legs. It is not done well; but you are surprised to find it done at all."

What's on trial here is the definition of marriage itself. How is it possible that an institution that for thousands of years has meant Boy + Girl = Babies is shifting to also mean Girl + Girl = Love—not just in Hawaii, but in every developed nation? The debate is, at its heart, about a very large question: What is marriage for?

Be careful: It's a trick question. Human beings, over and over, find sacred meaning in the pair bond, and from it tend to create and impose social roles. But, despite the way some conservatives cry "tradition!" like a Tevye chorus, how each society defines marriage shifts constantly over classes, regions and eras.

Think of every "fact" about marriage that our society takes for granted today. Is marriage between one man and one woman? Not for patriarch Jacob, who had 12 sons and one daughter via his two wives and two concubines. It is always a religious observance? Not for the Christian Church in its first few hundred years, when it had no marriage blessing because it saw the institution as secular. Is it always recognized by law? Not for centuries of European prole marriages that the law never deigned to recognize, because too little property was involved.

Does marriage always bind two intimate companions? Not for aristocratic marriages in more than one century and nationality, where spouses might see each other occasionally, meanwhile keeping separate incomes, visiting lists and wings in the estate. Is it always decided by the spouses-to-be? Not if the wedded pair had to depend on and contribute to the family income (as did most, until recently) or live under the patriarch's roof.

Right-wing rhetoric treats this history as a confident march toward perfect social forms (with perfection reached roughly 10 years before the particular rhetorician was born). But society is a work in progress. Marriage is—and always has been—variations on a theme, shifting so that it makes sense for each place, class and time.

So what makes sense in ours? To answer that, it's important to remember that today's "traditional" marriage was once considered shockingly, even offensively, private. Once upon a time, an individual marriage was just one nail holding together a larger family that functioned as a small but interdependent community. As those clans devolved into nuclear households

The Boston Globe, Focus Section, July 21, 1996. Copyright © E.J. Graff by permission.

(two parents and their children), the smaller family was accused by 19th-century social observers of instability and destructive individualism.

That same outrage arises every time public policy shifts more toward treating marriage as a haven for individuals' happiness. Around the turn of the last century, proposals for easing divorce brought tirades about selfishness and predictions of civilization's fall. Margaret Sanger's campaign in the 1920s to bring birth control to married women was charged with the "perversion of natural functions" and the spread of dire diseases. Not until 1940 did demographers finally declare the nuclear family as our standard household.

But could states make it mandatory? By 1951, the Supreme Court decided no; that to prevent the dismaying uncertainty of having couples married in one state though divorced in another, each state's civil divorce decrees must be recognized nationwide. And in 1965 the Supreme Court struck down the last laws forbidding marital birth control, formally snipping the link between sex and diapers. Most state marriage codes had been prefaced by a statement that marriage was for reproduction. But as the court wrote in Griswold vs. Connecticut, "Marriage is a coming together for better or for worse, hopefully enduring, and intimate to the degree of being sacred."

In other words, love is how we justify marriage today, not whether a couple can or will make babies.

These shifts fit our century's economic realities. Once upon a time, breach of promise suits were pursued with all the fervor a jilted CEO might bring to a canceled merger—because marriage defined one's financial future. And it's a truism by now that children are economic sacrifice, not a labor boon (however much they might be loved). Today Americans are work-units as mobile as cellular phones, making a living (or failing to) by making their own decisions about which talents or inclinations to trust. Trained from birth to ask

ourselves what we want to be when we grow up, how can Americans be expected to guide their marital—and sexual—hopes and lives by anything but that same inner voice?

The consequence? Just as society has expanded marriage's exit visas and eliminated its occupancy rules, it must now widen its entrance requirements—and for the same reasons. With legalized birth control, our nation's laws had recognized that the goal of married sex was now love, pleasure and that other sexual response so difficult to put into words—that temporary transcendence of self, that deep gratitude of belonging to another. Plenty of same-sex couples want to encircle that sexual joy with a gold band's optimistic, determined promises. When a couple decides to share responsibilities that go beyond their immediate desires, society awards them marriage's legal address—which allows a couple to make sensible contact with neighbors, insurers, courts, employers, schools and rental-car companies. How can that fairly be denied to same-sex pairs?

Many proponents of the federal Defense of Marriage Act—versions of which have been introduced in 36 state legislatures, passed in 15 and beaten back in 18—insist correctly that our nation's marriage laws are rooted in deep religious beliefs. But which religions? Every major religion today is debating same-sex marriage. Liberal denominations—Reconstructionist Judaism, Quakers, Unitarians and a host of individual congregations—increasingly bless same-sex pairs. Fundamentalist denominations—Orthodox Judaism, Southern Baptists (who only recently renounced their support for slavery), Catholicism and more—are loudly opposed.

The United States is a democracy, not a theocracy. Civil marriage—like any pluralist institution—must be one-size-fits-all, with plenty of room for differences and dissents.

Having run out of other justifications with which to prove to the Hawaii Supreme Court that barring same-sex is a "compelling state interest," the state of Hawaii, in this September's arguments, will charge that same-sex parents are bad for children. The implication, of course, is that lesbian and gay sex is so disgusting that children shouldn't be exposed to it. But most parents, same-sex parents included, rightly avoid letting their children catch them in bed.

Just because opponents are obsessed with what lesbians and gay men do in bed hardly means that the parents themselves are, or that it dominates household life. What dominates is getting kids ready for school, fed, cleaned, clothed and overseen while parents work, as in any family.

Some people can't rid their minds of propaganda, confusing homosexuality and pedophilia, despite the avalanche of facts: Most child sexual abuse involves adult men molesting girls. Life with (heterosexual) stepfathers does put girls at higher risk for sexual and physical abuse. But society treats step-parenting failures as individual problems, not as collective predictions.

Conservatives insist that the best parents are biological. If that's true, why not outlaw adoption or IVF practices? The fact is, being raised by someone other than two biological parents—whether that's two uncles or a British nanny—is hardly historical news. (Sure, remarried moms gave us Newt Gingrich and Bill Clinton, but that's not a serious objection.)

Every peer-reviewed study done to date shows that children raised by lesbian or gay parents are as well-adjusted as their peers on every developmental scale, from moral maturity to aggression, social closeness to self-esteem, with no more psychological or gender identity problems (and no more likely to be gay) than children of heterosexuals.

The revulsion some people feel at the idea of same-sex parents is often translated into the objection that it's unfair to let children be stigmatized by parents' homosexuality. It's a tautological argument: Marriage would help remove the stigma. Could anyone but Pharaoh imagine suggesting that, say, Jews should not have children because the kids will suffer anti-Semitism?

Hardly. It's every parent's job to teach children to handle ridicule and disrespect. And if lesbian and gay parents teach their children that there's no one right way to live, how can a pluralist society object? Whether to raise children by unpopular ideologies—from Amish Mennonites to survivalist home schoolers—is a decision that belongs to the parents, not the polis.

What does put those children at risk is the fact that their parents' bond is extra-legal. Same-sex parents need the protections granted any married pair—the ability to make school decisions, to protect the kids via family health policies and wills, to ensure visitation and support should the parents split. If marriage is in any way about children, then the children of lesbians and gay men need it too.

Allowing two people of the same sex to marry will shift the institution's message—away from reproductive determinism, to which the religious right would like us to return. Some people are unnerved to think that there are more choices in the world than their own. But once Hawaii opens marriage wider, marriage will stand instead for taking everyone's inner lives and desires seriously, for navigating life by heart. It is, after all, the American way.

E.J. Graff writes widely on lesbian and gay issues. She is working on a book, "What Is Marriage For?" to be published by Beacon Press. Debate over the legality of same-sex unions is prompting us to look at what defines the institution.

Questions for Discussion and Review

1. Think back over your life and pick the hardest choice you ever had to make. Was it a *moral* choice? Did it involve a decision about what is right and wrong? If the answer is yes, ask yourself whether it would have helped you to carry out a utilitarian-style calculation of pleasures and pains to yourself and others. Would Kant's rule—The Categorical Imperative—have helped you at all? How *did* you make the decision?

2. The central thesis of the theory of the healthy personality is that people with coherent, healthy, harmonious personalities will not act cruelly and unjustly. Certainly it is true that *some* immoral acts flow from disordered personalities, but is it reasonable to suppose that all do? Can there be a happy, well-adjusted mass murderer?

3. What do you think Kant's ethical theory tells us about the morality or immorality of abortion? Is it clear what utilitarianism tells us? Is it reasonable to pick your moral theory on the basis of what it tells you about issues, like abortion, on which you already have fixed views? Why? Why not? If you leave out any religious considerations, where do you think the truth lies on the question of the morality of abortion?

4. Are the moral experiences of women and men fundamentally different, in ways that would affect their interpretation and evaluation of choices and actions? If you have studied child development in a psychology course, can you draw on what you learned there to help clarify the dispute between the traditional moral theorists and Feminist theorists like Jaggar and Raugust? How would you develop an analogous critique based on racial differences?

THE ETHICAL DIMENSIONS OF MEDICINE

The Ethical Dimensions of Medical Decisions

As you may have read in the papers or seen on television, jobs are scarce in the academic world, especially for scholars in fields like philosophy. You don't see many ads these days looking for epistemologists or logicians. But strange as it may seem, in recent years, we *have* begun to see Help Wanted ads for *ethicists*, specifically for *medical ethicists*. Mind you, these are not ads placed by out-of-work Ph.D.'s in Philosophy hoping to snag some sort of employment in the health or business world. These are ads placed by serious hospitals or health maintenance organizations who say they will pay good money—very often more than you can make teaching philosophy—for men and women who are professional ethics experts. In a minute, we will try to figure out what sort of expertise an ethicist might possibly have that anyone would want to pay good money for. But first, let's try to understand why those hospitals and health maintenance organizations are so eager to put an ethicist on the payroll.

As we have just seen in the first part of this chapter, philosophers who write ethical theory talk rather abstractly about the moral dilemmas we face. When they do mention particular moral choices, the examples tend to be rather hastily made up, and very far from real life. The little example I invented about the young man deciding whether to leave home, for example. That is, I guess, a genuine moral decision that many young people have to make, but surely no one faced with that choice has ever made up a table of plus and minus pleasures and pains like the one on page 63 Just to give you an idea of how far out the examples can get in academic ethical theory, let me tell you about one that is all the rage these days in philosophy journals.

Suppose—these authors ask us—you found yourself in a situation in which you could save five lives by killing one person. Should you do it? For example, imagine you are standing on a little hill, overlooking a trolley line, and you see a trolley careening out of control and about to go over a cliff. You can see that the only way to stop the trolley and save those five people is to throw something onto the tracks to derail the trolley before it gets to the cliff. You look around for something big enough to throw, and the only thing you see is an innocent little five year old girl. If you pick her up and throw her onto the tracks, you will kill her and save the five lives. If you do nothing, she will live and the five will die. Which should you do?

No kidding. This really is the sort of thing ethical theorists talk about! Now, most of us never find ourselves in this sort of situation. I guess maybe someone, somewhere, has actually faced such a choice, but it isn't your average, everyday, make-a-decision-and-go-home-to-dinner sort of choice. So, I personally would be inclined to say that ethical theory written about "examples" like that one can't be taken seriously.

But the strange thing is that there *are* real decisions just as weird, just as impossible, just as gut-wrenching as that one, and there are thousands upon thousands of people who face them every day of their professional lives. I am speaking, of course, of doctors.

Let's talk about a real example, not a kooky made-up one. Consider the problems faced daily by the hospital committee charged with deciding which patient will be put on the list for kidney dialysis when a slot opens up. This is not a hypothetical philosophical exercise, conducted in a classroom for the purpose of illustrating certain general principles of ethical theory. It is a regular committee decision that results in one patient getting a chance to live, and other patients being forced to wait, and in some cases to die. How shall such a committee make its decisions? What should it take into account, and what should it ignore?

Should the committee pay any attention to the age of the patient? For example, should a fourteen year old boy, with maybe sixty-five years of life ahead of him, get preference over a seventy year old woman who, under the best of circumstances, has only ten years or so left? Should Whites be given preference over African-Americans, or African-Americans over Whites? Should rich people be offered a chance to buy their way to the head of the line, perhaps by paying off the poor people ahead of them on the list? If one of the patients has lived a virtuous life and another has been a bad person, should the good person get preference? Should the committee strive for a gender, ethnic, religious, and racial balance? Should they simply say first come, first served? How much weight should be given to the purely medical estimates of the likelihood that the dialysis will keep the patient alive? Suppose a young, virtuous, admirable candidate has very little chance of surviving, even with the dialysis, while an old, vicious reprobate has a very good chance? Should the patients themselves have some voice in the committee? What about their families? The community at large?

Throughout the 1960s, individual physicians, patient selection committees, and hospitals thus were forced to deal with the medical-moral dilemma of selecting a limited number of medically eligible candidates to receive dialysis, knowing that those patients not chosen would soon die unless a transplant was possible. The type of decision that recurrently had to be made—what many involved ruefully called "playing God"—was as follows: This month our hospital's dialysis unit has space for one new dialysis patient, but there are four medically eligible candidates. How do we select the recipient? Those responsible for allocating dialysis used a variety of selection methods, which were based on one or more of six principles of social justice that can be used to provide a moral basis for distributing scarce resources.

RENEE C. FOX, JUDITH P. SWAZEY, AND ELIZABETH M. CAMERON, *Problems in the Treatment of Renal Disease Patients**

1. A *meritarian* concept of social justice allocates limited goods or resources to individuals on the basis of their merits or deserts. Merits or deserts, in turn, can be defined by the distributors—for example, a dialysis selection committee—in many ways, such as a person's conduct, achievement, or contributions to society.

*From "Social and Ethical Problems in the Treatment of End-Stage Renal Disease Patients," by Renee C. Fox, Ph.D., Judith P. Swazey, Ph.D., and Elizabeth M. Cameron R.N. © Churchill Livingstone, New York. Reprinted by permission of the publisher.

2. A *needs* principle seeks to justly allocate a limited resource such as dialysis according to the essential needs of individuals, leaving for further definition the question of what constitutes "essential needs."

3. An *ability* principle distributes a scarce resource on the basis of various criteria concerning an individual's ability. For example, in a fee-for-service system ability to pay can be the determinant of who receives care, and a selection committee thus could narrow a pool of dialysis candidates by eliminating those who cannot afford to pay for treatment.

4. A principle of *compensatory justice* would distribute resources to those who have previously suffered social wrongs that deprived them of those resources, such as a lack of access to medical care because of a low socioeconomic status. (This is the principle of social justice underlying Medicaid insurance.)

5. A *utilitarian "ethometrics"* principle seeks to provide the greatest benefit or good for the greatest number of persons. This is the principle behind quantitative cost-benefit analyses for the provision of various forms of health care, which often founder in efforts to define what variables should constitute the "greatest good"—for example, economic, personal, social—and to quantitatively calculate noneconomic "goods" such as health status.

6. An *egalitarian* principle of social justice, in American society, is often viewed as the most morally acceptable way to distribute scarce resources. There are, however, many ways to formulate egalitarian principles, and it is seldom easy to specify just what is meant by them and consequently how one should act on them. In the arena of medical care, for example, many hold that we should "provide similar treatment for similar cases," which then leads to a panorama of questions about how one defines "similar treatment" and "similar cases." During the 1960s, a number of dialysis facilities selected patients by random lottery, believing that this form of egalitarian distribution was the fairest, most neutral way of determining who might live when not all could live.

As this brief discussion of the principles of social justice underlying the allocation of dialysis during the 1960s suggests, the need to make such decisions involves a host of complex, painful medical, moral, and social issues. None involved in selecting dialysis recipients welcomed their task, or were comfortable with the selection methods they adopted. All felt there was no really good way to make such decisions; rather, they sought to find what they felt was the "least worst" selection method.

Needless to say, rationing kidney dialysis is not the only medical problem that raises ethical questions. Let me list just a few of the types of everyday, real life decisions in which doctors, nurses, patients, family members, hospital administrators, and others are called on to think about the moral dimensions of their situation.

- Rationing scarce medical care of all sorts
- Deciding which patients get heart, kidney, or lung transplants when they become available
- Deciding whether to keep a terminally ill patient alive, even when the patient will never regain consciousness
- Deciding whether to tell a seriously ill patient the truth about his or her medical condition
- Deciding whether to have an abortion
- Deciding whether to perform an abortion
- Deciding whether to assist a patient who wants to die
- Deciding whether to use aborted fetuses for medical research that will save the lives of other patients
- Deciding whether to screen patients for genetically inherited diseases, and whether to tell them the results of the screening
- Deciding whether to use genetic techniques to influence the sex or other characteristics of a fetus
- Deciding whether patients should play a role in choosing their treatment

I think I can say with confidence that *every single person reading this chapter* will face one or more of these situations sometime in his or her life, either personally or in connection with a family member. What can ethical theory tell us that will help us, and the medical professionals, to make better decisions?

Well, let's get one thing clear right away. Philosophers specializing in ethical theory cannot make any of these decisions for us. When your sink is clogged up, you can call a plumber, step back, and let her unclog it. When your battery dies on a winter day, you can call the AAA and have them give you a jump-start. But if you are an intensive care unit physician trying to decide whether to keep a terminally ill patient alive by heroic means, you cannot call up the local university and have them send over an ethicist to take care of the matter.

This shouldn't surprise us. Remember what we learned from Socrates in Chapter 1. *The unexamined life is not worth living.* That is a snappy way of saying that each of us must make his or her own life choices, based on the clearest, most reflective, most critical thinking we can muster. No philosopher, minister, guru, or political ruler can make our life choices for us. And what is true of life in general is also true of the critical life-and-death choices that regularly arise in medicine. What a philosopher can do for us, as Socrates had the great wisdom to recognize almost 2500 years ago, is to assist us to think better about the choices we must make. As he put it, the philosopher can act as a midwife, assisting at the birth of ideas, but not herself actually producing those ideas. In the remainder of this chapter, I am going to try to play exactly that role. With the help of some selections from the writings of men and women who have thought deeply about the ethical dimensions of medicine, I am going to see whether I can help you to think a bit more clearly about a few of the many critical decisions that we must make in the field of medicine and biotechnology. You won't find any definitive answers here. Instead, if I am successful, you will begin to develop your own ability to look at a problem of medical ethics and see some of the complexities of it. Later in life, when you face one or another of these choices for yourselves, your parents, your children, or your partners, perhaps you will be able to think about it a bit more clearly. That is the most philosophy can do for you, but if the truth be told, that is a great deal.

One brief observation before we begin. Philosophers have been thinking and writing about ethics for two and a half millennia, but the literature devoted to medical ethics is no more than half a century old. There is a good reason for that odd fact. For most of human history, men and women have not been able to do more than say a prayer and hope when serious injury or illness strikes. That is why doctors have from time immemorial taken it as their first principle to do no harm. If you can't cure the patient, which for most of human history doctors couldn't, then at least don't make the patient worse.

In this century, however, medical science has suddenly advanced to a point where doctors can very definitely cure patients, whether with antibiotics and other wonder drugs, or with extraordinary surgical procedures, radiation therapy, and other miracles of modern medicine. That is why the average life expectancy for people in relatively wealthy societies has almost doubled in the past century. Now, once you *can* do something, there is no avoiding the question whether you *should* do it. If a patient in an irreversible coma is going to die regardless of what you do, then there is nothing for it but to arrange for the funeral. But if medical science can keep an irreversibly unconscious patient alive for years, as it now can, then we are forced to ask whether it should do so. And immediately, the hard questions about cost, scarce medical resources, the feelings of the family, and all the rest come up and just won't go away. So, in an odd way, Medical Ethics is a by-product of medicine's great success.

Now let us turn to some case studies. I have chosen three quite different sorts of problems to suggest something of the scope of the subject of medical ethics. These are: Is it ever morally right to withhold food and water from a hopelessly ill patient, which raises the issue of the moral principles that should guide the care-giver; Should we allow the purchase and sale of human organs for organ transplants, which raises many questions about the sanctity of the human body and the limits of the marketplace; and What should the doctor tell the patient, which raises issues of the rights of the patient and the responsibilities of the physician.

Withholding Food and Water

Doctors, nurses, orderlies, and hospital administrators are all trained to be care *givers*. When a patient is admitted to a hospital, they are supposed to bring all their knowledge, skill, and energy to bear on caring for that patient—curing him or her if possible, but at the very least alleviating pain and suffering. No doubt doctors and nurses sometimes fall short of that ideal. Anyone who has ever spent time as a patient in a hospital will have stories to tell of bad stretches in the middle of the night when no one answered the call button for what seemed like hours, or unfeeling attendants who were insensitive to one's pain. Nevertheless, I think we can all agree that hospitals, doctors, nurses, and attendants at least try to live up to their ideal of being caregivers. No ordinary doctor or nurse *tries* to make a patient worse, after all.

So what are we to think of the many, many cases in which the caregivers of a terminally, hopelessly ill patient decide to withhold care, so that the patient can die? And, what is even more important, what are the caregivers themselves to think of situations in which withholding care seems to be the right thing to do? Can it ever be right to withhold something as basic as food and water? Are there cases in which doctors should literally starve a patient to death? If medical science knows how to keep a patient alive, shouldn't it do so?

First of all, let us be absolutely clear about the nature of the cases. We are talking, for example, about a newborn infant who lacks organs necessary to survival and can be kept alive only by continual, heroic life-saving measures. We are talking about a terminally ill brain tumor patient who has slipped into an irreversible coma. We are talking about a patient so severely burned over so much of her body that doctors are unable to perform skin grafts or other procedures and cannot even find a way to keep the patient alive and without terrible pain for very long. We are very definitely *not* talking about a conscious, coherent, viable patient who is capable of communicating that he or she wants to be kept alive.

What sorts of ethical considerations arise cases like these? Let me briefly sketch just a few of the ethical questions that doctors and nurses must ask themselves as they decide what to do.

(a) First of all, there is the issue of *trust*. Hospitals are social institutions that exist for the purpose of caring for the sick. When you enter a hospital as a patient, you expect—you have a *right* to expect—that everyone in that hospital will try to help you get well, or at least that they will do what they can to enable you to suffer less. Even if you are brought into the hospital unconscious—say, after a car accident—you have a right to assume that the doctors and nurses will be care-givers, regardless of the fact that you weren't able to talk to them and tell them that you want to be cared for. Now, there is nothing in care-giving more basic than providing food and water. The doctors may not know how to treat whatever is wrong with you, but at least they can give you the food and water you need to stay alive. So it would seem that a hospital and its care-givers violate a fundamental principle of trust when they deliberately withhold food and water from a patient.

(b) Secondly, there is the issue of *knowledge.* In my description of the cases, I assume that doctors know with certainty that a patient cannot survive. I talk about a "terminally ill" patient in an "irreversible coma." But the most any doctor can honestly say is that it is extremely probable that the patient is terminally ill, and highly unlikely that the patient will come out of the coma. Is it right for doctors to withhold food and water from a patient on the basis of what is, after all, imperfect and incomplete knowledge?

(c) Third, there is the issue of *professional principles.* Doctors and nurses undergo long and rigorous training as care-givers. They are taught to make truly heroic personal sacrifices in order to provide care to their patients. Doctors are taught to work long hours when patients need them. Nurses are taught to check and recheck medications, in order to make absolutely certain that a patient is not harmed by a mistaken dosage. As they study and prepare for careers as care-givers, they learn to take a personal pride in their dedication to the welfare of their patients. All of us grumble from time to time about our doctors, but when someone collapses in a public place, and the call goes up, "Is there a doctor here?", we all feel that inner relief when a woman steps forward and says, quietly, "I am a doctor." Now, men and women who have been trained in this way feel a deep inward conflict when called upon to deny care rather than to give it. If society tells them that it is all right to withhold something as basic as food and water, will we be damaging the very professional principles that we admire so much in doctors and nurses? Will we be undermining the training on which all of us rely when we become patients?

So there are a number of very powerful moral reasons for condemning the withholding of food and water, even in cases that appear terminal, irreversible, hopeless. And these reasons involve just the sort of autonomy and respect for persons that we saw Kant emphasizing so strongly. But there are also a number of very powerful moral considerations that weigh on the other side, in favor of the withholding of food and water. And here too, some of the abstract issues of ethical theory that we took a look at in the first part of this chapter come into play. Consider just a few of them:

(a) First of all, we must confront once again the problem of *allocating scarce resources*. Terminally ill patients require a great deal of very skilled care just to keep them alive. The hospital beds they occupy, the nursing care they use, the doctor's time they need—all of those resources could be used to treat some other patient who has a chance of recovering. So long as we focus just on the terminally ill patient, it may seem heartless or even immoral to withhold the food and water needed for a few more days or weeks of life. But health care professionals know all too well that there are other patients waiting to be treated, and they have responsibilities to those people as well.

(b) Secondly, we must recognize the finiteness, *the limitations of medical science*. The great successes of the past century have made it easier for all of us to forget how little we can really do in the face of inevitable death. All people die, regardless of the heroic efforts of doctors and nurses. Isn't it better to accept that fact and find ways to make death dignified, even meaningful? Desperately keeping alive an infant born without the internal organs needed for survival is not *care-giving*. It is a kind of arrogance, a refusal to acknowledge the human condition. If doctors are being taught to keep patients alive at all costs, regardless of the patient's prospect for survival, then perhaps we should change medical education to include a dignified, resigned recognition of human mortality.

(c) And third, we must pay more attention to the *needs of the loved ones*. All human life is a cycle of childhood, adulthood, old age, and death. True human maturity, as Erik Erikson told us earlier in this chapter, is the recognition that "an individual life is the accidental coincidence of but one life cycle with but one segment of history; and that for [us] all human integrity stands or falls with the one style of integrity of which [we] partake." In some situations, the very best thing a doctor can do for the patient's family and friends is to help them to accept the death as an inevitable part of life, so that they can learn from the death and live their own lives with greater dignity and integrity.

All of these powerful considerations, pro and con, confront medical professionals each time they must deal with a patient for whom they can do no more. Set out like this in a textbook, (a) (b) (c) on one side, (a) (b) (c) on the other, they may look abstract and theoretical. But when you are a doctor or a nurse, standing in an Intensive Care Unit looking down at a woman in a coma, or a hopelessly burned man, or an infant on a respirator, these are anything but abstract and theoretical.

Here is an extended excerpt from a widely read treatment of the problem of withholding food and water, written by a Professor of Medicine at Dartmouth Medical School and a Professor of Religious Studies at the University of Virginia. As you will see, they are painfully conscious of the arguments on both sides of the issue, although they are not afraid to draw some conclusions at the end.

**JOANNE LYNN
AND JAMES F.
CHILDRESS,**
*Must Patients
Always Be Given
Food and Water?**

Many people die from the lack of food or water. For some, this lack is the result of poverty or famine, but for others it is the result of disease or deliberate decision. In the past, malnutrition and dehydration must have accompanied nearly every death that followed an illness of more than a few days. Most dying patients do not eat much on their own, and nothing could be done for them until the first flexible tubing for instilling food or other liquid into the stomach was developed about a hundred years ago. Even then, the procedure was so scarce, so costly in physician and nursing time, and so poorly tolerated that it was used only for patients who clearly could benefit. With the advent of more reliable and efficient procedures in the past few decades, these conditions can be corrected or ameliorated in nearly every patient who would otherwise be malnourished or dehydrated. In fact, intravenous lines and nasogastric tubes have become common images of hospital care.

Providing adequate nutrition and fluids is a high priority for most patients, both because they suffer directly from inadequacies and because these deficiencies hinder their ability to overcome other diseases. But are there some patients who need not receive these treatments? This question has become a prominent public policy issue in a number of recent cases. In May 1981, in Danville, Illinois, the parents and the physician of newborn conjoined twins with shared abdominal organs decided not to feed these children. Feeding and other treatments were given after court intervention, though a grand jury refused to indict the parents.[1] Later that year, two physicians in Los Angeles discontinued intravenous nutrition to a patient who had severe brain damage after an episode involving loss of oxygen following routine surgery. Murder charges were brought, but the hearing judge dismissed the charges at a preliminary hearing. On appeal, the charges were reinstated and remanded for trial.[2]

In April 1982, a Bloomington, Indiana, infant who had tracheoesophageal fistula and Down syndrome was not treated or fed, and he died after two courts ruled that the decision was proper but before all appeals could be heard.[3] When the federal government then

*Lynn and Childress, Part IV: 2: *Terminating Treatment for the Terminally Ill.* In *Life Choices: A Hastings Center Introduction to Bioethics* (pages 201–203, and 211). Edited by: Joseph H. Howell and William F. Sale. © by Georgetown University Press. Reprinted with permission from the publisher.

moved to ensure that such infants would be fed in the future,[4] the Surgeon General, Dr. C. Everett Koop, initially stated that there is never adequate reason to deny nutrition and fluids to a newborn infant.

While these cases were before the public, the nephew of Claire Conroy, an elderly incompetent woman with several serious medical problems, petitioned a New Jersey court for authority to discontinue her nasogastric tube feeding. Although the intermediate appeals court had reversed the ruling,[5] the trial court held that he had this authority since the evidence indicated that the patient would not have wanted such treatment and that its value to her was doubtful.

In all these dramatic cases and in many more that go unnoticed, the decision is made to deliberately withhold food or fluid known to be necessary for the life of the patient. Such decisions are unsettling. There is now widespread consensus that sometimes a patient is best served by not undertaking or continuing certain treatments that would sustain life, especially if these entail substantial suffering.[6] But food and water are so central to an array of human emotions that it is almost impossible to consider them with the same emotional detachment that one might feel toward a respirator or a dialysis machine.

Nevertheless, the question remains: should it ever be permissible to withhold or withdraw food and nutrition? The answer in any real case should acknowledge the psychological contiguity between feeding and loving and between nutritional satisfaction and emotional satisfaction. Yet this acknowledgment does not resolve the core question.

Some have held that it is intrinsically wrong not to feed another. The philosopher G.E.M. Anscombe contends: "For wilful starvation there can be no excuse. The same can't be said quite without qualification about failing to operate or to adopt some courses of treatment."[7] But the moral issues are more complex than Anscombe's comment suggests. Does correcting nutritional deficiencies always improve patients' well-being? What should be our reflective moral response to withholding or withdrawing nutrition? What moral principles are relevant to our reflections? What medical facts about ways of providing nutrition are relevant? And what policies should be adopted by the society, hospitals, and medical and other health care professionals?

In our effort to find answers to these questions, we will concentrate upon the care of patients who are incompetent to make choices for themselves.

Patients who are competent to determine the course of their therapy may refuse any and all interventions proposed by others, as long as their refusals do not seriously harm or impose unfair burdens upon others.[8] A competent patient's decision regarding whether or not to accept the provision of food and water by medical means such as tube feeding or intravenous alimentation is unlikely to raise questions of harm or burden to others.

What then should guide those who must decide about nutrition for a patient who cannot decide? As a start, consider the standard by which other medical decisions are made: one should decide as the incompetent person would have if he or she were competent, when that is possible to determine, and advance that person's interests in a more generalized sense when individual preferences cannot be known. . . .

Our conclusion—that patients or their surrogates, in close collaboration with their physicians and other caregivers and with careful assessment of the relevant information, can correctly decide to forego the provision of medical treatments intended to correct malnutrition and dehydration in some circumstances—is quite limited. Concentrating on incompetent patients, we have argued that in most cases such patients will be best served by providing nutrition and fluids. Thus, there should be a presumption in favor of providing nutrition and fluids as part of the broader presumption to provide means that prolong life. But this presumption may be rebutted in particular cases.

We do not have enough information to be able to determine with clarity and conviction whether withholding or withdrawing nutrition and hydration was justified in the cases that have occasioned public concern, though it seems likely that the Danville and Bloomington babies should have been fed and that Claire Conroy should not.

It is never sufficient to rule out "starvation" categorically. The question is whether the obligation to act in the patient's best interests was discharged by withholding or withdrawing particular medical treatments. All we have claimed is that nutrition and hydration by medical means need not always be provided. Sometimes they may not be in accord with the patient's wishes or interests. Medical nutrition and hydration do not appear to be distinguishable in any morally relevant way from other life-sustaining medical treatments that may on occasion be withheld or withdrawn.

The Buying and Selling of Human Organs

There have always been ways of making up for the loss of a leg, by means of crutches, or even of a hand, by means of the sort of metal hook that Captain Hook sported. But until quite recently, there has been nothing that medical science could do to provide some sort of substitute for one of the many vital internal organs the body needs to live. If a kidney, a lung, a liver, or a heart failed, the patient either died, or else, if the body had two of them [such as a kidney], got along with the remaining organ. If both of a patient's kidneys failed, then life depended on the dialysis machine forever.

In recent years, however, all that has changed. Miraculous as it seems to someone my age, who can remember a time when transplants were a matter of science fiction and fantasy, doctors can now actually take a functioning kidney, heart, liver, or lung out of one person and put it into a patient whose own organ has failed. In countless cases, men, women, and even tiny babies have received organ transplants that allow them to live reasonably full, functioning lives. No longer is it only the mad Dr. Frankenstein, in his Transylvanian castle, who snatches body parts from cadavers and constructs a monster out of them. Now, we see medical technicians rushing to a helicopter and transporting a still warm heart to a hospital hundreds of miles away where it is put into the chest of a dying patient and sewn up!

Well, as we have already observed, once doctors know how to do something heroic and technologically extraordinary, questions arise for which we seem to have no very good answers. Organ transplants are no exception. Here are just some of the previously unimaginable questions that must now be confronted and dealt with by doctors, nurses, hospital administrators, and legislators on a daily basis:

- Should we permit organ transplants?
- Who should get an organ when it becomes available?
- Should individuals be permitted, encouraged, even required to consent to the donation of their organs after they die?
- Should a market price be put on human organs?
- Should individuals be permitted to sell their organs to those needing transplants?
- Should doctors be permitted to harvest organs from dead people without their prior consent? [I really hate that use of the word "harvest," but that is the way people talk about organ transplants!]

All of these questions pose profound ethical problems, but the ones that trouble me the most concern the buying and selling of body parts. There is something obscene about the idea of a market in livers or the going price for hearts. I think it is morally admirable for a man or woman to choose to be an organ donor, declaring by a formal statement that his or her corneas, heart, liver, kidneys, and lungs can be removed at death and offered to patients who need them [even though, at this writing, I still have not actually taken the step of getting and signing an organ donor card]. But selling my body parts? Should I even be allowed to leave a little nest egg for my children by stipulating that they sell off parts of me before what is left gets buried?

If that doesn't bother you, how about allowing poor people to sell spare body parts to rich people who need transplants? Can it possibly be right to permit a desperately poor father to provide for his family by selling one of his two kidneys to a wealthy patient suffering from renal failure? Slavery seems benign by comparison!

And yet, and yet. Right now, homeless men keep alive by selling their blood to blood banks for $20 a pint. And surrogate mothers sell the use of their wombs to childless couples seeking a nurturing home for their fertilized ovum. Why shouldn't I be allowed to sell parts of my body, either before or after I die. It is my body, isn't it?

This is a perfect example of the point I have made several times—that modern medicine, by making previously unimaginable things possible, poses ethical dilemmas for which we simply are not prepared. Most of us—even ethical theorists—rely on our settled intuitions, or gut feelings [which is the same thing], to guide us through difficult ethical terrain. Those intuitions are the product of the accumulated experience of thousands of years of human history, during which men and women facing hard choices have struggled, puzzled, prayed, and argued about what to do. We have very strong intuitions about the relationships between husbands and wives, parents and children, the young and the old, the sick and the well. These intuitions are not always right—indeed, much of the most important ethical theory consists of challenges to those ancient intuitions. But they do give us somewhere to start, some fund of experience to draw on.

Organ transplants, however, are so new, so recent, that we have neither experience nor intuition concerning them. We are forced, therefore, to try to reason our way to decisions, with all the uncertainty and contradiction that seems to produce. Consider just a few of the arguments for and against the buying and selling of body parts that come to mind.

The first argument in favor of permitting the selling of organs is simply that my body is mine and I have a right to do with it what I choose. I have a right to be a body-builder, developing exaggerated muscles, and I also have a right to be a couch potato [though I may not have a right to expect society to give me medical care if I fail to look after myself]. I have a right to dye my hair, to cut my fingernails [or to grow them long], to risk my health in dangerous sports, and even—or so some people would say—to commit suicide. I have a right to choose to be embalmed, [so long as the process does not pose a health hazard to someone else], and I also have the right to be cremated at my death. Now, if I have a right to do all those things to and with my body, both before and after my death, then surely I also have the right to sell part of my body to someone willing to pay me for it. Unless it wants to invoke religious reasons for stopping me, what possible grounds could the state have for denying me the right to dispose of all or part of my body as I wish?

If I have the right to dispose of my body as I choose at my death, surely I have the right to give [i.e., donate] a part of my body to someone whose life it will save. And if I have the right to give my liver, lungs, or heart to a needy patient, why can't I sell the part and make some money in the transaction? No doubt it would be morally preferable for me to make a free gift of my body organs, just as it would be morally admirable for me to give away a large portion of my income to those in need. But however admirable either of those free gifts might be, surely I am not morally required to be generous, am I?

The second argument for permitting the buying and selling of body parts is that it would increase the number of available organs for transplanting. I am sure we can all agree that it would be better if millions of people agreed to donate their organs at death, but the hard fact is that they don't. As a result, tens of thousands of patients die who could be saved by a timely transplant. Doesn't it make sense at least to try marketing organs, in order to see whether it would stimulate an increase in donations? If you are still put off by the idea of the going price for a heart, imagine explaining to the parents of a dying child that her life could be saved by a transplant, and a heart could be made available if it were permissible to sell organs, but you are going to allow the child to die because you find the idea of buying and selling organs "troubling." Is it really more troubling than watching a patient die whom modern medicine could save?

But of course the arguments aren't all on one side. If they were, this would be a no-brainer. Perhaps the most powerful argument against the buying and selling of organs is the danger that such a practice would put unbearable pressures on the poor. Poverty itself is a moral outrage in a society that is capable of adequately feeding and housing everyone—at least some people would say that [and I am one of them]. But the hard fact is that there are tens of millions of poor people in this society, and the way things are going, we shall see more poor people, not fewer, as the years go by. Once people are confronted with the threat that they and their children will starve, the offer of money for their body parts is simply too tempting to turn down, even for some who are deeply offended by the idea. Markets have many advantages, but one of the worst disadvantages is that they put the poor at the mercy of the rich. It is bad enough that the rich can eat, drink, and be merry while the poor struggle to survive. Should the rich also have the right to bribe the poor to give up parts of their own bodies?

A second problem with buying and selling organs is that it turns a medical decision into an economic decision. A rich patient whose need for a transplant is not so desperate will go to the head of the line while a less wealthy patient in urgent need of the transplant will have to wait. A poor donor whose health really does not permit the giving up of a kidney will be led to make a medically unwise decision by the offer of large amounts of money. If organs are for sale, companies will spring up to make a profit out of the transactions, and the doctor's medically informed control over this heroic procedure will be lost to executives whose concern is the bottom line. Health care is already big business. Do we really want the financial pages of our newspapers to list the daily spot market prices for hearts, lungs, and livers?

It should be obvious from even this brief discussion that there are all sorts of legal as well as medical and ethical questions that spring up as soon as we begin to think about the sale of body parts. Judges often try to settle disputes about the selling of organs by applying the laws that govern ordinary property disputes, but that just seems to raise as many issues as it settles. In what sense, if any, is my body something I own? If I own my body, can I sell it to someone else? Does that make me a slave? If I can sell my kidney, can I also sell my heart, even though it will literally kill me to complete the transaction? If brain transplants ever become possible, should I be permitted to sell my brain? When I agree to sell my brain to a buyer and have it transplanted into her body, who is it who emerges from the operation? The buyer? Or me?

Well, enough science fiction! When Mary Shelley wrote *Frankenstein* more than a century ago, organ transplants were a matter of fictional imagination. By the time this edition is getting old, brain transplants may be on the horizon.

✸ What Should the Doctor Tell the Patient?

We have been discussing problems that are posed by the extraordinary medical advances of the past century, but there are some moral dilemmas facing doctors, nurses, and patients that have been with us for millennia. One of the most difficult is this: What should the doctor tell the patient? Even before doctors were actually able to do much in the way of curing disease, they had acquired expert knowledge that enabled them to tell, better than the patients themselves, what was likely to be the outcome of a bout of illness. A doctor who cannot cure tuberculosis, or relieve a stroke, or repair a dysfunctional kidney may nevertheless recognize how serious the patient's condition is. So for as long as there have been doctors and patients, the doctors have struggled with the decision of what to tell the patient and the family gathered around the sickbed.

The problem is most urgent when the doctor can see that the patient's condition is never going to improve—that he or she is dying. When the test results come back from the lab and the news is terminal cancer, should the doctor tell the patient, "You have three months to live?" Does a doctor have a right to withhold vital information from a patient or family members? If she does have that right, are there any circumstances in which she should exercise it? Or do patients have an absolute right to an honest answer when they ask, "How bad is it, Doc?"

This is one of those many cases in which a Utilitarian, dedicated to maximizing happiness, is likely to say one thing, whereas a Kantian, committed to truth-telling and individual autonomy, might say another. But there are, as always, complications. Twenty-five years ago, my physician saw a shadow on my lung x-ray, and made a provisional diagnosis that I had something called sarcoidosis. He sent me to New York City for some fancy tests, and sure enough, the experts said I had "asymptomatic sarcoidosis." That meant I didn't have any symptoms—no pains, no fever, nothing but the shadow on the x-ray. No treatment was indicated. My doctor just said he would monitor it yearly with chest x-rays, and in all probability it would go away of itself.

Well, I was much reassured, and promptly stopped worrying. Sure enough, the shadow disappeared after several years, and I never felt a thing. Some years later, I was sitting in a specialist's office, waiting for my wife, and I happened to pick up a big thick book lying on a shelf. It was a sort of medical encyclopedia of diseases. Out of curiosity, I looked up "sarcoidosis," and to my horror, discovered that in 17 percent of cases it is fatal! I very nearly had a retroactive heart attack.

Now, did my doctor do the right thing or the wrong thing by keeping from me the statistical fact that a significant percentage of sarcoid cases are fatal? He had already done everything that was medically indicated, sending me to specialists and allowing them to decide whether treatment was called for. There was nothing else I could have done, had I known how serious the condition might be. Had he told me, I would have suffered the tortures of the damned, to no useful effect whatsoever. There are even cases in which patients have suffered real heart attacks and other terrible consequences from being told the truth about their condition in plain English.

But there are at least some people—philosophers or not—who would argue that I had a right to know, and my doctor had a duty to tell me, regardless of the consequences. Interestingly, the first philosopher to comment on this issue was Plato, who argued that doctors should seek to educate their patients about medicine as part of their treatment, so that the patients can make rational choices when faced with medical prescriptions.

In this selection, two philosophers, Tom Beauchamp and Lawrence McCullough, explore some of the moral, legal, and medical issues intertwined in a real case, that of Bernard Berkey.

A Case Study: Herniated Disc Injury*

The following "informed consent" case was ultimately decided in a Los Angeles courtroom in 1970.

In 1961, Bernard Berkey suffered a neck injury, which became aggravated in 1962. Dr. Frank M. Anderson treated him on both occasions and conducted a neurological examination that revealed no obvious problem in the leg or back. Dr. Anderson thought the problem was probably in the neck and suggested a myelogram[9] to see if there was damage to the spinal cord. He said, "We have to get to the bottom of this." Mr. Berkey, according to his sworn and uncontested testimony, asked Dr. Anderson whether the myelogram would be similar to the electromyograms[10] he had undergone. Dr.

*From MEDICAL ETHICS by Beauchamp/McCullough, © 1984. Adapted by permission of Prentice-Hall, Inc., Upper Saddle River, NJ.

114

Anderson responded that myelograms were done for diagnostic and exploratory purposes. He said that patients experience minor discomfort when strapped to a cold table, which then is tilted in various directions to determine the extent of damage to the spinal system. Dr. Anderson was otherwise quite reassuring about the procedure; he said Mr. Berkey would "feel nothing" and promised to order an injection of a pain killer to eliminate any possible discomfort. There was little more to the patient-physician interchange during this discussion. Dr. Anderson did not mention that a myelogram involves a spinal puncture, which is *not* performed in electromyograms.

Dr. Robert E. Rickenberg performed the myelogram procedure, and Mr. Berkey later testified that the following events transpired during the procedure: He first felt a few innocuous "sticks." Then suddenly he felt an excruciating pain, as if someone were jamming an ice pick into his lower spine. Mr. Berkey said he had never experienced anything comparable to this pain, which then shot with intensity over his left side and left leg. He "let out a yell," as he later reported, but was told the pain would pass and was sent to rest for 24 hours. When he first stood up he found that he had what he called a "rubber leg": His leg buckled whenever he put weight on it. The next few weeks brought no significant improvement, and he was diagnosed as having "foot drop."[11]

He was examined by several doctors during this period, including Dr. Anderson. One physician, Dr. Faeth, noticed a compression of a nerve, which he judged to be "most probably" caused by a herniated disc.[12] Other possible causes, he later testified, included a tumor, adhesions around the nerve trunk, and the formation of a spur at the margin of the bone. Dr. Anderson was asked in court whether such a herniated disc injury could result from a myelogram. He responded that it could, but only under special circumstances such as "repeated injury with a large bore needle." Dr. Rickenberg testified that he had never heard of anyone developing foot drop as a result of a myelogram.

Mr. Berkey said that nothing whatever had been mentioned to him about the possibility of these levels of pain, injury, and subsequent loss of function. Neither Dr. Anderson nor Dr. Rickenberg had discussed their possible occurrence with Mr. Berkey. Neither physician denied Mr. Berkey's claim to this effect, except to note that they had told him it was a very important diagnostic procedure. Mr. Berkey sued them both—Dr. Rickenberg for negligent performance of the myelogram and Dr. Anderson for a failure to obtain informed consent before ordering the myelogram. The California court that heard an appeal in the case noted that different issues were involved in assessing each physician's actions, but that in each case the court's interest was exclusively in possible damages caused to Mr. Berkey by the responsible physician's action or inaction: "Regarding Dr. Anderson, the questions are whether he obtained the informed consent of his patient before ordering the myelogram and if not, what damages proximately resulted; and as to Dr. Rickenberg, whether there was negligence in administering the myelogram and, if so, whether the injury suffered was the proximate result of such negligence."[13]

The court noted, with regard to the suit against Dr. Anderson, that it is the "duty of a doctor" to explain fully the contemplated procedure and its possible consequences, as well as to obtain the patient's informed consent. If the patient proffered no consent whatever to the myelogram, this omission "would constitute a technical *battery*."[14] If Mr. Berkey had consented, but on the basis of an inadequate disclosure, then Dr. Anderson would be guilty of *negligence*.[15]

Dr. Anderson . . . held that other practicing physicians would not have explained such a remote risk of spinal injury under the circumstances and would have routinely ordered the diagnostic procedure. Dr. Anderson and his lawyer argued that this general standard of what other physicians routinely disclose establishes what *should* have been disclosed. Mr. Berkey and his lawyer, by contrast, argued that "the reasonable person's" needs for information set the standard, not simply what the community of physicians actually discloses. The court sided primarily with Mr. Berkey: "A physician's duty to disclose is not governed by the standard practice of the physicians' community, but is a duty imposed by law. . . . To hold otherwise would permit the medical profession to determine its own responsibilities to the patients in a matter of considerable public interest. Further, . . . Dr. Faeth testified that it was not standard practice in obtaining a patient's consent to a myelogram not to inform him that it involves a spinal puncture."[16]

Even their goal of helping or curing patients could not justify this apparent disrespect for patient autonomy. . . .

The Risks and Benefits of Disclosure

In modern medicine the nature and quality of communication in the patient-physician relationship tend to vary with the duration of prior contact, the state of the patient, and how well the physician relates to his or her patient and the patient's family. A patient's right to information ("to know the truth") and the physician's obligation to provide it have traditionally been thought to depend heavily on such situational factors. Most physicians believe that time constraints and other pressing obligations justify departures from such abstract, oversimplified principles as "Don't lie," "Don't deceive," or "Always tell the truth," when used as guides to determine appropriate levels of disclosure. . . . [A] strategy of nondisclosure or partial disclosure enjoys a prominent place throughout the history of medical ethics. . . .

The principal worry expressed in these historical writings about disclosures is that information might be harmful rather than helpful to seriously ill patients. For example, patients may become agitated as a consequence of full disclosure, sometimes leading to more complicated courses of recovery. This venerable hypothesis has its contemporary adherents, as the following influential statement by Elizabeth F. Loftus and James F. Fries indicates:

> A considerable body of psychological evidence indicates that humans are highly suggestible. Information has been found to change people's attitudes, to change their moods and feelings, and even to make them believe they have experienced events that never in fact occurred. This alone would lead one to suspect that adverse reactions might result from information given during an informed consent discussion.
>
> An examination of the medical evidence demonstrates that . . . not only can positive therapeutic effects be achieved by suggestion, but negative side effects and complications can similarly result. For example, among subjects who participated in a drug study after the usual informed consent procedure, many of those given an injection of a placebo reported physiologically unlikely symptoms such as dizziness, nausea, vomiting, and even mental depressions. One subject given the placebo reported that these effects were so strong that they caused an automobile accident. Many other studies provide similar data indicating that to a variable but often scarifying degree, explicit suggestion of possible adverse effects causes subjects to experience these effects. Recent hypotheses that heart attack may follow coronary spasm indicate physiological mechanisms by which explicit suggestions, and the stress that may be produced by them, might prove fatal. Thus, the possible consequences of suggested symptoms range from minor annoyance to, in extreme cases, death.
>
> If protection of the subject is the reason for obtaining informed consent, the possibility of iatrogenic harm [harm caused by a physician's treatment] to the subject as a direct result of the consent ritual must be considered.[17]

A recent Presidential Commission investigated such claims and concluded as follows: "Despite all the anecdotes about patients who committed suicide, suffered heart attacks, or plunged into prolonged depression upon being told 'bad news,' little documentation exists for claims that informing patients is more dangerous to their health than not informing them, particularly when the informing is done in a sensitive and tactful fashion. . . . There is much to suggest that therapeutic privilege has been vastly overused."[18]

Despite this cloud over the claims, physicians continue to report that many of their sick and dependent patients often find extensive disclosures of potential hazards frightening and incomprehensible. For example, Dr. Robert M. Soule, in response to Sissela Bok's views on lying to patients, argues as follows:

> She states there is no evidence that total candor does any harm to patients. Clinical experience simply doesn't bear this out. . . . Through the years I have seen too many examples of the lethal effect of total candor, including mental breakdowns and suicides by patients given a cold-turkey diagnosis.
>
> Years ago a Harvard report documented fatal ventricular fibrillation brought on by fright in healthy people. And a letter in the May 12, 1977, *New England Journal of Medicine,* cited two heart attacks—one fatal—after patients with no history of cardiac disease had been given full information for consent to noncardiac surgery. The authors said patients often complained they "could not sleep all night before their procedure because of preoccupation and concern.". . .
>
> Many times a conference with the family suggests a patient needs to be protected from the "whole truth.". . .
>
> In a crisis many people would prefer compassion to total frankness, which can have a devastating emotional impact.[19]

It is a matter of overwhelming importance that any generalizations . . . about physician behavior and patients' attitudes reflect the type of illness and degree of morbidity, as well as the context in which disclosures are made and the background of the patients involved. If a healthy patient wants information about the side effects of a prescribed drug or a parent seeks the results of a pediatrician's examination of a young child, we would not expect and would quickly condemn nondisclosure of relevant information. In such instances, a physician can relate to a patient or parent without the degree of emotional dependence that inevitably accompanies the state of sickness. Information can be freely dispatched without fear of undue alarm, let alone terror.

However, many patients with diseases such as metastatic cancer or endstage kidney disease face life-threatening circumstances that may inherently involve choices among alternative courses of treatment, each carrying terrifying risks. Here, any physician must employ managerial skills, taking into account the patient's need for information and ability to deal with it—as, for example, when the terminally ill cancer patient cannot accept the fact that his or her death is imminent, and thus refuses palliative treatment. Is it a primary responsibility of the physician to inform the patient that he or she has but a few months to live? Or is this only a rather wooden way of discharging legal responsibilities while failing the patient at a deeper moral level—for example, failing to help the patient come to grips with his or her mortality and the impact of his or her death on family and friends?

Both empirical evidence and philosophical argument suggest that considerations of risks and benefits of disclosure, as understood through the beneficence model, play an appropriate role in the physician's determination of moral responsibility. The perspective of medicine is invoked to determine the relative weight of harm full disclosure causes to some patients: They might refuse needed diagnostic or therapeutic interventions, suffer unnecessarily, or have more complicated courses of recovery. The physician assumes an obligation to avoid these harms while providing the benefits of medical care. Dr. Anderson's behavior in the diagnosis of Mr. Berkey's condition reflects this approach, even if his execution of it is flawed.

Review of argument and evidence on both sides . . . indicates that the basic issue in the management of medical information is how the physician should balance the goods and harms of various levels of disclosure. Under the professional community standard, as invoked by Dr. Anderson, the rationale is that of the beneficence model: Medicine's perspective should be used to determine the weight of the harms and goods of disclosure. By contrast, the *Berkey* court insisted that the perspective of the informed patient should determine the appropriate weighting—an approach that reflects the autonomy model. Because both perspectives have merit, we should expect that neither the law nor medical ethics will settle finally on a single directive. As we shall now see, the legal history of which *Berkey* is a key part does *not* result in the complete triumph of the patient-based perspective over the professionally based one. The result, instead, is a delicate tension in the law between the two perspectives.

Main Points in Chapter Two, Part Two

1. The dramatic advances in medicine over the last century have raised new and difficult ethical questions for doctors, nurses, and health professionals. Ethical theory can assist them in making their decisions, but cannot provide them with ready-made answers for the difficult questions they now must confront.

2. When trying to decide whether to withhold food and water from terminally ill and unconscious patients, doctors and nurses must weigh the sanctity of life and their professional commitments as care-givers against both the suffering of the families and the need for scarce resources to be allocated to other curable patients.

3. The development of organ transplant technology has forced the medical and legal professions to ask whether it is morally right, legal, or professionally acceptable for individuals to sell and buy human organs for transplant. The autonomy of the individual comes into conflict with the indirect, unintended market effects of the practice of selling organs.

4. One of the most ancient moral dilemmas faced by doctors is what to tell the patient. The moral autonomy of the individual seems to call for complete disclosure by the doctor. But the doctor's commitment to caring for the patient and his or her well-being may conflict with that autonomy.

NOTES

1. John A. Robertson, "Dilemma in Danville," *The Hastings Center Report* 11 (October 1981), 5–8.

2. T. Rohrlich, "2 Doctors Face Murder Charges in Patient's Death," L.A. *Times*, August 19, 1982, A–1; Jonathan Kirsch, "A Death at Kaiser Hospital," *California* 7 (1982), 79ff; Magistrate's findings, *California v. Barber and Nejdl*, No. A 925586, Los Angeles Mun. Ct. Cal., (March 9, 1983); Superior Court of California, County of Los Angeles,*California v. Barber and Nejdl*, No. AO 25586, tentative decision May 5, 1983.

3. *In re Infant Doe*, No. GU 8204–00 (Cir. Ct. Monroe County, Ind., April 12, 1982), writ of mandamus dismissed sub nom. *State ex rel. Infant Doe v. Baker*, No. 482 S140 (Indiana Supreme Ct. May 27, 1982).

4. Office of the Secretary, Department of Health and Human Services, "Nondiscrimination on the Basis of Handicap,"*Federal Register* 48 (1983), 9630–32. [Interim final rule modifying 45 C.F.R. #84.61]. See Judge Gerhard Gesell's decision, *American Academy of Pediatrics v. Heckler*, No. 83–0774, U.S. District Court, D.C., April 24, 1983; and also George J. Annas, "Disconnecting the Baby Doe Hotline," *The Hastings Center Report* 13 (June 1983), 14–16.

5. *In re Claire C. Conroy*, Sup Ct. NJ (Chancery Div-Essex Co. No. P-19083E) February 2, 1983; *In re Claire C. Conroy*, Sup Ct NJ (Appellate Div. No. 4-2483-82T1) July 8, 1983.

6. The President's Commission for the Study of Ethical Problems in Medicine and Biomedical and Behavioral Research, *Deciding to Forego Life-Sustaining Treatment* (Washington, D.C.: Government Printing Office, 1982).

7. G.E.M. Anscombe, "Ethical Problems in the Management of Some Severely Handicapped Children: Commentary 2," *Journal of Medical Ethics* 7 (1981), 117–124, at 122.

8. See e.g., the President's Commission for the Study of Ethical Problems in Medicine and Biomedical and Behavioral Research, *Making Health Care Decisions* (Washington, D.C.: Government Printing Office, 1982).

9. "Myelogram" literally means "graph of the spinal cord." During the myelogram, a large gauge, 2½-inch needle is inserted into the lumbar area (lower mid-back) of the spine, while the patient is prone and harnessed on a fluoroscopic table. Eight to ten cc's of spinal fluid are tapped for laboratory analysis, with the needle inserted into the subarachnoid space (just beneath a major covering membrane). An opaque substance (panopaque) is then introduced into the spinal canal through the needle. Tilting the table causes a flow of the substance in the spine, and this flow is captured by X-rays.

10. An electromyogram is a procedure used to study electrical activity in the muscle, to diagnose a variety of disorders. The procedure involves inserting needle electrodes into muscle tissue. This involves some discomfort, but poses only minor risks.

11. "Foot drop" means a falling of the foot because of paralysis of the ankle.

12. In a herniated disc, the pulpy body at the center of the disc protrudes through the surrounding fibrocartilage, forming a small sac.

13. *Berkey v. Anderson,* App. 82 Cal. Rptr. 67, p. 72.

14. Battery is an unconsented-to physical violence or constraint inflicted by one person on another.

15. Negligence is the omission of (or doing of) something that a reasonable person in the circumstances would do (or not do).

16. *Berkey v. Anderson,* p. 78.

17. Elizabeth F. Loftus and James F. Fries, "Informed Consent May be Hazardous to Health," *Science* 204 (6 April 1979): 11. The position and argument of Loftus and Fries have been subjected to important criticism. See Ruth Barcan Marcus, Bruce Kuklick, and Sacvan Bercovitch, Letter, *Science* 205 (17 August 1979): 644. These authors have shown its logical flaws, while important empirical limitations have been pointed to by Ruth Faden et al., "Disclosures of Information to Patients in Medical Care," *Medical Care* 19 (July 1981): 718–33, esp. 731, and Ruth Faden et al., "Disclosure Standards and Informed Consent," *Journal of Health Politics, Policy, and Law* 6 (1981): 255–84. Faden et al. show that there exists better evidence for the Loftus-Fries position than they themselves adduce, but that there exists equally powerful counterevidence.

18. President's Commission for the Study of Ethical Problems in Medicine and Biomedicine and Behavioral Research, *Making Health Care Decisions: The Ethical and Legal Implications of Informed Consent in the Patient-Practitioner Relationship* (Washington: U.S. Government Printing Office, 1982), vol. 1, p. 96.

19. Robert M. Soule, "The Case Against 'Total Candor'," *Medical World News* 20 (14 May 1979): 94.

CONTEMPORARY APPLICATIONS

Assisted Suicide

The abstract subtleties of ethical theory and the practical complexities of medical ethics come together with great urgency in the extremely controversial subject of assisted suicide. Can it ever be right, under any circumstances, for a doctor to help a patient to die? We are talking here about patients who are conscious, and capable of telling their doctors that they want to die. We are not talking about unconscious patients for whom a decision must be made. The issue has been on television and in the newspapers for several years now because of the activities of one man, a physician named Dr. Jack Kevorkian. Kevorkian, dubbed "Dr. Death" by the media, has assisted more than three dozen patients to die, usually by administering a lethal dose of medication or by helping the patient to breathe carbon monoxide. Again and again, state courts have tried Dr. Kevorkian for murder or some other crime, but as of the moment when I am writing this, he has always beaten the rap.

The ethical questions posed by physician-assisted suicide do not arise because of any modern advances in medical techniques. It has always been possible to help people to die, after all. The issues here go to the heart of ethical theory and practice, as well as to the very core of what it is to be a doctor. Do any of us have a moral right to commit suicide? Many philosophers have argued that we do not. Baruch Spinoza claimed that no one ever truly commits suicide, because people who kill themselves cannot possibly really understand what they are doing. They lack an "adequate idea" of their act. So, for example, a distraught child may think, "I will kill myself, and then everyone will be really sorry at my funeral." But the child is actually imagining the funeral, not realizing that if he kills himself, he won't be around to witness his family's grief. Kant insisted that it was irrational—self-contradictory—to commit suicide.

But even if we decide that each individual has a fundamental right to end his or her own life, that still does not tell us whether a doctor can, in good conscience, assist that suicide. Doctors are committed by their profession and their oath to save life, to relieve suffering, to act for the good of the patient. Can it ever be right for a doctor to take a life, even when asked to do so by the patient? In this pair of readings, you will find two opposed points of view. Notice that neither author thinks the issue is simple or clear-cut. This is one of those really hard cases that leads even strong opponents to recognize some merit in the contrary position.

ఌఌఌఌఌఌఌఌఌఌఌఌఌ

MAKE MINE HEMLOCK*
Ernest van den Haag

Before Christianity, governments were unconcerned with suicide, which was thought expedient in some circumstances and required by honor in others. However, with the coming of Christianity suicide became a sin, a violation of God's commandments. As unrepentant sinners, suicides were denied burial in consecrated ground and expected to end in Hell. Life was thought to be a gift from God, Who ordained its beginning and end. We possessed the life created by Him, but He owned it. Our possession could not license us to destroy what did not belong to us.

As the grip of Christianity weakened, this part of religion was secularized, as were many others. Suicide became a transgression against nature, not God, usually explained by mental derangement. Absent derangement, suicide was considered a crime against society, thought to own individuals more or less as God had been thought to before. Only in our time has it come to be believed that individuals collectively own society, rather than vice versa. They also are thought to own themselves. Without God (or slavery) no one else really could. Owners can dispose of what they own as they see fit. We thus each become entitled to control our life, including its duration, to the extent nature permits, provided that this control does not harm others in ways proscribed by law.

Very few people are inclined to commit suicide. But this hardly seems a good reason to prevent it, although sometimes it is asserted or implied that the unpopularity of suicide argues for its immorality and for preventing it. Yet, those who do not wish, or do not feel they have the moral right to, end their life can easily refrain. It is not clear on what grounds a government, or anyone else, could be entitled to prevent a competent person from controlling the duration of his or her life.

Although the foregoing view seems irrefutable, not everyone accepts it. It is contrary to tradition, wherefore many obstacles remain in the way of people who try to shorten their life. These obstacles can be nearly insurmountable for those who most wish to do so because of a disabling disease. They may be forced to go on living against their will. Even some healthy persons find the obstacles quite forbidding. They may have to jump out of windows, or use drugs which are difficult to obtain and of the specific effects of which they are not fully informed. Physicians and other experts, who do know the proper combination and quantities of drugs needed, usually refuse help, either because of moral objections or in fear of legal liabilities. They impose their own socially supported moral beliefs on patients who do not share them, but cannot act unaided. Dr. Jack Kevorkian is a rare and courageous exception.

To be sure, compassionate physicians may feel that terminal patients in extreme pain should be helped to end such pain. They may discreetly prescribe anesthetics which end suffering by ending life. There have been no successful prosecutions for this quasilegal practice, although some unsuccessful ones have been brought and physicians who prescribe painkillers in the required quantities assume some risk. Physicians also may withhold life-prolonging treatment at the directions of patients or of legal guardians. Patients do have a legal right to refuse any treatment—though the extent of that right is not well defined. However, merely withholding treatment still may lead to an unnecessarily prolonged, stressful, and perhaps painful way of dying.

Even physicians such as Dr. Kevorkian, willing to take major legal risks, have helped only patients who were incurable and, in most cases, had reached a terminal stage. This takes the decision on whether to end life out of the hands of a mentally competent patient and places it into the hands of a physician, who must decide that the patient is terminal enough, or has suffered enough, before helping him to die. He may also refuse to help at all.

Giving physicians (or any other persons) the authority to veto a patient's decision seems unwarranted. Physicians are trained in how to treat diseases so as to prolong life. They are not experts on whether or not to prolong it. There is no training for making such a decision. Indeed, physicians are taught *(primum non laedere)* always to prolong life. No respect is instilled for the patient's wishes, if he prefers to shorten his life. Yet, whether and when to end a person's life is a moral, not a medical, decision, for the patient to make, not the doctor. The physician's task is to inform the patient of his prognosis, perhaps to advise him, and, above all, to help him carry out his decision.

Imagine a 20-year-old patient hospitalized for a condition which, although incurable, is neither terminal nor acutely painful. In the patient's rational, carefully considered view his condition denies him the pleasures of life. He wants to die, but needs assistance. Since he is neither terminal nor suffering unbearable pain, most physicians would be unwilling to help and would run a major legal risk if they did. Again, imagine a 90-year-old who feels that life is of no further interest to him, although he is neither terminal nor in pain. He too will find it hard to persuade a physician to help him die if he cannot do so by himself.

For good or bad reasons, people commit suicide every day. Since many would-be suicides act on impulses which may turn out to be temporary, forcing a moderate delay seems in their interest and legitimate—but is not to be confused with preclusion. Imagine now a healthy young man who, perhaps influenced by Arthur Schopenhauer's philosophy, has decided to commit suicide. Before he has a chance to kill himself, a traffic accident leaves him paralyzed and hospitalized, incurable but not terminal. He now has additional reasons to end his life but is less able, perhaps altogether unable, to do so unless aided. Although we do not make it easy, we cannot prevent an able person from ending his life anytime he wants to. But we can prevent a disabled person from doing the same. Thus we add to the disability nature or accident has inflicted.

This seems odd because our compassionate society usually goes out of its way to help the disabled overcome whatever handicaps are in the way of their desires. Employers are legally compelled to hire disabled persons, schools to make special arrangements to teach them. Public buildings and transportation are made accessible to the wheelchair-bound. Yet, when it comes to suicide, we refuse to allow any assistance to the disabled. We exploit their disability to prevent them from doing what able-bodied persons can do. On all other occasions we try to compensate for the disadvantages nature inflicts on some. Yet when assistance is essential to enable the disabled to commit suicide, we threaten to prosecute anyone who helps them.

Despite the receding influence of religious ideas and our official unwillingness to impose them, and despite the precariousness of the notion that society has a compelling interest in preventing suicide, we continue to treat life as a social duty that individuals, however disabled, should not be helped to shirk. It is not clear to whom the duty to live could be owed. Once the government no longer legally recognizes God as the authority to which duties are owed, nature cannot have prescriptive authority to force unwilling persons to live, since such authority would have to come from God. Only society is left as the source of this alleged duty. But society cannot be shown to have a compelling interest in forcing persons to live against their will. Moreover, such an interest would hardly justify the cruelty involved. To be sure, the great majority has an instinctive wish to live. But why should we enforce the gratification of this wish on those who, for whatever reason, decide not to gratify it?

A Right to Die?

Since, from a secular viewpoint, the moral right to die can hardly be less fundamental than the moral right to live, our non-recognition of the former must flow from unacknowledged residual theological notions which we have officially renounced imposing on non-believers. Dimly realizing as much, most persons opposed to assistance in suicide tend to avoid moral arguments in favor of prudential arguments. These are of two kinds. The first questions the mental competence of individuals who want to hasten their death. The second questions the disinterestedness of persons willing to help them. We must also deal with questions about ending the life of persons who are in a terminal phase of disease, but not mentally competent to make decisions, and of persons in a permanent coma. These are particularly sticky questions, since ending the life of these two classes of patients would be homicide, justifiable or not, rather than suicide, since, by definition, the patients do not make the decision themselves.

How can we assess the mental competence of a physically disabled person who decides on suicide? The task is daunting but not impossible. First of all, prejudicial notions must be discarded. A patient who wants his life ended need not be mentally sick, clinically depressed, or temporarily deranged. The idea that he must be mentally sick merely justifies a conclusion foreordained by circular reasoning. Having discarded prejudicial notions, psychiatrists, using their customary methods, can ascertain whether the patient knows who and where he is, and whether his mental processes are realistic and logical to the normal degree. A conversation about what led to his decision is apposite as well. Reasonable opponents of suicide, religious or not, may be invited to participate where feasible. (The whole process could be videotaped if the patient's competence is controversial.) Beyond the judgment of the psychiatrist, based on these data, nothing is needed. The patient's decision should be accepted.

Intellectual competence is to be investigated, not what is sometimes referred to as emotional health. "Emotional health" is not a clinical concept, but a moral concept quite amorphous and subject to fashion. It allows the imposition of moral views on a patient who may be diagnosed as emotionally ill if he does not share them.

How can we make sure that no one will be pressed to end his or her life by self-interested relatives, friends, enemies, or caretakers? What about undue influence? Safeguards have long been developed to make sure that a patient's decisions about his last will are uncontaminated. These safeguards can be used as well to ensure that his decision about assisted suicide is independent. Where there are problems with the medical prognosis on which the patient's decision may depend, these must be dealt with by means of second or third opinions.

As for the terminal patient who is incompetent or unconscious, if he has provided instructions while competent, they should be followed. If he has not, the decision of relatives and legal guardians must be followed, unless there is evidence to make them suspect. If the situation is cloudy (or if the patient has no relatives) the hospital could name someone, preferably a physician familiar with the patient's syndrome, but practicing elsewhere, to make the decision. If his prognosis and decision agree with those of the treating physician there is no problem. If not, the two physicians will have to ask a third physician willing to decide within 36 hours. Decisions should be independent of the views of hospital administrators and allow ending life when there is no chance of regaining consciousness.

Sometimes an analogy between assisted suicide and abortion is suggested. Indeed, opponents of one usually oppose the other as well; in both cases the opposition may ultimately rest on traditional religious ideas even if the opponents are not religious. But the analogy is misleading. Abortion destroys a fetus with the consent of the mother and usually reflects her interests. The fetus does not make the decision and cannot be consulted. Conceivably the fetus could have an interest in survival. If allowed to develop, the fetus may be expected to desire and enjoy life. In contrast, assisted suicide shortens the life of a patient who has decided himself that prolongation does not serve his interests. Surely, the normal fetus could not be assumed to have an interest in self-destruction. The suicidal patient does. (Conflicts about abortion usually are about alleged fetal v. alleged maternal rights, with some denying fetal rights. But no one would deny that suicide patients are persons who have rights.)

Most arguments about assisted suicide can be dealt with in a reasonable, if not perfect, way. However, the "slippery slope" argument, though influential, is hard to deal with rationally. It suggests that, once we allow doctors to shorten the life of patients who request it, doctors could and would wantonly kill burdensome patients who do not want to die. This suggestion is not justified. The specter of Nazi practices is usually raised to make it credible. But Nazi practices were imposed on physicians and hospitals by political directives which did not evolve from any prior authority given physicians to assist in suicide. There was no "slippery slope." Nor can it be found elsewhere in medical practice. Physicians often prescribe drugs which, in doses greater than prescribed, would kill the patient. No one fears that the actual doses prescribed will lead to the use of lethal doses. No one objects to such prescriptions in fear of a "slippery slope." The "slippery slope" idea seems fortunately to be an unrealistic nightmare. Authorizing physicians to assist in shortening the life of patients who request this assistance no more implies authority to shorten the life of patients who want to prolong it, than authority for surgery to remove the gall bladder implies authority to remove the patient's heart.

Mr. van den Haag is a retired professor and psychoanalyst. He argues that unless there is a divine sanction, the law against suicide is without philosophical foundation.

ꕤ ꕤ ꕤ ꕤ ꕤ ꕤ ꕤ ꕤ ꕤ ꕤ ꕤ ꕤ

DEATH, BE NOT PROUD*
Robert P. George and William C. Porth, Jr.[†]

Darwin had his Huxley. Dr. Jack Kevorkian has at long last found his in the person of Professor

*From "Death, Be Not Proud" by Robert P. George and William C. Porth, Jr. from NATIONAL REVIEW, June 26, 1995, pp. 49–52. © 1995 by NATIONAL REVIEW, Inc., 150 East 35th Street, New York, NY 10016. Reprinted by permission.
[†]George and Porth take on Ernest van den Haag's argument for suicide in round two of our debate. Is there really a right to suicide? If so, is there a duty to assist in it?

Ernest van den Haag. In the June 12 issue of this journal, Professor van den Haag champions not only a legal right to commit suicide, but a right to demand medical assistance in doing so, praising Kevorkian as a "rare and courageous exception" to the refusal of most doctors to extend such "help." Granted that Dr. Kevorkian at least manifests the courage of his convictions, are we ready to embrace his vision not only as an acceptable medical ethic but as the basis for a new legal entitlement that would play its part in shaping the future of American society? Van den Haag is clearly ready, but the rest of us would do well to reflect a little more carefully on the implications of a sweeping right to death.

According to van den Haag, our failure to recognize a legal right to suicide is a remnant of the sway of Christianity over Western society. He even asserts that, before Christianity, governments were "unconcerned with suicide," deeming it either expedient or honorable. As in the analogous case of the wildly inaccurate historical account of abortion law given by Justice Blackmun in *Roe* v. *Wade,* bad history paves the way for bad political philosophy and deplorable law.

Suicide has been condemned and proscribed in a wide array of societies throughout history. To cite only a couple of instances predating the birth of Christ, suicide has always stood under a general condemnation in Jewish law, and Aristotle, in Book V of *Nicomachean Ethics,* addresses why the state punishes a man who kills himself (not merely why the state *should* punish him, it must be stressed, but why it in fact *does*). The philosophical rejection of suicide has also been widespread, although not universal, and it has only sometimes been dependent on the precepts of revealed religion, Christian or otherwise. As Kant observed, "Suicide is not abominable because God forbids it; God forbids it because it is abominable." Are millennia of law, tradition, and moral reasoning as undeserving of regard and as easily dismissed as Professor van den Haag imagines?

Even the foundational instrument of American democracy would have to go. According to the Declaration of Independence, each of us is endowed by our Creator with certain inalienable rights, including, notably, the right to life. Ought Americans to continue to credit this teaching? We can't if we accept van den Haag's notion of a freely alienable right to life, under which people would have the right to kill themselves and, indeed, to authorize others to kill them. "From a secular viewpoint," he declares, "the moral right to die can hardly be less funda-

mental than the moral right to live." So much for the inalienable right to life.

What of the Declaration's acknowledgment of the role of the "Creator"? Van den Haag makes short work of Him by denying the legitimacy of legislating on the basis of religiously informed moral judgments. He treats the inalienability of the right to life as nothing more than an "unacknowledged residual theological notion which we have officially renounced imposing on non-believers." This same stricture, he argues, eliminates even natural-law arguments against suicide: "Once the government no longer recognizes God as the authority to which duties are owed, nature cannot have prescriptive authority to force unwilling persons to live, since it would have to come from God."

Here, of course, van den Haag courts self-defeat. Natural law is not some oppressive external edict. It is the product of human reason directed to the eternal question of what it means to flourish fully as human beings. Such moral reasoning is foundational to any consideration of human rights. Either van den Haag's argument undercuts all moral claims, including his own claim of a moral right to commit suicide, or it proves nothing. If he is prepared to embrace moral subjectivism or relativism as a consequence of what he takes to be our "renunciation" of imposing "theological notions" on non-believers, then he has no basis for arguing that society does anything wrong in imposing its views on non-believers or violating what he takes to be people's moral rights, including their alleged moral right to kill themselves. But if he eschews subjectivism and relativism, then he will need to adduce some ground of moral rights which survives his own strictures against appealing to divine or natural law. Moral libertarians have been pushing this boulder up the hill for a long time now; it keeps rolling back and crushing them.

In any event, to van den Haag it "seems irrefutable, if religion is disregarded," that people have a right to kill themselves. His intellectual case for this alleged "right to die" is simple: 1) people own themselves; 2) owners can dispose of their property as they see fit; 3) people are therefore entitled to kill themselves, and even to engage the help of others in doing so.

Can People Be Owned?

Van den Haag's argument for the notoriously controversial proposition that individuals "own themselves" is that "without God (or slavery) no one else really could." Astonishingly, in view of its prominence in philosophical literature, the possibility seems not to have occurred to him that people are "owned" neither by themselves, nor by other people, nor (in any sense analogous to the human ownership of property) by God. People simply are not owned by anyone; nor, in any morally permissible way, can they be owned.

As subjects of moral rights and obligations, people are not chattels to be owned, traded, or disposed of as they or anyone else "sees fit." As *persons*, not merely *things*, human beings have intrinsic, not merely instrumental, value. Hence people possess a dignity to which rights attach that not even they have the moral authority to waive, i.e., *inalienable* rights.

In defending a right to commit suicide, van den Haag makes an implicit appeal to J. S. Mill's principle that people ought to be free to do as they please so long as they do not directly harm others. Mill himself, however, saw that his "harm principle" could not rationally be stretched to authorize people to "dispose of themselves as they see fit." For example, he famously denied that people have a moral right to sell themselves into slavery. Whatever is ultimately to be said for and against his philosophy of liberty, Mill stands with Jefferson, not van den Haag, on the question of inalienable rights.

Van den Haag's uncritical appeal to the idea of self-ownership renders his argument utterly unpersuasive. In fact, if people are the sorts of things that can be "owned" and "disposed of" as the owner "sees fit," then it is difficult to imagine what grounds could be given for believing that people have *moral* rights at all. And if people have no moral rights, then they cannot have what van den Haag calls the moral right to die. To treat the right to life as anything but inalienable ultimately undercuts all claims to moral rights.

Moreover, any theory of self-ownership, even one such as Locke's (which is far less imperialistic than van den Haag's), will have to identify the source of one's property interest in oneself. Mere "possession" cannot be enough. That provides no one with a morally compelling reason to refrain from, for example, seizing another and making him a slave. Obviously van den Haag cannot claim that God grants us title to ourselves; nor can he maintain that it derives from nature. Watch out, Professor, here comes that boulder!

The long and short of the matter is that van den Haag's argument for a moral right to die is anything but "irrefutable." It leaves untouched the most telling and—truth be told—the most obvious counterarguments, and rests on premises that eviscerate the moral force of the conclusions they are designed to support.

The shaky ground on which Professor van den Haag constructs his right to suicide becomes no stabler when he moves to the right to assistance in committing suicide. Here he contends that physicians who refuse to honor their patients' requests for help in killing themselves "impose their own socially supported moral beliefs on patients who do not share them, but cannot act unaided." Such a physician, according to van den Haag, exercises a "veto" over the patient's decision. And "giving physicians (or any other person) the authority to veto a patient's decision seems unwarranted."

So, in the Brave New World of Professor van den Haag, doctors who dissent from the new moral orthodoxy are guilty of imposing their morality on others simply by declining to do what they believe is morally wrong. What would a moral libertarian propose for dealing with people who insist on imposing their morality on others? Fines? License suspension or revocation? Some even more severe sanction? Whatever the solution, it would presumably take the form of some species of coercion designed to force dissenting physicians to get with the moral-libertarian program.

To be fair, van den Haag does not stipulate that he would *require* doctors to assist in suicides. But his argument tends nowhere else, since he maintains that it is a violation of a patient's rights to withhold such assistance. Obviously, though, government compulsion of doctors to assist in suicides could only result in the vindication of one putative moral right (that of a patient to kill himself) at the direct expense of another (that of a doctor to refrain from performing or facilitating such a killing). We therefore face the high irony that the assisted-suicide agenda diminishes the humanity of both patients and doctors: the former by treating their lives as disposable things; the latter, by treating them as mere instruments to carry out the wishes of their patients.

Part of van den Haag's error is his conception of the doctor's role. He sees it as essentially catering to the patient's desires. But there is no more reason to suppose that a doctor has a duty to gratify a patient's desire for death than that he has a duty to gratify his desire for the euphoria of addictive drugs. Physicians pledge themselves to promote human life and health. They have no right to *compel* a patient to act in service of those ends. But they themselves have a duty not to act against them. And they have a duty not to act except in accordance with their own expertise and professional judgment. Thus, a doctor should not infect a patient with a disease or amputate a healthy limb simply because an eccentric patient desires it. And if he should not do the lesser wrong of intentionally harming a patient's bodily well-being, he should not do

the greater wrong of intentionally destroying a patient's life.

Curiously, van den Haag does not expressly discuss why he hits upon doctors as the persons whom society should select to carry out the task of assisting would-be suicides. Certainly physicians possess a comprehensive knowledge of the vulnerabilities of human bodies. But one does not need all the training of an engineer to be a saboteur or the skill of an anatomist to be a butcher. Indeed, there is something more than faintly unsettling about asking the preservers of life to play so prominent a role in destroying it, much as if a government bent on iconoclasm insisted that painters and sculptors take the lead in smashing the images on which they had labored. If society decides to recognize a right of assisted suicide, the simplest way of implementing it might be to expand the duties of the mortician. He is already adept at using the syringe to withdraw and inject fluids. With a modicum of additional training he could administer a fatal injection and then have the body right at hand for his customary ministrations. The efficiencies of such a scheme are obvious, and even the title of "mortician" seems singularly apt.

As a further argument, van den Haag proposes that failure to provide assistance in committing suicide "discriminates" against those who, because of paralysis or some other disability, cannot destroy themselves unaided. This is a truly bizarre notion. Simply because government cannot prevent some people from transgressing its laws does not require it to assist others in doing so. The same is true of such harmful and even immoral conduct as government prudently declines to criminalize. For example, an ordinary adult may choose to drink himself into oblivion in the privacy of his home; but it does not follow that we discriminate against a quadriplegic who may be similarly inclined when the government does not provide him with a helper to purchase and ply him with alcohol.

Next Steps?

Professor van den Haag's final effort is to rebut prudential concerns which might make a society wary of legalizing assisted suicide, even if it were persuaded of its theoretical justification. Such concerns are legion, but van den Haag addresses only a few. These fall into four basic categories: difficulties in ensuring the mental competence of a would-be suicide, necessary safeguards against undue influence being used to persuade someone to accept being killed, the need for substituted decision-making for the unconscious and the incompetent, and the fear that acceptance of assisted suicide will lead to worse things.

The question of mental competence, van den Haag would handle by empowering psychiatrists, "using their customary methods," to rule upon the sanity of a person who elects to have himself killed. But there is no need to keep the process simple; so he suggests that "reasonable opponents of suicide, religious or not, may be invited to participate," and the "whole process" may be videotaped in controversial cases. Although van den Haag does not discuss the prospect, when two or more psychiatrists disagree, one must assume that the whole circus would end up before the courts, even if the mechanism for the competency hearing was such that it did not begin there. Isn't that an attractive prospect to add to the dockets of a medico-legal system already filled with acrimony and overloaded to the breaking point?

With respect to the fear of undue influence, van den Haag is far less specific. He assures us that "safeguards have long been developed to make sure that a patient's decisions about his last will are uncontaminated" and these "can be used as well to ensure that his decision about assisted suicide is independent." Yet he doesn't indicate what safeguards he may have in mind. Since the chief safeguard against undue influence upon testators is the right to challenge their wills during the probate process, this particular safeguard might come a little late for the weak and elderly relative who has been overzealously persuaded to call for the lethal injection. The only timely safeguard would seem to be another pre-suicide hearing, at which a different set of experts and lawyers could explore the possibility of undue influence.

Perhaps we are too pessimistic about the proliferation of these hearings. Since there is a tendency for many professional services to gravitate to where they can be adequately compensated, maybe these proceedings would reach full flower only when a Mellon or a Rockefeller contemplated ending it all. In the case of the middle class, and especially the poor, it may be that these hearings would be perfunctory, if not absent altogether. Many "unimportant" people might pass through the hands of the suicide facilitators in a brisk and efficient fashion. Alas, this prospect offers us strangely little reassurance.

Van den Haag's third prudential concern is the need for a proper mechanism for substituted decision-making, so that the mentally impaired and the comatose will not be denied the benefits of assisted suicide. Such a mechanism would not be a novelty in American society. Since the withholding of nutrition and hydration has been allowed to be directed by relatives in many instances under the guise of declining "medical treatment," one could say that we already have experience with one strain of third-party election of assisted suicide. The results are not encouraging. Apart from the moral objections to allowing someone to decide to have someone else killed, the number of cases in which our medical experts have proved to be wrong in their predictions is alarming. Professor van den Haag assures us that he would allow third-party election of assisted suicide only when there is no chance of a patient regaining consciousness. The problem is that medical science seems incapable of making this judgment with anything even remotely approaching accuracy. As Wesley J.

Smith reported in the aforementioned article, one study published in 1991 in the *Archives of Neurology* found that 58 per cent of patients with a "firm diagnosis" of being in a persistent vegetative state recovered consciousness within three years. Of course, such embarrassing statistics might tend to disappear if we were to embrace surrogate decision-making for assisted suicide, but this wouldn't mean that the errors would cease, only our painful consciousness of them. In this area, what would be an acceptable incidence of error? One per cent? One-tenth of one per cent? What would be a tolerable sacrifice for this questionable moral "progress"?

Slippery Slope

This brings us to a final area of prudential concern and the question perhaps most worth pondering: What sort of society would creation of a right to assisted suicide help us to become? Professor van den Haag is curtly dismissive of the notion that it would be likely to lead to moral deterioration and a slide from acceptance of suicide as a "rational" and legitimate choice to acceptance of "mercy killing" with or without the victim's consent and even to the disposal of those who desire to cling to life but whose desire is deemed selfish or irrational. But the slope becomes very slippery very fast as soon as a society begins acting on the proposition that some people are better off dead. We cannot forget that legalizing suicide means legitimizing the taking of an innocent human life, albeit one's own. And once a society has acknowledged as reasonable that there can be lives not worth living, and therefore rightly eliminated, only sentimentality stands in the way of embracing the concept of "*lebensunwertes Leben*"—"life unworthy of life."

We are well into our slide. Consider the widespread approval, discussed above, of depriving comatose patients of food and water. Consider recent proposals from the highest ranks of the American medical profession to allow harvesting of organs from anencephalic infants *before death*. Consider the even more "advanced" state of affairs in the Netherlands, where non-consensual euthanasia is common. Does all this appear to be anything but a perfectly logical progression? It is but a short step from judging that a person who is old, infirm, and in pain can rationally "choose death" to concluding that it is irrational for such a person to refuse to make that choice. As our population ages, government will face increased burdens in caring for the elderly. It is not unrealistic to fear that government may assume what began as a private prerogative, and move from making life-and-death decisions for the comatose, to making them for the insane, for the retarded, for those of less-than-average intelligence, and finally for those who are entirely rational and intelligent, but whose desire to cling to life brands them as obstinate, uncooperative, and just plain unreasonable. Are we then to rely on nothing but the heroism of individual doctors to restrain the abuses of government? If so, let us hope there are some "rare and courageous exceptions" among physicians of a rather different stripe from Dr. Jack Kevorkian.

Mr. George teaches legal and political theory at Princeton and is a lawyer. Mr. Porth is a lawyer and writer. They recently served as counsel to Mother Teresa on an amicus curiae brief asking the Supreme Court to reverse Roe v. Wade.

Questions for Discussion and Review

1. Have you or your family ever faced a really serious and difficult medical decision that raised ethical questions? How did you go about deciding what to do? Did you consider the relative value of alternative consequences [the Utilitarian approach], or did you focus on the rights of the different people involved [the Kantian approach]?

2. Do you think doctors and hospitals should consider whether patients have been good or bad persons when deciding who should get the next available heart or liver for transplant? Should they consider the age of the patients? How much they can contribute to society? Or should the organ transplants be distributed on a first-come first-served basis? Why?

3. If you were dying of an incurable disease, would you want to be told? Should you tell a friend or relative who has such a disease? Who has the right to make that decision?

4. As modern genetic techniques improve, doctors become more and more capable of determining who is at risk for various diseases, such as cancer, Alzheimer's, and multiple sclerosis. If doctors can predict who will become sick, but cannot cure the diseases or do anything to ward them off, do they have an obligation to give the information to their patients? Should they give that information to insurance companies or employers?

5. In this Section of Chapter Two, we have focused on the ethical dimensions of medical decisions, but similar ethical questions arise in other areas of human experience, such as business, the military, government, and education. See whether you can identify the sorts of ethical dilemmas that might come up in those areas, and try to figure out how the ethical theories you have studied could be applied to them.

JOHN STUART MILL

John Stuart Mill (1806–1873) was the most important English philosopher during the 125 years between the death of David Hume in 1776 and the turn of the twentieth century. Trained from his youth by his father, James Mill, to be a defender of the utilitarian doctrine of Jeremy Bentham and the Philosophical Radicals, Mill devoted his early years to an unquestioning support of his father's principles. After undergoing a severe emotional crisis in his twenties, Mill gave up the narrow doctrine of Bentham and became instead an eclectic synthesizer of the views of such diverse schools as the French utopian socialists and the German romantics.

Mill was active in the public life of England, first as an officer (and eventually head) of the great East India Company, a principal instrument of English economic expansion during the nineteenth century, and later as a member of Parliament. In addition to the books on moral and political topics which have established him as one of the leading advocates of liberalism, Mill also wrote a number of highly influential works on logic and the theory of knowledge, including A System of Logic *and* An Examination of Sir William Hamilton's Philosophy.

As a young man, Mill befriended Mrs. Harriet Taylor, with whom he maintained a close relationship until, after her husband's death, they were married in 1851. Mill believed Mrs. Taylor to be an enormously gifted thinker, and he was convinced that she would have made her mark on English letters had it not been for the powerful prejudice against women that operated then, as it does now. His relationship with Mrs. Taylor made Mill sensitive to the discrimination against women, with the result that he became one of the few philosophers to speak out on the matter. His discussion of the problem appears in a late work, The Subjection of Women, *published four years before his death.*

Social & Political Philosophy

- ✦ Mill and Classical Laissez-Faire Liberalism

- ✦ The Socialist Attack on Capitalism

- ✦ Rousseau and the Theory of the Social Contract

- ✦ The Pluralist Theory of the State

- ✦ The Racial Critique of the Social Contract Theory of the State

- ✦ *Contemporary Application: Affirmative Action*

❦ Mill and Classical Laissez–Faire Liberalism

Some, it is said, are born great; some achieve greatness; and some have greatness thrust upon them. To that saying we might add—and some are trained from birth for greatness. Of all the philosophers who have won for themselves a place in the ranks of the great, none was more carefully groomed, schooled, prodded, and pushed into greatness than the English empiricist and utilitarian thinker of the nineteenth century, John Stuart Mill. Never has a child been given less chance to "do his own thing," and never has a man defended with greater eloquence the right of every man and woman to be left free from the intrusions of well-meaning parents, friends, and governments. Though it would be wrong to reduce Mill's mature philosophical views to the level of mere psychological reflections on his childhood experiences, the temptation is irresistible to see in his adult career a reaction to the pressures of his youth.

Mill was born in 1806, at a time when a strong movement was developing to reform the political life of England. The intellectual leader of the movement was the same Jeremy Bentham whose utilitarian doctrines you encountered in Chapter 2. We took our first look at utilitarianism in its guise as a moral philosophy designed to lay down a principle for calculating what actions are right for an individual facing a decision. But Bentham's primary interest was in social issues, not in private morality. He conceived the Principle of Utility as a weapon in the attack on the traditions, privileges, laws, and perquisites of the English upper classes. So long as courts and governments could hide behind precedent, or immemorial custom, it was extremely hard to force them to admit the injustices and irrationalities of the social system. But once those ancient customs were put to the test of the Principle of Utility, it was immediately clear how badly they had failed to produce the greatest happiness for the greatest number.

One of Bentham's close friends and associates in the reform movement was a philosopher named James Mill; Mill was a thinker of considerable distinction, although he has long since been eclipsed by his more famous son. His writings on economics and moral philosophy erected a system, on Benthamite foundations, which served as a fortress from which the Philosophical Radicals, as they were called, sallied forth to do battle with the last remnants of the aristocratic hosts. Shortly after the birth of his son John Stuart, James Mill met Bentham and joined forces with him. Mill decided to train his son up as a soldier in the reform movement, and no medieval squire ever had a more rigorous preparation for combat. Little John Stuart began studying Greek at the age of three. His father surrounded him with Latin-speaking servants so that by the age of eight he could dig into that other ancient tongue. Logic was young John Stuart's fare at twelve, to be followed shortly by the study of the new science of political economy. Formal religion was deliberately omitted

JAMES MILL

James Mill (1773–1836) was a close friend and colleague of Jeremy Bentham, the founder of the doctrine known as utilitarianism. Mill led a group of English political reformers who believed that social justice and wise government required a broadening of the franchise to  include the industrial middle classes in England, and a thoroughgoing overhaul of the antiquated laws and governmental machinery which, in Mill's day, strongly favored the landed interests in England. Mill and the Philosophical Radicals, as his circle of supporters was called, succeeded in generating enough support to carry through a number of major reforms, culminating in the sweeping Reform Bill of 1832. Mill's son, the great John Stuart Mill, had this to say about his father's position in *The Autobiography of John Stuart Mill:*

So complete was my father's reliance on the influence of reason over the minds of mankind, whenever it is allowed to reach them, that he felt as if all would be gained if the whole population were taught to read, if all sorts of opinions were allowed to be addressed to them by word and by writing, and if by means of the suffrage they could nominate a legislature to give effect to the opinions they adopted.

from the curriculum, but the poor lad may be forgiven for having somewhat formed the notion that he was being raised by an orthodox utilitarian.

By the time he reached adulthood, John Stuart Mill was a brilliant, finely honed logical weapon in the armory of his father's political battles. He wrote attacks on the antiquated legal and political institutions of England, defending his points with straight utilitarian dogma.

Not surprisingly, Mill finally broke under the strain of this rigid doctrinaire discipline. At the age of twenty, he suffered an internal emotional crisis and began what was to be a lifelong reevaluation of the Benthamism of his father and his father's allies. Though it is always a mistake to sum up a great philosopher's work in a single phrase, we can get some general overview of Mill's subsequent intellectual development by saying that he spent his life struggling to broaden, deepen, and complicate the extremely simple philosophical theory into which he was initiated as a boy.

The doctrine of the reformers was clear, coherent, and attractively free from the mystifications which clouded the writings of the conservative defenders of the old order. As Bentham had laid it down, the only good in this world is pleasure; the only evil, pain. Human actions are goal-oriented, purposeful actions. Our desires determine what objects or experiences we choose as our goals, and reason aids us in discovering the most efficient path to those goals. The question, What ought I to do? is either a question of goals—What should I desire?—or else it is a question of means—How can I reach my goal most easily? But there is no point in disputing about desires. We either want something or we don't, and whatever pleasure we experience comes to us as the result of satisfying a desire. So the only questions worth debating are factual question of means: Is this the best was to satisfy my desire, or would that way be quicker, cheaper, easier?

If abstruse questions of natural rights and absolute goodness are to be disputed, then common men and women will be hard put to keep up with trained philosophers, lawyers, or theologians. But if Bentham is right, then the fundamental moral question is simply, Does it feel good? Is this experience pleasurable? Now each one of us is the best judge of whether he or she is feeling pleasure or pain, so utilitarianism has the effect of eliminating expertise and putting all men and women on an equal footing in moral debates. What is more, Bentham insisted, the only morally relevant distinction between pleasures and pains is a quantitative distinction of more and less. As Bentham put it, pushpin (a child's game) is as good as poetry, so long as it gives you an equal amount of pleasure. This doctrine too had the effect of leveling the social distinctions between the high- and low-born, for it had been easy for the cultivated upper classes to insist that they were privy to joys and sorrows too refined for the lower classes even to imagine. In these ways— by making each person the judge of his or her own happiness and by making quantity the only significant variable—utilitarianism provided a philosophical justification for a democratic social program.

All persons are basically prudent, rationally self-interested actors. That is to say, we seek to satisfy our desires in the most extensive and pleasurable way, and we use the resources available to us—money, talent, power—in the most efficient manner possible. But there are two great obstacles to fully rational self-interested action. The first of these, the target of the eighteenth-century enlightenment, is superstition. So long as people falsely believe that they have no right to satisfy their desires; so long as religion, or ancient custom, or class distinctions inhibit common men and women from using the resources they have for the achievement of their own happiness; so long, in short, as the reasoning power of the mind is clouded by fear, awe, and false belief—then just so long will the injustices and inequalities of society continue. The second obstacle is the ignorance which even enlightened men and women suffer of the facts of science and public affairs, ignorance of the most efficient means for pursuing legitimate satisfactions.

Education was the weapon utilitarians aimed at these twin enemies, superstition and ignorance. Education was to perform two tasks: first, to liberate enslaved minds from the superstitious religious and political dogmas of

> ⌒ **Laissez-Faire** Literally, to allow to do. Laissez-faire is the system of free market exchanges, with an absolute minimum of government control, which nineteenth-century liberals believed would result in the most efficient use of resources and the greatest material well-being for society. *Laissez-faire capitalism* refers to the early stage in the development of capitalism, when firms were small, owner-run, and controlled both in their purchases and in their sales by market pressures.

the past and, second, to introduce the liberated minds to the facts of science and society. An educated population could then be counted on to support wise public policy, for such policy would aim at the greatest happiness of the greatest number, and that simply meant their own happiness as private citizens. Thus utilitarianism combined a psychological theory of individual motivation with a moral theory of the good and an educational theory of enlightenment to produce what we today call a political theory of liberal democracy.

It remains to mention one last element of the utilitarian system, an element which may well have been the most important of all, namely the laissez-faire economic theory created by Adam Smith and David Ricardo and deployed by James Mill and his son in the great debates over public policy. This is not an economics textbook, and philosophy is hard enough all by itself, but at least a few words must be said about the laissez-faire theory in order to fill out Mill's position and set the stage for the powerful attacks which Karl Marx launched against it a very few years later.

The major fact of the end of the eighteenth century and the beginning of the nineteenth was, of course, the growth of mercantile and industrial capitalism. The key to the new capitalism was the systematic investment of accumulated wealth, or "capital," for the purpose of producing goods which could be sold at a profit in the marketplace. The individual who set the economic activity in motion was called an "entrepreneur," which is French for "undertaker" and means someone who undertakes to do something, not someone who buries someone (although critics of capitalism might have argued that there was indeed a connection between the two meanings). The capitalist undertook to rent the land, hire the labor, buy the raw materials, and bring together these factors of production in a process which resulted in finished goods. The goods were put on sale in a market where no law fixed the prices that must be paid or the profits that could be made. Adam Smith, in his famous treatise *The Wealth of Nations*, argued that if everyone were permitted to do the best he could for himself—worker, capitalist, merchant, and consumer—then the net result would be the most efficient use of the resources of the nation for the production of goods designed to satisfy human desires. The consumers would spend their money in the marketplace in such a way as to get the greatest pleasure for value. If one sort of product rose too high in price, they would shift to another, for paying all your money for a single piece of meat would be foolish when the same money could buy you fish, eggs, shoes, and a coat. The capitalists would pull their capital out of areas where too much was being produced, because as supply exceeded demand, they would be forced to drop their prices in order to unload their inventory, and profits would tumble. In the same way, if there were customers clamoring for a commodity that wasn't being produced, they would bid up the price in the market, drive up profits in that branch of business, and attract profit-seeking capitalists who would open new factories to "capitalize" on the unsatisfied demand.

Since happiness is pleasure and pleasure results from the satisfaction of desire, and consumers buy goods to satisfy desires, it follows that the capitalists trying to make a profit are at the same time actually working to make the consumers happy. They aren't *trying* to make them happy, of course! The capitalists, like all men and women, are rationally *self*-interested pleasure maximizers. But the genius of the new capitalist free market system was precisely that each person, seeking only his or her own good, automatically advanced the good of others. Thus selfishness could be counted on to do rationally and efficiently what altruism never quite managed—namely, to produce the greatest happiness possible for the greatest number of people. Here is how Adam Smith puts it in a passage that is much quoted and copied. Smith is actually in the midst of a discussion of restrictions on imports, but the thesis he enunciates has a quite general application:

ADAM SMITH,
The Wealth of
Nations

But the annual revenue of every society is always precisely equal to the exchangeable value of the whole annual produce of its industry, or rather is precisely the same thing with that exchangeable value. As every individual, therefore, endeavours as much as he can both to employ his capital in the support of domestic industry, and so to direct that industry that its produce may be of the greatest value; every individual necessarily labours to render the annual revenue of the society as great as he can. He generally, indeed, neither intends to promote the public interest, nor knows how much he is promoting it. By preferring the support of domestic to that of foreign industry, he intends only his own security; and by directing that industry in such a manner as its produce may be of the greatest value, he intends only his own gain, and he is in this, as in many other cases, led by an invisible hand to promote an end which was no part of his intention. Nor is it always the worse for the society that it was no part of it. By pursuing his own interest he frequently promotes that of the society more effectually than when he really intends to promote it. I have never known much good done by those who affected to trade for the public good. It is an affectation, indeed, not very common among merchants, and very few words need be employed in dissuading them from it.

ADAM SMITH

Adam Smith (1723–1790) was born in Scotland at a time when that small country was one of the liveliest intellectual centers in Europe. Like his countryman, David Hume, Smith wrote on a wide variety of problems in what we would now call the social sciences. His masterwork was a long, difficult, revolutionary study of the foundations of economic activity in a free market capitalist economy, entitled *Inquiry into the Nature and Causes of the Wealth of Nations.* With this book, Smith created the field of economics and laid the theoretical basis for the doctrine of laissez-faire, which still has wide support two centuries later. *The Wealth of Nations* was published in 1776, just at the time when the American colonies were declaring their independence of the English crown; and it is fitting that history should have linked these two events, for the Founding Fathers were deeply imbued with the laissez-faire spirit of individual freedom, minimal government, and the pursuit of rational self-interest.

Mill read widely in authors whose views were far removed from those of Bentham and his father. He learned from the Romantic critics of the reform movement even as he sought to counter their arguments. He studied the writings of such acute conservative observers as Alexis de Tocqueville, and even absorbed the lessons of the French socialists, though he seems not to have read or appreciated the more powerful theoretical assault mounted by the great German socialist Karl Marx. The breadth of his learning and his personal dissatisfaction with the narrow dogma of his father led Mill to doubt or even to deny some of the central tenets of utilitarian philosophy and social policy. Nevertheless, to the end of his life, his mind remained trapped within the confines of the principles he had been taught as a youth.

In at least *three* important ways, Mill questioned the theses of the orthodox reform doctrine. First, he denied Bentham's egalitarian insistence that any pleasure, in and of itself, is as good as any other (which, as we have seen, is a roundabout way of saying that any person is as good as any other). As far back as Plato, philosophers had argued that some pleasures were simply finer, higher, morally better than other pleasures. Usually, as we might expect, they claimed that the pleasures of the mind were superior to the pleasures of the body. Bentham was prepared to admit that some pleasures were more intense, or more long-lasting, or had more pleasant aftereffects than others. A quart of bad wine might give less pleasure than a sip of fine brandy. A night of drinking might be followed by such a horrendous morning after that the total experience would add up to a minus rather than a plus. Some pleasures, like some foods, might be acquired tastes, requiring knowledge and long practice before they could be properly appreciated. But after all this had been taken into account—and Bentham carefully did take it into account—utilitarianism still insisted that only quantity and not quality of pleasure mattered. Mill could not accept this teaching, fundamental though it was to the philosophy he had been trained to defend. He was stung by the critics of utilitarianism who made it out to be a brutish or degraded philosophy, a philosophy of the base appetites. In replying to their charge, he drew a distinction between higher and lower pleasures which fundamentally altered the significance and logical force of utilitarianism. Here is the passage, taken from an essay called "Utilitarianism" which Mill first published in a magazine and later as a short book.

"Gin Lane" by William Hogarth (1697–1765). Hogarth's famous engraving illustrates rather forcefully the negative consequences of a night of drinking! (The Metropolitan Museum of Art, Harris Brisbane Dick Fund, 1932.)

Higher and Lower Pleasures

Now such a theory of life excites in many minds, and among them in some of the most estimable in feeling and purpose, inveterate dislike. To suppose that life has (as they express it) no higher end than pleasure—no better and nobler object of desire and pursuit—they designate as utterly mean and groveling, as a doctrine worthy only of swine, to whom the followers of Epicurus were, at a very early period, contemptuously likened; and modern holders of the doctrine are occasionally made the subject of equally polite comparisons by its German, French, and English assailants.

When thus attacked, the Epicureans have always answered that it is not they, but their accusers, who represent human nature in a degrading light, since the accusation supposes human beings to be capable of no pleasures except those of which swine are capable. If this supposition were true, the charge could not be gainsaid, but would then be no longer an imputation; for if the sources of pleasure were precisely the same to human beings and to swine, the rule of life which is good enough for the one would be good enough for the other. The comparison of the Epicurean life to that of beasts is felt as degrading, precisely because a beast's pleasures do not satisfy a human being's conceptions of happiness. Human beings have faculties more elevated than the animal appetites and, when once made conscious of them, do not regard anything as happiness which does not include their gratification. . . .

It is quite compatible with the principle of utility to recognize the fact that some kinds of pleasure are more desirable and more valuable than others. It would be absurd that, while in estimating all other things quality is considered as well as quantity, the estimation of pleasure should be supposed to depend on quantity alone.

If I am asked what I mean by difference of quality in pleasures, or what makes one pleasure more valuable than another, merely as a pleasure, except its being greater in amount, there is but one possible answer. Of two pleasures, if there be one to which all or almost all who have experience of both give a decided preference, irrespective of any feeling of moral obligation to prefer it, that is the more desirable pleasure. If one of the two is, by those who are competently acquainted with both, placed so far above the other that they prefer it, even though knowing it to be attended with a greater amount of discontent, and would not resign it for any quantity of the other pleasure which their nature is capable of, we are justified in ascribing to the preferred enjoyment a superiority in quality so far outweighing quantity as to render it, in comparison, of small account.

Now it is an unquestionable fact that those who are equally acquainted with and equally capable of appreciating and enjoying both do give a most marked preference to the manner of existence which employs their higher faculties. Few human creatures would consent to be changed into any of the lower animals for a promise of the fullest allowance of a beast's pleasures; no intelligent human being would consent to be a fool, no instructed person would be an ignoramus, no person of feeling and conscience would be selfish and base, even though they should be persuaded that the fool, the dunce, or the rascal is better satisfied with his lot than they are with theirs. They would not resign what they possess more than he for the most complete satisfaction of all the desires which they have in common with him. If they ever fancy they would, it is only in cases of unhappiness so extreme that to escape from it they would exchange their lot for almost any other, however undesirable in their own eyes. A being of higher faculties requires more to make him happy, is capable probably of more acute suffering, and certainly accessible to it at more points, than one of an inferior type; but in spite of these liabilities, he can never really wish to sink into what he feels to be a lower grade of existence.

There are a number of tricky logical problems with the position Mill defends here, the complete analysis of which would carry us into some rather dry and technical regions of the theory of utility. But one problem springs instantly from the page at us. If not all pleasures are equal in quality, if some persons of more refined sensibility are better able to judge of the quality of pleasures, then the basic democratic one-person–one vote thrust of utilitarianism is lost. Instead of giving every person, however low in station or meager in education, an equal voice in the choice of the ends of social policy, special weight shall have to be accorded to the opinions of that educated minority who have tasted the elevated pleasures of the mind—to those who claim, from the height of their culture, that Bach is better than rock and cordon bleu better than cheeseburgers. The fact is that Mill does indeed exhibit just such an aristocratic bias in his political writings, both in regard to the privileged position of the upper classes within England and also in regard to England's privileged position in her colonies vis-à-vis the "subject races" not yet raised to her own level of culture. The cultural imperialism of Mill, as we may call it, is of course interesting as a fact about the man and his times. But it is also a first-rate example of the way in which an apparently trivial philosophical argument about a technical point can carry with it very large consequences for the most practical questions of politics.

Mill's second revision of his father's faith concerned the rationality and predictability of the laborers, capitalists, and consumers who interact in the marketplace. The doctrine of laissez-faire, with its emphasis on limited government intervention in the market and a removal of all regulations on trade and commerce depends upon two assumptions, as we have already seen. The first is that economic actors can be counted on to behave in a rationally self-interested manner, buying as cheaply as possible, taking the highest wages available, always looking for a profit; the second, which depended for its plausibility on the first, is that an economy run along laissez-faire lines and populated by rationally self-interested persons will maximize growth and production and thereby create the greatest happiness possible, within the limits of natural resources and technology, for the greatest number of people. In one of his major works, *Principles of Political Economy*, Mill denied the first of these two assumptions and thereby laid the theoretical groundwork for the rejection of the second.

First let us look at Mill's argument. Then we will consider its significance.

Under the rule of individual property, the division of the produce is the result of two determining agencies: Competition and Custom. It is important to ascertain the amount of influence which belongs to each of these causes, and in what manner the operation of one is modified by the other.

Political economists generally, and English political economists above others, have been accustomed to lay almost exclusive stress upon the first of these agencies; to exaggerate the effect of competition, and to take into little account the other and conflicting principle. They are apt to express themselves as if they thought that competition actually does, in all cases, whatever it can be shown to be the tendency of competition to do. This is partly intelligible, if we consider that only through the principle of competition has political economy any pretension to the character of a science. So far as rents, profits, wages, prices, are determined by competition, laws may be assigned for them. Assume competition to be their exclusive regulator, and principles of broad generality and scientific precision may be laid down, according to which they will be regulated. The political economist justly deems this his proper business: and as an abstract or hypothetical science, political economy cannot be required to do, and indeed cannot do, anything more. But it would be a great misconception of the actual course of human affairs, to suppose that competition exercises in fact this unlimited sway. I am not speaking of monopolies, either natural or artificial, or of any interferences of authority with the liberty of production or exchange. Such disturbing causes have always been allowed for by political economists. I speak of cases in which there is nothing to restrain competition; no hindrance to it either in the nature of the case or in artificial obstacles; yet in which the result is not determined by competition, but by custom or usage; competition either not taking place at all, or producing its effect in quite a different manner from that which is ordinarily assumed to be natural to it.

Since custom stands its ground against competition to so considerable an extent, even where, from the multitude of competitors

JOHN STUART MILL,
Principles of Political Economy

and the general energy in the pursuit of gain, the spirit of competition is strongest, we may be sure that this is much more the case
where people are content with smaller gains, and estimate their pecu-
niary interest at a lower rate when balanced against their case or
their pleasure. I believe it will often be found, in Continental Europe,
that prices and charges, of some or of all sorts, are much higher in
some places than in others not far distant, without its being possible
to assign any other cause than that it has always been so: the customers are used to it, and acquiesce in it. An enterprising competitor,
with sufficient capital, might force down the charges, and make his
fortune during the process; but there are no enterprising competitors;
those who have capital prefer to leave it where it is, or to make less
profit by it in a more quiet way.

Mill is saying that although the behavior of men and women in the market may be *predictable,* it is not *calculable.* The difference is fundamental, so
perhaps we should take a moment to explain it more clearly. Suppose I want
to open a snack shop, and I am trying to decide whether to locate downtown
or in a new mall being built on the edge of town. I know that the mall will
have a number of discount outlets selling well-known brands at very low
prices. If I can assume that consumers will be motivated solely by a desire to
minimize their expenditures for the goods they buy, then I can *calculate*
(without any special information about shopping habits in this area) that the
mall will be crowded with bargain-hunters. Since I want my snack shop to be
where the shoppers are, I will choose the mall.

But if Mill is right (as in fact he is), then a certain proportion of the
shoppers will go on shopping downtown, whether out of habit or because
they care enough about such nonmonetary things as the familiarity of the
stores. There is no way in the world that I can foresee just how many shoppers will be influenced enough by these factors to go downtown instead of to
the mall. I can observe shopping behavior in other towns and extrapolate to
this case, or do an opinion survey of shoppers, or in some other fashion try
to base my prediction on experience. With enough data, I may be able to *predict* what the shoppers will do, so that I can decide where to put my snack
shop. But there is no way that I can *calculate* their behavior.

So long as economic actors in the marketplace act in a rationally self-
interested way, I can calculate their actions without any prior knowledge of
their individual character, without elaborate collections of information about
their past behavior. All I need know is that (1) they seek to maximize profits
or enjoyments and (2) they will make use of the available information in a
rational attempt to achieve that maximization. I can then carry out in my
own head the same calculation they will carry out, and so I can calculate their
actions. But if they are influenced by what Mill calls *custom,* which is to say
by *irrational* tastes, habits, and preferences that deviate from the strict ratio-

nality of profit maximization, then I can only predict their behavior on the basis of vast quantities of systematically collected data about their past behavior. I cannot count on the "invisible hand" of the marketplace to direct their economic activities into the most productive areas. Capitalists may refrain, out of irrational habits or aversions, from shifting their capital into sectors of unmet market demand. Consumers may go on shopping at a more expensive store when identical goods are offered more cheaply next door. Workers may fail to quit low-paying jobs and move to better-paying jobs in labor-short industries.

The result will be a breakdown of the automatic mechanisms of the market and a need for scientifically controlled management of the economy by a central authority possessing both the information and the power to implement its judgments. In short, the slight revision which Mill makes in the classical theory of laissez-faire leads directly, although not immediately, to the modern managed economy of welfare-state capitalism.

Mill's third alteration in the radical philosophy of James Mill follows directly from the first, and concerns the government's right to interfere with the private lives of its citizens. In his famous essay, *On Liberty,* Mill argues for an absolute ban on all state or social intervention in the inner life of thoughts and feelings. But in the last chapter of the *Principles,* he takes a somewhat different line. To be sure, he says, "*Laisser-faire . . .* should be the general practice: every departure from it, unless required by some great good, is a certain evil." But in considering permissible departures, Mill concedes a very great deal indeed. Listen to him in this suggestive passage:

We have observed that, as a general rule, the business of life is better performed when those who have an immediate interest in it are left to take their own course, uncontrolled either by the mandate of the law or by the meddling of any public functionary. The persons, or some of the persons, who do the work, are likely to be better judges than the government, of the means of attaining the particular end at which they aim. Were we to suppose, what is not very probable, that the government has possessed itself of the best knowledge which had been acquired up to a given time by the persons most skilled in the occupation; even then, the individual agents have so much stronger and more direct an interest in the result, that the means are far more likely to be improved and perfected if left to their uncontrolled choice. But if the workman is generally the best selector of means, can it be affirmed with the same universality, that the consumer, or person served, is the most competent judge of the end? Is the buyer always qualified to judge of the commodity? If not, the presumption in favour of the competition of the market does not apply to the case; and if the commodity be one, in the quality of which society has much at stake, the balance of advantages may be in favour of some

JOHN STUART MILL,
Principles of Political Economy

mode and degree of intervention, by the authorized representatives of the collective interest of the state.

Now, the proposition that the consumer is a competent judge of the commodity, can be admitted only with numerous abatements and exceptions. He is generally the best judge (though even this is not true universally) of the material objects produced for his use. These are destined to supply some physical want, or gratify some taste or inclination, respecting which wants or inclinations there is no appeal from the person who feels them; or they are the means and appliances of some occupation, for the use of the persons engaged in it, who may be presumed to be judges of the things required in their own habitual employment. But there are other things of the worth of which the demand of the market is by no means a test; things of which the utility does not consist in ministering to inclinations, nor in serving the daily uses of life, and the want of which is least felt where the need is greatest. This is peculiarly true of those things which are chiefly useful as tending to raise the character of human beings. The uncultivated cannot be competent judges of cultivation.

We have been speaking thus far of Bentham, James Mill, and John Stuart Mill as "liberals," and that is indeed how they spoke of themselves. But as often happens in politics, as in other fields, words shift their meanings as time passes. No word shows this tendency more strikingly than the word "liberal."

"Liberal" comes from the same Latin root as "liberate," which means "to set free." The original, late eighteenth-century and early nineteenth-century liberals criticized the old order for its lack of "liberty," both political and economic. Men and women were not politically free to speak as they chose, to worship in their own manner, to assemble, to participate in the selection of their government, to help make the laws by which they were ruled. And they were also not free to buy and sell as they wished, to take jobs anywhere they could find them, to start businesses and sell their goods at whatever price they thought best.

Bentham and the Mills believed that these two kinds of unfreedom were connected. They argued, by means of their doctrine of utilitarianism, that the citizens of a nation should be free, "liberated," both to conduct their private lives as they chose *and* to conduct themselves in the marketplace, as employers or employees, buyers or sellers, consumers or producers, just as they saw fit. They argued that if the government would interfere as little as possible in either realm, men and women would be happier, and society as a whole would be better off.

Despite all his qualifications and revisions in the utilitarian creed, Mill remained faithful to its spirit. But powerful intellectual attacks were mounted on laissez-faire liberalism and utilitarianism. In the next section of this chapter, we shall listen to some of the voices of dissent. The attacks began as soon as industrial capitalism and its liberal defenders appeared. In the very first decades of the nineteenth century, Romantic conservative critics of industrialism and socialist critics of the capitalist organization of that industrialism appeared in England and on the Continent. But I do not want you to think that this is an ancient dispute, buried in dusty books written by men long dead. The very same argument continues today.

The Socialist Attack on Capitalism

The misery of the workers in the early factories, the squalor of the slums in which they and their families suffered, the gross contrast between their poverty and the wealth of the entrepreneurs provoked a flood of scathing condemnations of the new industrial order. Some of the criticisms were merely cries from the heart, but especially in France, a number of philosophers and economists made an effort to discover the underlying causes of the suffering created by capitalism. It was the German Karl Marx, however, who mounted the most sustained, thoroughgoing, and intellectually impressive critique of the institutions, economic theories, and philosophical rationalizations of industrial capitalism.

The genius of Marx's critique was that it met the liberal philosophy head on at its strongest point and turned its own arguments against itself. Liberalism and laissez-faire claimed to be rational doctrines, stripped of all superstitious mystification. Conservatives denied the primacy of reason and attempted instead to elevate imagination or tradition to the first place. But Marx accepted the challenge of liberalism. Industrial capitalism, he insisted, is not rational. Instead, it is profoundly irrational, and its claims to rationality, expressed in its economic theory and in its philosophy, are no more than an ideological rationalization designed to conceal the inner illogic of capitalism and thereby preserve a system which favors the interests of a few at the expense of the lives of many.

Marx begins his criticism of capitalism with an analysis of it. How does capitalism work? What is Marx's conception of the social and economic organization of a capitalist country? At first inspection, society at any one time seems an unorganized beehive of multifarious activities, without any system, pattern, or rationale. Agriculture, the arts, science, industry, government, religion, entertainment, marketing, war, charity, crime—the things men and women do are endless in number and variety. Merely to list all the categories of jobs being performed by someone or other is to lose oneself in a confusion of diversity. But Marx saw order in the chaos. He argued that in order to make sense of social life, we must distinguish a certain group of activities which are basic to the survival and reproduction of the human race. Each day, men and women work to transform nature into the food, clothing, and shelter they need to live. These economic activities form the base, or foundation, on which all else in the society rests. In order to distinguish the productive economic activities from the philosophical theorizing which his German idealist predecessors had made so much of, Marx called the productive elements of society its *material base*. In calling the base "material," he did not mean to suggest that it consisted of physical bodies rather than human thoughts, purposes, and plans, for even productive activities are intelligent, purposeful activities involving "ideas." Rather, Marx wanted to emphasize the fundamental role of economic production as opposed to philosophy, religion, or art.

The material base of a society consists of three layers. The first is the *means* of production—the raw materials, land, and energy resources with which men and women work. The second layer—the *forces* of production—includes the factories, machinery, technology, industrial knowledge, and accumulated skills of those who transform the means of production by their labor. The third and by far the most important layer of the material base is what Marx called the *social relationships of production*. Since everything in Marx's theory depends on this last element, we must take a few paragraphs to explain it in some detail.

Human beings are productive creatures, to be sure. But according to Marx, they are *socially* productive creatures. Men and women divide the labor among themselves, differentiating the process of production into a series of subjobs or specialties and then parceling these pieces of the total productive process out among different workers. Some people raise grain, others dig iron ore out of the ground. Others bake the grain into bread, and still others work the ore into tools and weapons. This *division of labor* requires also a system of exchange, for no one can live on the products of his or her own labor alone. The farmer needs the products of the carpenter, the carpenter needs the products of the metal worker, and the metal worker needs the grain grown by the farmer. The market is the system by which a never-ending chain of trades, or purchases and sales, distributes the products of labor among the members of society.

Although productive activity is cooperative, in the sense that there is a division of function and an exchange of products, it is by no means harmonious, equitable, or universally beneficent. Very early in human history, according to Marx, some men by force of arms succeed in seizing control over the vital means of production. They take the land, the streams, the mines, and the forests, and they prevent others from using them. Once these men have successfully asserted ownership of the means of production, they are in a position to extract a ransom from the rest of the men and women in the society. Pay me half of all you grow, the landholder says to the farmer, or I will not allow you to farm the land. The farmer has no choice, for if he does not farm, he starves. So two classes of people crystallize out of the social situation: the ruling class, which controls the means of production; and the underclass, which is forced to give up a part of the product of its labor in order to survive.

Cartoon: "Marx's theory of the structure of society." (Drawn for Robert Paul Wolff by Prentice Hall.)

At first, of course, the naked force which holds the underclass down is obvious to all. But as time passes and generations succeed one another, sheer custom and familiarity confer legitimacy on what was originally mere might. The rulers pass on the control of the means of production to their sons and daughters, who grow up believing that it is theirs by right. The free time which the rulers have—because they eat and drink and wear what they do not have to produce—permits them to develop a culture and style of life quite different from that of the laboring majority. Small wonder that even those in the underclass soon come to believe that the rulers are "different." They may not have been originally, but their descendants have certainly become so! As regular patterns of work, exchange, land ownership, and personal subordination develop, the rulers hold periodic courts to settle disputes that may have arisen in the enactment of those patterns. The decisions of these courts become the law of the land. Needless to say, the decisions rarely threaten the interests of the rulers, for it is they who convene the courts, they who sit on the bench, and they who enforce the orders of the courts with their soldiers. Nor is it surprising that the religious men and women of the society bless the rulers and their dominance. Churches are economically unproductive institutions, and they can survive only by sharing in that portion of the product which the rulers have taken from the laborers.

The system of relationships connecting those who control the means of production and those who do not is called by Marx the social relationships of production. It is the basic fact about a society, and from it grow such other, secondary facts as the structure of the law, and the dogmas of the dominant religion, and the underlying themes of the art and literature. Marx calls these subordinate or secondary features of a society its *superstructure,* conveying by this metaphor the notion that a society rests on, or is built on, that portion of it which is the "base." A more modern way of putting the same idea would be to say that the means, forces, and social relationships of production are the independent variables in a society and that the law, politics, art, religion, and philosophy are the dependent variables.

In the superstructure, the state occupies a central place, for it is the instrument the ruling class uses to maintain its domination of the rest of the society. As the character of the social relationships of production changes, so does the character of the state. Under feudalism, which is a system of production based on ownership of land, the state is controlled by the landed aristocracy, which employs it to maintain control of the agricultural workers (or "serfs") and to regulate the relationships between the great land holders (or "lords") and their subordinate tenants (or "vassals"). This same system of landholding also forms the basis for the military organization of the society, thereby combining the control of the means of production with the supply of the force to maintain that control. In an industrial system of production, where capital rather than land is central to the productive process, the class that owns the capital (the "capitalists") also controls the state. As Marx and his life-long collaborator, Friedrich Engels say in their most famous work, *The Communist Manifesto,* "The executive of the modern state is nothing but a committee for managing the common affairs of the whole bourgeoisie."

How, according to Marx, do societies change over time? At any given moment, we may speak of the ruling class and the underclass. But as new technology develops, as the division of labor is carried farther and farther, slow shifts take place in the material base. Within the feudal order, capitalism begins to grow. New ways of production and exchange give rise to new systems of relationships. At first, the changes seem minute by comparison with the overwhelming preponderance of economic activity. But little by little,

---

Bourgeoisie/Proletariat The *bourgeoisie* is the middle class consisting of factory owners, shop-keepers, bankers, financiers, and their associates. "Bourgeoisie" comes from the medieval term *bourg,* meaning walled city. Burghers, or bourgeois, were the inhabitants of a walled city—by extension, the merchants and master craftsmen who formed the economic elite of the city, as opposed to the aristocracy, whose wealth and power were based on landholdings. In Marx's writings, the *proletariat* is the urban population of wage-earning workers. The term "proletariat" comes from the old Latin word for the lowest class of people in Rome.

more men and women are drawn into the new patterns of economic activity. The economically progressive group, or class, is at first disadvantaged, for the rules have all been made to favor the dominant class. But as the real economic power of the progressive class grows, it begins to demand a place in the ruling circles of the society. It wants laws changed to help rather than hinder its economic interests. It wants a share of the power that comes from controlling the means of production.

Now Marx was an optimist, if by that we mean that he thought the human race was heading toward better times. But he was not a fool. It was perfectly obvious to him that whenever a growing class challenges the dominance of a ruling class, there is going to be violence. There was no way that capitalists could compromise their interests with the landed aristocrats of the old order; one of them was going to have to go. According to Marx, the two centuries of civil war and social upheaval beginning with the English Civil War, continuing on through the French and American revolutions, and ending with the American Civil War, were simply the protracted struggle between the landed aristocracy of the precapitalist order and the capitalist class which controlled the new industrial means of production.

This, in a very brief summary, is Marx's *analysis* of capitalism—how it emerged from feudalism, how it works, and what makes it change. Now we can take a look at his *criticism* of capitalism—what he thinks is wrong with it. As I suggested earlier, Marx's basic complaint against capitalism is that it is *irrational*. Indeed, Marx claims that industrial capitalism is irrational in two different ways. First, it is instrumentally irrational. That is to say, it systematically chooses inefficient means to attain the ends it claims to set for itself. The triumphant claim of Adam Smith and the other capitalist apologists had been that a free market profit system would make maximally efficient use of the resources and technology available to a society at any moment and that it would generate new economic production more expeditiously than any system of government management or tradition. Marx agreed that capitalism is unequaled at the task of production, but the very same capitalism is unable to solve the even more important problem of distributing what its factories have produced. In a capitalist system, production is for profit, not for use. If the capitalist cannot make a good return on his investment, he is forced to close up shop, even though there may be men and women in the society crying for the goods he produces. By the same token, as long as he is making a good profit, he goes on churning out goods regardless of whether they are high on society's list of genuine needs. The market is the distribution mechanism, which means that only consumers with cash in hand can buy what the capitalists have produced. But in order for the capitalist to make a high profit, he must keep his wages down, for—Marx argues—profits come out of the difference between the value of what the workers produce and the wages they are paid by their employers. So the same capitalist who cuts his workers' wages to the bone finds no one in the market with money to buy his products.

K A R L   M A R X

Karl Marx (1818–1883) is the founder of modern socialism. Born in Prussia, he studied philosophy and in his twenties joined a circle of young radical social critics and philosophers known as the Young Hegelians. After a number of years as a pamphleteer and intellectual agitator in Germany and France, Marx moved to London to escape political persecution. Once in England, he settled into a rather quiet life of scholarship, reflection, writing, and political organization. Throughout a lifetime of collaboration with Friedrich Engels (1820–1895), Marx systematically elaborated a full-scale economic, political, philosophical, historical, and moral critique of the industrial capitalist system which had developed first in England and then throughout the rest of Europe.

As a young man, Marx was inflamed with the revolutionary conviction that the capitalist order was on the brink of total collapse. After the failure of the workers' uprisings in 1848, and the reactionary turn of most Continental governments, Marx developed a deeper and more long-term analysis of the internal weaknesses of capitalism. Though his writings fill many volumes, there can be no doubt that the masterpiece of his life was the book called, simply, *Capital.*

Unlike many of his followers, Marx was always ready to alter his theories in the face of new evidence. Although he was certain in his youth that socialism could come only by way of a violent revolutionary overthrow of capitalist society and government, later in his life he concluded that in such countries as England and America socialism might come through the relatively peaceful avenue of political agitation and election.

Competition with other capitalists pushes each producer to cut prices and increase volume, in an attempt to seize a larger share of the market. The result is a cycle of overproduction, leading to layoffs, recession, depression, general misery, and then an upswing into new overproduction. Now, ever since people have been on the earth, natural disasters have afflicted them, blighting their crops, flooding their homes, striking them down with disease. But the depressions produced periodically in the nineteenth and twentieth centuries by capitalism are not natural disasters; they are man-made disasters, arising out of the inner irrationality of the capitalist system. Hunger has resulted not from crop failures, but from the inability of the market system to distribute what is produced. There has been famine in the midst of plenty; in America during the Great Depression of the 1930s, farmers were literally forced to plow piglets under with their tractors while millions hovered on the brink of malnutrition and actual starvation. These "inner contradictions" of capitalism, as Marx called them, are living evidence of the irrationality of that social system which the utilitarians had proclaimed the reign of reason.

Even this terrible instrumental irrationality of capitalism, however, is merely a means, as it were, to the substantive irrationality, the debasing inhumanity of capitalism as it is actually lived by industrial workers. You have all heard the term alienation. These days it has become a catchword and is used to apply to everything from psychic disorder to mere boredom. The term was first used by the German philosopher Georg F. W. Hegel and was taken over by Marx to describe what happens to men and women who labor under capitalism. Marx held that humans are by nature productive animals who live in this world by intelligently, purposefully transforming nature, in cooperation with their fellow humans, into commodities that can satisfy their needs and desires. In the process of production, men and women "externalize" themselves—that is, they make what was first a mere idea in their minds external to themselves in the form of an object or state of affairs which they create by their labor. The most important act of such self-externalizing creation is birth itself, but the same structure of creativity can be seen in the farmer's planning, planting, tending, and harvesting of a field of grain, in the carpenter's conceiving, cutting, fashioning, and finishing a piece of furniture, and also in an artist's sculpting of a statue or a poet's forming of a sonnet.

Men and women need productive, fulfilling labor in order to be truly happy, Marx thought. He rejected the utilitarian notion that happiness consists simply in the satisfaction of desire. But the process of "externalization," by which men and women embody themselves in their creations, in their transformations of nature and in their interactions with one another, can be corrupted and perverted. If the products of our labor are taken out of our control, if the very laboring process itself is turned into a kind of submission to superior force, then what we make will come to appear to us not as

> ⌒ **Marxism** The economic, political, and philosophical doctrines first set forth by Karl Marx and then developed by his disciples and followers. Although Marx himself considered his theories scientific, his followers have often treated them as a form of secular religion. The principal doctrines are: first, that capitalism is internally unstable and prone to fall into economic crises; second, that the profits of capitalist enterprises derive from the exploitation of the workers, who receive in wages less than they produce; third, that as capitalism develops, workers will tend to become more self-aware of their situation—and hence more likely to overthrow capitalism by force; and fourth, that the society that comes into existence after capitalism is destroyed will be socialist and democratic in its economic and political organization.

fulfillments of our needs but as oppressive enemies thwarting our human nature. What has been externalized will become *alien*. In short, healthy externalization will become destructive *alienation*.

Capitalism systematically frustrates our need for satisfying labor in every possible way, according to Marx. There is plenty of labor, to be sure. But it is not autonomous labor, it is not labor directed at satisfying genuine human needs, it is not healthful, fulfilling labor. It is competitive labor that sets worker against worker, worker against capitalist, and capitalist against capitalist. The very productivity of capitalism makes it a hell on earth, for at the moment in history when we first achieve the technology to raise ourselves above famine, sickness, and misery, the inner contradictions of our system of property plunge us into depths of suffering worse than anything that was known in the Middle Ages.

Here is just a short selection from Marx's essay on alienated labor from the unpublished and unfinished papers which are known today as the *Economic-Philosophic Manuscripts of 1844*.

KARL MARX,
Economic-Philosophic Manuscripts of 1844

What constitutes the alienation of labour? First, that the work is *external* to the worker, that it is not part of his nature; and that, consequently, he does not fulfill himself in his work but denies himself, has a feeling of misery rather than well-being, does not develop freely his mental and physical energies but is physically exhausted and mentally debased. The worker, therefore, feels himself at home only during his leisure time, whereas at work he feels homeless. His work is not voluntary but imposed, *forced labour*. It is not the satisfaction of a need, but only a means for satisfying other needs. Its alien character is clearly shown by the fact that as soon as there is no physical or other compulsion it is avoided like the plague. External labour, labour in which man alienates himself, is a labour of self-sacrifice, or mortification. Finally, the external character of work for the worker is shown by the fact that it is not his own work but work for someone else, that in work he does not belong to himself but to another person.

Alienation Alienation, according to Marx, is the condition of being at war with one's own nature, the products of one's labor, and one's fellow workers. Marx argued that capitalism undermines the human capacity for creative and productive work, making men and women unhappy in their work, dissatisfied in their leisure, and unable to fulfill their human potential. Marx derived the concept of alienation from German philosophers of the early nineteenth century.

What can be done about the irrationality and dehumanization of capitalism? Marx's answer, as you all know, was a revolution, a socialist revolution made by the workers against the capitalists. The revolution, Marx believed, would accomplish several things. First, it would overthrow the system of ownership of the means of production which, under capitalism, places in the hands of a few the accumulated technology, factories, raw materials, and machinery that have been produced collectively by the labor of generations of working men and women. Second, it would replace the system of production for profit in the marketplace by a system of production for the satisfaction of human needs. Men and women would collectively determine what they need and put their talents to work to produce it. The mere accident of profitability would no longer by permitted to govern decisions about capital investment and economic growth. It might be, for example, that a large profit can be made in the United States by building luxury housing for which there was no burning need, but that little or no profit can be made from the production of well-made, gracefully designed, low-cost housing. No matter. If the low-cost housing were needed, it would get first call on the available building materials and construction work force. Finally, the capitalist system of distribution through the market would be replaced by a rational and humane system of distribution for human need. Under capitalism, the ruling slogan might be "From each as much as you can get; to each as little as you can get away with giving." Under socialism, however, the ruling slogan would be "From each according to his ability; to each according to his work." When the final stage of communism is reached, Marx said, the slogan on society's banner would be "From each according to his ability; to each according to his need."

Collective ownership of the means of production, production for use rather than for profit, distribution for need rather than for ability to pay: with these changes, socialism would overcome the instrumental and substantive irrationality of capitalism and eliminate the alienation of human beings from their product, their labor, their own human nature, and their fellow workers.

Marx wrote in the middle of the nineteenth century, and it is now more than one hundred thirty years later. The last major depression was sixty years ago. In the major industrial nations, despite continuing inequalities of wealth,

> ⌒ **Socialism** An economic and social system based on collective social ownership of the means of production, rational planning of economic investment and growth, roughly equal distribution of goods and services, and production for the satisfaction of human need rather than for private profit. Modern socialism dates from the teachings of the French socialists of the early nineteenth century, but the leading socialist philosopher is the German, Karl Marx.

the workers enjoy a standard of living beyond Marx's wildest dreams. Governments have stepped in with active policies of budget management and monetary control to dampen the boom-to-bust swings which Marx saw as proof of the unstable inner nature of capitalism.

Earlier in the twentieth century, it looked to many people as though the world was going in the direction Marx predicted, although many modern socialists deny that the Soviet Union and its empire were truly socialist. But the Soviet Union is no more, and the nations of Eastern Europe are competing with one another to see which one can become truly capitalist the fastest. To be sure, China, with one-fifth of the world's population, calls itself Marxist, but even in that great country, the most rapid economic growth is taking place along the coast, in cities that have been permitted by the government to follow a capitalist economic path. So it would seem that Marx's dream of socialism is just one more outmoded fantasy, one more bit of nineteenth-century German metaphysics.

And yet, Marx's criticism of capitalism seems still to have some truth to it. In the United States, wealthiest of all the capitalist countries, millions of homeless men and women sleep on the streets, while entire buildings stand vacant because they do not have paying tenants. The government pays farmers billions of dollars *not* to grow food, while children go to bed hungry. Every day, we are told by newspaper reporters, politicians, and economists that the only way to get our country to grow economically is for all of us to go into the stores and buy "on credit" things we can't pay for. Meanwhile, half of America's black teenagers cannot find work, and this generation of young people has discovered that they will not even be able to live as well as their parents have.

The gap between rich and poor in wealthy countries like the United States is matched by the even bigger gap between rich nations and poor nations in the world as a whole. If we think of the entire planet Earth as a single society—a way of looking at things that comes naturally to those of us who have seen pictures of Earth from space—then the contrast between rich and poor, well-fed and hungry, hopeful and hopeless is as dramatic, as compelling, as overwhelming as the same contrast was for Marx in London, England, in the 1860s.

Perhaps socialism, as Marx conceived it, is not the *answer,* but the *question* he raised remains with us: how can men and women work together to create a world in which *all* people, not just the favored few, can live decent, meaningful lives? Even though the Cold War is over, it remains to be seen whether capitalism can provide a satisfactory answer to that question.

Rousseau and the Theory of the Social Contract

Thus far, we have been looking at some of the ways in which philosophers have answered the general question, What is the good society? We saw that moral problems of the just distribution of wealth are central to this subject.

In a way, social philosophy, as Plato suggested long ago, is ethics writ large—it is ethics in a social, rather than an individual, setting. But there is a very special set of questions associated with the study of the *state,* and it is to these questions that we now turn. Before we go any farther, we had best determine what we mean by a *state* and what philosophical problems are raised by states. Everywhere we look, across historical time and around the globe, men and women are organized into social groupings within defined territorial limits or borders. Within each one of these geographical units, there is some smaller group of people who rule, give orders, run things, use force to get others to obey—some group who makes and enforces laws. This smaller group is what we call the state. Sometimes the group that rules consists of a single person and his or her personal followers: a king or queen, a general or dictator, a priest or pope, plus a group of loyal underlings. Sometimes the group consists of a hereditary class, such as a military aristocracy. The group may be a political clique or party which has led a successful revolution against the previous rulers. It may even, as in our own country, be a large group of men and women who have been chosen in an election by a much larger group of citizens. But whoever makes the laws, gives the commands, and enforces them on everyone living within that territory *is* the state.

States may exist for any number of purposes: they may exist to carry out the tenets of a religious faith, to maintain general peace and security, to see to the well-being of some or all of the people within the territory, or to

"First of all, I would like to express my gratefulness to all those wonderful ancestors of mine who helped to make this glorious day possible." (Drawing by W. Miller, 1969, The New Yorker Magazine, Inc.)

ensure justice and tranquility. The state may even exist merely for the purpose of lining the pockets and satisfying the desires of itself, regardless of what the rest of the population wants or needs. There are so many different purposes for which states have existed that it is not much use to look for some basic or underlying function which all states perform insofar as they are states. Philosophers express this fact by saying that the state cannot be defined teleologically. That simply means that we cannot explain what a state is in terms of the goals (*telos* is Greek meaning "end" or "goal") at which it aims. But all states, regardless of who comprises them and no matter what purposes they pursue, have *two* characteristics in common. Once you understand these two characteristics, you will know what a state *is* and also what is the fundamental problem of political philosophy.

First, states everywhere and always use force to obtain obedience to their commands. Sometimes force takes the form of armed troops, police, jails and death rows. Sometimes merely the threat of force is enough to bring recalcitrant citizens into line. Economic threats can be used as effectively as the whip or the club. But behind the judge there always stands the police, and they are not there for ceremony only.

"Signing of The Constitution" by Albert Herter. The United States was the first state to actually be brought into existence by a social contract. (Brown Brothers.)

Force alone does not make a group of people into a state, however; for a band of robbers, an invading army, even a lone gunman holding you up on a dark street all use force to make you obey, and no one would call robbers, an army, or a mugger "the state." The second, more important, mark of the state is that as it issues its commands and shows its sword, it also claims to have the *right* to command and the *right* to be obeyed. Now a mugger does not claim the *right* to rob you. He says, "Your money or your life!"; he does not say, "Your money, for I have a right to it." But when the state sends you a bill for taxes, or commands you to report for induction into the armed forces, or orders you to stop at red lights and drive only with a valid license, it claims to have a right to your obedience. In the language of political philosophy, the state claims to be *legitimate*.

There is a wonderful scene in one of Shakespeare's plays *(Henry IV, Part 1)* in which a group of conspirators are planning their attack on the forces of the king. One of the group is a flamboyant Welsh chieftain named Glendower, who claims to have some magical powers in addition to some usable troops. At one point, in an effort to impress his fellow conspirators with the wonderfulness of his powers, he brags, "I can call spirits from the vasty deep." The leader of the conspiracy, Hotspur, is not very impressed, and he answers, "Why so can I, and so can any man/but will they come when you do call them?" The point, of course, is that it is one thing to make a claim, and quite another to get anybody to believe it.

The really remarkable thing about human beings is that they are so prone to accept the claims of legitimacy made by states that rule the territories in which they live. From time to time, people rebel against the state, and a few philosophers called anarchists have denied the state's claim to have a right to rule. But by and large, when states make laws and claim the right to enforce them, people believe their claim and obey *even when they aren't actually being forced to do so*. Those last few words are crucial, of course, for most of us "obey" a gunman who holds us up or an army that invades our city and points its guns at us. We "obey" because we don't want to get shot. Cynics might say that that is really the only reason anyone ever obeys the law, but all the historical and sociological evidence points in the opposite direction. Save in the most unusual circumstances, men and women obey the law more faithfully than the threat of punishment requires. They obey from habit, to be sure, but they also obey because they genuinely believe that the state has the right to command them. After all, they think, it is *the law*. How often has each of us done something or refrained from doing something merely because the law says that we must or mustn't? How, save by playing on this belief in the legitimacy of the law, could a single official or police officer control the behavior of a large crowd? How could several thousand overworked employees of the Internal Revenue Service collect taxes from 200 million Americans? How could a lieutenant lead a platoon of frightened soldiers into withering enemy fire? How, indeed, could an old and feeble king bend young, vigorous, ambitious dukes, princes, and generals to his will?

The belief in the legitimacy of the authority of the state is the glue that holds a political society together. It is, even more than armies or police or jails, the means by which the state gets its laws obeyed. So we may sum up the universal characteristics of states by saying that the state is *a group of people who claim the right to enforce obedience to their commands within a territory and succeed in getting most of the people in the territory to accept that claim*. A group of people who make a claim of this sort are said to be claiming *political authority*. So a state is a group of people who claim political authority and have their claim accepted by most of those against whom the claim is made.

Well, states claim political authority, and they get their claims accepted. But it is one thing to get other people to accept something you say; it is quite another to be right. I may claim to be a doctor, and if enough people believe me, I can open an office and start prescribing medicine. But that doesn't make me a doctor. My "patients" may fail to notice that I am not curing them, but even that does not make me a doctor. So too, a group may claim the right to rule, and the people may accept their claim, but that does not make their claim *true*.

The fundamental question of all political philosophy is obviously this: When does a group calling itself the state really have a *right* to command? Or, since that way of putting the question seems to assume that states sometimes have such a right, we can ask: Does any group of persons ever have the right to command?

The same question can be turned around to focus our attention on the person doing the obeying rather than the people doing the commanding. From my point of view as citizen, a state is a group of people who command me. If I believe that I have an obligation to obey their commands, then I consider them as constituting a legitimate state. Otherwise, I consider them tyrants. To the citizen, the fundamental question of political philosophy is: Do I ever have an obligation to obey the commands issued by some group calling itself the state?

⬠Legitimate Authority   Legitimate authority is the right to give commands that others have a moral obligation to obey. States claim legitimate authority when they say that they have a right to pass laws which citizens or subjects *ought* to obey, regardless of whether they are in danger of being caught for not obeying. Democratic states base their claim to legitimate authority on the fact that they are elected by the people whom they rule and, therefore, speak with the voice of the people.

Devout Catholic kissing the ring of Pope John Paul II.
The Roman Catholic Church demands obedience from
its communicants, as did the absolute monarchs of their
subjects. The distinctive mark of eighteenth-century
social contract theorists is their rejection of such
demands for obedience. (Sygma.)

In ancient and medieval times, the citizen's obligation to the ruler was considered to be limited and conditioned upon the ruler's just performance of his or her sovereign duties. But in the sixteenth and seventeenth centuries, in response to fundamental shifts in the relative power of the aristocracy, the monarchy, and the new middle class, the theory began to be put forward that the authority of the ruler is absolute. The king, it was said, is the sole possessor of the ultimate political authority—sovereignty, as it was called. All others in the society are unconditionally obligated to obey his commands. Usually, a religious justification was advanced for this claim—the king was considered God's representative on earth—but sometimes the theory of an original agreement or contract was also appealed to.

The unqualified claim of absolute kingly authority was unacceptable to the philosophers of the Enlightenment. A person who bows his head to God or his knee to the king merely makes himself the slave of another. In the words of Immanuel Kant, submission to the commands of another means a loss of autonomy, a denial of one's own reason.

So for the political philosophers of the seventeenth and eighteenth centuries, the question of obligation to the state became a new and more complicated question: Is there any way in which I can submit to the commands of a legitimate state without giving up my freedom and autonomy?

The man who asked this question more clearly and forcefully than anyone in the history of Western Philosophy was the eighteenth-century Swiss thinker Jean-Jacques Rousseau. Judgments differ among philosophers, as much as they do among the compilers of all-time baseball or football teams, but in my personal judgment, Jean-Jacques Rousseau is the greatest political philosopher who has ever lived. His claim to immortality rests upon one short book, *Of the Social Contract,* an essay scarcely more than a hundred pages long. In that brief, brilliant work, Rousseau formulates the fundamental question of the philosophy of the state and makes a valiant although ultimately unsuccessful effort to solve it. Why such fame, you might ask, if he failed to solve the problem? In philosophy, as in the sciences, the most important step frequently is to ask the right question, and although philosophers had been analyzing the nature of the state for more than 2,000 years before Rousseau, he was the first to see exactly what the problem was and to recognize how difficult it would be to solve.

For the philosophers of the state who struggled with the question of legitimate authority in the seventeenth and eighteenth centuries, the standard solution to the problem was the device which they call the social contract. The authority of the state, it was argued, can only be founded upon an agreement among all the persons who are to be ruled by the state. The idea of a contract, of course, was taken from the law, where it applied to an agreement between two parties for their mutual advantage. A buyer and seller in the marketplace make a contract with one another, according to which the seller will supply goods in such and such a quantity, and of so and so quality, and the buyer will pay so much money for them at a particular time. The heart and soul of a contract is what the lawyers call a *quid pro quo* or a "this for that;" each side must stand to benefit from the deal in order to make the contract binding. The right of either party to have the contract enforced on the other derives from two things: first, each party has freely promised to abide by the contract and so is bound by his or her word; second, each party benefits from the contract and so has an obligation to return the benefit to the other according to the agreed terms.

The social contract theorists, as they have become known, conceived the idea of tracing political obligation back to a contract or social agreement among all the members of the society. If each citizen could be imagined to have actually made such an agreement, then the riddle of legitimate state authority would be solved. First, it would then be possible to explain why, and under what conditions, the citizen has a duty to obey the law. Very sim-

JEAN-JACQUES ROUSSEAU

Jean-Jacques Rousseau (1712–1778) is one of the most paradoxical figures in modern European letters. Born in Geneva, Switzerland, he spent his early years in a succession of homes (his mother having died only a few days after his birth). At the age of sixteen, he converted to Catholicism, though he seems not to have been devout in any orthodox manner. After trying his hand at such tasks as music teacher and tutor, Rousseau finally found his true calling, which was to be a writer, a man of letters.

Rousseau's writings fall into two groups which seem entirely to contradict each other in their teachings. His autobiographical *Confessions*, his novels *Émile* and *La Nouvelle Heloise*, and his *Discourse on the Sciences and the Arts* all set forth in the most moving and powerful way the sentimental doctrine that our nature is inherently good, that civilization is the great corrupter, that feeling rather than reason is the proper guide to life, and that men and women will be naturally moral if only the impediments of cultivated life can be cleared away. But in his greatest work, *Of the Social Contact,* Rousseau argues in a spare and rigorously logical way for the proposition that the just state and morality itself arise from the exercise of our rational powers. Rousseau is thus an apostle both of sentiment—of feeling, of tears and sympathy—and also of reason.

It was the special genius of Rousseau that he saw the central question of political philosophy more clearly than anyone before him, and he expressed it with greater precision and force. Here are the words in which he framed the problem, taken from the sixth chapter of *Of the Social Contract:*

Where shall we find a form of association which will defend and protect with the whole common force the person and the property of each associate, and by which every person, while uniting himself with all, shall obey only himself and remain as free as before?

ply, he would have a duty to obey laws made by a state which he had freely contracted or agreed to bring into existence. If he says to the judge, "Who are you to command me? Who are you to threaten me with punishment if I fail to obey?" the judge will answer, "I am a representative of that state which you yourself promised to obey, when you signed the social contract." And if the citizen, still resistant, goes on to ask, "What have I received from my fellow citizens that I should keep the agreement I made with them?" the judge

> Social Contract A voluntary, unanimous agreement among all the people of a society to form themselves into a united political community and to obey the laws laid down by the government they collectively select. In seventeenth- and eighteenth-century political theory, the legitimacy claims of the state are said to rest on an actual or hypothetical social contract.

can answer, "You have received peace, social order, even-handed justice, and the benefits of a civilized society."

But even more important, if the citizen asks, "How can I obey this state I have brought into existence without forfeiting any autonomy and giving up my freedom?" the judge can answer, "In this state, and only in this state, those who obey remain free. For the state that makes the laws consists not of *some* of the people who live in this nation, but of all the people. The commands you obey are the very commands that you, as a citizen, have issued in your role as a law-maker. In this state, the law-obeyers and the law-makers are one. Through the device of a social contract, the people become the rulers." Indeed, since the traditional word for ruler is "sovereign," the social contract theory is a doctrine of people's sovereignty, or, as it is usually known, popular sovereignty. (That doesn't mean that people like it. It means that the people are sovereign. This is what Abraham Lincoln meant when he said that we live under a government that is by the people, as well as of and for the people.)

Here is how Rousseau describes the social contract. This passage directly follows the question quoted earlier:

JEAN-JACQUES ROUSSEAU, *Of the Social Contract*

The articles of this contract are so unalterably fixed by the nature of the act that the least modification renders them vain and of no effect; so that they are the same everywhere, and are everywhere tacitly understood and admitted, even though they may never have been formally announced; until, the social compact being violated, each individual is restored to his original rights, and resumes his native liberty, while losing the conventional liberty for which he renounced it.

The articles of the social contract will, when clearly understood, be found reducible to this single point: the total alienation of each associate, and all his rights, to the whole community; for, in the first place, as every individual gives himself up entirely, the condition of every person is alike; and being so, it would not be to the interest of any one to render that condition offensive to others.

Nay, more than this, the alienation being made without any reserve, the union is as complete as it can be, and no associate has any further claim to anything: for if any individual retained rights not enjoyed in general by all, as there would be no common superior to decide between him and the public, each person being in some points his own judge, would soon pretend to be so in everything; and thus would the state of nature be continued and the association necessarily become tyrannical or be annihilated.

Finally, each person gives himself to all, and so not to any one individual; and as there is no one associate over whom the same right is not acquired which is ceded to him by others, each gains an equivalent for what he loses, and finds his force increased for preserving that which he possesses.

If, therefore, we exclude from the social contract all that is not essential, we shall find it reduced to the following terms:

Each of us places in common his person and all his power under the supreme direction of the general will; and as one body we all receive each member as an indivisible part of the whole.

From that moment, instead of as many separate persons as there are contracting parties, this act of association produces a moral and collective body, composed of as many members as there are votes in the assembly, which from this act receives its unity, its common self, its life, and its will. This public person, which is thus formed by the union of all other persons, took formerly the name of "city," and now takes that of "republic" or "body politic." It is called by its members "State" when it is passive, "Sovereign" when in activity, and whenever it is compared with other bodies of a similar kind, it is denominated "power." The associates take collectively the name of "people": and separately, that of "citizens," as participating in the sovereign authority, and of "subjects," because they are subjected to the laws of the State. But these terms are frequently confounded and used one for the other, and it is enough that a man understands how to distinguish them when they are employed in all their precision.

Two problems arise immediately. First, it is going to be difficult to get everyone together when laws need to be made. How can the people obey only themselves if they don't personally make the laws? The usual solution both in political theory and in political practice is to institute a system of elected representatives. But Rousseau will have none of that. If the state is not kept small enough for everyone to participate in law-making, then so far as he is concerned, tyranny replaces liberty. Of course, that means that all citizens, and not just a few professionals, are going to have to pay attention to public affairs. But that is the price of freedom, Rousseau insists. As he says later on in *Of the Social Contract*.

As soon as men cease to consider public service as the principal duty of citizens, and rather choose to serve with their purse than with their persons, we may pronounce the State to be on the very verge of ruin. Are the citizens called upon to march out to war? They pay soldiers

"Revolutionary tribunal in the Abbaye." A meeting of the Jacobin club, a radical group that ruled France for a time during the Revolution. Maximilien Robespierre, the most famous revolutionary, was a leader of the Jacobin club from 1791 to 1792. (North Wind Picture Archives.)

for the purpose, and remain at home. Are they summoned to council? They nominate deputies, and stay at home. And thus, in consequence of idleness and money, they have soldiers to enslave their country, and representatives to sell it.

It is the hurry of commerce and of the arts, it is the greedy thirst of gain, and the effeminate softness and love of comfort, that occasion this commutation of money for personal service. Men give up a part of the profits they acquire in order to purchase leisure to augment them. Give money, and you will soon have chains. The word "finance" is a term of slavery; it is unknown in the true city. In a State truly free, the citizens do all with their own arms and nothing with their money; and, instead of purchasing exemption from their duty, they would even pay for fulfilling it themselves. My ideas on this subject are indeed very different from those commonly received; I even think the *corvées* [unpaid labor on roads and highways, required of French peasants before the revolution] are less an infringement upon liberty than taxes.

The better a State is constituted, the more do public affairs intrude upon private affairs in the minds of the citizens. Private concerns even become considerably fewer, because each individual shares so largely in the common happiness that he has not so much occasion to seek for it in private resources. In a well-conducted city, each member flies with joy to the assemblies; under a bad government, no one is disposed to bend his way thither, because no one is interested in proceedings where he foresees that the general will will not prevail, and in the end every man turns his attention to his own domestic affairs. Good laws lead on to better, and bad ones seldom fail to generate still worse. When once you hear some one say, when speaking of the affairs of the State, "What is it to me?" you may give over the State for lost.

It was the decline of patriotism, the activity of private interest, the immense extent of States, the increase of conquests, and the abuses of government, that suggested the expedient of having deputies or representatives of the people in the assemblies of the nation. These representatives are the body to which, in certain countries, they have dared to give the name of the "Third Estate," as if the private interest of the two other orders deserved the first and second rank, and the public interest should be considered only in the third place.

Sovereignty cannot be represented for the same reason that it cannot be alienated; its essence is the general will, and that will must speak for itself, or it does not exist: it is either itself or not itself: there is no intermediate possibility. The deputies of the people, therefore, are not and cannot be their representatives; they can only be their commissioners, and as such are not qualified to conclude anything definitively. No act of theirs can be a law, unless it has been ratified by the people in person; and without that ratification nothing is a law. The people of England deceive themselves when they fancy they are free; they are so, in fact, only during the election of members of parliament: for, as soon as a new one is elected, they are again in chains, and are nothing. And thus, by the use they make of their brief moments of liberty, they deserve to lose it.

The second problem is how to make decisions when there is disagreement. The natural solution that springs to our minds is to take a vote and let the majority rule. We have become so accustomed to deciding questions by majority vote that it sometimes seems as though little children learn to vote in school before they learn how to count the votes. But Rousseau had the clarity of mind to see that majority rule presents a very serious obstacle to freedom. I may promise, in the original unanimous contract, to abide by the vote of the majority. But in so doing, I seem simply to be agreeing to a sort of voluntary slavery. If I vote against a proposed law, believing that it is a bad law, contrary to the national interest, then how can I be said to "obey only myself and remain as free as before," when I am forced to submit to it? Rousseau has an extremely subtle answer to this question. First read what he has to say, and then we can talk about it a bit.

> There is one law only which, by its nature, requires unanimous consent; I mean the social compact: for civil association is the most voluntary of all acts; every man being born free and master of himself, no person can under any pretense whatever subject him without his consent. To affirm that the son of a slave is born a slave is to pronounce that he is not born a man.
>
> Should there be any men who oppose the social compact, their opposition will not invalidate it, but only hinder their being included: they are foreigners among citizens. When the State is instituted, residence constitutes consent; to inhabit a territory is to submit to the sovereignty.
>
> Except in this original contract, a majority of votes is sufficient to bind all the others. This is a consequence of the contract itself. But it may be asked how a man can be free and yet forced to conform to the will of others. How are the opposers free when they are in submission to laws to which they have never consented?
>
> I answer that the question is not fairly stated. The citizen consents to all the laws, to those which are passed in spite of his opposition, and even to those which sentence him to punishment if he violates any one of them. The constant will of all the members of the State is the general will; it is by that they are citizens and free. When any law is proposed in the assembly of the people, the question is not precisely to enquire whether they approve the proposition or reject it, but if it is conformable or not to the general will, which is their will. Each citizen, in giving his suffrage, states his mind on that question; and the general will is found by counting the votes. When, therefore, the motion which I opposed carries, it only proves to me that I was mistaken, and that what I believed to be the general will was not so. If my particular opinion had prevailed, I should have done what I was not willing to do, and, consequently, I should not have been in a state of freedom.

Something very tricky is going on in this passage. How can I be free when I don't get what I voted for? Earlier in *Of the Social Contract,* Rousseau put his point even more dramatically. A citizen who refuses to obey the general will, he said, must be compelled to do so. "This in fact only forces him to be free." What on earth can Rousseau have meant?

The full answer would take a book by itself, but we can say a few things to clear away some of the mystery. Rousseau believed that the people have a right to make laws only as long as they are genuinely attempting to legislate in the public interest rather than in their own individual and private interests. Now, if the majority could be counted on always to be right about the general good, then no one in the minority would want his or her view to become law. For if I want what is for the general good, and if the majority is always right about the general good, and if I am in the minority, then what I mistakenly wanted is *not* for the general good, and hence not what I really want. And if freedom is getting what you really want, then only by being forced to abide by the majority can I really be free!

There is a flaw in the argument, of course. The majority may always aim at the general good, but it does not always aim accurately. More often than not, even when every citizen is seeking what is best for all, the truth will be seen only by one citizen or a few. Rousseau confused aiming at and hitting the target.

Americans have a vested interest in the theory of the social contract, with all its flaws, because we are the first nation ever actually to bring itself into existence as a state by means of a real, historical, explicit contract. We call it our Constitution, but what the Founding Fathers actually wrote was the first operative social contract. When it was ratified in 1788, there came into being for the first time in Western history a state truly founded upon a contract.

Although the theory of the social contract has dominated liberal political theory since the seventeenth century, it has been subjected to a number of powerful criticisms. The most obvious objection is that, save for the special case of the United States, no actual state has ever been brought into existence by such an explicit contractual agreement among the citizens-to-be. Hence, the theory does not provide any justification at all for the claims of even the most "democratic" governments.

But the mere historical absence of a contract is not the worst of the problems confronting social contract theories. Even if a group of men and

⌒ **The General Will**   A term invented by Jean-Jacques Rousseau to describe the decision by the citizens of a republic to set aside their private and partisan concerns and instead collectively aim at the general good. According to Rousseau, to say that a society "has a general will" is to say that all the members of the society are public-spiritedly aiming at the general good in their political actions and deliberations. Rousseau was very pessimistic about the possibility of ever achieving a general will.

President Clinton gestures while giving his State of the Union address, Thursday, January 23, 1996, on Capitol Hill. (Photograph: Greg Gibson. AP/Wide World Photos.)

women have indeed contracted together, some time in the dim past, to submit themselves to the collective will of all, that still leaves those of us in the present generation without any reason for obeying the commands of the state. After all, I am not bound by the marriage contracts or the business contracts made by my ancient ancestors; why should I be bound by whatever political contracts they may have made?

To this, the social contract theorists answer that each of us, upon reaching the legal age of adulthood, implicitly signs his or her own name to that original contract by remaining in the country, living under its laws, and entering actively into its legal arrangements. John Locke, the spiritual father of our Constitution, especially emphasizes the owning of property in this selection from his most famous political work, the *Second Treatise of Government.*

JOHN LOCKE,
*Second Treatise
of Government*

Every man being, as has been shown, naturally free, and nothing being able to put him into subjection to any earthly power but only his own consent, it is to be considered what shall be understood to be sufficient declaration of a man's consent to make him subject to the laws of any government. There is a common distinction of an express and a tacit consent, which will concern our present case. Nobody doubts but an express consent of any man entering into a society makes him a perfect member of that society, a subject of that government. The difficulty is, what ought to be looked upon as a tacit consent, and how far it binds, *i.e.,* how far any one shall be looked on to have consented, and thereby submitted to any government, where he has made no expressions of it at all. And to this I say that every man that hath any possession or enjoyment of any part of the dominions of any government doth thereby give his tacit consent, and is as far forth obliged to obedience to the laws of that government during such enjoyment as any one under it; whether this his possession be of land to him and his heirs for ever, or a lodging only for a week; or whether it be barely traveling freely on the highway; and in effect it reaches as far as the very being of any one within the territories of that government.

To understand this the better, it is fit to consider that every man when he at first incorporates himself into any commonwealth, he, by his uniting himself thereunto, annexes also, and submits to the community those possessions which he has or shall acquire that do not already belong to any other government; for it would be a direct contradiction for any one to enter into society with others for the securing and regulating of property, and yet to suppose his land, whose property is to be regulated by the laws of the society, should be exempt from the jurisdiction of that government to which he himself, and the property of the land, is a subject. By the same act, therefore, whereby any one unites his person, which was before free, to any commonwealth, by the same he unites his possession, which was before free, to it also; and they become, both of them, person and possession, subject to the government and dominion of that commonwealth as long as it hath a being. Whoever therefore from thenceforth by inheritance, purchases, permission, or otherwise, enjoys any part of the land so annexed to, and under the government of that commonwealth, must take it with the condition it is under, that is, of submitting to the government of the commonwealth under whose jurisdiction it is as far forth as any subject of it.

But since the government has a direct jurisdiction only over the land, and reaches the possessor of it (before he has actually incorporated himself in the society), only as he dwells upon, and enjoys that: the obligation any one is under, by virtue of such enjoyment, to submit to the government, begins and ends with the enjoyment; so that whenever the owner, who has given nothing but such a tacit consent to the government, will by donation, sale, or otherwise, quit the said possession, he is at liberty to go and incorporate himself into any other commonwealth, or to agree with others to begin a new one *(in vacuis locis)* in any part of the world they can find free and unpossessed. Whereas he that has once by actual agreement and any express declaration given his consent to be of any commonwealth is perpetually and indispensably obliged to be and remain unalterably a subject to it, and can never be again in the liberty of the state of

J O H N L O C K E

John Locke (1632–1704) had a philosophical career which was, in a sense, the reverse of David Hume's. Locke's great works were not published until close to his sixtieth year, and they were received almost immediately with great acclaim. During the troubled times in England which followed the restoration of the Catholic monarchy (in 1660) after the English Civil War, Locke sided with the moderate faction which sought to limit the power of the king and bring the throne under some control by Parliament. In 1689, one year after the so-called Glorious Revolution, which established a limited monarchy in England, Locke published a pair of long essays on the subject of the foundations of the authority of the state. The second of these essays, known now as the *Second Treatise of Government,* is the most important single document in the literature of constitutional democracy. Appearing when it did, the *Second Treatise* naturally was interpreted as a justification for the new regime of William and Mary, for it defended the sort of limited monarchy, hedged round with parliamentary restraints, which the English people adopted as their form of government in 1688. Actually, we now know that the two *Treatises* were written in the early 1680s, some years before the change in government took place.

The next year, 1690, Locke published a massive work on the foundations of human knowledge, the *Essay Concerning the Human Understanding.* (See Chapter 6.) The *Essay* is the foundation of the school of philosophy known as empiricism. Locke's arguments profoundly affected Berkeley, Hume, and the other British philosophers who followed him. The work was very soon translated into French and had a major influence as well on Continental thought. A century later, Immanuel Kant was to acknowledge it as one of the most important influences on his own thinking.

nature; unless, by any calamity, the government he was under comes to be dissolved, or else by some public acts cuts him off from being any longer a member of it.

You may wonder how a person can enter into a contract by "tacit consent." Don't I have to actually *say* that I am making a contract in order to do so? Locke here is relying on the ancient legal principle that when a person, over a period of time, acts in such a way as to give other persons a reasonable expectation that she will continue so to act, and if she benefits from that unspoken understanding, then she has made a "quasi-contract," which the law will enforce just as it will an explicit, spoken contract.

But Locke's argument depends on the assumption that a citizen can pick up and leave if he or she is dissatisfied with the laws of the state under which he or she lives. In Locke's day (the late 1600s) that was still possible. The Pilgrims who came to America, and many millions who followed them, were exercising precisely that option. Today, however, emigration requires visas and passports, no matter where you want to go. Every square foot of inhabitable earth is claimed by some state or other, so that the most anyone can do is to go from the rule of one state to the rule of another. Under this condition, it is harder and harder to see what truth there is in the theory of the implicit, or tacit, contract.

The Pluralist Theory of the State

The theory of the social contract takes it for granted that the political world is made up of individuals and of the state—nothing more. Rousseau and the classical liberal social contract theorists think that the individual comes first, and that it is many individuals, acting together, who create the state by their social contract. They see a direct relationship between the individual and the state—a relationship of the sort philosophers call "immediate" or sometimes "unmediated." Both words—"immediate" and "unmediated"—convey the same idea, which is that there is nothing in between "mediating" the individual and the state.

In the late nineteenth and twentieth centuries, however, a new view was put forward of the relationship between the individual and the state. According to this view, all of us, children and grown-ups, men and women, old and young, belong to many different *groups,* such as neighborhoods, churches, labor unions, fraternities, women's groups, gun enthusiasts' groups, farmers' groups, chambers of commerce, ethnic groups, hobbyists' groups, and so on. No one ever actually confronts the state as an individual, except perhaps when he or she is on trial in a court of law. It is always groups of people who work, as groups, to influence legislation, persuade judges, sway presidents, and in general to get the state to favor their needs, interests, or desires.

So society is really made up of groups, on this view, not individuals. Even the state is a group, like any other. Indeed, the state is actually many groups, not just one. It is the career civil servants in the state capital or Washington; it is the members of Congress; it is the men and women who serve as judges in the federal, state, or municipal courts; it is the leaders and workers of the political parties; it is the staffers who work for members of Congress, and who keep their jobs only so long as their bosses get re-elected.

To understand politics, this pluralist or group theory of the state says, you must study the way groups are formed and the way they interact. Just reading social contract theorists or the Constitution will not help you to understand what really goes on—how decisions are made, how power is wielded, who really governs.

One of the clearest statements of the pluralist theory was set forth in a book, *The Group Basis of Politics,* by a professor of government named Earl Latham. Here is how he summarizes this theory in the first chapter of his book:

> The chief social values cherished by individuals in modern society are realized through groups. The number is countless, and the variety of these social groupings is abundant and complex. No aspect of the life of the individual is untouched by them. Modern man is literally conducted from the cradle to the grave by groups, for he is born in a family, goes to school in organized classes, goes to church, perhaps, plays with boyhood gangs, joins fraternities, works for a corporation, belongs to various associations, cultural, civic, professional and social, and is carried off to his immortal reward by a business enterpriser with the solemnity appropriate to such ceremonies. . . .
>
> The utilitarians made the same assumptions about the nature of the political community that they made about the nature of the economic community. The liberal philosophy of a John Stuart Mill rejected the doctrines of natural law and right that were so familiar to the eighteenth century but retained the feeling that the chief political problems were those that involved the singular individual on the one hand and the "state" on the other. All other and intermediate associations and groupings were dissolved, blanked, and obscured— a kind of sunken hinterland between two dominating mountainous battlements. This exaggerated individualism not only abstracted man from his social environment; it made him more sentient, more responsive to the gentle but compelling dictates of reason, more enlightened about his affairs than the facts justified. . . .
>
> But utilitarian theories did not entirely dominate the field of political speculation. . . .
>
> The principal attack, in England at least, upon the political speculations of the philosophic idealists was made by a group of writers professing pluralist doctrines. . . . The state, said the pluralists, is merely one association among a host of associations both as fact and right, which, far from absorbing the entire allegiance of the individual, has to compete with conflicting group loyalties, some of which are invincible. Most people think of themselves first as members of their clubs, lodges, unions, or parishes, and only incidentally as members of the state. The state, therefore, is merely one group among many, without superior right to dominate other associations. . . .

The apparatus of the state, through its manifold offices—legislatures, councils, agencies, departments, courts, and other forums—maintains a system of instrumentalities for the writing and enforcement of the formal rules by which society is governed. But all of these instrumentalities are themselves groups, and they possess a sense of group belonging and identification which is very strong. In what respect are these groups different from the more numerous groups outside the structure of public government? In a political sense they are not different at all, but are the same. They exhibit all the internal social and political characteristics of group forms in that infinite universe of plural forms outside the state apparatus. . . .

The legislature referees the group struggle, ratifies the victories of the successful coalitions, and records the terms of the surrenders, compromises, and conquests in the form of statutes. Every statute tends to represent compromise because the process of accommodating conflicts of group interest is one of deliberation and consent. The legislative vote on any issue tends to represent the composition of strength, i.e., the balance of power, among the contending groups at the moment of voting. What may be called public policy is the equilibrium reached in this struggle at any given moment, and it represents a balance which the contending factions of groups constantly strive to weight in their favor. In this process, it is clear that blocs of groups can be defeated. In fact they can be routed. Such groups do not possess a veto on the proposals and acts that affect them. What they do possess when they are defeated is the right to make new combinations of strength if they are able to do so, combinations that will support a new effort to rewrite the rules in their favor. This process is fully in accord with the American culture pattern which rates high in the characteristics of optimism, risk, experimentalism, change, aggressiveness, acquisitiveness, and a colossal faith in man's ability to subdue and bend nature to his desire. The process is dynamic, not static; fluid, not fixed. Today's losers may be tomorrow's winners.

Latham's description of politics certainly sounds a good deal more like what goes on in the United States than what Rousseau and Locke have to say. But there remains a very important question to which he provides no answer: This may be the way things *do* work in this country, but is it the way they *should* work? Is a pluralist political system a good thing?

The Founding Fathers—the men who wrote our Constitution—did not think so. In fact, in a famous essay published during the debates over the ratification of the Constitution, James Madison, later our fourth president, condemned what Latham calls "interest groups" as *factions*. Madison actually thought that one of the greatest advantages of the new Constitution was precisely that it would undermine the effects of factions. "Among the numerous advantages promised by a well-constructed Union," Madison wrote in the

Tenth *Federalist Paper*, "none deserves to be more accurately developed than its tendency to break and control the violence of factions." By a faction, he went on, "I understand a number of citizens, whether amounting to a majority or minority of the whole, who are united or actuated by some common impulse or passion, or of interest, adverse to the rights of other citizens, or to the permanent and aggregate interests of the community." This is exactly what Latham means by an interest group.

What did Madison have against factions? Very simply, they are out for their own particular interest, rather than for the larger interest of the community as a whole. Farmers want laws that help farmers, regardless of who else must pay. The same can be said for entrepreneurs, workers, gun owners, importers, exporters, Southerners, Northerners, Easterners, and Westerners. So long as citizens think, act, and vote as members of interest groups rather than as members of the whole community, the true interests of the society will be ignored in the struggle for partisan advantage.

Now, Latham was perfectly well aware of Madison's objections to factions. The Tenth *Federalist Paper* is one of the most widely read texts of American political theory. So, was he simply describing the way government now works? Or is there an argument *in favor* of interest group politics that can respond to Madison's fears?

Let me suggest just such an argument, based on a combination of the traditional contract belief in the sovereignty of the people and the modern story about the role of interest groups in American politics.

According to the social contract theorists, the people speak every two or four years at election time. But the business of governing goes on daily, week in and week out, year after year. Thousands of important decisions are made, many of them about issues that never even arose during the election campaign. If voters only get to express their will on election day, how can their representatives know, between elections, what their will is? And if the elected representatives don't know the will of their constituents, how can they truly be *representatives?*

The interest group theory steps in at this point to fill the gap between elections. In a democracy like ours, citizens are politically active every day, not just on election day. Through their letter writing, lobbying, political fundraising, and other activities, groups of citizens communicate their desires to their representatives, who are then able truly to *represent* their constituents.

Television pundits may look down their noses at lobbying and letter-writing campaigns, but these are, according to the pluralist theory of democracy, the legitimate and essential means by which the will of the people is translated into the law of the land. Wipe out "factions"—put a stop to interest group politics—and true democracy dies. All that remains is a token, meaningless, once-every-four-years vote.

The argument in favor of the interest group theory is even stronger. When I vote in an election, all I can do is vote "yes" or "no." Now, there are some proposals I don't care very much about, even though on balance I may be in favor. Others matter deeply to me, so much so that I might consider them life-or-death issues. I cannot express the intensity of my preference through a vote, because my "yes" counts no more and no less than your "no," even if for you it is life-or-death and for me it is no big deal.

But there *is* a way that I can express the intensity of my feeling about an issue, and that is by the amount of money I am willing to give or the amount of time I am willing to spend on that issue. If gun control is the heart and soul of my political life, I can spend all my spare time working for a gun control law (or against it, as the case may be). At the same time, if I care only a little bit about the environment, I can pay my annual $25 dues to the local environmentalist club and forget about it until next year.

Thus, interest group politics permits me to give effective expression to the *complexity, specificity,* and *intensity* of my interests, something mere electoral politics can never do.

If interest group politics has this much going for it, what can be said against it? At least one thing, quite important. In order to express the intensity of your interest through political action, you must have resources to make that intensity known to your representatives. You must have the money, the time, and the skill to bring pressure to bear on a senator or representative, a mayor, or a governor. But as we all know, the resources in our society are very unevenly distributed. If you own a newspaper, or have a job that permits you to take time off for lobbying; if you have enough money to make a big donation to a political campaign; in short, if you are one of the affluent members of society, then your interests are going to get a much more attentive hearing from the elected representatives. And this will distort the process of interest expression, giving some people an advantage that outweighs the greater intensity of interest of the poorer people opposed to you.

So the pluralist theory of democracy does not make place for a fair expression of the interests of all. And that, you will recall, was precisely what the utilitarians claimed democracy would accomplish.

Nevertheless, the pluralist theory clearly takes into account the way American democracy actually works in the modern world, and it answers at least some, but certainly not all, of James Madison's objections to *factions*.

The Racial Critique of the Social Contract Theory of the State

Since the eighteenth century, the theory of the Social Contract has been the leading philosophical story in Western thought about the nature, origin, and justification of the State. Our own nation was organized by the Founding Fathers on the principle of Consent of the Governed—which means that those who seek to rule must have the consent of those whom they claim to rule. The *Social Contract* is supposed to embody that consent.

In the early days of the Social Contract theory, some philosophers actually talked as though they thought people had gathered together and made a formal agreement with one another—in a clearing in the woods, maybe. But for the most part, the Social Contract were conceived either as an ideal—what *would* be the case if everything was exactly as it should be—or else merely as a way of expressing the central principle that the rulers must have the consent of the governed if their rule is to be legitimate. It is this belief that lies behind the modern emphasis on Democracy and Free Elections. There seems to be very broad agreement throughout the world that states must go to the people for approval and endorsement if they are to be legitimate.

Social Contract theory is really very simple and straightforward, or so it seems. A group of people living together in some part of the world decides that it would be mutually beneficial for them to get together and set up a government—perhaps to protect the whole community against outside attack, perhaps to provide common social services, such as fire and police protection, perhaps to launch some collective projects too big for any private individuals to undertake, like the building of a national highway network, or the exploration of space. They agree to unite their forces and submit themselves to a common government. If they need laws, they, or their representatives, enact them. Periodically, the people review the performance of their representatives and tell them, in elections, whether they can continue serving the public. If a majority of the people believes that their representatives have been doing a good job, they give them another turn. If they are dissatisfied, they turn them out and replace them with a new set of representatives.

From time to time, people from other part of the world may ask permission to live in the community. If they want to settle permanently, then they can become citizens, which means joining themselves to the contract along with those already included. If they are just visiting, then they must agree to abide by the laws the community has established for as long as they stay.

All this sounds lovely. Clear, simple, persuasive. But a growing number of critics have started to point out that this lovely picture doesn't actually correspond at all to what goes on in the real world. The most powerful critique I know is the one advanced by a young West Indian philosopher named Charles Mills who currently teaches at the University of Illinois in Chicago. Mills' criticism of Social Contract theory takes the form of a competing story, which he calls the Racial Contract This Racial Contract, he says, comes a great deal closer to describing the way the world really works. According to Mills, the theory of the Social Contract is actually a bit of camouflage designed to conceal from view what has been going on in the world since the seventeenth century.

To put Mills' story in a nutshell, the theory of the Social Contract conveniently forgets to mention the people of color—slaves, colonials, original inhabitants—over whom the participants in the Social Contract exercise forcible control. The Founding Fathers made a contract with one another, but it was not merely a contract about how they would behave toward one another. It was also an agreement that they would own slaves, who were not permitted to participate in this "contract" at all. It was also an agreement that they would together drive the Native Americans out of the land where they had been living, land that the Founding Fathers had decided would be theirs. Mills writes: "The Racial Contract is obviously not a contract to which the nonwhite subset of humans can be a genuinely consenting party (though, depending on the circumstances, it may sometimes be politic to pretend that this is the case); rather it is a contract *between* those categorized as white *over* the nonwhites, who are thus the objects rather than the subjects of the agreement."

Sometimes this Racial Contract is open, aboveboard, and completely explicit. The Constitution of the United States, for example, states for all to see that a slave does not count for as much as a free man, but instead counts for 3/5 of a free man or woman. In South Africa, under the apartheid regime that has finally been overthrown, nonwhites were officially denied the vote, citizenship, the right to own property, and even the right to remain within the limits of the white cities after sundown. In this century, throughout the world, one could see signs posted that read "No natives or dogs allowed."

At other times, the Racial Contract has been invisible to the white majority [although never to people of color, who knew quite well what was going on in the world.] Right now, our own Supreme Court hands down decisions outlawing affirmative action on the grounds that differentiations according to race or color have no place in American society, as though it was not obvious to anyone with eyes to see that America is elaborately segregated and sorted by skin color. Mills insists that it "would be a fundamental error to see racism as *anomalous,* a mysterious *deviation* from Enlightenment European humanism. Rather, "he says, "it needs to be realized that *European* [and American—RPW] *humanism usually meant that only Europeans were human."*

Those of us who are white find it hard to imagine how the world looks to someone who is Black, Brown, Red, or Yellow. [I use these terms as a shorthand for referring to the various categories into which people are currently classified, but of course there is something a little bit weird about describing people as Black, Brown, White, Red, or Yellow. Only the stick figures in children's crayon drawings are really these colors. But that is one more example of what Mills is talking about.] It is hard for all of us to become self-aware of the ways in which the racial definition of the world by European/American whites has shaped our thinking. Perhaps I can begin to help you to see it by talking about something we all share—movies.

How many of you have seen one of those marvelous old voyage-to-darkest-Africa movies complete with wild animals, impenetrable jungles, and stiff-upper-lip British types maintaining their upper class calm in the midst of savage darkness? My all-time favorite is *King Solomon's Mines* with Stewart Granger and Deborah Kerr. [I actually saw the movie when it first came out, but I am hoping some of you have seen it on late-night cable somewhere. A much more sophisticated, upscale version which came out only a few years ago, is the modern re-make of the old Tarzan movies, called *Greystoke*.]

All those movies have the same plot, basically. A safe, secure, middle-class man or woman starts out in safe, secure, thoroughly manageable England[for some reason it is always England], and launches on a long, difficult, dangerous trip to the heart of darkest Africa. The first part of the trip, by boat or plane, is easy, getting as far as a city on the East Coast of Africa. Then the adventurer hooks up with a white Big Game Hunter or guide, who is an old Africa hand and speaks some Swahili. He rounds up some bearers, who then set off, singing their native songs, carrying all manner of junk into the bush. The adventurer, despite looking very healthy, carries nothing, except maybe a rifle. The farther into the jungle they go, the harder the going gets, with bearers deserting for unnamed superstitious reasons, wild animals turning up to threaten the party, and menacing natives surfacing in fearsome headdresses and war paint. Eventually, after many trials and tribulations, during which they become thoroughly exhausted and almost die, they reach their destination, which is either a fabulous treasure or else the remains of the adventurer's husband or brother. Then the whole party turns around and makes its way back to civilization. The closer they get to the coastal city from which they began, the easier the going gets, until finally, everyone is back in England, safe and secure, and the movie ends.

Now when you stop and think about it, there is something very odd about this scenario. East Africa is no more or less hospitable to the people who live there than London is to the people who live *there*. To be sure, if you grew up in East Africa, you would find London traffic hard to get used to, and London streets utterly confusing. But East Africa wouldn't be confusing, dark, ominous, or impenetrable to you. It would be your *home*. You would be able to move about in it with the same ease with which a native Londoner makes her way through the streets of London. Everyone in the world is born and brought up somewhere, and to each of us, that place is home—familiar, manageable, and unmysterious. The movie, by presenting London as safe and secure and East Africa as mysterious, reinforces the assumptions on which the Racial Contract is founded. The movie is telling you that Londoners are civilized, while the Masai are savages. It is telling you that the very physical space of London is safe, familiar, and within the Social Contract, while the physical space of East Africa is wild, savage, and outside the contract.

If you are White, all of this may come as a total shock. Indeed, you may think it must be an exaggeration, an emphasizing of something that was important a hundred years ago, but surely doesn't make that much difference any more. If you are Black or Brown or Yellow or Red, none of this will come as any surprise at all. The only surprise may be that someone bothers to put it in a college textbook, as though it was news. That divide, separating those of us who are White from everyone else in the world, is part of what Charles Mills [who is Black] is talking about.

The following excerpt, taken from a long paper called "The Racial Contract," soon to be a book, will give you some idea of Mills' argument. Perhaps it will also get a good argument going in your class!

> The Racial Contract manifests itself [politically] in white resistance to anything more than the *formal* extension of the terms of the social contract [to nonwhites] (and often to that also.) Whereas before it was denied that nonwhites *were* equal persons, it is now pretended that nonwhites *are* equal abstract persons who can be fully included in the polity merely by extending the scope of the moral operator, without any fundamental change in the arrangements that have resulted *from* the previous system of explicit *de jure* racial privilege. Sometimes the new forms taken by the Racial Contract will be transparently exploitative, for example the "Jim Crow" contract, where the claim of "separate but equal" was patently ludicrous. But others —the job discrimination contract, the restrictive convenant—will be harder to prove. Nonwhites will then find that race is, paradoxically, both everywhere and nowhere, structuring their lives, but not formally recognized in political/moral theory. But in a racially-structured polity, the only people who can find it psychologically possible to deny the centrality of race are those who are racially-privileged, for whom race is invisible precisely because the world is structured around them, whiteness is the ground against which the figures of other races appear. The fish does not see the water, and whites do not see the racial nature of a white polity because it is natural to them, the element in which they move.
>
> The Racial Contract shows that we need another alternative way of theorizing the state: the racial, or white-supremacist state, whose function *inter alia* will be to safeguard the polity as a white or white-dominated polity. The liberal-democratic state of classic contractarianism will use force only to protect its citizens, thereby abiding by the terms of the social contract, who delegated the moralized force to it so that it could guarantee the safety not to be found in the state of nature. By contrast, the state established by the Racial Contract will by definition *not* be neutral, since its purpose will be to bring about the conformity to the terms of the Racial Contract of the sub-person population, who will obviously have no reason to accept these terms voluntarily, since the contract is an exploitation contract.
>
> Now by its relative silence on the question of race, conventional moral theory would lead the unwary student with no experience of the world—the visiting anthropologist from Arcturus, say—to think that deviations from the ideal have been contingent, random, theoretically

opaque or not worth the trouble to theorize. This suggests that all people have generally tried to live up to the norm, but, given inevitable human frailty, have sometimes fallen short. But this is, in fact, simply false. Racism and racially-structured discrimination have not been *deviations* from the norm; they have *been* the norm, not merely in the statistical sense of *de facto* distribution patterns, but in the formal codified sense of being written down and proclaimed *as such*.

The Racial Contract thus generates its own peculiar moral and empirical epistemology. In the standard accounts of the moral epistemology of contractarianism, it is natural law which provides us with a moral compass, [as] in the traditional version of Locke—the light of reason implanted in us by God so we can discern objective right or wrong. But the requirements of "veridical" cognition, factual and moral, in a racial polity are in a sense more demanding, in that officially-sanctioned reality is divergent from actual reality. In the first phase of the Racial Contract, the racial restructuring is *acknowledged and endorsed,* so that whites will not be able to permit themselves to see nonwhites as fully human; in the second phase of the Racial Contract, the racial structuring is *denied,* so that whites will not be able to permit themselves to see the systematic advantaging and disadvantaging of individuals by racial membership. *Thus in both phases the Racial Contract prescribes for its signatories an epistemology of nescience, a particular pattern of global and localized cognitive dysfunctions (which are psychologically functional) producing the ironic outcome that whites will in general be unable to understand the world they themselves have made.*

Nonwhites have always (at least in first encounters) been bemused or astonished by the *invisibility* of the Racial Contract to whites, the fact that whites have routinely talked in universalist terms even when it has been quite clear that the scope has been limited to themselves. Correspondingly, nonwhites, with no vested material or psychic interest in the Racial Contract—objects rather subjects of it, viewing it from outside rather than inside, sub-persons rather than persons—will be able to see its terms quite clearly. Thus, the hypocrisy of the racial polity will be most transparent to its victims.

What does it require for a sub-person to assert himself or herself politically? It means, to begin with, "challenging the white ontology that has deemed one a body impolitic," an entity not equipped to enter this arena in the first place. So in a sense one has to fight an internal battle before even advancing on to the ground of external combat. One has to overcome the internalization of sub-personhood prescribed by the Racial Contract, and recognize one's own humanity, resisting the official category of despised aboriginal, natural slave, colonial ward. One has to learn the basic self-respect that can casually be assumed by Kantian persons, those privileged by the Racial

Contract, but which is denied to sub-persons. Particularly for blacks, ex-slaves, the importance of developing self-respect and demanding respect from whites will be crucial. *"Negroes want to be treated like men:"* writes James Baldwin in the 1950's. "A perfectly straightforward statement, containing only seven words. People who have mastered Kant, Hegel, Shakespeare, Marx, Freud, and the Bible find this statement utterly impenetrable."

The Main Points in Chapter Three

1. John Stuart Mill devoted his life to applying the principle of utilitarianism to social questions. In the course of his writings, he revised the principle in three ways:

    a. He distinguished lower and higher pleasures.
    b. He recognized the role of habit or custom in economic life.
    c. He denied the right of the state to interfere in the private lives of men and women.

2. The utilitarians defended the free market or laissez-faire principle that consumers and producers should be free to make bargains in the marketplace without government interference.

3. Socialists like Karl Marx criticized capitalism for exploiting the working class, for corrupting the work process so that it became a source of pain and suffering rather than fulfillment, and for driving the economy into ever-greater business crises. Marx claimed that a socialist revolution would put an end to capitalism by placing ownership and control of the society's means of production in the hands of the working class.

4. The pluralist theory of American democracy takes account of the interest group political activity that goes on between elections. It claims that through such political activity, the complexity and intensity of the interests of citizens are given expression.

5. Classical Social Contract theory and its modern variants completely ignore the white domination and exploitation of nonwhite peoples, which has been a central fact of world history for the past four centuries. An alternative model of the state, called by Charles Mills the Racial Contract, seeks to capture and understand that fact.

CONTEMPORARY APPLICATION

Affirmative Action

Almost a century ago, W. E. B. Du Bois wrote, "The problem of the Twentieth Century is the problem of the color line." That prophetic statement, uttered more in sadness than in bitterness, has proved all too true. The century that now draws to a close has been as twisted and tortured by racial oppression and division as the century that preceded it. With a new millennium about to dawn, America remains divided by race. I have visited South Africa a number of times over the past ten years. At first, what impressed and troubled me most was the legal oppression of people of color, the laws forbidding Africans even to sleep in the big white cities unless they were house servants [and even then, required by law to live in little huts not physically connected to the house in which the white people live!] But after I had traveled back and forth a few times, it began to dawn on me that America is as racially divided and segregated as South Africa. There is really no more mingling of the races there than here—less, indeed, in some respects.

Over many years, the United States Government has taken a number of steps to remove some of the legal obstacles placed in the way of African-Americans. People of color were guaranteed the right to vote—a right granted them shortly after the end of the Civil War and then forcibly taken away again in little more than a decade. The Armed Forces were integrated by a presidential Executive Order, and the Government's own rules segregating federally funded housing were rescinded. Eventually, in an historic decision of the Supreme Court emerging from decades of legal struggle by Black lawyers and plaintiffs, segregated schools were declared unconstitutional.

But despite these victories, for which many men and women gave their lives, deep inequities in employment, housing, and education continued to distort American society. To correct some of these inequities, the Government, some thirty years ago, began to require colleges, universities, corporations, and public agencies to take positive steps to correct the imbalance in the opportunities accorded people of color. Because these steps went beyond merely the removal of legal barriers, requiring employers and others to be pro-active in the redressing of racial imbalances, they came to be called "Affirmative Action." The idea behind the phrase was that those in a position to open doors to people of color must act affirmatively by offering opportunities, not merely negatively by removing barriers.

From the outset, there has been enormous opposition to Affirmative Action. Those of you only beginning to become aware of the public world must not make the mistake of supposing that Affirmative Action was ever universally accepted or endorsed. But for several decades, the weight of the Federal Government was put behind a variety of affirmative efforts to rectify racial imbalances and inequities. And to a considerable extent, the programs had at least some success. Countless African-Americans, Latinos, and Asian-Americans have secured educations and jobs that could only have been opened to them by the sorts of governmental programs labeled as "Affirmative Action."

In recent years, however, opposition to Affirmative Action has been growing stronger. With the shift of both the judiciary and the Federal Government toward the more conservative end of the political spectrum, a number of Affirmative Action programs have either been cut back or terminated. In the four selections included here, we can hear the debate as it is now being conducted all across this country. Speaking for Affirmative Action is a well-known Professor of Literature, Stanley Fish. James Q. Wilson, an expert on urban sociology, takes what we can call a modified negative position, arguing that under some circumstances there are good reasons for limited Affirmative Action. The strongly negative position is presented first by Thomas Sowell, a conservative economist, and then by Linda Chavez, Director of the U. S. Commission on Civil Rights during the Reagan administration.

ఆ ఆ ఆ ఆ ఆ ఆ ఆ ఆ ఆ ఆ ఆ ఆ ఆ

REVERSE RACISM OR HOW THE POT GOT TO CALL THE KETTLE BLACK*
Stanley Fish

In America "whites once set themselves apart from blacks and claimed privileges for themselves while denying them to others," the author writes.

"Now, on the basis of race, blacks are claiming special status and reserving for themselves privileges they deny to others. Isn't one as bad as the other? The answer is no."

*From "Reverse Racism or How the Pot Got to Call the Kettle Black" by Stanley Fish. *Atlantic Monthly*, November 1993, Vol. 272, No. 5, pp. 128–136. Reprinted with permission from Stanley Fish, Professor of English and Law, and Executive Director of the Duke University Press.

I take my text from George Bush, who, in an address to the United Nations on September 23, 1991, said this of the UN resolution equating Zionism with racism: "Zionism . . . is the idea that led to the creation of a home for the Jewish people. . . . And to equate Zionism with the intolerable sin of racism is to twist history and forget the terrible plight of Jews in World War II and indeed throughout history." What happened in the Second World War was that six million Jews were exterminated by people who regarded them as racially inferior and a danger to Aryan purity. What happened after the Second World War was that the survivors of that Holocaust established a Jewish state—that is, a state centered on Jewish history, Jewish values, and Jewish traditions: in short, a Jewocentric state. What President Bush objected to was the logical sleight of hand by which these two actions were declared equivalent because they were both expressions of racial exclusiveness. Ignored, as Bush said, was the *historical* difference between them—the difference between a program of genocide and the determination of those who escaped it to establish a community in which they would be the makers, not the victims, of the laws.

Only if racism is thought of as something that occurs principally in the mind, a falling-away from proper notions of universal equality, can the desire of a victimized and terrorized people to band together be declared morally identical to the actions of their would-be executioners. Only when the actions of the two groups are detached from the historical conditions of their emergence and given a purely abstract description can they be made interchangeable. Bush was saying to the United Nations, "Look, the Nazis' conviction of racial superiority generated a policy of systematic genocide; the Jews' experience of centuries of persecution in almost every country on earth generated a desire for a homeland of their own. If you manage somehow to convince yourself that these are the same, it is you, not the Zionists, who are morally confused, and the reason you are morally confused is that you have forgotten history."

A Key Distinction

What I want to say, following Bush's reasoning, is that a similar forgetting of history has in recent years allowed some people to argue, and argue persuasively, that affirmative action is reverse racism. The very phrase "reverse racism" contains the argument in exactly the form to which Bush objected: In this country whites once set themselves apart from blacks and claimed privileges for themselves while denying them to others. Now, on the basis of race, blacks are claiming special status and reserving for themselves

privileges they deny to others. Isn't one as bad as the other? The answer is no. One can see why by imagining that it is not 1993 but 1955, and that we are in a town in the South with two more or less distinct communities, one white and one black. No doubt each community would have a ready store of dismissive epithets, ridiculing stories, self-serving folk myths, and expressions of plain hatred, all directed at the other community, and all based in racial hostility. Yet to regard their respective racisms—if that is the word—as equivalent would be bizarre, for the hostility of one group stems not from any wrong done to it but from its wish to protect its ability to deprive citizens of their voting rights, to limit access to educational institutions, to prevent entry into the economy except at the lowest and most menial levels, and to force members of the stigmatized group to ride in the back of the bus. The hostility of the other group is the result of these actions, and whereas hostility and racial anger are unhappy facts wherever they are found, a distinction must surely be made between the ideological hostility of the oppressors and the experience-based hostility of those who have been oppressed.

Not to make that distinction is, adapting George Bush's words, to twist history and forget the terrible plight of African-Americans in the more than 200 years of this country's existence. Moreover, to equate the efforts to remedy that plight with the actions that produced it is to twist history even further. Those efforts, designed to redress the imbalances caused by long-standing discrimination, are called affirmative action; to argue that affirmative action, which gives preferential treatment to disadvantaged minorities as part of a plan to achieve social equality, is no different from the policies that created the disadvantages in the first place is a travesty of reasoning. "Reverse racism" is a cogent description of affirmative action only if one considers the cancer of racism to be morally and medically indistinguishable from the therapy we apply to it. A cancer is an invasion of the body's equilibrium, and so is chemotherapy; but we do not decline to fight the disease because the medicine we employ is also disruptive of normal functioning. Strong illness, strong remedy: the formula is as appropriate to the health of the body politic as it is to that of the body proper.

At this point someone will always say, "But two wrongs don't make a right; if it was wrong to treat blacks unfairly, it is wrong to give blacks preference and thereby treat whites unfairly." This objection is just another version of the forgetting and rewriting of history. The work is done by the adverb "unfairly," which suggests two more or less equal parties, one of whom has been unjustly penalized by an incompetent umpire. But blacks have not simply been treated unfairly; they have been subjected first to decades of slavery, and then to decades of second-class citizenship, widespread legalized discrimination, economic persecution, educational deprivation, and cultural stigmatization. They have been bought, sold, killed, beaten, raped, excluded, exploited, shamed, and scorned for a very long time. The word "unfair" is hardly an adequate description of their experience, and the belated gift of "fairness" in the form of a resolution no longer to discriminate against them legally is hardly an adequate remedy for the deep disadvantages that the prior discrimination has produced. When the deck is stacked against you in more ways than you can even count, it is small consolation to hear that you are now free to enter the game and take your chances.

A Tilted Field

The same insincerity and hollowness of promise infect another formula that is popular with the anti-affirmative-action crowd: the formula of the level playing field. Here the argument usually takes the form of saying "It is undemocratic to give one class of citizens advantages at the expense of other citizens; the truly democratic way is to have a level playing field to which everyone has access and where everyone has a fair and equal chance to succeed on the basis of his or her merit." Fine words—but they conceal the facts of the situation as it has been given to us by history: the playing field is already tilted in favor of those by whom and for whom it was constructed in the first place. If mastery of the requirements for entry depends upon immersion in the cultural experiences of the mainstream majority, if the skills that make for success are nurtured by institutions and cultural practices from which the disadvantaged minority has been systematically excluded, if the language and ways of comporting oneself that identify a player as "one of us" are alien to the lives minorities are forced to live, then words like "fair" and "equal" are cruel jokes, for what they promote and celebrate is an institutionalized unfairness and a perpetuated inequality. The playing field is already tilted, and the resistance to altering it by the mechanisms of affirmative action is in fact a determination to make sure that the present imbalances persist as long as possible.

One way of tilting the field is the Scholastic Aptitude Test. This test figures prominently in Dinesh D'Souza's book *Illiberal Education* (1991), in which one finds many examples of white or Asian students denied admission to colleges and universities even though their SAT scores were higher than the scores of some others—often African-Americans—who were admitted to the same institution. This, D'Souza says, is evidence that as a result of affirmative-action policies colleges and universities tend "to depreciate the importance of merit criteria in admissions." D'Souza's assumption—and it is one that many would share—is that the test does in fact measure *merit*, with merit understood as a quality objectively determined in the same way that body temperature can be objectively determined.

In fact, however, the test is nothing of the kind. Statistical studies have suggested that test scores reflect income and socioeconomic status. It has been demonstrated again and again that scores vary in relation to cultural background; the test's questions assume a certain uniformity in educational experience and lifestyle and penalize those who, for whatever reason, have had a different experience and lived different kinds of lives. In short, what is being measured by the SAT is not absolutes like native ability and merit but accidents like birth, social position, access to libraries, and the opportunity to take vacations or to take SAT prep courses.

Furthermore, as David Owen notes in *None of the Above: Behind the Myth of Scholastic Aptitude* (1985), the "correlation between SAT scores and college grades . . . is lower than the correlation between weight and height; in other words you would have a better chance of predicting a person's height by looking at his weight than you would of predicting his freshman grades by looking only at his SAT scores." Everywhere you look in the SAT story, the claims of fairness, objectivity, and neutrality fall away, to be replaced by suspicions of specialized measures and unfair advantages.

Against this background a point that in isolation might have a questionable force takes on a special and even explanatory resonance: the principal deviser of the test was an out-and-out racist. In 1923 Carl Campbell Brigham published a book called *A Study of American Intelligence,* in which, as Owen notes, he declared, among other things, that we faced in America "a possibility of racial admixture . . . infinitely worse than that faced by any European country today, for we are incorporating the Negro into our racial stock, while all of Europe is comparatively free of this taint." Brigham had earlier analyzed the Army Mental Tests using classifications drawn from another racist text, Madison Grant's *The Passing of the Great Race,* which divided American society into four distinct racial strains, with Nordic, blue-eyed, blond people at the pinnacle and the American Negro at the bottom. Nevertheless, in 1925 Brigham became a director of testing for the College Board, and developed the SAT. So here is the great SAT test, devised by a racist in order to confirm racist assumptions, measuring not native ability but cultural advantage, an uncertain indicator of performance, an indicator of very little except what money and social privilege can buy. And it is in the name of this mechanism that we are asked to reject affirmative action and reaffirm "the importance of merit criteria in admissions."

FOR THE TAKING

And always, the damp blonde curls
on her temples
and bountifully down to her shoulder blades,
the rich loose curls all summer mixed with sand
and sweat,
and the rare, voluptuous double
curve of her nether lip—most children lose
that ripeness before
they can talk—and the solemn forehead,
which betokens thought and, alas
for her, o-
bedience, and the pure, unmuddied line
of the jaw, and the peeling brown shoulders—
she was always
a child of the sun . . . This
was his sweet piece of luck, his
find,
his renewable turn-on,
and my brown-and-golden sister at eight-
and-a-half
took to hating her body and cried
in her bath, and this was years,
my bad uncle did it
for years, in the back of the car,
in the basement where he kept his guns,
and we
who could have saved her, who knew

what it was in the best of times
to cross
the bridge of shame, from the body un-
encumbered to the body on the
block,
we would be somewhere mowing the lawn
or basting the spareribs right
outside, and—how
many times have you heard this?—we
were deaf and blind
and have
ever since required of her that she
take care of us, and she has,
and here's
the worst, she does it for love.

—Linda Gregerson

The Reality of Discrimination

Nevertheless, there is at least one more card to play against affirmative action, and it is a strong one. Granted that the playing field is not level and that access to it is reserved for an already advantaged elite, the disadvantages suffered by others are less racial—at least in 1993—than socioeconomic. Therefore shouldn't, as D'Souza urges, "universities . . . retain their policies of preferential treatment, but alter their criteria of application from race to socioeconomic disadvantage," and thus avoid the unfairness of current policies that reward middle-class or affluent black at the expense of poor whites? One answer to this question is given by D'Souza himself when he acknowledges that the overlap between minority groups and the poor is very large—a point underscored by the former Secretary of Education Lamar Alexander, who said, in response to a question about funds targeted for black students, "Ninety-eight percent of race-specific scholarships do not involve constitutional problems." He meant, I take it, that 98 percent of race-specific scholarships were also scholarships to the economically disadvantaged.

Still, the other two percent—nonpoor, middle-class, economically favored blacks—are receiving special attention on the basis of disadvantages they do not experience. What about them? The force of the question depends on the assumption that in this day and age race could not possibly be a serious disadvantage to those who are otherwise well positioned in the society. But the lie was given dramatically to this assumption in a 1991 broadcast of the ABC program *Prime-Time Live.* In a stunning fifteen-minute segment reporters and a camera crew followed two young men of equal education, cultural sophistication, level of apparent affluence, and so forth around St. Louis, a city where neither was known. The two differed in only a single respect: one was white, the other black. But that small difference turned out to mean everything. In a series of encounters with shoe salesmen, record-store employees, rental agents, landlords, employment agencies, taxicab drivers, and ordinary citizens, the black member of the pair was either ignored or given a special and suspicious attention. He was asked to pay more for the same goods or come up with a larger down payment for the same car, was turned away as a prospective tenant, was rejected as a prospective taxicab fare, was treated with contempt and irritation by clerks and bureaucrats, and in every way possible was made to feel inferior and unwanted.

The inescapable conclusion was that alike though they may have been in almost all respects, one of these young men, because he was black, would lead a significantly lesser life than his white counterpart: he would be housed less well and at greater expense; he would pay more for services and products when and if he was given the opportunity to buy them; he would have difficulty establishing credit; the first emotions he would inspire on the part of many people he met would be distrust and fear; his abilities would be discounted even before he had a chance to display them; and, above all, the treatment he received from minute to minute would chip away at his self-esteem and self-confidence with consequences that most of us could not even imagine. As the young man in question said at the conclusion of the broadcast, "You walk down the street with a suit and tie and it doesn't matter. Someone will make determinations about you, determinations that affect the quality of your life."

Of course, the same determinations are being made quite early on by kindergarten teachers, grade school principals, high school guidance counselors, and the like, with results that cut across socioeconomic lines and place young black men and women in the ranks of the disadvantaged no matter what the bank accounts of their parents happen to show. Racism is a cultural fact, and although its effects may to some extent be diminished by socioeconomic variables, those effects will still be sufficiently great to warrant the nation's attention and thus the continuation of affirmative-action policies. This is true even of the field thought to be dominated by blacks and often cited as evidence of the equal opportunities society now affords them. I refer, of course, to professional athletics. But national self-congratulation on this score might pause in the face of a few facts: A minuscule number of African-Americans ever receive a paycheck from a professional team. Even though nearly 1,600 daily newspapers report on the exploits of black athletes, they employ only seven full-time black sports columnists. Despite repeated pledges and resolutions, major-league teams have managed to put only a handful of blacks and Hispanics in executive positions.

Why Me?

When all is said and done, however, one objection to affirmative action is unanswerable on its own terms, and that is the objection of the individual who says, "Why me? Sure, discrimination has persisted for many years, and I acknowledge that the damage done has not been removed by changes in the law. But why me? I didn't own slaves; I didn't vote to keep people on the back of the bus; I didn't turn water hoses on civil-rights marchers. Why, then, should I be the one who doesn't get the job or who doesn't get the scholarship or who gets bumped back to the waiting list?"

I sympathize with this feeling, if only because in a small way I have had the experience that produces it. I was recently nominated for an administrative post at a large university. Early signs were encouraging, but after an interval I received official notice that I would not be included at the next level of consideration, and subsequently I was told unofficially that at some point a decision had been made to look only in the direction of women and minorities. Although I was disappointed, I did not conclude that the situation was "unfair," because the policy was obviously not directed at me—at no point in the proceedings did someone say, "Let's find a way to rule out Stanley Fish." Nor was it directed even at persons of my race and sex— the policy was not intended to disenfranchise white males. Rather, the policy was driven by other considerations, and it was only as a by-product of those considerations—not as the main goal—that white males like me were rejected. Given that the institution in question has a high percentage of minority students, a very low percentage of minority faculty, and an even lower percentage of minority administrators, it made perfect sense to focus on women and minority candidates, and within that sense, not as the result of prejudice, my whiteness and maleness became disqualifications.

I can hear the objection in advance: "What's the difference? Unfair is unfair: you didn't get the job; you didn't even get on the short list." The difference is not in the outcome but in the ways of thinking that led up to the outcome. It is the difference between an unfairness that befalls one as the unintended effect of a policy rationally conceived and an unfairness that is pursued as an end in itself. It is the difference between the awful unfairness of Nazi extermination camps and the unfairness to Palestinian Arabs that arose from, but was not the chief purpose of, the founding of a Jewish state.

The New Bigotry

The point is not a difficult one, but it is difficult to see when the unfairness scenarios are presented as simple contrasts between two decontextualized persons who emerge from nowhere to contend for a job or a place in a freshman class. Here is student A; he has a board score of 1,300. And here is student B; her board score is only 1,200, yet she is admitted and A is rejected. Is that fair? Given the minimal information provided, the answer is of course no. But if we expand our horizons and consider fairness in relation to the cultural and institutional histories that have brought the two students to this point, histories that weigh on them even if they are not the histories' authors, then both the question and the answer suddenly grow more complicated.

The sleight-of-hand logic that first abstracts events from history and then assesses them from behind a veil of willed ignorance gains some of its plausibility from another key word in the anti-affirmative-action lexicon. That word is "individual," as in "The American way is to focus on the rights of individuals rather than groups." Now, "individual" and "individualism" have been honorable words in the American political vocabulary, and they have often been well employed in the fight against various tyrannies. But like any other word or concept, individualism can be perverted to serve ends the opposite of those it originally served, and this is what has happened when in the name of individual rights, millions of individuals are enjoined from redressing historically documented wrongs. How is this managed? Largely in the same way that the invocation of fairness is used to legitimize an institutionalized inequality. First one says, in the most solemn of tones, that the protection of individual rights is the chief obligation of society. Then one defines individuals as souls sent into the world with equal entitlements as guaranteed either by their Creator or by the Constitution. Then one pretends that nothing has happened to them since they stepped onto the world's stage. And then one says of these carefully denatured souls that they will all be treated in the same way, irrespective of any of the differences that history has produced. Bizarre as it may seem, individualism in this argument turns out to mean that everyone is or should be the *same*. This dismissal of individual difference in the name of the individual would be funny were its consequences not so serious: it is the mechanism by which imbalances and inequities suffered by millions of people through no fault of their own can be sanitized and even celebrated as the natural workings of unfettered democracy.

"Individualism," "fairness," "merit"—these three words are continually misappropriated by bigots who have learned that they need not put on a white hood or bar access to the ballot box in order to secure their ends. Rather, they need only clothe themselves in a vocabulary plucked from its historical context and made into the justification for attitudes and policies they would not acknowledge if frankly named.

ෂ ෂ ෂ ෂ ෂ ෂ ෂ ෂ ෂ ෂ ෂ ෂ ෂ

SINS OF ADMISSION*
James Q. Wilson

Good Affirmative Action and Bad

Affirmative action—by which I mean selecting persons based on their group membership—is not one program but many and has consequences that range from acceptable to intolerable. We understand these distinctions intuitively. When a television commercial displays white and black actors or when a political party endorses candidates from a variety of ethnic backgrounds, no one complains—even though this is, literally, affirmative action. But should someone suggest that the musicians in a major symphony orchestra or the players in the National Basketball Association be chosen to create a specific racial balance, most people would be outraged.

The difference, of course, has to do with the purposes of the organizations. Television commercials and party candidates are chosen chiefly to attract support from customers and voters. Everyone expects organizations trying to sell something to cater to the preferences of those who might buy. But top-ranked musicians and athletes are selected exclusively on the basis of merit.

The debate over affirmative action in contracts, university admissions and public employment is in large measure a debate over what set of standards ought to govern achievement in these enterprises. The strongest defenders of affirmative action argue that these organizations have a representative as well as a technical function, while the toughest critics claim that the latter greatly outweighs the former.

Consider undergraduate admissions. A plausible proposal might run as follows: given the growing importance of college education in the life of the nation and the uncertainty attached to conventional measures of merit, one might defend the modest use of racial preferences as a way of increasing participation of underrepresented groups in educated society without doing serious harm to the quality of the university. One might, by the same token, take into account other nonintellectual attributes like athletic or musical ability.

But as one moves up through the university experience—to medical and law schools and onto a faculty—academic ability becomes the dominant criterion. Excellence at teaching and research are overwhelmingly important tests for faculty recruitment; no one proposes that law or medical schools admit athletes or musicians. Furthermore, three or four years of college training ought to have given students with natural abilities but subpar elementary and secondary educations a chance to catch up.

This guideline—race and ethnicity as a factor for 18 year olds but not after—might provide a reasonable basis on which to "mend, not end" affirmative action. Unfortunately, preference programs, as administered today, make no such distinctions—affirmative action is at least as pervasive in admissions to law and medical schools as in college, if not more so.

UCLA's undergraduate admissions are based on two sets of criteria: academic (grades, test scores) and supplemental ("socio-economic or educational disadvantage"). For each, students are ranked from one (the highest) to six (the lowest). The admissions office admits between 40 and 60 percent of the student body strictly on academic grounds. The next group consists of people whose combined academic and supplemental ranking gives them a high total score. In this combined mark, being disadvantaged may count for more than being smart; a student can have an academic ranking as low as five and still get in if his or her disadvantage rating is at

*From "Sins of Admission" by James Q. Wilson. *The New Republic*, July 8, 1996, Vol. 215, No. 2, Issue 4, pp. 12–16. Reprinted with permission from *The New Republic*.

the top. The final group—the "read" group, meaning their files are closely read—are those whose rankings, academic and supplemental, are low.

In 1994, UCLA admitted 6,801 students as part of its academic-only criteria. Of these seventy-seven, or about 1 percent, were African Americans. The African American students admitted in the first, academic, group had an average SAT score nearly 300 points higher than blacks admitted in the latter two groups, and their high-school grades were half a grade higher. Among those not chosen on purely academic grounds, 19 percent were African Americans, and another 51 percent were Latino. These second two categories have effectively become ethnicity driven.

The evidence is equally clear for the fall of 1995. Eighty-one percent of Asians and Caucasians admitted had academic rankings of one or two, but only 10 percent of the Asians and 1 percent of the Caucasians were in the top two supplemental ranks. For Mexican-American and African American applicants, less than 13 percent of those admitted had academic ranks of one or two, but more than 97 percent were in the top two supplemental ranks.

Once admitted, disparities remain. Among white and Asian American students, at least 80 percent graduate within five years. Among African American students, less than half do so. In the UCLA class admitted in 1990, Caucasians had an average grade of just over a "B" while African Americans averaged just above a "C."

A common defense of these disparities is that athletic ability or alumni connections already count in admissions and, therefore, race should, too. But this misses the point. Race, according to the Supreme Court, is a suspect classification subject to strict scrutiny. Athletic prowess (or musical ability, or rich parents) are not suspect classifications and do not require strict judicial scrutiny. If these traits were treated legally the same as race, then I could sue the Boston Red Sox for denying me my lifelong ambition of playing second base for them simply because I can't hit, an untalented violinist could sue the New York Philharmonic to get a seat in the string section, and rich parents could demand scholarships for their children. One cannot easily correct this problem by abandoning the judicial protection given race; to do that would permit colleges and employers to discriminate against blacks. To the extent race deserves special constitutional protection, it cannot be equated with other principles of classification.

The famous opinion of Justice Lewis Powell in the *Bakke* case, decided in 1978, is still supposedly the basis for racial preference in American law: race, despite its special status, can be a "plus factor" in admissions so long as it is not the decisive one. Yet, at the University of California today, strictly academic admissions would admit a 1 percent black student body (down from 7 percent currently), while the supplemental categories admit students of whom only a tiny fraction are white or Asian. The contrast between the two systems is not a "plus" factor. It is decisive.

The evidence from medical school is the same. Ellen and Jerry Cook—she teaches at the University of California at San Diego (UCSD)—have compared graduates of UCSD who applied to that university's medical school between 1987 and 1993. The *only* students admitted with MCAT scores below the sixtieth percentile or with college grades below 3.0 were from affirmative action groups. Furthermore, a separate study showed that students from poorer families received no advantage per se; the only criteria for preference was race and ethnicity. The result was that UCSD admitted students based on two different distributions of abilities—one curve consisted of almost all the affirmative action students, another (barely overlapping) curve consisted mostly of whites and Asians. This although both had access to the same undergraduate education.

Much the same pattern exists in law schools. If you have an LSAT score below the ninetieth percentile and college grades below 3.5, you are vastly more likely to be admitted into UCLA Law School if you are black or Hispanic than if you are white or Asian. One study, done unofficially by a student who cracked the law school's secrecy codes, suggests that the grades received by black students during their first year are significantly lower than those received by whites.

The costs of professional school racial preference are greater than those of undergraduate colleges in part because 18 year olds have a wider range of available opportunities. High-school students wanting to enter a good university have more choices than do those wanting to enter the considerably smaller number of good law or medical schools. By the same token, the costs to society of admitting less qualified students into these select institutions is greater.

In California, four Under-Represented Minority groups (URMs) are generically entitled to affirmative action: African Americans, Native Americans, Mexican-Americans and mainland Puerto Ricans. Let us suppose for a moment that African Americans belong there because of past discrimination and the legacy of slavery. But on what grounds are Mexican-Americans on the list and other Hispanics numerous in California—Guatemalans, El Salvadorans, Cubans —not? At one time Asians were the object of the bluntest possible discrimination in California— many could not own land or serve on a jury— and Japanese-Americans were exiled to inland camps during World War II. Yet Asians do not make the list and, indeed, lose space in universities owing to the preferences given to URMs. The Vietnamese came to this country poor after a war in which we were a major participant, but URM graduates applying for admission to California medical schools were 2.7 times as likely

to be accepted as Vietnamese students despite the fact that the grades of most of the rejected Vietnamese were higher than those of most of the accepted URMs.

One argument often cited in favor of university affirmative action is its support among faculty. And, indeed, last year the UCLA faculty legislative assembly did vote by a margin of six to one to criticize the State Regents for abandoning racial preferences. (Although when the assembly's vote was sent out on a mail ballot to all faculty members, support for its position fell from six to one to three to two, and to even lower margins at other UC campuses.) But even this does not prove faculty support for racial preference, since some faculty may have objected to the *way* the Regents made their decision, rather than to the principle of color-blindness itself. In 1995 the California Association of Scholars polled faculty opinion in the nine California public universities. Designed by the Roper Center for Public Opinion Research, the central question was this: Should the university "grant preferences to women and certain racial and ethnic groups in admissions, hiring and promotions?" Most faculty said no.

Just as affirmative action is more costly for professional schools than undergraduate colleges, it is more problematic at some colleges than others. At Harvard, with its pick of the country's top high-school students, white and black, the racial gap on college entrance scores was modest. But the scarcity of academically prepared blacks means that the best universities skim off the top. The result is that other universities—including the very good public universities in California—take a chance admitting students who may be unprepared to tackle college-level work, and may not graduate at all.

Affirmative action has lost its moorings. Colleges legitimately want a diverse student body, but their definition of diversity is limited to ethnicity, excludes ideology and favors some but not other ethnic groups. Law and medical schools want to produce more attorneys and physicians of certain ethnicities, but they can only do this by denying—not modifying, but denying—equal access to more talented applicants, thereby lowering the quality of the professionals they produce. This inevitably·has consequences for consumers of medicine and legal assistance.

As universities become more competitive overall while lowering the standards by which they admit certain students, they increasingly produce anger and frustration among those hardworking young people who have upheld demanding standards themselves and expect their universities to do the same. Even worse, the very professional schools that have long made a special claim to excellence have abandoned that claim—to the dismay of all those who once believed them.

James Q. Wilson, a professor at the University of California-Los Angeles, is author of The Moral Sense *(The Free Press).*

ఌఌఌఌఌఌఌఌఌఌఌఌఌఌ

THE "Q" WORD*
Thomas Sowell

Affirmative Action Produced Polarization and Violence in Some Countries, Including Civil War in Sri Lanka.

Now that affirmative action is coming under fire politically and may be outlawed in some states, or perhaps even nationally, look for lots of word games by its advocates as they try to confuse the issues.

The big word game is denial that affirmative action means group quotas. Historically, it began meaning something else—but so did such terms as Catholic, communist and magazine. What matters is not these excursions down memory lane but what it is that people are for or against today.

What people are opposed to are group quotas instead of decisions based on individual performance. But of course the word "quota" has set off its own round of evasive word games.

The clever alternative to quotas is "goals," a more flexible version of quotas. By shifting the issue to flexibility versus rigidity, advocates of affirmative action evade the fundamental question: whether applicants for jobs, colleges, or a thousand other things are to be judged according to their own individual qualifications or according to some numerical standard of group representation.

Old-fashioned name-calling is another word game often invoked in discussions of affirmative action. "Racist" has long been tried and true in this role, but its overuse has weakened its sting and sometimes produces more boredom than anything else.

A related charge against minority critics of affirmative action is to claim that they have themselves benefited from affirmative action and are narrow and selfish in wanting to deny those benefits to others like themselves. Since it is impossible to prove a negative, supposedly this kind of word game should always be successful.

But, for the sake of argument, let us assume that this charge is 100 percent correct in all cases. What follows? If I have benefited from a war, should my position on issues of peace and war be determined forever after by what bene-

---

*From "The 'Q' Word" by Dr. Thomas Sowell, *Forbes*, April 10, 1995, p. 61. Reprinted by permission of FORBES Magazine. © Forbes Inc., 1995.

fited me personally, rather than by what is best overall? This would be raising personal bias to the level of a principle.

One of the many unfortunate consequences of affirmative action has been that many minorities and females have no definitive way to know whether, or to what extent, they got where they are by their own efforts. Those of us old enough to have begun our careers before affirmative action began may be spared this particular burden, but, by and large, group quotas stigmatize even legitimate achievements.

Just recently a black youngster in a California high school who had received early admission to a prestigious college was told by a white classmate that this was due to racial preferences. The white classmate had been turned down—and had lower SATs than the black student. Just as "racism" has become a blanket excuse for individual failure available to minorities, so affirmative action has become a blanket excuse for individual failure available to white males.

The word "preferences" spawns a whole family of word games.

"There were once preferences for white males," we are told. So why such an objection now to preferences that offset that?

If it was wrong to have preferences for white males, then two wrongs do not make a right. And if it is all right to have preferences for various other groups now, why was it wrong to have had preferences for white males in the past?

In academia, the argument is that preferential admission for alumni children, football players and the like all preceded preferences for minority applicants to college. This might be a reasonable argument if the issue were whether minority students are benefiting too much in college.

The tragic fact, however, is that three-fourths of minority students are failing to graduate, often from colleges where they should never have been admitted in the first place. These include youngsters with test scores and other qualifications that would make them candidates for the dean's list in the average American college. They are simply going to the wrong schools.

Perhaps the most fraudulent of all the word games has been the claim that affirmative action is a "temporary" measure. Such claims have been made for affirmative action in countries around the world. Yet group preferences have not only persisted but spread over time to encompass more activities, more institutions and more groups.

By and Large, Group Quotas Stigmatize Even Legitimate Achievements

Even where explicit cut-off dates were written into the law, as in India and Pakistan, these laws were extended again and again, long past the original cut-off date. South Africa is the only country that has ended racial preferences—for whites, in this case—and that after more than a century.

That is not most people's idea of "temporary." Nor do Americans need to go to the brink of civil war before repealing a policy that has produced polarization and intergroup violence in other countries, including even civil war in Sri Lanka.

Dr. Thomas Sowell is an economist and a senior fellow at the Hoover Institution in Stanford, Calif.

ಜಿ ಜಿ ಜಿ ಜಿ ಜಿ ಜಿ ಜಿ ಜಿ ಜಿ ಜಿ ಜಿ ಜಿ ಜಿ

PORK BARREL QUOTAS*
Linda Chavez

When my oldest son graduated from high school a few years ago, he was inundated with college recruitment letters. Several offered him generous scholarships *without even seeing* his school transcripts or getting any idea of his financial need. His zip code alone should have told them he lived in an affluent suburban community. He was unlikely to have encountered any social or economic disadvantage. But the colleges' only interest was that he would make their Hispanic numbers look good. The irony is that he is just one-quarter Hispanic.

(We turned down all the offers.)

My family's experience as middle-class beneficiaries of affirmative action is not exceptional. Senate majority leader Bob Dole recently ordered a study by the Congressional Research Service of 168 federal affirmative action programs. The service found there were no fewer than 19 separate programs just to benefit minority bankers. Other programs included set-asides for minority contractors who run multimillion-dollar businesses. This is nothing more than pork barrel politics with a fancy name—affirmative action.

As affirmative action begins to unravel, after nearly 30 years of virtually unquestioned acceptance by the Washington elite, the rhetoric of those who want to save the programs has reached hysterical pitch.

"When the trains come, you'll be shoved right in there with me. And your political views won't protect you either," the Reverend Jesse Jackson warned me as we sat waiting to tape a TV show on affirmative action. At first, I thought it was the kind of barb I've grown used to getting from the civil rights establishment since the days when I was a Reagan Administration offi-

cial. Then I realized he was serious. He really believes the current national mood on affirmative action means an American Kristallnacht is near for minorities.

Jackson is not alone. Representative Charles Rangel (D–N.Y.) says, "When I compare this to what happened in Germany, I hope that you will see the similarities to what is happening to us." Representative Major Owens (D–N.Y.), referring to Republican critics of affirmative action, says: "[They] are practicing genocide with a smile; they're worse than Hitler." Pulitzer Prize-winning author Toni Morrison, commenting on the possible dismantling of affirmative action, says, ". . . the descent into a final solution is not a jump. It's one step and then another and then another."

This grotesque hyperbole will have less effect than it would have had even a few years ago. The civil rights establishment has lost the moral high ground in the debate over racial justice. America today is not the Deep South of 1963, when civil rights leaders were beaten, hosed down and sometimes killed for the right to sit at a lunchroom counter. And most Americans know it.

It's not surprising, given the passions aroused by the subject, that some politicians want to figure out a way to save affirmative action without incurring the political risk that defending it would cost them. In a series of meetings with civil rights leaders in mid-March, President Clinton was said to be looking for a "third way" between defending the status quo and abolishing all race- and sex-based preferences.

I have news for him. There is no "third way." Compromise on this issue is impossible. Quotas are a zero-sum game. Any effort to preserve them will leave their victims injured and mad.

Since there is no third way, there are only two alternatives: Get rid of quotas or preserve them pretty much as they are. Therefore, a terrific fight is shaping up. Defenders of affirmative action will throw up as many roadblocks as they can. They are not without resources.

*From "Pork Barrel Quotes" by Linda Chavez. *Forbes*, April 24, 1995, p. 112. Reprinted by permission of FORBES Magazine. © Forbes Inc., 1995.

Recently, California Assembly Speaker Willie Brown told me on CNN *& Co.* that he expects to defeat the California Civil Rights Initiative, which would bar all racial preferences in the state, if it makes it to the ballot next year. I was incredulous. I offered to fly to California and buy him a steak dinner if he did block the measure. On air, I asked if he was serious.

Brace Yourself for Extreme and Divisive Rhetoric as the Fight Over So-called Affirmative Action Heats Up.

"Wait until Levi Strauss and Bechtel weigh in," he said. "They're committed to diversity." He may be right about corporate support for the quota system. Many in the corporate world long ago made their Faustian bargain with racial preferences.

But they should reconsider. So long as we continue to count by race, ethnicity and gender and to distribute benefits and preferences accordingly, civil rights will be a hollow and corrupt substitute for equal opportunity.

Linda Chavez is president of the Center for Equal Opportunity and former director of the U.S. Commission on Civil Rights, under Ronald Reagan.

Questions for Discussion and Review

1. According to Mill, we should judge public policies on the basis of their tendency to produce the greatest happiness for the greatest number. Select one of the issues currently being debated in the United States—drug policy, abortion policy, the balanced budget—and try to analyze it in terms of the tendency of the competing proposals to promote the greatest happiness. Is it possible to analyze public policies in this way? What are some of the problems? Does Mill's way of thinking clarify the issues for you?

2. Mill claims that we, the public, are good judges of consumer goods, but poor judges of cultural and intellectual goods, such as books, music, and art. Do you agree? Is it, in your experience, easier for you to judge the value of a consumer good such as a car, a VCR, or a quart of milk? Or is it easier to judge the value of a novel, a movie, or a CD record? In this age of advertising, with millions of competing consumer goods, do we need government regulation to protect us? What about medicines and drugs? Are we, as consumers, good judges of their value? If we turn over the job of evaluating commodities to the state, how do we guarantee that the state will protect us?

3. In the United States today, barely half of the eligible voters bother to vote in a general Presidential election. In non-Presidential years, the turn out is even smaller. What would Rousseau or Locke say about this fact? Does it call into question the legitimacy of the officials who are elected? If I do not

bother to vote, am I morally bound to obey the laws passed by the representatives who get elected?

4. Underlying the justification of representative democracy is the assumption that individual voters sometimes get what they want and sometimes don't. But suppose some voters, for example Black or Latino voters, are permanent losers. They vote, but their candidates never get elected, because everyone votes along racial lines and they are in the minority. Are they still morally bound to obey the laws passed by the representatives who do get elected? If you think the answer is No, what changes in the system of elections might give all segments of a society a chance to be represented?

5. Charles Mills claims that there is a Racial Contract among White people to oppress and exploit non-White people. If your Philosophy class has both White and non-White students in it, have a discussion in which each student is asked to describe how he or she experiences American society. See whether Mill is right that the perceptions of White and non-White people are radically different. How do you think Rousseau and Locke would respond to Mills' thesis?

PLATO

Plato (427?–347 B.C.) is one of the immortal geniuses of philosophy. Born in Athens to a wealthy and politically influential aristocratic family, he was closely associated as a young man with Socrates, who died when Plato was in his late twenties. When the democracy was restored, Plato's family fell out of favor, and his hostility to demo-cratic government is reflected in a number of his works. At some time after Socrates' death, perhaps as much as fifteen years or more, Plato started to write dialogues in which moral, political, religious, cosmological, logical, and other subjects were explored. In the early Dialogues, Socrates is always the principal speaker, and there is some reason to suppose that Plato's picture of Socrates' personality and doctrines bears a close resemblance to the actual historical man who was his teacher. Later on, however, the Dialogues clearly come more and more to reflect Plato's own philosophical investigations, and in the works that he composed last, Socrates disappears altogether as a character.

Retreating from public life, Plato founded a school at his home in Athens, called the "Academy," and the word has since then meant a school or university. Many of the most gifted philosophers of the day worked or studied at the Academy, including the other great genius of ancient thought, Aristotle. Eventually, the Academy became an independent institution, and it continued in existence for almost 900 years before it was finally closed by the Roman emperor Justinian in A.D. 529.

Plato's greatest work was the Republic, *a dialogue on the nature of justice, but much of his work in later life was devoted to mathemat-ics and cosmology, and members of the Academy made significant contributions to formal logic and to such mathematical fields as solid geometry.*

Philosophy of Art

❧ Plato's Attack on the Poets

Here is a short parable: There was a singer with a clear, strong, beautiful voice, whose songs were so lovely that people would come from miles around to hear him sing. The singer was a thoughtful, compassionate man whose heart was troubled by the poverty and misery of the people for whom he sang. After much reflection, he concluded that the people should rise up and change their condition. And he realized that his songs, because of their loveliness, were a distraction to the people, making them forget for the moment the real causes of their misery. He decided to tell the people what he had discovered, but alas, they would only listen to him when he sang. So he wrote a song about the misery of the people and the dangerousness of lovely songs. But because he was a great singer, his song was a lovely song, and the people, listening to it, were soothed and distracted from their misery, and so did nothing.

Plato was just such a singer of philosophical songs, and nothing is more poignant or paradoxical than his attitude toward the great works of art which he himself created. You have several times met Socrates in these pages, always in his role as the principal character in Plato's Dialogues (his "philosophical songs"). But Plato, the artist himself, is not to be confused with the dramatic character who sometimes speaks for him in his Dialogues, any more than the real historical Socrates should be confused with that character. Socrates wrote nothing himself, as Plato's own portrait of him tells us; but Plato wrote a great deal, and so he was forced to ask himself, as every artist must, whether artistic creation is good or evil, whether a life spent in the forming of artworks is a life well-spent, what indeed the function of art is in human life and society, and whether there is a place for art in the good society.

Since Plato's Dialogues, at least as we encounter them today, are classified as philosophical works rather than as works of art, it might be worth saying a few words about what sets them off from all the other philosophical works which no one would dream of calling "artistic." A philosophical dialogue is easy enough to write, if all you care about is getting the arguments down on paper. Just put your own theories in the mouth of one character—call her Ms. Wise—and whatever objections you can think of in the mouth of a second character—"The Fool," perhaps—and then write the whole thing down as though it were a play. The result will not exactly be beautiful, but as long as it has two characters in it, you can call it a dialogue. A number of great and not-so-great philosophers have actually written some of their philosophy in roughly this way, including the seventeenth-century Dutch metaphysician Baruch Spinoza, who was no artist at all, and the eighteenth-century Irish cleric George Berkeley, who wasn't either.

But Plato's Dialogues are quite another thing altogether. Their artistic brilliance results from Plato's ability to do three things at the same time, and to do them all superbly. First, his Dialogues are not shadowboxing, or put-up jobs. Plato constructs real arguments, in which Socrates' opponents score points and make philosophical moves that are genuinely persuasive. Second, the characters in the Dialogues are not cardboard figures, two-dimensional pop-ups with name tags attached. They are fully realized human beings, with feelings, passions, characteristic ways of speaking. Some of them run on in great long speeches; others are mulish, grudging, giving nothing in an argument and resisting even the most obvious implications of their own statements. Some are dignified old men, full of years and self-confident in an awareness that they are nearing the end of life with their honor unsullied; others are eager, ambitious young men, out to score a quick knockout over Socrates and make their reputations. Most of the characters in the Dialogues were apparently modeled after real people, and the original readers presumably could judge how skillfully Plato had caught their characters in his portraits. But for those of us who read the Dialogues two millennia later, it matters only that they are completely successful artistic creations.

Finally, Plato accomplishes the most difficult creative feat of all—he makes the personalities and speech of his characters actually exemplify, and thereby provide evidence for, the philosophical theories he is trying to expound. His characters are not merely believable; they are just what they ought to be, given the philosophy they are expressing, if Plato's own theories are true. This fit between character and belief is designed by Plato as an expression of the central thesis of his philosophy: the doctrine that the metaphysical order of the universe is mirrored in the inner psychic order of the soul. Plato bases his philosophy upon a distinction between *appearance* and *reality,* a distinction that turns up over and over in many different guises throughout his works (indeed, we can quite accurately say that although the distinction *appears* in many different forms, it is *really* always the same distinction, and that is just one more example, Plato would say, of the distinction between appearance and reality). For example, a straight stick looks bent when half of it is put in water (because of the refraction of light). Sugar may seem good to a diabetic even though it would really make him sick. A tricky argument may look correct, but really be invalid. A devil may appear to be an angel of the Lord, but really be a messenger from Satan. It may seem smart to cheat on an exam, even though it is really dumb. Popular opinion may sound wise, but really be foolish.

In all these cases, and countless others besides, there is an image, a belief, an action, a feeling, which seems to be right, true, good, accurate, veridical, or healthy but is really wrong, false, evil, misleading, fallacious, or harmful. The ability to tell the difference between the two is always, according to Plato, a matter of some sort of knowledge, and the power or part of the soul whose job it is to make that distinction is *reason*. Reason tells us that the stick is really straight, even though it looks bent; reason tells the diabetic not to eat the apparently good sugar; reason finds the flaw in the valid-looking argument; and reason shows us when the easy way—cheating, or going along with popular opinion—is in the end the harmful, destructive way.

As these examples suggest, knowledge of reality, and the ability to distinguish it from misleading appearance, is more than just "book learning." You can study the principles of optics in the classroom, but you need some common sense and the power of observation to tell when to apply the formulas to a real stick in some real water. The diabetic patient can carefully write down his doctor's instructions not to eat candy, but he needs a quite different kind of knowledge and a much stronger power of reason to apply those instructions when temptation appears in the guise of a rich, tasty dessert. Socrates needed more than just a "philosophical" understanding of justice to resist the chance to escape from his punishment by the Athenians and instead remain, calm and resigned, to drink the hemlock.

According to Plato, a woman who has some true opinions but does not really understand what makes them true will *look* wise as long as she doesn't get into morally difficult or complicated situations, but she will not *really be* wise. We are liable to confuse her good habits and her true opinions with real knowledge until we see her come unstuck in a crunch. Then we will realize that we were deceived and that what we took for real wisdom was only its appearance. So too, a man who mouths current arguments without really having thought them through for himself will sound very knowledgeable until we press him with some hard questions. Then we will discover that his knowledge is only appearance. Worst of all, according to Plato, a person who has no systematic grasp of the true good for humanity will not be able to tell what is going to make her truly happy and so will do what looks pleasant but is ultimately harmful. She will allow herself to be flattered into betraying a trust, or beguiled away from the hard work that brings real satisfaction, or frightened by imagined evils into shameful or dishonorable deeds.

Plato weaves his philosophical theory about appearance and reality together with his psychological insights into human character to produce a series of persuasive and fundamentally true portraits in his Dialogues. (Needless to say, he deliberately intends the dramatic persuasiveness of his characters—their appearance—to reveal, rather than conceal, the truth about their souls—their reality.)

One example may make all this a bit clearer. In the Dialogue entitled *Gorgias,* there are three characters who argue with Socrates. The first is the title character, a traveling public speaker and teacher named Gorgias; the second is a young disciple named Polus; and the third is the hot-headed, brilliant Callicles. Now Plato sees Gorgias as one of those decent human beings who personally would not do anything shameful or wicked, but who does not really have rational knowledge of the right moral principles. In fact, although in his own life he is an upright person, the philosophy he expounds is totally false. Plato thinks that Gorgias is dangerous, because his pupils tend to do as he says, not as he does. Instead of imitating the decency and honorableness of

Gorgias' private life, his pupils listen to his relativistic moral arguments and act on them in the law courts and public life of Athens. Plato presents Gorgias as a man who is stuffily self-confident, easily trapped into logical contradictions, but personally horrified at the thought that anyone would take his philosophy as an excuse for dishonorable behavior. Plato lets him off rather easily in the Dialogue, because he respects Gorgias' personal decency as a human being, while nevertheless condemning the confusion of his thought. When Polus, the young disciple, enters the argument in Gorgias' place, the tone changes immediately. Polus is one of those impressionable young men who have been misled by Gorgias' statements and insufficiently impressed by Gorgias' actual character. Polus argues better than Gorgias, because he is not restrained—as Gorgias is—by a well-developed sense of what it is fitting and proper to maintain in a moral argument. Gorgias cannot bring himself to say something he knows to be wrong merely to make a point in a debate, but Polus is not so hesitant. Nevertheless, since he is merely repeating things he has heard in current conversation, without any deep thought, he is easily refuted by Socrates. But Plato permits Socrates to make fun of Polus, thereby expressing his moral evaluation of Polus as compared with Gorgias. When Callicles jumps into the debate to replace Polus, a real tension develops between him and Socrates. Callicles really believes, as he says, that might makes right, that there are no universal rational principles binding the weak and the strong, the ordinary and the extraordinary, to a single standard of conduct. This total confusion (as Plato sees it) is mirrored in the disorder of Callicles' soul. He rants, he shouts, he grows abusive, he loses whatever dignity he may have possessed. In short, his personality exhibits precisely that breakdown of true reason which his philosophy also reveals. The Dialogue becomes, at one and the same time, an argument between two philosophies and a contrast between two personalities. The truth of Socrates' position is shown as much by his composure, his ironic self-deprecation, his inner peace, as it is by the forcefulness of his arguments.

Now let me connect up the parable at the beginning of the chapter with Plato's theory of appearance and reality and this long example from the *Gorgias* of Plato's artistic skill. Strange and paradoxical as it may seem, Plato actually believed, on the basis on his theoretical distinction between appearance and reality, that artistic creations were *appearances* and that as such they led us away from knowledge and away from a proper inner harmony of the soul. And like the singer in the parable, Plato expressed this conviction in a series of artistic works of such beauty that the attention of his audience is turned away from the message rather than toward it!

Our first selection in this chapter is, once again, from the *Republic*. It contains Plato's reasons for believing that art is misleading and harmful and, therefore, that it ought not to be permitted a place in the ideal society he is sketching. In much of this selection, Plato seems to be talking about what philosophers call metaphysics, or the study of the forms and

Plato criticized art for misrepresenting reality. Here are three paintings by the Frenchman Auguste Renoir, the American Jackson Pollock, and the Spaniard Pablo Picasso. All three would claim that they are successfully capturing some aspect of reality that a photograph fails to reveal. Auguste Renoir, "Oarsmen at Chatou." (**left**) French (1841–1919) Canvas, 32″ × 39$\frac{1}{2}$″. (0.813 × 1.003) Courtesy of National Gallery of Art, Washington, D.C.; Gift of Sam A. Lewisohn, 1951. Jackson Pollock, "Echo" (Number 25, 1951). (**below left**) Enamel paint on canvas, 7′8″ × 72″. Collection, The Museum of Modern Art, New York. Acquired through the Lillie P. Bliss Bequest. Pablo Picasso, "Three Musicians," 1921. (Summer) (**below**) Collection, The Museum of Modern Art, New York. Mrs. Simon Guggenheim Fund. Oil on canvas, 6′7″ × 7′3$\frac{3}{4}$″ (200.7 × 222.9 cm).

nature of being, as much as about art. This interconnection of the different branches of philosophy is typical of the work of the great philosophers, and you should not be misled by the organization of this book into supposing that philosophy consists of a number of separate subfields locked away in watertight compartments. Indeed, the distinction between appearance and reality also bears directly on John Stuart Mill's claim, in Chapter 3, that some pleasures are higher or truer or better than others. Plato held the same view, and he defended it precisely by saying that some pleasures are *more real* than others.

Plato's objections to art focus on two distinct but related questions: First, does art give us knowledge, or does it mislead us about the nature of reality? and, second, does art help us to achieve a proper, harmonious inner psychic order, or does it stir up our emotions and destroy the rule of reason within the personality? Plato convicts art on both counts. Art leads us away from reality rather than toward it, he claims, and it destroys our psychic harmony rather than reinforcing it. These twin issues, of the truthfulness of art and the psychological effect of art on the audience, run through all the philosophies of art that we shall be examining in this chapter.

Plato's Philosophy of Art

Can you tell me what is meant by representation in general?

. . . shall we proceed as usual and begin by assuming the existence of a single essential nature or Form for every set of things which we call by the same name? . . .

Then let us take any set of things you choose. For instance there are any number of beds or of tables, but only two Forms, one of Bed and one of Table. . . .

And we are in the habit of saying that the craftsman, when he makes the beds or tables we use or whatever it may be, has before his mind the Form of one or other of these pieces of furniture. The Form itself is, of course, not the work of any craftsman. . . .

Now what name would you give to a craftsman who can produce all the things made by every sort of workman?

He would need to have very remarkable powers!

Wait a moment, and you will have even better reason to say so. For, besides producing any kind of artificial thing, this same craftsman can create all plants and animals, himself included, and earth and sky and gods and the heavenly bodies and all the things under the earth in Hades.

That sounds like a miraculous feat of virtuosity.

Are you incredulous? Tell me, do you think there could be no such craftsman at all, or that there might be someone who could create all these things in one sense, though not in another? Do you not see that you could do it yourself, in a way?

In what way, I should like to know.

PLATO,
Republic

There is no difficulty; in fact there are several ways in which the thing can be done quite quickly. The quickest perhaps would be to take a mirror and turn it round in all directions. In a very short time you could produce sun and stars and earth and yourself and all the other animals and plants and lifeless objects which we mentioned just now.

Yes, in appearance, but not the actual things.

Quite so; you are helping out my argument. My notion is that a painter is a craftsman of that kind. You may say that the things he produces are not real; but there is a sense in which he too does produce a bed.

Yes, the appearance of one.

And what of the carpenter? Were you not saying just now that he only makes a particular bed, not what we call the Form or essential nature of Bed?

Yes, I was.

If so, what he makes is not the reality, but only something that resembles it. It would not be right to call the work of a carpenter or of any other handicraftsman a perfectly real thing. . . .

We must not be surprised, then, if even an actual bed is a somewhat shadowy thing as compared with reality.

True.

Now shall we make use of this example to throw light on our question as to the true nature of this artist who represents things? We have here three sorts of bed: one which exists in the nature of things and which, I imagine, we could only describe as a product of divine workmanship; another made by the carpenter; and a third by the painter. So the three kinds of bed belong respectively to the domains of these three: painter, carpenter, and god.

Yes.

Now the god made only one ideal or essential Bed, whether by choice or because he was under some necessity not to make more than one; at any rate two or more were not created, nor could they possibly come into being.

Why not?

Because, if he made even so many as two, then once more a single ideal Bed would make its appearance, whose character those two would share; and that one, not the two, would be the essential Bed. Knowing this, the god, wishing to be the real maker of a real Bed, not a particular manufacturer of one particular bed, created one which is essentially unique.

So it appears.

Shall we call him, then, the author of the true nature of Bed, or something of that sort?

Certainly he deserves the name, since all his works constitute the real nature of things.

And we may call the carpenter the manufacturer of a bed?

Yes.

Can we say the same of the painter?

Certainly not.

Then what is he, with reference to a bed?

I think it would be fairest to describe him as the artist who represents the things which the other two make.

Very well, said I; so the work of the artist is at the third remove from the essential nature of the thing?

Exactly.

The tragic poet, too, is an artist who represents things; so this will apply to him: he and all other artists are, as it were, third in succession from the throne of truth.

Just so.

We are in agreement, then, about the artist. But now tell me about our painter: which do you think he is trying to represent—the reality that exists in the nature of things, or the products of the craftsman?

The products of the craftsman.

As they are, or as they appear? You have still to draw that distinction.

How do you mean?

I mean: you may look at a bed or any other object from straight in front or slantwise or at any angle. Is there then any difference in the bed itself, or does it merely look different?

It only looks different.

Well, that is the point. Does painting aim at reproducing any actual object as it is, or the appearance of it as it looks? In other words, is it a representation of the truth or of a semblance?

Of a semblance.

The art of representation, then, is a long way from reality; and apparently the reason why there is nothing it cannot reproduce is that it grasps only a small part of any object, and that only an image. Your painter, for example, will paint us a shoemaker, a carpenter, or other workman without understanding any one of their crafts; and yet, if he were a good painter, he might deceive a child or a simple-minded person into thinking his picture was a real carpenter, if he showed it to them at some distance.

. . . the content of this poetical representation is something at the third remove from reality, is it not?

Yes.

On what part of our human nature, then, does it produce its effect?

What sort of part do you mean?

Let me explain by an analogy. An object seen at a distance does not, of course, look the same size as when it is close at hand; a straight stick looks bent when part of it is under water, and the same thing appears concave or convex to an eye misled by colours. Every sort of confusion like these is to be found in our minds; and it is this weakness in our nature that is exploited, with a quite magical effect, by many tricks of illusion, like scene-painting and conjuring.

. . . Instead of trusting merely to the analogy from painting, let us directly consider that part of the mind to which the dramatic element in poetry appeals, and see how much claim it has to serious worth. We can put the question in this way. Drama, we say, represents the acts and fortunes of human beings. It is wholly concerned with what they do, voluntarily or against their will, and how they fare, with the consequences which they regard as happy or otherwise, and with their feelings of joy and sorrow in all these experiences. That is all, is it not?

Yes.

And in all these experiences has a man an undivided mind? Is there not an internal conflict which sets him at odds with himself in his conduct, much as we were saying that the conflict of visual impressions leads him to make contradictory judgments? However, I need not ask that question; for, now I come to think of it, we have already agreed that innumerable conflicts of this sort are constantly occurring in the mind. But there is a further point to be considered now. We have said that a man of high character will bear any stroke of fortune, such as the loss of a son or of anything else he holds dear, with more equanimity than most people. We may now ask: will he feel no pain, or is that impossible? Will he not rather observe due measure in his grief?

Yes, that is nearer the truth.

Now tell me: will he be more likely to struggle with his grief and resist it when he is under the eyes of his fellows or when he is alone?

He will be far more restrained in the presence of others.

Yes; when he is by himself he will not be ashamed to do and say much that he would not like anyone to see or hear.

Quite so.

What encourages him to resist his grief is the lawful authority of reason, while the impulse to give way comes from the feeling itself; and, as we said, the presence of contradictory impulses proves that two distinct elements in his nature must be involved. One of them is law-abiding, prepared to listen to the authority which declares that it is best to bear misfortune as quietly as possible without resentment, for several reasons: it is never certain that misfortune may not be a blessing; nothing is gained by chafing at it; nothing human is matter for great concern; and, finally, grief hinders us from calling in the help we most urgently need. By this I mean reflection on what has happened, letting reason decide on the best move in the game of life that the fall of the dice permits. Instead of behaving like a child who goes on shrieking after a fall and hugging the wounded part, we should accustom the mind to set itself at once to raise up the fallen and cure the hurt, banishing lamentation with a healing touch.

Certainly that is the right way to deal with misfortune.

And if, as we think, the part of us which is ready to act upon these reflections is the highest, that other part which impels us to dwell upon our sufferings and can never have enough of grieving over them is unreasonable, craven, and faint-hearted.

Yes.

Now this fretful temper gives scope for a great diversity of dramatic representation; whereas the calm and wise character in its unvarying constancy is not easy to represent, nor when represented is it readily understood, especially by a promiscuous gathering in a theatre, since it is foreign to their own habit of mind. Obviously, then, this steadfast disposition does not naturally attract the dramatic poet, and his skill is not designed to find favour with it. If he is to have a popular success, he must address himself to the fretful type with its rich variety of material for representation.

Obviously.

We have, then, a fair case against the poet and we may set him down as the counterpart of the painter, whom he resembles in two ways: his creations are poor things by the standard of truth and reality, and his appeal is not to the highest part of the soul, but to one which is equally inferior. So we shall be justified in not admitting him into a well-ordered commonwealth, because he stimulates and strengthens an element which threatens to undermine the reason. As a country may be given over into the power of its worst citizens while the better sort are ruined, so, we shall say, the dramatic poet sets up a vicious form of government in the individual soul: he gratifies that senseless part which cannot distinguish great and small, but regards the same things as now one, now the other; and he is an image-maker whose images are phantoms far removed from reality.

Quite true.

One final word on the paradox of the parable of the singer before we move on to the views of other philosophers. Plato feared that art would lead us away from reality, rather than toward it. Considering how famous Plato has become, how widely his works have been read and studied in both the West and the East, it is tempting to dismiss his fears as foolish. But the fact is that in a peculiar way, Plato's own success is evidence that he was right. Through the dramatic power of Plato's art, Socrates has become an immortal figure of Western thought. When we read the Dialogues today, all of us—

students and trained philosophers alike—instinctively cast Socrates as the hero and his opponents as the villains of the drama. This encourages us to accept Socrates' (and Plato's) doctrines without properly criticizing them or evaluating them. In other words, we treat Socrates in exactly the way that the ancient Athenians treated Gorgias and the other popular speakers. We are swayed by Plato's art rather than persuaded by his arguments. Now, Socrates took what we today would call a conservative political position, and his opponents—at least according to some scholars—were the "liberals" of their society. Strange as it may seem, many modern philosophers whose own political opinions are liberal still treat Socrates as the good guy and Gorgias or Protagoras or Thrasymachus or Callicles as the bad guys. In short, they are so beguiled by the beauty of Plato's song that they do not reflect, calmly and rationally, on its words. That is just the danger Plato saw and warned of when he banned the artists from his ideal Republic.

Aristotle's Defense of the Poets

Plato was not yet thirty when Socrates died. Later in life, he founded a school or center for mathematical, cosmological, and philosophical investigation called the Academy. Far and away the most distinguished "student" at the Academy, if we can speak of students at all, was a man named Aristotle. There are many students of philosophy who consider Aristotle the greatest philosopher of all. St. Thomas Aquinas, the medieval theologian who figures so prominently in the development of Catholic doctrine, had so high an opinion of Aristotle that he referred to him simply as "the philosopher," as if there were no other. When you think about it, the odds must be simply astronomical against such a sequence of teachers and students as Socrates, Plato, and Aristotle.

Aristotle was not at all gifted artistically as Plato was, though in his youth he tried his hand at writing some dialogues. His temperament was rather that of a scientist, and the writings which we have today by him are actually treatises or lecture notes for the teaching he did at the Academy. Because they were written for a specialized audience rather than for the general public, they are very condensed, rather dry, and sometimes hard to follow if you aren't already pretty well up on what Aristotle is talking about. The range of Aristotle's investigations was simply staggering. In addition to his great work in logic, he wrote on systematic comparative political science, moral philosophy, cosmology, psychology, biology, astronomy, and physics, and he even developed several proofs for the existence of a "prime mover," or God. In Athens at that time, the public theater was an important part of the religious and civic as well as cultural life of the people, and the annual performances of the tragedies written by the great Greek playwrights were a focus of public interest. Aristotle wrote a short treatise on the subject of

ARISTOTLE

Aristotle (384–322 B.C.) is the most influential figure in the history of Western philosophy. Born in Stagira, a Greek colony on the Aegean Sea, he came to Athens as a very young man to study with Plato in the school known as the Academy. He remained a student and member of the Academy for twenty years, leaving only in 347 B.C. on Plato's death. Eventually, he founded his own school, where he lectured on a range of subjects so broad that he must have been virtually a one-man faculty. In addition to his major philosophical discoveries in the fields of logic, metaphysics, and the theory of knowledge. Aristotle did an enormous amount of empirical work on problems of astronomy, biology, comparative politics, and anatomy.

Aristotle is remembered today for his philosophy, but during his middle life, after leaving Plato's Academy and before founding his own school, he spent seven years as a tutor to the young prince who was to become Alexander the Great. Alexander, heir to the throne of Macedonia, eventually conquered the entire Greek world and pushed his military campaigns as far east as India. Aristotle persuaded Alexander to send back biological specimens and other data from his explorations.

Although much of Aristotle's work has been surpassed by later investigators in the 2,000 years and more since his death, some of his writings, particularly those in the areas of psychology and the theory of art, remain as suggestive and useful today as they were in ancient times.

tragedy. We know that little work today as *Poetics*, and despite its brevity, it is much read and quoted, for it has had a wide and deep influence throughout the ages on philosophical theories about art.

For our purposes, Aristotle's treatise is interesting because of its defense of art against the twofold attack of his teacher, Plato. Recall the charge that Plato had leveled against poetry: it leads us away from truth, and it disorders the soul. Aristotle does not say a great deal about these two criticisms, but he indicates rebuttals to both. First, consider the claim that art misleads us by offering nothing more than imperfect copies of the world of the senses, which is itself no better than an imperfect copy or realization of the ideal standards of beauty, goodness, and justice which Plato calls the Forms or Ideas. If I want to know the true nature of a circle, I had better turn my eyes away from physical objects and reflect instead upon the pure definitions of mathematical

> ☞ **Catharsis**   Literally, a cleansing or purging. Aristotle uses the term to describe the effect on us of powerful dramatic performances. By watching a play whose events arouse fear and pity within us, he thought, we are purged of those emotions, so that we leave the theater liberated or cleansed. The opposing view is that such plays (and, by extension, movies and television programs) arouse in us feelings we otherwise wouldn't have, and shouldn't have, such as certain aggressive and sexual feelings.

forms. It is bad enough that my inadequate intelligence sometimes needs the aid of wheels, coins, and other imperfectly round objects which I encounter in life. I will simply stray farther from the truth if I fix my eyes on a picture of a wheel. The same is true for the knowledge of the human soul. True or ideal justice has never been achieved by a living man or woman, so I can learn very little about the eternal standard of justice through an examination of the lives of even the noblest men and women. What can a tragedian do, save conjure up for me on the stage an admittedly imperfect imitation of an admittedly imperfect character. I might as well try to get a feel for fine cowhide by looking at a photograph of imitation leather!

Not so, Aristotle replies. Plato is right in insisting that we should seek a knowledge of the unchanging, universal forms of justice, beauty, and goodness, but he is wrong in supposing that art merely provides us with imperfect copies of particular instances of those universal forms. Great artists have the ability, through their art, to grasp the universal that lies within the particular, and to present it to us in such a way that we achieve a greater knowledge than we would otherwise have. When Shakespeare creates for us the character of Hamlet (needless to say, this is my example, not Aristotle's), he shows us, through the particularities of the vacillations and inner conflicts of one young prince, some universal truths about fathers and sons, sons and mothers, intellect and will, thought and action. Plato to the contrary notwithstanding, we are wiser for seeing a performance of *Hamlet* than we would be were we to travel back in time and meet the real man on whom the play is based.

The dispute between Plato and Aristotle is partly a disagreement about art, of course, but it is, at a deeper level, a disagreement about metaphysics. Plato seems to have held that the universal, eternal, unchanging Forms actually exist independently of the particular, time-bound, changing objects and events which fitfully and inadequately embody them. (I say, "seems to have held," because this is a subject on which scholars differ.) In other words, Plato believed that there is a reality which transcends the appearances of the senses and the world of space, time, and physical things. True knowledge was for him, therefore, a rational understanding of that transcendent realm of universal Forms. Aristotle, on the other hand, held that the universal Forms are completely embodied in the particular things of the world of space and time. True knowledge does indeed consist of a grasp of those forms, and Plato was certainly right that we must penetrate the changing particularity of this and that moment or event in order to get at the universal truths. But because the universals are embodied in the particulars—because true circularity is to be found within actual circular things, true rationality within actual rational creatures, true beauty within actual works of art, our attention should be focused even more intently on those particular instances rather than directed entirely away from them toward an independent realm of eternal Forms.

Aristotle's answer to Plato's second charge rests on a point of psychology rather than metaphysics. Plato was afraid that tragedy would arouse uncontrollable passions in the audience and thereby disarrange the proper harmony of the soul. It would weaken the ascendency of the rational forces within the personality and release erotic and aggressive elements that are destructive and deluding. Aristotle argued that just the opposite is the case. Since those harmful passions are present anyway, far better to release them in the controlled setting of the drama than to bottle them up entirely. In art, we experience those terrible feelings vicariously, through our identification with the characters in the play. When they suffer, triumph, love, hate, rage, and mourn, we in the audience do also. When the play ends, we experience a catharsis and are purged of the pent-up passions without having expressed them in the terrible deeds that the playwright has depicted on the stage. We leave the theater calmed, not aroused.

All this seems thin, bloodless, "academic" until we realize that exactly the same debate now rages in America about violence and sex in our movies and television shows. Does the portrayal of violence make our children more prone to act violently in their real lives, or does it drain away the violence that lies within all of us, giving it a safe, harmless outlet? Does sadomasochistic pornography stimulate its viewers to commit sex crimes, or does it divert passions which otherwise would lead to rape or mutilation?

The following brief selections from Aristotle's *Poetics* will give you some sense of his approach to the analysis and justification of art, but they will hardly settle such a host of difficult and controversial questions. In the remainder of this chapter, we shall take a look at a number of other conceptions of the nature and rationale of art. Perhaps somewhere in this debate you will find your own answer to Plato's question: Does art have a legitimate place in the good society?

Aristotle's Philosophy of Art

From what we have said it will be seen that the poet's function is to describe, not the thing that has happened, but a kind of thing that might happen, i.e., what is possible as being probable or necessary. The distinction between historian and poet is not in the one writing prose and the other verse—you might put the work of Herodotus

ARISTOTLE,
Poetics

into verse, and it would still be a species of history; it consists really in this, that the one describes the thing that has been, and the other a kind of thing that might be. Hence poetry is something more philosophic and of graver import than history, since its statements are of the nature rather of universals, whereas those of history are singulars. . . .

A tragedy, then, is the imitation of an action that is serious and also, as having magnitude, complete in itself; in language with pleasurable accessories, each kind brought in separately in the parts of the work; in a *dramatic,* not in a narrative form; with incidents arousing pity and fear, wherewith to accomplish its catharsis of such emotions. . . .

We assume that, for the finest form of Tragedy, the Plot must be not simple but complex; and further, that it must imitate actions arousing fear and pity, since that is the distinctive function of this kind of imitation. It follows, therefore, that there are three forms of Plot to be avoided. (1) A good man must not be seen passing from happiness to misery, or (2) a bad man from misery to happiness. The first situation is not fear-inspiring or piteous, but simply odious to us. The second is the most untragic that can be; it has not one of the requisites of Tragedy; it does not appeal either to the human feeling in us, or to our pity, or to our fears. Nor, on the other hand, should (3) an extremely bad man be seen falling from happiness into misery. Such a story may arouse the human feeling in us, but it will not move us to either pity or fear; pity is occasioned by undeserved misfortune, and fear by that of one like ourselves; so that there will be nothing either piteous or fear-inspiring in the situation. There remains, then, the intermediate kind of personage, a man not pre-eminently virtuous and just, whose misfortune, however, is brought upon him not by vice and depravity but by some error of judgment, of the number of those in the enjoyment of great reputation and prosperity; e.g., Oedipus, Thyestes, and the men of note of similar families. The perfect Plot, accordingly, must have a single, and not (as some tell us) a double issue; the change in the hero's fortunes must be not from misery to happiness, but on the contrary from happiness to misery; and the cause of it must lie not in any depravity, but in some great error on his part; the man himself being either such as we have described, or better, not worse, than that. . . .

The tragic fear and pity may be aroused by the Spectacle; but they may also be aroused by the very structure and incidents of the play—which is the better way and shows the better poet. The Plot in fact should be so framed that, even without seeing the things take place, he who simply hears the account of them shall be filled with horror and pity at the incidents; which is just the effect that the mere recital of the story in *Oedipus* would have on one. To produce this same effect by

A portrait of a scene from William Shakespeare's "*Hamlet.*" Hamlet
speaks to the skull of Yorick. Undated portrait. Terrible though the
events of the play are, Aristotle would claim that in watching them
unfold, we are purged of powerful and potentially destructive emotions.
(Corbis–Bettmann.)

means of the Spectacle is less artistic, and requires extraneous aid.
Those, however, who make use of the Spectacle to put before us that
which is merely monstrous and not productive of fear, are wholly out of
touch with Tragedy; not every kind of pleasure should be required of a
tragedy, but only its own proper pleasure.

The tragic pleasure is that of pity and fear, and the poet has to
produce it by a work of imitation; it is clear, therefore, that the

causes should be included in the incidents of his story. Let us see, then, what kinds of incident strike one as horrible, or rather as piteous. In a deed of this description the parties must necessarily be either friends, or enemies, or indifferent to one another. Now when enemy does it on enemy, there is nothing to move us to pity either in his doing or in his meditating the deed, except so far as the actual pain of the sufferer is concerned; and the same is true when the parties are indifferent to one another. Whenever the tragic deed, however, is done within the family—when murder or the like is done or meditated by brother on brother, by son on father, by mother on son, or son on mother—these are the situations the poet should seek after.

Romanticism

The most powerful and influential aesthetic movement of the past several centuries, both in England and on the continent of Europe, is undoubtedly romanticism. In the late eighteenth century, poets, painters, and philosophers of art rebelled against the style and tenets of the neoclassicism which had until then dominated the theory and practice of art. Neoclassicism exalted order, proportion, reason, and the subordination of the creative artist to objective principles of aesthetic taste. In England especially, neoclassicism looked back to the calm gravity of the art and language of the great period of Roman culture known—after the Emperor Caesar Augustus—as the Augustan Age. The English romantic poets overturned all the entrenched tenets of neoclassical art, and in doing so carried out a revolution whose effects are still being felt today even beyond the confines of the world of art and literature.

The key to the romantic rebellion was two reversals or denials of the traditional doctrine. First, the romantics denied the supremacy of *reason* in art and life. Instead, they insisted that the power of creative *imagination* is the highest human faculty. From Plato on, philosophers and students of art had insisted that reason is our primary organ of knowledge, our source for whatever truth we can attain. The romantics granted the power of reason to accumulate knowledge of the ordinary, or work-a-day sort. But for deep insight

Romanticism The late eighteenth-century and nineteenth-century movement in art and literature that stressed the powerful expression of feeling and the free play of imagination over the observation of formal limits on artistic creativity. The term comes originally from the late medieval term *romance*, meaning a poem, play, or story written in the local popular language, such as French, rather than in Latin.

A portrayal by the French romantic painter Delacroix of Jacob struggling
with the Angel. (See the Book of Genesis, Chapter 32.) Fresco in Church
of St. Sulpice, Paris. (Corbis–Bettmann.)

into the inner being of humanity and nature, for a grasp of that eternal,
unchanging realm beyond the world of the senses, artistic imagination is necessary.

The second reversal was the substitution of the subjective for the objective as the test and source of true knowledge. Philosophers traditionally had
dismissed the subjective, the particular, the individual, as lacking in value or
cognitive significance. What mathematics or philosophy or science could val-
idate as universally and objectively true, independently of the momentary
subjective state of the individual investigator, could be accepted as established. But the intense fleeting feeling of the lone artist could not possibly

WILLIAM WORDSWORTH

William Wordsworth (1770–1850) was one of the leading poets of the English romantic movement. In his youth, he traveled to France and became an enthusiastic supporter of the revolution. After fathering an illegitimate child by a French woman, Marie Anne Vallen, he returned to England and eventually settled in Somerset, near Samuel Coleridge. During the last years of the old century and the first years of the new, Coleridge and Wordsworth wrote a series of poems, entitled *Lyrical Ballads,* which remain among the classic works of romanticism.

In middle life, Wordsworth turned against the liberal views of his youth and became increasingly conservative. He continued to write poetry throughout his lifetime, but he never achieved the heights of his early work. In 1843, he was named Poet Laureate of England, succeeding Robert Southey.

serve as a conduit of important truth. The romantics turned this traditional view on its head. They insisted that the most intense and momentary emotional states of the most extraordinary individuals are our glimpse of the infinite, our window on eternity.

Plato was suspicious of poets and the poetic impulse, because he believed that the act of artistic creation had more than a touch of madness about it. Poets were, in popular Greek opinion, possessed by the gods, and certainly their moments of inspiration bore little resemblance to the quiet rational progress of dialectical philosophical argument. Art, Plato said, could not put us in touch with the eternal because it was irrational. The romantics turned Plato completely around and asserted that art *can* put us in touch with the eternal precisely *because* it is ecstatic, subjective, emotionally intense, and in that sense irrational. The great irony of the romantics is that they considered themselves neo-Platonists!

One of the finest statements of the romantic philosophy is, as you might expect a poem, namely, the ode by William Wordsworth entitled "Intimations of Immortality from Recollections of Early Childhood." I would have liked to use it as our selection, but since this is a philosophy text, I have instead selected a portion of the preface which Wordsworth wrote for a book of verse entitled *Lyrical Ballads.* Ask your English teacher to read Wordsworth's ode with you.

A Romantic Poet Defines Poetry

. . . All good poetry is the spontaneous overflow of powerful feelings: and though this be true, Poems to which any value can be attached were never produced on any variety of subjects but by a man who, being possessed of more than usual organic sensibility, had also thought long and deeply. For our continued influxes of feelings are modified and directed by our thoughts, which are indeed the representatives of all our past feelings; and, as by contemplating the relation of these general representatives to each other, we discover what is really important to men, so, by the repetition and continuance of this act, our feelings will be connected with important subjects, till at length, if we be originally possessed of much sensibility, such habits of mind will be produced, that, by obeying blindly and mechanically the impulses of those habits, we shall describe objects, and utter sentiments, of such a nature, and in such connexion with each other, that the understanding of the Reader must necessarily be in some degree enlightened, and his affections strengthened and purified. . . .

However exalted a notion we would wish to cherish of the character of a Poet, it is obvious, that while he describes and imitates passions, his employment is in some degree mechanical, compared with the freedom and power of real and substantial action and suffering. So that it will be the wish of the Poet to bring his feelings near to those of the persons whose feelings he describes, nay for short spaces of time, perhaps, to let himself slip into an entire delusion, and even confound and identify his own feelings with theirs; modifying only the language which is thus suggested to him by a consideration that he describes for a particular purpose, that of giving pleasure. Here, then, he will apply the principle of selection which has been already insisted upon. He will depend upon this for removing what would otherwise be painful or disgusting in the passion; he will feel that there is no necessity to trick out or to elevate nature: and, the more industriously he applies this principle, the deeper will be his faith that no words, which his fancy or imagination can suggest, will be to be compared with those which are the emanations of reality and truth.

But it may be said by those who do not object to the general spirit of these remarks, that, as it is impossible for the Poet to produce upon all occasions language as exquisitely fitted for the passion as that which the real passion itself suggests, it is proper that he should consider himself as in the situation of a translator, who does not scruple to substitute excellencies of another kind for those which are unattainable by him; and endeavours occasionally to surpass his original, in order to make some amends for the general inferiority to which he feels that he must submit. But this would be

WILLIAM WORDSWORTH, *Preface to the Lyrical Ballads*

to encourage idleness and unmanly despair. Further, it is the language of men who speak of what they do not understand; who talk of Poetry as of a matter of amusement and idle pleasure; who will converse with us as gravely about a *taste* for Poetry, as they express it, as if it were a thing as indifferent as a taste for rope-dancing, or Frontiniac or Sherry. Aristotle, I have been told, has said, that Poetry is the most philosophic of all writing: it is so: its object is truth, not individual and local, but general, and operative; not standing upon external testimony, but carried alive into the heart by passion; truth which is its own testimony, which gives competence and confidence to the tribunal to which it appeals, and receives them from the same tribunal. Poetry is the image of man and nature. The obstacles which stand in the way of fidelity of the Biographer and Historian, and their consequent utility, are incalculably greater than those which are to be encountered by the *Poet* who comprehends the dignity of his art. The Poet writes under one restriction only, namely, the necessity of giving immediate pleasure to a human Being possessed of that information which may be expected from him, not as a lawyer, a physician, a mariner, an astronomer, or a natural philosopher, but as a Man. Except this one restriction, there is no object standing between the Poet and the image of things; between this, and the Biographer and Historian, there are a thousand.

Tolstoy's Religious Defense of Art

The romantics follow Plato, Aristotle, and most other philosophers of art in assigning instrumental value to art, but their conception of its instrumentality leads them to emphasize the unusual rather than the ordinary, the outstanding rather than the commonplace. The characteristic romantic image of the artist is the gifted, tortured genius, alone in his garret, unappreciated by the multitudes but nevertheless tearing great works of art quivering from his breast.

Just about the most completely opposite conception of art and the artist was put forward by another great literary figure, the Russian novelist Leo Tolstoy. You have all heard of Tolstoy's immortal novel, *War and Peace,* though in all likelihood very few of you have plowed your way through that immensely long book. Tolstoy is an extraordinary figure in literature and philosophy. He was born in 1828 into the Russian aristocracy and served in the army as a young man. When he was only thirty-eight, he published *War and Peace,* his great novel of Russian life and thought during the period of the Napoleonic wars. Some time later, he underwent a deep religious conversion

C O U N T   L E O   T O L S T O Y

Count Leo Tolstoy (1828–1910) is one of the immortal geniuses of European literature. He and Feodor Dostoyevsky have, in their novels, given us matchless pictures of Russian life in the nineteenth century. In his youth, Tolstoy served in the czar's army, seeing action as the commander of a battery in the Crimean War (1854–1856). He retired to his family's estates and began his career as a writer. His masterpiece, *War and Peace,* was published in 1866. It is a panoramic story of Russian life and thought during the great struggle of Russia against Napoleon.

In 1876, Tolstoy underwent a profound spiritual conversion to a form of Russian Orthodox Christianity that emphasized the virtues of the simple life and hard, physical labor. He worked alongside the peasants in the fields of his estates, while continuing to write novels and essays. Among the works of this later period in his life are *Anna Karenina,* which was begun before his conversion and completed in 1877; *The Death of Ivan Ilyich;* and the essay on the nature of art from which the selection in this book is taken.

and adopted a life of peasant simplicity. Out of his conversion emerged a new, simplified Christian faith and a rejection of the cultivated aesthetic sensibilities which he himself had contributed to in his earlier writings. Thirty years after the publication of *War and Peace,* in 1896, Tolstoy gave formal philosophical expression to his new conception of art and life in an essay entitled *What Is Art?*

Tolstoy argues that there are two basic means by which human beings communicate with one another. The first is speech, by which men and women communicate their *thoughts;* the second is art, by which they communicate their *feelings.* Each of us has the capacity to communicate feelings by arousing them in others. We not only tell our listeners that we are sad, we actually arouse feelings of sadness in them, sometimes by reporting what it is that has made us sad, sometimes by the tone of our voice, sometimes by looks, gestures, or other means of expression. Feelings are infectious. When one person laughs, others laugh too. When one cries, others cry. Tolstoy describes art in this way:

To evoke in oneself a feeling one has experienced, and having evoked it in oneself, then, by means of movements, lines, colors, sounds, or forms expressed in words, so to transmit that feeling that others may experience the same feeling—this is the activity of art.

Art is a human activity consisting in this, that one man consciously, by means of certain external signs, hands on to others feelings he has lived through, and that other people are infected by these feelings and also experience them.

The stronger the degree of infectiousness of art, the better the art is, Tolstoy maintains. And the fundamental source of infectiousness—the quality in the artist which enables him or her to spark a contagion of feeling in the audience—is not reason nor imaginative brilliance, nor metaphysical insight, nor extraordinary creativity, but simply *sincerity*. Honesty of feeling is directly apprehended and responded to by an artist's audience.

So far as the content of the work of art is concerned, Tolstoy—as you might expect—turns the usual canons of aesthetic judgment upside down. Common subjects are best, for they will enable the artist to reach the largest audience. The purpose of art is to unite humanity through shared feeling. Art that relies on specialized knowledge or highly refined taste will exclude rather than include, divide rather than unite. If a work of art is so specialized that men and women can respond to it emotionally only after long training and cultivation, then it will mark off the few from the many and place obstacles in the way of a union of all humanity.

If sincerity and universality of emotional appeal are the criteria of greatness in art, then obviously some so-called artistic "masterpieces" are going to get pretty low marks. Sure enough, Tolstoy downgrades some of the works of music, literature, and painting that had been held up for generations as perfect examples of great art, and in their place offers peasant stories, folk music, and other arts of the common people.

There is one last element in Tolstoy's aesthetic theory which we have not yet mentioned—namely, the *religious* dimension of art. In the following selection from *What Is Art?* Tolstoy draws upon his analysis of art as a means for the communication of feeling and as an instrument for uniting human beings in a universal community, in order to lay the foundations for a religious justification of art.

Tolstoy's Philosophy of Art

In every period of history, and in every human society, there exists an understanding of the meaning of life which represents the highest level to which men of that society have attained, an understanding defining the highest good at which that society aims. And this understanding is the religious perception of the given time and society. And this religious perception is always clearly expressed by some ad-

These two paintings illustrate the difference between the formalism of high art and the vibrant immediacy of folk art. John Hesselius (American, 1728–1778). *"Charles Calvert,"* 1761, oil on canvas; 50¼ x 40 ¼." The Baltimore Museum of Art. Gift of Alfred R. and Henry C. Riggs in memory of General Lawrason Riggs. Folk art portrait of Sussanna M. and Mary L. Murdock, painted in 1830 by "N.M." National Museum of American History, Smithsonian Institution.

vanced men, and more or less vividly perceived by all the members of the society. Such a religious perception and its corresponding expression exists always in every society. If it appears to us that in our society there is no religious perception, this is not because there really is none, but only because we do not want to see it. And we often wish not to see it because it exposes the fact that our life is inconsistent with that religious perception.

Religious perception in a society is like the direction of a flowing river. If the river flows at all, it must have a direction. If society lives, there must be a religious perception indicating the direction in which, more or less consciously, all its members tend. . . .

I know that according to an opinion current in our times religion is a superstition which humanity has outgrown, and that it is therefore assumed that no such thing exists as a religious perception, common to us all, by which art, in our time, can be evaluated. I know that this is the opinion current in the pseudocultured circles of today. People who do not acknowledge Christianity in its true meaning because it undermines all their social privileges, and who, therefore, invent all kinds of philosophic and aesthetic theories to hide from themselves the meaninglessness and wrongness of their lives, cannot think otherwise. These people intentionally, or sometimes unintentionally, confusing the conception of a religious perception think that by denying the cult they get rid of religious perception. But even the very attacks on religion and the attempts to establish a life-conception contrary to the religious perception of our times most clearly demonstrate the existence of a religious perception condemning the lives that are not in harmony with it.

If humanity progresses, i.e., moves forward, there must inevitably be a guide to the direction of that movement. And religions have always furnished that guide. All history shows that the progress of humanity is accomplished not otherwise than under the guidance of religion. But if the race cannot progress without the guidance of religion—and progress is always going on, and consequently also in our own times—then there must be a religion of our times. So that, whether it pleases or displeases the so-called cultured people of today, they must admit the existence of religion—not of a religious cult, Catholic, Protestant, or another, but of religious perception—which, even in our times, is the guide always present where there is any progress. And if a religious perception exists among us, then our art should be appraised on the basis of that religious perception; and, as has always and everywhere been the case, art transmitting feelings flowing from the religious perception of our time should be chosen from all the indifferent art, should be acknowledged, highly esteemed, and encouraged, while art running counter to that perception should be condemned and despised, and all the remaining indifferent art should neither be distinguished nor encouraged. . . .

Christian art, i.e., the art of our time, should be catholic in the original meaning of the word, i.e., universal, and therefore it should unite all men. And only two kinds of feeling do unite all men: first, feelings flowing from the perception of our sonship to God and of the brotherhood of man; and next, the simple feelings of common life, accessible to every one without exception—such as the feeling of merriment, of pity, of cheerfulness, of tranquillity, etc. Only these two kinds of feelings can now supply material for art good in its subject matter. . . .

Beethoven's *Ninth Symphony* is considered a great work of art. To verify its claim to be such, I must first ask myself whether this work transmits the highest religious feeling. I reply in the negative, for music in itself cannot transmit those feelings; and therefore I ask myself next, Since this work does not belong to the highest kind of religious art, has it the other characteristic of the good art of our time—the quality of uniting all men in one common feeling: does it rank as Christian universal art? And again I have no option but to reply in the negative; for not only do I not see how the feelings transmitted by this work could unite people not specially trained to submit themselves to its complex hypnotism, but I am unable to imagine to myself a crowd of normal people who could understand anything of this long, confused, and artificial production, except short snatches which are lost in a sea of what is incomprehensible. And therefore, whether I like it or not, I am compelled to conclude that this work belongs to the rank of bad art. It is curious to note in this connection that attached to the end of this very symphony is a poem of Schiller's which (though somewhat obscurely) expresses this very thought, namely, that feeling (Schiller speaks only of the feeling of gladness) unites people and evokes love in them. But though this poem is sung at the end of the symphony, the music does not accord with the thought expressed in the verses; for the music is exclusive and does not unite all men, but unites only a few, dividing them off from the rest of mankind.

And just in this same way, in all branches of art, many and many works considered great by the upper classes of our society will have to be judged. By this one sure criterion we shall have to judge the celebrated *Divine Comedy* and *Jerusalem Delivered,* and a great part of Shakespeare's and Goethe's works, and in painting every representation of miracles, including Raphael's *Transfiguration,* etc.

Whatever the work may be and however it may have been extolled, we have first to ask whether this work is one of real art or a counterfeit. Having acknowledged, on the basis of the indication of its infectiousness even to a small class of people, that a certain production belongs to the realm of art, it is necessary, on the basis of the indication of its accessibility, to decide the next question. Does this work belong to the category of bad, exclusive art, opposed to religious perception, or to Christian art uniting people? And having acknowledged an article to belong to real Christian art, we must then, according to whether it transmits the feelings flowing from love to God and man, or merely the simple feelings uniting all men, assign it a place in the ranks of religious art or in those of universal art.

Only on the basis of such verification shall we find it possible to select from the whole mass of what in our society claims to be art those works which form real, important, necessary spiritual food, and to separate them from all the harmful and useless art and from the counterfeits of art which surround us. Only on the basis of such verification shall we be able to rid ourselves of the pernicious results of harmful art and to avail ourselves of that beneficent action which is the purpose of true and good art and which is indispensable for the spiritual life of man and of humanity.

HERBERT MARCUSE

Herbert Marcuse (1898–1979) was born in Berlin. He was one of the original members of the famous Frankfurt School of Social Research which flourished in Germany in the years before World War II. After fleeing to the United States to escape the Nazis, Marcuse became a major voice on the left. During the 1960s, he was the most widely quoted radical critic of American capitalist society. His best-known books include *Eros and Civilization* and *One-Dimensional Man.*

❧ Marcuse and the Uses of Negation

Plato says that art is negative, disruptive, antirational and, therefore, that it ought to be banned from the good society. Aristotle, Wordsworth, and Tolstoy all in their different ways say that good art is positive, constructive, and ought to play an important role in social life. Our next theory of art turns these views upside down in a startling, apparently contradictory way. Herbert Marcuse argues that great art is negative, destructive, irrational and, *therefore,* is a valuable element in human life! Why on earth would anyone praise art for having precisely the qualities that other philosophers have considered worthy of condemnation? To put the question in its most paradoxical form. What is positive about being negative?

Marcuse begins his argument with a puzzle that doesn't at first seem to have anything to do with art. Why is it that the most dramatic, outrageous, powerful words and ideas so rapidly become domesticated and acceptable in America today, *without changing anything along the way?* Sixties radicals called America imperialist, and decent people everywhere were horrified. Several years later, Senator J. William Fulbright referred in passing to America's imperialist foreign policy on a television interview program and none of the newscasters thought it worth commenting on. Black militants shout "Power to the people!" and "nice folks" cringe in their beds. Next season, "Power to the people!" is a liberal Democratic campaign slogan, and soon thereafter a Richard Nixon campaign promise. Avant-garde artists violate every canon of artistic sensibility in a last-ditch effort to repudiate the plastic culture of Madison Avenue capitalism, and Madison Avenue reproduces their most outrageous productions as decorations for its advertisements. Woodstock begins as a cry of protest against Middle America and ends as the name of a bird in *Peanuts*. How can this be? Is nothing sacrilegious? Can modern American society absorb anything into itself without changing? Must every protest turn into this year's fad and next year's ancient history?

To answer these questions, Marcuse draws on the psychological theory of the origins of the ego and of civilization which Sigmund Freud set forth in *Civilization and Its Discontents,* and which Marcuse revised and developed in *Eros and Civilization.* Freud argued that the objective, "un-get-over-able" constraints of the real world force each infant to, as he put it, substitute the reality principle for the pleasure principle. Because the physical world won't always fit itself to our desires, and also because we all inevitably get into interpersonal conflicts, particularly those fueled by sexual desire, we are forced to regulate or deny entirely some of our strongest desires. The psychic means for the regulation, Freud suggested, are repression, sublimation, and fantasy, of which repression is the first and most important. Thus is generated the realm of the "unconscious," populated by wishes, impulses, desires, loves, and hatreds which cannot be expressed and acted out in the real world. Civilization itself, our organized collective life, rests upon a foundation of repression, for not even the most miraculous technical wonders or the most flexible social arrangements can gratify the infantile wishes that lie beneath the conscious surface in every adult man and woman.

Repression/Sublimation   Two terms from the psychological theories of Sigmund Freud referring to the primitive operations of the human mind. *Repression* is the forcible pushing out of consciousness of desires, wishes, thoughts, or feelings that the mind considers bad, dangerous, or otherwise unacceptable. According to Freud, what is repressed does not go away, but remains, with all its emotional power, in the unconscious portion of the mind. *Sublimation* is the redirecting of sexual or aggressive energies into socially or morally acceptable channels—for example, aggressive energies directed away from physical violence and into philosophical arguments, or sexual energies diverted from immediate sexual activity into flirting.

Two features of the content and structure of the unconscious are crucial to Marcuse's analysis. First, the unconscious is timeless. The thwarted desires and fears which reside there retain their power across decades of real-world time, returning again and again irrespective of changes in the world which originally thwarted them. A mother who loses her child grieves, mourns, and eventually becomes reconciled to the loss. Time heals her wounds, and the objective passage of events places the loss further and further behind her. The child whose mother dies before he or she can cope with the loss may repress the grief and anger, so that half a century later, the anger at the mother's desertion will recur as strongly, albeit in transmuted forms. In particular, all of us carry with us unrelinquished infantile desires for the sorts of total, immediate, ecstatic satisfaction which as tiny babies we imagined we could, in our omnipotence, command.

Second, the content of the unconscious has a thoroughly ambivalent character. In the unconscious is to be found everything that reality (either natural or social) has decreed to be bad, inefficient, worthless, dirty, ugly, hostile, shameful. But the wishes and desires that fill the unconscious retain their power, even though they have been denied fulfillment. Part of the self—the part that identifies with society, reality, adulthood, and the world—hates, loathes, feels shame for what is repressed. That is the part of the self that cannot acknowledge a fascination with its own feces, or sexual desire for objects deemed socially inappropriate, or laziness, or messiness, or the urge to inflict pain and suffering. But another part of the self secretly delights in the content of the repressed. And what is more, it delights in the repressed *because* it is repressed. So we have the men and women who can only enjoy illicit sex; or, rather less dramatically, we find the familiar folk character of the perpetual child who refuses to grow up— Pan, Til Eulenspiegel, and Peter Pan.

Marcuse accepts Freud's fundamental claim that repression is essential to civilization. But in a brilliant deployment of one of Marx's key notions, he revises Freud's theory of repression by introducing a distinction between necessary repression and surplus repression. Necessary repression is simply that kind and amount of repression that is required at any stage of social development in order to carry on the struggle for existence. It involves, for example, denying ourselves part of the harvest even when we are hungry so that we have seed for the next planting; it involves forcing ourselves to continue laboring at painful tasks because of our rational recognition that hunger, disease, danger, and death may result if we let up too soon. But some repression, Marcuse argues, is not required by the objective constraints of reality. Rather, it is required by the specific system of domination and submission that exists in society at that moment in history. In short, some repression serves only to protect the favored position of the rulers by restraining the subjects from rising up and overthrowing their masters. That repression is "surplus repression," and human progress consists in eliminating surplus repression while simultaneously decreasing the amount of necessary repression through technological advance. Indeed, Marcuse argues, at a time when our technology should permit us considerably to relax the bonds of necessary repression, through the shortening and lightening of the workday, through the relaxation of work discipline, and so forth, surplus repression grows greater and greater so that the total burden of repression suffered in modern industrial society is not appreciably lighter than that suffered in technically less advanced societies. The purpose of that ever-increasing portion of surplus repression is, Marcuse claims, to maintain the ever more manifestly unjustifiable dominance of the ruling sectors of our society.

The concept of surplus repression is one of those brilliant insights which are too often rejected by hard-headed social scientists because they prove difficult to quantify or operationalize. How would we measure the relative proportions of necessary and surplus repression in an individual psyche? Indeed, how could we ever show of a single instance of repression that it was unnecessary, and hence surplus? I don't know the answer to these questions, but I remain convinced that Marcuse has his finger on a fundamental fact here, and that to the extent that it is fuzzy or imprecise, we should struggle to clarify it rather than use the unclarity as an excuse for rejecting it.

Now, with the notion of surplus repression, and the theory of the unconscious, we can sketch Marcuse's theory of the function of negative thinking and thereby approach his analysis of the function of art. Briefly, his position is this: The repressed content of the unconscious in all of us exists as a permanent psychic pool or source of opposition to the established order of society. We all construct powerful defenses against this repressed content within ourselves, using such familiar mechanisms as denial, projection, and transference. When a rebellious member of society violates some taboo by uncovering a part of the body that is supposed to be concealed; or by using, in public, language that is supposed to be used only in private; or by defying canons of dress, decorum, or deference, he or she provokes a response that is exaggerated all out of proportion. The rest of us recoil from the temporary and perhaps insignificant breach of the rules of repression because it provokes the ever-present desire within us to liberate ourselves from the same rules, and we can control that desire only by clamping down on the transgressor. A struggle over bare nipples or long hair or even an insolent, slouching way of standing becomes a struggle between the repressed content and the forces of civilization.

If all the actual repression were necessary repression, then it would be clear that the rebel should be contained, however sympathetically we might acknowledge that he or she speaks for a part of each of us. Marcuse's claim, however, is precisely that not all of the repression is necessary, that some of it is surplus, unnecessary, and that in the interest of human happiness it ought to be eliminated. But—and this is the key to his entire theory—in order to generate sufficient emotional energy in enough people to conquer the surplus repression inflicted by our society, it is necessary to tap the ubiquitous, irrational, infantile desire for a release from all repression. To put it bluntly, you must promise people an impossible liberation from necessary repression in order to get them to struggle for the elimination of the merely surplus repression. To get us to the barricades, it is not enough to say, "Workers of the world, unite! After the revolution you shall suffer only necessary repression." Instead, you must say, "Workers of the world, unite! After the revolution you shall be free." And each projects his or her own fantasy of absolute freedom, a daydream both inevitable and unfulfillable.

The revolutionary role of negative, oppositional styles of artistic expression is precisely to tap the reservoir of repressed desires, to draw on the permanent opposition within us to necessary repression, and thereby to fuel the fight against surplus repression. The artist's image of liberation is necessary, and illusory. The particular content of the rebellion against the established order of aesthetic canons is not crucial. In one social setting, the expletive "damn" will have as much effect as total nudity in another. The point is that no matter what is permitted, there remains both a repressed content that is denied and a longing to express it that can be tapped. The fight always appears to be about the particular artistic rule that has been broken, but it is always really about the existence of repression itself. If the rebellion is successful, surplus repression is reduced, but that success is always perceived as a failure by the participants themselves, because they must sooner or later relinquish their fantasy of total liberation.

The social function of art is thus to keep alive the possibility of what Marcuse calls transcendence. By transcendence, he does not mean, as Plato or Wordsworth might, the passing from this world of space, time, and objects to a higher, eternal realm of forms or ideal entities. Rather, he means the imaginative leap beyond the given social world, with its repressions, oppressions, and reality-oriented sacrifices, to the conception of possible future social orders in which some of the repressed libidinal energy has been liberated. In thus adding a second "dimension" to our existence, Marcuse claims, art helps us to escape the one-dimensionality of present society. But it is not art's job to draw us blueprints of the future. It must simply keep alive those repressed dreams of liberation and gratification whose energies, blocked but not diminished, will fuel the revolutions that reduce surplus repression and bring us closer to conditions of genuine human happiness.

In this selection, we listen to Marcuse talking about the "negative" function of great art. Despite the difficulty of his philosophical language, I think you will be able to see here some of the themes I have been discussing in the last few pages.

The Negative Function of Art

The achievements and the failures of this society invalidate its higher culture. The celebration of the autonomous personality, of humanism, of tragic and romantic love appears to be the ideal of a backward stage of the development. What is happening now is not the deterioration of higher culture into mass culture but the refutation of this culture by the reality. The reality surpasses its culture. Man today can do more than the culture heros and half-gods; he has solved many insoluble problems. But he has also betrayed the hope and destroyed the truth which were preserved in the sublimations of higher culture. To be sure, the higher culture was always in contradiction with social reality, and only a privileged minority enjoyed its blessings and represented its ideals. The two antagonistic spheres of society have always coexisted: the higher culture has always been accommodating, while the reality was rarely disturbed by its ideals and its truth.

Today's novel feature is the flattening out of the antagonism between culture and social reality through the obliteration of the oppositional, alien, and transcendent elements in the higher culture by virtue of which it constituted *another dimension* of reality. This liquidation of *two-dimensional* culture takes place not through the denial and rejection of the "cultural values," but through their wholesale incorporation into the established order, through their reproduction and display on a massive scale. . . .

In contrast to the Marxian concept, which denotes man's relation to himself and to his work in capitalist society, the *artistic alienation* is the conscious transcendence of the alienated existence—a "higher level" or mediated alienation. The conflict with the world of progress, the negation of the order of business, the antibourgeois elements in bourgeois literature and art are neither due to the aesthetic lowliness of this order nor to romantic reaction—nostalgic consecration of a disappearing stage of civilization. "Romantic" is a term of condescending defamation which is easily applied to disparaging avant-garde positions, just as the term "decadent" far more often denounces the genuinely progressive traits of a dying culture than the real factors of decay. The traditional images of artistic alienation are indeed romantic in as much as they are in aesthetic incompatibility with the developing society. This incompatibility is the token of their truth. What they recall and preserve in memory pertains to the future: images of a gratification that would dissolve the society which suppresses it. . . .

The tension between the actual and the possible is transfigured into an insoluble conflict, in which reconciliation is by grace of the oeuvre as *form:* beauty as the "promesse de bonheur." In the form of the oeuvre, the actual circumstances are placed in another dimension

HERBERT MARCUSE, *One-Dimensional Man*

where the given reality shows itself as that which it is. Thus it tells the truth about itself; its language ceases to be that of deception, ignorance, and submission. Fiction calls the facts by their name and their reign collapses; fiction subverts everyday experience and shows it to be mutilated and false. But art has this magic power only as the power of negation. It can speak its own language only as long as the images are alive which refuse and refute the established order. . . .

Whether ritualized or not, art contains the rationality of negation. In its advanced positions, it is the Great Refusal—the protest against that which is. The modes in which man and things are made to appear, to sing and sound and speak, are modes of refuting, breaking, and recreating their factual existence. But these modes of negation pay tribute to the antagonistic society to which they are linked. Separated from the sphere of labor where society reproduces itself and its misery, the world of art which they create remains, with all its truth, a privilege and an illusion.

In this form it continues, in spite of all democratization and popularization, through the nineteenth and into the twentieth century. The "high culture" in which this alienation is celebrated has its own rites and its own style. The salon, the concert, opera, theater are designed to create and invoke another dimension of reality. Their attendance requires festive-like preparation: they cut off and transcend everyday experience.

Now this essential gap between the art and the order of the day, kept open in the artistic alienation, is progressively closed by the advancing technological society. And with its closing, the Great Refusal is in turn refused; the "other dimension" is absorbed into the prevailing state of affairs. The works of alienation are themselves incorporated into this society and circulate as part and parcel of the equipment which adorns and psychoanalyzes the prevailing state of affairs. Thus they become commercials—they sell, comfort, or excite.

Art for Art's Sake

Plato claims that art is harmful, both intellectually and emotionally. Aristotle replies that art teaches and purges, that it aids us in acquiring knowledge of universal truths and in maintaining the proper internal order of our psyches. Though they seem to disagree fundamentally, nevertheless they are united in believing that the art should be judged according to the positive or negative value of its effects on us. Most philosophers who have reflected on the value of art have judged it in this way, as useful or harmful for some purpose. But one group of defenders of art, repelled by the merely instrumental conception of art, developed the view that art needs no justification outside itself, that art should be encouraged, valued, cherished for itself alone. The slogan of this group, who lived and wrote in the nineteenth century, was "art for art's sake." It might be interesting to spend a few moments looking at the "art for art's sake" doctrine.

The central notion that we need here is a distinction, long current in philosophy, between what is sometimes called *instrumental value* and *instrinsic value*. Human beings are purposive creatures. They have goals or ends or purposes which they pursue by choosing what seem to them to be appropriate means. Very often, when we describe something as valuable, or useful, or good, we simply mean that it is especially helpful to us in achieving some purpose or getting to some goal that we have. If I call a car a good car, I probably mean that it runs smoothly, or rarely breaks down, or uses relatively little gas. In short, I mean that it is a useful means or *instrument* for doing what I want to do, which may be to get somewhere fast, or safely, or cheaply, or reliably. If I say that a good education is the most valuable gift that parents can give their child, I probably mean that in the modern world, a good education will be more useful to that child in achieving his or her goals than anything else. Someone who replies that strong character is even more valuable than a good education will probably mean that certain strengths of personality turn out to make more difference in the adult world than formal book learning or credits and degrees.

A good car is good *for* doing something; an education is valuable as a means *to* something; character will be a source of strength *for* some end. All these, and countless other things besides, are valuable as means or instruments, which is to say that they have instrumental value. Now, if you stop and think about it for a moment, it should be obvious that you will never consider something valuable *as a means* unless there is something else that you consider just plain valuable in itself. If there is nothing you want for *itself*, nothing you like or desire or consider worthy *in and of itself*, then it would make no sense to value other things simply as "useful." Suppose, for example, that you are quite happy right where you are and have no desire whatsoever to go anywhere else. A friend comes along and says, "Now that road there is a really great road. You ought to take a ride down it." You

---

☞ **Intrinsic Value/Instrumental Value** To say that something has *intrinsic value* is to say that it is valuable, good, worthwhile, purely for itself alone, regardless of what it may produce or lead to. Some people say that pleasure has intrinsic value, others that beauty does, still others that moral goodness does. *Instrumental value* is the value something has as a means, or instrument, for producing or getting something else. A tool or instrument that is useful for some purpose is said to be instrumentally valuable.

say, "Why should I take a ride down it? I don't want to go where it leads."
And she answers, "It doesn't matter! It's such a great road, you ought to
take it anyway." Well, your friend is either joking, or she is crazy. As the old
saying goes, a bargain isn't a bargain unless it is a bargain for you. And a
road isn't a good road for you unless it is a good road to somewhere you
want to go.

Or you might go into a hardware store to buy a hammer so that you can
hang some pictures. But even if the store has nothing better than a mediocre
hammer and a really great sale on saws, the sensible thing to do is to buy the
hammer. You don't want "a good tool." You want a tool that is *good for* whatever you want to do, which in this case is to hang some pictures.

By contrast, things which are good in themselves, rather than being
good for something else, are said to have intrinsic value. That simply means
that their merit, value, goodness, or whatever is possessed by them independently of anything else in the world. One way to make this point about something that has intrinsic value is to say that it would be valuable even if nothing else in the world existed. A road has only instrumental value, for if there
were nothing in the world but that road—and in particular, if there were no
place at the other end of it—who would value it as a road? Similarly, if there
were no nails, no pictures to hang, nothing to hit, who would value a hammer? But when something has intrinsic value, it retains that value even in the
absence of other objects, places, events, or states of affairs with regard to
which it might be useful.

Is there anything at all that has intrinsic value? Well, we might argue
that unless *something* has intrinsic value, then nothing has instrumental
value. If one thing is useful for getting another, and that other is not valuable
in itself, but simply useful for getting a third thing, and so on and on, we get
into what is sometimes called "an infinite regress." It is like the ancient Hindu
theory that the world rests on the back of an elephant, which stands on the
back of a giant sea turtle, which swims in an enormous ocean. The obvious
question is, What is the ocean in? So something must have intrinsic value, if
anything is to have any sort of value at all.

We have already encountered two philosophical candidates for the title
of things having intrinsic value, although we didn't use that language when
we met them. Immanuel Kant said that humanity is an end in itself, and that
is another way of claiming that *humanity* has intrinsic value. And Jeremy
Bentham said that the only good thing is *pleasure,* by which he obviously
meant that pleasure was the only thing that is intrinsically valuable. In the
nineteenth century, Walter Pater, Clive Bell, and Oscar Wilde, all of them
British, argued that art has intrinsic value, that it is valuable in and of itself.
Wilde carried this view to such lengths that he ended by reversing the usual
order of priority between life and art. Instead of saying, as most philosophers
have, that art is valuable insofar as it contributes to life, Wilde argued that
life acquired value by contributing to art! In this selection from his book,

Intentions, Wilde summarizes his doctrine. Incidentally, Wilde was a gifted and successful playwright, as well as a thoughtful philosopher of art. You probably know the old joke that those who can, do, and those who can't, teach. Sometimes a third line is added: and those who cannot even teach, philosophize. But in this chapter, most of the philosophers we read are also able practitioners of some form of artistic creation.

CYRIL. . . . But in order to avoid making any error I want you to tell me briefly the doctrines of the new aesthetics.

VIVIAN. Briefly, then, they are these. Art never expresses anything but itself. It has an independent life, just as Thought has, and develops purely on its own lines. It is not necessarily realistic in an age of realism, nor spiritual in an age of faith. So far from being the creation of its time, it is usually in direct opposition to it, and the only history that it preserves for us is the history of its own progress. Sometimes it returns upon its footsteps, and revives some antique form, as happened in the archaistic movement of late Greek Art, and in the pre-Raphaelite movement of our own day. At other times it entirely anticipates its age, and produces in one century work that it takes another century to understand, to appreciate and to enjoy. In no case does it reproduce its age. To pass from the art of a time to the time itself is the great mistake that all historians commit.

The second doctrine is this. All bad art comes from returning to Life and Nature, and elevating them into ideals. Life and Nature may sometimes be used as part of Art's rough material, but before they are of any real service to art they must be translated into artistic conventions. The moment Art surrenders its imaginative medium it surrenders everything. As a method Realism is a complete failure, and the two things that every artist should avoid are modernity of form and modernity of subject matter. To us, who live in the nineteenth century, any century is a suitable subject for art except our own. The only beautiful things are the things that do not concern us. It is, to have the pleasure of quoting myself, exactly because Hecuba is nothing to us that her sorrows are so suitable a motive for a tragedy. Besides, it is only the modern that ever becomes old-fashioned. M. Zola sits down to give us a picture of the Second Empire. Who cares for the Second Empire now? It is out of date. Life goes faster than Realism, but Romanticism is always in front of Life.

The third doctrine is that Life imitates Art far more than Art imitates Life. This results not merely from Life's imitative instinct, but from the fact that the self-conscious aim of Life is to find expression, and that Art offers it certain beautiful forms through which it may realise that energy. It is a theory that has never been put forward before, but it is extremely fruitful, and throws an entirely new light upon the history of Art.

OSCAR WILDE,
Intentions

CHAPTER 4

OSCAR WILDE

Oscar Wilde (1854–1900) was a brilliant Irish play-wright and novelist whose super-aesthetic mannerisms typified the movement known as "art for art's sake." He wrote *The Picture of Dorian Gray,* which was made many years later into a truly scary horror film, and the much revived play *The Importance of Being Earnest.* In Gilbert and Sullivan's delightful light opera, *Patience,* the character of Bunthorne is a take-off on Wilde.

It follows, as a corollary from this, that external Nature also imitates Art. The only effects that she can show us are effects that we have already seen through poetry, or in paintings. This is the secret of Nature's charm, as well as the explanation of Nature's weakness.

The final revelation is that Lying, the telling of beautiful untrue things, is the proper aim of Art. But of this I think I have spoken at sufficient length. And now let us go out on the terrace, where "droops the milk-white peacock like a ghost," while the evening star "washes the dusk with silver." At twilight nature becomes a wonderfully suggestive effect, and is not without loveliness, though perhaps its chief use is to illustrate quotations from the poets. Come! We have talked long enough . . .

The Main Points in Chapter Four

1. Plato criticized the poets of classical Greece on the ground that they presented mere imitations or copies of reality that took their listeners farther away from the truth. He thus raised a question—about the value or purpose of art—that has been debated ever since.

2. Plato's great disciple and pupil, Aristotle, defended the poets, saying that through their tragedies we are able to experience powerful emotions of anger and pity, and purge our souls of them.

3. In the nineteenth and twentieth centuries, a number of artists rejected the notion that art must justify itself, saying that art is valuable simply for its own sake—that it is *intrinsically* valuable.

4. Against the art-for-art's-sake school, we may counterpose a number of theories about what art is good for, what it can accomplish that other forms of human activity can not. *Romanticism,* for example, claims that art puts us in touch with a realm that transcends the sphere of ordinary life. The romantics conceived of the artist as an unusual individual whose powerful creative imagination sets him or her off from the general run of humanity.

5. In contrast to the romantics, the great Russian novelist Tolstoy said that true art is the expression of what is universal in human experience, and in that way has the religious purpose of uniting us and bringing us into relation to God.

6. The most unusual defense of art in the history of the debate comes from twentieth-century social theorists like Herbert Marcuse who defend art as an expression of the *negative,* and *oppositional,* in human personality and society. Art, Marcuse claims, is thus a medium of social revolution.

CONTEMPORARY APPLICATION

Pornography and Art

Twenty-four hundred years ago, Plato began the debate over the role of the arts in a good society, and the argument has raged without stop ever since. In recent decades, the focus of the debate in the United States has been pornography and obscenity, with complicated legal questions of constitutional rights getting tangled up with the more traditional disagreements about the good and bad effects of art. A great deal of attention, of course, has been concentrated on the impact of explicit sexuality and violence on the young. For every psychologist who testifies that boys and girls are made more violent or more sexually promiscuous by what they see on television, in movies, and on the newsstands, there is another one ready to prove that such vicarious sexual or violent experience actually drains away destructive passions and leaves children less prone to commit antisocial acts. It all sounds very much like a modern-dress replay of the dispute between Plato and Aristotle!

Frequently, the psychological and legal arguments dominate the discussion so completely that we lose sight entirely of the original issue, which is the proper role or function for art. But sometimes, even today, the debate rises to an impressive level of philosophical generality. Our first pair of readings is actually a legal opinion handed down by a judge in a famous obscenity trial and the dissenting opinion of another member of the same bench who saw the matter differently. At issue was the long, complex, experimental novel *Ulysses* by the twentieth-century Irish author James Joyce. In an effort to capture the complexity and immediacy of daily experience, Joyce experimented with what has come to be known as "stream of consciousness" exposition. As his characters go about their business on a single day in Dublin, Ireland, we hear the flow of their inner thoughts and associations, in addition to their public conversation. Not surprisingly, their thoughts are less inhibited, more concerned overtly with sex, than is their outer behavior.

The novel was published in Paris in 1922, having already caused a considerable stir there. A decade later, the novel was imported into the United States, where the distributor was charged with disseminating obscene materials. The ensuing trial was enlivened, as were subsequent trials of other supposedly obscene materials, by expert testimony from literary critics, who were called upon to give their professional judgment as to the intention of the author. Although the justices made no reference to classical philosophy in their official opinions, it is obvious that they had in mind exactly the same sorts of considerations that exercised Plato and Aristotle, among others.

What is the proper role, or function, of art? Does a work of art injure us or improve us when it provokes strong sexual or aggressive feelings? Should art be judged by its effects on us? Ought there to be one standard for literary works written with "elevated" artistic intentions and a different standard for works written purely to arouse? Does it matter, indeed, what the author's intention was, or should we attend only to the effect of the work on its readers? All of these traditional issues in the philosophy of art, and others besides, were raised by the justices in the case.

The *Ulysses* case was tried more than sixty years ago, during the Great Depression. You might think that with everything that has happened since—World War II, television, X-rated movies, the sixties, drugs, rock-and-roll—these issues would be long dead. Not so! Some years ago, an exhibit of photographs by the gay artist Robert Mapplethorpe caused an enormous stir and led members of Congress to place restrictions on the support provided by the National Endowment for the Arts to painters, sculptors, poets, and other artists. Our last two brief selections bring you up-to-date with a pro and con opinion on this episode in the twenty-four-hundred-year-old debate about art and the state.

❧ ❧ ❧ ❧ ❧ ❧ ❧ ❧ ❧ ❧ ❧ ❧ ❧

THE ULYSSES CASE OPINIONS

Judge Woolsey: I have read "Ulysses" once in its entirety and I have read those passages of which the Government particularly complains several times. In fact, for many weeks, my spare time has been devoted to the consideration of the decision which my duty would require me to make in this matter.

"Ulysses" is not an easy book to read or to understand. But there has been much written about it, and in order properly to approach the consideration of it, it is advisable to read a number of other books which have now become its satellites. The study of "Ulysses" is, therefore, a heavy task.

The reputation of "Ulysses" in the literary world, however, warranted my taking such time as was necessary to enable me to satisfy myself as to the intent with which the book was written, for, of course, in any case where a book is claimed to be obscene it must first be deter-

mined, whether the intent with which it was written was what is called, according to the usual phrase, pornographic—that is, written for the purpose of exploiting obscenity.

If the conclusion is that the book is pornographic that is the end of the inquiry and forfeiture must follow.

But in "Ulysses," in spite of its unusual frankness, I do not detect anywhere the leer of the sensualist. I hold, therefore, that it is not pornographic.

In writing "Ulysses," Joyce sought to make a serious experiment in a new, if not wholly novel, literary genre. He takes persons of the lower middle class living in Dublin in 1904 and seeks not only to describe what they did on a certain day early in June of that year as they went about the City bent on their usual occupations, but also to tell what many of them thought about the while.

Joyce has attempted—it seems to me, with astonishing success—to show how the screen of consciousness with its ever-shifting kaleidoscopic impressions carries, as it were on a plastic palimpsest, not only what is in the focus of each man's observation of the actual things about him, but also in a penumbral zone residua of past impressions, some recent and some drawn up by association from the domain of the subconscious. He shows how each of these impressions affects the life and behavior of the character which he is describing.

What he seeks to get is not unlike the result of a double or, if that is possible, a multiple exposure on a cinema film which would give a clear foreground with a background visible but somewhat blurred and out of focus in varying degrees.

To convey by words an effect which obviously lends itself more appropriately to a graphic technique, accounts, it seems to me, for much of the obscurity which meets a reader of "Ulysses." And it also explains another aspect of the book, which I have further to consider, namely, Joyce's sincerity and his honest effort to show exactly how the minds of his characters operate.

If Joyce did not attempt to be honest in developing the technique which he has adopted in "Ulysses" the result would be psychologically misleading and thus unfaithful to his chosen technique. Such an attitude would be artistically inexcusable.

It is because Joyce has been loyal to his technique and has not funked its necessary implications, but has honestly attempted to tell fully what his characters think about, that he has been the subject of so many attacks and that his purpose has been so often misunderstood and misrepresented. For his attempt sincerely and honestly to realize his objective has required him incidentally to use certain words which are generally considered dirty words and has led at times to what many think is a too poignant preoccupation with sex in the thoughts of his characters.

The words which are criticized as dirty are old Saxon words known to almost all men and, I venture, to many women, and are such words as would be naturally and habitually used, I believe, by the types of folk whose life, physical and mental, Joyce is seeking to describe. In respect of the recurrent emergence of the theme of sex in the minds of his characters, it must always be remembered that his locale was Celtic and his season Spring.

Whether or not one enjoys such a technique as Joyce uses is a matter of taste on which disagreement or argument is futile, but to subject that technique to the standards of some other technique seems to me to be little short of absurd.

Accordingly, I hold that "Ulysses" is a sincere and honest book and I think that the criticisms of it are entirely disposed of by its rationale.

Furthermore, "Ulysses" is an amazing *tour de force* when one considers the success which has been in the main achieved with such a difficult objective as Joyce set for himself. As I have stated, "Ulysses" is not an easy book to read. It is brilliant and dull, intelligible and obscure by turns. In many places it seems to me to be disgusting, but although it contains, as I have mentioned above, many words usually considered dirty, I have not found anything that I consider to be dirt for dirt's sake. Each word of the book contributes like a bit of mosaic to the detail of the picture which Joyce is seeking to construct for his readers.

If one does not wish to associate with such folk as Joyce describes, that is one's own choice. In order to avoid indirect contact with them one may not wish to read "Ulysses"; that is quite understandable. But when such a real artist in words, as Joyce undoubtedly is, seeks to draw a true picture of the lower middle class in a European city, ought it to be impossible for the American public legally to see that picture?

To answer this question it is not sufficient merely to find, as I have found above, that Joyce did not write "Ulysses" with what is commonly called pornographic intent. I must endeavor to apply a more objective standard to his book in order to determine its effect in the result, irrespective of the intent with which it was written.

The statute under which the libel is filed only denounces, in so far as we are here concerned, the importation into the United States from any foreign country of "any obscene book." . . . It does not marshal against books the spectrum of condemnatory adjectives found, commonly, in laws dealing with matters of this kind. I am, therefore, only required to determine whether "Ulysses" is obscene within the legal definition of that word.

The meaning of the word "obscene" as legally defined by the Courts is: tending to stir the sex impulses or to lead to sexually impure and lustful thoughts. . . .

Whether a particular book would tend to excite such impulses and thoughts must be tested by the Court's opinion as to its effect on a person with average sex instincts—what the French would call *l'homme moyen sensuel*—who plays, in this branch of legal inquiry, the same role of hypothetical reagent as does the "reasonable man" in the law of torts and "the man learned in the art" on questions of invention in patent law.

The risk involved in the use of such a reagent arises from the inherent tendency of the trier of facts, however fair he may intend to be, to make his reagent too much subservient to his own idiosyncrasies. Here, I have attempted to avoid this, if possible, and to make my reagent herein more objective than he might otherwise be, by adopting the following course:

After I had made my decision in regard to the aspect of "Ulysses," now under consideration, I checked my impressions with two friends of mine who in my opinion answered to the above stated requirement for my reagent.

These literary assessors—as I might properly describe them—were called on separately, and neither knew that I was consulting the other. They are men whose opinion on literature and on life I value most highly. They had both read "Ulysses," and, of course, were wholly unconnected with this cause.

Without letting either of my assessors know what my decision was, I gave to each of them the legal definition of obscene and asked each whether in his opinion "Ulysses" was obscene within that definition.

I was interested to find that they both agreed with my opinion: that reading "Ulysses" in its entirety, as a book must be read on such a test as this, did not tend to excite sexual impulses or lustful thoughts but that its net effect on them was only that of a "somewhat tragic and very powerful commentary on the inner lives of men and women. . . .

Judge Manton: I dissent. . . . Who can doubt the obscenity of this book after a reading of the pages referred to, which are too indecent to add as a footnote to this opinion? Its characterization as obscene should be quite unanimous by all who read it. . . .

Ulysses is a work of fiction. It may not be compared with books involving medical subjects or description of certain physical or biological facts. It is written for alleged amusement of the reader only. The characters described in the thoughts of the author may in some instances be true, but, be it truthful or otherwise, a book that is obscene is not rendered less so by the statement of truthful fact . . . nor can that case be taken to mean that the book is to be judged as a whole. If anything, the case clearly recognizes that the statute forbade it to be carried in the mails. Congress did not intend that the question as to the character of the paper should depend upon the opinion or belief of the person who, with knowledge or notice of its contents, assumed the responsibility of putting it in the mails of the United States. The evils that Congress sought to remedy would continue and increase in volume if the belief of the accused as to what was obscene, lewd, and lascivious were recognized as the test for determining whether the statute has been violated. Every one who uses the mails of the United States for carrying papers or publications must take notice of what, in this enlightened age, is meant by decency, purity, and chastity in social life, and what must be deemed obscene, lewd, and lascivious.

Congress passed this statute against obscenity for the protection of the great mass of our people; the unusual literator can, or thinks he can, protect himself. The people do not exist for the sake of literature, to give the author fame, the publisher wealth, and the book a market. On the contrary, literature exists for the sake of the people, to refresh the weary, to console the sad, to hearten the dull and downcast, to increase man's interest in the world, his joy of living, and his sympathy in all sorts and conditions of men. Art for art's sake is heartless and soon grows artless; art for the public market is not art at all, but commerce; art for the people's service is a noble, vital, and permanent element of human life.

The public is content with the standard of salability; the prigs with the standard of preciosity. The people need and deserve a moral standard: it should be a point of honor with men of letters to maintain it. Masterpieces have never been produced by men given to obscenity or lustful thoughts—men who have no Master. Reverence for good work is the foundation of literary character. A refusal to imitate obscenity or to load a book with it is an author's professional chastity.

Good work in literature has its permanent mark: it is like all good work, noble and lasting. It requires a human aim—to cheer, console, purify, or ennoble the life of people. Without this aim, literature has never sent an arrow close to the mark. It is by good work only that men of letters can justify their right to a place in the world.

Under the authoritative decisions and considering the substance involved in this appeal, it is my opinion that the decree should be reversed.

Source: *From U.S. District Court opinion,* One Book Called Ulysses, *rendered December 6, 1933, in the Southern District of New York.*

౩ ౩ ౩ ౩ ౩ ౩ ౩ ౩ ౩ ౩ ౩ ౩ ౩

Now let us turn to two contemporary thinkers who take up the debate over pornography in a deliberately philosophical manner. We begin with an attack on censorship by the late poet, novelist, social critic, and philosopher Paul Goodman. Goodman was trained at the University of Chicago in the philosophy of Plato and Aristotle, a fact that shows in everything he subsequently wrote. Goodman faces the issue of pornography head on, by challenging the usually unexamined assumption that it is harmful to arouse powerful sexual passions. He also points out, quite rightly, that there is something absurd and insulting in saying both that Joyce was a great writer and that he did not intend to arouse the feelings that his novel so obviously and successfully arouses! Such a defense is a little like defending a great magician by saying that he didn't mean to fool us.

౩ ౩ ౩ ౩ ౩ ౩ ౩ ౩ ౩ ౩ ౩ ౩ ౩

PORNOGRAPHY, ART, AND CENSORSHIP
Paul Goodman

Present thinking about obscenity and pornography is wrongheaded and damaging. In order to protect vital liberties, the higher, more intellectual courts often stand out against the police, the post-masters, and popular prejudice; yet since they don't give the right reasons, the issues are never settled. And worse, the courts lend themselves to the sexual attitude which, at this moment in our history, creates the very "hardcore" pornography that is objected to. That is, the court corrupts, it helps the censors corrupt. It ought to give light and provide leadership, and instead it stands in the way of progress. And worst of all, finally, by misunderstanding the nature of art and speech, the court emasculates them and prevents them from playing their indispensable social role. . . .

Judge Woolsey's method in clearing *Ulysses* is as follows: he defines the obscene as the pornographic, as "tending to stir the sex impulses or to lead to sexually impure and lustful thoughts," and he proceeds to show that the book does neither but "is a sincere and serious attempt to devise a new literary method for the observation and description of mankind." Let us postpone the literary criticism till the next section, but here stop short at the definition of obscenity.

The notion that sexual impulse or stirring sexual impulse is a bad thing comes from an emotional climate in which it was generally agreed that it would be better if sexuality did not overtly exist, when people bathed and slept fully clothed, and a bull was called a hecow. Then anything which was sexual in public, as by publication of "detailed representation in words or pictures," violated society's self-image and was certainly obscene. In our times such a notion cannot define obscenity. The pornographic is not *ipso facto* the obscene. As Judge Jerome Frank pointed out in 1949, "No sane man thinks that the arousing of normal sexual desires is socially dangerous." We live in a culture where all High Thought insists on the beauty and indeed hygienic indispensability of sexual desires, and where a vast part of commerce is busy in their stimulation. . . .

Let me proceed to a philosophical question raised by these decisions, which is, in my opinion, even more important for our society than the sexual matter: what is the nature of speech and art? To protect their "serious" books, the courts attempt to distinguish speech as communication of an idea or even as talking *about* a subject, from speech as an action doing something to its speaker, subject, and hearer. This is the tactic of Woolsey when he devotes most of his opinion to Joyce's "new method for the observation and description of mankind". . . .

Woolsey's doctrine is insulting to the artist. He says that the book did "not tend to excite lustful thoughts, *but* the net effect was a tragic and powerful commentary" (italics mine). Surely the author wants to say, "It is lustful among other things, and *therefore* its net effect is tragic."

In our culture an artist is expected to move the reader; he is supposed to move him to tears, to laughter, to indignation, to compassion, even to hatred; but he may not move him to have an erection or to mockery of public figures making a spectacle of themselves. Why not? By these restrictions we doom ourselves to a passionless and conformist community. Instead of bracketing off the "classics," as especially the British courts do—indeed, the legal definition of a classic seems to be a "nonactionable obscenity"—let us pay attention to the classical pornography and we shall see that it is not the case, as the court feels obliged to prove, that a work has a "net" social use despite its sexual effect, but rather that the pornography, in a great context and spoken by a great soul, *is* the social use. Aristophanic comedy was still close to a seasonal ritual to encourage rebelliousness and lead to procreation. Rabelais is disgraceful like a giant baby, and this *is* the Renaissance. Catullus teaches us the callous innocence of highborn youth, free of timidity and pettiness; and Tom Jones is a similar type, with a dash of English sentimentality. If we may believe their preludes, both the *Arabian Nights* and the *Decameron* are cries of life in the face of death; and in our times Jean Genet, one of our few fine writers, is pornographic and psychopathic because only so, he tells us, can he feel that he exists in our inhuman world. But apart from these lofty uses, there are also famous pornographic books made just for fun, since sex is a jolly subject.

Source: *Paul Goodman, selections from "Pornography, Art, and Censorship," from* Commentary *(March 1961). Copyright © 1961 by Paul Goodman. Reprinted from* Utopian Essays and Practical Proposals, *by Paul Goodman, by permission of Random House, Inc.*

᭟᭟᭟᭟᭟᭟᭟᭟᭟᭟᭟᭟᭟᭟

For a while, the anticensorship side of the debate had the good publicity. Very few people want to defend censorship of political, religious, or moral opinions, and it is difficult to say exactly when a novel, a play, or a movie ceases to be "political" and becomes simply a commercial exploitation of sex and violence. In our next selection, however, we encounter a serious, thoughtful defense of censorship from a thinker who, like Plato, takes the moral health of the body politic as the highest good. The key to Walter Berns's defense of censorship is his provocative question, "What if, contrary to what is now so generally assumed, shame is natural to man . . . ?" In other words, What if it is natural to be aroused by sex and violence, *and equally natural to feel the moral emotion of shame for being aroused?* What if the primary role of society is not to release our natural impulses, but to restrain them, not to make us shameless but to strengthen, direct, and use our shame for humanly good purposes! In that case, it will be no defense of pornographic books that we all have a "natural" desire to read them. Quite to the contrary, that fact will simply make it all the clearer that society must help us to control that ugly side of our souls.

I have deliberately given the procensorship side of the debate the lion's share of space here because I suspect that your sympathies will lie with Paul Goodman. As John Stuart Mill pointed out, there is much to be gained from forcing ourselves to face arguments that contradict our own opinions.

᭟᭟᭟᭟᭟᭟᭟᭟᭟᭟᭟᭟᭟

PORNOGRAPHY VS. DEMOCRACY: THE CASE FOR CENSORSHIP
Walter Berns

The case against censorship is very old and very familiar. Almost anyone can formulate it without difficulty. One has merely to set the venerable Milton's *Areopagitica* in modern prose, using modern spelling, punctuation, and examples. This is essentially what the civil libertarians did in their successful struggle, during the past century, with the censors. The unenlightened holder of the bishop's imprimatur, Milton's "unleasur'd licencer" who has never known "the labour of book-writing," became the ignorant policeman or the bigoted school board member who is offended by "Mrs. Warren's Profession," or the benighted librarian who refuses to shelf *The Scarlet Letter,* or the insensitive customs official who seizes *Ulysses* in the name of an outrageous law, or the Comstockian vigilante who glues together the pages of every copy of *A Farewell to Arms* she can find in the bookstore. The industrious learned Milton, insulted by being asked to "appear in Print like a punie with his guardian and his censors hand on the back of his title to be his bayle and surety," was replaced by Shaw, Hawthorne, Joyce, or Hemingway, and those who followed in their wake, all victims of the mean-spirited and narrow minded officials who were appointed, or in some cases took it upon themselves, to judge what others should read, or at least not read. The presumed advantage of truth when it grapples with falsehood became the inevitable victory of "enduring ideas" in the free competition of the market. With these updated versions of old and familiar arguments, the civil libertarians have prevailed.

They prevailed partly because of the absurdity of some of their opposition, and also because of a difficulty inherent in the task their opponents set for themselves. The censors would proscribe the obscene, and even assuming, as our law did, that obscene speech is no part of the speech protected by the First Amendment to the Constitution, it is not easy to formulate a rule of law that distinguishes the nonobscene from the obscene. Is it the presence of four-letter words? But many a literary masterpiece contains four-letter words. Detailed descriptions of sexual acts? James Joyce provides these. Words tending to corrupt those into whose hands they are likely to fall? But who is to say what corrupts or, for that matter, whether anything corrupts or, again, what is meant by corruption? Is it an appeal to a "prurient interest" or is it a work that is "patently offensive"? If that is what is meant by the obscene, many a "socially important work," many a book, play, or film with "redeeming social value," would be lost to us. The college professors said so, and if college professors do not know the socially important, who does? Be that as it may, they succeeded in convincing the Supreme Court, and the result was the complete rout of the "forces of reaction." To the college professors, therefore, as well as to the "courageous" publishers and the "public-spirited" attorneys who had selflessly fought the cases through the courts, a debt of gratitude is owed by the lovers of Shaw, Hawthorne, Joyce and Hemingway—and others too numerous to detail here. In the same spirit one might say that never has there been such a flourishing of the arts in this country. . . .

Just as it is no simple task to formulate a rule of law that distinguishes the nonobscene from the obscene, it is still more difficult to distinguish the obscene from the work of genuine literary merit. In fact, it is impossible—and our failure to understand this may be said to be a condition, if not a cause, of our present situation. Our laws proscribe obscenity as such and by name, and we are unwilling to admit that great literary and dramatic works can be, and frequently are, obscene. In combination these two facts explain how it came about that we now have, with the sanction of the law, what is probably the most vulgar theatre and literature in history. The paradox is readily explained. The various statutes making up the law have made obscenity a criminal thing, and our judges assume that if a work of art is really a work of art, and not vulgar rubbish, it cannot be obscene. Thus, Judge Woolsey, in his celebrated opinion in the *Ulysses* case, recounts how he had asked two literary friends whether the book was obscene within the legal definition, which he had explained to them, and how they had both agreed with him that it was not. But of course *Ulysses* is obscene. Not so obscene as an undoubted masterpiece, Aristophanes' "Assembly of Women," for example, which would not be a masterpiece—which would not be anything—were its obscenity removed, but obscene nevertheless.

The trouble stems from the fact that the Tarrif Act of 1930 would exclude "obscene" books from the country, and Judge Woolsey, being a sensible man, did not want this to happen to *Ulysses*. So he fashioned a rule to protect it. But the same rule of law protects *The Tropic of Cancer,* because according to the rule's necessarily clumsy categories, the latter is no more obscene than the former, however it compares on another scale and whatever the aesthetic distances separating its author, Henry Miller, and James Joyce as writers. Eventually, and for the same reason, the protection of the law was extended to *Trim, MANual,* and *Grecian Guild Pictorial,* the homosexual magazines involved in a case before the Supreme Court in 1962, and then to *Fanny Hill.* . . .

Underlying this unfortunate development is the familiar liberal idea of progress. Rather than attempt to inhibit artists and scientists, the good polity will grant them complete freedom of expression and of inquiry, and will benefit collectively by so doing. What is good for the arts and sciences is good for the polity: this proposition has gone largely unquestioned among us for 200 years now. The case for censorship rests on its denial, and can be made only by separately examining its parts. What is good for the arts and sciences? What is good for the polity? The case for censorship arises initially out of a consideration of the second question.

The case for censorship is at least as old as the case against it, and, contrary to what is usually thought today, has been made under decent and even democratic auspices by intelligent men. To the extent to which it is known today, however, it is thought to be pernicious or, at best, irrelevant to the enlightened conditions of the twentieth century. It begins from the premise that the laws cannot remain indifferent to the manner in which men amuse themselves, or to the kinds of amusement offered them. . . .

We turn to the arts—to literature, films, and the theatre, as well as to the graphic arts . . . for the pleasure to be derived from them, and pleasure has the capacity to form our tastes and thereby to affect our lives. It helps determine the kind of men we become, and helps shape the lives of those with whom and among whom we live. So one can properly ask: Is it politically uninteresting whether men derive pleasure from performing their duties as citizens, fathers, and husbands or, on the other hand, from watching their laws and customs and institutions being ridiculed on the stage? Whether the passions are excited by, and the affections drawn to, what is noble or what is base? Whether the relations between men and women are depicted in terms of an eroticism wholly divorced from love and calculated to destroy the capacity for love and the institutions, such as the family, that depend on love? Whether a dramatist uses pleasure to attach men to what is beautiful or to what is ugly? We may not be accustomed to thinking of these things in this manner, but it is not strange that so much of the obscenity from which so many of us derive our pleasure today has an avowed political purpose. It would seem that the pornographers know intuitively what liberals have forgotten, namely, that there is indeed a "causal relationship . . . between word or pictures and human behavior." At least they are not waiting for behavioral science to discover this fact.

The purpose is sometimes directly political and sometimes political in the sense that it will have political consequences intended or not. This latter purpose is to make us shameless, and it seems to be succeeding with astonishing speed. Activities that were once confined to the private scene—to the "ob-scene," to make an etymological assumption—are now presented for our delectation and emulation in center stage. Nothing that is appropriate to one place is inappropriate to any other place. No act, we are to infer, no human possibility, no possible physical combination or connection, is shameful. . . . Nothing prevents a dog from enjoying sexual intercourse in the marketplace, and it is unnatural to deprive men of the same pleasure, either actively or as voyeurs in the theatre. Shame itself is unnatural, a convention devised by hypocrites to inhibit the pleasures of the body. We must get rid of our "hang-ups."

The Importance of Shame

But what if, contrary to what is now so generally assumed, shame is natural to man, in the sense of being an original feature of human existence? What if it is shamelessness that is unnatural, in the sense of having to be acquired? What if the beauty that men are capable of knowing and achieving in their living with each other derives from the fact that man is naturally a "blushing creature," the only creature capable of blushing? . . .

To speak in a manner that is more obviously political, there is a connection between self-restraint and shame, and therefore a connection between shame and self-government or democracy. There is, therefore, a political danger in promoting shamelessness and the fullest self-expression or indulgence. To live together requires rules and a governing of the passions, and those who are without shame will be unruly and unrulable; having lost the ability to restrain themselves by observing the rules they collectively give themselves, they will have to be ruled by others. Tyranny is the natural and inevitable mode of government for the shameless and self-indulgent who have carried liberty beyond any restraint, natural and conventional.

Such, indeed, was the argument made by political philosophers prior to the twentieth century, when it was generally understood that democracy, more than any other form of government, required self-restraint, which it would inculcate through moral education and impose on itself through laws, including laws governing the manner of public amusements. It was the tyrant who could usually allow the people to indulge themselves. Indulgence of the sort we are now witnessing did not threaten his rule, because his rule did not depend on a citizenry of good character. Anyone can be ruled by a tyrant, and the more debased his subjects the safer his rule. A case can be made for complete freedom of the arts among such people, whose pleasures are derived from activities divorced from their labors and any duties associated with citizenship.

One who undertakes to defend censorship in the name of the arts is obliged to acknowledge that he has not exhausted his subject when he has completed that defense. What is missing is a defense of obscenity. What is missing is a defense of the obscenity employed by the greatest of our poets—Aristophanes and Chaucer, Shakespeare and Swift—because it is impossible to believe, it is unreasonable to believe, that what they did is indefensible; and what they did, among other things, was to write a good deal of obscenity. Unfortunately, it would require a talent I do not possess to give a sufficient account of it.

They employed it mainly in comedy, but their purpose was not simply to make us laugh. Comedy, according to Aristotle, makes us laugh at what is ludicrous in ugliness, and its purpose is to teach, just as tragedy teaches by making us cry before what is destructive in nobility. The latter imitates what is higher, the former what is lower, but they are equally serious; Aristotle discussed both, and Shakespeare, for example, was a comic as well as a tragic poet.

Those aspects of his soul that make man truly human and distinguish him from all other beings—higher or lower in the natural order of things—require political life. And no great poet ever denied this. Man's very virtues, as well as their counterparts, his vices, require him to be governed and to govern; they initiate demands that can be met only in political life—but the poet knows with Rousseau that the demands of human virtue cannot be fully met in political life because they transcend political life. The poet knows the beauty of that order beyond the polity; he reminds us that there is an order outside the conventional and that we are part of that natural order, as well as of the conventional. Shakespeare knows with Rousseau that there is a tension between this natural order and the conventional or legal order, and his purpose is to resolve it, at least for some men, at the highest possible level. These men must first be shown that this world of convention is not the only world, and here is where obscenity may play a part—that beyond Venice there is Portia's Belmont, the utopia where the problems that plague Venice do not exist. Obscenity can be used to ridicule the conventional. But it is used in the name of the natural, that order outside the conventional according to which the conventional may be criticized and perhaps, if only to an extent, reformed. Obscenity in the hands of such a poet can serve to *elevate* men, elevate them, the few of them, above the conventional order in which all of us are forced to live our mundane lives. Its purpose is to teach what is truly beautiful—not what convention holds to be beautiful—and to do so by means of pleasure, for obscenity can be pleasurable.

How to express in a rule of law this distinction between the justified and the unjustified employment of obscenity is no simple task. That I have admitted and willingly concede. I have also argued that it cannot be done at all on the premise from which our law has proceeded. I have, finally, tried to indicate the consequences of a failure to maintain the distinction in the law: not only will we no longer be able to teach the distinction between the proper and the improper, but we will no longer be able to teach—and will therefore come to forget—the distinction between art and trash. Stated otherwise, censorship, because it inhibits self-indulgence and supports the ideal of propriety and impropriety, protects political democracy; paradoxically, when it faces the problem of the justified and unjustified use of obscenity, censorship also serves to maintain the distinction between art and trash and, therefore, to protect art and, thereby, to enhance the quality of this democracy. We forgot this. We began with a proper distrust of the capacities of juries and judges to make sound judgments in an area that lies outside their professional competence; but led by the Supreme Court we went on improperly to conclude that the judgments should not be made because they cannot be made, that there is nothing for anyone to judge. No doubt the law used to err on occasion; but democracy can live without "Mrs. Warren's Profession," if it must, as well as without *Fanny Hill*—or to speak more precisely, it can live with the error that consigns "Mrs. Warren's Profession" to under-the-counter custom along with *Fanny Hill*. It remains to be seen whether the true friend of democracy will want to live in the world without under-the-counter custom, the world that does not know the difference between "Mrs. Warren's Profession" and *Fanny Hill*.

Source: *Walter Berns, "Pornography vs. Democracy: The Case for Censorship,"* The Public Interest *(Winter 1971). Reprinted by permission of the author and the Public Affairs Conference Center, Kenyon College.*

☙ ☙ ☙ ☙ ☙ ☙ ☙ ☙ ☙ ☙ ☙ ☙ ☙

Finally, here are two brief comments on the Mapplethorpe debate: one by Meg Greenfield, writing on the "liberal" side for *Newsweek*, and the other by William F. Buckley, writing on the "conservative" side in the magazine he founded, *The National Review*. You might be interested to learn that the director of a Cincinnati art gallery in which the exhibit appeared was acquitted of all charges at a trial held after these two comments were published.

☙ ☙ ☙ ☙ ☙ ☙ ☙ ☙ ☙ ☙ ☙ ☙ ☙

SUMMER STORM
Meg Greenfield

The summer's much debated exhibit of Robert Mapplethorpe's photographs—some beautiful, some revolting—drew huge crowds at a private gallery in Washington, having earlier been expelled from the august Corcoran Gallery. This predictable surge of interest and popularity showed that *all* the parts in the classic drama among artist, patron and public were in good working order. As is mandated by tradition, the artists were raising hell about repression, the patron—government in this case—was raising hell about the artists, and the public was thronging in unprecedented numbers to avail itself of the denounced works of art.

What may be distinctive to our time and culture is the earnestness of the argument over whether the Mapplethorpe photographs and other current offending works are in fact art. Sometimes, in our age of scienceism gone mad, it seems as if people believe that a panel of experts, such as those who decide on government grants to painters and so forth, have some pure scientific method of determining whether the object before them qualifies as art. These panels' deliberations are made to sound like laboratory findings soon to be disclosed in the *New England Journal of Medicine*. In this they are as close as we get to those European "academies" once so famous for their ruthlessness as arbiters of suitable artistic expression.

In our day the need for certification of this kind is probably made more acute by the anarchy of our total artistic product and the consequent inability of socially ambitious would-be collectors to know whether or not they should buy the blob before them and, equally important, whether or not for future tax purposes it will be considered the real thing. But it is not the distinctiveness of our time that interests me. Rather it is the traditional, familiar, commonplace nature of the tensions now being argued over as if they had never existed before. At the heart of the controversy is the relationship of artist and patron, especially if the patron is the state.

We are supersensitive, as we should be, to the perils of state intrusion into the artist's choice of subject, style, message. And we are very suspicious of artists overtly engaged in the glorification of the state or the promotion of its political interests. There is good reason for this too. In the centuries before art became so generally detached from public sponsorship and public purposes, the state was more likely to inspire transcendent works—I will enter the Aeneid, a hymn to the Emperor Augustus and a fancied-up propaganda-type history of Rome as Exhibit A. But as often as not in our time, when art has long since gone its private way, the result of state intervention is something foolish or hideous or oppressive—or, in rare cases, all three, like the infamous architecture of the Ital-

ian Fascists and the "socialist realism" of the Soviet state.

It is a curious fact that although the American government ultimately does much more to influence art in this country through its educational, tax and construction policies than through its direct-grant endowment programs, it is the latter programs that draw the fire. This is surely because the transaction of artist and official is so much more clearly delineated here. And though these transactions between artist and official is so smoothly for the most part, as we have seen this summer, the calm on both sides is about a quarter of an inch deep and conceals—barely—a latent, at-the-ready mutual hysteria.

Thus some in the art world seem to be making wild demands for license to do whatever they want on taxpayer subsidy and characterizing all resistance to this as police-state brutality. And some in Congress, notably Sen. Jesse Helms, are proposing a truly absurd and repressive denial of funds from federal art programs to anything much more controversial than Little Bo-peep. It seems obvious to me that the Helms effort should be resoundingly defeated. And my guess is that if it is, everyone will retract his horns a little and stop going out of his way to challenge the other side. But the socially defiant nature of our contemporary art will not change, and neither will the socially conservative nature of most of the people who go into government, and, above all, neither will the inherently unhappy relationship between artist and patron.

Patron and Genius

In the famous 1775 preface to his Dictionary, Samuel Johnson let his ungenerous patron, the Earl of Chesterfield, have it: "Seven years, my Lord, have now passed, since I waited in your outward rooms, or was repulsed from your door; during which time I have been pushing on my work through difficulties . . . and have brought it at last to the verge of publication, without one act of assistance, one word of encouragement, or one smile of favor." It's all there: the resentment, the contempt, the humiliation of one who knows himself to be the intellectual superior of a patron from whom he has to beg favors and who has a more exalted place in the society than he.

Sometimes there is a sickly exchange of obsequiousness—the patron buttering up a genius whose work he doesn't really understand, the genius buttering up the moneybags for whom he has disdain. The romantic painter and poet William Blake spent several years in the pay of a dilettante named William Hayley, who himself wrote horrible poems with names like "The Grateful Snake," and who, when he wasn't flattering Blake, was trying to bend him away from his vast, unconventional talent. "I am determin'd to be no longer Pester'd with his Genteel

Ignorance & Polite Disapprobation," Blake wrote to a friend. But soon enough we find Blake addressing the abominated Hayley this way: "You, Dear Sir, are one who has my Particular Gratitude, having conducted me thro' Three that would have been the Darkest Years that ever Mortal Suffer'd . . ."

Who can be happy or even rational in these circumstances? You are trapped in dependence on one you think a fool, if you are the artist; you are condescended to and defied by one who only feigns gratitude to you for gifts given, if you are the patron, and unceremoniously told to butt out. Why *should* the course of this untrue love run smooth? I think we should all get together and work to defeat Senator Helms's awful legislation—and then sit back and relax until, as it surely will, it happens again.

Source: *Meg Greenfield, "Summer Storm,"* Newsweek, *September 4, 1989.*

ఉఉఉఉఉఉఉఉఉఉఉఉ

SHUTTERBUGGERY
William F. Buckley

The Mapplethorpe uproar roars on, even though the controversial photo exhibit, which includes plenty of explicit perversity, has been removed from its scheduled site to a small gallery under purely private auspices. The predictable cries of censorship are ringing off the Capitol walls, and everyone from George Will to *The Village Voice* has been sneering at the philistinism of Jesse Helms for introducing a measure to deny federal funding to filthy art.

The funny thing is, Helms is right. The monster from North Carolina seems to be the only public figure who truly appreciates Robert Mapplethorpe's art. It has fallen to him to point out not only that the Emperor is wearing no clothes but that he is performing unnatural acts. To say

this is not to disparage Mapplethorpe's art but to specify it.

That Mapplethorpe (who died of *AIDS* in March) was wondrously gifted is undeniable. His arresting portraits of clothed people and his subtly gorgeous still-lifes would have made his reputation, if not as many headlines, without benefit of sodomy.

But it was intrinsic to Mapplethorpe's art to try to aestheticize the obscene. He deliberately chose subjects that shock the normal sense of decency and displayed them for the sake of their abstract form. He counted on and exploited the dual reaction to create tension in the viewer: what is indecent and immoral becomes stunningly beautiful. And, thus, especially disturbing.

But to pretend the obscenity isn't *there*—that it exists only in the dirty mind of Jesse Helms— is as false to the pictures as to deny their beauty.

Some of the acts Mapplethorpe photographs would cause comment at a hairdressers' convention. Which is simply to say, we have a right to be shocked when someone tries to shock us.

But is it art? Yes, yes, it's art, maybe great art—and so what? Great artistry may be used immorally, just as a saintly artist may produce banality. There is no strict correlation between the moral and the aesthetic, and there is no need for morality to grovel before the claims of Art. Anyone who wants to subsidize a Mapplethorpe is free to do so. The public should be free not to.

Source: *William F. Buckley, "Shutterbuggery,"* National Review, *September 1, 1989.*

Questions for Discussion and Review

1. There is overwhelming evidence that art, in some form or other, occurs in every human society, however technologically primitive or advanced. In short, art is *natural* to human beings. Does that, by itself, prove that art is a good thing? Might something that is natural and universal nevertheless be a bad thing, something to be repressed or stamped out?

2. It is easy enough to see in what sense a realistic painting is a representation, or image, or mere appearance, of the object it pictures. But what representational relation, if any, does music bear to the world? We are accustomed to separating out some artistic activities as belonging to what are called the *fine* arts. That distinction, however, only dates back to the fifteenth and sixteenth centuries. Is there any important difference between ballet, opera, classical music, poetry, sculpture, and painting on the one hand, and fairy tales, folk songs, rock music, macramé, basket weaving, and leather work on the other?

3. One of the principal charges against pornography is that its sole purpose is to arouse prurient desires in its readers or viewers. In defense of the civil rights of pornographers, some people respond that pornography has a political or social purpose. But what is wrong with arousing prurient desires?

4. Most pornography in American society portrays women in degrading fashion, and that fact has led many feminists to argue that pornography violates the rights of women and should be banned. Now, pornography, almost without exception, is bad art, whatever else it is. But suppose we are confronted with a great work of art that is also morally objectionable, because of its representation of women, or Jews, or the Irish, or working people, or because of its attack on religion, or on democracy. Should our *moral* objections take precedence over our *aesthetic* judgments?

5. If Marcuse is correct, art performs a valuable social function precisely by being negative, offensive, a reproach to decent people. If that is true, then don't we destroy art's positive function by *tolerating* it?

SØREN KIERKEGAARD

Søren Kierkegaard (1813–1855) was the founder and most brilliant spokesman of the style of philosophizing known as "existentialism." His life was devoted to an unending inward reflection on human existence and the terror and uncertainty which each of us experiences in the face of his or her own death. Kierkegaard was deeply religious, though he rejected what he felt to be the superficial, self-satisfied Lutheranism of his native Denmark. In a series of books, some on philosophical topics, others more directly religious in their focus, he redefined the nature of faith, making it radically subjective and totally alien to the processes of ordinary systematic reason. Kierkegaard was a witty, brilliantly provocative writer. His works abound in complex ironies which are challenges to the reader. He seems always to seek to unsettle his readers, to put us off balance and thereby force us to examine our lives as Kierkegaard had examined his own. One of his many literary devices to achieve this was the practice of publishing his books under pseudonyms. The Philosophical Fragments, *for example, was published with its author listed as "Johannes Climacus." Farther down on the page, there appeared the statement, "Responsible for publication: S. Kierkegaard." By this and other devices, Kierkegaard hoped to block any attempt by his readers to classify his position and pigeonhole him, for Kierkegaard was convinced that such techniques of systematic professional philosophy were merely ways of defusing a book and making it safe.*

As he himself pessimistically predicted, Kierkegaard has fallen into the hands of professors and systematizers, and even his challenge to established philosophy has itself come to be treated merely as one more philosophy, namely, existentialism. Kierkegaard would have laughed, or perhaps he would have wept, to see his struggle with death and eternity reduced to an "ism."

C H A P T E R

Philosophy of Religion

- ✦ Kierkegaard's Encounter with Faith

- ✦ Can We Prove That God Exists?

- ✦ William Paley: The Argument from Design

- ✦ St. Thomas Aquinas: The Cosmological Argument

- ✦ St. Anselm: The Ontological Argument

- ✦ The Problem of Evil

- ✦ *Contemporary Application: Creationism vs. Evolution*

Kierkegaard's Encounter with Faith

Søren Kierkegaard was born in 1813 to a father fifty-six and a mother forty-four. His early life and education were very closely supervised by his father, who demanded both a scholarly mastery of classical languages and a highly charged imaginative appreciation of the literature his young son read. The young Søren had laid upon him the full weight of the guilt which extreme Pietist Protestantism so often inflicted upon its communicants. Although Kant and Kierkegaard thus had roughly the same sort of religious upbringing, Kierkegaard completely lacked Kant's quiet inner confidence and peace. He reacted first against the torment of his religious training by plunging himself into a life of physical self-indulgence, eating, drinking, dressing the dandy. But these distractions could not free him from the black gloom which hung over him, and he decided finally to return to his studies and become a pastor.

The dramatic turning point in Kierkegaard's private life was his engagement, and then the breaking of it, to seventeen-year-old Regine Olson. Kierkegaard wrote endlessly of his feelings for Regine, of the philosophical significance of marriage, love, and the problems of such a life commitment, but one cannot help thinking that she was more important to him as a subject for meditation than as a real, live woman. After pouring out a series of essays and books on aesthetic, moral, and religious topics, Kierkegaard died at the relatively early age of forty-two.

Kierkegaard's inner emotional life, his lifelong struggle with religious faith, and his reaction to the dominant Hegelian philosophy of his day are all so intimately intertwined that it is very difficult to speak of any one without immediately bringing in all three. There is hardly space in an introductory text of this sort to explore the subject fully, but a few systematic remarks may be helpful to you. I especially want you to develop an interest in Kierkegaard because, in my opinion, he is, after the immortal Plato, the most gifted artist among all the important philosophers who have come down to us in the Western tradition. If you pick up one of his books, many of which are easily available in paperback editions, you will find him profound, troubling, witty, touching, and in the end deeply rewarding.

The passionate center of Kierkegaard's thought and life is his confrontation with the ever-present terror of existential dread—the obsessive, unavoidable fact of my own impending death, the infinity of the universe, and the meaninglessness of my own brief life in comparison. Every man, woman, and child faces these terrible, fundamental facts of the human condition. We may deny them, flee from them, repress them, distract ourselves to escape from them, but always they are there, at the edge of consciousness, waiting to return in the darkness of night. The first lesson Kierkegaard teaches us, both in his books and by his life, is that this dread of death and meaninglessness must be faced, confronted, not shoved aside again and again. If I may speak personally—and the greatest honor we can pay to Kierkegaard is precisely to be honest, each one of us, about our own encounter with the fear of death—I first came face to face with this dread as a teenager. I was obsessed with fears of death, and the more I thrust them from my mind, the more intensely they returned. In my case, the fear was not of pain, or age, or sickness, but simply of nonbeing. The more I turned the thought over in my mind, the closer my own eventual death seemed to come, until finally I would seize any distraction to divert my attention from what was, and of course still is, an unavoidable fate.

For Kierkegaard, the dread of death was both heightened and complicated by the hope of eternal life which the religion of his fathers held out to him. All of you have heard the expression, "Trust in the Lord." But how many of you have actually asked yourselves what it means to "trust in the Lord"? What does it mean to "believe in" God, to have faith in Him?

Well, what it *doesn't* mean is believing *that* God exists! In our increasingly nonreligious society, when a person says that she "believes in God," we automatically assume that she means that she believes there is such a thing as God. But in the Judeo-Christian religious tradition, particularly in the extremely individualistic Protestant sort of Christianity that was Kierkegaard's heritage, the phrase "belief in God" has quite a different meaning. To believe in God, to trust in Him, to have faith in Him, means to believe that He will keep His promise to humanity; it is to have faith that He will keep the pact, or covenant, that He made with the beings He created. That pact is testified to first in what we call the Old Testament, and then again in a renewed form in the New Testament.

The promise, of course, is the promise of salvation, of a life after death, of true happiness, of fruitfulness, of a union of the soul with God. (Needless to say, long books could be written on the various interpretations that Jews, Christians, and Muslims have placed upon this notion of a covenant with God. The version I am summarizing here is something like what Kierkegaard would have learned and brooded upon.) According to the Old Testament, God made a promise to Noah, and He repeated it to Abraham. He renewed it again and again, despite the failure of the Hebrews to keep His Law and follow His commands. Finally, God embodied that Law (or Word or Logos) in the Person of Jesus Christ, in order that His offer of salvation might be made once more. With the birth, suffering, and death of Jesus, God sealed His free gift of eternal life. As the price of that blessedness, He asked only faith, an unstinting, unconditioned, unqualified belief by us that He would keep His promise of this free gift.

Other Christian traditions had emphasized the role of right behavior, or "good works," either as part of the price of salvation or else as worldly evidence of one's true belief. But the Pietist strain of Protestantism placed a very heavy emphasis upon the pure possession of that unconditioned faith in God.

Abraham and Isaac, with the Angel. A drawing, by the great seven-teenth-century Dutch artist Rembrandt, of Abraham preparing to sacri-fice his only son, Isaac, at God's command. In one of his most power-ful books, *Fear and Trembling,* Kierkegaard interpreted the story of Abraham and Isaac as an evidence of Abraham's perfect faith in the Lord. (Undated engravings. Corbis–Bettmann.)

So it was that for Kierkegaard, the central religious problem quite naturally became the problem of faith.

You might think, on first reflection, that the Christian message would be a very welcome message indeed! After all, life is short, bedeviled by suffering, terminated by the absolute finality of unavoidable death. It was good enough news to be told, in the Old Testament, that God would grant life everlasting to those who kept His commandments. But we are weak, imperfect creatures, and it soon became clear that doing God's bidding was a task too hard for us, even with the promise of salvation to lead us on. He took upon Himself, in the Person of His Son, the atonement for *our* sins, and offered to us the price-

> ⌢ **Faith** In Christianity, trust that God will keep the promise He made to the Israelites in the Old Testament and renewed to all mankind in the New Testament (hence, "trust in the Lord"). Originally, the promise was to make the Israelites fruitful and populous. In the New Testament, the promise is of life eternal in heaven. According to some Christians, men and women are unable to have and sustain this trust without the miraculous help of God.

less pearl of salvation for the merest asking. All we needed to do was believe that we would receive it. What could possibly be better news than that? Small wonder that this message was called the Gospel, which means "good news." Small wonder too that those who spread the message were called evangelists, which means "bringers of good news."

But strange to tell, the glad tidings of God's free gift have brought fear, dread, doubt, torment, and tortured self-examination to countless hearers, among them Søren Kierkegaard. The gift is so great, the price so small—and yet, the price of faith must be paid freely, unhesitatingly, without doubts or second thoughts. Therein lie the seeds of terror. Do I truly believe? Is my faith pure? Can I trust in the Lord, or is there lurking deep within my heart a doubt that so great a gift will be conferred on so undeserving a creature as myself? Out of this inner hell Kierkegaard tore the writings by which we remember him. His doubts and fears concerned his very *existence* as an individual, mortal creature longing to believe in God's promise, not the abstract, impersonal logical relationships among disembodied forms, or "essences." Hence, Kierkegaard's way of thinking has come to be called existentialist. Indeed, Kierkegaard is universally acknowledged to be the first true existentialist philosopher. Whether he would have appreciated such a categorization and sterilization of his inner torment is of course not so clear.

In his lifelong struggle with the problem of faith, Kierkegaard did battle with three enemies, against whom he turned not only his considerable philosophical and theological gifts, but also a brilliant, convoluted, ironic wit. The first of his enemies was the established Christianity of his own day, the solid, comfortable, Sunday-sermon Lutheranism of nineteenth-century Denmark. Like so many passionate prophets before him, Kierkegaard accused the established church of mouthing empty formulae which were neither lived nor understood. Sin, redemption, damnation, salvation—all were the subjects of elegant sermons and pious attitudes which did not for a moment interfere with the secular, weekday activities of this world. Kierkegaard once observed that just as it is hard to jump up in the air and land exactly on the spot from which one began, so too it is hard to become a Christian when one has been born a Christian. He meant that those who were born into Christianity, who were baptized, confirmed, and raised in the official emptiness of its dogmas

> **Existentialism** The philosophical doctrine, associated originally with Søren Kierkegaard, according to which our being as subjective individuals (our *existence*) is more important than what we have in common objectively with all other human beings (our *essence*). Of primary concern for Kierkegaard was his relationship to God. Later existentialists emphasized the individual's creation of himself or herself through free individual choices.

and rituals, might actually find it more difficult to take the message of Christianity seriously than would a pagan to whom the divine promise came as wonderful, terrible, astonishing news. Kierkegaard devoted many of his books to a sustained effort to breathe new existential significance into the familiar phrases and concepts of Christian theology.

His second enemy was the complacent middle-class culture of his society, the "bourgeois" culture of solid tradesmen and lawyers—sound, self-confident people who disdained anyone so odd, so passionate, so disruptive as Kierkegaard. The word "bourgeois" has drifted into our vocabulary these days as a catch-all term for what we in America call "middle-class" life, but in nineteenth-century Europe, it had a much richer, more resonant set of associations. Historically, a "bourgeois," or a "burgher," was simply a resident of a "bourg" or "burg," which in the late Middle Ages was a walled city. By extension, the word came to mean a member of the urban merchant class, and also a "freeman" or citizen of one of the cities whose charter came from the king rather than from the feudal aristocracy. The burghers of the European cities were men of substance, solid citizens, true to their word in business deals, extremely conservative in their family relationships, jealous of their rights as city leaders, forward-looking in commerce, and quite often supporters of a strong monarchy against the ancient and dispersed powers of the landed aristocracy. For the burghers of Copenhagen, religion was first of all a matter of propriety, of respectability, and only then a matter of conscience or salvation. One dressed in one's finest clothes on Sunday and went with one's family to church; one sat in a front pew, purchased at great expense, where one was seen by one's neighbors. One listened piously to the sermon, which, though heavy on damnation, was conveniently light on social responsibility, and then one returned to one's substantial townhouse for a good Sunday dinner.

As you can imagine, the unthinking religiosity, the self-satisfied complacency of the solid citizens of Denmark made Kierkegaard furious. Many of his most spectacular literary tricks and devices, and particularly his extremely heavy irony, are aimed at puncturing that complacency and somehow reaching the real human beings behind those masks.

The final enemy was the official philosophy of Kierkegaard's day, the vast, pompous, elaborate philosophical systems constructed by the disciples

A nineteenth-century bourgeois gentleman and lady friend as the painter Toulouse-Lautrec saw them. "The Englishmen at the Moulin Rouge," Toulouse–Lautrec, Henry Raymond de French (1864–1901). Oil on cardboard. H. 33³/₄ W. 26 in. Signed (lower left): T–Lautrec. (Courtesy of The Metropolitan Museum of Art, Bequest of Miss Adelaide Milton de Groot (1876–1967), 1967.)

and followers of the great German philosopher Georg Hegel. The Hegelian philosophy, as it was expounded by the professors of Europe, put itself forward as the objective, impersonal, purely rational, totally systematic, absolutely final truth about just about everything. It was turgid, jargon-filled, and completely self-confident. It claimed to wrap up space, time, eternity, being, history, man, the state, and God in one vast metaphysical synthesis that simultaneously answered all our questions about the universe and also—rather conveniently—demonstrated the superiority of precisely the social and religious system then dominant in European society.

In short, Kierkegaard's three enemies were really one and the same enemy in different disguises. The Christianity of his day was bourgeois Christianity, buttressed and justified by the official philosophical system. The burghers were Establishment Christians, who—though they knew precious little philosophy—were justified and rationalized by that same philosophy. And the philosophy, though it claimed to be the purest product of reason, was a thoroughgoing justification of the reign of the burghers and the ascendency of their religion.

Karl Marx, facing this very same union of religion, philosophy, and the ascendent bourgeoisie, turned his attack on the social and economic consequences, for Marx was a secular man, concerned with this-worldly issues of justice, poverty, and work. Kierkegaard, before all else a man of God, attacked the same union of forces on its religious front. He cared nothing at all for worldly happiness or misery. Rather, he brushed all secular considerations aside and instead demanded that the good Christians of Denmark begin to pay to eternal life as much attention as they regularly gave to a daily profit.

Kierkegaard's onslaught was complex and subtle and, hence, is impossible to summarize in a few paragraphs. Two ideas lie at the heart of his religio-philosophical message, and we can at least take a first step toward understanding them. These notions are the inwardness, or subjectivity, of truth, and the irrational, unarguable "leap of faith." Now, that sounds more like a Hegelian mouthful than a bit of biting wit, so let us take a look at each.

"You seem troubled, Brother Timothy. Is anything worrying you? I mean, besides the sins of the world, the vanities of mankind, and that sort of thing."
(Cartoon by Stevenson, © 1960 The New Yorker Magazine, Inc.)

The Hegelian philosophers put their doctrines forward as *rational* and *objective*. They were, in a way, like today's scientists. All of you have noticed, I imagine, that there is a very big difference in the teaching style and approach of science professors as compared with professors of literature or philosophy. In a literature class, you are encouraged to express your own "interpretation" of Dickens or Mailer or Shakespeare. In a philosophy class —I hope!—you are prompted to think out your own position, to develop your own arguments, and to defend whatever point of view you think closest to the truth. But nobody teaches calculus or physics that way! Can you imagine a physics quiz with questions like "Write a ten-minute essay on your impressions of Boyle's law" or "Take a position for or against relativity and defend it—in your answer, make reference to the text." Hardly! Scientists quite confidently assume that their knowledge is objective, and that what they teach is a matter neither of "opinion" nor of personality. In the same way, the Hegelian philosophers represented themselves as objective, rational discoverers of the truth. Their private fears, hopes, terrors, and joys were no more a part of their philosophy, they thought, than would a modern biochemist's neuroses be a part of her theory of DNA. To be sure, readers might be curious, in a gossipy way, about the personal lives of the great philosophers, just as we today like to read stories about Albert Einstein. But no one would suppose for a moment that there was any important scientific connection between those delightful or depressing glimpses into the scientist's private life and the scientific truth of his theories.

In a total reversal of the received philosophical-scientific opinion of his day, Kierkegaard argued that Truth is Subjectivity. In other words, he denied the objective impersonality of truth and insisted, instead, that all truth must be inward, dependent upon the subject, particular rather than universal, personal rather than interpersonal or impersonal.

When Kierkegaard says that Truth is Subjectivity, he is denying the ancient philosophical doctrine that the truth of an idea or a statement consists in its conformity to an independent object. When I say, "That is a very good picture of Jim," I mean that the picture looks like Jim, that it resembles, or copies, or conforms to the objective nature of Jim's body. When I say, "It is true that Sacramento is the capital of California," I mean that the real world—California, in this case—actually has the characteristics that my statement says it has. In other words, truth is conformity to the objective state of things in the world. Or, Truth is Objectivity. If this familiar conception of truth is correct, then the truth of a statement or belief depends only on the relationship between the statement or belief and the world, *not* on the relationship between the statement or belief and the person who thinks it. If Truth is Objectivity, then it doesn't matter, so far as truth is concerned, whether I believe Sacramento to be the capital of California passionately, calmly, tentatively, with all my heart, or simply because a friend told me so.

Kierkegaard doesn't care about the capitals of states or nations, of course. He cares about salvation, the Christian message. And when it comes to salvation, *how* you believe is as important as *what* you believe, he thought. The Hegelian system builders wanted to treat the Christian message as though it were merely one subpart of their grand structure of objective knowledge. So "Jesus died for my sins" would be treated by them as more or less on a par with "Space is three dimensional and homogeneous." Each statement would be true if it corresponded correctly to the objective state of things, false otherwise. But that treatment of the promise of salvation as "objective" is precisely wrong, Kierkegaard insisted. Truth does not consist in the proper relationship between the belief and the *object;* rather, it consists in the proper relationship between the belief and the *subject,* the individual human being who holds that belief. *How* he or she holds it is the criterion of its truth. In order for the belief to be true, it must be held passionately, unconditionally, absolutely without inner reservation or doubt.

But—and here we come to the second of Kierkegaard's great ideas, the "leap of faith." That belief in God's promise of eternal life can have no rational justification, no evidence, no proof. Theologians since the time of Aristotle have sought to *prove* the existence of God, to prove the truth of this or that religious doctrine. Sometimes they used evidence of their senses—what they could see, hear, and touch. At other times, they erected abstract arguments of pure logic, deducing the absolute, objective truth of Christianity (or Islam, or Judaism). But Kierkegaard believed that all such attempts at rational justification are doomed to total failure. The absolute gap between finite man and infinite God makes any rational bridge building between the two on man's part futile. God may reach down to man, though how He can manage that is beyond our comprehension. But man can no more reason his way into the presence of God than a mathematician, by doggedly adding unit to unit, can calculate his way to infinity.

Because reason is inadequate to the task of supporting our belief in God's promise, Kierkegaard said, our only hope is an absolutely unconditional leap of faith. I must take the plunge and say, with all my heart, *Credo*—I believe.

Can't we perhaps look for a little bit of support from reason? Mightn't reason at least show that God's promise is probable? That the weight of the evidence inclines us toward God's promise? That a reasonable person could tend to believe God's promise?

Not a bit of it! That is just what a solid, smug merchant or a pompous, self-important professor would say. Can't you just imagine the two of them sitting in front of the fire, the burgher after a long day at the counting house, the professor after a day of serious, important lectures. The burgher leans back in his comfortable chair, puffs a bit on his pipe (one wouldn't want to speak too quickly on such matters—it might show a lack of seriousness), and then asks, "Is it your opinion that the weight of the evidence, objectively and impartially considered, inclines us to the view that God has promised us eternal life rather than eternal death?" The professor takes a sip of beer, strokes his beard thoughtfully, and answers, "Well, on the one hand, Hegel, in the *Phenomenology of Mind,* seems to suggest that God does make such a promise; but on the other hand, Kant, in the *Critique of Pure Reason,* argues that we cannot know with certainty that such a promise has been made. In the light of recent research which I understand has been reported in the latest issue of the Berlin *Journal of Metaphysics,* I would judge professionally that the answer is a qualified yes."

Both the subjectivity of truth and the leap of faith are central to the writings of Kierkegaard. The *Concluding Unscientific Postscript to the Philosophical Fragments* is Kierkegaard's major systematic exposition of his philosophical theology. The title, in typical Kierkegaardian fashion, is an elaborate joke. The *Philosophical Fragments* is short—not quite one hundred pages. The *Postscript,* on the other hand, runs to more than five hundred pages. By calling his most important work a mere "postscript" to the *Fragments,* a lengthy p.s. to a short letter, so to speak, Kierkegaard was laughing at the self-important philosophers of his day. The word "unscientific," of course, is another dig at the Hegelian systematizers, who called everything they did "scientific."

The *Philosophical Fragments* deals with the contrast between secular truth and religious truth, between the objective and the subjective, between reason and faith, between wisdom and salvation. Kierkegaard imagines all these contrasts as gathered together into the person of Socrates, who is the greatest of all teachers, and Jesus, who is not a teacher in the rational sense, but the Saviour. Kierkegaard's argument goes like this (yes indeed, Kierkegaard uses arguments to show us that arguments cannot be used in matters of faith! I leave it to you to determine whether there is a contradiction in his mode of procedure): Secular knowledge of morality is something that can be learned through rational self-reflection. Teachers like Socrates help us to bring our moral knowledge to consciousness by probing questions that force us to justify our beliefs. But since in some sense this moral knowledge already lies within each of us, a teacher—even so great a teacher as Socrates—is merely helpful; if we had to, we could get along without one. As philosophers say, a teacher is "accidental" rather than "essential." But salvation is a matter of the fate of my soul. It is a matter of my *existence,* not merely of my state of knowledge. And salvation is not something I can acquire on my own if I am forced to do so. Salvation requires that God reach down and lift me up to His Kingdom. Somehow, the gulf between myself and God must be crossed. Thus salvation is totally different from the acquisition of wisdom, for there is no gulf to be crossed on the road to wisdom. I need only look carefully and critically enough inside myself.

Jesus is God's instrument for bridging the gulf between Himself and myself. Jesus is the Saviour. And since salvation concerns my *existence,* the actual, historical reality of Jesus is all-important. You see, it doesn't really matter to me whether Socrates ever actually lived. Once I have learned from Plato's Dialogues how to engage in Socratic questioning, it would make no difference if I were to discover that the Dialogues were a hoax and that there never had been any Socrates. But if God never actually became Man in the form of Jesus Christ, if Christ never died for my sins, then I am damned rather than saved. The mere Idea of the Saviour isn't enough. I need to be absolutely certain that God did actually become Man, that He really died for my sins, that God did renew His free gift to me through His only begotten Son.

But just because I need so desperately to know that Jesus really lived, I am hopelessly at a loss for evidence or argument sufficient to my need. Can I rest comfortably in the belief that I have been promised eternal life, when the evidence for my belief is merely probable, merely the sort of evidence that an historian or a philosopher can produce? No, too much is at stake: Salvation is everything; it is eternity of life rather than death. I am reduced by my terror and my need to infinite concern for something that defies rational grounding. In short, I am reduced to an absolute *leap of faith.*

When Kierkegaard tells us that we must make a *leap of faith,* he is not at all suggesting that such a leap is frivolous, or random, or something that just pops into my head. Quite to the contrary, Kierkegaard believes that we must prepare for this leap, as a ballet dancer might prepare during half a lifetime for an exquisite leap on stage. We must turn our backs on all the solid, substantial, everyday pleasures and concerns that tie most men and women, leaden, to the ground and make it impossible for them to take the leap of faith. We must cultivate a special relationship to life, to the universe, to God, in order even to attempt the leap. Thus, the leap is not *irrational* in the sense of being silly or mindless. But it *is* an act that cannot be grounded in argument, proof, or step-by-step justification. There is no such thing, Kierkegaard thinks, as having a little bit of faith.

In the following passage from the *Concluding Unscientific Postscript,* Kierkegaard tries to help us to understand what is involved in *faith.* The text, which comes from a section entitled "The Subjective Thinker," focuses on the contrast between the sort of relationship I could have to some other human being, such as Socrates, and my unique relationship to the divine Saviour, Jesus.

SØREN KIERKEGAARD, *Concluding Unscientific Postscript to the Philosophical Fragments*

Faith and One's Relationship to Others and to God
The mode of apprehension of the truth is precisely the truth. It is therefore untrue to answer a question in a medium in which the question cannot arise. So for example, to explain reality within the medium of the possible, or to distinguish between possibility and reality within possibility. By refraining from raising the question of reality from the aesthetic or intellectual point of view, but asking this question only ethically, and here again only in the interest of one's own reality, each individual will be isolated and compelled to exist

for himself. Irony and hypocrisy as opposite forms, but both expressing the contradiction that the internal is not the external, irony by
seeming to be bad, hypocrisy by seeming to be good, emphasize the
principle anent the contemplative inquiry concerning ethical inwardness, that reality and deceit are equally possible, and that deceit can
clothe itself in the same appearance as reality. It is unethical even to
ask at all about another person's ethical inwardness, in so far as such
inquiry constitutes a diversion of attention. But if the question is
asked nevertheless, the difficulty remains that I can lay hold of the
other's reality only by conceiving it, and hence by translating it into
a possibility; and in this sphere the possibility of a deception is
equally conceivable. This is profitable preliminary training for an ethical mode of existence: to learn that the individual stands alone.

It is a misunderstanding to be concerned about reality from the
aesthetic or intellectual point of view. And to be concerned ethically
about another's reality is also a misunderstanding, since the only
question of reality that is ethically pertinent, is the question of one's
own reality. Here we may clearly note the difference that exists
between faith *sensu strictissimo* on the one hand (referring as it does
to the historical, and the realms of the aesthetic, the intellectual) and
the ethical on the other. To ask with infinite interest about a reality
which is not one's own, is faith, and this constitutes a paradoxical
relationship to the paradoxical. Aesthetically it is impossible to raise
such a question except in thoughtlessness, since possibility is aesthetically higher than reality. Nor is it possible to raise such a question
ethically, since the sole ethical interest is the interest in one's own
reality. The analogy between faith and the ethical is found in the infinite interest, which suffices to distinguish the believer absolutely from
an aesthetician or a thinker. But the believer differs from the ethicist
in being infinitely interested in the reality of another (in the fact, for
example, that God has existed in time). . . .

Precisely in the degree to which I understand a thinker I become
indifferent to his reality; that is, to his existence as a particular individual, to his having really understood this or that so and so, to his
actually having realized his teaching, and so forth. Aesthetic and
speculative thought is quite justified in insisting on this point, and it
is important not to lose sight of it. But this does not suffice for a
defense of pure thought as a medium of communication between
man and man. Because the reality of the teacher is properly indifferent to me as his pupil, and my reality conversely to him, it does not
by any means follow that the teacher is justified in being indifferent
to his own reality. His communication should bear the stamp of this
consciousness, but not directly, since the ethical reality of an individual is not directly communicable (such a direct relationship is exem-
plified in the paradoxical relation of a believer to the object of his

faith), and cannot be understood immediately, but must be understood indirectly through indirect signs.

When the different spheres are not decisively distinguished from one another, confusion reigns everywhere. When people are curious about a thinker's reality and find it interesting to know something about it, and so forth, this interest is intellectually reprehensible. The maximum of attainment in the sphere of the intellectual is to become altogether indifferent to the thinker's reality. But by being thus muddle-headed in the intellectual sphere, one acquires a certain resemblance to a believer. A believer is one who is infinitely interested in another's reality. This is a decisive criterion for faith, and the interest in question is not just a little curiosity, but an absolute dependence upon faith's object.

The object of faith is the reality of another, and the relationship is one of infinite interest. The object of faith is not a doctrine, for then the relationship would be intellectual, and it would be of importance not to botch it, but to realize the maximum intellectual relationship. The object of faith is not a teacher with a doctrine; for when a teacher has a doctrine, the doctrine is *eo ipso* more important than the teacher, and the relationship is again intellectual, and it again becomes important not to botch it, but to realize the maximum intellectual relationship. The object of faith is the reality of the teacher, that the teacher really exists. The answer of faith is therefore unconditionally yes or no. For it does not concern a doctrine, as to whether the doctrine is true or not; it is the answer to a question concerning a fact: "Do you or do you not suppose that he has really existed?" And the answer, it must be noted, is with infinite passion. In the case of a human being, it is thoughtlessness to lay so great and infinite a stress on the question whether he has existed or not. If the object of faith is a human being, therefore, the whole proposal is the vagary of a stupid person, who had not even understood the spirit of the intellectual and the aesthetic. The object of faith is hence the reality of the God-man in the sense of his existence. But existence involves first and foremost particularity, and this is why thought must abstract from existence, because the particular cannot be thought, but only the universal. The object of faith is thus God's reality in existence as a particular individual, the fact that God has existed as an individual human being.

Christianity is no doctrine concerning the unity of the divine and the human, or concerning the identity of subject and object; nor is it any other of the logical transcriptions of Christianity. If Christianity were a doctrine, the relationship to it would not be one of faith, for only an intellectual type of relationship can correspond to a doctrine. Christianity is therefore not a doctrine, but the fact that God has existed.

The realm of faith is thus not a class for numskulls in the sphere of the intellectual, or an asylum for the feeble-minded. Faith constitutes a sphere all by itself, and every misunderstanding of Christianity may at once be recognized by its transforming it into a doctrine, transferring it to the sphere of the intellectual. The maximum of attainment within the sphere of the intellectual, namely, to realize an entire indifference as to the reality of the teacher, is in the sphere of faith at the opposite end of the scale. The maximum of attainment within the sphere of faith is to become infinitely interested in the reality of the teacher.

Can We Prove That God Exists?

When students are introduced to the study of philosophy, one of the standard moves is to go through what are usually referred to as the "proofs of the existence of God." This is a set of arguments, developed over the past 2,000 years by many different philosophers, which purport to demonstrate that there is, or exists, an infinite, omnipotent, omniscient, benevolent creator of the universe who goes by the name of God. When I teach an introduction to philosophy, I try to slip the proofs for the existence of God in just before Christmas in the fall semester, and just before Easter in the spring semester. It seems fitting, somehow.

Is anyone ever convinced by the proofs? Well you may ask! I have, from time to time, started off my presentation of them by asking how many members of the class believe in God. I mean by that, of course, how many believe that there is a God, not how many believe that He will keep His promise of eternal life. Anyway, I count the hands, and then I present one of the proofs. Usually, I try out what is called the Cosmological Argument, and sometimes I go right into the real number one proof, which is called the Ontological Argument. (We'll get to these in a minute. Don't despair!) After running through the proof, I ask whether there are any objections or criticisms. Usually there aren't any (how many students are going to tell their professor that they think he is crazy?). Then I ask for another show of hands on those who believe in God. Now, it is the most peculiar thing, but even though no one ever objects to my proofs or raises any doubts, not a single person is ever converted to the faith by them! I don't think I have convinced a single, solitary nonbeliever in all the years I have been proving the existence of God. Next I run through the standard refutations for the proofs. (In philosophy, there is an argument against just about everything that there is an argument for.) Same result. I never make agnostics out of the believers, any more than I have made believers out of the agnostics.

When you stop and think about it, there is really something wonderful and mad about a finite, mortal man or woman undertaking to *prove* that God exists. It is as though the philosopher rears up on her hind legs and says, "God! You may be out there, You may exist, but unless You fit into my syllogisms, unless You follow from premises, unless You are a theorem in my system, I won't acknowledge Your existence!" When it comes to sheer effrontery, to what the Greeks called *hubris* and the Jews call *chutzpah*, there just isn't anything to match it.

Philosophers have never been known for their humility, and a fair number of great ones have had a shot at proving the existence of God. Aristotle tried it, and so did St. Thomas Aquinas. Occam had a proof, Descartes had several, Spinoza came up with some, and even William James, the American pragmatist, offered his own rather odd version of reasons for believing in the existence of God. In this section, we are going to take a close look at the three most famous proofs. These aren't all the proofs, by any means, but they will give you a good idea of some of the different tactics that philosophers have used over the ages. The three proofs are called the *Argument from Design,* the *Cosmological Proof,* and the *Ontological Proof.* We will examine the version of the Argument from Design offered by the eighteenth-century English philosopher William Paley; the Cosmological Argument as it was set forth by the great medieval theologian St. Thomas Aquinas; and the Ontological Argument in its original version as stated by the man who thought it up, the eleventh-century logician St. Anselm. Since David Hume and Immanuel Kant are the two best proof-for-existence-of-God-refuters who have ever lived, we will look at their refutations together with the proofs. Here we go. Don't be surprised if you hear Kierkegaard laughing at us along the way!

William Paley: The Argument from Design

Our first proof for the existence of God is at once the most obvious, the most natural, the most ancient, the most persuasive, the easiest to understand, and—alas—the philosophically weakest! The **Argument from Design** is quite simple. We observe that certain man-made objects exhibit an internal purposive organization, a fitting of parts to the function of the whole. In a watch, to take the example that Paley himself uses, the various springs and pins and hands are all made precisely to serve the purpose of keeping and telling time. This rational, purposive order in the watch is the direct result of the conscious, rational, pur-

---

 Argument from Design   The attempt to prove the existence of God by demonstrating the high degree of organization and purposive order in the universe, and arguing that such design must be the product of an intelligent, powerful, purposeful creator. The argument is very old but had a wide popularity in the eighteenth century.

WILLIAM PALEY

William Paley (1743–1805) was an English church-man whose writings in defense of Christianity were widely read and much admired in the eighteenth and nineteenth centuries. Paley was a defender of utilitarianism in moral philosophy and of the truths of revelation in theology (a position known as *theism*). His book *Natural Theology* was a systematic presentation of the so-called Argument from Design for the existence of God, an argument which David Hume had vigorously attacked in his *Dialogues Concerning Natural Religion.*

posive activity of its creator, the watchmaker. From the character of the watch, we naturally infer the existence of a watchmaker, whether we actually know him or not. If you show me a watch (or a chair or a painting or even a simple stone axe) and say, "It is so old that no one can remember who made it," I would never dream of saying, "Perhaps no one made it." The intelligence of its creation inheres in its internal organization. The watch is, if you will permit a bad pun, intelligently produced on the face of it. Well, Paley argues (and so have countless other theologians and philosophers over the ages), nature is more wonderfully organized than the most subtle human contrivance. The human eye far exceeds a camera in sensitivity and fidelity of reproduction; the human brain cannot be duplicated by the most sophisticated computer; the merest one-celled microscopic organism exhibits a biochemical complexity and adaptation that taxes the analytic powers of all science. Who can doubt for a moment that nature has its Creator, an intelligent, purposeful, all-powerful Maker, who in His infinite wisdom has adjusted means to end, part to whole, organ to organism, throughout the whole of space and time?

The technical name for this is an *argument from analogy.* You have probably encountered ratios or proportions in high school math—problems like: "Eight is to four as six is to *x*. Solve for *x*." When I was in school, the way to state that mathematically was either like this: 8:4::6:*x*, or else like this: 8/4 = 6/*x*. The solution, of course is *x* = 3. The same sort of "analogy" turns up in aptitude tests. "Fire engine is to fire department as _____ is to police department." The answer is "police car." The point is that if we already know the relationship between one pair of things (such as the numbers 8 and 4, or a fire engine and the fire department), then when we are presented with only one member of another pair, we may be able to figure out what the other member of the pair is (3 in the math example, or a police car in the other case). Now all this may seem like baby talk to you, but philosophers frequently build powerful arguments from what look like very simple pieces.

Paley and the other arguers from design draw up two sorts of analogies. The first is between an artificially constructed object and its human maker, on the one hand, and a particular organism or bit of natural organization and its divine Creator, on the other. So we get

Watch is to watchmaker as the human eye is to *x*.   *x* = God.

The other analogy is between an artificially constructed object and its human maker, on the one hand, and the whole universe and its divine Creator, on the other. So this time we get

Watch is to watchmaker as the universe is to *x*.   *x* = God.

Here is Paley's own statement of the argument. Because he tends to be rather wordy, I have edited it down to the bare bones.

WILLIAM
PALEY,
Natural Theology

In crossing a heath, suppose I pitched my foot against a *stone,* and were asked how the stone came to be there, I might possibly answer, that for any thing I knew to the contrary it had lain there for ever, nor would it, perhaps, be very easy to show the absurdity of this answer. But suppose I had found a *watch* upon the ground, and it should be inquired how the watch happened to be in that place, I should hardly think of the answer which I had before given, that for any thing I knew the watch might have always been there. Yet why should not this answer serve for the watch as well as for the stone; why is it not as admissible in the second case as in the first? For this reason, and for no other, namely, that when we come to inspect the watch, we perceive—what we could not discover in the stone—that its several parts are framed and put together for a purpose, e.g. that they are so formed and adjusted as to produce motion, and that motion so regulated as to point out the hour of the day; that if the different parts had been differently shaped from what they are, or placed after any other manner or in any other order than that in which they are placed, either no motion at all would have been carried on in the machine, or none which would have answered the use that is now served by it. . . .

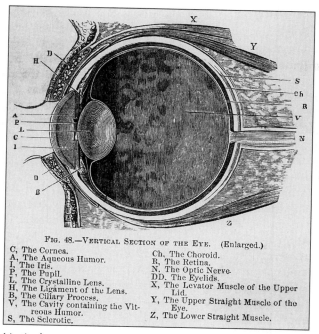

FIG. 48.—VERTICAL SECTION OF THE EYE. (Enlarged.)

C, The Cornea.
A, The Aqueous Humor.
I, The Iris.
P, The Pupil.
L, The Crystalline Lens.
H, The Ligament of the Lens.
B, The Ciliary Process.
V, The Cavity containing the Vit-
reous Humor.
S, The Sclerotic.

Ch, The Choroid.
R, The Retina.
N, The Optic Nerve.
DD, The Eyelids.
X, The Levator Muscle of the Upper
Lid.
Y, The Upper Straight Muscle of the
Eye.
Z, The Lower Straight Muscle.

Vertical cross-section of the eye. Undated illustration. The complexity of the human eye, the exact fitting of its structure to the purpose of sight, was viewed by many scientifically minded theologians as evidence of the existence and benevolence of God. (Corbis–Bettmann.)

This mechanism being observed—it requires indeed an examination of the instrument, and perhaps some previous knowledge of the subject, to perceive and understand it; but being once, as we have said, observed and understood, the inference we think is inevitable, that the watch must have had a maker—that there must have existed, at some time and at some place or other, an artificer or artificers who formed it for the purpose which, we find it actually to answer, who comprehended its construction and designed its use. . . .

Were there no example in the world of contrivance except that of the eye, it would be alone sufficient to support the conclusion which we draw from it, as to the necessity of an intelligent Creator. It could never be got rid of, because it could not be accounted for by any other supposition which did not contradict all the principles we possess of knowledge—the principles according to which things do, as often as they can be brought to the test of experience, turn out to be true or false. . . .

If other parts of nature were inaccessible to our inquiries, or even if other parts of nature presented nothing to our examination but disorder and confusion, the validity of this example would remain the same. If there were but one watch in the world, it would not be less certain that it had a maker. If we had never in our lives seen any but one single kind of hydraulic machine, yet if of that one kind we understood the mechanism and use, we should be as perfectly assured that it proceeded from the hand and thought and skill of a workman, as if we visited a museum of the arts, and saw collected there twenty different kinds of machines for drawing water, or a thousand different kinds for other purposes. Of this point each machine is a proof independently of all the rest. So it is with the evidences of a divine agency. The proof is not a conclusion which lies at the end of a chain of reasoning, of which chain each instance of contrivance is only a link, and of which, if one link fail, the whole falls; but it is an argument separately supplied by every separate example. An error in stating an example affects only that example. The argument is cumulative, in the fullest sense of that term. The eye proves it without the ear, the ear without the eye. The proof in each example is complete, for when the design of the part, and the conduciveness of its structure to that design is shown, the mind may set itself at rest; no future consideration can detract any thing from the force of the example.

This argument has an antique sound, of course. It was written almost 200 years ago, after all. But the principle underlying it is one we use today in interplanetary exploration. When astronauts first walked on the moon, they looked of course for evidences of intelligent life, though they didn't really expect to find such evidences on an atmosphereless body. Now how on earth (or elsewhere) could they possibly tell what would be evidence of intelligent life? Having no advance knowledge of the sorts of creatures that might inhabit other parts of the universe, by what signs could the astronauts infer their existence and presence? The answer is obvious. Any sort of device, or instrument, or machine that exhibited some purposive internal organization, and that seemed not to grow naturally in that environment, would permit them to infer by analogy the existence of some (presumably) nonhuman intelligent maker.

Anyone who has been enraptured, bemused, or awestruck by the wonder of nature will appreciate the psychological force of the Argument from Design. Can the order of planets, stars, and galaxies, the underlying simplicity and regularity of natural forces, the exquisitely delicate adjustment of part to part in living things really just *be*? Must there not be some intelligence directing, organizing, creating this vast interconnected universe?

Well, maybe so, but the Argument from Design won't prove it! There are basically two things wrong with the Argument from Design. First, even if it is correct, it doesn't prove what Paley and most other Christian, Jewish, or Muslim theologians want it to prove. And, second, it doesn't really prove

Proofs for the Existence of God

Argument from design

Premise: The purposive organization of man-made objects is evidence of the intelligence and purpose of the maker.

Premise: The world contains many natural objects (animals, plants, the human eye, and so on) whose organization is clearly purposive and the world itself is purposively organized.

Conclusion: By analogy, there must exist a maker of the universe who has made it according to a plan. That world-maker, or Creator, is God.

Cosmological argument

Premise: We know, by the evidence of our senses, that in the world some things are moved.

Premise: Everything that is moved must be caused to move by something else.

Argument: If each thing that moves is in turn moved by something that itself moves, which in its turn requires a cause of motion that itself moves, then there will nowhere be a first mover, and hence no motion at all. But there is motion.

Conclusion: Hence, there must be a first mover that is not itself moved. That first mover is what we call God.

Ontological argument

Premise: I possess the idea of a being than which no greater can be conceived. That idea includes within it everything that belongs essentially to such a being.

Premise: To exist in actuality is greater than merely to be possible.

Argument: The idea of that, than which nothing greater can be conceived, includes the idea of its existence, which thus belongs to it necessarily.

Conclusion: Hence, that, than which nothing greater can be conceived, exists, and it is this that we call God.

much of anything at all. The first point is liable to slip by us because we are so mesmerized by the word "God." In the great Western religions, God is conceived as an infinite, eternal, omnipotent (infinitely powerful), omniscient (all-knowing) creator of the universe. But the most that the Argument from Design can prove, even if it is sound, is that there is a *very* long-lived (not eternal), very powerful (not omnipotent), very wise (not omniscient) world organizer who has worked up the raw materials of space, time, and matter into a reasonably well-integrated machinelike universe. After all, the watchmaker does not create his materials; he merely fashions them to his purposes. And the human eye is not infinitely complex, it is just a good deal more complex than a camera. So if the analogy is taken strictly, we can at best demonstrate the existence of a conscious, purposeful, powerful, very knowledgeable, very old worldmaker. But if we label that worldmaker "God," then we may mistakenly slip into identifying him or her or it with the God of the Old and New Testaments, the God of the great Western religions, the God who lays down commandments, punishes the wicked, offers the free gift of eternal life, and so forth. And absolutely nothing in the analogy justifies any of those conclusions.

But the argument isn't very sound, as David Hume pointed out in one of his most brilliant works, the *Dialogues Concerning Natural Religion.* Hume actually wrote the *Dialogues* in the 1750s, twenty years before his death in 1776, but he was prevailed upon by his friends (including the economist and philosopher Adam Smith) to withhold them from publication, because the forcefulness of their attack on received religious opinions would open Hume to condemnation. Eventually, they were brought out posthumously in 1779 by his nephew. The work is a three-person discussion of all the principal arguments for the existence of God; in which first one character and then another comes to the fore. In the subtlety of their development and pacing, the *Dialogues* have something of the quality of a Baroque trio, and I think it may fairly be said that Hume is the only great philosopher after Plato to use the dialogue form to its full literary effect. The work is in twelve parts, and this selection comes from Part Two. The speaker is the skeptic, Philo:

DAVID HUME,
*Dialogues
Concerning
Natural Religion*

In reality, CLEANTHES, continued he, there is no need of having recourse to that affected skepticism, so displeasing to you, in order to come at this determination. Our ideas reach no farther than our experience: We have no experience of divine attributes and operations: I need not conclude my syllogism: You can draw the inference yourself. And it is a pleasure to me (and I hope to you too) that just reasoning and sound piety here concur in the same conclusion, and both of them establish the adorably mysterious and incomprehensible nature of the supreme Being. . . .

What I chiefly scruple in this subject, said PHILO, is not so much, that all religious arguments are by CLEANTHES reduced to experience, as that they appear not to be even the most certain and irrefragable of that inferior kind. That a stone will fall, that fire will burn, that the earth has solidity, we have observed a thousand and a thousand times; and when any new instance of this nature is presented, we draw without hesitation the accustomed inference. The exact similarity of the cases gives us a perfect assurance of a similar event; and a stronger evidence is never desired nor sought after. But wherever you depart, in the least, from the similarity of the cases, you diminish proportionably the evidence; and may at last bring it to a very weak *analogy*, which is confessedly liable to error and uncertainty. After having experienced the circulation of the blood in human creatures, we make no doubt that it takes place in Titius and Maevius: But from its circulation in frogs and fishes, it is only a presumption, though a strong one, from analogy, that it takes place in men and other animals. The analogical reasoning is much weaker, when we infer the circulation of the sap in vegetables from our experience that the blood circulates in animals; and those, who hastily followed that imperfect analogy, are found, by more accurate experiments, to have been mistaken.

If we see a house, CLEANTHES, we conclude, with the greatest certainty, that it had an architect or builder, because this is precisely that species of *effect,* which we have experienced to proceed from that species of cause. But surely you will not affirm, that the universe bears such a resemblance to a house, that we can with the same certainty infer a similar cause, or that the analogy is here entire and perfect. The dissimilitude is so striking, that the utmost you can here pretend to is a guess, a conjecture, a presumption concerning a similar cause; and how that pretension will be received in the world, I leave you to consider. . . .

Were a man to abstract from every thing which he knows or has seen, he would be altogether incapable, merely from his own ideas, to determine what kind of scene the universe must be, or to give the preference to one state or situation of things above another. For as nothing, which he clearly conceives, could be esteemed impossible or implying a contradiction, every chimera of his fancy would be upon an equal footing; nor could he assign any just reason, why he adheres to one idea or system, and rejects the others, which are equally possible.

Again; after he opens his eyes, and contemplates the world, as it really is, it would be impossible for him, at first, to assign the cause of any one event, much less, of the whole of things or of the universe. He might set his fancy a rambling; and she might bring him in an infinite variety of reports and representations. These would all be possible; but being all equally possible, he would never, of himself, give a satisfactory account for his preferring one of them to the rest. Experience alone can point out to him the true cause of any phenomenon.

Although Hume's refutation stands pretty well on its own feet, it also draws upon the more fundamental criticisms which Hume developed of causal reasoning of all sorts. In Chapter 6, we will have an opportunity to examine the reasons for his skepticism concerning any attempt to infer causes from effects or effects from causes.

St. Thomas Aquinas: The Cosmological Argument

Christian theologians derive their beliefs about God from two sources. The first is *revelation,* consisting of those truths which God has revealed to us through the holy writings of the Old and New Testaments or through His miraculous appearance to particular individuals. Revelation must of course be interpreted, and therein lies the origin of many learned disputes and bloody wars. But everyone agrees that the *fact* of revelation is simply a miracle, to be taken on faith. The second source is *reason,* our natural human power of analysis, argument, observation, and inference. We must wait for revelation. We cannot make it happen, and we cannot predict when or where God will reveal Himself. But reason is our own instrument, and we can deploy it at will to seek out the origins of the universe and the existence and nature of a Creator. The greatest of all the rational theologians, by universal agreement, is the thirteenth-century Christian philosopher St. Thomas Aquinas. His elaboration and codification of the rational metaphysical basis for Christian theology remains to this day the dominant intellectual influence in the Roman Catholic Church. The philosophy known as Thomism is an enduring monument of medieval intellectual architecture, as impressive in its way as the great Cathedral of Notre Dame in Paris.

Aquinas actually offers five separate *proofs* for the existence of God in his most important work, the *Summa Theologica.* The first three of these are variations of the same argument, and we shall examine them all together. In each case, Aquinas begins with some fact about the world: the first argument takes off from the fact that things *move* in the world around us; the second from the fact that every event that is observed to take place is made to happen, or is caused, by something else that precedes it; the third from the fact that there are at least some things in the world whose existence is not necessary, which are, in metaphysical language, "possible."

Aquinas then reasons that the observed motion, or event, or possible thing, is the last in a chain of motions or causes or possible things, and he

"La Creazione dell'uomo." God's creation of Adam, as rendered by the great Italian painter Michelangelo. (Alinari/Art Resource)

asserts that such a chain cannot reach back endlessly to prior motions, to earlier causes, to other possible things on which this thing depends for its existence. Somewhere, the chain must end, with a mover that is not itself also moved by something else, with a cause that is not itself caused by yet another cause, with a being whose existence is not merely possible but necessary. That first mover, first cause, or necessary being, is God.

If the task of proving the existence of God weren't such a serious business, we might say that the **Cosmological Argument** is a very sophisticated answer to the four-year-old's questions, "Where did I come from, Mommy?" Now a straight answer would be, "You came from inside Mommy's womb." And after a few more details have been added, that answer usually satisfies a four-year-old. Eventually, the obvious follow-up question will occur to a six- or seven-year-old, namely, "Where did you come from, Mommy?" A somewhat longer story about Grandma and Grandpa should handle that one. But sooner or later, a bright child is going to start brooding on the *real* problem. Maybe I came from Mom and Dad, each of whom came in turn from a mother and father; maybe the earliest human mothers and fathers evolved through a combination and mutation and selection from prehuman mam-

> ☞ **Cosmological Argument**   The attempt to prove the existence of God by starting with the mere fact of motion, or change, or the existence of things in the universe, and then arguing that these must have their origin in a being that does not move, or does not change, or does not merely happen to exist. The earliest form of the argument is to be found in the writings of Aristotle.

mals, who in turn evolved from reptiles, or what have you; and maybe life itself sprang up spontaneously through chance rearrangements of amino acid-like compounds, which in turn emerged from the stuff of which the earth was formed, but *damn it,* somewhere the buck has got to stop! If there isn't anything that was *first,* then how can there be anything at all? If the existence of each particular thing is to be explained by saying that it came from some preceding thing, then we have no explanation at all. We just have a chain that leads so far back into the misty past that finally we get tired of asking, and mistake our fatigue for an answer. In short, an "infinite regress" is no answer at all. We might just as well have answered the very first question by saying, "Shut up and don't ask silly questions!"

So we might summarize Aquinas' proofs by saying that if the universe makes any sense at all, if it is through and through rational, then there must be a necessary being, a first mover, a first cause. Here are the three proofs as Aquinas stated them. Notice that he doesn't waste any words. He proves the existence of God three times in the space it takes Plato to introduce one of the characters in a Dialogue.

ST. THOMAS
AQUINAS,
Summa
Theologica

The existence of God can be proved in five ways.

The first and more manifest way is the argument from motion. It is certain and evident to our senses, that in the world some things are in motion. Now whatever is moved is moved by another, for nothing can be moved except it is in potentiality to that towards which it is moved; whereas a thing moves inasmuch as it is in act. For motion is nothing else than the reduction of something from potentiality to actuality. But nothing can be reduced from potentiality to actuality, except by something in a state of actuality. Thus that which is actually hot, as fire, makes wood, which is potentially hot, to be actually hot, and thereby moves and changes it. Now it is not possible that the same thing should be at once in actuality and potentiality in the same respect but only in different respects. For what is actually hot cannot simultaneously be potentially hot; but it is simultaneously potentially cold. It is therefore impossible that in the same respect and in the same way a thing should be both mover and

ST. THOMAS AQUINAS

St. Thomas Aquinas (1225–1274) is the greatest intellectual figure of the high medieval culture that flourished in Europe during the thirteenth century. Aquinas was an Italian theologian and philosopher who spent his life in the Dominican Order, teaching and writing. His writings, which run to many volumes, set forth in extremely systematic form a full-scale theory of God, man, and the universe. The official dogma of the Church, as established by revelation and interpretation of holy scriptures, was combined by Aquinas with the secular metaphysical doctrines of Aristotle and the post-Aristotelian Greek and Roman philosophers.

Aquinas' philosophical synthesis of philosophy and theology became the accepted teaching of the Roman Catholic Church. It is known today as Thomism, and in various forms it continues to exercise a profound intellectual influence both on Church doctrine and on the philosophical work of Catholic and non-Catholic thinkers.

moved, i.e., that it should move itself. Therefore, whatever is moved must be moved by another. If that by which it is moved be itself moved, then this also must needs be moved by another, and that by another again. But this cannot go on to infinity, because then there would be no first mover, and consequently, no other mover, seeing that subsequent movers move only inasmuch as they are moved by the first mover, as the staff moves only because it is moved by the hand. Therefore it is necessary to arrive at a first mover, moved by no other, and this everyone understands to be God.

The second way is from the nature of efficient cause. In the world of sensible things we find there is an order of efficient causes. There is no case known (neither is it, indeed, possible) in which a thing is found to be the efficient cause of itself; for so it would be prior to itself, which is impossible. Now in efficient causes it is not possible to go on to infinity, because in all efficient causes following in order, the first is the cause of the intermediate cause, and the intermediate is the cause of the ultimate cause, whether the intermediate cause be several, or one only. Now to take away the cause is to take away the effect. Therefore, if there be no first cause among efficient causes, there will be no ultimate, not any intermediate, cause. But if in efficient causes it is possible to go on to infinity, there will be no first efficient cause, neither will there be an ultimate effect, nor any intermediate efficient causes; all of which is plainly false. Therefore it is necessary to admit a first efficient cause, to which everyone gives the name of God.

The third way is taken from possibility and necessity, and runs thus. We find in nature things that are possible to be and not to be, since they are found to be generated, and to be corrupted, and consequently, it is possible for them to be and not to be. But it is impossible for these always to exist, for that which can not-be at some time is not. Therefore, if everything can not-be, then at one time there was nothing in existence. Now if this were true, even now there would be nothing in existence, because that which does not exist begins to exist only through something already existing. Therefore, if at one time nothing was in existence, it would have been impossible for anything to have begun to exist; and thus even now nothing would be in existence—which is absurd. Therefore, not all beings are merely possible, but there must exist something the existence of which is necessary. But every necessary thing either has its necessity caused by another, or not. Now it is impossible to go on to infinity in necessary things which have their necessity caused by another, as has been already proved in regard to efficient causes. Therefore we cannot but admit the existence of some being having of itself its own necessity, and not receiving it from another, but rather causing in others their necessity. This all men speak of as God.

Hume has an answer to these arguments as well as to the argument from design. In Part IX of his *Dialogues,* he considers a version which reasons from cause and effect to the existence of a first cause, whose existence must therefore be necessary. It is thus a combination of the second and third of Aquinas' proofs. Hume's refutation, put this time into the mouth of the character named Cleanthes, begins with a paragraph that is also a refutation of the third great proof, the ontological argument. More of that a little later.

DAVID HUME,
Dialogues
Concerning
Natural Religion

I shall begin with observing, that there is an evident absurdity in pretending to demonstrate a matter of fact, or to prove it by any arguments *a priori.* Nothing is demonstrable, unless the contrary implies a contradiction. Nothing, that is distinctly conceivable, implies a contradiction. Whatever we conceive as existent, we can also conceive as non-existent. There is no Being, therefore, whose non-existence implies a contradiction. Consequently there is no Being, whose existence is demonstrable. I propose this argument as entirely decisive, and am willing to rest the whole controversy upon it.

It is pretended that the Deity is a necessarily existent Being; and this necessity of his existence is attempted to be explained by asserting that, if we knew his whole essence or nature, we should perceive it to be as impossible for him not to exist as for twice two not to be four. But it is evident, that this can never happen, while our faculties remain the same as at present. It will still be possible for us, at any time, to conceive the non-existence of what we formerly conceived to exist; nor can the mind ever lie under a necessity of supposing any object to remain always in being: in the same manner as we lie under a necessity of always conceiving twice two to be four. The words, therefore, *necessary existence,* have no meaning; or, which is the same thing, none that is consistent.

But farther, why may not the material universe be the necessarily existent Being, according to this pretended explication of necessity? We dare not affirm that we know all the qualities of matter, and for aught we can determine, it may contain some qualities, which, were they known, would make its non-existence appear as great a contradiction as that twice two is five. I find only one argument employed to prove, that the material world is not the necessarily existent Being; and this argument is derived from the contingency both of the matter and the form of the world. "Any particle of matter," it is said, "may be *conceived* to be annihilated; and any form may be *conceived* to be altered. Such an annihilation or alteration, therefore, is not impossible." But it seems a great partiality not to perceive, that the same argument extends equally to the Deity, so far as we have any conception of him; and that the mind can at least imagine him to be non-existent, or his attributes to be altered. It must be some unknown, inconceivable qualities, which can make non-existence appear impossible, or his attributes unalterable. And no reason can be assigned, why these qualities may not belong to matter. As they are altogether unknown and inconceivable, they can never be proved incompatible with it.

Add to this, that in tracing an eternal succession of objects, it seems absurd to inquire for a general cause or first Author. How can any thing, that exists from eternity, have a cause, since that relation implies a priority in time and a beginning of existence?

In such a chain too, or succession of objects, each part is caused by that which preceded it, and causes that which succeeds it. Where then is the difficulty? But the *whole,* you say, wants a cause. I answer, that the uniting of these parts into a whole, like the uniting of several distinct counties into one kingdom, or several distinct members into one body, is performed merely by an arbitrary act of the mind, and has no influence on the nature of things. Did I show you the particular causes of each individual in a collection of twenty particles of matter, I should think it very unreasonable, should you afterwards ask me, what was the cause of the whole twenty. This is sufficiently explained in explaining the cause of the parts.

⚛ St. Anselm: The Ontological Argument

Here it is, the most famous, the most mystifying, the most outrageous and irritating philosophical argument of all time! Read it carefully and see what you think.

ST. ANSELM,
Proslogion

And so, Lord, do thou, who dost give understanding to faith, give me, so far as thou knowest it to be profitable, to understand that thou art as we believe; and that thou art that which we believe. And, indeed, we believe that thou art a being than which nothing greater can be conceived. Or is there no such nature, since the fool hath said in his heart, there is no God? (Psalms XIV. 1). But, at any rate, this very fool, when he hears of this being of which I speak—a being than which nothing greater can be conceived—understands what he hears, and what he understands is in his understanding; although he does not understand it to exist.

For, it is one thing for an object to be in the understanding, and another to understand that the object exists. When a painter first conceives of what he will afterwards perform, he has it in his understanding, but he does not yet understand it to be, because he has not yet performed it. But after he has made the painting, he both has it in his understanding, and he understands that it exists, because he has made it.

Hence, even the fool is convinced that something exists in the understanding, at least, than which nothing greater can be conceived. For, when he hears of this, he understands it. And whatever is understood, exists in the understanding. And, assuredly that, than which nothing greater can be conceived, cannot exist in the understanding alone. For, suppose it exists in the understanding alone: then it can be conceived to exist in reality; which is greater.

Therefore, if that, than which nothing greater can be conceived, exists in the understanding alone, the very being, than which nothing greater can be conceived, is one, than which a greater can be conceived. But obviously this is impossible. Hence, there is no doubt that there exists a being, than which nothing greater can be conceived, and it exists both in the understanding and in reality.

And it assuredly exists so truly, that it cannot be conceived not to exist. For, it is possible to conceive of a being which cannot be conceived not to exist; and this is greater than one which can be conceived not to exist. Hence, if that, than which nothing greater can be

ST. ANSELM

Saint Anselm (1033–1109) was born in Italy and was trained there for the priesthood. In 1093, he was appointed Archbishop of Canterbury in England by the Norman king William Rufus. His most important philosophical work is the *Proslogion,* in which he set forth a startling and radically new proof for the existence of God. The proof, known now as the Ontological Argument, has been defended over the past nine centuries by Descartes, Spinoza, and others. St. Thomas Aquinas, on the other hand, claimed it was not a valid proof, and he rejected it.

This drawing shows the ceremony in which Anselm (standing, with hand raised) was appointed Archbishop of Canterbury by the king.

conceived, can be conceived not to exist, it is not that, than which nothing greater can be conceived. But this is an irreconcilable contradiction. There is, then, so truly a being than which nothing greater can be conceived to exist, that it cannot even be conceived not to exist; and this being thou art, O Lord, our God.

So truly, therefore, dost thou exist, O Lord, my God, that thou canst not be conceived not to exist; and rightly. For, if a mind could conceive of a being better than thee, the creature would rise above the Creator, and this is most absurd. And, indeed, whatever else there is, except thee alone, can be conceived not to exist. To thee alone, therefore, it belongs to exist more truly than all other beings, and hence in a higher degree than all others. For, whatever else exists does not exist so truly, and hence in a less degree it belongs to it to exist. Why, then, has the fool said in his heart, there is no God (Psalms XIV. 1), since it is so evident, to a rational mind, that thou dost exist in the highest degree of all? Why, except that he is dull and a fool?

Whenever I read the **Ontological Argument,** I have the same feeling that comes over me when I watch a really good magician. Nothing up this sleeve; nothing up the other sleeve; nothing in the hat; presto! A big, fat rabbit. How can Anselm pull God out of an idea? At least the Argument from Design and the Cosmological Argument start from some actual fact about the world, whether it is the apparently purposeful organization of living things, or the motion of bodies in space, or whatever. But the Ontological Argument starts from a mere idea in the mind of the philosopher and undertakes to prove, from that idea alone, that there must actually be something corresponding to the idea. The argument makes no use at all of facts that might be gathered by observation or analysis of the world. Philosophers call an argument of this sort an *a priori* argument. Propositions that can be known to be true without consideration of factual support, merely from an analysis of the concepts involved in the judgments, are called propositions *knowable a priori,* or simply, "*a priori* propositions."

Now, philosophers have for a long time held that there are *a priori* propositions, or propositions whose truth can be known merely from a consideration of their meaning. For example, consider the proposition, "If an aardvark is a mammal, then it bears its young live." Is that true? Well, your first reaction might be to ask yourself whether you know what an aardvark is, or maybe to look it up in the encyclopedia. But stop and think about it for a moment. A mammal is an animal that bears its young live rather than laying eggs. That is what we *mean* when we call something a mammal. This is part of the definition of the word "mammal." So if anything is to be classified as a mammal, it will have to be the sort of thing that bears its young live. Otherwise we wouldn't call it a mammal; we would call it something else, or even just say that we don't have a word for it. If you think about it, you will realize that you can decide about the truth of my proposition without knowing anything about aardvarks, indeed without ever having heard the word "aardvark" before. Whatever aardvarks are, "If an aardvark is a mammal, then it bears its young live." In short, you can know the truth of the proposition *a priori,* or even more briefly, it is an *a priori* proposition.

But are there any aardvarks? Ah well, that is quite another question. My *a priori* proposition only tells me that if there are any, and if they are mammals, then they bear their young live. It doesn't tell me whether there are any. Indeed, it doesn't even tell me whether aardvarks are mammals. It just says, *if* there are aardvarks and they are mammals, then they bear their young live. Propositions that can be known to be true merely on the basis of the meanings of the words used in them are called tautologies, and you can make up tautologies all day long, with no more material to work with than the English language.

> **Ontological Argument**   The attempt to prove the existence of God by starting with nothing more than the mere concept of the most perfect being. The argument is extremely controversial and has been rejected as invalid by many religious philosophers, including the leading medieval proponent of the Cosmological Argument, St. Thomas Aquinas.

The Ontological Argument seems to depend on a tautology too. First, Anselm *defines* the word "God" as meaning "a being than which nothing greater can be conceived." Then, he argues that this concept, of a greatest being, must include the notion that the being cannot be conceived not to exist. In other words, he argues that when we spell out the definition of "God" as "a being than which nothing greater can be conceived," we will find that the definition includes the characteristic "necessarily existing," just as when we spell out the definition of "mammal," we find that it includes the notion "bearing its young live."

Well, "Mammals bear their young live" is a tautology; it is true by definition; we can know it to be true merely by understanding the words used in the statement. It follows from the definition. So too, Anselm claims, "God necessarily exists" is a tautology; it too is true by definition; it too can be known merely through an understanding of the words used in the statement. But there is one enormous difference. The statement about mammals, and all the other ordinary tautologies that have ever been thought up, say nothing about whether something *exists*. Ordinary tautologies just tell us that *if* there are any things fitting a certain definition, *then* they have the following characteristics. If there are mammals, then they bear their young live; if there are any bachelors, then they are unmarried (because "bachelor" means "unmarried man"); if there are any triangles, then they have three angles; and so forth. The Ontological Argument is the only case in which a tautology is used to prove that something—namely, God—exists.

Now of course philosophers who use the Ontological Argument are perfectly well aware that this is a very special and peculiar sort of tautology. If they can prove the existence of God this way, why can't I use the same trick to prove the existence of a perfect horse, or a necessarily existent ox, or a mosquito than which none greater can be conceived? Their answer is that God is different from all the other beings in or out of the universe, and that God's existence is a different sort of existence from the existence of every created thing. God is infinite, all other things are finite; God's existence is necessary, the existence of every other thing is merely contingent; God is perfect, all else is imperfect; and God's existence follows *a priori* from His definition, whereas the existence of every other thing, since it depends ultimately on God and not on itself alone, follows *not* from its own definition but only from God's act of creation.

The Ontological Argument remains to this day one of the most controversial arguments in all of philosophy. Some very devout theologians, including St. Thomas Aquinas, have believed that it was wrong, invalid, a confusion. Several of the greatest philosophers of the seventeenth century, including Descartes and Spinoza, thought it was valid and developed their own versions of it. In his great *Critique of Pure Reason,* Immanuel Kant offered an elaborate refutation of the argument which for more than a hundred years was thought to have permanently laid it to rest. In this century, however, there has been a revival of philosophical interest in the Ontological Argument, and philosophers like myself, who grew up thinking that Kant had once and for all finished it off, now find the technical journals full of new versions of the Ontological Argument, in which the latest tools of formal logic are used to give the old warhorse some new life.

Let us wind up this discussion of proofs for the existence of God with Kant's refutation of the Ontological Argument. This is a difficult passage, harder even than the argument itself, which was no breeze. Please don't expect to understand everything Kant is saying. I have been studying Kant for forty-five years, and I am not sure what he means sometimes. But read through this selection two or three times, with the aid of your professor. Kant always repays hard work, and his treatment of the Ontological Argument is one of his most brilliant efforts.

One bit of explanation before you begin. Kant asks whether the proposition "God exists" is an *analytic* or a *synthetic* proposition. An analytic proposition, according to Kant, is a statement which merely spells out, or *analyzes,* what is already contained in the subject of the statement. For example, the proposition "Triangles have three angles" tells us nothing new about triangles. All it does is repeat what is already contained in the idea of a triangle. Synthetic propositions, on the other hand, add something to what is contained in the idea of the subject of the proposition. "Bachelors are unhappy" is synthetic (whether or not it is true!), because being unhappy is *not* part of what we mean by being a bachelor. "Bachelors are unmarried" is analytic, however, for being unmarried *is* part of what we mean by being a bachelor. Kant argues, as you will see, that any proposition which asserts the existence of something must be a synthetic proposition. He thinks that this claim successfully undermines the Ontological Argument.

IMMANUEL KANT,
Critique of Pure Reason

Kant's Critique of the Ontological Argument
Notwithstanding all these general considerations, in which every one must concur, we may be challenged with a case which is brought forward as proof that in actual fact the contrary holds, namely, that there is one concept, and indeed only one, in reference to which the not-being or rejection of its object is in itself contradictory, namely, the concept of the *ens realissimum.* It is declared that it possesses all reality, and that we are justified in assuming that such a being is possible (the fact that a concept does not contradict itself by no means proves the possibility of its object: but the contrary assertion I am for the moment willing to allow). Now "all reality" includes existence; existence is therefore contained in the concept of a thing that is possible. If, then, this thing is rejected, the internal possibility of the thing is rejected—which is self-contradictory.

My answer is as follows. There is already a contradiction in introducing the concept of existence—no matter under what title it may be disguised—into the concept of a thing which we profess to be thinking solely in reference to its possibility. If that be allowed as legitimate, a seeming victory has been won: but in actual fact nothing at all is said: the assertion is a mere tautology. We must ask: Is the proposition that *this* or *that thing* (which, whatever it may be, is allowed as possible) *exists,* an analytic or a synthetic proposition? If it is analytic, the assertion of the existence of the thing adds nothing to the thought of the thing; but in that case either the thought, which is in us, is the thing itself, or we have presupposed an existence as belonging to the realm of the possible, and have then, on that pretext, inferred its existence from its internal possibility—which is nothing but a miserable tautology. The word "reality," which in the concept of the thing sounds other than the word "existence" in the concept of the predicate, is of no avail in meeting this objection. For if all positing (no matter what it may be that is posited) is entitled reality, the thing with all its predicates is already posited in the concept of the subject, and is assumed as actual; and in the predicate this is merely repeated. But if, on the other hand, we admit, as every reasonable person must, that all existential propositions are synthetic, how can we profess to maintain that the predicate of existence cannot be rejected without contradiction? This is a feature which is found only in analytic propositions, and is indeed precisely what constitutes their analytic character.

I should have hoped to put an end to these idle and fruitless disputations in a direct manner, by an accurate determination of the concept of existence, had I not found that the illusion which is caused by the confusion of a logical with a real predicate (that is, with a predicate which determines a thing) is almost beyond correction. Anything we please can be made to serve as a logical predicate; the subject can even be predicated of itself; for logic abstracts from all content. But a *determining* predicate is a predicate which is added to the concept of the subject and enlarges it. Consequently, it must not be already contained in the concept.

"Being" is obviously not a real predicate; that is, it is not a concept of something which could be added to the concept of a thing. It is merely the positing of a thing, or of certain determinations, as existing in themselves. Logically, it is merely the copula of a judgment. The proposition, "God is omnipotent," contains two concepts, each of which has its object—God and omnipotence. The small word "is" adds no new predicate, but only serves to posit the predicate *in its relation* to the subject. If, now, we take the subject (God) with all its predicates (among which is omnipotence), and say "God is," or "There is a God," we attach no new predicate to the concept of God, but only posit the subject in itself with all its predicates, and indeed posit it as being an *object* that stands in relation to my *concept.* The

content of both must be one and the same; nothing can have been added to the concept, which expresses merely what is possible, by my thinking its object (through the expression "it is") as given absolutely. Otherwise stated, the real contains no more than the merely possible. A hundred real thalers do not contain the least coin more than a hundred possible thalers. For as the latter signify the concept, and the former the object and the positing of the object, should the former contain more than the latter, my concept would not, in that case, express the whole object, and would not therefore be an adequate concept of it. My financial position is, however, affected very differently by a hundred real thalers than it is by the mere concept of them (that is, of their possibility). For the object, as it actually exists, is not analytically contained in my concept, but is added to my concept (which is a determination of my state) synthetically; and yet the conceived hundred thalers are not themselves in the least increased through thus acquiring existence outside my concept.

The Problem of Evil

The two approaches to religion that we have been looking at in this chapter—the subjective, faith-based approach, and the objective, rational approach—meet head-on in the greatest test to religious faith and rational theological doctrine, the problem of evil.

The problem is simplicity itself to state, but devilishly difficult to solve. God, according to the Judeo-Christian and Islamic teachings, is infinitely powerful, infinitely wise, and infinitely loving. God knows all, can do all, and means well. But the world is full of misery, pain, natural disaster, and human evil. And worst of all, God's special creatures, human beings, must one and all face death. Indeed, as the American poet Emily Dickinson protested in a number of her most powerful poems, God calls us to love him, to seek him, to worship him, and then arranges matters so that we must die before we can be gathered into his bosom. What sort of loving God is this?

Couldn't God have arranged things so that innocent little children wouldn't die painfully in car crashes? Couldn't an all-powerful, all-wise God have figured out a way to create a world without cancer, plague, or AIDS? Do we really have to have earthquakes, floods, and famines? Couldn't God at least have managed a world without mosquitoes?

The problem is as old as religious faith itself. Here is the way it was posed by David Hume, in the *Dialogues Concerning Natural Religion* that you have already met in this chapter. Cleanthes and Philo have been talking about the variety of miseries and afflictions faced by human beings. Philo then poses the problem. This passage is taken from the Tenth Dialogue:

And is it possible, *Cleanthes,* said *Philo,* that after all these reflections, and infinitely more, which might be suggested, you can still persevere in your anthropomorphism, and assert the moral attributes of the deity, his justice, benevolence, mercy, and rectitude, to be of the same nature with these virtues in human creatures? His power we allow is infinite: Whatever he wills is executed: But neither man nor any other animal is happy: Therefore he does not will their happiness. His wisdom is infinite: He is never mistaken in choosing the means to any end: But the course of nature tends not to human or animal felicity: Therefore it is not established for that purpose. Through the whole compass of human knowledge, there are no inferences more certain and infallible than these. In what respect, then, do his benevolence and mercy resemble the benevolence and mercy of men?

Epicurus's old questions are yet unanswered. Is he willing to prevent evil, but not able? then is he impotent. Is he able, but not willing? then is he malevolent. Is he both able and willing? whence then is evil?

Omnipotent, omniscient, benevolent. *Omnipotent* simply means "having all power," "capable of doing everything and anything." If God is omnipotent, then we cannot explain the existence of pain, suffering, misery, and evil by saying that God just wasn't strong enough to stop them from happening. *Omniscient* means "all-knowing." If God is omniscient, we cannot explain away the evil in the world by saying that God just didn't know about it, but would have done something if He had only known. *Benevolent* means "wishing good" or "intending to do good." If God is benevolent, then we cannot explain the evil in the world by saying that God just doesn't care about us, or even actively wants us to suffer.

And there it is. As Epicurus says, if God is willing to prevent evil (benevolent) but not able, then He is not omnipotent. If He is able (omnipotent) but not willing, then He is not benevolent. (And, though Epicurus doesn't add this, since many philosophers consider omniscience just a part of omnipotence, if God is able to prevent evil, and willing to prevent evil, then He must not know about it, in which case He is not omniscient.) What can a faithful Christian, Jew, or Muslim possibly say in response to this challenge?

The great seventeenth-century logician, mathematician, physicist, and philosopher Gottfried Leibniz devoted considerable energy to the problem of evil. He began with the premise that this world, since it was created by an infinite and benevolent God, must be the very best world that it was possible to create. In effect, Leibniz imagines God before the Creation turning over in His Divine Mind all the possible worlds that He might bring into existence. Clearly, if He thought it would be better to create no world at all, He would have simply refrained from creating one. And among all the logically possible worlds He could create, obviously He would choose the best one, since He is infinitely good. What is more, since He is infinitely wise, whatever He thinks must be true! So, this world is the best of all possible worlds. If we cannot see that, then it is *we* who are imperfect, not God. Here is one of Leibniz's many statements of this idea, taken from a work entitled *A Vindication of God's Justice Reconciled with His Other Perfections and All His Actions.*

> The infinite wisdom of the Almighty allied with his boundless goodness has brought it about that nothing better could have been created, everything taken into account, than what God has created. As a consequence all things are in perfect harmony and conspire in the most beautiful way: the formal causes or souls with the material causes or bodies, the efficient or natural causes with the final or moral causes, and the realm of grace with the realm of nature.
>
> Whenever, therefore, some detail of the work of God appears to us reprehensible, we should judge that we do not know enough about it and that according to the wise who would understand it, nothing better could even be desired.
>
> Hence it follows, furthermore, that there is no greater felicity than to serve so good a master, and that we should therefore love God above everything else and trust him without reservation. . . .
>
> *Physical good and evil* occur in this life as well as in life hereafter. There is much complaint that *in this life* human nature is exposed to so many evils. Those who feel this way fail to consider that a great part of this evil is the effect of human guilt. In fact, they do not recognize with sufficient gratitude the divine goods of which we are the beneficiaries, and pay more attention to our sufferings than to our blessings.
>
> Others are particularly dissatisfied with the fact that physical good and evil are not distributed in proportion to moral good and evil, or in other words, that frequently the just are miserable while the unrighteous prosper.
>
> To these complaints there are two answers: the first, given by the Apostle, namely, that the afflictions of this life are nothing compared with the future glory, which will be revealed to us. The second, which Christ Himself has suggested, in an admirable parable: If the grain falling to the soil did not die, it would not bear fruit.
>
> Thus our afflictions not only will be largely compensated, but they will serve to increase our felicity. These evils are not only profitable, but indispensable.

This is just about the best that the rationalist tradition in religious thought can manage with regard to the problem of evil. God is infinite, the world is perfect, and we just can't see the big picture well enough to recognize that fact.

The only alternative, so far as I can see, is to turn away from rational explanations entirely, and simply submit oneself to the majesty of God, accepting without question His world, and giving oneself up to worship of Him. To a believer like Kierkegaard, clever philosophical reconciliations of God's omnipotence, omniscience, and benevolence are expressions of just the sort of attitude toward religious faith that takes us farther from God.

In an odd way, the problem of evil is a sort of twin to the proofs for the existence of God. No nonbeliever has ever been transformed into a believer by one of those proofs. And no true believer has ever lost his or her faith because of the problem of evil. In the end, I suspect, these are both philosophical topics that are intriguing and fun to chew over, not pathways to or from faith.

The Main Points in Chapter Five

1. The nineteenth-century Danish philosopher Søren Kierkegaard struggled throughout his life to come to terms with the Protestant Christianity of northern Europe, focusing in complex ways on such religious concepts as *faith, the Saviour, sin,* and *dread.* His many writings were at one and the same time an exploration of the experience of religious faith and a critique of the middle-class society in which he lived.

2. Rejecting the teachings of Hegel, who was the leading philosophical influence of that time, Kierkegaard asserted that truth lies in what is *subjective, inward,* and *immediate,* not *objective* and *universal.* Kierkegaard's approach to these central questions of human existence has come to be called existentialism.

3. For several thousand years, philosophers have argued about whether it is possible to actually prove the existence of a divine and infinite being— God. The arguments designed to prove that God exists have traditionally been grouped under three headings:

   a. The *Argument from Design* seeks to prove that there is a God by pointing to the evidences in nature of purpose or design and then reasoning that they must be the result of an intelligent, purposive designer, namely God. William Paley, in the late eighteenth century, gave the most elaborate version of this argument, although in one form or another it goes all the way back to ancient times.

   b. St. Thomas Aquinas' *Cosmological Argument* starts from the fact there is motion in the world, or from the fact that things in the world come into being and pass away, and then reasons that there must be a first cause of motion, or a first unalterable cause of existence, which itself has no higher cause and neither comes to be nor passes away.

c. St. Anselm's *Ontological Argument* begins with the mere *concept* of an infinite being and argues that from a logical analysis of the concept, we can conclude that something corresponding to the concept—an infinite being, or God—*must* exist. The Ontological Argument, which dates from the middle ages, has been the subject of a very vigorous debate in philosophy for the past seven centuries.

4. The problem of evil poses the question: How can a God who is all-powerful, all-wise, and all-good permit so much pain, suffering, and evil in the world?

CONTEMPORARY APPLICATION

Creationism vs. Evolution

In the beginning, religion and science went hand in hand. The early creation myths which form such an important part of most religions are at one and the same time religious accounts of God's relationship to the human race and scientific theories of the origin of the cosmos. As we saw in Chapter 1, early Greek speculations about the nature and origin of our world were one of the two great sources of what we now call philosophy.

There has always been a certain tension between science and religion, to be sure. The Carthaginian church father Tertullian, who lived and wrote in the early third century after Christ, rejected the "science" of the Greek philosophers with a dramatic declaration of faith: *Credo, quia absurdum est!* I believe *because* it is absurd. Religious faith, he insisted, was utterly divorced from the rational science of the philosophers.

Nevertheless, Tertullian was very much in the minority. For the first eighteen hundred years of the Christian era, the scientific explanation of the natural world—both in the heavens and on earth—seemed perfectly compatible with the teachings of the church and the word of the Bible. Descartes, Leibniz, Locke, and Kant, among the philosophers we have encountered, believed that they could square their religious faith with what reason and the senses told them about the world around them.

In the end, the greatest challenge to this harmony of science with religion came not from physics or chemistry, but from biology. It was the theory of evolution, as developed and taught most effectively by Charles Darwin, that produced a crisis in the ancient relationship between faith and reason.

Darwin himself was a quite pious and unrevolutionary naturalist, whose most impressive work consisted of painstaking observations of a variety of animal and plant species. But his theory of evolution, as set forth in his two most famous books, *The Origin of Species* and *The Descent of Man,* hit nineteenth-century European and American society like an earthquake. Needless to say, the focus of the controversy was Darwin's claim that the human species itself had descended, by a process of evolution and natural selection, from nonhuman species. A great deal was made of the notion that human beings were descended from monkeys, something that Darwin in fact never asserted. But it didn't really matter whether he traced our ancestry back to apes or to some slightly less disreputable sort of creatures. What caused all the fuss was the claim that we are simply a part of nature—not lifted up above the other inhabitants of the earth, not formed in God's image, not separated once and for all from everything else in the universe by our immortal souls—just animals.

As you might expect, reactions to Darwin's revolutionary theories varied. Some religious thinkers insisted that evolution posed no problem for the believing Christian. The story of the Creation at the beginning of the Book of Genesis could, with suitable interpretations, be made quite compatible with the latest evolutionary speculations. Other divines took a slightly different line. Science and the revealed truths of the Bible, they said, were like trains running on separate tracks. Science told us whatever reason and observation could discover about the natural world, and the Bible told us of God's plan for the human race and His divine commandments. So long as we rendered unto God what was God's, we could go on poking about with fossils and such to our heart's content.

But in the heartland of American Christianity, in that portion of the United States known to this day as "the Bible belt," where an unswerving belief in the literal truth of the Bible was the litmus test of true faith, neither of these compromises held any appeal. Fundamentalist Christians, particularly Protestants, rejected evolution as absolutely incompatible with the teachings of their faith.

At first, efforts were made simply to exclude the theory of evolution from the textbooks and classrooms. In several states, including Tennessee, laws were passed making it a crime to teach the theory of evolution in public schools. In 1925, a schoolteacher, John Scopes, was actually prosecuted and convicted under one such law.

In recent years, however, Bible literalists, or fundamentalists, have taken a quite different tack in their fight against evolutionary theories. Evolution, they now insist, is simply one explanation of the origin of species, and the teachings of the Bible, which they label creationism, is a second theory, equally legitimate, which ought in all fairness to be given equal time in public education.

The posing of creationism as an alternative to evolution raises the debate to a level of genuine philosophical significance, for it forces the defenders of the evolutionary teaching to ask themselves exactly what they think science is, what they think religion is, and what relation they think the two ought to bear to one another. It is that debate which we encounter in the pair of selections reproduced here.

The creationism/evolution debate frequently becomes extremely technical, for the creationists, despite their rejection of evolution, know all the ins and outs of the fossil evidence quite as well as the evolutionists. Sometimes, however, as in these selections, the basic issue of religion versus science emerges clearly without the confusing fog of paleontological detail. The first selection is by Dr. Duane T. Gish, the leading spokesperson of the creationist school. Dr. Gish holds a Ph.D. in biochemistry from the University of California at Berkeley and spent two decades doing scientific research at Cornell University and elsewhere before taking up a position as Associate Director of the Institute for Creation Research. His opponent in this confrontation, Mark Ridley, was teaching at Oxford University in England when these passages were written.

Obviously, the creation/evolution debate raises questions which belong in half a dozen branches of philosophy. In the context of the issues we have been discussing in this chapter, it might be especially useful to consider the way in which the debate calls into question the relationship between faith and reason. Are religious faith in the revealed truth of the Bible and rational scientific explanations of the natural world compatible with one another? If the answer is yes, then how do we explain away the apparent conflicts between the story of Genesis and the accounts of cosmologists and biologists? If faith and reason are incompatible, to which shall we give precedence? These selections may start you thinking about the issues.

₰ ₰ ₰ ₰ ₰ ₰ ₰ ₰ ₰ ₰ ₰ ₰ ₰

EVOLUTION? THE FOSSILS SAY NO!
Duane T. Gish

The general theory of organic evolution, or the evolution model, is the theory that all living things have arisen by a materialistic evolutionary process from a single source which itself arose by a similar process from a dead, inanimate world. This theory may also be called the molecule-to-man theory of evolution.

The creation model, on the other hand, postulates that all basic animal and plant types (the created kinds) were brought into existence by acts of a supernatural Creator using special processes which are not operative today.

Most scientists accept evolution, not as a theory, but as an established fact. . . . Almost all science books and school and university texts present evolution as an established fact. These considerations alone convince many people that molecule-to-man evolution has actually occurred.

The proponents of evolution theory adamantly insist that special creation be excluded from any possible consideration as an explanation for origins on the basis that it does not qualify as a scientific theory. On the other hand, they would view as unthinkable the consideration of evolution as anything less than pure science. In fact, as already

mentioned, most evolutionists insist that evolution must no longer be thought of as a theory, but must be considered to be a fact. In spite of this attitude, however, not only is there a wealth of scientific support for rejecting evolution as a fact, but evolution does not even qualify as a scientific theory according to a strict definition of the latter.

What criteria must be met for a theory to be considered as scientific in the usually accepted sense? . . . A definition of science given by the Oxford Dictionary is:

A branch of study which is concerned either with a connected body of *demonstrated truths* or with *observed facts* systematically classified and more or less colligated by being brought under general laws, and which includes trust-worthy methods for the discovery of new truth within its own domain. [Emphasis added.]

Thus, for a theory to qualify as a scientific theory, it must be supported by events, processes, or properties which can be observed, and the theory must be useful in predicting the outcome of future natural phenomena or laboratory experiments. An additional limitation usually imposed is that the theory must be capable of falsification. That is, it must be possible to conceive some experiment, the failure of which would disprove the theory.

It is on the basis of such criteria that most evolutionists insist that creation be refused consideration as a possible explanation for origins. Creation has not been witnessed by human observers, it cannot be tested experimentally, and as a theory it is nonfalsifiable.

The general theory of evolution also fails to meet all three of these criteria, however. It is obvious, for example, that no one observed the origin of the universe, the origin of life, the conversion of a fish into an amphibian, or an ape into a man. No one, as a matter of fact, has ever observed the origin of a species by naturally occurring processes. Evolution has been *postulated*, but it has never been *observed* . . . .

In view of the above, it is incredible that most leading scientists dogmatically insist that the molecules-to-man evolution theory be taught as a fact to the exclusion of all other postulates. Evolution in this broad sense is unproven and unprovable and thus cannot be considered as fact. It is not subject to test by the ordinary methods of experimental science—observation and falsification. It thus does not, in a strict sense, even qualify as a scientific theory. It is a postulate and may serve as a model within which attempts may be made to explain and correlate the evidence from the historical record, that is, the fossil record, and to make predictions concerning the nature of future discoveries.

Creation is, of course, unproven and unprovable by the methods of experimental science. Neither can it qualify, according to the above criteria, as a scientific theory, since creation would have been unobservable and would as a theory be nonfalsifiable. In the scientific realm, creation is, therefore, as is evolution, a postulate which may serve as a model to explain and correlate the evidence related to origins. Creation is, in this sense, no more religious nor less scientific than evolution. In fact to many well-informed scientists, creation seems to be far

superior to the evolution model as an explanation for origins. . . .

The evolutionist's view of man . . . is in direct contrast to the Biblical view of man, found, for example, in Psalm 100, verse 3: "Know ye that the Lord he is God: it is he that hath made us and not we ourselves; we are his people and the sheep of his pasture." The Bible does indeed reveal that there is a living God who has created us and who controls our destiny.

Furthermore, a God who is great enough to create and control this universe is great enough, once having given His revelation to man, to preserve that revelation free from error. This preservation was not dependent upon man, but succeeded in spite of man. In this revelation, found in the first two chapters of Genesis in the Bible, the account of creation is recorded in a grand but concise fashion.

Not all evolutionists are materialistic atheists or agnostics. Many evolutionists believe in God and some even believe the Bible to be the Word of God. They believe that evolution was God's method of creation, that God initiated the process at the molecular level and then allowed it to follow its natural course. The Biblical and scientific evidence, however, tells just as strongly against theistic evolution as it does against any other form of evolution.

The first two chapters of Genesis were not written in the form of parables or poetry but present the broad outlines of creation in the form of simple historical facts. These facts directly contradict evolution theory. The Bible tells us that at one time in history there was a single human being upon the earth—a male by the name of Adam. This is in basic contradiction to evolution theory because, according to that theory, populations evolve, not individuals. After God had formed Adam from the dust of the ground, the Bible tells us that He used some portion from Adam's side (in the King James version this is translated as "rib") to form Eve. This, of course, cannot be reconciled with any possible evolutionary theory concerning the origin of man.

The New Testament Scriptures fully support this Genesis account. For example, in I Corinthians 11:8 we read, "Man is not of the woman, but the woman of the man." By any natural reproductive process, man is always born of a woman. We all have mothers. This Biblical account can, therefore, be referring only to that unique time in history when God created woman from man, just as described in Genesis 2:21,22.

It is apparent that acceptance of creation requires an important element of faith. Yes, it is true, creationists do have faith, and that faith is vitally important. In Hebrews 11:6 we read "But without faith it is impossible to please Him, for he that cometh unto God must believe that He is, and that He is a rewarder of them that diligently seek Him." This faith is an intelligent faith, supported both by Biblical revelation and the revelation found in nature. While the *theories* and *opinions* of some scientists may contradict the Bible, there is no contradiction between the *facts* of science and the Bible.

Of course, belief in evolution also requires a vitally important element of faith. According to one of the most popular theories on the origin of the universe, all energy and matter of the universe was once contained in a plasma ball of electrons, protons, and neutrons (how it got there, no one has the faintest notion). This huge cosmic egg then exploded—and here we are today, several billion years later, human beings with a three-pound brain composed of 12 billion neurons each connected to about 10 thousand other neurons in the most complicated arrangement of matter known to man. (There are thus 120 trillion connections in the human brain.)

If this is true, then what we are and how we came to be were due solely to the properties inherent in electrons, protons, and neutrons. To believe *this* obviously requires a tremendous exercise of faith. Evolution theory is indeed no less religion nor more scientific than creation.

The question is, then, who has more evidence for his faith, the creationist or the evolutionist? The scientific case for special creation . . . is much stronger than the case for evolution. The more I study and the more I learn, the more I become convinced that evolution is a false theory and that special creation offers a much more satisfactory interpretive framework for correlating and explaining the scientific evidence related to origins.

Source: *Duane T. Gish,* Evolution: The Fossils Say No. *Reprinted by permission of Master Book Publishers.*

꒫ ꒫ ꒫ ꒫ ꒫ ꒫ ꒫ ꒫ ꒫ ꒫ ꒫ ꒫ ꒫

IS EVOLUTION TRUE?
Mark Ridley

The first problem of evolution is whether it is itself true. Although almost all biologists are now agreed on the answer, it cannot be taken for granted. Both common sense and many of the high authorities of history (if not of the present) testify to the immutability of species. To take common sense, species do seem—if you do not look too far and wide—always to reproduce their kind: cows reproduce cows, robins robins, and oaks oaks; cows do not reproduce robins, or even horses. What facts and arguments can disprove the authority of common sense and history? . . .

The best evidence of evolution would be to see it in action. This has been achieved under both natural and artificial conditions. Naturally occurring evolutionary change is studied by the school of ecological genetics, which has many discoveries to its credit. The best known is the case of the peppered moth in Great Britain. This moth exists in two main forms, a dark one and a light one. Before the Industrial Revolution the light form was much the commoner; but through the nineteenth century, in industrial areas, the dark form gradually increased in numbers, to become the commoner form. A comparable degree of evolutionary change has been studied in many other species. In all of them, the appearance of the species has changed through time: they have evolved and been seen to evolve. Similar changes can be produced artificially. A new generation that differs from its predecessor can easily be produced by breeding selectively from certain forms in a population. If one breeds, for instance, from only the larger mice of a population, the next generation will have a larger average weight. The evolutionary change can be watched as it takes place. The observation will favour the theories of evolution and of transformism, but will count against separate creation. . . .

Species are not immutable. New species can be artificially made from old ones. We can also see the species category being violated in nature. If the same species is studied in different places, it will be found to differ slightly from place to place. The spatial rate of change is (usually) insensibly slow, but the extreme forms can be so different that they were classified (before the geographic connection was known) as different species. Normally it is not known whether the extremes do behave as separate reproductive species, because they are too far apart ever to try to mate. But sometimes the geographic extremes do meet. Then we can see whether they behave as separate species. This is the case where the geographic distribution is in the form of a ring. The distribution of the herring gull around the North Pole forms a ring. As we look at the herring gull, moving westwards from Great Britain to North America, we see gulls that are recognizably herring gulls, although they are a little different from the British form. We can follow them, as their appearance gradually changes, as far as Siberia.

At about this point in the continuum the gull looks more like the form that in Great Britain is called the lesser black-backed gull. From Siberia, across Russia, to northern Europe, the gull gradually changes to look more and more like the British lesser black-backed gull. Finally, in Europe, the ring is complete; the two geographically extreme forms meet, to form two perfectly good species: the herring and lesser black-backed gull can be both distinguished by their appearance and do not naturally interbreed.

The gulls are not the only example, but they are enough to make the point. . . . If observation were confined to northern Europe, the two gulls would look like two ordinary species. One might imagine that they had separate origins. But what of all the insensible gradations between the two around the North Pole? A creationist could hardly argue that *all* the gradations were separately created, for if the argument is pursued it must lead to the absurd conclusion that all individuals were separately created, because all individuals differ to some extent. We know that conclusion to be absurd, for individual organisms are not separately created out of the air or in the ground; they originate in the reproduction of other individuals. At some arbitrary point between individual differences and the species difference, the creationist will have to declare that up to this point normal individual variation is permitted, but beyond it something altogether different happened. At that point some process of the separate origin of species did its work.

The error of the creationist argument is in this case obvious. If the differences within the herring gull species were evolutionary, the difference between the herring gull and lesser black-backed gull must be as well. If evolution can produce the difference between gulls in Canada and eastern Siberia, it can surely also produce the difference between gulls in east and in west Siberia. But in many other cases, if less obviously, the creationist error is the same. There is a continuous gradation from individual variation, through geographical variation, through such levels as the subspecies, through the species level, and up through the Linaean hierarchy of genus, family, order, class, phylum. It is difficult to argue convincingly that evolution takes place up to some point in this hierarchy (such as within the species), but separate creation is necessary to produce larger differences. The degrees of difference are a continuum. If any point on the continuum is chosen as the limit of evolution, a paradox immediately arises. If evolution can produce all the changes up to that point, why can it not produce the tiny change from one side of the point to the other? . . .

We now come to the final argument for evolution: the fossil record. The fossil record offers two candidate arguments for evolution. One is the direct observation of evolutionary change over geological time. Because geological time lasts longer than the life of any single human being we might hope that the fossil record would show more extensive evolutionary change than those cases of directly observed evolution that we have dealt with. The second kind of geological argument steps back from observations of single evolutionary lineages, to consider the pattern of the fossil record as a whole. This leads to the argument from what Darwin called (in a chapter title) "the geological succession of organic beings." Let us consider the two in turn.

The fossil record of evolutionary change within single evolutionary lineages is very poor. If evolution is true, species originate through changes of ancestral species: one might expect to be able to see this in the fossil record. In fact it can rarely be seen. In 1859 Darwin could not cite a single example. He attributed the absence of examples to the incompleteness of the fossil record. Thus the chapter of *On the Origin of Species* in which

he considers this first geological argument is entitled "On the imperfections of the geological record." There are now some cases in which evolutionary change can be seen in the fossil record. A few dozen could be listed. But the most striking thing about them is their rarity. This being so, the first geological argument cannot provide a strong argument for evolution. With the accumulation of evidence it may become a powerful argument; but at present it is not. Nor, of course, is the rarity of observable evolution in the fossil record an argument against evolution. That rarity is exactly what an evolutionist would expect if the fossil record contained many gaps: and it is known that the fossil record is very incomplete. . . .

The second geological argument is more successful. For this argument we retreat from the evolutionary change of single lineages, to look instead at the distribution of the main animal groups in time. Take the vertebrates as an example. Fish first appear in the fossil record before amphibians, amphibians appear before reptiles, reptiles appear before mammals, with a clear sequence of progressively more mammal-like reptiles, in the right order, in between; the first mammals appear before the smaller sub-groups of mammals, such as apes; humans appear only about a million years ago. This sequence is exactly what the theory of evolution predicts. In order for a mammal to evolve from a fish it would have to go through amphibian, then reptilian, and then mammal-like reptilian stages; the evolutionist therefore expects these groups to appear in the fossil record in the order they do. Conversely, he would be very worried if they appeared in some other order. Creationist critics of evolution have therefore made a great song and dance about purported fossil human footprints from the Cretaceous, contemporary with the dinosaurs. If such footprints really did exist, they would seriously challenge evolution. The evolutionary descent of humans fits in well with the fossil record if humans originated a few million years ago. Before that there is a good sequence of general ancestral forms: there are anthropoid apes, and then, moving backwards in time, more generalized primate forms, more generalized mammals, and so on. . . .

We have now completed a summary of the main arguments for evolution. We have only been through the main classes of evidence: the number of examples could be multiplied by a large factor. We could also have considered another powerful argument for evolution. No sensible alternative is known. . . . There is a mechanism to explain evolution. It is called natural selection, and is utterly inconsistent with separate creation. . . . Natural selection created species by modifying existing ones, not by creating them from nothing. The absence of any coherent alternative to natural selection as a mechanism of creating species is by itself a powerful reason for accepting evolution.

Our first problem of evolution, I believe, is solved. The accumulation of facts and arguments on the side of evolution is so great that it can no longer be considered an open question. It is best that our beliefs should be rationally based: it is well worth knowing what the case for evolution is. But once the case has been examined, it is not really possible for anyone (who is not a fanatic) to doubt what the conclusion must be.

Source: *Mark Ridley,* The Problems of Evolution, *Oxford: Oxford University Press, 1983, pp. 2–14.*

Questions for Discussion and Review

1. Have you ever had an experience that you could properly describe as religious? I have in mind not only dramatic experiences like visions and conversions, but also more commonplace, socially embedded experiences such as receiving communion, becoming *bar mitzvah,* serving as a godparent for a young relative, or even simply attending religious services. Think about that experience, and ask yourself: Did it put you in touch, do you think, with a realm outside of, or different from, the everyday world? What significance did the experience have for you? Did it change your life? Why? Why not? What would change your life?

2. Read through the proofs for the existence of God carefully. Think about them. Do any of them convince you? If the answer is no (and it usually is), then what purpose do you think those proofs serve? Would it make a difference to you if the proofs were beefed up, made better? How would Jesus have responded to attempts to prove the existence of God?

3. Let us suppose you reject the proofs for the existence of God, and even reject the claim that there is a God. How then do you explain the fact that there is a universe? Do we need an explanation for the fact that we exist? Why is there in general something, and not nothing?

4. Suppose we make contact with an alien race on a distant planet and discover that they, like us, worship a divine being who has revealed himself to them in a set of holy writings. Suppose that when we finally learn how

to translate their language into ours, it turns out that their holy writings and the New and Old Testaments say roughly the same things. Would that prove that there is a God? Suppose, on the other hand, that they have no cultural practice that looks even remotely like religion. Would that undermine the claims of our religion? Why?

5. How do you suppose Kierkegaard would react to the creationism/evolution controversy? Would he think that we needed more scientific data to settle the dispute? Why? Why not? At the present time, a team of editors is slowly publishing the complete papers of the greatest scientist of the twentieth century, Albert Einstein. If it turns out, down the road, that Einstein secretly believed in Creationism, would that be evidence that it is correct? What *would* be evidence that one or the other theory is correct?

RENÉ DESCARTES

René Descartes (1596–1650) is universally recognized among philosophers as the first great figure of the modern age. Born in a small town in Touraine, France, Descartes was educated by the Jesuits, and he remained throughout his life a devoted Catholic. His early interest was principally in mathematics and physics, two fields in which exciting new work was being done by many Continental and English thinkers. In his early twenties, perhaps as the result of a dramatic trio of dreams, Descartes conceived the grandiose plan of formulating an entirely new system of science founded upon mathematics. Though he never accomplished this impossible task, his many contributions to mathematics and physics place him in the forefront of seventeenth-century science.

Descartes' primary concern throughout his life was with problems of methodology, justification, and certainty. His first work was entitled Rules for the Direction of the Mind, *and in it he sought to establish the proper procedures by which a question could be investigated without the danger of error or confusion. His most famous work,* Meditations on First Philosophy, *was immediately recognized as a dramatic challenge to all established philosophy and science. It was circulated widely throughout Europe and provoked a series of objections, to which Descartes wrote extended replies. In these objections and replies, we can see a number of profound and dramatic debates unfolding, in which such famous thinkers as Hobbes, Gassendi, and Arnauld locked horns with Descartes.*

Although Descartes was deeply influenced by the scholastic philosophy which had preceded him, the problems he posed, the questions he raised, and the demands he made for absolute subjective certainty in knowledge served to undermine the influence of the 2,000-year-old tradition of Aristotelian philosophizing. Virtually all the great philosophy written during the 150 years following Descartes' death can be seen as an attempt to answer the questions raised by the brilliant, iconoclastic Frenchman.

Theory of Knowledge

- ✦ Descartes' Method of Doubt

- ✦ Rationalism and Empiricism: Two Responses to Cartesian Doubt

- ✦ Leibniz and Rationalism

- ✦ Hume and Empiricism

- ✦ Kant's Resolution of the Rationalism/Empiricism Debate

- ✦ *Contemporary Application: Virtual Reality*

❧ Descartes' Method of Doubt

If you have been working your way through this book carefully, reading and thinking, discussing the problems it raises with your teacher and your fellow students, you should by now be getting some feel for what philosophy is and how philosophers think. And if I have been at all successful, then philosophy ought to seem a fairly sensible sort of business to you. Perhaps philosophical questions aren't exactly what your mind would turn to if you had a few spare moments caught in a traffic jam or if you couldn't sleep late at night, but at least it is easy enough to understand how reasonable men and women might get genuinely worked up about them. What rules should I use to decide the hard moral choices that life poses for me? How should the wealth of a society be divided up among its members? Do I have an obligation to obey the state, even when I believe that its laws are unjust? These may not be everyone's questions, but they are surely questions worth asking. Some of them even get asked in political campaigns, in hospital emergency wards, in law courts, or in the front lines of a war.

In this chapter, the situation changes dramatically. We are going to take a look at the philosophical attempts to deal with questions that some of you may think are just plain crazy. Suppose a friend of yours asks whether you and he really did go to the movies last night or whether he just dreamed it. A little odd, perhaps, but people do have very lifelike dreams; I have myself on a couple of occasions had dreams so real that afterwards I wasn't entirely sure whether they had actually happened or not. You wouldn't think your friend was being *philosophical,* but on the other hand you wouldn't think he was crazy either. Suppose he went on to wonder, in absolute seriousness, whether everything that had ever happened to him was a dream, whether his childhood, his adolescence, his school days, his fights with his parents, his first romance, his first trip away from home, his coming to college, and his standing right there in front of you were *all just dreams.* If he were dead serious, not just kidding around or trying to get a rise out of you, then about now you would start edging toward the phone, trying to figure out how you could call the school psychiatrist without getting your friend too upset. People who really aren't sure whether their whole lives have been dreams "need help," as the saying goes.

Suppose another friend said, as the two of you were waiting for an elevator, that she couldn't really be sure that she needed an elevator to get back down to the first floor. Maybe if she stepped out the window, she would be able simply to fly down. Suppose, indeed, that she expressed doubt about whether she could ever tell what would happen next—whether she would drown if she held her head under water, whether her finger would burn if she held it in a flame, whether her books would fall down or up if she let them go. She might even admit that she wasn't sure there was anyone else in the whole world besides herself, though of course there might be a lot of human-looking bodies that made speechlike noises and acted in peoplelike ways. Well, once again, you would probably think that either the whole act was a put-on, or your friend was in the midst of a bad trip, or else that it was time for the shrink. You certainly wouldn't think that she was simply doing philosophy!

From the beginning of the seventeenth century until the present day, some of the most brilliant thinkers ever to grace the cultural and intellectual life of Western civilization have devoted their best philosophical efforts to just such questions as the ones we have been imagining your friends to be asking. And though I would be the first to admit that philosophers have suffered their share of mental illness, there is no reason at all to suspect that any of these great thinkers was mentally unsound when he wrote his philosophy. (Rousseau was more than a little odd, but we won't be talking about him in this chapter.) The greatest challenge any teacher of philosophy faces is to present the epistemological theories of the seventeenth- and eighteenth-century theorists of knowledge in such a way that students not only understand the arguments but also understand why in heaven's name sane people worried about such peculiar problems.

The theory of knowledge is the heart and soul of the philosophy that has been written since the beginning of the seventeenth century. All of the most important philosophers—Descartes, Leibniz, Locke, Berkeley, Hume, Kant—set epistemological investigations at the center of their work. If we cannot understand what made them take so seriously the questions that seem odd to us today, then we cannot really understand philosophy as it has been done during the past four centuries. In the second place, the strange-seeming problems of the modern theory of knowledge (in philosophy, anything since 1600 is called "modern") connect directly with one of the dominant cultural and intellectual developments of the postmedieval world—namely, the steady movement toward a radical individualism in religion, in politics, in art, and in literature, as well as in philosophy. Though the epistemological puzzles of seventeenth- and eighteenth-century philosophy seem bizarre or unintuitive on first inspection, they have deeply influenced the way painters painted; the way poets wrote; the way theologians reinterpreted the Word of God; and even the way economists, political scientists, and sociologists have explained our collective social life. So like it or not, we are in for some complicated philosophy in this chapter.

By common agreement, the man who started the new theory of knowledge on its way in philosophy was a Frenchman, born in 1596, named René Descartes. Indeed, though Descartes wrote a number of important works during his fifty-four years, in which mathematics, physics, and other subjects as well as philosophy were discussed, we can even name the precise piece of philosophy that marks the beginning of modern philosophy as we study it today. That honor clearly belongs to a seventy-page work entitled *Meditations on First Philosophy,* published by Descartes in 1641.

The seventeenth century was an age of scientific giants, and among the truly great thinkers whose efforts created what we know today as modern science, only the German Gottfried Leibniz and the Englishman Isaac Newton can stand with Descartes. You have probably already met Descartes, or at least spent some time working with one of his contributions to knowledge, for it was he who invented what is called analytic geometry. (That is why, when you draw a graph and plot points on it, you are said to be using "Cartesian" coordinates.)

Descartes was born three-quarters of a century after Martin Luther had begun the Protestant Reformation by nailing his famous theses to the church door in Wittenberg. Descartes himself was, and remained throughout his life, a Roman Catholic, and his early education was received from the Jesuits. Nevertheless, if the essence of the Protestant Reformation was the rejection of the religious authority of the institution of the Church and the emphasis on the primacy of individual conscience, then it is clear that Descartes was, intellectually and emotionally, an extreme protestant. The keynote of his life work was a thoroughgoing rejection of received opinion, established doctrine, and the authority of the ancients and a thoroughly individualistic insistence upon accepting only those truths which his own reason could certify to be correct.

In his early twenties, Descartes' interest turned to mathematics and physics, fields which at that time were dominated by concepts and methods almost 2,000 years old. Exciting new work was being done in both areas, and Descartes, like many young scientific geniuses, moved immediately to the scientific frontier. On the night of November 10, 1619, Descartes, then twenty-three, had a series of three dreams which seem to have transformed his life. He spoke and wrote of them ever after as the turning point in his career. I am not going to try my hand at armchair dream interpretation. As Freud made very clear when he first described the psychoanalytic method of interpreting dreams, you cannot figure out what a dream meant to the person who had it unless you can get that person actually to talk to you about the dream. There isn't any code book of dream symbols in which you can look up the meaning of falling, or a mirror, or whatever. But Descartes himself interpreted his dreams as a sign that he was to spend his life establishing a new, unified theory of the universe based upon mathematics—what we today would call mathematical physics.

The important part of Descartes' plan, for our purposes, is not the new science he developed, but his conception of the *method* by which he was to proceed. Descartes devoted a great deal of thought to problems of intellectual and scientific method, and his contributions in this field are, if anything, more revolutionary than his actual mathematical and scientific work itself. Descartes published nothing while he was young, despite the fact that he had made a number of important discoveries in his twenties and thirties. In 1637, when he was past forty, he brought out his first published work, appropriately titled "Discourse on the Method of Rightly Conducting the Reason and

Seeking for Truth in the Sciences." In this partly autobiographical, partly philosophical work, he lays down a set of four rules which he claims are sufficient to guide the mind in whatever inquiry it may undertake. Here are the rules, as Descartes stated them:

> The first of these was to accept nothing as true which I did not clearly recognize to be so: that is to say, carefully to avoid precipitation and prejudice in judgments, and to accept in them nothing more than what was presented to my mind so clearly and distinctly that I could have no occasion to doubt it.
>
> The second was to divide up each of the difficulties which I examined into as many parts as possible, and as seemed requisite in order that it might be resolved in the best manner possible.
>
> The third was to carry on my reflections in due order, commencing with objects that were the most simple and easy to understand, in order to rise little by little, or by degrees, to knowledge of the most complex, assuming an order, even if a fictitious one, among those which do not follow a natural sequence relatively to one another.
>
> The last was in all cases to make enumerations so complete and review so general that I should be certain of having omitted nothing.

RENÉ DESCARTES,
Discourse on Method

They don't seem like much when you first read them, do they? Avoid prejudice, don't take anything on faith, be careful, tackle questions a step at a time, be orderly, and so forth. It sounds more like instructions to an army filing clerk or the directions for assembling an outdoor barbecue grill than a great revolution in philosophy. Indeed, Leibniz once remarked rather sarcastically that Descartes' famous "method" boiled down to saying "Take what you need, and do what you should, and you will get what you want." But first impressions are often wrong (as Descartes himself pointed out), and in this case Leibniz was being more clever than wise.

The real importance of Descartes' method lies in two of its features and a consequence that follows from those two. Since what follows may be easier to understand if you have some labels to attach to it, let me start by telling you that Descartes' method is both a *method of inquiry* and a *method of doubt,* and that the combined consequence of these two methods is to set in motion a philosophical transformation known as the *epistemological turn.* Now, if you have carefully underlined these three terms in red or yellow or blue, we can try to make some sense out of them.

First, Descartes' method is a method of inquiry. In other words, it is a method for finding things out and making sure that you get them right; it is not a method for proving what you already know, or for setting forth your knowledge in the most systematic way. Think for a moment about traditional Euclidean geometry. On the first page of a geometry book (at least this was so when I went to school), you find definitions, axioms, and postulates. These are the simplest, or the most fundamental part of the geometric theory, but they are hardly the first things that a real mathematician would think up if she were doing geometry. Then come the theorems, each one neatly set forth, step by step, from the axioms or previously proved theorems down to what is to be proved, Q.E.D. That may be the way Euclid rearranged his proofs once he had thought them up, but it surely isn't the way he discovered them! Most likely, when he wanted to prove something (say, the theorem that the line bisecting the apex of an isosceles triangle is perpendicular to the base), he drew a diagram, fiddled around with the lines, looked to see whether there was anything that was equal to anything else, worked his way up from the conclusion and down from the premises, until the proof finally fell into place. So his *method of inquiry*—his way of finding something out—was very different from his method of proof or exposition. Descartes' rules for the mind are obviously intended as guides for someone who is trying to solve a problem or analyze a phenomenon. In other words (and this is going to turn out to be very important indeed), he adopts the point of view of someone who does not yet know anything but is trying by the use of his or her intelligence to discover something, rather than the point of view of a teacher or expert who is quite sure he or she knows something and is simply trying to explain it to someone else.

Second, Descartes' method is a method of doubt. His first rule is "to accept nothing as true which I do not clearly recognize to be so." Just how radical this rule will be depends on how we interpret the phrase "clearly recognize." If Descartes merely wants us to stop and think before we say we are sure, as a quiz show contestant might pause before answering the jackpot question, then obviously that rule is not going to produce any great intellectual revolution. But as you shall see in a few pages, when you read part of the *Meditations on First Philosophy,* Descartes had much more in mind. When he tells us not to accept anything unless we can "clearly recognize" it as true, he means that we should refuse to accept anything, however sure we once were of it, however many people believe it, however obvious it seems, unless we can be *absolutely certain that it is one hundred percent right.* If there is the slightest, the wildest, the farthest-out chance that it just might be false, then we are not to accept it. Now that opens up quite a can of worms! For example, I am quite sure that Washington, D.C., is the capital of the United States of America. If you ask me how I can be so sure, I will tell you that I have read it in history and government books, that I have heard Washington referred to a thousand times on television as "our nation's capital," that I have visited Washington and actually sat for a day in the visitors' gallery of the Senate, and so forth. But does that make it absolutely, one hundred percent certain? Couldn't I be wrong? It isn't likely that I am wrong, but is it logically possible? Maybe the books were wrong; maybe the television commentators were wrong; maybe I was actually in Philadelphia when I thought I was in Washington; indeed, maybe there is a great conspiracy afoot to fool me into thinking that Washington is the capital. I can't imagine why anyone would go to all that trouble, but it *is* possible. Put it this way: I could write a science fiction story about such a conspiracy; and although you might say it wasn't very plausible, you couldn't say that the story was a total impossibility.

Well, you protest, if Descartes is going to interpret "clearly recognize" like that, then just about everything anyone has ever believed will go out the window! I might as well doubt that there is even a United States, or an earth, or a human race, or space and time and the universe. If I am going to refuse to accept things like that, then maybe I ought to start doubting that two plus two is four. After all, if a giant conspiracy might be underway to trick me into believing that Washington is the capital of the United States, then maybe some mysterious, evil, powerful demon is reaching into my mind and tricking me into thinking that two plus two is four when really it is five. Maybe every time I take two objects and place them next to two more, that demon sneaks one of them away, so that as I count them up, I get only four instead of five, which is the right number!

Strange as it may sound, this is just what Descartes has in mind. When he says accept *nothing* that isn't certain, he means *nothing*. But, you object, that is madness! We have to start somewhere. Why, if I am going to doubt everything that has even the most minute bit of possible uncertainty attached to it, then I might even have to doubt my own existence! Perhaps I don't exist either; maybe that evil demon is fooling me about myself as well as about simple arithmetic! No, says Descartes, with one of the most dramatic reversals in all philosophical literature. Doubt all else, but you cannot doubt your own existence. That, and nothing but that, is the true foundation, the unshakable first principle, the rock on which all the rest of your knowledge shall be raised up. How does he manage to prove that I cannot rationally doubt my own existence, when he has erected a standard of certainty so strict that literally everything else that I have ever believed fails to meet it? You shall see when you read the *Meditations*. I do not want to spoil the effect of the argument by giving it away. Descartes' proof of his own existence is one of the high points in the history of philosophy. It is also, in a way, the high point of unbridled individualism in Western civilization. Imagine a philosopher who proposes to base the entire edifice of scientific, mathematical, and religious knowledge *not* on the collective learning and wisdom of humanity, *not* on the evidence of the laboratory, *not* on the existence of God, *not even* on the first principles of logic, *but simply on the fact of his own existence!*

When the method of inquiry is combined with the method of doubt, a transformation in the central nature of philosophy is begun. That transformation, which I am calling the epistemological turn, took a century and a half to complete. Not until Kant's *Critique of Pure Reason* was the epistemological turn brought to its end; thereafter, all philosophy was so changed that the very questions philosophers asked, as well as the answers they gave, looked little like what was written before the *Meditations.* The epistemological turn is a very simple, but tricky, notion. Even after you have it, you find it slipping away from you. Like Einstein's notion of relativity, or a Picasso painting, it makes you see familiar things in an entirely new way.

The heart of the *epistemological turn* is a simple reversal in order of two basic questions. From the ancient pre-Socratic cosmologists up to the time of Descartes, philosophers put questions about what exists, about the nature of the universe, before questions about what I can know to exist, about what I can know the nature of the universe to be. That is to say, philosophers considered questions of *being* to take precedence over questions of *knowing.* Aristotle, for example, called the essays in which he discussed questions of being "essays on first philosophy." He didn't mean that these very difficult, very abstract essays were the first sorts of philosophy a student should read. He meant that questions about the nature of being were the logically first, or most fundamental, or most basic questions to be dealt with.

To be sure, Aristotle and many of his predecessors and followers discussed the nature of knowledge. They talked about the nature of the mind, the role of the senses (sight, hearing, touch, and so forth) in knowledge, the role of reasoning, the limits of human knowledge, and countless other topics. But they considered these *epistemological* questions to be secondary, less important than questions about the nature of God, the reality of space and time, and all the other topics dealt with in "first philosophy," or as we call it today, metaphysics. So we can sum up philosophy prior to Descartes by saying that in it, *metaphysics took precedence over epistemology.*

Descartes' two methods—the method of inquiry and the method of doubt—had the effect of reversing this order of precedence. Properly understood and carried out with a consistency and rigor which Descartes himself never achieved, these two methods forced philosophers to set aside questions of being until they had dealt with the questions of knowing. And that fact in turn changed the meaning of the questions about being, so that by the time the revolution begun by Descartes had run its course, old-style metaphysics was finished, and new-style epistemology had taken its place as "first philosophy." Let us see how Descartes' two methods began this transformation.

 ☞ **Epistemological Skepticism**   The doctrine that no adequate justification can be given for any of our beliefs about the world, not even for apparently rock-solid beliefs that there is a physical world, that I have a body, that the sun will rise tomorrow, or that fire causes heat. The aim of epistemological skepticism is to focus our attention on the relationship between our beliefs and their justification, not actually to get us to stop believing.

First, as we have noted, the method of inquiry tells us to adopt the point of view of someone who is ignorant but is trying to learn, rather than the point of view of someone who knows something and is trying to explain. What is more, it teaches us to take questions in an orderly manner, not moving on to the next until we have settled the first. There is an old case in the English common law, going back to the Middle Ages, which illustrates the hidden force of Descartes' rule. Jones sued Smith for damages, claiming that Smith had borrowed a water jug from him and had returned it broken. Smith's defense was a classic of what we now call "stonewalling." "First," he argued, "the jug does not exist; second, I didn't borrow it; third, it was whole when I returned it; and fourth, it was cracked when I borrowed it." Smith wasn't out of his mind. He was simply saying to Jones, "Before I am going to pay you any money, you are going to have to prove every single item in your story. You must prove that the jug even exists; then you must prove that I borrowed it; then you must prove that I didn't return it whole; and then you must prove that it wasn't cracked when I borrowed it, but was cracked when I returned it." Now the legal point of this story is that proving one of these points might be a good deal harder than proving another, and Jones must prove them all in order to collect damages. If he threw the jug away after it was returned broken, then he may have trouble proving that it ever existed. Even if he kept the pieces, he may have trouble proving that it wasn't already cracked when he lent it to Smith. And so on. When the defense in a court case agrees not to dispute some assertion by the prosecution about the facts of the case, it is called "stipulating." Descartes' first rule tells us not to stipulate anything.

For example, at the beginning of his book entitled *Physics,* Aristotle says that the subject matter of physics is motion, or rather things in motion. If anyone wants to deny that there is motion in the world (as some philosophers in fact had denied), then a book on physics is not the right place to argue with him or her. "We physicists," Aristotle writes, "must take for granted that the things that exist by nature are, either all or some of them, in motion. . . . No man of science is bound to solve every kind of difficulty that may be raised, but only as many as are drawn falsely from the principles of the science." But Descartes adopts the opposite view. Before we can do physics, we must prove that there are bodies in motion in space. Once we have established that, we can appeal to the experiments and observations, deductions and proofs, which scientists have developed in their study of nature. But until we have shown that nature exists—until we have, like Jones, proved that there is a jug—we must set aside such investigations. We shall not stipulate the universe.

The second half of Descartes' method—the method of doubt—makes things ten times worse, of course. Having refused to stipulate anything, even the existence of the world, Descartes now insists that the standard of proof be absolute certainty. In a court of law, the jury is asked whether the case has been proved "beyond a reasonable doubt." There is a whole lot of difference between absolute certainty and beyond a reasonable doubt. I am pretty sure that my car won't turn into a boa constrictor and squeeze me to death while I am putting on my seat belt. I am sure enough of it to bet my life on it every day when I drive somewhere. My conviction goes way beyond any reasonable doubt. But if Descartes asks me whether I can be *certain* that my car won't turn into a boa, I must answer that of course I cannot rule it out as absolutely impossible. I can, after all, imagine some weird planet across the galaxy in which cars turn into boa constrictors. In a way, that isn't much stranger than the fact that caterpillars turn into butterflies.

Combining the two methods seems to drive us into the corner which philosophers call "skepticism." If we can't move on to point B until we have proved point A, and if in order to prove point A, we must establish it with absolute certainty, then it looks as though we will have a very hard time proving any point at all. Instead of wandering all over the universe, studying the stars, the planets, the origins of life, the workings of the human body, the laws of society, or the movement of the tides, we are going to be huddled in a corner, trying to figure out how to take step A, so that we can take step B.

Now, if your car is working, you go on trips and look at the scenery. But if your car won't run, you open the hood and inspect the motor. So too, if your logical engine is in good working order, then you cruise through the world of knowledge, looking at one interesting field after another; but if your logical engine breaks down—if your rules of inquiry and proof don't permit you to move with ease from one truth to another—then you stop, raise the lid on your mind (which is, after all, your logical engine), and take a good hard look to see what is wrong. In short, you start analyzing and examining the process by which you come to know anything. Epistemology is the study of the way in which we know, the rules by which we reason, the limits of what we can know, and the criteria or standards we use for judging whether a supposed piece of knowledge really is knowledge. If we follow Descartes' rule, we cannot take a scientific or metaphysical trip through the universe until we have checked out our means of transportation—our knowing process itself—and made sure that it will take us where we want to go.

Descartes himself never realized the full magnitude of the revolution that his two methods were to produce. He thought of himself as laying the basis for a new, unified system of scientific knowledge free of all reliance on tradition, the wisdom of the ancients, or the old concepts of Aristotelian metaphysics. But he seems still to have supposed that questions of being would take precedence over questions of knowing. In the *Meditations*, after the section which you are about to read, he went on to offer "proofs" for the existence of God, of the physical universe, and of all the other things he had so carefully doubted at the beginning of the essay. It remained for later philosophers, both on the continent of Europe and in Great Britain, to draw out the deeper implications of the process which Descartes started.

Here now are selections from the First and Second Meditations.

Meditation I

It is now some years since I detected how many were the false beliefs that I had from my earliest youth admitted as true and how doubtful was everything I had since constructed on this basis; and from that time I was convinced that I must once and for all seriously undertake to rid myself of all the opinions which I had formerly accepted, and commence to build anew from the foundation, if I wanted to establish any firm and permanent structure in the sciences.

Now for this object it is not necessary that I should show that all of these are false—I shall perhaps never arrive at this end. But inasmuch as reason already persuades me that I ought no less carefully to withhold my assent from matters which are not entirely certain and indubitable than from those which appear to me manifestly to be false, if I am able to find in each one some reason to doubt, this will suffice to justify my rejecting the whole. And for that end it will not be requisite that I should examine each in particular, which would be an endless undertaking; for owing to the fact that the destruction of the foundations of necessity brings with it the downfall of the rest of the edifice, I shall only in the first place attack those principles upon which all my former opinions rested.

All that up to the present time I have accepted as most true and certain I have learned either from the senses or through the senses; but it is sometimes proved to me that these senses are deceptive, and it is wiser not to trust entirely to any thing by which we have once been deceived.

But it may be that although the senses sometimes deceive us concerning things which are hardly perceptible, or very far away, there are yet many others to be met with as to which we cannot reasonably have any doubt, although we recognize them by their means. For example, there is the fact that I am here, seated by the fire, attired in a dressing gown, having this paper in my hands and other similar matters. And how could I deny these hands and this body are mine, were it not perhaps that I compare myself to certain persons, devoid of sense, whose cerebella are so troubled and clouded by the violent vapours of black bile, that they constantly assure us that they think they are kings when they are really quite poor, or that they are clothed in purple when they are really without covering, or who imagine that they have an earthenware head or are nothing but pumpkins or are made of glass. But they are mad, and I should not be any the less insane were I to follow examples so extravagant.

At the same time I must remember that I am a man, and that consequently I am in the habit of sleeping, and in my dreams representing to myself the same things or sometimes even less probable

RENÉ DESCARTES, *Meditations on First Philosophy*

things, than do those who are insane in their waking moments. How often has it happened to me that in the night I dreamt that I found myself in this particular place, that I was dressed and seated near the fire, whilst in reality I was lying undressed in bed! At this moment it does indeed seem to me that it is with eyes awake that I am looking at this paper, that this head which I move is not asleep, that it is deliberately and of set purpose that I extend my hand and perceive it; what happens in sleep does not appear so clear nor so distinct as does all this. But in thinking over this I remind myself that on many occasions I have in sleep been deceived by similar illusions, and in dwelling carefully on this reflection I see so manifestly that there are no certain indications by which we may clearly distinguish wakefulness from sleep that I am lost in astonishment. And my astonishment is such that it is almost capable of persuading me that I now dream.

Now let us assume that we are asleep and that all these particulars, e.g. that we open our eyes, shake our head, extend our hands, and so on, are but false delusions; and let us reflect that possibly neither our hands nor our whole body are such as they appear to us to be. At the same time we must at least confess that the things which are represented to us in sleep are like painted representations which can only have been formed as the counterparts of something real and true, and that in this way those general things at least, i.e. eyes, a head, hands, and a whole body, are not imaginary things, but things really existent. For, as a matter of fact, painters, even when they study with the greatest skill to represent sirens and satyrs by forms the most strange and extraordinary, cannot give them natures which are entirely new, but merely make a certain medley of the members of different animals; or if their imagination is extravagant enough to invent something so novel that nothing similar has ever before been seen, and that then their work represents a thing purely fictitious and absolutely false, it is certain all the same that the colours of which this is composed are necessarily real. And for the same reason, although these general things, to wit, [a body,] eyes, a head, hands, and such like, may be imaginary, we are bound at the same time to confess that there are at least some other objects yet more simple and more universal, which are real and true; and of these just in the same way as with certain real colours, all these images of things which dwell in our thoughts, whether true and real or false and fantastic, are formed.

To such a class of things pertains corporeal nature in general, and its extension, the figure of extended things, their quantity or magnitude and number, as also the pace in which they are, the time which measures their duration, and so on.

That is possibly why our reasoning is not unjust when we conclude from this that Physics, Astronomy, Medicine, and all other sciences which have as their end the consideration of composite things, are very dubious and uncertain; but with Arithmetic, Geometry, and other sciences of that kind which only treat of things that are very simple and very general, without taking great trouble to ascertain whether they are actually existent or not contain some measure of certainty and an element of the indubitable. For whether I am awake or asleep, two and three together always form five, and the square can never have more than four sides, and it does not seem possible that truths so clear and apparent can be suspected of any falsity [or uncertainty].

Nevertheless I have long had fixed in my mind the belief that an all-powerful God existed by whom I have been created such as I am. But how do I know that He has not brought it to pass that there is no earth, no heaven, no extended body, no magnitude, no place, and that nevertheless [I possess the perceptions of all these things and that] they seem to me to exist just exactly as I now see them? And, besides, as I sometimes imagine that others deceive themselves in the things which they think they know best, how do I know that I am not deceived every time that I add two and three, or count the sides of a square, or judge of things yet simpler, if anything simpler can be imagined? But possibly God has not desired that I should be thus deceived, for He is said to be supremely good. If, however, it is contrary to His goodness to have made me such that I constantly deceive myself, it would also appear to be contrary to His goodness to permit me to be sometimes deceived, and nevertheless I cannot doubt that He does permit this.

I shall then suppose, not that God who is supremely good and the fountain of truth, but some evil genius not less powerful than deceitful, has employed his whole energies in deceiving me; I shall consider that the heavens, the earth, colours, figures, sound, and all other external things are nought but the illusions and dreams of which this genius has availed himself in order to lay traps for my credulity; I shall consider myself as having no hands, no eyes, no flesh, no blood, nor any senses, yet falsely believing myself to possess all these things; I shall remain obstinately attached to this idea, and if by this means it is not in my power to arrive at the knowledge of any truth, I may at least do what is in my power [i.e. suspend my judgment], and with firm purpose avoid giving credence to any false thing, or being imposed upon by this arch deceiver, however powerful and deceptive he may be. . . .

Meditation II

The Meditation of yesterday filled my mind with so many doubts that it is no longer in my power to forget them. And yet I do not see in what manner I can resolve them; and, just as if I had all of a sud-

den fallen into very deep water, I am so disconcerted that I can neither make certain of setting my feet on the bottom, nor can I swim
and so support myself on the surface. I shall nevertheless make an
effort and follow anew the same path as that on which I yesterday
entered, i.e. I shall proceed by setting aside all that in which the least
doubt could be supposed to exist, just as if I had discovered that it
was absolutely false; and I shall ever follow in this road until I have
met with something which is certain, or at least, if I can do nothing
else, until I have learned for certain that there is nothing in the world
that is certain. Archimedes, in order that he might draw the terrestrial globe out of its place, and transport it elsewhere, demanded only
that one point should be fixed and immoveable; in the same way I
shall have the right to conceive high hopes if I am happy enough to
discover one thing only which is certain and indubitable.

I suppose, then, that all the things that I see are false; I persuade
myself that nothing has ever existed of all that my fallacious memory
represents to me. I consider that I possess no senses; I imagine that
body, figure, extension, movement and place are but the fictions of
my mind. What, then, can be esteemed as true? Perhaps nothing at
all, unless that there is nothing in the world that is certain.

But how can I know there is not something different from those
things that I have just considered, of which one cannot have the
slightest doubt? Is there not some God, or some other being by whatever name we call it, who puts these reflections into my mind? That
is not necessary, for is it not possible that I am capable of producing
them myself? I myself, am I not at least something? But I have
already denied that I had senses and body. Yet I hesitate, for what
follows from that? Am I so dependent on body and senses that I cannot exist without these? But I was persuaded that there was nothing
in all the world, that there was no heaven, no earth, that there were
no minds, nor any bodies: was I not then likewise persuaded that I
did not exist? Not at all; of a surety I myself did exist since I persuaded myself of something [or merely because I thought of some-
thing]. But there is some deceiver or other, very powerful and very
cunning, who ever employs his ingenuity in deceiving me. Then without doubt I exist also if he deceives me, and let him deceive me as
much as he will, he can never cause me to be nothing so long as I
think that I am something. So that after having reflected well and
carefully examined all things, we must come to the definite conclusion that this proposition: I am, I exist, is necessarily true each time
that I pronounce it, or that I mentally conceive it.

But I do not yet know clearly enough what I am, I who am certain that I am; and hence I must be careful to see that I do not impru-
dently take some other object in place of myself, and thus that I do
not go astray in respect of this knowledge that I hold to be the most

certain and most evident of all that I have formerly learned. That is why I shall now consider anew what I believed myself to be before I embarked upon these last reflections; and of my former opinions I shall withdraw all that might even in a small degree be invalidated by the reasons which I have just brought forward, in order that there may be nothing at all left beyond what is absolutely certain and indubitable.

Rationalism and Empiricism: Two Responses to Cartesian Doubt

When Descartes summarized his proof for his own existence in Latin, he used the phrase *Cogito, ergo sum,* which means "I think, therefore I am." So his proof has come to be known in philosophical shorthand as the Cogito Argument. If you read the selection from the *Meditations* carefully, you will realize that "I think, therefore I am" is not exactly what Descartes says. Instead, he says something slightly but very significantly different, namely, "The proposition, I exist, is necessarily true each time I pronounce it." Pronouncing or asserting the proposition is crucial, because it is the asserting that guarantees its truth. The point is that if the proposition is being *asserted,* then someone must be doing the asserting, and if I am asserting it, then that someone must be me. Needless to say, I cannot use this proof to establish the existence of anyone else. Suppose, for example, that I try to prove my wife's existence by saying, "The proposition, She exists, is necessarily true each time I pronounce it." Well, that just won't work. The fact that I pronounce or assert that she exists in no way guarantees that she does. But it does guarantee that I exist! In fact, my asserting any proposition, true or false, about myself or about anything else, guarantees that I exist, because I am the subject, the asserter, the conscious thinker of the proposition. And—this is the key point—assertions cannot simply hang in midair with no one asserting them. When a proposition is asserted, it must be asserted *by* someone.

Incidentally, I hope you realize that Descartes' Cogito Argument only proves his existence to him; it doesn't prove his existence to you or to me.

> **Solipsism**   Literally, the belief that I am the only person in the universe. Somewhat more generally, solipsism is an extreme form of epistemological skepticism which refuses to acknowledge the existence of anything other than my own mind. Some philosophers have even argued that I cannot be sure of anything but my own mind *right now,* since my memories might also be mistaken.

"The proposition, Descartes exists, is necessarily true each time I pronounce it" doesn't hold water at all. Descartes can use his new argument to prove his existence to himself, I can use his argument to prove my existence to myself, and each of you can use his argument to prove your own existence to yourself. But no one can use the argument to prove someone else's existence. This fact about the Cogito Argument has two important consequences for subsequent epistemology. First, it drives each philosopher into the position called solipsism; that is, the individual subject knows its own existence prior to, and better than, anything else and perhaps knows the existence of nothing but itself. Second, it turns the attention of philosophers away from the *objects* of knowledge, the things that we know about, and toward the *subject* of knowledge, the mind that does the knowing. Later in this chapter, we shall see that this pair of implications of the Cogito Argument is used by Kant in his effort to find a way out of the skepticism and solipsism of the Cartesian position.

Descartes got himself, and us, into the skeptical solipsist box in the First Meditation by doubting everything that was not known with certainty. He proceeded, you will recall, by adopting a criterion of certainty so strict that in the end, nothing save the assertion of his own existence could meet its requirements. In surveying the multitude of his beliefs, furthermore, Descartes divided them into two major groups: those which he thought he knew on the basis of the evidence of his own senses and those which he thought he knew on the basis of reasoning with general concepts. In this way, two central problems are raised by the argument in the First Meditation. The first is the problem of *certainty*. What criterion of truth should we adopt as the standard against which to measure our various knowledge claims? The second is the problem of the sources of knowledge. Insofar as we know anything, is our knowledge based upon the evidence of the senses, upon abstract reasoning, or upon some combination of the two? The philosophy of the 150 years following the publication of the *Meditations* was very largely a series of variations on these two themes.

Descartes himself offered preliminary answers to the questions of certainty and the sources of knowledge in the latter part of the Second Meditation. Before taking our leave of him, and moving on to survey the attempts of his successors to deal with the problems he raised, perhaps we ought to see what he had to say about them. On the problem of certainty, he offered two criteria, two tests of the certainty of an assertion. Here is what he says:

> I am certain that I am a thing which thinks; but do I not then likewise know what is requisite to render me certain of a truth? Certainly in this first knowledge there is nothing that assures me of its truth, excepting the clear and distinct perception of that which I state, which would not indeed suffice to assure me that what I say is true, if it could ever happen that a thing which I conceived so clearly and distinctly could be false; and accordingly it seems to me that already

I can establish as a general rule that all things which I perceive very clearly and very distinctly are true.

Clearness and distinctness aren't much as a hedge against the far-reaching skepticism fostered by the method of doubt. How can I be sure that I really perceive a proposition clearly or distinctly? It is no good saying that it really, truly *seems* clear and distinct to me. After all, it really, truly seems to me that I am awake, but as Descartes himself pointed out, I might nonetheless be mistaken. Later on, after using the clearness and distinctness test to prove the existence of God, Descartes turns around and uses the goodness of God as a proof that clearness and distinctness are adequate criteria of certainty. A good God, he argues, would not deceive me! Well, that is about as obvious a case of arguing in a circle as you will find in the writings of great philosophers, and I think we can agree that having posed the problem of certainty, Descartes didn't really have a solution to it.

As for the sources of our knowledge, Descartes came down foursquare on the side of reason rather than the senses. That is what you would expect from someone whose dream it was to create a mathematical physics. In place of observation and the collecting of data from sight, smell, hearing, and touch, Descartes wanted a universal system of science derived from logical and mathematical premises and proved by rigorous deduction.

In order to persuade his readers of the primacy of reason in our acquiring of knowledge, Descartes uses what is called a "thought experiment." That is, he asks us to imagine with him a situation—in this case, that he is sitting near his fire with a piece of wax in his hand—and then he tries to get us to see, through an analysis of the situation, that our methods of reasoning or of acquiring knowledge must have a certain character. Philosophers frequently argue in this way when they are trying to establish some general proposition rather than to prove a particular fact. The thought experiment isn't supposed to be evidence, in the modern scientific sense. Rather, it is merely a device for exploring the logical or conceptual relationships between different ideas. Here is Descartes' thought experiment to show that our knowledge comes from understanding or reason or the mind, rather than through the senses.

Let us begin by considering the commonest matters, those which we believe to be the most distinctly comprehended, to wit, the bodies which we touch and see; not indeed bodies in general, for these general ideas are usually a little more confused, but let us consider one body in particular. Let us take, for example, this piece of wax: it has been taken quite freshly from the hive, and it has not yet lost the sweetness of the honey which it contains; it still retains somewhat of the odour of the flowers from which it has been culled; its colour, its figure, its size are apparent; it is hard, cold, easily handled, and if you strike it with the finger, it will emit a sound. Finally all the things

Meditations on First Philosophy

which are requisite to cause us distinctly to recognize a body, are met with in it. But notice that while I speak and approach the fire what remained of the taste is exhaled, the smell evaporates, the colour alters, the figure is destroyed, the size increases, it becomes liquid, it heats, scarcely can one handle it, and when one strikes it, no sound is emitted. Does the same wax remain after this change? We must confess that it remains; none would judge otherwise. What then did I know so distinctly in this piece of wax? It could certainly be nothing of all that the senses brought to my notice, since all these things which fall under taste, smell, sight, touch, and hearing, are found to be changed, and yet the same wax remains.

Perhaps it was what I now think, viz. that this wax was not that sweetness of honey, nor that agreeable scent of flowers, nor that particular whiteness, nor that figure, nor that sound, but simply a body which a little while before appeared to me as perceptible under these forms, and which is now perceptible under others. But what, precisely, is it that I imagine when I form such conceptions? Let us attentively consider this, and, abstracting from all that does not belong to the wax, let us see what remains. Certainly nothing remains excepting a certain extended thing which is flexible and movable. But what is the meaning of flexible and movable? Is it not that I imagine that this piece of wax being round is capable of becoming square and of passing from a square to a triangular figure? No, certainly it is not that, since I imagine it admits of an infinitude of similar changes, and I nevertheless do not know how to compass the infinitude by my imagination, and consequently this conception which I have of the wax is not brought about by the faculty of imagination. What now is this extension? Is it not also unknown? For it becomes greater when the wax is melted, greater when it is boiled, and greater still when the heat increases, and I should not conceive [clearly] according to truth what wax is, if I did not think that even this piece that we are considering is capable of receiving more variations in extension than I have ever imagined. We must then grant that I could not even understand through the imagination what this piece of wax is, and that it is my mind alone which perceives it. I say this piece of wax in particular, for as to wax in general it is yet clearer. But what is this piece of wax which cannot be understood excepting by the [understanding or] mind? It is certainly the same that I see, touch, imagine, and finally it is the same which I have always believed it to be from the beginning. But what must particularly be observed is that its perception is neither an act of vision, nor of touch, nor of imagination, and has never been such although it may have appeared formerly to be so, but only an intuition of the mind, which may be imperfect and confused as it was formerly, or clear and distinct as it is at present according as my attention is more or less directed to the elements which are found in it, and of which it is composed.

The debate over Descartes' problems soon resolved itself into a conflict between two more or less unified schools of thought, the Continental rationalists and the British empiricists. (Since this makes it sound a bit like an international soccer match, let me explain that those are labels we put on the two groups today; they themselves did not go about wearing T-shirts saying "Continental Rationalist" or "British Empiricist.") The rationalists accepted Descartes' demand for certainty, agreed with his view that logic and mathematics were the model for all true knowledge, and sought to discover ways of establishing the principal propositions of science and metaphysics with as much certainty as the truths of the syllogism or geometry possessed. They sought proofs for the existence of God (using some that had been around for quite a while, such as the cosmological and ontological proofs that we have already examined); they offered demonstrations of the fundamental principles of the new physics; and they pursued Descartes' dream of a universal system of knowledge. Like Descartes, they downgraded the senses as a source of knowledge and instead claimed that all valid knowledge claims must rest upon the operations of reason.

The empiricists also accepted Descartes' demand for certainty, but in progressively more sweeping attacks on the knowledge claims of the rationalists, they argued that nothing could meet that demand. David Hume, the most brilliant and thoroughgoing of the empiricists, produced devastating proofs that neither the theorems of science nor the beliefs of common sense could possibly qualify as knowledge when measured against Descartes' own standard of certainty.

The empiricists also challenged the rationalists' reliance upon reason as the sole source of knowledge. First John Locke, in his *Essay Concerning the Human Understanding,* and then Hume, in *A Treatise of Human Nature,* insisted that all the ideas in the human mind must ultimately be derived from the sights, sounds, smells, feels, and tastes of our sense organs. Reason, they argued, could do no more than rearrange and sort the materials provided to the mind by sensation. This subordination of reason to the senses was one of the most powerful weapons in the empiricists' assault on the systems of science and metaphysics erected by the rationalists.

If you have managed to follow our discussion of epistemology thus far, it should be obvious to you that there is much more to be discussed in the theory of knowledge than we can hope to touch on in the remainder of this chapter. Rather than mentioning everyone and everything without explaining anything, therefore, I shall limit myself to *three* areas. First, we shall take a brief look at Gottfried Leibniz's attempt to deal with the criteria of certainty, and his very important distinction between what he calls truths of reasoning and truths of fact. Then, we shall examine David Hume's attempt to reduce all the contents of the mind to data of the senses, and his analysis of the criterion of certainty, so that we can understand the full force of his skeptical attack on the claims of science and common sense. And, finally, I will try to explain how Immanuel Kant sought to overcome the division between the rationalists and the empiricists by compromising their dispute over the sources of knowledge and the criteria of certainty. If you can get all that under your belt, then you will have had quite enough philosophy for one chapter!

⚒ Leibniz and Rationalism

Descartes' tests of certainty were clearness and distinctness. These essentially psychological criteria tell us very little about the structure of knowledge, about the kinds of knowledge claims that can meet the test of certainty and the kinds that cannot. After all, any belief might, upon inspection, turn out to be conceived clearly and distinctly, or at least it might seem to be. I think I clearly and distinctly apprehend that two things added to two things make a total of four things; but I also think I clearly and distinctly apprehend that I am seated now at a desk in my office, with a computer in front of me and a chair under me.

In place of Descartes' psychological tests, Leibniz offered logical criteria of truth and certainty. All truths, he proposed, could be divided into two sorts. The first are truths that can be known merely by application of a fundamental principle of logic called the **law of contradiction.** When we state some truth, we do so by making an assertion. "Two plus two equals four" is an assertion; "Washington, D.C., is the capital of the United States" is an assertion; "$E = mc^2$" is an assertion. Any declarative statement in its ordinary usage makes an assertion. If I have one assertion, I can make another, opposite assertion simply by denying the first. So from "Two plus two equals four" I can make "It is not the case that two plus two equals four." From "Washington, D.C., is the capital of the United States" I can make "It is not the case that Washington, D.C., is the capital of the United States." The denial of an assertion is called *negation,* and since "It is not the case that" is a little clumsy to keep repeating, philosophers and logicians shorten it to "not." The negation of "Two plus two equals four" would thus be "Not two plus two equals four," and so on.

If you think about it for a moment, you will see that a statement and its negation cannot both be true. Maybe Washington is our capital—maybe it isn't—but there is just no way that it can both be and not be our capital. Logicians express this in very general form by saying that for any statement, it cannot be the case that both the statement and its negation are true. Because two statements are said to "contradict" one another if they cannot both be true, this general principle about statements and their negations is called the law of contradiction. There is another law of logic which usually goes along with the law of contradiction, according to which for any statement, either it is true or else its negation is true. There is no third possibility, no middle ground. This law is called the law of the excluded middle. So logic teaches us that no matter what statement we are thinking about, either it is true or its negation is true, but not both.

According to Leibniz, truths of reasoning are those statements which we can know to be true merely by using the law of contradiction (and the law of the excluded middle, although he doesn't mention it). For example, suppose a fast-talking door-to-door salesman tries to push a fifteen-volume encyclopedia on you. "This encyclopedia is absolutely free," he says, "You only pay ten dollars per volume." Now you don't have to know anything about encyclopedias to be certain that he isn't telling you the truth. All you have to do is whip out your trusty law of contradiction and perform the following process of reasoning:

— Number one, you say this encyclopedia is absolutely free.

— Number two, you say I must pay ten dollars per volume for it.

— But "free" means "I don't have to pay."

— So you are saying that I don't have to pay, and I do have to pay.

— Or, as we logicians put it, I do have to pay and not I do have to pay.

— And that violates the law of contradiction, so it must be false. What is more, with a quick application of the law of the excluded middle, I can draw the absolutely certain conclusion that

— Either I have to pay or I do not have to pay, so stop the fast talk and tell me which it is.

Truths of reasoning are nice, because we can know them to be certain merely by application of these two simple laws, but they leave a good deal to be desired. Thus, my bit of reasoning doesn't tell me whether I have to pay. It just tells me that either I have to or I don't, but not both. Truths that cannot be certified by appeal to the laws of logic are called truths of fact by

---

⌢ Law of Contradiction/Law of the Excluded Middle   The two basic laws of formal logic. The *Law of Contradiction* states that a statement and its contradictory cannot both be true. For example, the statement, "Fire is hot" may be true, and it may be false. Its contradictory, "It isn't the case that fire is hot" may be true, and it may be false. But it cannot be that *both* the statement *and* its contradictory are true. The *Law of the Excluded Middle* says that for any statement, *either* it is true *or* its contradictory is true. Thus, either fire is hot, or it is not the case that fire is hot.

Leibniz. They include most of what we ordinarily call *knowledge*. To establish their truth, we must appeal to a quite different principle, which Leibniz labeled the principle of sufficient reason. Here is the passage from his short summary work, *The Monadology*, in which he defined and distinguished the two sorts of truths.

GOTTFRIED LEIBNIZ,
The Monadology

Our reasoning is based upon two great principles: first, that of Contradiction, by means of which we decide that to be false which involves contradiction and that to be true which contradicts or is opposed to the false.

And second, the principle of Sufficient Reason, in virtue of which we believe that no fact can be real or existing and no statement true unless it has a sufficient reason why it should be thus and not otherwise. Most frequently, however, these reasons cannot be known by us.

There are also two kinds of Truths: those of Reasoning and those of Fact. The Truths of Reasoning are necessary, and their opposite is impossible. Those of Fact, however, are contingent, and their opposite is possible. When a truth is necessary, the reason can be found by analysis in resolving it into simpler ideas and into simpler truths until we reach those which are primary. . . .

There are finally simple ideas of which no definition can be given. There are also the Axioms and Postulates or, in a word, the primary principles which cannot be proved and, indeed, have no need of proof. These are identical propositions whose opposites involve express contradictions.

But there must also be a sufficient reason for contingent truths or truths of fact; that is to say, for the sequence of the things which extend throughout the universe of created beings, where the analysis into more particular reasons can be continued into greater detail without limit because of the immense variety of the things in nature and because of the infinite division of bodies. There is an infinity of figures and of movements, present and past, which enter into the efficient cause of my present writing, and in its final cause there are an infinity of slight tendencies and dispositions of my soul, present and past.

And as all this detail again involves other and more detailed contingencies, each of which again has need of a similar analysis in order to find its explanation, no real advance has been made. Therefore, the sufficient or ultimate reason must needs be outside of the sequence or series of these details of contingencies, however infinite they may be.

It is thus that the ultimate reason for things must be a necessary substance, in which the detail of the changes shall be present merely potentially, as in the fountainhead, and this substance we call God.

Valid Arguments	
1. Major Premise	All dogs are mammals.
Minor Premise	All poodles are dogs.
CONCLUSION	All poodles are mammals.
2. Major Premise	Some band members are freshmen.
Minor Premise	No freshmen are frat members.
CONCLUSION	Some band members are not frat members.

Invalid Arguments	
1. Major Premise	Some dogs are affectionate.
Minor Premise	Some affectionate animals are cats.
CONCLUSION	Some dogs are cats.
2. Major Premise	Some preserves are not marmalade.
Minor Premise	All marmalade is made from oranges.
CONCLUSION	Some preserves are made from oranges.

The first two arguments are "valid"—that means that the conclusion follows from the premises. Can you figure out why they are valid? The second two arguments are not valid. The conclusion does not follow from the premises (even though, in the fourth argument, the conclusion happens to be true). How can we tell whether an argument is valid or invalid?

As you can see, Leibniz thought that when it came to truths of fact, such as the laws of physics or the facts of history, we could only certify them by an indirect appeal to God. The skeptical opponents of the rationalists had very little faith in the proofs for the existence of God, so you can imagine that they were not much impressed by this sort of justification for scientific theories. (Hume's objections to some of those proofs appeared in Chapter 5.)

Hume and Empiricism

The first major assault on the Continental rationalists was launched by the Englishman John Locke, whose theory of the social contract you have already encountered. Locke hit upon a simple but very powerful strategy for attacking the claims by Descartes and others that reason alone could provide us with knowledge. Instead of examining our knowledge claims directly, Locke suggested, let us instead ask from what source we derive the ideas which we use in stating these knowledge claims. Scientists and metaphysicians had been accustomed to express their theories by statements using terms like "matter," "space," "time," "substance," "cause," "necessary," "possible," "object," and "self." In addition, of course, they used more familiar terms like "red," "hard," "round," and "sweet." If our knowledge claims make any sense at all, Locke argued, then these words must correspond to ideas in our minds. Otherwise, we will simply seem to be saying something, but really we won't be asserting anything at all. (This is what humorists do when they write nonsense verse. Lewis Carroll, the author of *Alice in Wonderland,* wrote a poem that begins, "Twas brillig, and the slithy toves did gyre and gimble in the wabe." That sounds as though it ought to mean something, but it doesn't, because "words" like "brillig" and "toves" don't correspond to any ideas in our minds.)

According to Locke, the mind is a tabula rasa when we are born. He compares it to a piece of white paper on which experience writes. Here, from his *Essay Concerning the Human Understanding* (Book II, Chapter 1), is his statement of this famous doctrine:

> Let us then suppose the mind to be, as we say, white paper, void of all characters, without any ideas;—How comes it to be furnished? Whence comes it by that wide store which the busy and boundless fancy of man has painted on it with almost endless variety? Whence has it all the *materials* of reason and knowledge? To this I answer, in one word, EXPERIENCE. In that all our knowledge is founded; and from it ultimately derives itself.

That doesn't sound like such a brilliant philosophical strategy when you first hear it. Indeed, it sounds positively obvious. But in the hands of Locke, of George Berkeley, and especially of David Hume, it turned out to be a crusher. To see why this is so, think for a moment about all the statements that philosophers and theologians have asserted over the ages about God. Every one of those statements uses the idea of God somehow. For example, one statement is that God exists; a second is that God is omnipotent; a third is that God has promised us eternal life if only we will obey His laws; and so forth. If we follow Locke's suggestion, instead of asking directly what evidence there is for these statements, we will instead ask, Is there an *idea* of God in our minds corresponding to the word "God" which is used in each of the statements? And following Locke's theory of the blank white paper, we will ask whether the idea of God has come to us through our eyes, our ears, our fingertips, our noses, or our other sense organs. As soon as you put the question that way, it is obvious that we couldn't have derived the idea of God from any sensory sources. God is supposed to be infinite, but we can only see, hear, feel, and taste finite things. God is supposed to be eternal, but we cannot see or hear or feel something that exists outside time, or even something that exists in time forever and ever. God is supposed to be omnipotent, but the most our senses could ever show us is something very powerful, not something infinitely powerful. So it would seem to follow simply and directly from Locke's strategy that *we do not really have an idea of God at all!* We have the word "God" and we make up what we think are meaningful statements using it, but all that talk about God turns out to have no more meaning that Lewis Carroll's poem about slithy toves. (Incidentally, Locke himself did not draw his antireligious conclusion from his theory of ideas, and he would have been horrified by it.)

⌒ **Tabula Rasa** Literally, blank tablet. The term was used by John Locke to summarize his claim that the mind comes into life blank or empty, and is written on by experience as though it were a clay or wax tablet waiting to be marked by a writing stylus. Locke was arguing against the widely held view that the mind comes to experience with ideas which are built into it (or "hard-wired," as computer types like to say).

Since the last paragraph may have whipped by a bit fast, let's stop a moment and be sure that we understand what the argument is really saying. Lewis Carroll's poem isn't *false;* it is *meaningless,* because it uses "words" which don't correspond to ideas in our minds and hence have no meaning. A statement has to mean something before we can ask whether it is true or false. Philosophical books are full of arguments about the truth or falsehood of various theological, metaphysical, and scientific theories. But Locke's attack cuts these arguments off at the knees. Before two philosophers can even begin to argue about the existence of God, they must show that their words have meaning. According to Locke, that means showing that the words correspond to ideas in our minds which have been derived from the senses. So by his strategy of looking to the sources of our ideas, together with his doctrine of the mind as a blank sheet of paper written on by experience, Locke shifted the whole debate into a new channel.

Locke's weapon, incidentally, is a double-edged sword. If the theory proves that we do not even have a coherent idea of God, then one possible conclusion is that all our talk about God is nonsense, and all our theories of religion meaningless. But another possible conclusion is that since his theory implies such a ridiculous notion, it must itself be false! It comes down to deciding which is harder to believe. If I do have an idea of God, then it cannot have come through my senses, so I am going to have to explain how the mind can acquire ideas which it does not derive from sense experience; on the other hand, if all my ideas are derived from sense experience, then I cannot have an idea of God, so I am going to have to explain why so many apparently reasonable people firmly believe that they have such an idea, and why people who talk about God think they are making sense and not nonsense.

The empiricist who carried Locke's strategy to its logical conclusion was David Hume. As you will recall from Chapter One, Hume conceived the plan, when still a very young man, of writing a full-scale theory of the human mind along the lines of Isaac Newton's enormously successful theory of the physical universe. In the very opening pages of *A Treatise of Human Nature,* Hume adopts Locke's strategy and stakes out his own version of the "white paper" principle. In the following selection, remember that Hume uses the word "perception" to mean any content of the mind. He then divides perceptions

GEORGE BERKELEY

George Berkeley (1685–1753) was an Irish philosopher and cleric who is remembered as the defender of a philosophical position known as "idealism." Berkeley's most important philosophical works, including his *Treatise Concerning the Principles of Human Knowledge* and *Three Dialogues Between Hylas and Philonus*, were all written before his thirtieth birthday. Berkeley defended the view that the only things that could be known to exist are human minds, the ideas in these minds, and God. This doctrine is opposed to the view, defended by Hobbes and others, that physical bodies are the only things that exist ("materialism").

Berkeley spent three years in the New World, seeking to found a college in the Bermudas. Though his plans were never carried out, he did leave his philosophical library to the then recently founded Yale College in New Haven, Connecticut.

into those which come directly from our senses and those which we form from our impressions by copying, rearranging, and otherwise altering them.

DAVID HUME,
*A Treatise of
Human Nature*

Perceptions: Impressions and Ideas

All the perceptions of the human mind resolve themselves into two distinct kinds, which I shall call IMPRESSIONS and IDEAS. The difference betwixt these consists in the degrees of force and liveliness with which they strike upon the mind, and make their way into our thought or consciousness. Those perceptions, which enter with most force and violence, we may name *impressions;* and under this name I comprehend all our sensations, passions and emotions, as they make their first appearance in the soul. By *ideas* I mean the faint images of these in thinking and reasoning; such as, for instance, are all the perceptions excited by the present discourse, excepting only, those which arise from the sight and touch, and excepting the immediate pleasure or uneasiness it may occasion. I believe it will not be very necessary to employ many words in explaining this distinction. Every one of himself will readily perceive the difference betwixt feeling and thinking. The common degrees of these are easily distinguished; tho' it is not impossible but in particular instances they may very nearly approach to each other. Thus in sleep, and in fever, in madness, or in any very violent emotions of soul, our ideas may approach to our impressions: As on the other hand it sometimes happens, that our impressions are so faint and low, that we cannot distinguish them from our ideas. But notwithstanding this near resemblance in a few instances, they are in general so very different, that no-one can make a scruple to rank them under distinct heads, and assign to each a peculiar name to mark the difference.

There is another division of our perceptions, which it will be convenient to observe, and which extends itself both to our impressions and ideas. This division is into SIMPLE and COMPLEX. Simple perceptions or impressions and ideas are such as admit of no distinction nor separation. The complex are the contrary to these, and may be distinguished into parts. Tho' a particular colour, taste, and smell are qualities all united together in this apple, 'tis easy to perceive they are not the same, but are at least distinguishable from each other.

Having by these divisions given an order and arrangement to our objects, we may now apply ourselves to consider with the more accuracy their qualities and relations. The first circumstance, that strikes my eye, is the great resemblance betwixt our impressions and ideas in every other particular, except their degree of force and vivacity. The one seem to be in a manner the reflexion of the other, so that all the perceptions of the mind are double, and appear both as impressions and ideas. When I shut my eyes and think of my chamber, the ideas I form are exact representations of the impressions I felt; nor is there any circumstance of the one, which is not to be found in the other. In running over my other perceptions, I find still the same resemblance and representation. Ideas and impressions appear always to correspond to each other. This circumstance seems to me remarkable, and engages my attention for a moment.

Upon a more accurate survey I find I have been carried away too far by the first appearance, and that I must make use of the distinction of perceptions into *simple and complex,* to limit this general decision, *that all our ideas and impressions are resembling.* I observe, that many of our complex ideas never had impressions, that corresponded to them, and that many of our complex impressions never are exactly copied in ideas. I can imagine to myself such a city as the *New Jerusalem,* whose pavement is gold and walls are rubies, tho' I never saw any such. I have seen *Paris;* but shall I affirm I can form such an idea of that city, as will perfectly represent all its streets and houses in their real and just proportions?

I perceive, therefore, that tho' there is in general a great resemblance betwixt our complex impressions and ideas, yet the rule is not universally true, that they are exact copies of each other. We may next consider how the case stands with our simple perceptions. After the most accurate examination, of which I am capable, I venture to affirm, that the rule here holds without any exception, and that every simple idea has a simple impression, which resembles it; and every simple impression a correspondent idea. That idea of red, which we form in the dark, and that impression, which strikes our eyes in sunshine, differ only in degree, not in nature. That the case is the same with all our simple impressions and ideas, 'tis impossible to prove by a particular enumeration of them. Everyone may satisfy himself in this point by running over as many as he pleases. But if any one should deny this universal resemblance, I know no way of convincing him, but by desiring him to shew a simple impression that has not a correspondent idea, or a simple idea, that has not a correspondent impression. If he does not answer this challenge, as 'tis certain he cannot, we may from his silence and our own observation establish our conclusion.

Thus we find, that all simple ideas and impressions resemble each other; and as the complex are formed from them, we may affirm in general, that these two species of perception are exactly correspondent. Having discover'd this relation, which requires no farther examination, I am curious to find some other of their qualities. Let us consider how they stand with regard to their existence, and which of the impressions and ideas are causes, and which effects.

The *full* examination of this question is the subject of the present treatise; and therefore we shall here content ourselves with establishing one general proposition. *That all our simple ideas in their first appearance are deriv'd from simple impressions, which are correspondent to them, and which they exactly represent.*

Hume's style is not nearly as technical or forbidding as that of Aristotle, Descartes, Leibniz, or Kant, but you mustn't be misled into supposing that his arguments are therefore less powerful. The few simple principles which he lays down in the opening pages of the *Treatise* turn out to be more than enough to destroy some of the most impressive systems built up by his philosophical predecessors. There are three key points to notice in the passage you have just read. The first, of course, is Hume's adoption of the "white paper" theory. The second is what is sometimes called the copy theory of ideas. According to Hume, all our ideas are either straight copies of sense impressions or combinations and rearrangements of copies of sense impressions. When we are confronted with some metaphysical statement, therefore, we need not ask immediately whether it is true or false. Instead, we may simply examine the words in which it is expressed and ask whether they correspond to ideas in our minds. If we do have such ideas, then either they will be copies of sense impressions or they will be constructed out of copies of sense impressions by combinations and rearrangements. We have already seen what a blow this doctrine can be to the claim that we have an idea of God. The third important point is that Hume has an "atomic" theory of the contents of the mind. That is to say, he conceives of the mind as containing little indivisible

A centaur being driven by a Bacchant; after an ancient painting found in the Herculaneum. Undated engraving. (Corbis–Bettmann.)

Louis the XIV on horseback with the symbol of Victory. Painting by P. Mignard. Castle Versailles. (Corbis–Bettmann.)

"atomic" bits of sensation, plus indivisible copies of those bits of sensation, plus what we might call "molecular" combinations of atomic sensations. But unlike chemical molecules, the combinations of atomic sensations don't have any properties that the atomic components lack.

Since all the contents of the mind can be divided into atomic units, it follows that we can always distinguish one unit from another. In addition, Hume says, the mind has the power to "separate" two units of sensation from one another by imagining one away while keeping the other in mind. For example, when I look at a horse, I can distinguish my visual perception of its head from my visual perception of its body. Therefore, I can at least *imagine* the head without the body, or the body without the head. That power of "separating" impressions in imagination, and then recombining the parts in new ways, is of course what we all do when we imagine giants, or unicorns, or little green men, or anything else we have not actually seen. Hume summarizes this third point, a bit later on in the *Treatise,* in two principles:

1. Whatever objects are different are distinguishable.

2. Whatever objects are distinguishable are separable by thought and imagination.

By means of these two principles, which follow directly from his copy theory of ideas and his atomic theory of the contents of the mind, Hume constructs an argument which at one blow wipes out all metaphysics, all natural science, and just about all our commensense beliefs about the world. Here is the entire argument, as it appears in the *Treatise.*

DAVID HUME,
A Treatise of
Human Nature

'Tis a general maxim in philosophy that whatever begins to exist, must have a cause of existence. This is commonly taken for granted in all reasonings, without any proof given or demanded. 'Tis suppos'd to be founded on intuition, and to be one of those maxims, which tho' they may be deny'd with the lips, 'tis impossible for men in their hearts really to doubt of. But if we examine this maxim by the idea of knowledge above-explain'd, we shall discover in it no mark of any such intuitive certainty; but on the contrary shall find, that 'tis of a nature quite foreign to that species of conviction.

All certainty arises from the comparison of ideas, and from the discovery of such relations as are unalterable, so long as the ideas continue the same. These relations are *resemblance, proportions in quantity and number, degrees of any quality, and contrariety;* none of which are imply'd in this proposition: *Whatever has a beginning has also a cause of existence.* That proposition therefore is not intuitively certain. At least any one, who wou'd assert it to be intuitively certain, must deny these to be the only infallible relations, and must find some other relation of that kind to be imply'd in it; which it will then be time enough to examine.

But here is an argument, which proves at once, that the foregoing proposition is neither intuitively nor demonstrably certain. We can never demonstrate the necessity of a cause to every new existence, or new modification of existence, without shewing at the same time the impossibility there is, that any thing can ever begin to exist without some productive principle; and where the latter proposition cannot be prov'd, we must despair of ever being able to prove the former. Now that the latter proposition is utterly incapable of a demonstrative proof, we may satisfy ourselves by considering, that as all distinct ideas are separable from each other, and as the ideas of cause and effect are evidently distinct, 'twill be easy for us to conceive any object to be nonexistent this moment, and existent the next, without conjoining to it the distinct idea of a cause or productive principle. The separation, therefore, of the idea of a cause from that of a beginning of existence, is plainly possible for the imagination; and consequently the actual separation of these objects is so far possible, that it implies no contradiction nor absurdity; and is therefore incapable of being refuted by any reasoning from mere ideas; without which 'tis impossible to demonstrate the necessity of a cause.

Accordingly we shall find upon examination, that every demonstration, which has been produc'd for the necessity of cause, is fallacious and sophistical. All the points of time and place, say some philosophers, in which we can suppose any object to begin to exist, are in themselves equal; and unless there be some cause, which is peculiar to one time and to one place, and which by that means determines and fixes the existence, it must remain in eternal suspense; and the object can never begin to be, for want of something to fix its beginning. But I ask; Is there any more difficulty in supposing the time and place to be fix'd without a cause, than to suppose the existence to be determin'd in that manner? The first question that occurs on this subject is always, *whether* the object shall exist or not: The next, *when* and *where* it shall begin to exist. If the removal of a cause be intuitively absurd in the one case, it must be so in the other: And if that absurdity be not clear without a proof in the one case, it will equally require one in the other. The absurdity, then, of the one supposition can never be a proof of that of the other, since they are both upon the same footing, and must stand or fall by the same reasoning.

The second argument, which I find us'd on this head, labours under an equal difficulty. Every thing, 'tis said, must have a cause; for if any thing wanted a cause, *it* wou'd produce *itself*; that is, exist before it existed; which is impossible. But this reasoning is plainly unconclusive; because it supposes, that in our denial of a cause we still grant what we expressly deny, *viz.* that there must be a cause; which therefore is taken to be the object itself; and that, no doubt, is an evident contradiction. But to say that any thing is produc'd, or to express myself more properly, comes into existence, without a cause, is not to affirm, that 'tis itself its own cause; but on the contrary in excluding all external causes, excludes *a fortiori* the thing itself which is created. An object, that exists absolutely without any cause, certainly is not its own cause; and when you assert, that the one follows from the other, you suppose the very point in question, and take it for granted, that 'tis utterly impossible any thing can ever begin to exist without cause, but that upon the exclusion of one productive principle, we must still have recourse to another.

'Tis exactly the same case with the third argument, which has been employ'd to demonstrate the necessity of a cause. Whatever is produc'd without any cause, is produc'd by *nothing;* or in other words, has nothing for its cause. But nothing can never be a cause, no more than it can be something, or equal to two right angles. By the same intuition, that we perceive nothing not to be equal to two right angles, or not to be something, we perceive, that it can never be a cause; and consequently must perceive, that every object has a real cause of its existence.

I believe it will not be necessary to employ many words in shewing the weakness of this argument, after what I have said of the foregoing. They are all of them founded on the same fallacy, and are deriv'd from the same turn of thought. 'Tis sufficient only to observe, that when we exclude all causes we really do exclude them, and neither suppose nothing nor the object itself to be the causes of the existence; and consequently can draw no argument from the absurdity of these suppositions to prove the absurdity of that exclusion. If every thing must have a cause, it follows, that upon the exclusion of other causes we must accept of the object itself or of nothing as causes. But 'tis the very point in question, whether every thing must have a cause or not; and therefore, according to all just reasoning, it ought never to be taken for granted.

They are still more frivolous, who say, that every effect must have a cause, because 'tis imply'd in the very idea of effect. Every effect necessarily pre-supposes a cause; effect being a relative term, of which cause is the correlative. But this does not prove, that every being must be preceded by a cause; no more than it follows, because every husband must have a wife, that therefore every man must be marry'd. The true state of the question is, whether every object, which begins to exist, must owe its existence to a cause; and this I assert neither to be intuitively nor demonstratively certain, and hope to have prov'd it sufficiently by the foregoing arguments.

It doesn't take much imagination to see how deeply Hume's argument cuts. We can hardly get out of bed in the morning without implicitly relying on a host of causal beliefs. I believe that when I swing my legs over the side of the bed, they will naturally fall down toward the floor. (As astronauts have discovered, that is a belief which turns out to be false once we get away from the gravitational pull of the earth.) I believe that when I take a drink of water, it will cause my thirst to be abated. I believe that when I push the light switch, it will cause the lights to go on. The simplest propositions of physics, chemistry, and biology either are, or else depend upon, causal judgments.

Hume himself did not believe that it was psychologically possible for human beings to suspend their belief in causal judgments for very long. Although he was absolutely convinced that no adequate justification could ever be found for our beliefs, he also thought that we were naturally so constituted that we believe anyway. In a much quoted passage from the end of the First Book of the *Treatise*, Hume tells how he disperses the clouds of gloom and doubt that settle over him when he follows out the logical conclusions of his powerful arguments.

> Most fortunately it happens, that since reason is incapable of dispelling these clouds, nature herself suffices to that purpose, and cures me of this philosophical melancholy and delirium, either by relaxing this bent of mind, or by some avocation, and lively impression of my senses, which obliterate all these chimeras. I dine, I play a game of backgammon, I converse, and am merry with my friends; and when after three or four hours' amusement, I wou'd return to these speculations, they appear so cold, and strain'd, and ridiculous, that I cannot find in my heart to enter into them any farther.

Kant's Resolution of the Rationalism/ Empiricism Debate

Immanuel Kant was not content to flee from the skepticism into which Hume had plunged philosophy by his wholesale destruction of causal beliefs. If Hume's arguments were accepted, then I could not even be sure that anything at all existed outside my own mind. Descartes' fanciful notion that his whole life was a mere dream might be true, as far as philosophers could prove. It was, Kant said, a "scandal to philosophy and to human reason in general that the existence of things outside us . . . must be accepted merely on *faith,* and that if anyone thinks good to doubt their existence, we are unable to counter his doubts by any satisfactory proof." So Kant decided to return to Descartes' starting point, the Cogito, or "I think." He wanted to see whether he could derive directly from that fundamental premise an argument that would avoid the skepticism and solipsism that seemed to be implied by the powerful attacks of the British empiricists.

As we have seen, Descartes' philosophical investigation raised two basic problems: the problem of certainty and the problem of the sources of knowledge. But Kant realized that the Cogito argument raised an even more fundamental issue which both the rationalists and the empiricists had tended to ignore. The conclusion of Descartes' argument, you will recall, was the following:

> This proposition: I am, I exist, is necessarily true each time that I pronounce it, or that I mentally conceive it.

On the basis of this conclusion, Descartes went on to argue that he was essentially a "thing that thinks." Descartes' successors concentrated on the criteria to be used in judging the truths of what the mind thinks, and they concentrated on the sources of the ideas with which the mind thinks, but they paid much less attention to the central fact that the mind, in thinking, is *conscious*. Trees are not conscious, rocks are not conscious, even calculating machines are not conscious, but the mind is. It occurred to Kant that perhaps a proof of our scientific beliefs in the existence of physical objects and in causal connections between them could be based on the mere fact of consciousness. Such a proof would certainly be very hard to find, for the mere fact of consciousness isn't much to go on in proving anything as large-scale as the truth of science. But if he could find such a proof, Kant would have an answer to anyone who wanted to challenge the claims of reason, even someone prepared to go as far in the direction of skepticism as David Hume.

Descartes had simply accepted consciousness as an indisputable, directly observable, inexplicable fact. I know that I am conscious because I can think about my own thoughts and become aware of myself thinking about them. This self-awareness or self-consciousness is clearly central to the mind's operation; what is more, it is directly self-confirming. Even an evil demon could not trick me into thinking I was conscious when I wasn't, because if I thought anything at all, it would have to be the case that I was conscious. So instead of the premise "I think" as the starting point of all philosophy, Kant instead adopted the slightly different premise "I am conscious." But introspection reveals, and logical analysis confirms, that my consciousness has a certain basic structure or characteristic: it is unified into a *single* consciousness. All

---

⌒**Unity of Consciousness**   A phrase invented by Immanuel Kant to describe the fact that the thoughts and perceptions of any given mind are bound together in a unity by being all contained in one consciousness. Kant claimed that this fact—the *unity* of individual consciousness—could only be explained by postulating a fundamental mental activity of holding together, or "synthesizing," those thoughts and perceptions.

the thoughts, impressions, beliefs, expectations, hopes, and doubts that I have are *my* thoughts, and so on. They occur in *my* consciousness, and that consciousness is a single consciousness, or—to put it somewhat differently—the consciousness of a single subject, a single center of thought. Kant described this fundamental fact as the unity of consciousness. In order to show the connection between what he was doing and what Descartes had done, Kant invoked Descartes' language when he stated his own basic premise. In the central section of the *Critique of Pure Reason,* as he started the argument which he hoped would refute the skeptics and reinstate science as objectively justified, Kant stated his premise in the following way:

> It must be possible for the "I think" to accompany all my representations.

This was his way of saying that all the contents of my consciousness are bound up in a unity of consciousness.

Kant argued that the *unity* of my thoughts and perceptions could not be a given fact of my experience. The individual thoughts and impressions might just be brute facts of consciousness, but their unity could only be explained by some unifying act of the mind itself. Kant claimed that when my mind unifies its various thoughts and perceptions, when it holds them all together in a single consciousness and thinks of them all as *my* thoughts, it follows a certain set of *rules*. These rules are rules for holding thoughts together in the mind, and he gave them the technical name "categories." The only way in which I can think all of my thoughts as unified in a single consciousness is by following the rules or categories for holding thoughts together. Kant claimed that the categories are innate in the human mind; we are all born with them, he said, and we cannot change them.

What are these rules, or categories? Well, it turns out—if Kant is right—that they are just exactly those crucial concepts which play so large a role in the metaphysics, mathematics, and physics that Hume and the skeptics were attacking. Among the categories are such central concepts as substance, cause and effect, unity, plurality, possibility, necessity, and reality.

It may not look as though Kant moved very far toward an answer to Hume, but stop and reflect for a moment on what he is saying. Descartes claimed I could be conscious of my own thoughts, and even conscious of their unity *as* my thoughts, without knowing whether they were really accurate or truthful thoughts about substances, causation, and a world independent of my mind. In other words, Descartes admitted that my subjective knowledge of my own thoughts was better established than any claims I might make about a world of objects. Locke, Hume, and other critics of the rationalists accepted Descartes' starting point—they agreed that I could know the contents of my own mind—but they threw doubt on all Descartes' attempts to move from that purely subjective knowledge to anything further.

Kant turned the whole argument around by denying Descartes' first premise. I cannot know the contents of my own mind unless I first unify them into a single consciousness, he said. And that means that I must first have applied the categories to them, for those categories are the rules for unifying contents of consciousness. Now the categories are precisely the concepts (substance, cause, etc.) which we use in making objective judgments about the world outside the mind. So Kant concluded that I could not even be subjectively conscious, à la Descartes, unless I had first put my thoughts and perceptions together in ways that would allow me to make objective judgments about them. Descartes' nightmare of life as an endless dream is an epistemological impossibility, Kant argued.

But Kant paid a price for his solution to the problem of skepticism. It might very well be that my objective concepts were guaranteed to apply to my experiences—it might, in short, be a sure thing that I would encounter substances related to one another causally—but such knowledge as I obtained through the use of the categories would not and could not be knowledge of the world as it really is in itself. Rather, my knowledge must be merely of a world of things as they appear to me.

We have already encountered the distinction between appearance and reality in the philosophy of Socrates and Plato, you will recall. But Plato claimed that we could, by the use of our reason, gain knowledge of true reality. Kant, by contrast, insists that we can only obtain knowledge of appearance, even though such knowledge is real knowledge, and not—as the skeptics claimed—error or unfounded belief.

The dispute between the rationalists and the empiricists was changed by Kant's new theory of the unity of consciousness. Even though many subsequent philosophers rejected his distinction between appearance and reality, they continued to ponder the problem of the nature of consciousness, a problem that Descartes had discovered and that Kant had substantially deepened by his arguments.

The Main Points in Chapter Six

1. In the seventeenth century, the great French mathematician, scientist, and philosopher René Descartes changed the course of philosophy by raising a fundamental question about what we can know, and how we know it. Descartes' *method of doubt* called into question every belief that could not be demonstrated with absolute certainty. Descartes was able to show that most of the mathematical, scientific, religious, and everyday beliefs we have really cannot stand up to that kind of examination.

2. Descartes' systematic doubt brought to center stage a question that philosophers had discussed for a very long time: How do we learn about

the nature of things, through our physical senses or by reasoning? Philosophers who think sensation is the source of knowledge are called *empiricists*. Philosophers who think reason is the source of knowledge are called *rationalists*. The seventeenth and eighteenth centuries saw a complicated debate between empiricists and rationalists, in which physics, mathematics, theology, and logic were called into play.

3. Descartes himself was a rationalist, as was the German Leibniz. The most original empiricists were a number of British philosophers, including John Locke, George Berkeley, and David Hume. These British Empiricists pushed Descartes' skeptical arguments farther than he had himself and thereby called into question the validity of the proof for the existence of God, the basic propositions of physics, and even the theorems of mathematics.

4. The most radical of the empiricists was David Hume, whose *A Treatise of Human Nature*, published in 1739 to 1740, raised skeptical doubts about even the unity and existence of the self.

5. By the middle of the eighteenth century, the empiricists and rationalists had fought one another to a draw, philosophically speaking. At this point, the greatest philosopher since Plato and Aristotle, Immanuel Kant, came forward to try to resolve the conflict and get philosophy out of the dead end it was in. Kant's great work, the *Critique of Pure Reason*, published in 1781, transformed philosophy by changing our understanding of knowledge, consciousness, the self, and the relation between what we know and the way things are.

6. Using the old Platonic distinction between *appearance* and *reality*, Kant argued that we in fact never have knowledge of reality, but only of things as they appear to us, and that the mind itself contributes the form in which we know appearances. As Kant said in perhaps his most famous statement, "The mind is itself the lawgiver to nature."

CONTEMPORARY APPLICATION

Virtual Reality

Ever since Jules Verne published his great science fiction yarn, *Twenty Thousand Leagues Under the Sea,* about a boat that could actually submerge and travel for months without surfacing, the real world has been imitating the literary imagination. When I was a boy, many decades ago, the comic book detective Dick Tracy spoke into a wrist telephone. Today, as I drive down the highway, I see people carrying on telephone conversations while steering with one hand. Even that most impossible of all science fiction dreams, walking on the moon, is now a reality. Indeed, it happened so long ago that my students these days have heard about it from their parents.

For some time now, very sophisticated philosophers have been arguing about a quite fanciful, imaginary situation that sounds straight out of science fiction. It goes by the bizarre name of "brains in vats." Hilary Putnam, a distinguished philosopher of mathematics asked what it would be like if an evil scientist removed my brain from my body and kept it alive in a tub of nutrient fluids, feeding sensory inputs to it through electrical connections. Putnam used this weird idea to explore some rather tricky issues in the philosophy of mind.

Another distinguished philosopher, Daniel Dennett, took issue with Putnam, arguing that the sort of complete hallucination Putnam was talking about would be impossible. The first two readings in this Contemporary Application are selections from the discussions by Putnam and Dennett.

But neither of these philosophers realized that hardly before the ink was dry on their articles, science would produce a device that goes a long way toward creating the brains-in-a-vat situation they were arguing about. The name for this device is "virtual reality," a futuristic helmet that projects images onto an internal visor and responds to movements of the eyes, hands, or body of the person wearing the device. The effect is to make it seem as though you have entered a television world. Looking straight ahead, perhaps, you see a tree-lined walk. Turn your head to the left, and into view come the trees on your left. Walk two steps forward, and the trees look larger, just as they would if they were really there. *Except that there is nothing there but images on the inside of the helmet visor!*

The latest wrinkle is a pair of virtual reality helmets that allow two people to enter the same imaginary space or virtual reality, and even to play ball in it. The makers promise that before too long, you will be able to climb into a body suit and make virtual love to an imaginary, but quite visible, partner. It sounds too much like the Holodeck on the Enterprise for comfort.

Our last selection discusses the new virtual reality devices directly. But this is one chapter where you must view the accompanying video to get the full flavor of the discussion. How about a virtual reality philosophy class, in which you can carry on debates with an imaginary Socrates? If you ask a question the imaginary Socrates can't answer, do you suppose the helmet would short out?

ꙮ ꙮ ꙮ ꙮ ꙮ ꙮ ꙮ ꙮ ꙮ ꙮ ꙮ ꙮ ꙮ ꙮ

THE CASE OF THE BRAINS IN A VAT
Hilary Putnam

Here is a science fiction possibility discussed by philosophers: imagine that a human being (you can imagine this to be yourself) has been subjected to an operation by an evil scientist. The person's brain (your brain) has been removed from the body and placed in a vat of nutrients which keeps the brain alive. The nerve endings have been connected to a super-scientific computer which causes the person whose brain it is to have the illusion that everything is perfectly normal. There seem to be people, objects, the sky, etc; but really all the person (you) is experiencing is the result of electronic impulses travelling from the computer to the nerve endings. The computer is so clever that if the person tries to raise his hand, the feedback from the computer will cause him to "see" and "feel" the hand being raised. Moreover, by varying the program, the evil scientist can cause the victim to "experience" (or hallucinate) any situation or environment the evil scientist wishes. He can also obliterate the memory of the brain operation, so that the victim will seem to himself to have always been in this environment. It can even seem to the victim that he is sitting and reading these very words about the amusing but quite absurd supposition that there is an evil scientist who removes people's brains from their bodies and places them in a vat of nutrients which keep the brains alive. The nerve endings are supposed to be connected to a super-scientific computer which causes the person whose brain it is to have the illusion that . . .

When this sort of possibility is mentioned in a lecture on the Theory of Knowledge, the purpose, of course, is to raise the classical problem of skepticism with respect to the external world in a modern way. *(How do you know you aren't in this predicament?)* But this predicament is also a useful device for raising issues about the mind/world relationship.

Instead of having just one brain in a vat, we could imagine that all human beings (perhaps all sentient beings) are brains in a vat (or nervous systems in a vat in case some beings with just a minimal nervous system already count as "sentient"). Of course, the evil scientist would have to be outside—or would he? Perhaps there is no evil scientist, perhaps (though this is absurd) the universe just happens to consist of automatic machinery tending a vat full of brains and nervous systems.

This time let us suppose that the automatic machinery is programmed to give us all a *collective* hallucination, rather than a number of separate unrelated hallucinations. Thus, when I seem to myself to be talking to you, you seem to yourself to be hearing my words. Of course, it is not the case that my words actually reach your ears—for you don't have (real) ears, nor do I have a real mouth and tongue. Rather, when I produce my words, what happens is that the efferent impulses travel from my brain to the computer, which both causes me to "hear" my own voice uttering those words and "feel" my tongue moving, etc., and causes you to "hear" my words, "see" me speaking, etc. In this case, we are, in a sense, actually in communication. I am not mistaken about your real existence (only about the existence of your body and the "external world," apart from brains). From a certain point of view, it doesn't even matter that "the whole world" is a collective hallucination; for

you do, after all, really hear my words when I speak to you, even if the mechanism isn't what we suppose it to be. (Of course, if we were two lovers making love, rather than just two people carrying on a conversation, then the suggestion that it was just two brains in a vat might be disturbing.)

Source: *Hilary Putnam,* Reason, Truth, and History, *Cambridge University Press, 1981, pp. 5–7.*

ఌ ఌ ఌ ఌ ఌ ఌ ఌ ఌ ఌ ఌ ఌ ఌ ఌ

THE BRAIN IN THE VAT
Daniel Dennett

Suppose evil scientists removed your brain from your body while you slept, and set it up in a life-support system in a vat. Suppose they then set out to trick you into believing that you were not just a brain in a vat, but still up and about, engaging in a normally embodied round of activities in the real world. This old saw, the brain in the vat, is a favorite thought experiment in the toolkit of many philosophers. It is a modern-day version of Descartes's evil demon, an imagined illusionist bent on tricking Descartes about absolutely everything, including his own existence. But as Descartes observed, even an infinitely powerful evil demon couldn't trick him into thinking he himself existed if he didn't exist: *cogito ergo sum,* "I think, therefore I am." Philosophers today are less concerned with proving one's own existence as a thinking thing (perhaps because they have decided that Descartes settled that matter quite satisfactorily) and more concerned about what, in principle, we may conclude from our experience about our nature, and about the nature of the world in which we (apparently) live. *Might* you be nothing but a brain in a vat? Might you have *always* been just a brain in a vat? If so, could you even conceive of your predicament (let alone confirm it)?

The idea of the brain in the vat is a vivid way of exploring these questions, but I want to put the old saw to another use. In the standard thought experiment, it is obvious that the scientists would have their hands full providing the nerve stumps from all your senses with just the right stimulations to carry off the trickery, but philosophers have assumed for the sake of argument that however technically difficult the task might be, it is "possible in principle." One should be leery of these possibilities in principle. It is also possible in principle to build a stainless-steel ladder to the moon, and to write out, in alphabetical order, all intelligible English conversations consisting of less than a thousand words. But neither of these are remotely possible in fact and sometimes an *impossibility in fact* is theoretically more interesting than a *possibility in principle,* as we shall see.

Let's take a moment to consider, then, just how daunting the task facing the evil scientists would be. We can imagine them building up to the hard tasks from some easy beginnings. They begin with a conveniently comatose brain, kept alive but lacking all input from the optic nerves, the auditory nerves, the somatosensory nerves, and all the other afferent, or input, paths to the brain. It is sometimes assumed that such a "deafferented" brain would naturally stay in a comatose state forever, needing no morphine to keep it dormant, but there is some empirical evidence to suggest that spontaneous waking might still occur in these dire circumstances. I think we can suppose that were you to awake in such a state, you would find yourself in horrible straits: blind, deaf, completely numb, with no sense of your body's orientation.

Not wanting to horrify you, then, the scientists arrange to wake you up by piping stereo music (suitably encoded as nerve impulses) into your auditory nerves. They also arrange for the signals that would normally come from your vestibular system or inner ear to indicate that you are lying on your back, but otherwise paralyzed, numb, blind. This much should be within the limits of technical virtuosity in the near future—perhaps possible even today. They might then go on to stimulate the tracts that used to innervate your epidermis, providing it with the input that would normally have been produced by a gentle, even warmth over the ventral (belly) surface of your body, and (getting fancier) they might stimulate the dorsal (back) epidermal nerves in a way that simulated the tingly texture of grains of sand pressing into your back. "Great!" you say to yourself: "Here I am, lying on my back on the beach, paralyzed and blind, listening to rather nice music, but probably in danger of sunburn. How did I get here, and how can I call for help?"

But now suppose the scientists, having accomplished all this, tackle the more difficult problem of convincing you that you are not a mere beach potato, but an agent capable of engaging in some form of activity in the world. Starting with little steps, they decide to lift part of the "paralysis" of your phantom body and let you wiggle your right index finger in the sand. They permit the sensory experience of moving your finger to occur, which is accomplished by giving you the kinesthetic feedback associated with the relevant volitional or motor signals in the output or efferent part of your nervous system, but they must also arrange to remove the numbness from your phantom finger, and pro-

vide the stimulation for the feeling that the motion of the imaginary sand around your finger would provoke.

Suddenly, they are faced with a problem that will quickly get out of hand, for just how the sand will feel depends on just how you decide to move your finger. The problem of calculating the proper feedback, generating or composing it, and then presenting it to you in real time is going to be computationally intractable on even the fastest computer, and if the evil scientists decide to solve the real-time problem by precalculating and "canning" all the possible responses for playback, they will just trade one insoluble problem for another: there are too many possibilities to store . . .

It is a familiar wall these scientists have hit; we see its shadow in the boring stereotypes in every video game. The alternatives open for action have to be strictly—and unrealistically—limited to keep the task of the world-representers within feasible bounds. If the scientists can do no better than convince you that you are doomed to a lifetime of playing Donkey Kong, they are evil scientists indeed.

There is a solution of sorts to this technical problem. It is the solution used, for instance, to ease the computational burden in highly realistic flight simulators: use *replicas* of the items in the simulated world. Use a real cockpit and push and pull it with hydraulic lifters, instead of trying to simulate all that input to the seat of the pants of the pilot in training. In short, there is only one way for you to store for ready access that much information about an imaginary world to be explored, and that is to use a *real* (if tiny or artificial or plaster-of-paris) world to store its own information! This is "cheating" if you're the evil demon claiming to have deceived Descartes about the existence of absolutely everything, but it's a way of actually getting the job done with less than infinite resources.

Descartes was wise to endow his imagined evil demon with *infinite* powers of trickery.

Although the task is not, strictly speaking, infinite, the amount of information obtainable in short order by an inquisitive human being is staggeringly large. Engineers measure information flow in bits per second, or speak of the *bandwidth* of the channels through which the information flows. Television requires a greater bandwidth than radio, and high-definition television has a still greater bandwidth. High-definition smello-feelo television would have a still greater bandwidth, and *interactive* smello-feelo television would have an astronomical bandwidth, because it constantly branches into thousands of slightly different trajectories through the (imaginary) world. Throw a skeptic a dubious coin, and in a second or two of hefting, scratching, ringing, tasting, and just plain looking at how the sun glints on its surface, the skeptic will consume more bits of information than a Cray supercomputer can organize in a year. Making a *real* but counterfeit coin is child's play; making a *simulated* coin out of nothing but organized nerve stimulations is beyond human technology now and probably forever.[1]

One conclusion we can draw from this is that we are not brains in vats—in case you were worried. Another conclusion it seems that we can draw from this is that strong hallucinations are simply impossible! By a strong hallucination I mean a hallucination of an apparently concrete and persisting three-dimensional object in the real world—as contrasted to flashes, geometric distortions, auras, afterimages, fleeting phantom-limb experiences, and other anomalous sensations. A strong hallucination would be, say, a ghost that talked back, that permitted you to touch it, that resisted with a sense of solidity, that cast a shadow, that was visible from any angle so that you might walk around it and see what its back looked like.

Hallucinations can be roughly ranked in strength by the number of such features they have. Reports of *very* strong hallucinations are rare, and we can now see why it is no coincidence that the credibility of such reports seems, intuitively, to be inversely proportional to the strength of the hallucination reported. We are—and should be—particularly skeptical of reports of very strong hallucinations because we don't believe in ghosts, and we think that only a real ghost could produce a strong hallucination. . . .

But if *really* strong hallucinations are not known to occur, there can be no doubt that convincing, multimodal hallucinations are frequently experienced. The hallucinations that are well attested in the literature of clinical psychology are often detailed fantasies far beyond the generative capacities of current technology. How on earth can a single brain do what teams of scientists and computer animators would find to be almost impossible? If such experiences are not genuine or veridical perceptions of some real thing "outside" the mind, they must be produced entirely inside the mind (or the brain), concocted out of whole cloth but lifelike enough to fool the very mind that concocts them.

[1]The development of "virtual reality" systems for recreation and research is currently undergoing a boom. The state of the art is impressive, electronically rigged gloves that provide a convincing interface for "manipulating" virtual objects, and head-mounted visual displays that permit you to explore virtual environments of considerable complexity. The limitations of these systems are apparent, however, and they bear out my point: it is only by various combinations of physical replicas and schematization (a relatively coarse-grained representation) that robust illusions can be sustained. And even at their best, they are experiences of virtual surreality, not something that you might mistake for the real thing for more than a moment. If you really want to fool someone into thinking he is in a cage with a gorilla, enlisting the help of an actor in a gorilla suit is going to be your best bet for a long time.

Source: *Daniel Dennett*, Consciousness Explained, *Little Brown & Co., 1991, pp. 3–7.*

࿐ ࿐ ࿐ ࿐ ࿐ ࿐ ࿐ ࿐ ࿐ ࿐ ࿐ ࿐ ࿐ ࿐

COULD LIFE, SEX AND DEATH BECOME JUST PART OF THE COMPUTER REVOLUTION, ASKS PAT COYNE

Computer graphics have become part of everyday life. Within a decade, they have invaded TV, the military, games, advertising, Hollywood and even high Euro-art, with Peter Greenaway's *Prospero's Books.* From the most rudimentary beginnings—simulated ping-pong on the mono screens of machines like the Sinclair Z80 with a bare four kilobytes of memory—computer graphics programmes now run on some of the most powerful machines in the world, creating illusions that first mirror and then better reality. Take, for example, the $100-million movie, *Terminator 2: Judgment Day,* with its villain sliding between prison bars, melting and reforming into dozens of different shapes, all done not with the use of trick photography, but digital manipulation.

The buzzword now is interactive. It is not enough to sit passively and watch electronic wonders being displayed before your eyes. You must take part. At its simplest, this means computer games, a herd of demonic hedgehogs zipping through hoops and pipes in an effort to escape obliteration.

One step up is the home interactive system, such as the CD-i being marketed by Phillips, which combines all the electronic gadgets in the home—TV, video, CD player, camcorder—under the control of a computer. This allows the user to mix and match, pulling in pictures from the TV, adding graphics or video from the camcorder and music from the CD, speeding up or slowing the action and, at least in theory, allowing everybody to produce their own original electronic art.

But the real focus of interest is now virtual reality, the creation of whole new, sensory worlds. At its simplest, the subject is fitted with sensors to hands and body and provided with a helmet, inside which are two small TV screens that give him or her a stereoscopic view of the new reality. Inside that world, there need be no constraints. You can fly, jump impossible distances, perform incredible feats, visit Mars or Jupiter, do whatever pleases you.

At the moment, virtual reality graphics and action are relatively crude, but that is simply a function of computer powers. As computers become more powerful, and programs and sensors more sophisticated, the differences between actual and virtual reality will become smaller and smaller, perhaps ultimately vanishing. After all, what the brain experiences as sensations are actually electronic and chemical stimuli, which can, at least in principle, be duplicated.

What then? Why confine the sensors to limbs and head? The most obvious next step is virtual sex, or teledildonics as it is becoming known in the (as yet, virtual) trade. So far, computer porn has been confined to still pictures circulated on floppy disks or downloaded from bulletin boards, which, even at super-VGA resolutions, are fairly tame stuff. But now we have the possibility of the digital equivalent of the inflatable doll, infinitely more sophisticated and capable of being programmed to cater for the most exotic of tastes. Will we be able to rent the electronic versions of our favorite movie or TV actors to enjoy their bodies, just as we now rent their videos?

Indeed, teledildonics holds out the ultimate in choice—an infinite variety of safe sex. Turn your TV camera on a crowd, pick out someone that you fancy and allow the camera long enough to gather all the necessary data—shape, looks, colouring, body rhythms and so on. Perhaps do a vox pop interview to capture the modalities of voice and facial expression. Download the data to the computer and allow it to calculate all the necessary parameters, set your own passion levels, preferred positions, duration of activity and timing of orgasm and then double-click the mouse cursor on the icon.

For those brave enough to seek the ultimate in virtual experience, there will be, sooner or later, the "snuff" program. Already, the computer games charts are stuffed with a huge variety of beat-'em-up and shoot-'em-up games, in which the players are encouraged to visit mayhem on their opponents using guns, missiles, fists, feet and anything else capable of being pressed into service. Virtual reality offers the logical extension of such games. You can stalk your prey in the setting of your choice, armed with your favorite weapons (or use bare hands if that is your fancy). Aim a gun, and direction, trajectory and recoil will all be faithfully calculated. The computer will be primed with the tensile strengths of flesh and bone and arterial systolic pressures to produce the most realistic simulation of wounds, rendered in 24-bit colour, with over 16 million shades, more than the human eye is capable of distinguishing. The screams of the victim will be synthesized in 20-channel stereo and algorithms emulating the human metabolism will give a realistic prognosis—life or death. Mission accomplished, you can remove the helmet and relax with another part of your electronic emporium, perhaps a Chopin prelude. After all, it won't be real, will it?

Source: *Coyne, Pat,* Dielectrics (Could life, sex and death become just part of the computer revolution?) *New Statesman & Society v. 6, p. 31, March 19, 1993.*

Questions for Discussion and Review

1. These are strange times, what with *The National Enquirer* regularly featuring stories about people who say they have been kidnapped by aliens, and the actress Shirley MacLaine reporting that in a previous life she was stomped to death by a white elephant. On the other hand, in recent decades we have also seen live television transmissions from the moon and electron microscope photographs of individual atoms. *How* can we tell the difference between truth and fiction? Are the people crazy who refused to believe their own eyes and said that the pictures of men on the moon were faked?

2. Reflect for a bit about all the things you think you know: state capitals, historical events, details of the private lives of rock stars, the difference between reptiles and mammals, how much a Chevy sedan costs, what a Big Mac is really made of. How do you *know* these things? If you were forced to defend any of these beliefs, how would you go about it? Could you produce arguments, evidence, reasons, proof? If not, then is it sensible for you to believe them anyway?

3. The great epistemologists of the seventeenth and eighteenth centuries were, one must admit, a little mad, what with their dreams of settling once

and for all, by a philosophical investigation, the limits of human knowledge. Is there *any* way of determining whether there are limits beyond which human knowledge cannot go? Would it help us to know more about the structure and functioning of our sense organs? Would a deeper insight into computers make any difference?

4. Imagine that the virtual reality equipment eventually becomes so good that it can simulate sound, smell, taste, and touch as well as sight when you are wearing it. Imagine, too, that the programming becomes so elaborate that you can have week-long virtual reality experiences, not just brief encounters. Under those circumstances, would you be willing to give up real world interactions with other people and settle for virtual reality fantasies? Why? Why not? What is there about an engagement with the real world that is missing from a virtual reality experience? Remember: everything we know about the world comes originally through our senses. Or does it?

5. Is anything that happens in a virtual reality experience moral or immoral? What about two-person virtual reality experiences? Suppose the equipment becomes so complex that a whole community could be hooked up to it. Would there be political implications? What is *reality* anyway?

FRANCIS BACON

Francis Bacon (1561–1626) was both a major figure in the early modern development of science and an important player in English politics during the reigns of Queen Elizabeth I and King James I. Bacon was related to influential public figures on both his mother's and his father's side. After pursuing studies at the University of Cambridge and in Paris, he returned to England to take up a career in law. Throughout his life, Bacon remained involved with legal matters, rising eventually to hold two of the most important legal positions in the nation: Solicitor General and Attorney General. In addition, Bacon sat as a member of Parliament for four different constituencies. In the turbulent politics of Elizabethan and Jacobean England, where a wrong move could literally cost you your head, Bacon managed to survive, and to flourish, until 1621, when charges of bribery and mismanagement of funds drove him from public life. He died, in 1626, without ever obtaining from the king the full pardon he sought.

Bacon's published works were many and quite varied, including literary essays as well as scientific and philosophical works. He conceived a systematic work on a grand scale, called the Instauratio Magna, *which was intended to reestablish all human knowledge on a sound foundation. In the first part of the* Instauratio, *called the* Novum Organum, *or* New Organon, *Bacon set down the method which, in his view, would provide a satisfactory basis for the expansion of our knowledge of nature. It is this work, more than any other, that influenced subsequent thinkers and secured his reputation as a major figure in the philosophy of science.*

Bacon has achieved a second sort of fame, posthumously, in the strange world of Shakespearean scholarship. Odd as it may sound, there are serious students of Elizabethan literature who claim that, in addition to his many other accomplishments, Francis Bacon wrote the plays and sonnets attributed to William Shakespeare. If it were true, it would undoubtedly make him the most artistically gifted philosopher in the long history of the subject!

Philosophy of Science

❧ The Place of Science in the Modern World

The four modern thinkers whose works, more than those of any others, have made our world what it is today are Charles Darwin, Karl Marx, Albert Einstein, and Sigmund Freud. Darwin, whose theory of evolution threw nineteenth-century European society into turmoil with its claim that human beings had descended from lower orders of animals, laid the foundations for modern biology. Marx was the greatest of the nineteenth-century socialist theoreticians (although not the only one, by any means) and the inspiration for the communist movement that has played a central role in the economics and politics of half of the world. Einstein was the mathematical and scientific genius whose theories of special and general relativity created modern physics, paving the way for atomic energy, nuclear weapons, and the modern speculations about the origins and shape of the universe. And Sigmund Freud was a medical doctor who single-handedly created psychoanalysis and gave to the modern world the concept of the unconscious and a clinically grounded theory of the psychosexual development of human personality.

There are a great many things we might say about these four giants of the nineteenth and twentieth centuries. All four of them were men. All four were white (which is to say, Caucasian—very few people are actually *white!*). Three of them—Marx, Einstein, and Freud—spoke German as their native language. The same three were Jewish by background (although Marx's father converted to Christianity, for career reasons, before Karl was born). Two of them had the first same name ("Karl" and "Charles" are the same name in different languages). And no two of them knew each other, even though there was a brief period of three years, from 1879–1882, when all four were alive.

But what is most striking about this quartet of world-shaking figures is that three of them—Darwin, Einstein, and Freud—were scientists, and the fourth—Marx—thought that "scientific" was the highest word of praise he could apply to his economic, historical, and political theories.

It probably won't surprise you, at first, that three of the four dominant thinkers of the past century have been scientists. We have grown accustomed to the domination of science in our lives. Whether as an endless source of new technological miracles (such as the home computer on which I am writing these words) or as the force that brought nuclear weapons into the world to terrify us, science shapes, directs, and consumes our lives.

But it has not always been that way. Indeed, the rise of science to this position of pre-eminence is really only about a century old. If you had asked an Athenian of the fourth century B.C., or a Chinese mandarin of the eighth century of the modern era, or the king of France in the thirteenth century, or, indeed, if you had asked any of the Founding Fathers of the American Republic in the 1780s, who the thinkers were who had most decisively formed their eras, they would almost certainly have named religious and ethical figures, such as Jesus, Confucius, or Calvin; or, perhaps, political leaders—Pericles, Caesar Augustus, Charlemagne, Genghis Khan: or possibly great artists, such as Homer, Sophocles, Shakespeare. They might *even* have named philosophers. But scientists? There weren't any, to speak of, and those thinkers who engaged in what we today would call scientific speculation were more likely to be known for something other than their "science."

What *is* science? How does it achieve the extraordinary successes that have set it above all other disciplines and activities in the modern world? What sort of knowledge, if any, does science give us, and in what way does it operate? How do we know what is genuine science, and what is not? A look at your college catalogue will give you a list of what are today accepted as *sciences:* physics, chemistry, zoology, botany, microbiology, and the rest. But what about some of the activities, bodies of knowledge claims, disciplines— call them what you will—that do not turn up in a college catalogue? What of astrology, phrenology, dianetics, *I Ching,* freemasonry, Zoroastrianism, and all those other odd affairs that are advertised in the back pages of not-quite-respectable magazines?

In this chapter, we are going to try to get at least a preliminary understanding of the nature of science by looking at the debates that have raged during the past four centuries over the nature of this central activity of the modern world. We will start back in the time of Queen Elizabeth I, when William Shakespeare was writing his plays and sonnets, for that is where our story begins. Very quickly, however, we shall find ourselves in the twentieth century, for as science has come to dominate our lives, the debates over its nature have grown steadily more vigorous and wide-ranging.

We are now well into the last decade of the second millennium of the modern era. Before you graduate from college, the world will confront the year 2001—something which, only a short time ago, was the subject of science fiction, not of life. It is absolutely certain that your lives will be transformed by science many times over as the twenty-first century unfolds. Your encounter with philosophy in this book will be a success if it leaves you thinking about what science is, and what it will become.

Francis Bacon and the Foundations of Scientific Method

The late sixteenth and early seventeenth centuries were a time of dramatic developments in our understanding of the universe, and of the place of the earth in that universe. In 1543, Nicholas Copernicus scandalized the learned world by asserting that the sun, and not the earth, is the center of the solar system. The planets, he said, revolve about the sun, which remains unmoving

at the center. Copernicus was by no means the first thinker to put forward
this claim, but ever since the time of Aristotle, in the fourth century before
Christ, it had been almost universally agreed that the earth was the hub about
which the sun, the moon, the planets, and the stars rotated. Indeed, this theory had become a part of the official doctrine of the Roman Catholic Church,
with the result that Copernicus and later astronomers found themselves in
religious hot water, not merely intellectual hot water, for their revolutionary
hypothesis.

Within less than a century, a flood of other astronomical works
appeared in which ever more powerful and astonishing theories of the heavens were put forward. The Danish astronomer, Tycho Brahe, conducted
observations in the late 1500s, which his even more brilliant student,
Johannes Kepler, published early in the new century. Kepler himself formu-
lated several general propositions, or laws, about the motions of the planets,
including the revolutionary claim that the planets actually travel in elliptical
orbits, not circular orbits, around the sun. In 1632, the Italian physicist and
astronomer Galileo Galilei published a set of Dialogues in which he defended
Copernicus's claim about the revolution of the planets around the sun.

I want you to try to think your way back to the way things were in the
late sixteenth and early seventeenth centuries. Today, we have seen so many
television pictures of the earth from satellites and space shuttles, we have seen
so many diagrams of the solar system and of the galaxy of which it is a part,
that it is very hard for us to imagine what it was like to live at a time when
even the brightest scientists couldn't really tell which was the truth—the earth
going around the sun, or the sun going around the earth.

At first, there were tremendous disputes about these new theories. Without sophisticated instruments, like modern telescopes and space vehicles, it
was unclear just what the truth was. It is not at all surprising, therefore, that
along with the arguments about the nature of the universe, a new kind of
debate began—about what *method* we should use to investigate the universe.
In short, questions of *scientific method* began to play an important part along
with questions about *scientific fact*.

The most important contributor to this growing debate, at the beginning of the seventeenth century, was an extraordinary Englishman named
Francis Bacon. Bacon was a man of many parts, as they used to say. He was
a learned scholar of the law; a skilled politician in the very complicated and
dangerous world of Queen Elizabeth and her successor, King James; a pol-
ished and witty essayist; the holder of several of the most important political
offices in the England of his day. Strange though it may sound, he is actually
thought by some to have been the real author of the three dozen plays attributed to William Shakespeare. But most important of all, Bacon was a systematic thinker who undertook to lay the methodological foundations for the
new science of his day. He pulled together all of his speculations on scientific
method in a great work which he called the *Novum Organum* (in English,

The New Organon). An organon is a system of scientific investigation, a method for discovering truths about the world, and Bacon thought he could state, once and for all time, how such investigation should be carried out.

The secret to scientific investigation, Bacon claimed, was to make a systematic collection of observations about the world and then to tabulate them and arrange them in ways that would enable us to discover the hidden nature of the phenomena we wish to understand. In this day of federally funded science, when the newspapers casually report the expenditure of billions of dollars for a supercollider and hundreds of millions of dollars for genetic research, it may not come as much of a surprise to you to hear that Bacon believed in *observation*. What else, you might ask. But in Bacon's day, very few students of nature thought that the way to learn about the world was patiently to collect observations. Indeed, the greatest intellectual successes up to that time had been in fields like mathematics and logic, in which observation played no role at all.

We must also remember that for Bacon, observation meant looking, listening, tasting, smelling, and touching with our unaided senses. The time of elaborate scientific *instruments* was still far in the future. The primitive telescopes that were beginning to come into use were so weak and unreliable that it was an open question how much better they were than the naked eye.

In Book I of *The New Organon,* Bacon laid out for us the fundamental controversy that dominated discussion about scientific method for the next two centuries. "There are and can be only two ways of searching into and discovering truth," he said.

> The one flies from the senses and particulars to the most general axioms, and from these principles, the truth of which it takes for settled and immovable, proceeds to judgment and to the discovery of middle axioms. And this way is now in fashion. The other derives axioms from the senses and particulars, rising by a gradual and unbroken ascent, so that it arrives at the most general axioms last of all. This is the true way, but as yet untried.

If we recall the discussion in Chapter 6, we can see that Bacon is presenting us with the old and fundamental conflict between *rationalism* and *empiricism*. In his view, the rationalists move immediately to very general axioms, which are set forth systematically as the starting point for elaborate deductions. This is exactly what happens in mathematics, where the method works very well indeed. For example, those of you who studied geometry in high school will remember that first you were given some definitions, axioms, and postulates, and then you began deducing conclusions, or propositions, such as the proposition that the interior angles of a triangle equal two right angles.

But successful though this method may be in mathematics, Bacon was convinced that it was all wrong in the exploration of nature. Instead, he said, we must start from the evidence of our senses and proceed very, very slowly, from particular observations to tentative generalizations or hypotheses. Then, instead of rushing into deductions and elaborate system-building, we must go back to nature and test our generalizations with more evidence of the senses. Eventually, if we are careful (and lucky), we will arrive at the end of this process at some general truth which we can hang onto with confidence.

To show us exactly what he has in mind, Bacon sets out an elaborate example, designed to arrive at a scientific understanding of *heat*. Here is how he introduces his examination in *The New Organon:*

> The investigation of forms proceeds thus: a nature being given, we must first of all have a muster or presentation before the understanding of all known instances which agree in the same nature, though in substances the most unlike. And such collection must be made in the manner of a history, without premature speculation or any great amount of subtlety. For example, let the investigation be into the form of heat.

What is Bacon saying here? Well, first of all, Bacon believes that in nature there are certain *forms,* such as heat, light, whiteness, heaviness, hardness, and so forth. The job of science is to learn exactly what these forms are and thereby to gain the ability to change and manipulate nature so that it can be used to satisfy human needs. "A nature being given"—that is to say, once we have posed the question, What is *heat* (for example)—we begin by systematically collecting all the examples we can find of that form—what Bacon calls a "muster or presentation." If heat is what we are trying to understand, we collect as many examples as possible of heat, from the widest possible variety of situations: hot metal, hot water, the hot sun, a hot forehead of someone who is sick, a hot ember from a dying fire, a stick that becomes hot after it is rubbed very hard with another stick, and so on.

Once we have made our collection, Bacon says, we make a list of all the instances of heat and contrast it with another list of as many examples as we can find of lack of heat—an ice cube, a chilly day, a cold wind, water fresh from a spring, and so on.

With these two lists before us, we now try out a series of guesses, or hypotheses, about what heat is, checking them against our two lists to see whether they fit the facts.

For example, suppose someone offers the suggestion that heat is a kind of fluid that is in things that are hot. Well, that certainly fits the case of hot water, which is liquid, and it might even fit the case of the hot forehead of a sick person, because she might have a hot fluid inside her. But it doesn't fit the case of the hot dry sand of the desert. So that guess is contradicted by the evidence, and rejected.

Little by little, according to Bacon, we zero in on the true nature of heat by checking and rechecking what he calls the Tables of Presence and Absence (i.e., presence of heat and absence of heat). We can then take a next step and make up what Bacon calls Tables of Increase and Decrease (lists of cases in which things get hotter [increase] or colder [decrease]). Suppose we are working with the guess that heat is somehow connected with things getting smaller. We check this against our Table of Increase and find that as a volume of air is heated in a balloon, it gets bigger. That is sufficient to rule out the theory that heat is connected with things getting smaller.

Well, you get the idea. Eventually, after a good many pages, Bacon comes up with the following theory about heat, which, as it happens, is pretty close to the mark:

> If in any natural body you can excite a dilating or expanding motion, and can so repress this motion and turn it back upon itself that the dilation shall not proceed equably, but have its way in one part and be counteracted in another, you will undoubtedly generate heat.

There are three important things to notice about what Bacon says in this little passage. All of them will turn out to be crucial to the discussion of this chapter.

First: The "forms" whose nature science investigates are, according to Bacon, familiar, everyday characteristics of things that are readily accessible to the five senses. Heat, weight, solidity, whiteness—these are the *subjects* of scientific discovery. Compare this with modern science, which investigates things—atoms, genes, galaxies, electricity—which we cannot see with the naked eye and wouldn't even know about without complicated scientific equipment and even more complicated theories.

Second: The "muster or presentation"—that is to say, the list of instances of what we are investigating—is to be "made in the manner of a history, without premature speculation or any great amount of subtlety." What Bacon means is that the scientist is to make up the list by just *describing* the instances of heat without any prior scientific assumptions about what heat is, or where it is likely to be found. As much as possible, the scientist is to approach experience with an open mind, recording whatever presents itself to her senses. The point of this procedure is to avoid prejudicing the outcome by unintentionally building any of the scientist's presuppositions into the list of facts.

To see why Bacon thinks that this is so important, consider a controversy that has been raging in the world of television sports reporting in recent years. Careful monitoring of broadcasts of professional football games reveals that descriptions like "smart," "clever," "savvy," "intelligent," "always in there thinking," and the like are regularly applied to *white* ball players who make good plays, while *black* star players are equally regularly described as "natural athletes," "very physical," and so forth. The prejudice of the sportscasters leads them to see instances of intelligence in the play of white athletes but not in the play of black athletes. If someone watching these broadcasts were to make up Tables of Presence and Absence of intelligence from these descriptions, he would come to the completely incorrect conclusion that intelligence in sports is somehow connected with race. The problem would lie *not* with his reasoning, but with the original muster of facts on which that reasoning was based.

So, Bacon insists, the initial collection of facts must be made "in the manner of a history, without premature speculation."

Third: The purpose of the entire scientific investigation, as Bacon's conclusion about heat makes clear, is to use knowledge to gain the power to change nature. Bacon doesn't tell us what heat *is.* He tells us how to *generate* heat—in other words, how to produce it. He tells us that "The true and lawful goal of the sciences is none other than this: that human life be endowed with new discoveries and powers."

Let us take a closer look at the second of these three points, for it came to be central to subsequent debates about scientific method. The collection of observations with which scientific theorizing begins is to be made, as far as possible, in an unprejudiced manner. The facts are to be set down by observers who do not allow their own prior beliefs or expectations, their own scientific theories, to color their descriptions. For example, even if a physicist firmly believes that the temperature of a gas *increases* as it is compressed into a smaller volume, he must not allow that belief to alter the way he reads the thermometer when he compresses a gas and observes its temperature. An astronomer may be absolutely certain, on the basis of some prior theory, that an eclipse of the sun will occur at precisely 10:04 A.M. on June 13, 1998, but as she carefully observes the onset of the eclipse and checks the time against her watch, she must not allow her expectations to affect her report of the time at which the eclipse starts.

Now, here is the point of these apparently innocuous remarks. If observations are unaffected by, uncolored by, the theories of the scientists who make them, then those observations will continue to serve as a legitimate basis for theorizing *even after the theoretical beliefs of the original observers have been disproved.* If the observations are, as we now say, theory neutral, which means that they are completely independent of any theories about what makes the world tick, then scientists even centuries later can continue to use those observations as part of the collection or muster on which they base their own theorizing.

Quite clearly, the immediate implication of this "theory neutrality" is that the pile of observations will grow steadily bigger over time, as more and more new observations are added to the list, *and none are thrown out.* And so, we can conclude that science will progress toward a greater and greater understanding of nature in a steady, unbroken, upward direction. Today's scientists will have available to them everything that previous generations of scientists have observed, plus whatever new observations they add to the collection. And tomorrow's scientists will be better off still, for they will add new observations to the ever-growing store.

This sort of one-directional progress, onward and upward, is certainly not typical of other spheres of human activity. I daresay very few serious students of politics, or art, or religion would be prepared to claim that those fields exhibit steady upward progress. Are we in the United States confident that today's politicians are superior to Abraham Lincoln or the Founding Fathers? Would many Christians claim that today's religious leaders are superior to Jesus, the Disciples, and St. Paul? Does anyone think today's composers are a distinct improvement over Beethoven and Bach, that today's playwrights have advanced beyond Sophocles or Shakespeare?

And yet, when it comes to science, we all automatically assume that even mediocre scientists today know vastly more than the most brilliant scientists of only a generation ago. Francis Bacon had the great foresight to see, at the very beginning of the modern scientific era, that this claim of unidirectional progress in science must rest firmly on the base of an ever-expanding body of theory-neutral, unbiased observations.

Now turn this idea around. Suppose it should turn out that theory-neutral observation is impossible—that every observer, no matter how honest, objective, and careful, unavoidably brings to the process of observation a set of theoretical presuppositions that shape and color the observations. In *that* case, it may turn out that science is rather more like religion, art, or politics than we thought—changing, but not unambiguously progressing to better, more inclusive theories of the world.

The Relation Between Theory and Observation

The great scientific advances of the early modern period—the late fifteenth to the early eighteenth centuries—were capped by the greatest achievement of classical physics, and by one of the handful of truly immortal accomplishments of the human mind: Sir Isaac Newton's *Mathematical Principles of Natural Philosophy* (in Latin, *Philosophiae Naturalis Principia Mathematica*), usually referred to simply as the *Principles*. It is obviously impossible to summarize a work of this sort, although if you have studied physics in high school or in college, you have certainly encountered Newton's theories in one form or another. Galileo had worked out a theory that described the motions of bodies on the earth—a theory, as physicists put it, of terrestrial motion. Kepler, as we have noted, propounded a number of laws that described the motions of planets around the sun—a theory of celestial motion. From ancient times up to the seventeenth century, philosophers and physicists believed that objects on earth were fundamentally different from heavenly bodies—made of

S I R   I S A A C   N E W T O N

Sir Isaac Newton (1642–1727) was the greatest physicist of the modern age. Newton did revolutionary work on the laws of optics in addition to inventing the calculus and achieving a theoretical unification of the theories of Galileo and Kepler.

a different stuff, obeying different laws. Newton proved that *both* Galileo's laws of terrestrial motion *and* Kepler's laws of celestial motion could be derived mathematically from the very same set of three elementary principles, using a new mathematics that he had invented, known today as calculus.

This extraordinary theoretical achievement had a profound effect on the methodological debate over the proper role of observation and pure theory in the study of nature, for Newton proceeded in his *Principles* by abstract mathematical deduction, not by what Bacon had called a "muster" of observational data. The balance was thus tilted in favor of the rationalist side of the debate.

To be sure, the rationalists freely acknowledged that observation of nature had a role to play, but they insisted that observation must be *guided* by theory. It was not enough, they argued, just to collect data and pile it up into vast Tables, as Bacon proposed. Instead, the observations had to take the form of what we today call "experiments."

The word "experiment" comes from a Latin word meaning "to try," and that sense of a trial, a test, conveys just exactly how experiments are different from mere observations. When I perform an experiment, I already have in mind some theory or hypothesis that I am testing. That tentative idea guides me in making the test and focuses my attention on the particular aspects of the situation that I suspect are important. When I merely observe, however, with no theory in mind. I have no guide to tell me what to pay attention to and what to ignore.

Suppose, for example, that I planted a rose bush in my garden last fall, and now, after the winter, it has died. I want to figure out why. I can simply *observe* the plant and the garden and write down everything I notice. But in that case, I am likely to end up with an enormous number of observations and no way of sorting them out. I will jot down the condition of the soil, the average number of cars that pass by on the road each day, whether there is a Democrat or a Republican in the White House, how much it snowed last winter, what species of birds are nesting in nearby trees, how much it has rained this spring, and so forth. Even with Bacon's Tables of Presence and Absence, I am not likely to figure out why my rose bush has died.

When I do an *experiment,* on the other hand, I start with a hypothesis—some idea in mind that I want to test. For example, I may guess that the survival of the rose bush depends on how acid the soil is. I then compare the acidity of my soil with the acidity of the soil of my neighbor, whose rose bushes did not die. I may even alter the acidity of half of my rose bed and leave the other half alone, to perform what scientists today call a "controlled experiment." I am still observing, notice, but now my observations are guided and shaped by a prior theory.

Otto von Guericke's most celebrated experiment on air pressure utilizing the Magdeburg hemispheres to demonstrate the power of a vacuum before Emperor Ferdinand III in 1657. Copper engraving from his *Experiments Nova*, Amsterdam, 1672. (The Granger Collection.)

❧ Thomas Kuhn's Theory of Scientific Revolutions

Thus far, we have said a good deal about how scientists *ought* to proceed (Bacon's "muster of known instances"), but very little at all about how real, working scientists actually go about doing their scientific research, day by day. Strange as it may seem, despite the fact that many of the classical and modern philosophers of science were themselves accomplished scientists, sometimes even major scientific figures of their age, until recently very little was written about the real conduct of science.

One problem, which shows up again and again, is the tendency of philosophers of science to assume, without argument, that the scientists in past debates who turned out to be right were, in their own time, obviously the best scientists, and that their opponents were just dodos. For example, we now know that the earth is round (or, more precisely, an oblate spheroid—flattened at the poles) and that the earth revolves around the sun. That is what Copernicus said in the sixteenth century. His opponents were the supporters of the so-called Ptolemaic theory, named after the ancient Egyptian astronomer Ptolemy, according to which the earth is fixed in the heavens and does not move. Since we know that all the arguments and evidence are now on Copernicus's side, it is natural for philosophers of science to suppose that the Ptolemaists were just bad scientists who couldn't recognize sound arguments and clear evidence when they saw it.

But the truth is actually very different, as modern historians of science began to realize when they took a careful look at the documents of the time and reconstructed the debates as they actually took place. If you think about it, it isn't really surprising to learn that the supporters of the Ptolemaic system were by and large a serious, intelligent, careful group of people who had some good arguments and facts on their side. As a matter of historical fact, given the rather primitive state of astronomical observation in the early sixteenth century, the Ptolemaists actually did a slightly *better* job of predicting and explaining the observed positions of heavenly bodies than the Copernican system did!

Very much the same sort of situation turned up again and again as historians of science began to do detailed studies of scientific debates in earlier times. For example, in the great debate over the nature of combustion between the British chemist Joseph Priestley and the French chemist Antoine Lavoisier, Priestley's theory of "phlogiston" lost out to Lavoisier's "oxygen." We now know that Lavoisier was right, but Priestley's experiments were just as careful, just as scientific, just as reasonable as were Lavoisier's.

Historians of science also began to notice that scientific development did not exhibit quite the sort of slow, steady, straight-line upward progress that philosophers of science seemed to describe. Instead, in any given science, the historical evidence suggested a more uneven process, with long periods of

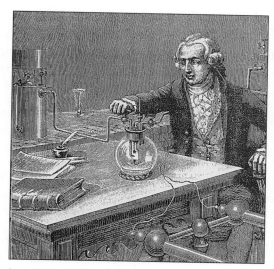

Lavoisier, Antoine Laurent, 1743–1794. French chemist. Lavoisier experimenting to determine the composition of water by igniting a mixture of hydrogen and oxygen with an electric spark. Line engraving, French, 19th century. (The Granger Collection.)

quiet, incremental development being punctuated with brief, dramatic periods of change in which, within a very short time, the whole picture with which scientists were working apparently was transformed.

Putting these historical results together with some of his own research, the American historian of science Thomas Kuhn startled the philosophical and scientific world in 1962 with a short monograph entitled *The Structure of Scientific Revolutions*. Ranging over 2,000 years of scientific history, but focusing especially on the developments in theoretical physics and chemistry of the past four centuries, Kuhn painted an extremely persuasive picture of the shape and course of scientific development which differed dramatically from virtually everything that countless philosophers of science had been saying. Kuhn's book itself revolutionized the philosophy of science and called into question the two proudest boasts of science: first, that science gives us the *truth* about what nature really is; and second, that science, unlike art, philosophy, religion, or politics, is *progressive,* securing an ever-greater store of truths about nature and building steadily on the work of past scientists.

Kuhn tells his story with the aid of three interconnected concepts: Normal Science, Paradigm, and Scientific Revolution. Here is how Kuhn introduces the first two of these ideas.

In this essay, "normal science" means research firmly based upon one or more past scientific achievements, achievements that some particular scientific community acknowledges for a time as supplying the foundation for its further practice. Today such achievements are recounted, though seldom in their original form, by science textbooks, elementary and advanced. These textbooks expound the body of accepted theory, illustrate many or all of its successful applications, and compare these applications with exemplary observations and experiments. Before such books became popular early in the nineteenth century (and until even more recently in the newly matured sciences), many of the famous classics of science filled a similar function. Aristotle's *Physica,* Ptolemy's *Almagest,* Newton's *Principia* and *Opticks,* Franklin's *Electricity,* Lavoisier's *Chemistry,* and Lyell's *Geology*—these and many other works served for a time implicitly to define the legitimate problems and methods of a research field for succeeding generations of practitioners. They were able to do so because they shared two essential characteristics. Their achievement was sufficiently unprecedented to attract an enduring group of adherents away from competing modes of scientific activity. Simultaneously, it was sufficiently open-ended to leave all sorts of problems for the redefined group of practitioners to resolve.

Achievements that share these two characteristics I shall henceforth refer to as "paradigms," a term that relates closely to "normal science." By choosing it, I mean to suggest that some accepted examples of actual scientific practice—examples which include law, theory, application, and instrumentation together—provide models from which spring particular coherent traditions of scientific research. These are the traditions which the historian describes under such rubrics as "Ptolemaic" astronomy (or "Copernican"), "Aristotelian dynamics" (or "Newtonian"), "corpuscular optics" (or "wave optics"), and so on. The study of paradigms, including many that are far more specialized than those named illustratively above, is what mainly prepares the student for membership in the particular scientific community with which he will later practice. Because he there joins men who learned the bases of their field from the same concrete models, his subsequent practice will seldom evoke overt disagreement over fundamentals. Men whose research is based on shared paradigms are committed to the same rules and standards of scientific practice. That commitment and the apparent consensus it produces are prerequisites for normal science, i.e., for the genesis and continuation of a particular research tradition.

Notice the difference between the way Bacon speaks about science and the way Kuhn speaks about it. For Kuhn, science is something done by real men (and women, though he doesn't say so)—people who are born into a particular culture at a particular time, learn their science out of textbooks and in classrooms, and then practice what they have learned in laboratories. Kuhn is interested in the human processes by which real scientists learn their craft and pass it on to others.

Kuhn's picture of real-world science (not science as we find it in textbooks or in the writings of philosophers of science) is this: in each branch or sub-branch of science, such as astronomy, during times of "normal science," there are a few models ("paradigms") of actual scientific work that are so striking, so successful in solving the problems that scientists in that field are working on, so persuasive as pictures of how to do science, that all the ordinary scientists in the field imitate those models and try to solve the puzzles that remain by applying or adapting the methods that the author of the paradigm introduced. When they are first getting into the field, these everyday, average scientists (many of whom, of course, may be very gifted and brilliant men and women) either study those models in school or else read them on their own. These paradigms come to be the accepted picture of what the world is like and how to study it.

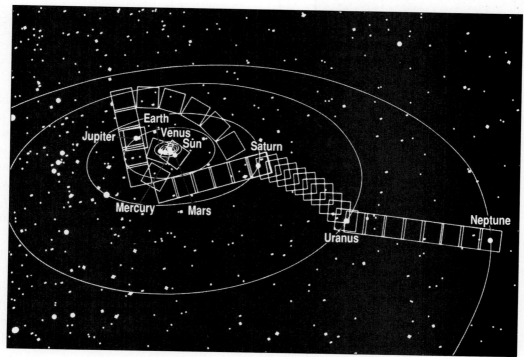

A computerized composite photo of the solar system produced by the Voyager space probe as it left the solar system, showing all but the outermost planet. We are now able to see that our system has the structure postulated by Copernicus, Galileo, and Newton. (NASA Headquarters.)

THOMAS S. KUHN

Thomas S. Kuhn (1922–1996) was educated at Harvard University, where he spent three years as a junior fellow and five years as a member of the faculty. He also held teaching positions at the University of California at Berkeley, Princeton University, and at the Massachusetts Institute of Technology. In addition to his major work, *The Structure of Scientific Revolutions,* Kuhn published *The Copernican Revolution: Planetary Astronomy in the Development of Western Thought* (1957) and *Black-Body Theory and the Quantum Discontinuity, 1894–1912* (1978).

Normal scientists are puzzle-solvers, working out answers to problems that no one has yet solved. Normal science is based upon paradigms, or models, which are precise and clear enough to tell scientists what the world should look like, but which are not so complete and finished as to leave no unsolved puzzles for normal scientists to tackle. If they are too loose and ill-defined, they fail to create the context of expectation and investigation within which the normal science can proceed. But if they are too finished off, too closed, they will generate no new problems for solution and attract no followers.

Notice that Kuhn talks about paradigms attracting followers, not about theories being proven right by logic or evidence or both. Science, he is telling us, is a human activity like any other. A theory succeeds, it takes hold, it becomes a paradigm for future work, by attracting supporters, followers, adherents. Kuhn is deliberately using a language to talk about science that is usually reserved for historical descriptions of political or religious or artistic movements.

But first, we must introduce the third key term in Kuhn's story—"scientific revolutions." Scientific revolutions, Kuhn suggests in *The Structure of Scientific Revolutions,* are "noncumulative developmental episodes in which an older paradigm is replaced in whole or in part by an incompatible new one." In this passage, excerpted from two different sections of Kuhn's work, we get his account of the process by which this "paradigm shift" occurs.

Anomaly and the Emergence of Scientific Discoveries
Normal science is a highly cumulative enterprise, eminently successful in its aim, the steady extension of the scope and precision of scientific knowledge. In all these respects it fits with great precision the most usual image of scientific work. Yet one standard product of the scientific enterprise is missing. Normal science does not aim at novelties of fact or theory and, when successful, finds none. New and unsuspected phenomena are, however, repeatedly uncovered by scientific research, and radical new theories have again and again been invented by scientists. History even suggests that the scientific enterprise has developed a uniquely powerful technique for producing surprises of this sort. If this characteristic of science is to be reconciled with what has already been said, then research under a paradigm must be a particularly effective way of inducing paradigm change. That is what fundamental novelties of fact and theory do. Produced inadvertently by a game played under one set of rules, their assimilation requires the elaboration of another set. After they have become parts of science, the enterprise, at least of those specialists in whose particular field the novelties lie, is never quite the same again.

The Response to Crisis
Let us then assume that crises are a necessary precondition for the emergence of novel theories and ask next how scientists respond to their existence. Part of the answer, as obvious as it is important, can be discovered by noting first what scientists never do when confronted by even severe and prolonged anomalies. Though they may begin to lose faith and then to consider alternatives, they do not renounce the paradigm that has led them into crisis. They do not, that is, treat anomalies as counterinstances, though in the vocabulary of philosophy of science that is what they are. In part this generalization is simply a statement from historic fact, based upon examples like those given above and, more extensively, below. These hint what our later examination of paradigm rejection will disclose more fully: once it has achieved the status of paradigm, a scientific theory is declared invalid only if an alternate candidate is available to take its place. No process yet disclosed by the historical study of scientific development at all resembles the methodological stereotype of falsification by direct comparison with nature. That remark does not mean that scientists do not reject scientific theories, or that experience and experiment are not essential to the process in which they do so. But it does mean—what will ultimately be a central point—that the act of

THOMAS KUHN,
The Structure of Scientific Revolutions

judgment that leads scientists to reject a previously accepted theory is always based upon more than a comparison of that theory with the world. The decision to reject one paradigm is always simultaneously the decision to accept another, and the judgment leading to that decision involves the comparison of both paradigms with nature and with each other.

Though history is unlikely to record their names, some men have undoubtedly been driven to desert science because of their inability to tolerate crisis. Like artists, creative scientists must occasionally be able to live in a world out of joint. But that rejection of science in favor of another occupation is, I think, the only sort of paradigm rejection to which counterinstances by themselves can lead. Once a first paradigm through which to view nature has been found, there is no such thing as research in the absence of any paradigm. To reject one paradigm without simultaneously substituting another is to reject science itself. That act reflects not on the paradigm but on the man. Inevitably he will be seen by his colleagues as "the carpenter who blames his tools."

As Kuhn notes, it is extremely difficult for a scientist who has grown up in one paradigm to shift over to a new one. Those of us who are not scientists at all may have trouble understanding why this is so difficult, but that is because we have not adopted the habits of thought, the manual skills, the very body language that characterize one paradigm or the other. Changing one's paradigm, for a scientist, must be at least as difficult as changing one's backhand for a professional tennis player, or one's bowing arm for a violinist. It may be almost as difficult as, say, giving up the law as a profession and becoming a doctor. What is called for is not so much learning new things as adopting an entirely new way of looking at the world. It is hardly surprising, then, that during times of dramatic paradigm conflict in a branch of science, it is the young apprentices who most easily take up a newly proposed paradigm. Nor should we be surprised that some scientists, even very great ones, steadfastly refuse to the end of their lives to adopt a new paradigm, even after it has virtually swept the field. Perhaps the best recent example of this phenomenon is the great physicist Albert Einstein, who found the Quantum Theory of his contemporary Max Planck so fundamentally contrary to his way of conceiving the world that he refused to consider it an acceptable new theory, choosing instead to treat it as a temporary ad hoc approximation until a satisfactory "classical" interpretation could be found.

In a postscript to his book, written seven years after its first publication, Kuhn responded to critics who accused him of portraying scientific change as an irrational process, determined by subjective factors rather than by evidence and argument. Kuhn rejected this criticism, pointing out that in his view, paradigm change occurs in response to experimental evidence or theoretical calculation and is carried out by argument, reasoning, counterargument, and new experimentation—precisely the sorts of activities that his critics presumably considered appropriate scientific behavior.

But Kuhn acknowledged—indeed, he insisted—that precisely because paradigm *change* does not take place *within* a single paradigm, but instead consists of a struggle between competing paradigms, the arguments between proponents of the opposed paradigms cannot possibly appeal to the clearly defined rules of a common paradigm to resolve their dispute.

Kuhn's critics were not entirely wrong, however, for it is clear that his conception of science differed radically from the tradition we looked at in the earlier sections of this chapter. The crucial theme, as I noted when we were discussing Bacon, is that what counts as scientific *facts* is independent of the theories a scientist advances to explain or predict the facts. Hence, the foundation of observation, on which scientific theory builds, is solid and ever-growing. But Kuhn rejected this basic tenet of the modern philosophy of science, arguing instead on the basis of the historical evidence that when a paradigm shift takes place, there is actually a corresponding shift in what counts as a scientific fact as well.

The result is that if there are two competing paradigms, we can no longer say that whichever one explains all the facts that the other explains, and more besides, wins. The most we can say—and this, I think, is what really has unsettled so many of Kuhn's readers—is that after a time, one paradigm wins the allegiance of virtually all the new young scientists, while those who used to adhere to the other paradigm retire, or die, or get redefined as "not scientists."

Science as a Social Institution

In the last section, Thomas Kuhn introduced the idea that science is a social practice, an activity carried on by groups of men and women whose interactions with one another in the classroom, in the laboratory, and through their publications shape who they are and what they believe. We saw him talking about times of scientific crisis and controversy, when some scientists choose one paradigm, much as if they were supporting a political party, and other scientists choose a competing paradigm which they defend with their research.

This recognition, that science, like politics, the economy, marriage, art, and religion, is a *social* institution, is the distinctive mark of the most recent work being done in the philosophy of science. Let us conclude this chapter by taking a look at some of the implications of the fact that science is a social institution.

First of all, what do we *mean* by calling science a "social institution"? We mean that science is an activity or a practice that is organized into social roles, such as research scientist, science student, science professor, science journal editor, laboratory assistant, and so forth. We mean, too, that science is carried on in established places—the laboratory, the research institute, the university—and is regulated, paid for, and run by bureaucratic structures—by committees, professional associations, international congresses, state and federal bureaus, and university departments. There are certain marks or symbols by which participants in the institution of science recognize one another and are recognized by outsiders—Ph.D. degrees, lab coats, "nerd packs" (the uncomplimentary slang name for the little plastic pen holder that engineers especially use to keep ink from staining their shirt pockets).

We also mean that science as a social institution has certain norms or standards of behavior that are passed on from established to novice scientists and are enforced, officially or unofficially, by members of the profession.

But we mean something much deeper and more important than all of this, for at base, what we mean is that the character, performance, accomplishments, and role of an individual scientist can only be properly understood and evaluated when seen in the context of the total social practice of which he or she is a part.

Suppose, for example, that we are trying to evaluate the performance of an individual scientist—to decide whether she is doing good science, as it were. Following Bacon, we might look at how she assembles her muster of facts, and what sorts of conclusions she derives from them. Kuhn introduces a *social* consideration by asking whether she is engaged in normal science within a paradigm, or is struggling to formulate a revolutionary new paradigm. But this does not tell us how her relationship to other scientists bears on the value or scientific propriety of her apparently individual research. We have not yet captured the *social* dimension of the scientific enterprise.

To see exactly how the social aspect of science might enter into our evaluation and understanding of the performance of an individual scientist, but without going into the elaborate detail of a real scientific research project, let us choose a *non*scientific example, which will make the very same point. (I am indebted to Robert J. Ackermann for this very useful illustration.) Imagine that a little brother and sister have gotten themselves lost in the woods and that the whole town in which they live has turned out to search for them. (I want to compare the lost children to a fact that a group of scientists is trying to discover, and the town searchers to the scientific community engaged in research in this area of science.)

How should the anxious townspeople undertake a search for the lost children? One thing is perfectly obvious: they *shouldn't* do it as isolated, individual searchers. Instead, they should organize a *group* search based on a plan for the whole town. If each man or woman in the town sets out by him- or herself to search for the children, the result will probably be something like this: Mr. Jones will say to himself, "The most likely place for those kids to have gone is the old swimming hole in the north quadrant of the woods, so I will look there." Ms. Smith will say to herself, "The most likely place for those kids to have gone is the old swimming hole in the north quadrant of the woods, so I will go there," and so on, until the whole town is hunting in the same little corner of the woods! Now, the old swimming hole may very well *be* the *most* likely place, but it surely isn't the *only* place. So it would obviously be better for at least some of the townspeople to try the less likely places, just in case one of them is where the children are. Indeed, if there are enough searchers, it would make sense to send at least someone to the *least* likely place, just to make sure.

Cartoon: "Search." When organizing a search for children lost in the woods, the best plan is to send searchers into all parts of the woods, not just into the part where the children are most likely to be. Similarly, when scientists are trying to solve a problem, it makes sense to have researchers working on a wide variety of solutions, not just on the one that is most promising. It is really the entire search party that finds the lost children, not just the particular searcher who happens to stumble upon them. (Drawn for Robert Paul Wolff by Prentice Hall.)

There are several different ways in which the searchers can be spread out through the woods in accordance with the probabilities of where the children are. One way is for the mayor to get a map of the woods, divide it up into sections, make some estimates of the probability that the children are in each segment (after consulting with the Boy Scout troop leader, the fire captain, and a few other town bigwigs), and then assign searchers to different segments as they report for the search. Another way is simply to let people sign up for segments as they arrive and leave it to late-comers to select segments of the woods that aren't yet spoken for. In this case, instead of getting official estimates of the probabilities, the search organizers will rely on the common knowledge in the town of the nature of the woods. There will, of course, be significant differences of opinion among the towns-people about which the likeliest segments are, and that will affect who goes where.

Some parts of the woods will be much easier to get to than others, and it may be necessary to motivate people to try the more inaccessible segments, either by a cash reward for the person who finds the children, or simply by the promise of publicity and general praise. Those setting out relatively late in the search may decide to gamble on trying a very unlikely piece of woods, thinking to themselves that if they head for the old swimming hole, they will be stumbling over other searchers and probably not get credit for finding the children even if that is where they are.

Now, let us suppose that the search is successful, and the children are found, *not* by the old swimming hole, perhaps, but at the camp grounds, which was everybody's second choice as the likeliest place. When Molly Johnson emerges from the woods, leading the two exhausted children, everyone starts to cheer, the TV cameras capture the moment, microphones are shoved in Molly's face, and nobody bothers even to say thank you to all the weary searchers who straggle out of remote segments of the woods after the flares are set off announcing that the children have been found.

The town reporter, writing the story up for the news wires, might very well ask himself the following obvious, but totally inappropriate question: What were the special techniques Molly used that distinguish her from all the unsuccessful searchers and enabled her to find the children? What can we learn from her success for future searches?

The answer, of course, is *nothing!* Molly didn't use any special techniques; she wasn't privy to secrets of the search that enabled her to be the one to find the children. She just happened to be looking in the segment of the woods where the children actually were. In a very real sense, it wasn't Molly who was successful; it was the whole search of which she was simply one part.

Now, if the search was organized by the mayor, then it makes a certain amount of sense to give him the credit. But suppose the town used the second method of organization mentioned above—suppose individual searchers took their cues from those who set out before them, without any organization or even much communication among the searchers. In that case, the only thing we can say is that the structure of the *institution* of the search was successful, that the search as a social practice is effectively arranged so as to maximize the likelihood of finding lost children.

Two final points, before we return to the subject of science as a social institution. First: Even though we cannot reasonably conclude that Molly was doing something special that enabled her rather than any of the other searchers to find the children, nevertheless we certainly can make judgments about whether she was following proper procedures in searching. We can observe that she made marks on the trees as she proceeded so as to be able to tell whether she was doubling back on herself, that she observed safety pre-cautions so that she herself wouldn't get hurt, and so forth. This doesn't dis-tinguish her from most of the other searchers, of course, since they did the same thing, and it doesn't at all explain why *she* found the children. But it does serve to distinguish her, and the other genuine searchers, from some foolish thrill-seekers who blundered into the woods unprepared and had themselves to be rescued when they got lost.

Second: The search could, of course, have had an unhappy outcome. The children might, against all the odds, have wandered into the *least* likely place of all, to which only one searcher went, and they might therefore have been overlooked until they died of exposure. That failure, however, would not by itself prove that the search was poorly organized or based on the wrong search principles, nor surely would it show that any particular searcher had in any way searched incorrectly. When you are dealing with probabilities, unhappy outcomes are an unavoidable fact of life. What is more, we cannot even say that a successful search *must* have been properly conducted! After all, even if all the townspeople rushed to the old swimming hole and left the rest of the woods unsearched, if that was where the children actually were, they would have been found; and everyone would have been happy, even though any sensible person could see that the search, as a search, was a shambles.

Well, by now, the relation of this long story to science must be obvious. A group of researchers, looking, let us suppose, for a cure for AIDS, is like a town searching in the woods for lost children, except that the researchers can-not even be sure there is a cure to be found. The sensible way to organize the scientific search for a cure for AIDS is to put relatively more researchers and research dollars into the most promising areas, but still to put some money and some research teams into even the least likely areas, on the off chance that that is where the cure lies. The search for a cure must be seen as a large social effort, not as a collection of individual efforts, and any philosophical or methodological evaluation of the scientific efforts of particular AIDS researchers can only be carried out in the context of an evaluation of the entire social effort to find a cure.

The task of distributing resources to different research projects can be guided centrally, perhaps by the National Institutes of Health, or it can be left to the choices of individual researchers, who make their decisions in part on the basis of the prior choices by other research teams already in the field. In practice, of course, a combination of these two different methods is always at work in the real world of modern science.

When cures finally are found—as we all hope and pray they will be—inevitably the particular research teams who make the discoveries will receive public acclaim, perhaps the Nobel Prize, certainly lasting fame. But, like Molly Johnson, they may simply be good, solid, competent searchers who happened to be looking in the right place. And where they are looking *may* be the result of their shrewd insight and scientific judgment, or it may simply be a result of the fact that when they came on the scene, that was a spot that no other team had yet headed for. Only a conception of science as a social institution can guide us to the correct evaluations of individual scientific efforts.

But if you have been reading carefully, you may have noticed that our elaborate searching-the-woods example still does not do justice to what is, perhaps, the most controversial element in Thomas Kuhn's theory. If scientific research is like looking for lost children in the woods, then the implication is that there really are facts to be discovered (just as there really are children to be found), and that we can unambiguously know when we have found them (just as we can surely tell whether the children have been rescued). Where is there room, in this example, for the idea of competing paradigms? The children-in-the-woods example fits Kuhn's description of normal science, with its focus on puzzles to be solved (children to be found), but it does not seem to fit his account of paradigm shifts.

Rather than trying to fuss with the example, stretching it and cutting it here and there to fit Kuhn's theory, it would be best just to recognize that to understand the social dimensions of paradigm shifts, we need different examples. We can say that when a paradigm shift takes place, one of the things up for grabs is the very definition of what will count as a problem, what will count as a scientific fact, and what will count as a solution to a problem.

The most unsettling and controversial element in all this is the notion that social factors can play a role in determining what is and what is not a scientific fact. Bacon clearly thought that a scientific fact is simply a careful, bias-free observation, made either with our unaided senses or else with such simple devices as telescopes or magnifying glasses. We might be able to increase the usefulness of our muster of facts by arranging experiments in a laboratory, but even then, there could be no dispute about whether something *is* a fact, only a disagreement about what the fact means, or whether it is important.

Nothing in the methodological speculations of Bacon or Kuhn fundamentally challenges the independent reality of scientific facts, although some of Kuhn's remarks come very close. But some recent work in the philosophy and history of science is changing that four-centuries-old assumption, and it might be appropriate to conclude this chapter by saying a few words about this truly unsettling new thinking.

How does something come to be established as a fact in science? The outsider, not initiated into the actual practices of modern scientific research, might quite naturally suppose that the correct answer goes like this: a statement about the world comes to be established as a scientific fact by its being shown to be a description of a state of affairs (e.g., the electrical charge on an ion, the boiling point of water, the molecular structure of DNA) which is confirmed by the observations, calculations, and theoretical interpretations of a number of competent scientists, working independently of one another in the same field of investigation.

But the truth is rather significantly different. What happens, it now appears, is something like this: a scientist writes a research report in the socially appropriate fashion (right sorts of footnotes, correct tone and language, proper credentials as a research investigator, etc.) and submits it to a recognized, referred journal—a periodical publication that other scientists consider to be respectable, which publishes papers only after they have been sent to other respectable scientists who read the papers anonymously and judge whether they are worthy of publication.

Once the paper is published, it is either cited in the papers written by other researchers in the same field, or it is not. If it is not, the statements in it drop out of sight and do not become scientific facts. If it *is* cited, then there is a chance that the statements in it will become scientific facts. A while later, new papers on the same subject are written by other researchers who, along the way to staking *their* claims about what is and isn't a fact, cite the paper we are considering. They may report that they have replicated the original experiments, with the same results. Or they may simply cite the paper in support of further claims which they are advancing.

If the future research continues in a direction that incorporates the claim we are considering, eventually through repeated citations it acquires the status of a *fact* and is henceforth used by other researchers, perhaps even without citation, as the basis for their own experiments and analyses.

What you will see immediately from this description is that it is a matter of *social* convention whether something is a scientific fact. There is no other test save acceptance by the scientific community, as signalled by citation, replication, and eventual incorporation into the canon of well-known "facts." But surely airplanes fly, lightbulbs light, heart transplant operations work, atomic bombs explode! That is a matter of fact, not of convention, agreement, or social determination.

To be sure. But the fact that atomic bombs explode does not, of itself, settle the debates in atomic physics, any more than the fact that sixteenth-century sailors made it home to port while navigating by the stars proved that their astronomical theories were correct. In the contemporary application at the end of this chapter, we shall see how the social dimension of science as an established institution interacts with laboratory observation and experiment to determine what is, and what is not, a scientific fact.

The Main Points in Chapter Seven

1. Francis Bacon proposed to lay a solid foundation for our scientific study of nature by beginning with a theory-neutral "muster" of observations, on which theories could then be built. Bacon's method is central to the school of philosophy called empiricism. According to Bacon, science can progress to greater and greater knowledge because it rests on an evergrowing foundation of observations.

2. Thomas Kuhn rejected the traditional picture of science as progressing steadily and evenly toward ever greater knowledge, arguing instead that science changes by a series of revolutions, in which old pictures or paradigms lose out to new ones. On Kuhn's view, it is quite unclear whether there is one-direction progress in science, since the change from old paradigms to new ones is so great that there is no common ground between them on which to base a judgment.

3. Recent work in the philosophy of science has emphasized the social and institutional structure of science, rather than portraying science as something done by isolated individuals. Judgments about the value of scientific research are ultimately social judgments rather than logical ones.

CONTEMPORARY APPLICATION

Cold Fusion

In this time of scientific miracles, when every month seems to bring a new disease cure, and each year a new consumer item that, ten years ago, was the stuff of comic strips, you might think that no announcement by a scientist, however extraordinary, would cause more than the slightest ripple of interest in the public press. But in March 1989, the world was shocked into total attention by a press conference held in Salt Lake City, Utah. Two obscure research chemists, neither of them known at all outside of his scientific specialty, announced that they had achieved something called "cold fusion" in a cheap, table-top laboratory experiment, using equipment that might be found in a reasonably well-stocked high-school laboratory. The two scientists were Stanley Pons of the University of Utah, in Salt Lake City, and Martin Fleischmann of the University of Southampton, in England.

To say that this announcement caused a sensation is putting it mildly indeed. As our two readings make clear, the entire worldwide scientific community went into a sort of panic overdrive trying to confirm or disconfirm the claim. Physicists have been trying to achieve fusion for years, using enormous, expensive, sophisticated equipment. It was as though a couple of amateurs, using home chemistry sets, had announced a cure for cancer, AIDS, and the common cold, all rolled into one, for twenty-five cents a pill!

What is cold fusion? Indeed, what is *fusion*, cold or hot? You will get a better idea from these two selections, but perhaps a few preliminary words would be helpful.

The matter in our world is made up of atoms. At the center of each atom is a nucleus, consisting of small particles called neutrons and protons. It takes a good deal of energy to hold these particles together. Under normal circumstances, that energy is tied up, or bound, in the nucleus along with the particles. For a long time, scientists have known that if they could find a way to release some of that bound-up energy, they would have a source of very great energy indeed.

There are essentially two ways to do this, *fission* and *fusion*. Fission means splitting a very heavy atomic nucleus into several smaller parts. It turns out that when you split certain very heavy atoms, the sum total of the bound-up energy in the parts is less than the bound-up energy in the original nucleus. The difference gets released. That is exactly what happens when a plutonium atomic bomb explodes. Millions of plutonium atoms break apart, and large amounts of extra binding-energy are released.

Salt Lake City, March 24. Fusion Researchers B. Stanley Pons, left, and Martin Fleischmann display the large-scale model of the flask in which they say they created sustained nuclear fusion. (AP/Wide World Photos.)

The second way to get at some of that bound-up energy is fusion. When two very small atoms of hydrogen join together, or *fuse*, to form one helium atom, there is some binding energy left over, which gets released. This is the process that is going on all the time in the sun. As you can tell from the heat of the sun, a *great* deal of energy is released in this way.

When scientists tried to release the energy in heavy atoms by breaking them apart, it turned out that they were helped by the fact that really heavy atoms, like plutonium, are unstable already and more-or-less ready to break up, if they are given a little shove. That is why the fission bomb was invented first, during World War II. But fusion, the other possible source of atomic energy, requires unbelievably high temperatures to trigger the process—temperatures so hot that they occur on earth only in the interior of an atomic explosion. That is why the incredibly powerful hydrogen bomb couldn't be developed until physicists had a fission bomb to set it off. The experiments with controlling fusion reactions all involved very expensive, very sophisticated attempts to create the enormous temperatures needed to trigger fusion. Without those temperatures, fusion will not take place.

Or so everybody thought! You can see why the Pons-Fleischmann announcement was such a bombshell. Not only did they claim to be able to produce fusion without expensive equipment. They said that fusion was taking place in their laboratory at *room temperature*.

What issues does the cold fusion story raise for us in this chapter on the Philosophy of Science? Obviously, it raises questions about how one confirms or disconfirms a scientific theory, how one makes scientific observations, and what the relationship is between them. But in addition, the cold fusion episode raises fascinating questions about the social structure of science. Part of the story is a territorial dispute between physicists and chemists. The physicists think they own atomic energy as a theoretical issue, and they were not amused by two *chemists* butting in. What is more, in the academic pecking order, physicists think of themselves as above mere chemists, whom they tend to see as glorified cooks stirring mixtures of ingredients over a laboratory flame. Then too, institutional snobbery played a clear role. The University of Utah is a state university, and not a very high-status one at that. If some scientists at Princeton or Harvard or Caltech or MIT had announced cold fusion, the reaction of the scientific community would have been very different indeed. But Utah? Southampton? Really!

Notice too the revolutionary role of instantaneous worldwide communications in the cold fusion story. Fax machines spread copies of scientific reports literally at the speed of light. An experiment performed in the morning in the United States could be reported that afternoon to scientists in Australia, Germany, the Soviet Union, or Italy. What some commentators have called the "Global Village" already exists in the world of science.

The question of cold fusion is still open, although it is no longer on the front pages of newspapers. It may be decades before a new consensus emerges about the possibility of this revolutionary source of energy.

ఒ ఒ ఒ ఒ ఒ ఒ ఒ ఒ ఒ ఒ ఒ ఒ ఒ

COLD FUSION
F. David Peat

The Utah Bombshell
On March 23, 1989, two chemists called a press conference at the University of Utah in Salt Lake City. The announcement they made was staggering. In the words of one scientist, "It is as important as the discovery of fire."

"Simple experiment results in sustained N-fusion at room temperature for first time. Breakthrough process has potential to provide inexhaustible source of energy," read the headlines in the University of Utah's press release. Martin Fleischmann and B. Stanley Pons claimed to have done nothing less than create nuclear fusion in a test tube. Using apparatus that can be found in a school laboratory, they had harnessed the power of the sun. For over 100 hours, Fleischmann and Pons had created pure energy in a tiny glass jar. The fuel they were using was as abundant as seawater.

Controlled nuclear fusion has been a dream for decades. If fusion power could be harnessed, unlimited energy would be available to the whole world. But everyone believed that controlled fusion power lay decades away and demanded massive equipment, experiments on an international scale, and funds of tens of billions of dollars a year. Now two chemists had done the whole thing in a small basement laboratory.

Within hours of the Utah announcement, the entire scientific community was in a state of shock. Physicists, chemists, and engineers talked to each other over computer networks. Fax machines spewed out letters and page upon page of calculations. The wire services buzzed. Scientists from one of the United States' major laboratories sat glued to a television set, trying to learn more about Fleischmann and Pons's discovery from a TV news item.

Science had never been done this way before. Scientific conferences and publications tend to be planned long in advance, so over the following days, scientists could only rely upon news reports for current information. Graduate students worked around the clock to duplicate the Fleischmann and Pons experiment. Distinguished scientists dropped their research projects and began to build fusion cells. In Canada, Ontario Hydro, the world's major supplier of heavy water—the fuel that had been used by Fleischmann and Pons in their cell—was inundated by telephone calls from laboratories, companies, and even schoolchildren who wanted to try the fusion experiment.

Everyone was getting "fusion fever." Things were becoming so frantic that one Nobel Prize winner cautioned that science was in danger of falling into chaos because the "due process" of scientific investigation—which requires a methodical peer review of any new discovery—had been bypassed.

Science was very much in the news as, with each edition, major newspapers carried updates of the fusion story. As the next weeks went by, one laboratory would announce a confirmation of the Fleischmann and Pons experiment, while another would claim that nothing spectacular had happened when it had attempted to replicate the experiment. One theoretician would prove that the whole thing was a storm in a teacup, simply the result of a well-known chemical reaction that had no potential as a new energy source. Another would offer proof of novel nuclear reactions producing immense energy with very little radiation.

In short, no one really knew what to think. Except, that is, for the financial speculators who were prepared to make a killing on the power of rumor alone. Futures on palladium (the metal that had been used in the Fleischmann and Pons experiment) rose to a five-year high before retreating.

In a news statement released on March 31, a few days after their original press conference, Pons and Fleischmann left no doubt of what they had achieved. The experiment had generated an abundant supply of energy, they said, that persisted for over 100 hours. All this using a fuel that is present in ordinary water. And this was only the beginning, for Fleischmann and Pons believed that the process could be scaled up to solve the energy problems of the human race for incalculable centuries to come.

Many experienced scientists, however, could not believe that so much energy could be produced in a test tube. Robert Cohen, director of UCLA's Institute of Plasma and Fusion Research, declared that if this energy was really being produced by conventional nuclear fusion, then the amount of radiation released in the process would have killed everyone in the laboratory.

The whole idea of Utah's cold fusion sounded crazy. It did not agree with what everyone took to be the laws of nuclear physics. "It's got to be wrong," said Stanley Luckhardt, a physicist with MIT's fusion group. "I'm afraid we'll look like idiots if we are seen trying this thing." Said that group's head, Ronald R. Parker, "My first reaction was that it was incredible. In fusion research there are always crackpot claims to produce fusion in a simple way. It always turns out that a little green man from Mars told them how to do it. When I heard this, I thought . . . here's another one, but for some reason the *Wall Street Journal* bit on this one."

A matter of days after the original announcement by Fleischmann and Pons, the cold-fusion plot took on a sudden twist. A second group announced that it had discovered room-temperature fusion: moreover, this bombshell came from a university only forty miles away, in Provo, Utah. The announcement from Brigham Young University was more guarded in its claims. To begin with, although BYU's scientists had not seen the same large amounts of heat being produced as had the University of Utah team, radioactive particles (neutrons) were certainly detected. Group leader Steven E. Jones said, "The discovery of cold nuclear fusion . . . opens the possibility, at least, of a new path to fusion energy."

In fact, it would later become known that the group from Brigham Young University, including a scientist from the University of Arizona, had been working along the same track as the University of Utah team for several years. By now, rumors were beginning to circulate that the two groups already knew about each other's work, that a grant application made by Pons and Fleischmann had been sent to Steven Jones as an independent referee, and that an agreement had been made to announce cold fusion on the same day. Claims were also made that the two teams had been collaborating with each other, as well as, contrarily, that the two universities were involved in a heavy competition. The major question that people had begun to ask themselves was why Fleischmann and Pons had jumped the gun and gone to the press before Jones and his team from Brigham Young University. Was this a race for the Nobel Prize, or were some vital patents at stake?

Whatever the story, the announcement from Brigham Young University at first sight appeared to be an independent corroboration of Fleischmann and Pons's work. Now scientists were prepared to take the whole thing a bit more seriously. In the words of Carl Henning from the Lawrence Livermore National Laboratory, "While it's too early to say for sure, the general opinion is that there may be something in it."

Over the next few weeks, hopes were to rise and fall as evidence of new experiments from the United States, the Soviet Union, Italy, India, Czechoslovakia, and the United Kingdom began to come in over the wire services. At first some reports appeared to confirm the Fleischmann and Pons phenomenon; then others questioned that anything out of the ordinary was happening. By mid-April different laboratories were making, almost daily, conflicting claims. Was the promise of nuclear fusion slipping through our fingers? Or was it simply a matter of time before the final, crucial confirmation appeared? . . .

Implications
Within a month of the first cold-fusion announcement, scientists at the University of Utah were talking in terms of scaled-up fusion reactors and cold-fusion systems for use in trucks and automobiles. While Steven Jones at Brigham Young University was cautioning that current attempts at cold fusion were simply a small step on the way toward a long-term goal, Pons and Fleischmann's colleagues were already thinking in terms of the engineering challenges involved in building large-scale power systems.

A number of scientists now agree that there must be something to cold fusion. What is still being hotly debated is the scale of the whole process. There does appear to be evidence of some low levels of fusion, possibly fracto-fusion, in palladium and titanium electrodes. But this is a long way from anything approaching heat production. Some believe that years and even decades of hard work are needed to produce competitive cold-fusion energy, while others maintain that cold fusion simply operates below the margin and can never compete with other forms of energy. The optimists have no time for debate. For them, cold-fusion energy has already arrived, and with each new experiment, the amount of power generated is increased. If the optimists are correct—and that is still a big if—then cold fusion will indeed be the most significant scientific discovery since fire.

But such a cheap and abundant new energy source attacks a number of vested interests. This could spell trouble. The first to react were the physicists, who felt that their whole understanding of nuclear reactions was being turned upside down—and this was being done not by fellow physicists but by a bunch of chemists! This cold-fusion revolution generated animosity and frustration as some scientists attacked what they felt was a fusion hoax.

But the implications of cold fusion go far beyond the scientist's laboratory. If cheap cold-fusion energy is ever achieved on a large scale, then it will revolutionize not only the energy industry but also the whole web of international politics and trade tied to it. The global effect of this new energy source is so great as to be unpredictable—in fact, we have little in the past to compare it with.

A major new source of energy would have a destabilizing effect nationally and internationally. Already, some scientists have begun to worry about the official reaction to this breakthrough. Research on cold fusion has so far been carried out freely, but some scientists began to worry about whether the U.S. government would suddenly step in. At the time of the Manhattan Project (the building of the U.S. atomic bomb), wide legislation was enacted to control the use and possession of radioactive substances. In essence, the government could clamp down, at a moment's notice, on cold-fusion research within the United States. But in the first months of cold-fusion fever, the exact opposite was happening, with the Department of Energy actively encouraging conferences and research.

Another scare story involved the reaction of power companies. One version, carried on the computer networks, came from "an engineer at a Midwestern power company" who claimed that cold fusion had badly shaken the industry. It is difficult to confirm the accuracy of this story, but the fact that it was being circulated demonstrates the unease that some people were beginning to feel. The power companies had already discussed ways to head off the potential catastrophe of individuals and private interests developing their own energy sources, the engineer reportedly claimed. One approach would be to control the production and possession of deuterium and heavy water, but this looked too difficult to enforce. Another plan was to urge authorities to act on the grounds that the processes involved in cold fusion would be potentially hazardous if they got into too many hands.

But by the time of the Los Alamos conference in late May 1989, nearly every university in the United States and many others throughout the world had an interest in cold fusion. It was simply too late to put the lid on.

The most active group interested in the control of information on cold fusion was not the government or power companies but patent lawyers. The University of Utah was attempting, at all costs, to hold onto the potential of its invention, and that meant having cast-iron patents. The law firms retained by the University of Utah, as well as the patent lawyers operating for other universities and laboratories, were desperately trying to keep the lid on cold fusion.

Patents are complicated things. A drug company, for example, may spend hundreds of millions of dollars and years of research on developing a new drug. But patenting that particular molecule or chemical process is not sufficient. Suppose that a related chemical can do the job just as well or almost as well: it will not be covered by the patent, and a rival company will be free to manufacture it. Whenever a new drug is marketed, drug companies must spend a great deal of effort in researching and patenting the potential of all related molecules and chemical processes. The aim is to own an umbrella of patents that block any competition.

The same is true about the Fleischmann and Pons discovery. It is one thing to patent a Pons and Fleischmann cell, but what about the Frascati discovery in which deuterium gas was pumped into titanium? What if some other metal or new design of fusion cell proved to be as effective, and its use is not included in the Utah patent description? The lawyers had to cover all possible situations.

Scientists who had been unable to duplicate the Pons and Fleischmann result were already beginning to wonder whether there was a secret missing ingredient in the experiment. When Fleischmann and Pons refused to come up with details on request, this only heightened their suspicion. If there really was a magical missing step, this could well be the key to the Utah patent application. Provided that only Fleischmann and Pons knew the secret, their patent would be secure.

But how specific was that magical ingredient? A patent disclosure has to spell out all the details. It is no use talking about "a pinch of chemicals"; the exact composition of the fusion cell has to be spelled out. Moreover, the device has to be shown to work. Some researchers were beginning to wonder whether Fleischmann and Pons really knew what they were doing. It was certainly true that they could get their cells to work most of the time, but did they know enough to make a totally secure patent disclosure?

For the University of Utah, this patent application must have seemed like a Holy Grail. And, like the grail of Arthurian legend, there was always the chance that it would vanish into thin air just as it came within grasp. Too many people were working on cold fusion, and too many speculations were flying around. This is why the lawyers were beginning to be concerned about the wide availability of information on cold fusion—if too many people talked about what was going on, then applying for a patent would be impossible.

Source: *F. David Peat,* Cold Fusion, *Contemporary Books, 1989.*

ఴ ఴ ఴ ఴ ఴ ఴ ఴ ఴ ఴ ఴ ఴ ఴ ఴ

COLD FUSION, PRO-FUSION, AND CON-FUSION

John G. Cramer

As I write this column in early May, the cold fusion "discovery" of Prof. G. Stanley Pons of the University of Utah and Prof. Martin Fleischmann of Great Britain's Southampton University had just been featured on the covers of both *Time* and *Newsweek*. Pons and Fleischmann (P&F) claimed in a March 23 press conference and in papers submitted to *Nature* and to the *Journal of Electrochemistry,* that by electrolyzing heavy water using a 4 millimeter diameter rod of palladium, a noble metal that readily absorbs large quantities of hydrogen, they have achieved nuclear fusion at room temperature. Soon after the announcement, the price of palladium on the commodities market soared from about $120 per troy ounce to about $180. The announcement also produced a veritable scientific gold-rush, with scientists at laboratories around the world (including my own) scrambling to obtain palladium and heavy water to test this amazing effect.

That happened almost six weeks ago, but an unresolved question remains: is P&F cold fusion a real effect, an out-of-the-blue solution to the world's pressing need for energy, or is it perhaps another demonstration of humanity's boundless capacity for self-delusion, particularly when the prospect of limitless free energy is involved? Perhaps *you*, reading this column several months from now, will know the answer. I do not. At my laboratory at the University of Washington we are still carefully monitoring a cell that is electrolyzing heavy water, searching for some indication of excess heat, neutrons, gamma rays, or tritium. After several weeks of this, we have seen no hint of the P&F effect. But we will continue for weeks or months more, until the issue is resolved.

What might be called the "P&F Credibility Coefficient" has gone through wild swings recently. In the past week it (and the stock market) moved in the downward direction. It reached soaring heights of enthusiasm when European laboratories (Hungary, Moscow, Frascati) reported confirmations, and other U.S. laboratories (Brigham Young, Brookhaven, Georgia Tech, Texas A&M, and Stanford) made announcements including some staged press conference spectaculars to announce preliminary evidence in support of the effect. There have been plummets into the depths of depression as some of these confirming results were discreetly retracted (by Brookhaven, Georgia Tech, and Texas A&M) and as a growing number of other laboratories revealed their inability to confirm the Utah results. Two condensed-matter graduate students from my department at the University of Washington contributed to these P&F mood swings. At a university-sponsored and nationally televised press conference last month they announced the observation of a "mass 5 fusion signature" from heavy water electrolysis which they felt might be deuterium-tritium molecular ions from fusion-produced tritium. Several weeks later, after further testing, they submitted a paper reporting evidence that their "signature" was more likely to be a triple deuterium-deuterium-hydrogen molecular ion unrelated to cold fusion. This week at the American Physical Society Meeting in Baltimore, the P&F Credibility Index sank to a new low because of the absence of any confirming experiments reported at the meeting and the detailed dissection of the flaws in the P&F experiment by Prof. Nathan Lewis, a physical chemist from Caltech.

Because of these ongoing controversies and uncertainties and because of the delay between writing and the publication of this column, I can't give a timely discussion of the recent results of cold fusion, so I am stuck with writing about history. I'll start with the physics of cold fusion, then look at past "discoveries" in fusion and other areas, and finally consider the sociology of science as revealed by the present controversy.

Nuclear fusion is the primary energy source of the Sun, where high temperatures and pressures drive the fusion of hydrogen into helium. Here on Earth we would like to make fusion a primary energy source as well, but, with the exception of thermonuclear explosions, we have yet to master the trick. What we would *like* is to bring two deuterium nuclei (1 proton + 1 neutron each) close enough together so that they would fuse, forming a single helium nucleus (2 protons + 2 neutrons) accompanied by the release of about five million times more energy than could be obtained from any chemical reaction.

There are several problems with achieving this. First, both deuterons are electrically charged, so there is a large electrical force pushing them apart. A way must be found to overcome this force and bring the deuterons close enough to fuse. The second problem is that a fusion process must simultaneously obey the laws of conservation of energy and conservation of momentum. Because of this dual requirement, d + d fusion reactions that make helium-3 + neutron or hydrogen-3 + proton should be far more probable than helium-4 + gamma ray. Normal d + d fusion should therefore be a prodigious source of fast neutrons and the secondary gamma rays from energetic protons. In other words, fusion should make lots of radiation.

In the P&F experiment, the energy released would require a speedup of the d + d fusion rate by a factor of about a trillion (the ratio of one dollar to the U.S. National Debt). At the same time, their fusion process would have to make at least a billion times fewer neutrons and gamma rays than would be expected from a normal fusion reaction.

Therefore, to explain the P&F effect we would need the help of the Tooth Fairy (or her equivalent) at least twice. She would have to wave her wand once to make the fusion happen at all, and she must wave it again to make the radiation go away. Some theoretical physicists have explored possible non-Tooth-Fairy mechanisms for doing this. All the proposals seem unlikely. The least unlikely suggests that the palladium crystal lattice is somehow bringing the deuterons close enough to fuse and is also absorbing the recoil momentum from the reaction, allowing the produced helium-4 nucleus to receive the full fusion energy. Even this explanation is not consistent with observations, however, because the 24 MeV helium nuclei thereby created should make gamma rays that are not observed.

Controlled nuclear fusion has had a checkered history that does nothing to give one confidence in the validity of the present claims. In 1923 two German chemists, Fritz Paneth and Kurt Peters, revealed that they had achieved fusion using a method very similar to P&F, the electrolysis of heavy water using a palladium electrode. Within a year they published a retraction. In 1951 Argentine President Juan Perón revealed to the world that his protegé, physicist Ronald Richter, had produced "controlled liberation of atomic energy" through a new fusion process. Within a year Richter was imprisoned for having deceived his benefactor. In 1956 Luis Alvarez, who later won the Nobel Prize for his work in particle physics, reported achieving low temperature fusion, using mu mesons, but he later reported that the reaction rate had been seriously overestimated and was not useful for energy production. In 1958 the British Nobel Laureate Sir John Cockcroft announced "he was 90% certain" that controlled fusion had been produced using his ZETA machine. Later he announced that he had been mistaken and that only a very small amount of energy had been produced.

In the history of physics these are only a few of the succession of scientific "discoveries" that proved incorrect. In recent times, the announcements of the "discoveries" of superheavy elements, tachyons, "anomalons," magnetic monopoles (twice), and free quarks (twice) have all proved incorrect. These wrong results often involved effects that were barely within the realm of measurability, and many of them required special materials or the use of highly specialized apparatus and techniques that could not be readily duplicated.

The F&P experiment, while seemingly simple and straightforward, has some of these characteristics. Pons revealed recently that one must use palladium rods that are cast rather than extruded or forged, and that even among the cast rods tested, only a fraction show excess heat. He also asserted that the electrolysis must be continued for several months before any release of excess heat can be expected. These requirements make it very difficult to compare the negative results at other laboratories with the Utah results. Any experiments initiated after the P&F announcement can have been in operation for only a few weeks and many of these have used forged rather than cast rods.

There are other details of the F&P experiment that are controversial:

- Conventional wisdom is that in heat measurements it is important to stir the solution so that the temperature in the solution is as uniform as possible. F&P do *not* stir their solution, arguing that it is not necessary since the bubbles from the electrolysis provided enough agitation. Tests at my own and other laboratories show that this assumption is wrong. The gas bubbles do not mix the solution, very strong temperature gradients are present, and F&P have placed their temperature sensor near the hottest part of the solution. This may explain part of their "extra heat."

- Conventional wisdom is that one should always do a *controlled* experiment, matching a system where the effect is expected against a system where it is not. In the F&P case the obvious choice is to compare the electrolysis of H_2O with that of D_2O, connecting the cells in series so the same current passes through them and adjusting the electrolytes so that they have the same voltage drops. F&P did not do this. Their "control" is a D_2O electrolysis cell with a "dead" palladium rod, one that, for some unknown reason, does not show excess heat.

- Conventional wisdom is that one should measure the electrical power input by multiplying the current through the cell by the voltage drop across the cell. F&P, in computing the input power, do not use the voltage across the cell (and indeed may not even measure it). Instead they use an estimated "representative" voltage drop of about 0.5 volts in their power calculations.

These controversial aspects of their procedures, together with the unusual way in which their results were publicized and their reluctance to allow other scientists to view or test their apparatus, have made it very difficult to take their results at face value. At the APS Meeting it was stated that scientists at Los Alamos National Laboratory, after extensive discussions with Pons, are skeptical of his methods of estimating energy. Work at Harwell Laboratory in Great Britain, where Fleischmann is a consultant, have thus far failed to confirm the Utah results. Time will tell, but the world grows impatient for a believable confirmation of the effect.

Many SF [science fiction] stories often involve the discovery of some revolutionary new physical effect, and SF authors must describe the impact of the discovery on the scientific community, the government, and the public. Whether the F&P effect is true or false, it represents an interesting testing ground for assessing such reactions. In my novel *Twistor*, I described a revolutionary scientific breakthrough that, near the climax of the book, is very rapidly revealed to the scientific community through the use of computer networks. This is a relatively new aspect of scientific communication. After the initial F&P announcement, preprints of scientific papers from Utah, Brigham Young, and other institutions spread like wildfire through the scientific community by means of computer networks and fax machines. Those with networks access had new ideas and new results within minutes after they were put on the nets.

Curiously, the P&F controversy also revealed some fundamental differences in attitude between the community of chemists and of physicists. Physicists, finding the production of fusion energy without radiation too hard to swallow, demanded more information and tended to blame the excess energy on bad measurements and chemical effects (like catalysis of evolved deuterium). Chemists, perhaps placing more trust in the reputations of P&F, tended to scold the physicists for not taking chemical results seriously. They revelled in the vision of a tabletop experiment done in a dishpan by two obscure electrochemists that achieved what billions of dollars and decades of research by an army of physicists working on magnetic confinement fusion and plasma physics had not.

Certain university administrators seemed more interested in securing patent rights, holding press conferences, and lobbying Congress for special grants than in supplying information or facilitating scientific inquiry. Pons and Fleischmann testified before the House Science, Space and Technology committee and requested $25 million to pursue their research. The press, in its characteristic fashion, lavished page space and air time on those with claims of confirmations and new effects while nearly ignoring those who expressed skepticism or caution in accepting unconfirmed results and untested speculations. The Department of Energy, the funding agency for magnetic fusion research, ordered its national laboratories to set up cold fusion research task forces. Industrial firms were, at last report, negotiating with University of Utah officials for inside information on cold fusion.

It all seems very much . . . like a science fiction novel.

Source: *John G. Cramer, "The Alternate View: Cold Fusion, Pro-fusion, and Con-fusion,"* Analog Science Fiction/Science Fact, *1989.*

Questions for Discussion and Review

1. Suppose you were part of a space exploration team that had landed on a distant planet, where you had no idea what the local conditions were like, whether there was anything alive, what life would look like if you found it. How would you go about learning something about this entirely new environment? How would you interpret your instrument readings? How would you check to see whether the physical and chemical laws you knew from earth worked there?

2. Thomas Kuhn published *The Structure of Scientific Revolutions* in 1962. Have there been any "scientific revolutions" in the three decades since that time? Is the development of computers a "revolution" in Kuhn's terms? What about space travel? Why? Why not?

3. If the final test of a scientific theory is its acceptance by the community of men and women who are called "scientists," does that mean that *anything* is acceptable science so long as enough of the right people agree with it? Does that mean there is no such thing as scientific *truth*? How, if at all, does science differ from politics, or art, or religion, in that case?

THOMAS HOBBES

Thomas Hobbes (1588–1679) was (in my opinion) the most power-ful political theorist and the most accomplished literary stylist ever to write philosophy in English. Born at the very moment when rumors were flooding England of a threatened attack by the powerful Span-ish navy, Hobbes grew up in the age of Shakespeare and Queen Eliz-abeth I. In his earlier years, he served as tutor to the young Earl of Devonshire, and in his thirties, he met the great scientific philosopher Francis Bacon (see Chapter 7).

By the time Hobbes was approaching the age of fifty, the political struggles between the Catholic House of Stuart and the Puritans were becoming more and more heated. Fearing for his life, Hobbes exiled himself to Paris in 1640, just as the English Civil War was breaking out. In 1651, with the English King Charles I executed by the Puritans and the royalist cause seemingly lost, Hobbes published his greatest work, Leviathan, *in which he set forth in the most ele-gant and compact manner his theory of matter, perception, desire, the social contract, and the state.*

At the end of 1651, Hobbes returned to England. Although he is commonly considered a supporter of the Stuart monarchy (which was restored in 1660), Hobbes actually managed to alienate both sides in the great struggle. The royalists viewed him with suspicion because he claimed that the absolute authority of the king is derived from the will of the people; the Puritans considered him an enemy because he taught that social peace can come only from an absolute submission to the will of a king.

After his return to England at the age of sixty-three, Hobbes lived another twenty-eight years, writing a series of major works that earned him great renown. He died in 1679, only a few years before the second great upheaval in English politics, the so-called Glorious Revolution of 1688. Hobbes is perhaps best remembered for his famous description of life in a society without a strong ruler as "soli-tary, nasty, brutish, and short." The political events of the twentieth century have made him once again a writer much looked to for insight into our social and political condition.

Metaphysics and Philosophy of Mind

❊ What Is Metaphysics?

Some years ago, there appeared a listing in the Yellow Pages of the Manhattan telephone book, between "Metals" and "Meteorologists," for "Metaphysician." A gentleman who shall remain nameless had hung out his shingle in Greenwich Village and was apparently prepared to offer his metaphysical services for a fee to all comers. The listing has disappeared from subsequent editions of the Yellow Pages, but I continue to wonder just what services he offered, and what his clients imagined they were going to get when they sought him out.

What *is* metaphysics? Or should we ask, What *are* metaphysics? The term itself is a sheer historical accident. As you already know, Aristotle wrote a set of essays on fundamental problems concerning the most basic classifications or categories of being and the most general concepts by means of which we can think about what is. He called his discussions *First Philosophy,* not because they were about things most easily understood, but because they were about fundamentals. Several centuries after Aristotle's death, when other philosophers commented on Aristotle's arguments, they found that the essays on first philosophy came after the book on physics in the edition or manuscript with which they worked. Because the essays had no name, they were referred to in Greek as *"ta meta ta physika biblia,"* which is to say "the books which come after the physics." Eventually, this was shortened to *The Metaphysics,* and the topics dealt with under this title were dubbed "metaphysics." Unfortunately, over the centuries the prefix "meta" has acquired the bogus sense of "super" or "going beyond" or "transcending sense perception." So metaphysics is thought somehow to deal with what transcends physics, with what is supernatural, occult, mysterious. Perhaps that is what our Greenwich Village metaphysician's clients expected—a touch of the beyond.

In philosophy, metaphysics is not really a single field or discipline, but rather a catch-all for a number of problems whose scope and significance are so broad that they seem to have implications for virtually every other field of philosophy. Let me mention just a few of the questions that are dealt with by philosophers under the heading of "metaphysics." You will very quickly see why this branch of philosophy was for so long considered truly fundamental.

First, there are the basic questions: What sorts of things are there? What are the categories into which whatever is can be sorted? Physical bodies in

> ☞ **Metaphysics** In modern philosophy, the study of the most fundamental principles of the nature of things. The term derives from an early description of the set of essays by Aristotle, called by him "First Philosophy," which came after the Physics in an edition of Aristotle's works (*ta meta ta physika,* or "after the Physics").

space? Minds? Properties of things, such as size, shape, color, smell, hardness, and taste? Events, such as the moving of a body from one place to another, or the growth of a tree from a seed, or the change in color of a leaf as it dies and browns? Ideas in a mind, thoughts, feelings, sense perceptions? How many different categories are there? Can some of these sorts of things be reduced to instances of other sorts? Is there one correct set of general categories for classifying things? What shall we say of peculiar things, like the number three, which doesn't seem to *exist,* in any ordinary sense, but on the other hand can hardly be said not to exist? (It would certainly sound odd to say there is no such thing as the number three!)

Then there are more particular questions: What is space, and what is time? Are they dimensions? Containers in which things exist and happen? Relations among things? Forms of our perception of things? Can there be space in which nothing exists—a void, as it is called by philosophers and scientists? Can there be a stretch of time in which absolutely nothing happens? Could there be totally empty time, in which nothing happens and nothing even exists? What sense does it make to speak of "empty" time and "empty" space, as though they were huge boxes waiting to be filled up?

Is there such a thing as a soul? Is it made out of physical matter, and if not, what then is it? Is the soul the same as the mind? Can a soul exist without relation to a body? How? Do souls continue to exist after the body dies? Did they exist before they were associated with, or planted in, bodies? What *is* the relationship of the soul to the body? Is the mind the same as the brain? Is the body just an idea in the mind?

Does the past exist? If not, then does nothing exist save whatever there is right now at this very moment? If the past does exist, then where is it? Is there some other universe of past things? What about future things as well? Is there a whole assortment of possible worlds alongside this actual one that we live in? Does it make any sense at all to say that something has *possible* existence?

Are all my actions absolutely causally determined by what has gone before, or am I free in some sense to choose among a variety of alternative actions available to me? If I am determined to act as I do, then can I also consider myself responsible for what I do? If I am free, what is the nature of my freedom? What sort of thing am I, that I should have this strange capacity to act freely?

Why is there anything at all in the universe? Why is there in general something and not nothing? Is the universe fundamentally absurd, or does it make some sort of rational sense? Was it created? Has it existed from all eternity? Can I even imagine a satisfactory *reason* for the universe? Does the universe stretch infinitely away from me in space? Will it go on existing forever?

And last, but of course hardly least: Is there an infinite, omnipotent, omniscient creator of all that is—a God?

Well, no one can accuse metaphysics of wasting its time on trivia! But how are we to get a handle on a field this vast in the confines of a single chapter?

Following the practice of previous chapters, we shall begin by focusing on the life and thought of a single great philosopher, Thomas Hobbes, one of the most provocative thinkers ever to write in English. Although Hobbes wrote on many subjects, including the theory of the social contract and the nature of the state, we shall focus on his *metaphysical* theories, which we can describe in a word as materialism.

After getting a general idea of how Hobbes saw the world, and human beings in the world, we shall look at one of the oldest and most challenging metaphysical questions, the problem customarily referred to by philosophers as "free will and determinism." Hobbes, as we shall see, held a very controversial and uncompromising position on this question.

Finally, we shall look at a selection of brief passages from twentieth-century writers in which some very odd things are said about the relation of mind to body.

By the time we are done, you should have a pretty good idea of what metaphysics is, and how some of the great thinkers have approached its most puzzling problems.

❧ Hobbes' Materialism

The well-known American logician and philosopher Willard van Orman Quine, in one of his most famous essays, written almost half a century ago, begins with the following tongue-in-cheek observation.

> A curious thing about the ontological question is its simplicity. It can be put in three Anglo-Saxon monosyllables: "What is there?" It can be answered, moreover, in a word—"Everything"—and everyone will accept this answer as true. However, this is merely to say that there is what there is. There remains room for disagreement over cases; and so the issue has stayed alive down the centuries.

Quine is quite right; the issue has indeed stayed alive down the centuries. By and large, philosophers have argued not about particular *things*, but rather about what *sorts* of things there are. And simple as that little three-word question may look, it has turned out to be uncommonly difficult to find an answer that everyone can agree on.

Here are some of the sorts of things philosophers have said there are: physical bodies, including big ones like the stars and the planets, middle-sized ones like trees, houses, and the human body, and very small ones, such as atoms; minds, or souls, or spirits—not only the human mind, but also angels, devils, world-souls, and of course God; numbers, geometric shapes (triangles, squares, and so forth), logical relationships such as if-then, or, and not; sense perceptions, such as smells, tastes, sounds, sights, and feels; emotions, like anger, love, jealousy, and affection; properties or characteristics of bodies, such as softness, hardness, solubility, density, and elasticity; and even imaginary or fictional things, such as the Starship Enterprise, Superman, and Alf the alien.

If you look back over the past 2,000 years of Western philosophy, for each one of these kinds of things, you can find at least one major thinker who argued for their existence. Democritus believed that physical bodies exist (as did lots of other philosophers, of course); Leibniz believed that minds or souls exist; Plato believed that numbers and logical relationships exist; Hume believed that sense perceptions exist; and Meinong believed that possible objects like Alf exist (in some curious sense of existing).

But simplifying for the sake of getting a handle on this confusion, we can say that there have been essentially three dominant positions in the whole history of the debate, to which philosophers have attached the titles *materialism, idealism, and dualism.* Materialism is the theory that physical objects in space are all there is—everything else, even mind or spirit, on closer examination, turns out to be just combinations of physical objects. Idealism is the theory that minds or spirits are all there is—everything else, even physical body, turns out on closer examination to be just minds, or ideas in minds. Dualism (by now you ought to be able to figure this one out) is the theory that there are *two* fundamentally different kinds of things in the world—bodies and minds—neither of which can be reduced to, or analyzed into, the other.

The ancient Greek atomists whom we discussed briefly in Chapter 1 were materialists. They believed that everything, even soul or spirit, consists of very small, very fine bits of physical matter, which they called "atoms." Thomas Hobbes, writing 2,000 years after the time of those early philosophers, defended exactly the same theory. Hobbes was the most brilliant, insightful, consistent materialist since the time of ancient Greece. Let us begin by taking a look at Hobbes' materialism.

Hobbes has no serious difficulty explaining the physical universe in terms of atoms. Following the ancient thinkers, he describes the world as made up of very tiny atoms that are constantly moving about, bumping into one another like billiard balls. Allowing for 300 years of scientific advance, we still take essentially the same view today.

The problem for Hobbes or any other materialist is how to explain the human mind and its operations without ever appealing to anything except atoms in motion. How can we give a purely physical, atomistic explanation of desire, aversion, choice, deliberation, sensation, language, and such personality traits as courage, greed, or pride?

Hobbes's answer is both very modern and very puzzling. When light strikes my eye or sound strikes my ear, the atoms in the eye or ear begin to vibrate—to move. That motion is then communicated to the atoms next to them, and is passed along, by a chain reaction, until the atoms in the brain start to vibrate. The vibrating of the atoms in the brain is what we call sight or sound, seeing or hearing. When I think about something, all that happens is that certain atoms vibrate in a particular fashion.

Think, if you will, of Commander Data on the television show *Star Trek: The Next Generation*. Data is an android, and as we discover periodically when Geordie lifts up a flap on his head for repairs, he is essentially a very complicated, very sophisticated electronic machine. Many of the most provocative *Star Trek* episodes deal with the puzzling question, Is Data alive? Is he a person? The last episode of the 1992–93 season even confronted the question, Can Data feel emotions?

Hobbes' answer, if he were suddenly transported to the twentieth century, would be: Data is as alive as any of us, for we are all nothing more than very complicated machines.

Now, on the face of it, this doesn't sound quite right. We are surrounded today by extremely complicated machines, some of which—such as the computer on which I am writing these words—can perform wonders in a fraction of a second. But I don't think my computer is alive, nor do I suppose that my car, my toaster, my VCR, or my telephone answering machine is alive. They are all very complicated machines, but they are not alive. What is more, I don't think they get closer and closer to being alive, the more complicated they become.

The real test for a materialist like Hobbes is not explaining complicated machines—or, since there weren't any complicated machines in Hobbes' day, explaining complicated physical things like an eclipse, or combustion, or the human eye. No, the real test is explaining what seems most distinctively human, namely desires, aversions, choice, deliberation, and action. No one thinks a computer, however complicated, *desires* anything. It simply operates whatever programs are loaded into it.

Hobbes recognized that desire, deliberation, and choice—in a word, will—posed the greatest challenge to his philosophy, and he faced the problem head on. Here is a selection from his most important book, *Leviathan,* in which he undertakes to explain these most human of all our capacities and characteristics.

There be in Animals, two sorts of *Motions* peculiar to them: One called *Vitall;* begun in generation, and continued without interruption through their whole life; such as are the course of the *Bloud,* the *Pulse,* the *Breathing,* the *Concoction, Nutrition, Excretion,* &c; to which Motions there needs no help of Imagination: The other is *Animall motion,* otherwise called *Voluntary motion*; as to go, to *speak,* to *move* any of our limbes, in such manner as is first fancied in our minds. That Sense, is Motion in the organs and interiour parts of mans body, caused by the action of the things we See, Heare, &c; And that Fancy is but the Reliques of the same Motion, remaining after Sense, has been already sayd in the first and second Chapters. And because *going, speaking,* and the like Voluntary motions, depend always upon a precedent thought of *whither, which way,* and *what;* it is evident, that the Imagination is the first internall beginning of all Voluntary

Motion. And although unstudied men, do not conceive any motion at all to be there, where the thing moved is invisible; or the space it is moved in, is (for the shortnesse of it) insensible; yet that doth not hinder, but that such Motions are. For let a space be never so little, that which is moved over a greater space, whereof that little one is part, must first be moved over that. These small beginnings of Motion, within the body of Man, before they appear in walking, speaking, striking, and other visible actions, are commonly called ENDEAVOUR.

This Endeavour, when it is toward something which causes it, is called APPETITE, or DESIRE; the later, being the generall name; and the other, oftentimes restrayned to signifie the Desire of Food, namely *Hunger* and *Thirst*. And when the Endeavour is fromward something, it is generally called AVERSION. . . .

That which men Desire, they are also sayd to LOVE: and to HATE those things, for which they have Aversion. So that Desire, and Love, are the same thing; save that by Desire, we always signifie the Absence of the Object; by Love, most commonly the Presence of the same. So also by Aversion, we signifie the Absence; and by Hate, the Presence of the Object.

Of Appetites, and Aversions, some are born with men; as Appetite of food, Appetite of excretion, and exoneration, (which may also and more properly be called Aversions, from somewhat they feele in their Bodies;) and some other Appetites, not many. The rest, which are Appetites of particular things, proceed from Experience, and triall of their effects upon themselves, or other men. For of things wee know not at all, or believe not to be, we can have no further Desire, than to taste and try. But Aversion wee have for things, not onely which we know have hurt us; but also that we do not know whether they will hurt us, or not.

Those things which we neither Desire, nor Hate, we are said to *Contemne:* CONTEMPT being nothing else but an immobility, or contumacy of the Heart, in resisting the action of certain things; and proceeding from that the Heart is already moved otherwise, by other more potent objects; or from want of experience of them.

And because the constitution of a mans Body, is in continuall mutation; it is impossible that all the same things should alwayes cause in him the same Appetites, and Aversions; much lesse can all men consent, in the Desire of almost any one and the same Object. . . .

As, in Sense, that which is really within us, is (as I have sayd before) onely Motion, caused by the action of externall objects, but in apparence; to the Sight, Light and Colour; to the Eare, Sound; to the Nostrill, Odour, &c; so, when the action of the same object is continued from the Eyes, Eares, and other organs to the Heart; the reall effect there is nothing but Motion, or Endeavour; which consisteth in Appetite, or Aversion, to, or from the object moving.

Although Hobbes writes with great style, his English is of the seventeenth century, and you may therefore find it a bit hard to follow. Let me summarize what he is telling us in the passage you have just read.

There is nothing in the world but atoms moving about, and atoms, like all physical bodies, can move up or down, backward or forward, fast or slow—and nothing else. When I see a table with food on it, what is happening is that atoms from the food on the table (Hobbes didn't know that light is a form of electromagnetic radiation) are moving into my eyes, where they start the atoms in my retinas and my optic nerves moving. Eventually, the atoms in a portion of my brain vibrate as a result of that motion in the eye, and that is what I call "seeing the food on the table."

Now, sometimes, these vibrations in my brain trigger vibrations in the nerves leading to my arms and legs; the muscles in my arms and legs contract, and I reach for the food, or start walking toward it. That, according to Hobbes, is what we call "desiring the food." On other occasions (perhaps because the food is rotting, and gives off a particular smell that agitates my nose), I start moving away from the food. That, says Hobbes, is what we call "having an aversion to the food," or perhaps "disliking the food."

Sometimes, of course, I vacillate between moving toward the food and moving away from it. Perhaps I am hungry, even though the food is rotting. So first the atoms in my brain agitate the nerves in such a way that I start to move toward it; then the atoms in my brain agitate the nerves in such a way that I start to move away from it. For a while, I go on like that, leaning toward it, leaning away from it, leaning toward it, leaning away from it. That, Hobbes says, is what we call "deliberating" or "deciding."

Finally, the atoms in my brain that are triggering movement toward the food get the better of the atoms in the brain that are triggering movement away, and my body makes a decisive move for the food on the table. That, says Hobbes, is what we call "willing," or "determining the will."

Put as I have just done, this all sounds horribly simple-minded. Surely desire, aversion, deliberation, and will are something more than that! But think about it for a minute. I can complicate the story considerably with some modern scientific jargon from the field of neurophysiology, and no doubt a complete explanation is going to be much, much more elaborate than anything Hobbes can tell us. But at bottom, won't it just be a story about atoms bumping into other atoms? Or, if you wish, electric currents passing along nerve pathways? Won't it be, when all is said and done, a *materialistic* explanation? After all, what else could the final explanation possibly be?

So in principle, Data *is* a human being. Or at least, he can become a human being once his neural circuitry gets complicated enough. The only real difference between Data and me is that Data's insides are wires and transistors, whereas mine are nerve cells and fluids. My body is wet and his is dry, as scientists these days like to say. But both Data and I—and you, of course—

are physical beings, all of whose behavior must in principle be explainable in purely materialistic terms.

We are going to have a good deal more to say about this fascinating and troubling idea in the remainder of this chapter, but it might be a good idea right now to consider one of the principal objections to Hobbes' story, an objection we can label *the consciousness objection.*

The consciousness objection goes like this. The defining characteristic of all minds—the "essence," as some philosophers put it—is *consciousness.* I am aware of myself, of my own thoughts, feelings, pains, pleasures, hopes, fears, deductions, and sense impressions. As Descartes said in the *Meditations,* I am a thing that thinks. Now computers aren't conscious. They are not aware of themselves. They are simply complicated combinations of transistors, circuitry, and other hardware. When I say that a computer is "calculating" something, or checking my grammar, I am speaking very loosely. I do the same sort of thing when I say that my car "doesn't want to start this morning." I don't actually suppose that my car sits there in the garage saying to itself, "It is cold outside. I think I won't turn over." I understand that the charge in the battery is low. I am just saying, in a sort of shorthand way, that the car is behaving *as though* it were conscious.

Exactly the same is true of a computer, although the physics of what is happening may be more complicated. When I type this sentence on my computer, I am actually causing a series of electric currents to be sent through the circuitry. Eventually, the cathode ray tube in the monitor sends a stream of particles to the screen in the shape of letters. But there is no consciousness in the computer of the words being formed, let alone of the ideas those words stand for.

So Data isn't conscious; he (for it, as a character in one episode insists on saying) is simply a very advanced machine. We humans are conscious, no doubt the higher animals are conscious, and for all we know there are beings elsewhere in the universe who are conscious. And that shows that we, the higher animals, and those other beings, if they exist, *are not merely material things.*

That is the objection, and it certainly does have an initial plausibility. I *am* conscious, and I cannot see how that consciousness can simply be the same thing as a complicated electrical pattern in my nerve cells. But Hobbes, or any other materialist, has a very powerful comeback. If the mind is *not* some arrangement of matter, he may ask, what else could it possibly be? I started out as a nonconscious sperm fused with a nonconscious egg. As I grew and developed, I became more and more physically complicated. My organs and nervous system developed before I was born. At some point, either before or after birth (for this discussion, it doesn't matter which), I developed consciousness, and finally *self-consciousness*—an awareness of my own awareness.

I can always explain this development by appeal to the religious notion of a soul, but if I want a purely naturalistic, scientific explanation, my only option seems to be to explain consciousness as a certain level of complexity of my physical body. In short, Hobbes appears to be right.

❦ Free Will and Determinism

We turn first to one of the oldest and most difficult problems in all of philosophy, the conflict between *free will* and *determinism*. The problem is this: I think of myself as free, at least within some limits, to choose what I will do, and how I will do it. Give me enough money to buy an ice cream cone, and I think of myself as free to choose vanilla, chocolate, or strawberry. Present me with a college course catalogue, and I deliberate about precisely which courses to enroll for. Even if I am confined to my bed with a broken leg, physically able to do little more than turn my head to the right or to the left, I think of myself as free to choose which way I will turn, or even whether I will turn at all.

The notion that I am free to choose is important to me when I am trying to decide what to do, for it wouldn't make much sense to trouble myself with deciding unless I were really free to choose. It is also important when I am trying to judge whether I am responsible for what I do. I consider myself responsible for deciding to run a red light, because I am aware of having chosen to do it. But I do not consider myself responsible for the beating of my heart, because I don't think I could choose whether to have it beat or not.

So, some things are within my choice, and some are not. I am free to choose among the things that are within my choice, and hence I can be held responsible for what I have chosen. Without this notion of freedom and choice, our whole legal system seems to make no sense, nor does any of our ethical and political deliberation.

But even as I tell myself that I am *free to choose,* I am also aware that I am a physical being like any other, and that the movements of my arms and legs, the sounds I utter, everything I do, can be traced to physical causes in my nervous system, my muscles, my bones, and my other organs. And I am accustomed to thinking of physical movements of that sort as *causally determined,* not free. If I trigger an electrical impulse in a nerve cell, the impulse travels along the cell and causes a muscle to contract. If I shine light on the retina of my eye, a series of physical reactions is set up that results in my seeing a colored light. I can "choose" to close my eye, of course, but even that is accomplished by a causal sequence that takes impulses from the brain and sends them to the muscles controlling my eyelids.

Hobbes, as we have seen, is a materialist. He argues that all things, including thoughts in our minds, consist of the motions of atoms. And the motions of atoms obey the universal laws of physics, in which there seems to be no room for *choice* or *freedom.* So Hobbes denies that there is any sort of free will, in the sense described above.

According to Hobbes, here is what actually happens. First, atoms from outside the body strike the various sense organs of the body (eyes, ears, etc.), setting up sympathetic vibrations in the nerve cells, which are carried to the brain. Then the brain atoms rattle about, bumping into one another, triggering little beginning motions toward or away from something outside the body. These to-ings and fro-ings, these bumpings and reboundings, are what I call *thinking about what I am going to do,* or *deliberating.* So long as this process is going on, I am under the illusion that I am "free," because the motions are too small and quick for me to observe them. Eventually, the atoms bump into each other in such a way that a message is sent back down the nerve cells to the muscles, and I move (I go to the store and buy some chocolate ice cream, perhaps). I now tell myself that I have *freely chosen* to buy the chocolate ice cream, but in fact my "choice" is as rigorously determined by the law of physics as any movement of balls on a billiard table.

Perhaps I can make Hobbes' theory a bit clearer, and also a bit more believable, with the help of one of Hobbes' countrymen, Jonathan Swift, who published his great satire, *Gulliver's Travels,* just seventy-five years after Hobbes published *Leviathan.*

Do you remember that in *Gulliver's Travels,* Lemuel Gulliver travels first to a land of very small people, the Lilliputians, and then to a land of very big people, the Brobdingnagians? Swift is rather careful about his proportions, and while the Lilliputians are exactly one-twelfth the size of normal

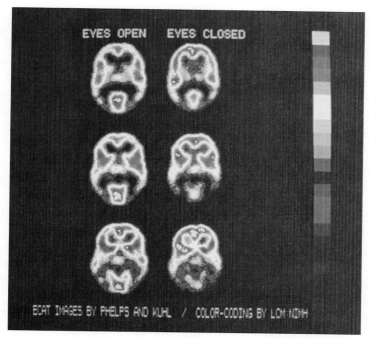

Positron Image. The CAT scan (short for computerized axial tomography) has made it possible for physicians to get a three-dimensional picture of the brain—but not, of course, to get a picture of the mind. (U.S. Dept. of Health and Human Services—Admin. on Children, Youth, and Families.)

humans, the Brobdingnagians are exactly twelve times as big. So in comparison to Gulliver, who is six feet tall, they are seventy-two feet tall.

Now, let us suppose (this is not actually in the book, of course) that the Brobdingnagians played dominoes, and were especially fond of setting up long rows of dominoes so that when the first was tipped over, each of the remaining dominoes would be knocked over in turn. (I assume you have all seen this sort of thing, or have even done it yourselves.) The Brobdingnagian dominoes, of course, would be enormous—three feet long. And let us also suppose that Gulliver has brought along a set of his own dominoes, which are the normal length—three inches each.

Gulliver, we may imagine, sets up a display of dominoes for the amusement of the Brobdingnagians, who also, by the way, do not have very good eyesight. In fact, while they can see their own dominoes well enough from their great height, Gulliver's dominoes are too small for them to be able to pick out.

Gulliver sets up a long row of big Brobdingnagian dominoes, and then carefully arranges the last in the series so that when it falls, it just barely brushes the first of a long row of normal-sized dominoes. These are set to fall over, one after another, until the very last hits a hair-triggered big domino, which starts a second row of Brobdingnagian dominoes falling.

O.K. There is our imaginary experiment, all set up. A row of big dominoes, then a row of small ones, and then another row of big dominoes. The Brobdingnagians sit down on their enormous chairs, and tell Gulliver to begin the demonstration. He shoves the first big three-foot domino over, and one by one the dominoes begin to fall.

Now, what actually happens, of course, is that each domino is knocked over by the one just before it. *But that is not what the Brobdingnagians see!* They see the first run of big dominoes fall, but the middle run of small dominoes is too small for them to see, so for a while, as far as they can tell, nothing at all is happening. Then suddenly (or so it seems to them) the first big domino in the second run falls over, apparently without having been pushed, and the second run starts falling, one after the other.

To the Brobdingnagians, it looks as though the second run of dominoes started falling freely, spontaneously, without having been caused to fall. *And that is exactly the way our very own actions appear to us.* Because our eyes are not able to see the tiny brain atoms pushing and shoving, we mistakenly think that our movements are spontaneous, free, uncaused. In fact, they are just as rigorously determined by the previous movements of atoms as the second run of big dominoes was by the fall of the little dominoes in between.

To be sure, Hobbes admits that we use words like "freedom" and "choice" and "deliberation," but upon close examination, these words turn out to refer to physically determined motions of atoms, for that is all there is in the world. According to Hobbes, when I say that a man is *free,* all I mean is that nothing external to him stood in the way of his doing what he was inclined to do. But his inclination itself is of course causally determined, as is everything in the natural world. Here is how Hobbes explains "freedom."

LIBERTY, or FREEDOME, signifieth (properly) the absence of Opposition; (by Opposition, I mean externall Impediments of motion;) and may be applyed no lesse to Irrationall, and Inanimate creatures, than to Rationall. For whatsoever is so tyed, or environed, as it cannot move, but within a certain space, which space is determined by the opposition of some externall body, we say it hath not Liberty to go further. And so of all living creatures, whilest they are imprisoned, or restrained, with walls, or chayns; and of the water whilest it is kept in by banks, or vessels, that otherwise would spread it selfe into a larger space, we use to say, they are not at Liberty, to move in such manner, as without those externall impediments they would. But when the impediment of motion, is in the constitution of the thing it selfe, we use not to say, it wants the Liberty; but the Power to move; as when a stone lyeth still, or a man is fastned to his bed by sicknesse.

And according to this proper, and generally received meaning of the word, A FREE-MAN, *is he, that in those things, which by his strength and wit he is able to do, is not hindred to doe what he has a will to.* . . . From the use of the word Freewill, no liberty can be inferred to the will, desire, or inclination, but the liberty of the man; which consisteth in this, that he finds no stop, in doing what he has the will, desire, or inclination to doe.

Feare and Liberty are consistent; as when a man throweth his goods into the Sea for *feare* the ship should sink, he doth it neverthelesse very willingly, and may refuse to doe it if he will: It is therefore the action, of one that was *free:* so a man sometimes pays his debt, only for *feare* of Imprisonment, which because no body hindred him from detaining, was the action of a man at *liberty.* And generally all actions which men doe in Commonwealths, for *feare* of the law, or actions, which the doers had *liberty* to omit.

Liberty and *Necessity* are Consistent: As in the water, that hath not only *liberty,* but a *necessity* of descending by the Channel: so likewise in the Actions which men voluntarily doe; which (because they proceed from their will) proceed from *liberty;* and yet because every act of mans will, and every desire, and inclination proceedeth from some cause, and that from another cause, which causes in a continuall chaine (whose first link in the hand of God the first of all causes) proceed from *necessity.* So that to him that could see the connexion of those causes, the *necessity* of all mens voluntary actions, would appeare manifest.

Although Hobbes was unusual, among philosophers of the seventeenth and eighteenth centuries, in defending materialism, he was by no means alone in denying that human beings have a will that is free of external determinations. David Hume takes the same view in his *Treatise of Human Nature*, although, as we shall see very shortly, he manages at the same time to get a dig in at Hobbes.

In Hume's day—the 1700s—it was commonplace for philosophers and scientists to grant the absolute determination of physical events, but at the same time to claim that human actions are freely chosen. Hume pointed out that no one in actual practice really believes any such thing. We go through the day making predictions about the behavior of those around us, and very often bet our lives on the accuracy of those predictions. When I drive down a two-way street (my example, of course, not Hume's), at every moment I am predicting that the people driving toward me will not suddenly decide to veer into my lane and crash into my car. When I fly in a commercial airplane, I bet my life that the pilot will perform in a totally expected fashion, taking off and landing in accordance with the rules and practices of safe navigation. When I buy a meal at a restaurant, I depend on the chef not to poison me.

All these beliefs about the behavior of others are instances of causal judgments, Hume says, and we all consider them quite as reliable as our judgments about the boiling point of water or the properties of sodium. But that is just another way of saying that we consider the behavior of people to be causally determined, just as the behavior of physical bodies is. Hume puts the point this way:

> Shou'd a traveller, returning from a far country, tell us, that he had seen a climate in the fiftieth degree of northern latitude, where all the fruits ripen and come to perfection in the winter, and decay in the summer, after the same manner as in *England* they are produc'd and decay in the contrary seasons, he would find few so credulous as to believe him. I am apt to think a traveller wou'd meet with as little credit, who shou'd inform us of people exactly of the same character with those in *Plato's Republic* on the one hand, or those in *Hobbes's Leviathan* on the other. There is a general course of nature in human actions, as well as in the operations of the sun and the climate. There are also characters peculiar to different nations and particular persons, as well as common to mankind. The knowledge of these characters is founded on the observation of an uniformity in the actions, that flow from them; and this uniformity forms the very essence of necessity.

In the face of these arguments, it will obviously require a very strong counterattack to defend the notion of the freedom of the human will. The strongest response in the entire philosophical literature comes from Immanuel Kant, whose ideas you met in the previous chapter.

At the very end of Chapter 6, we saw that Kant tried to resolve the conflict between the empiricists and the rationalists by appealing to the old distinction between appearance and reality. Our scientific and mathematical knowledge, he said, is knowledge only of appearance, not of independent reality. Even mathematical physics gives us knowledge only of how things appear to us in space and time. How they are in themselves is forever a closed book to us.

Confronted by the conflict between the determinism of science and morality's demand for freedom and responsibility, Kant adopts a similar position. The realm of appearance, the world of mathematics and science, is through and through determined, he argues. Thus far, Kant agrees completely with Hobbes and Hume. But the realm of independent reality stands outside the chain of natural causation. In that realm, a different kind of determination holds sway, what Kant calls "rational determination." And in that realm—or, as he sometimes puts it, from that standpoint—we are free, not causally determined.

To be sure, our freedom is not license or a mere absence of determination. That, Kant insists, is impossible. But in the realm of independent reality,

Immanuel Kant. Immanuel Kant tried to resolve conflict between empiricists and rationalists by appealing to the distinction between appearance and reality. (PH College Archives.)

we are self-determined, obeying only laws that our reason gives to itself. We are thus lawgivers to ourselves, or *autonomous* ("the Greek auto-nomos" means "giving law to oneself"). Here is Kant's clearest statement of his position:

IMMANUEL KANT,
Critique of Pure Reason

If appearances were things in themselves, and space and time forms of the existence of things in themselves, the conditions would always be members of the same series as the conditioned; and thus, in the present case, as in the other transcendental ideas, the antinomy would arise, that the series must be too large or too small for the understanding. But the dynamical concepts of reason, with which we have to deal in this and the following section, possess this peculiarity that they are not concerned with an object considered as a magnitude, but only with its existence. Accordingly we can abstract from the magnitude of the series of conditions, and consider only the dynamical relation of the condition to the conditioned. The difficulty which then meets us, in dealing with the question regarding nature and freedom, is whether freedom is possible at all, and if it be possible, whether it can exist along with the universality of the natural law of causality. Is it a truly disjunctive proposition to say that every effect in the world must arise *either* from nature *or* from freedom; or must we not rather say that in one and the same event, in different relations, both can be found? That all events in the sensible world stand in thorough-going connection in accordance with unchangeable laws of nature is an established principle of the Transcendental Analytic, and allows of no exception. The question, therefore, can only be whether freedom is completely excluded by this inviolable rule, or whether an effect, notwithstanding its being thus determined in accordance with nature, may not at the same time be grounded in freedom. The common but fallacious presupposition of the *absolute reality* of appearances here manifests its injurious influence, to the confounding of reason. For if appearances are things in themselves, freedom cannot be upheld. Nature will then be the complete and sufficient determining cause of every event. The condition of the event will be such as can be found only in the series of appearances; both it and its effect will be necessary in accordance with the law of nature. If, on the other hand, appearances are not taken for more than they actually are; if they are viewed not as things in themselves, but merely as representations, connected according to empirical laws, they must themselves have grounds which are not appearances. The effects of such an intelligible cause appear, and accordingly can be determined through other appearances, but its causality is not so determined. While the effects are to be found in the series of empirical conditions, the intelligible cause, together with its causality, is outside the series. Thus the effect may be regarded as free in respect of its intelligible cause, and at the same time in respect of appearances as resulting from them according to the necessity of nature.

The Mind and the Body: Some Puzzles and Odd Cases

One of the enduring subjects of philosophical speculation and puzzlement is the relationship of the mind to the body. As we have seen, Hobbes held that the mind is simply a complicated assortment of physical atoms all moving about, this way and that. The ancient atomists from whom Hobbes is intellectually descended believed that the soul, or spirit, or life is a very fine mist of particularly small atoms that leave the body as it breathes its last.

Throughout the history of reflection on this subject, purely philosophical arguments about logical possibilities, general categories of being, and the nature of substance have been all mixed up with detailed observations of people. Sometimes the observations reveal very strange things indeed. Speaking in modern terms, we can say that discussions of the relation of mind to body have, from the very beginning, mixed philosophy with psychology. So it seemed like a good idea, in this section, to present some remarkable case studies reported by an equally remarkable man, Dr. Oliver Sacks. One of his earliest books was made into a movie, starring Robin Williams as the good doctor. It will give you some idea about Sacks if I tell you that he is even stranger than Robin Williams!

Here are three brief case studies reported by Sacks. In each case, a real patient has some neurological problem—a purely physical problem—that results in a very weird distortion of mental functioning. Each of the cases deserves some special comment.

The first case, "The Man Who Fell out of Bed," shows that my easy, casual, unquestioned conception of *my* body actually rests on a very complex psychophysical interaction that can get fouled up in really peculiar ways by some injury or disease of the nervous system. The speculative arguments of

Cartoon. (By permission of Johnny Hart and Creators Syndicate, Inc. Creators Syndicate, Inc.)

Descartes and other "dualists" (people who think there are two sorts of things in the world, minds and bodies) don't begin to take into account cases as strange as this one.

The second case, "Eyes Right!," raises a different sort of philosophical problem. Many philosophers have argued that certain pairs of ideas, such as right/left, up/down, awake/asleep, and even good/bad, are "contrast terms" that depend on one another for their meaning. We simply could not have the idea of right without also having the idea of left, they have argued. Now here is an actual woman who, in some clinical sense, has a firm grasp on the idea of right but can't seem to keep the idea of left in her head.

The last case concerns the question of whether a full-blown hallucination is possible. Some philosophers, such as Daniel Dennett (see the previous chapter), claim that a genuine complete hallucination is impossible. "A Passage to India" does not *disprove* Dennett's claim, of course, but it should at least make us think twice about pronouncing from our armchairs what is possible and impossible in human experience.

The Man Who Fell out of Bed

When I was a medical student many years ago, one of the nurses called me in considerable perplexity, and gave me this singular story on the phone: that they had a new patient—a young man—just admitted that morning. He had seemed very nice, very normal, all day—indeed, until a few minutes before, when he awoke from a snooze. He then seemed excited and strange—not himself in the least. He had somehow contrived to fall out of bed, and was now sitting on the floor, carrying on and vociferating, and refusing to go back to bed. Could I come, please, and sort out what was happening?

When I arrived I found the patient lying on the floor by his bed and staring at one leg. His expression contained anger, alarm, bewilderment and amusement—bewilderment most of all, with a hint of consternation. I asked him if he would go back to bed, or if he needed help, but he seemed upset by these suggestions and shook his head. I squatted down beside him, and took the history on the floor. He had come in, that morning, for some tests, he said. He had no complaints, but the neurologists, feeling that he had a "lazy" left leg—that was the very word they had used—thought he should come in. He had felt fine all day, and fallen asleep towards evening. When he woke up he felt fine too, until he moved in the bed. Then he found, as he put it, "someone's leg" in the bed—*a severed human leg,* a horrible thing! He was stunned, at first, with amazement and disgust—he had never experienced, never imagined, such an incredible thing. He felt the leg gingerly. It seemed perfectly formed, but "peculiar" and cold. At this point he had a brainwave. He now realised what had happened: *it was all a joke!* A rather monstrous and improper, but a very original, joke! It was New Year's Eve, and everyone was celebrating. Half the staff were drunk; quips and crackers were flying; a carnival scene. Obviously one of the nurses with a macabre sense of humour had stolen into the Dissecting Room and nabbed a leg, and then slipped it under his bedclothes as a joke while he was still fast asleep. He was much relieved at the explanation; but feeling that a joke was a joke, and that this one was a bit much, he threw the damn thing out of the bed. But—and at this point his conversational manner deserted him, and he suddenly trembled and became ashen-pale—*when he threw it out of bed, he somehow came after it—and now it was attached to him.*

"Look at it!" he cried, with revulsion on his face. "Have you ever seen such a creepy, horrible thing? I thought a cadaver was just dead. But this is uncanny! And somehow—it's ghastly—it seems stuck to me!" He seized it with both hands, with extraordinary violence, and tried to tear it off his body, and, failing, punched it in an access of rage.

"Easy!" I said. "Be calm! Take it easy! I wouldn't punch that leg like that."

"And why not?!" he asked, irritably, belligerently.

"Because it's *your* leg," I answered. "Don't you know your own leg?"

He gazed at me with a look compounded of stupefaction, incredulity, terror and amusement, not unmixed with a jocular sort of suspicion, "Ah Doc," he said, "You're fooling me! You're in cahoots with that nurse—you shouldn't kid patients like this!"

"I'm not kidding," I said. "That's your own leg."

He saw from my face that I was perfectly serious—and a look of utter terror came over him. "You say it's my leg, Doc? Wouldn't you say that a man should know his own leg?"

"Absolutely," I answered. "He should know his own leg. I can't imagine him *not* knowing his own leg. Maybe *you're* the one who's been kidding all along?"

"I swear to God, cross my heart, I haven't . . . A man *should* know his own body, what's his and what's not—but this leg, this *thing*"—another shudder of distaste—"doesn't feel right, doesn't feel real—and it doesn't *look* part of me."

"What *does* it look like?" I asked in bewilderment, being, by this time, as bewildered as he was.

"What does it look like?" He repeated my words slowly. "I'll tell you what it looks like. *It looks like nothing on earth.* How can a thing like that belong to me? I don't know where a thing like that belongs. . . ." His voice trailed off. He looked terrified and shocked.

"Listen," I said. "I don't think you're well. Please allow us to return you to bed. But I want to ask you one final question. If this—

this thing—is *not* your left leg" (he had called it a "counterfeit" at one point in our talk, and expressed his amazement that someone had gone to such lengths to "manufacture" a "facsimile") "then where is your own left leg?"

Once more he became pale—so pale that I thought he was going to faint. "I don't know," he said. "I have no idea. It's disappeared. It's gone. It's nowhere to be found . . ."

Eyes Right!

Mrs S., an intelligent woman in her sixties, has suffered a massive stroke, affecting the deeper and back portions of her right cerebral hemisphere. She has perfectly preserved intelligence—and humour.

She sometimes complains to the nurses that they have not put dessert or coffee on her tray. When they say, "But, Mrs. S., it is right there, on the left," she seems not to understand what they say, and does not look to the left. If her head is gently turned, so that the dessert comes into sight, in the preserved right half of her visual field, she says, "Oh, there is it—it wasn't there before." She has totally lost the idea of "left," with regard to both the world and her own body. Sometimes she complains that her portions are too small, but this is because she only eats from the right half of the plate—it does not occur to her that it has a left half as well. Sometimes, she will put on lipstick, and make up the right half of her face, leaving the left half completely neglected: it is almost impossible to treat these things, because her attention cannot be drawn to them ("hemi-inattention"—see Battersby 1956) and she has no conception that they are wrong. She knows it intellectually, and can understand, and laugh; but it is impossible for her to know it directly.

Knowing it intellectually, knowing it inferentially, she has worked out strategies for dealing with her imperception. She cannot look left, directly, she cannot turn left, so what she does is to turn right—and right through a circle. Thus she requested, and was given, a rotating wheelchair. And now if she cannot find something which she knows should be there, she swivels to the right, through a circle, until it comes into view. She finds this signally successful if she cannot find her coffee or dessert. If her portions seem too small, she will swivel to the right, keeping her eyes to the right, until the previously missed half now comes into view; she will eat this, or rather half of this, and feel less hungry than before. But if she is still hungry, or if she thinks on the matter, and realises that she may have perceived only half of the missing half, she will make a second rotation till the remaining quarter comes into view, and, in turn, bisect this yet again. This usually suffices—after all, she has now eaten seven-eighths of the portion—but she may, if she is feeling particularly hungry or obsessive, make a third turn, and secure another sixteenth of her portion (leaving, of course, the remaining sixteenth, the left sixteenth, on her plate). "It's absurd," she says, "I feel like Zeno's arrow—I never get there. It may look funny, but under the circumstances what else can I do?"

It would seem far simpler for her to rotate the plate than rotate herself. She agrees, and has tried this—or at least tried to try it. But it is oddly difficult, it does not come naturally, whereas whizzing round in her chair does, because her looking, her attention, her spontaneous movements and impulses, are all now exclusively and instinctively to the right.

Especially distressing to her was the derision which greeted her when she appeared only half made-up, the left side of her face absurdly void of lipstick and rouge. "I look in the mirror," she said, "and do all I see." Would it be possible, we wondered, for her to have a "mirror" such that she would see the left side of her face on the right? That is, as someone else, facing her, would see her. We tried a video system, with camera and monitor facing her, and the results were startling, and bizarre. For now, using the video screen as a "mirror," she did see the left side of her face to her right, an experience confounding even to a normal person (as anyone knows who has tried to shave using a video screen), and doubly confounding, uncanny, for her, because the left side of her face and body, which she now saw, had no feeling, no existence, for her, in consequence of her stroke. "Take it away!" she cried, in distress and bewilderment, so we did not explore the matter further. This is a pity because, as R. L. Gregory also wonders, there might be much promise in such forms of video feedback for such patients with hemi-inattention and left hemi-field extinction. The matter is so physically, indeed metaphysically, confusing that only experiment can decide.

A Passage to India

Bhagawhandi P., an Indian girl of 19 with a malignant brain tumour, was admitted to our hospice in 1978. The tumour—an astrocytoma—had first presented when she was seven, but was then of low malignancy, and well circumscribed, allowing a complete resection, and complete return of function, and allowing Bhagawhandi to return to normal life.

This reprieve lasted for ten years, during which she lived life to the full, lived it gratefully and consciously to the full, for she knew (she was a bright girl) that she had a "time bomb" in her head.

In her eighteenth year, the tumour recurred, much more invasive and malignant now, and no longer removable. A decompression was performed to allow its expansion—and it was with this, with weakness and numbness of the left side, with occasional seizures and other problems, that Bhagawhandi was admitted.

She was, at first, remarkably cheerful, seeming to accept fully the fate which lay in store, but still eager to be with people and do things, enjoy and experience as long as she could. As the tumour inched forward to her temporal lobe and the decompression started to bulge (we put her on steroids to reduce cerebral edema) her seizures became more frequent—and stranger.

The original seizures were *grand mal* convulsions, and these she continued to have on occasion. Her new ones had a different character altogether. She would not lose consciousness, but she would look (and feel) "dreamy"; and it was easy to ascertain (and confirm by EEG) that she was now having frequent temporal-lobe seizures, which, as Hughlings Jackson taught, are often characterised by "dreamy states" and involuntary "reminiscence."

Soon this vague dreaminess took on a more defined, more concrete, and more visionary character. It now took the form of visions of India—landscapes, villages, homes, gardens—which Bhagawhandi recognised at once, as places she had known and loved as a child.

"Do these distress you?" we asked. "We can change the medication."

"No," she said, with a peaceful smile, "I like these dreams—they take me back home."

At times there were people, usually her family or neighbours from her home village; sometimes there was speech, or singing, or dancing; once she was in church, once in a graveyard; but mostly there were the plains, the fields, the rice paddies near her village, and the low, sweet hills which swept up to the horizon.

Were these all temporal-lobe seizures? This first seemed the case, but now we were less sure; for temporal-lobe seizures . . . tend to have a rather fixed format: a single scene or song, unvaryingly reiterated, going with an equally fixed focus in the cortex. Whereas Bhagawhandi's dreams had no such fixity, but presented ever-changing panoramas and dissolving landscapes to her eye. Was she then toxic and hallucinating from the massive doses of steroids she was now receiving? This seemed possible, but we could not reduce the steroids—she would have gone into coma and died within days.

And a "steroid psychosis," so-called, is often excited and disorganised, whereas Bhagawhandi was always lucid, peaceful and calm. Could they be, in the Freudian sense, phantasies or dreams? Or the sort of dream-madness (oneirophrenia) which may sometimes occur in schizophrenia? Here again we could not be certain; for though there was a phantasmagoria of sorts, yet the phantasms were clearly all memories. They occurred side by side with normal awareness and consciousness (Hughlings Jackson, as we have seen, speaks of a "doubling of consciousness"), and they were not obviously "over-cathected," or charged with passionate drives. They seemed more like certain paintings, or tone poems, sometimes happy, sometimes sad, evocations, revocations, visitations to and from a loved and cherished childhood.

Day by day, week by week, the dreams, the visions, came oftener, grew deeper. They were not occasional now, but occupied most of the day. We would see her rapt, as if in a trance, her eyes sometimes closed, sometimes open but unseeing, and always a faint, mysterious smile on her face. If anyone approached her, or asked her something, as the nurses had to do, she would respond at once, lucidly and courteously, but there was, even among the most down-to-earth staff, a feeling that she was in another world, and that we should not interrupt her. I shared this feeling and, though curious, was reluctant to probe. Once, just once, I said, "Bhagawhandi, what is happening?"

"I am dying," she answered. "I am going home. I am going back where I came from—you might call it my return."

Another week passed, and now Bhagawhandi no longer responded to external stimuli, but seemed wholly enveloped in a world of her own, and, though her eyes were closed, her face still bore its faint, happy smile. "She's on the return journey," the staff said. "She'll soon be there." Three days later she died—or should we say she "arrived," having completed her passage to India?

The Main Points in Chapter Eight

1. *Metaphysics* is the philosophical study of the fundamental nature of the things that exist. In the seventeenth century, Hobbes put forward a modern version of the ancient theory that the universe is composed of tiny indivisible bits of matter, or atoms. By means of his atomic theory of matter, Hobbes sought to explain the way human beings think, feel, choose, and act.

2. Clinical evidence from medicine shows us that damage to one or another part of the nervous system can result in very strange distortions of our conception of our own bodies, in ways philosophers might find it very hard to imagine by means of thought experiments.

3. One of the central problems posed by the relation between mind and body is *freedom of the will.* Hobbes was a determinist, arguing that all our actions are determined by the motions of atoms. Kant used the distinction between appearance and reality to try to show that the determinism of science could be made compatible with the freedom demanded by morality.

CONTEMPORARY APPLICATION

Do Computers Think?

According to Aristotle, man is a rational animal. Rationality, he argued, is the distinguishing mark of human beings, the "specific difference" that sets us off from all other animals. In the 2,000 years since Aristotle offered his definition, philosophers have called attention to a number of other characteristics that seem to set humans apart: the fact that we play games, that we laugh, that we kill members of our own species, and of course the fact that we speak. Nevertheless, again and again one returns to rationality, for being able to think, to reason, does seem to be what makes us most fully human.

Descartes says, "I am a thing that thinks," thereby making thought his defining characteristic. Animals, he holds, are merely machines, for they have no consciousness, no thought processes. For most philosophers, it is the power of thought that has distinguished us from all other beings, and thought most often means some form of reasoning.

What do I mean when I say that I am rational? Well, one answer is that I can calculate. I can count objects, I can do sums, multiply two numbers together, or divide one by the other, or add or subtract them. The ability to perform computations has always seemed to philosophers to be central to what we mean when we say we are rational.

A second answer, closely associated with the first, is that I can perform logical deductions. Tell me that all men are mortal, and that Socrates is a man, and I can work it out that Socrates is mortal. From the premise that no woman has ever been elected president, and the premise that Zachary Taylor was the twelfth president, I can deduce that Zachary Taylor was not a woman. Many philosophers, impressed by the similarities between this sort of reasoning and arithmetic computations, have tried to find some way to represent logical deductions as a sort of calculation.

A third answer to the question, What do I mean when I say that I am rational?, is that I learn from experience. I observe, I remember, and I generalize from past experiences so that I am better prepared to face the future. The first time I see fire, I may reach out to touch it, but very quickly I will learn that fire burns, and from then on I will be careful with it. Over time, I and my fellow humans acquire elaborate, complex systems of knowledge based on observation and generalization, with the aid of which we can transform the world around us.

Yet a fourth answer is that I can act in accordance with rules rather than merely behaving instinctively or in response to immediate stimuli. To be rational is to be able to follow a plan, play a game, conform to directions. Or, some philosophers have argued, to be rational is to be able to make up new rules, devise new games, formulate new plans, in the service of some end or goal or purpose.

Finally, to be rational, philosophers like Kant have said, is to be self-aware, self-conscious, capable not only of thinking, but also of thinking that one is thinking.

For two millennia, philosophers have puzzled over the nature of rationality without having to worry very much about whether humans are the only rational creatures in the universe. To be sure, God was assumed to possess reason to the highest degree, and angels, if one included them in one's world, also were rational. But among the things of this world, only human beings could be said to calculate or compute, to make logical deductions, to learn from experience, to make and follow rules, or to be self-conscious.

All this has changed drastically in the past twenty years or so with the invention of the high-speed, sophisticated computer. Computers can calculate faster, more accurately, and with greater precision than humans ever could. Computers can also perform logical deductions. Indeed, the basic structure of a computer is modeled on a branch of logic known as Truth Function theory, or the First Order Predicate Calculus (believe it or not, those of you who know how to write simple computer programs, in BASIC or FORTRAN or Pascal, actually know quite a lot of logic without realizing it!). Computers can learn from experience, and they follow rules with great success. Computers are now capable of playing chess as well as a Grandmaster, which means better than all but one tenth of one percent of the serious tournament players in the United States.

Or so it seems! Do computers actually perform arithmetic calculations? Well, they look as though they do. If I punch in "5" and "+" and "7" and hit the appropriate button, the computer prints "12" on the screen. Hasn't it added five and seven to get twelve? What else is there to doing arithmetic calculations?

One answer that springs to mind is consciousness. When I do a sum, I think to myself, "five plus seven, that's twelve." I am aware of what I am doing. Indeed, I am *self*-aware. That is to say, I am aware that I am aware. And that, as Descartes and Kant agreed, is what distinguishes me from a mere machine.

Can we be sure, then, that a computer is *not* self-aware, not conscious? We could ask it, of course, but what would we do if it assured us that it *was* quite aware of what it was doing? This is the point at which the British mathematician and logician Alan Turing steps into the picture. Turing specialized in thinking up hypothetical situations—"thought experiments," they are called—that help us to reason about questions which puzzle or confuse us.

In this dialogue, written by Douglas Hofstadter, we are introduced to a test Turing thought up to determine whether a computer can think. In the course of the imaginary discussion among three young people, many of the knottiest philosophical issues of rationality, consciousness, and the nature of the self are posed and explored. Because this selection contains within it not one, not even just two, but three sides of the question, I have decided to include it alone. The dialogue ends with a question, not an answer. That is the most appropriate way for a philosophical debate to end!

Incidentally, in the ABC video that accompanies this chapter, the Grandmaster Patrick Wolff who appears is my son.

౿ ౿ ౿ ౿ ౿ ౿ ౿ ౿ ౿ ౿ ౿ ౿ ౿

METAMAGICAL THEMAS
Douglas Hofstadter

The participants in the following dialogue are Chris, a physics student; Pat, a biology student; and Sandy, a philosophy student.

Chris: Sandy, I want to thank you for suggesting that I read Alan Turing's article "Computing Machinery and Intelligence." It's a wonderful piece and certainly made me think—and think about my thinking.

Sandy: Glad to hear it. Are you still as much of a skeptic about artificial intelligence as you used to be?

Chris: You've got me wrong. I'm not against artificial intelligence: I think it's wonderful stuff—perhaps a little crazy, why not? I simply am convinced that you A.I. advocates have far underestimated the human mind, and that there are things a computer will never, ever be able to do. For instance, can you imagine a computer writing a Proust novel? The richness of imagination, the complexity of the characters—

Sandy: Rome wasn't built in a day!

Chris: In the article Turing comes through as an interesting person. Is he still alive?

Sandy: No, he died back in 1954, at just 41. He'd only be 67 this year, although he is now such a legendary figure it seems strange to think that he could still have been living today.

Chris: How did he die?

Sandy: Almost certainly suicide. He was homosexual and was much persecuted for it. In the end it apparently got to be too much and he killed himself.

Chris: Sad.

Sandy: Yes, it certainly is. What saddens me is that he never got to see the amazing progress in computing machinery and computing theory that has taken place.

Pat: Hey, are you going to clue me into what this Turing article is about?

Sandy: It is really about two things. One is the question "Can a machine think?"—or rather "Will a machine ever think?" The way Turing answers the question—he thinks the answer is yes, by the way—is by batting down a series of objections to the idea, one after another. The other point he tries to make is that the question as it stands is not meaningful. It's too full of emotional connotations. Many people are upset by the suggestion that people are machines, or that machines might think. Turing tries to defuse the question by casting it in less emotional terms. For instance, what do you think, Pat, of the idea of thinking machines?

Pat: Frankly, I find the term confusing. You know what confuses me? It's those ads in the newspapers and on TV that talk about "products that think" or "intelligent ovens" or whatever. I just don't know how seriously to take them.

Sandy: I know the kind of ads you mean, and they confuse a lot of people. On the one hand we're given the refrain "Computers are really dumb; you have to spell everything out for them in complete detail," and on the other we're bombarded with advertising hype about "smart products."

Chris: That's certainly true. Do you know that one company has even taken to calling its products "dumb terminals" in order to stand out from the crowd?

Sandy: That's clever, but it just plays along with the trend toward obfuscation. The term electronic brain always comes to my mind when I'm thinking about this. Many people swallow it completely, and others reject it out of hand. It takes patience to sort out the issues and decide how much of it makes sense.

Pat: Does Turing suggest some way of resolving it, some kind of I.Q. test for machines?

Sandy: That would be interesting, but no machine could yet come close to taking an I.Q. test. Instead Turing proposes a test that theoretically could be applied to any machine to determine whether or not it can think.

Pat: Does the test give a clear-cut yes-or-no answer? I'd be skeptical if it claimed to.

Sandy: No, it doesn't claim to. In a way that's one of its advantages. It shows how the borderline is quite fuzzy and how subtle the whole question is.

Pat: And so, as is usual in philosophy, it's all just a question of words.

Sandy: Maybe, but they're emotionally charged words, and so it's important, it seems to me, to explore the issues and try to map out the meanings of the crucial words. The issues are fundamental to our concept of ourselves, so we shouldn't just sweep them under the rug.

Pat: So tell me how Turing's test works.

Sandy: The idea is based on what he calls the imitation game. A man and a woman go into separate rooms and can be interrogated by a third party via some sort of teletype set-up. The third party can address questions to either room but has no idea which person is in each room. For the interrogator the idea is to determine which room the woman is in. The woman, by her answers, tries to help the interrogator as much as she can. The man, however, is doing his best to bamboozle the interrogator, by responding as he thinks a woman might. And if he succeeds in fooling the interrogator—

Pat: The interrogator only gets to see written words, eh? And the sex of the author is supposed to shine through? It sounds like a good challenge. I'd certainly like to take part in it someday. Would the interrogator know either the man or the woman before the test began? Would any of them know the others?

Sandy: That would probably be a bad idea. All kinds of subliminal cueing might occur if the interrogator knew one or both of them. It would certainly be best if all three people were totally unknown to one another.

Pat: Could you ask any questions at all, with no holds barred?

Sandy: Absolutely. That's the whole idea.

Pat: Don't you think, then, that pretty quickly it would degenerate into sex-oriented questions? I can imagine the man, overeager to act convincing, giving away the game by answering some very blunt questions that most women would find too personal to answer, even through an anonymous computer connection.

Sandy: It sounds plausible.

Chris: Another possibility would be to explore traditional sex-role differences, such as asking about dress sizes and so on. The psychology of the imitation game could get pretty subtle. I suppose it would make a difference if the interrogator were a woman instead of a man. Don't you think that a woman could spot some telltale differences more quickly than a man?

Pat: If so, maybe *that's* how to tell a man from a woman.

Sandy: H'm. . . . That's a new twist. In any case I don't know if this original version of the imitation game has ever been seriously tried out, in spite of the fact that it would be relatively easy to do with modern computer terminals. I have to admit, though, that I'm not at all sure what it would prove, whichever way it turned out.

Pat: I was wondering about that. What would it prove if the interrogator—say a woman —couldn't tell correctly which person was the woman? It certainly wouldn't prove that the man *was* a woman.

Sandy: Exactly. What I find funny is that although I fundamentally believe in the Turing test, I'm not sure what the point is of the imitation game, on which it is founded.

Chris: I'm not any happier with the Turing test as a test for thinking machines than I am with the imitation game as a test for femininity.

Pat: From what you say I gather the Turing test is a kind of extension of the imitation game, only involving a machine and a person in separate rooms.

Sandy: That's the idea. The machine tries its hardest to convince the interrogator that it is the human being, and the human tries to make it clear that he or she is not the computer.

Pat: Except for your loaded phrase "the machine tries," this sounds very interesting. But how do you know that this test will get at the essence of thinking? Maybe it's testing for the wrong things. Maybe, just to take a random illustration, someone would feel that a machine was able to think only if it could dance so well that you couldn't tell it was a machine. Or someone else could suggest some other characteristic. What's so sacred about being able to fool people by typing at them?

Sandy: I don't see how you can say such a thing. I've heard that objection before, but frankly it baffles me. So what if the machine can't tap dance or drop a rock on your toe? If it can discourse intelligently on any subject you want, then it has shown it can think. It has shown it to me, at least. As I see it, Turing has drawn, in one clean stroke, a clear division

between thinking and other aspects of being human.

Pat: Now *you're* the baffling one. If you couldn't conclude anything from a man's ability to win at the imitation game, how could you conclude anything from a machine's ability to win at the Turing game?

Chris: Good question.

Sandy: It seems to me that you could conclude *something* from a man's win at the imitation game. You wouldn't conclude he was a woman, but you could certainly say he had good insights into the feminine mentality (if there is such a thing). Now, if a computer could fool someone into thinking it was a person, I guess you'd have to say something similar about it—that it had good insights into what it's like to be human, into the human condition, whatever that is.

Pat: Maybe, but that isn't necessarily equivalent to thinking, is it? It seems to me that passing the Turing test would merely prove some machine or other could do a very good job of *simulating* thought.

Chris: I couldn't agree more with Pat. We all know that fancy computer programs exist today for simulating all sorts of complex phenomena. In physics, for instance, we simulate the behavior of particles, atoms, solids, liquids, gases, galaxies and so on. But no one confuses any of those simulations with the real thing.

Sandy: In his book *Brainstorms* the philosopher Daniel Dennett makes a similar point about simulated hurricanes.

Chris: That's a nice example too. Obviously what goes on inside a computer when it's simulating a hurricane is not a hurricane. The machine's memory doesn't get torn to bits by 200-mile-an-hour winds, the floor of the machine room doesn't get flooded with rainwater, and so on.

Sandy: Oh, come on—that's not a fair argument. In the first place the programmers don't claim the simulation really *is* a hurricane. It's merely a simulation of certain aspects of a hurricane. But in the second place you're pulling a fast one when you imply that there are no downpours or 200-mile-an-hour winds in a simulated hurricane. To *us* there aren't any, but if the program were incredibly detailed, it could include simulated people on the ground who would experience the wind and the rain just as we do when a hurricane hits. In their minds—or, if you'd rather, in their *simulated* minds—the hurricane would be not a simulation but a genuine phenomenon complete with drenching and devastation.

Chris: Oh, boy—what a science-fiction scenario! Now we're talking about simulating entire populations, not just a single mind.

Sandy: Well, look, I'm simply trying to show you why your argument that a simulated McCoy isn't the real McCoy is fallacious. It depends on the tacit assumption that any old observer of the simulated phenomenon is equally able to assess what's going on. In fact it may take an observer with a special vantage to recognize what is going on. In this case it takes special "computational glasses" to see the rain and the winds.

Pat: Computational glasses? I don't know what you're talking about.

Sandy: I mean that to see the winds and the wetness of the hurricane you have to be able to look at it in the proper way. You—

Chris: No, no, no! A simulated hurricane isn't wet! No matter how much it might seem wet to simulated people, it won't ever be *genuinely* wet. And no computer will ever get torn apart in the process of simulating winds.

Sandy: Certainly not, but you're confusing levels. The laws of physics don't get torn apart by real hurricanes, either. In the case of the simulated hurricane, if you go peering at the computer's memory expecting to find broken wires and so forth, you'll be disappointed. But look at the proper level. Look into the *structures* that are coded for in the memory. You'll see that some abstract links have been broken, some values of variables radically changed and so on.

There's your flood, your devastation. It is real, only a little concealed, a little hard to detect.

Chris: I'm sorry, I just can't buy it. You're insisting that I look for a new kind of devastation, one never before associated with hurricanes. That way you could call *anything* a hurricane as long as its effects, seen through your special glasses, could be called floods and devastation.

Sandy: Right—you've got it! You recognize a hurricane by its *effects*. You have no way of going in and finding some ethereal essence of hurricane, some "hurricane soul" right in the middle of the storm's eye. It's the existence of a certain kind of *pattern*—a spiral storm with an eye and so forth—that makes you say it's a hurricane. Of course, there are a lot of things you'll insist on before you call something a hurricane.

Pat: Well, wouldn't you say that being an *atmospheric* phenomenon is one prerequisite? How can anything inside a computer be a storm? To me a simulation is a simulation is a simulation.

Sandy: Then I suppose you would say that even the *calculations* computers do are simulated, that they are fake calculations. Only people can do genuine calculations, right?

Pat: Well, computers get the right answers, so their calculations are not exactly fake, but they're still just *patterns*. There's no understanding going on in there. Take a cash register. Can you honestly say that you feel it is *calculating* something when its gears turn on one another? A computer is just a fancy cash register, as I understand it.

Sandy: If you mean that a cash register doesn't feel like a schoolkid doing arithmetic problems, I'll agree. But is that what calculation means? Is that an integral part of it? If it is, then contrary to what everybody has thought up to now we'll have to write a very complicated program to perform *genuine* calculations. Of course, such a program will sometimes get careless and make mistakes and will sometimes scrawl its answers illegibly, and it will occasionally doodle on its paper. It won't be any more reliable than the store clerk who adds up your total by hand. Now, I happen to believe eventually such a program could be written. Then we'd know something about how clerks and school-kids work.

Pat: I can't believe you would ever be able to do it.

Sandy: Maybe, maybe not, but that's not my point. You say a cash register can't calculate. It reminds me of another favorite passage of mine from Dennett's *Brainstorms*. It goes something like this: "Cash registers can't really calculate; they can only spin their gears. But cash registers can't really spin their gears, either; they can only follow the laws of physics." Dennett said it originally about computers; I modified it to refer to cash registers. And you could use the same line of reasoning in talking about people: "People can't really calculate; all they can do is manipulate mental symbols. But they aren't really manipulating symbols; all they are doing is firing various neurons in various patterns. But they can't really make their neurons fire; they simply have to let the laws of physics make the neurons fire for them." Et cetera. Don't you see how this reductio ad absurdum would lead you to conclude that calculation doesn't exist, hurricanes don't exist, nothing at a level higher than particles and the laws of physics exists? What do you gain by saying a computer only pushes symbols around and doesn't truly calculate?

Pat: The example may be extreme, but it makes my point that there is a vast difference between a real phenomenon and any simulation of it. This is true for hurricanes and even more so for human thought.

Sandy: Look, I don't want to get too tangled up in this line of argument, but let me try one more example. If you were a radio ham listening to another ham broadcasting in Morse code and you were responding in Morse code, would it sound funny to you to refer to "the person at the other end"?

Pat: No, that would sound okay, although the existence of a person at the other end would be an assumption.

Sandy: Yes, but you wouldn't be likely to go and check it out. You're prepared to recognize personhood through those rather unusual channels. You don't have to see a human body or hear a voice. All you need is a rather abstract manifestation—a code. What I'm getting at is this. To "see" the person behind the dits and dahs, you have to be willing to do some *decoding,* some interpretation. It's not direct perception: it's indirect. You have to peel off a layer or two to find the reality hidden in there. You put on your radio ham's glasses to see the person behind the buzzes. It's the same with the simulated hurricane. You don't see it darkening the machine room; you have to decode the machine's memory. You have to put on special memory-decoding glasses. *Then* what you see is a hurricane.

Pat: Oh ho! Talk about fast ones. In the case of the short-wave radio there's a real person out there, somewhere in the Fiji Islands or wherever. My decoding act as I sit by my radio simply reveals that that person exists. It's like seeing a shadow and concluding there's an object out there casting it. One doesn't confuse the shadow with the object, however. With the hurricane there's no real storm behind the scenes, making the computer follow its patterns. No, what you have is just a shadow hurricane without any genuine hurricane. I simply refuse to confuse shadows with reality.

Sandy: All right. I don't want to drive the point into the ground. I even admit it is pretty silly to say that a simulated hurricane *is* a hurricane. I just wanted to point out that it's not as silly as you might think at first blush. And when you turn to simulated thought, you've got a very different matter on your hands from simulated hurricanes.

Pat: I don't see why. You still have to convince me. . . .

Chris: I would want to see if the program could understand jokes. That would be a real test of intelligence.

Sandy: I agree that humor probably is an acid test for a supposedly intelligent program, but equally important to me—perhaps more so—would be to test its emotional responses. So I would ask it about its reactions to certain pieces of music or works of literature—particularly my favorite ones.

Chris: What if it said, "I don't know that piece," or even "I have no interest in music"? What if it avoided all emotional references?

Sandy: That would make me suspicious. Any consistent pattern of avoiding certain issues would raise serious doubts in my mind about whether I was dealing with a thinking being.

Chris: Why do you say that? Why not say you're dealing with a thinking but unemotional being?

Sandy: You've hit on a sensitive point. I simply can't believe emotions and thought can be divorced. To put it another way, I think emotions are an automatic by-product of the ability to think. They are required by the very nature of thought.

Chris: Well, what if you're wrong? What if I produced a machine that could think but not emote? Then its intelligence might go unrecognized because it failed to pass *your* kind of test.

Sandy: I'd like you to point out to me where the boundary line between emotional questions and nonemotional ones lies. You might want to ask about the meaning of a great novel. This requires an understanding of human emotions. Is that thinking or merely cool calculation? You might want to ask about a subtle choice of words. For that you need an understanding of their connotations. Turing uses examples like this in his article. You might want to ask for advice about a complex romantic situation. The machine would need to know a lot about human motivations and their roots. If it failed at this kind of task, I would not be much inclined

to say that it could think. As far as I am concerned, the ability to think, the ability to feel and consciousness are just different facets of one phenomenon, and no one of them can be present without the others. . . .

Chris: I still can't see that intelligence has to involve emotions. Why couldn't you imagine an intelligence that simply calculates and has no feelings?

Sandy: A couple of answers here. Number one, any intelligence has to have motivations. It's simply not the case, whatever many people may believe, that machines could think any more objectively than people do. Machines, when they look at a scene, will have to focus and filter the scene down into some preconceived categories, just as a person does. And that means seeing some things and missing others. It means giving more weight to some things than to others. This happens on every level of processing.

Pat: I'm not sure I'm following you.

Sandy: Take me right now, for instance. You might think I'm just making some intellectual points, and I wouldn't need emotions to do that. But what makes me *care* about these points? Why did I stress the word "care" so heavily? Because I'm emotionally involved in this conversation. People talk to one another out of conviction, not out of hollow, mechanical reflexes. Even the most intellectual conversation is driven by underlying passions. There's an emotional undercurrent to every conversation. It's the fact that the speakers want to be listened to and understood, and respected for what they are saying. . . .

Pat: How can you think of a computer as a conscious being? I apologize if this sounds like a stereotype, but when I think of conscious beings, I just can't connect that thought with machines. To me consciousness is connected with soft, warm bodies, silly though it may sound.

Chris: That *does* sound odd coming from a biologist. Don't you deal with life in terms of chemistry and physics enough for all magic to seem to vanish?

Pat: Not really. Sometimes the chemistry and physics simply increase the feeling that there's something magical going on in there. Anyway, I can't always integrate my scientific knowledge with my gut feelings.

Chris: I guess I share the trait.

Pat: So how do you deal with rigid preconceptions like mine?

Sandy: I'd try to dig down under the surface of your concept of machines and get at the intuitive connotations that lurk there, out of sight but deeply influencing your opinions. I think we all have a holdover image from the Industrial Revolution that sees machines as iron contraptions moving under the power of some chugging engine. Maybe that's even how the computer inventor Charles Babbage saw people. After all, he called his geared computer "the analytical engine."

Pat: Well, I certainly don't think people are just fancy steam shovels or even electric can openers. There's something about people, something that—that—they've got a kind of *flame* inside them, something alive, something that flickers unpredictably, wavering, uncertain—but something *creative.*

Sandy: Great! That's just the sort of thing I wanted to hear. It's very human to think that way. Your flame image makes me think of candles, of fires, of thunderstorms with lightning dancing all over the sky. But do you realize just that kind of thing is visible on a computer's console? The flickering lights form chaotic sparkling patterns. It's such a far cry from heaps of lifeless, clanking metal. It *is* flame-like, by God! Why don't you let the word "machine" conjure up images of dancing patterns of light rather than of giant steam shovels?

Chris: That *is* a powerful image, Sandy. It does change my sense of mechanism from being matter-oriented to being pattern-oriented. It makes me try to visualize the thoughts in my

mind—these thoughts right now, even—as a huge spray of tiny pulses flickering in my brain.

Sandy: That's quite a poetic self-portrait for a spray of flickers to have come up with!

Chris: But still I'm not totally convinced that a machine is all I am. I admit my concept of machines probably *does* suffer from anachronistic subconscious flavors, but I'm afraid I can't change such a deeply rooted sense in a flash.

Sandy: At least you do sound open-minded. And to tell the truth part of me does sympathize with the way you and Pat view machines. Part of me balks at calling myself a machine. It *is* a bizarre thought that a feeling being like you or me might emerge from mere circuitry. Do I surprise you?

Chris: You certainly surprise me. So tell us—*do* you believe in the idea of an intelligent computer or don't you?

Sandy: It all depends on what you mean. We've all heard the question, "Can computers think?" There are several possible interpretations of this (apart from the many interpretations of the word "think"). They revolve around different meanings of the words "can" and "computer."

Pat: Back to word games again.

Sandy: That's right. First of all, the question might mean, "Does some present-day computer think, right now?" To that I would immediately answer with a loud no. Then it could be taken to mean, "Could some present-day computer, if it was suitably programmed, potentially think?" That would be more like it, but I would still answer, "Probably not." The real difficulty hinges on the word "computer." The way I see it, "computer" calls up an image of just what I described earlier: an air-conditioned room with rectangular metal boxes in it. But I believe progress in computer architecture will eventually make that vision outmoded.

Pat: Don't you think computers as we know them will be around for a while?

Sandy: Sure, there will have to be computers in today's image around for a long time, but advanced computers—maybe no longer called computers—will evolve and become quite different. Probably, as with living organisms, there will be many branchings in the evolutionary tree. There will be computers for business, computers for schoolkids, computers for scientific calculations, computers for systems research, computers for simulation, computers for rockets going into space and so on. Finally, there will be computers for the study of intelligence. It's really only these last that I'm thinking of—the ones with the maximum flexibility, the ones people are deliberately attempting to make smart. I see no reason for these staying fixed in the traditional image. They will probably soon acquire as standard features some rudimentary sensory systems, at first mostly for vision and hearing. They will need to be able to move around, to explore. They will have to be physically flexible. In short, they will have to become more self-reliant, more animal-like.

Chris: It makes me think of the robots R2D2 and C3PO in *Star Wars.*

Sandy: As a matter of fact I don't think of anything like them when I visualize intelligent machines. They are too silly, too much the product of a film designer's imagination. Not that I have a clear vision of my own. But I do think it is necessary, if people are realistically going to try to imagine an artificial intelligence, to go beyond the limited, hard-edged picture of computers that comes from seeing what we have today. The only thing all machines will always have in common is their underlying mechanicalness. That may sound cold and inflexible, but what could be more mechanical—in a wonderful way—than the working of the DNA and enzymes in our cells?

Pat: To me what goes on inside cells has a wet, slippery feel to it and what goes on inside machines is dry and rigid. It's connected with the fact that computers don't make mistakes,

that computers do only what you tell them to do. At least that's my image of computers. . . .

Sandy: I guess I'm a strange sort of advocate for machine intelligence. To some degree I straddle the fence. I think machines won't really be intelligent in a humanlike way until they have something like that biological wetness or slipperiness to them. I don't mean *literally* wet—the slipperiness could be in the software. But biological-seeming or not, intelligent machines will in any case be machines. We shall have designed them, built them—or grown them! We shall understand how they work, at least in some sense. Possibly no one person will really understand them, but collectively we shall know how they work.

Pat: It sounds as if you want to have your cake and eat it too.

Sandy: You're probably right. What I'm getting at is that when artificial intelligence comes, it will be mechanical and yet at the same time organic. It will have the same amazing flexibility that we see in life's mechanisms. And when I say mechanisms, I *mean* mechanisms. DNA and enzymes and so on really *are* mechanical and rigid and reliable. Don't you agree, Pat?

Pat: I have to. But when they work together, a lot of unexpected things happen. There are so many complexities and rich modes of behavior that all the mechanicalness adds up to something very fluid.

Sandy: For me it's an almost unimaginable transition from the mechanical level of molecules to the living level of cells. But it's what convinces me that people are machines. The thought makes me uncomfortable in some ways, but in other ways it is exhilarating.

Chris: If people are machines, how come it's so hard to convince them of the fact? Surely if we are machines, we ought to be able to recognize our own machine-hood.

Sandy: You have to allow for emotional factors here. To be told you're a machine is in a way to be told that you're nothing more than your physical parts, and it brings you face to face with your own mortality. That's something no one finds easy to confront. But beyond the emotional objection, to see yourself as a machine you have to jump all the way from the bottom-most mechanical level to the level where the complex lifelike activities take place. If there are many intermediate layers, they act as a shield and the mechanical quality becomes almost invisible. I think when intelligent machines come, that's how they will seem to us—and to themselves!

Pat: I once heard a funny idea about what will happen when we eventually have intelligent machines. When we try to implant that intelligence into devices we'd like to control, their behavior won't be so predictable.

Sandy: They'll have a quirky little "flame" inside, maybe?

Pat: Maybe.

Chris: And what's so funny about that?

Pat: Well, think of military missiles. The more sophisticated their target-tracking computers get, according to this idea, the less predictably they will function. Eventually you'll have missiles that will decide they are pacifists and will turn around and go home and land quietly without blowing up. We could even have smart bullets that turn around in mid-flight because they don't want to commit suicide.

Sandy: A lovely thought.

Chris: I'm very skeptical about all this. Still, Sandy, I'd like to hear your predictions about when intelligent machines will come to be.

Sandy: It probably won't be for a long time that we'll see anything remotely resembling the level of human intelligence. It rests on too awesomely complicated a substrate—the brain—for us to be able to duplicate it in the foreseeable future. That's my opinion, anyway.

Pat: Do you think a program will ever pass the Turing test?

Sandy: That's a pretty hard question. I guess there are various degrees of passing such a test,

when you come down to it. It's not black and white. First of all it depends on who the interrogator is. A simple-minded person might be totally taken in by some programs today. But secondly it depends on how deeply you are allowed to probe.

Pat: Then you could have a range of Turing tests—one-minute versions, five-minute versions, hour-long versions. Wouldn't it be interesting if some official organization sponsored a periodic competition, like the annual computer-chess championships, for programs to try to pass the Turing test?

Chris: The program that lasted the longest against some panel of distinguished judges would be the winner. Perhaps there could be a big prize for the first program that can fool a famous judge for, say, 10 minutes.

Pat: What would a program do with a prize?

Chris: Come now, Pat. If a program's good enough to fool the judges, don't you think it's good enough to enjoy the prize?

Pat: Sure—particularly if the prize is an evening out on the town, dancing with the interrogators.

Sandy: I'd certainly like to see something like that established. I think it could be hilarious to watch the first programs flop pathetically.

Pat: You're pretty skeptical, aren't you? Well, do you think any computer program today could pass a five-minute Turing test, given a sophisticated interrogator? . . .

Chris: If you could ask a computer just one question in the Turing test, what would it be?

Sandy: Um—

Pat: I've got one. How about "If you could ask a computer just one question in the Turing test, what would it be?"

Source: *Douglas R. Hofstadter,* Metamagical Themas: Questing for the Essence of Mind and Pattern. © 1985 by *Basic Books, Inc. Reprinted by permission of the publisher.*

Questions for Discussion and Review

1. What *are* minds? It is easy enough to find objections to the leading philosophical theories, but very hard indeed to come up with an alternative. Does it make any sense to say that my mind is a substance with neither spatial location nor mass? On the other hand, does it make sense to identify my mind with the brain, the heart, the nervous system, or some other anatomical structure?

2. Let us suppose, for the sake of argument, that one or another of the three theories of mind/body relation discussed in the chapter is true. How could we go about deciding which one it was? Would scientific evidence help us? Logical analysis? Inner reflection?

3. Every time we decide that there is some distinctively human capacity that computers cannot imitate, someone invents a way for computers to imitate it! By the time you are my age (sixty-three at this writing), computers may very well be walking, talking, designing houses, writing music, and who knows what else! At what point down the road do we have to start worrying about whether computers should have the vote?

4. Can computers *feel?* Can they love, hate, desire, yearn? Suppose we can build a computer that *imitates* all these human emotional responses and *looks* rather human besides. Should we be allowed to marry computers? Kill them (that is, turn them off)? Hire them? Ought we to pay them at least minimum wage? Why? Why not?

APPENDIX: HOW TO WRITE A PHILOSOPHY PAPER

Introduction

Most of you will be called on to submit one or more papers as part of the written work for your course in philosophy, and this requirement may well have you stumped. Even though you have, by now, read at least a few chapters of this book, and participated in a number of classes, you may have no idea at all about how to write a paper in philosophy. No doubt, you wrote papers in high school for English courses, perhaps also for social studies courses, even for science courses. But philosophy is something quite different. Where do you start? What sort of library research should you do, if any? Should you put down your own ideas, those of your professor, ideas you have found in your course reading? Are you expected to come up with your *own* philosophy?

This appendix is designed to answer these questions. I will give you a simple, clear, almost foolproof way of writing a satisfactory philosophy paper; I will give you some tips and hints and warnings that may help you to avoid the most common problems in writing philosophy papers; I will take you through a careful critique and analysis of a real course paper written just recently by one of my students at the University of Massachusetts (who shall remain anonymous, of course!); and I will then rewrite the student paper so that you can see how the author could have improved it.

If you read this appendix carefully, and follow its guidelines when writing papers for your philosophy course, I am absolutely certain that you will write good papers, from which you will learn a great deal *About Philosophy*.

A Simple, Foolproof Method for Writing Philosophy Papers

A philosophy paper is a defense of a *thesis*, in which the thesis is *explained* and *analyzed*, *arguments* are given in support of the thesis, possible *objections* to the thesis are stated and examined, and *responses* are given to the objections. A philosophy paper thus has five parts:

1. The statement of the thesis

2. The analysis and explanation of the thesis

3. The arguments in support of the thesis

4. The examination of objections to the thesis

5. The response to the objections

The simplest and most foolproof way to write a philosophy paper is to organize it in precisely this order: Thesis, Analysis of Thesis, Arguments for Thesis, Objections to Thesis, and Response to Objections. It isn't necessary to stick to this order, of course, and after you get good at writing philosophy papers, you may want to experiment with other systems of organization. But if you have never written a philosophy paper before, and you aren't really quite sure what you are doing, it might be a good idea to stick to this structure. It can't lose!

Let's take a close look at each of these five elements in turn.

1. The Thesis

A philosophy paper is a defense of a thesis, so the first step is to get clear what a thesis is. A *thesis* is a statement that makes some clear, definite assertion about the subject under discussion. For example, if the topic of your paper, the subject under discussion, is *the morality of abortion,* here are some of the many *theses* you might choose to defend:

Abortion is morally wrong under all circumstances.

A woman has an absolute right to decide whether to have an abortion.

Abortion is morally right only to save the life of the mother.

Each of these is a clear, definite statement that takes a position on the morality of abortion, a position that the rest of the paper will attempt to defend.

Let's try another example. Suppose the subject under discussion is *the existence of a Supreme Being.* Among the theses you might choose to defend are these:

There is no God but Allah.

It is logically impossible for there to be a Supreme Being.

Human beings are incapable of determining whether there is a Supreme Being.

Now let's look at some examples of things that look like theses, but aren't:

The scientific status of astrology

Abortion, pro and con

Why I believe in God

These aren't *theses* because they don't *assert* anything. All three of these are what we might call *topics*. You can certainly write a philosophy paper about one of these topics, but you must first choose a *thesis* about the topic, a thesis that you will defend in the paper. By the way, watch out especially for fake theses like the third one ("Why I believe in God"). A philosophy paper is not a personal report of how you feel or what you believe. It is an *argument* for a thesis.

Those of you who took part in formal debate team competitions in high school may think that all of this looks very much like a debate. You are absolutely right. Philosophy *is* very much like debating.

One more word about the thesis of your paper. Learning to do philosophy is a lot like learning to play basketball or tennis. You can't learn if you just stand on the sidelines and watch other people. So writing a philosophy paper is a way of getting in some philosophy practice. When you pick the thesis of your paper, don't think that you must pick something you deeply believe, something you would be willing to die for! Just choose a clear, simple, straightforward thesis that you think you can do a good job of defending. No one will be mad at you if you defend the other side of the question a week later.

But whatever you do, don't pick a wishy-washy thesis that hedges your bets, like "There is much to be said on both sides of the abortion question," or "There are good arguments for and against the existence of God." Take a stand, plant your feet squarely on the ground, and argue for your thesis as well as you can.

Since we have already used the example of the morality of abortion, let's continue to use it. For the remainder of this appendix, our thesis will be:

Abortion is morally wrong under all circumstances whatsoever.

2. The Analysis and Explanation of the Thesis

The first step in the defense of a thesis is to explain what you mean by it. Since we are using as an example the thesis "Abortion is morally wrong under all circumstances whatsoever," we must state exactly what we mean by the term "abortion," by the phrase "morally wrong," and by the qualifying clause "in all circumstances whatsoever." This may seem like a trivial exercise to you, but watch out! In philosophy, a lot can get loaded into an innocent-looking definition.

For example, we will want to make it clear that by "morally wrong" we mean something quite different from "against the law" or "legally wrong." It is one thing to argue that abortion, suitably defined, violates some state or federal law in the United States or elsewhere. It is quite another thing to argue that abortion is morally wrong, that it violates some principle that all persons ought to abide by. If we are arguing about the law, we shall have to cite the criminal codes, judicial decisions, Supreme Court opinions, or law books. But if we are arguing about what is right and wrong, then we shall have to appeal to some other sorts of considerations—*unless we want to claim that "morally wrong" and "legally wrong" are one and the same, which would itself be a very powerful, highly debatable claim.*

How shall we understand "in any circumstances"? Are we claiming that abortion is wrong even in cases in which the pregnancy resulted from incest or rape? Do we mean that abortion is wrong even if the fetus cannot possibly survive, and the mother will die without the abortion? Are we claiming that abortion is wrong even if prenatal testing reveals that the fetus has a fatal congenital disease and cannot survive for more than a few hours after birth?

Notice: At this stage we are not *arguing,* we are just explaining what we mean by the thesis. And since it is our thesis, we can interpret it any way we wish. But how we interpret the thesis will shape the rest of the paper, for it will determine what sorts of arguments we give and what sorts of objections we must consider. For example, if we interpret "in any circumstances" to mean "even if the pregnancy resulted from rape," then we will have to consider the objection that a woman should not be required against her will to risk her life. But if we exclude pregnancies resulting from rape, then that isn't an objection against our position, so we don't have to consider it in this paper.

You can begin to see how the paper will be shaped and determined by how we interpret our thesis. That is why explaining and analyzing the thesis is such an important step, one we must take before moving on to the arguments.

For purposes of our discussion, let us agree to interpret our thesis in the following way (remember, this is just one of countless possible interpretations—not in any sense the *right* interpretation, just the interpretation we have chosen in order to write this paper):

> "Abortion is morally wrong under all circumstances whatsoever" means "Terminating a human pregnancy at any stage before birth, so long as the fetus is alive, violates the objective and universal principles of Judeo-Christian morality, and is therefore wrong without exception for rape, incest, danger to the life of the mother, or any other circumstance, including even a circumstance in which the abortion might save the lives of many other innocent people."

Notice that I have interpreted "morally wrong" to mean "contrary to the objective and universal principles of Judeo-Christian morality." Needless to say, that is not the only way "morally wrong" can be interpreted. We might also have interpreted it to mean "in conflict with the Principle of Utilitarianism," or "incompatible with the Categorical Imperative." Let me repeat: *You can choose any thesis you wish, and interpret it in any plausible manner you wish, so long as you make it clear to your reader what you are doing.*

Before moving on to the main body of your paper, which is the Argument for the Thesis, review what you have written. Make sure that you have stated a genuine thesis (not just a topic), and that you have explained clearly what that thesis means. Here, as always, you must try very hard to put yourself into the mind of your reader, and ask whether he or she will understand exactly what your thesis means. Reading what you have written as your reader will read it is actually the hardest part of all writing. *You* may think you know what you have in mind, but unless you put it down on paper clearly, precisely, and accurately, your reader won't have a clue. One way to check on yourself is to give what you have written to a friend and ask him or her to tell you what he or she thinks you have said. Don't give any hints, and don't argue. If your friend doesn't understand what you have written in the same way you understand it, then there is probably something wrong with what you have written. (Choose an intelligent friend!)

3. The Arguments in Support of the Thesis

We have come to the heart of the paper—the arguments for the thesis. This is where you show your stuff. You have got to come up with arguments that are designed to persuade your reader that your thesis is true. What is an argument? To put it as simply as possible, an argument for a thesis is a reason for believing that the thesis is true. There are many different sorts of reasons you can give in support of a thesis. In the next few paragraphs, we will take a brief look at some of the most important. Just remember: When you are putting forward an argument in support of your thesis, ask yourself, "If I didn't already believe my thesis, would this reason convince me that the thesis is true? Would it at least make me more inclined to believe that it is true? Would it tend to convince a reasonable reader who is open-minded enough so that he or she is willing to listen to reasons?" If the answer is yes, then you have your hands on a genuine argument. If the answer is no, then leave it out of the paper, and look for a better argument.

Let's take a look at some very simple examples. Philosophy may strike you as pretty difficult, but like many difficult things, it is made up of simple parts. Don't try to be too fancy! Just look for straightforward arguments that tend to support your thesis.

If you are trying to show that abortion is morally wrong, you might begin by arguing that abortion is the taking of an innocent life, and the taking of an innocent life is morally wrong. This is an example of what is perhaps the most widely used form of argument—what we can call *instantiation*. "Instantiation" means "giving an instance of." In this case, we have appealed to the general rule:

⟶ Taking an innocent life is morally wrong.

Then we have argued that abortion is an *instance* of this general rule— it is the taking of an innocent life. If we spell out our argument completely, it looks like this:

⟶ Taking an innocent life is morally wrong.

⟶ Abortion is the taking of an innocent life.

⟶ Therefore, abortion is morally wrong.

This argument, in turn, is an instance of a very general form of argument that looks like this:

All *A* are *B* (where *A* = acts of taking an innocent life, and *B* = morally wrong acts)
C is *A* (where *C* = abortion, and *A* again = acts of taking an innocent life.)
Therefore *C* is *B* (i.e., abortion is a morally wrong act).

The point is that *if C* is an *A*, and *if* all *A*'s are *B*'s, then *C must be a B*. Arguments of this sort are sometimes called *syllogisms*. In the Middle Ages, philosophers spent a great deal of time analyzing such arguments in order to figure out which kinds were good arguments and which kinds were not.

Instantiation, or showing that the matter under discussion is an instance of a general rule, is a technique of argument that can be used in a very wide variety of circumstances. Notice that if it is to be convincing to your reader, then your reader must already be persuaded that the taking of an innocent life is morally wrong. Otherwise, even though your reader agrees that abortion is the taking of an innocent life, he or she won't be led to the conclusion that it is morally wrong.

A second form of argument, which in a sense is the reverse of instantiation, is *generalization*. Suppose you are trying to persuade your reader that the taking of an innocent life is morally wrong, as a first step toward springing the above argument, and thereby proving that abortion is morally wrong. You might proceed like this (imagine yourself actually talking to your reader):

⟶ Will you agree that shooting down someone walking along the street is morally wrong? Yes.

⟶ Will you agree that bombing civilians who happen to live near a war zone is morally wrong? Yes.

➤ Will you agree that smothering a baby in its crib is morally wrong? Yes.

➤ Can you see that what all these cases have in common, *what makes them all morally wrong,* is the fact that they are cases of taking an innocent life [crucial step here—you must get your reader to agree to this]?

➤ Well [now your trap snaps shut on your reader], if what makes these three acts morally wrong is the fact that they are cases of taking an innocent life, if that is *why* they are wrong, then it follows by simple parity of reasoning that *any* act that is the taking of an innocent life must also be wrong. In other words, Taking an innocent life is morally wrong.

The trick here is figuring out just what it is that all three cases have in common, in virtue of which they are morally wrong. If you fix on some other characteristic, which isn't, so to speak, the *wrong-making* characteristic, then you won't come up with a defensible generalization. For example, the person gunned down in the street, the civilians near the war zone, and the baby in the crib might all be Americans, or male, or Caucasian, or rich, or they might all have the same astrological sign. But none of those things is what makes the killing of them morally wrong. What makes the killing of them morally wrong is the fact that they are innocent—that is, they haven't done anything to warrant being killed, they just happened to be there. If the person gunned down in the street *isn't* innocent, if she is a serial murderer on her way to commit yet another heinous crime, then maybe it wouldn't be wrong to kill her, for killing her would not be the taking of an innocent life.

So, we now have two kinds of arguments, which you can use singly or together, in your attempt to convince your reader that your thesis is true: instantiation and generalization.

A third form of argument, especially useful in replying to an opponent's objections, is the *counterexample.* A counterexample is a particular case—an instantiation—designed to show that an opponent's generalization is wrong. Suppose, for example, that your opponent, trying to show that abortion is morally right, argues that a pregnant woman has a right to have an abortion because having an abortion is choosing to do something with your own body, and (here comes the generalization) *Persons have an absolute right to do with their own bodies whatever they choose.* You can try to come up with a *counterexample* to this generalization that will show that it is not in fact a true universal principle.

For example, you might point out that using your hands to strangle someone you don't like is an example of doing with your body (your hands) whatever you choose, and yet your opponent surely will not agree that you have an absolute right to strangle someone you don't like. Now, your opponent may, of course, just reply, with an absolutely straight face, "Of course you have a right to strangle someone you don't like," but that is not likely!

More probably, your opponent will point out that this is an example (strangling someone) that involves inflicting injury on someone else in addition to doing what you choose with your own body, and that makes it different from abortion. In this case, your opponent is appealing to a slightly different principle, namely, *Persons have an absolute right to do with their own bodies whatever they choose,* **so long as they do not injure others.**

Now you can respond by pointing out that abortion *does* involve injury to another person, namely to the fetus. This is an example of yet a fourth technique of argument, which we can call *counter-instantiation*—showing that a case is not an instance of the generalization your opponent has cited, but is in fact an instance of a different generalization. Your opponent can now respond that a fetus is not a person, and hence that abortion doesn't fall under the generalization you have just invoked.

Notice that this last move—arguing that the fetus isn't a person—involves two more kinds of arguments that play a role in philosophical debates: *citing facts* and *drawing conceptual distinctions.* When your opponent says the fetus is not a person, he or she may be calling attention to facts (the fetus is not biologically fully developed, it cannot live independently of the mother's body, etc.) that tend to show that it is in fact different from the things we usually call persons. This is an example of citing facts. In addition, your opponent may be pointing out that the concept *person,* which plays a central role in the generalization you have invoked, cannot properly be applied to a fetus. This is an example of drawing a conceptual distinction.

Well, you are beginning to get the idea. In this central part of your paper, your job is to produce arguments in support of your thesis, using instantiation, generalization, counterexample, counter-instantiation, citing of facts, drawing conceptual distinctions, and any of the other forms of argument you can find. The success of your paper, to a very considerable extent, will depend on how well you can think up arguments in support of your thesis.

There is no set of rules that will produce good arguments. This is a skill you have to learn through practice. Just keep one idea clearly in mind: What makes an argument a good one is its ability to persuade an intelligent, reasonable reader or listener who doesn't already agree with your thesis. If you test arguments against that standard, you will be able to judge whether they are good.

4. The Examination of Objections to the Thesis

This is the part of your paper in which you put yourself into an imaginary opponent's shoes and try to figure out what objections he or she might raise to your thesis. The techniques you use in this exercise are precisely the ones we have just been looking at in the previous section: instantiation, generalization, counterexample, counter-instantiation, and so forth. The trick—and it is a very difficult trick—is to think up the *strongest* objections you can to your thesis. Don't just put up some cream-puff objections that anyone can knock over!

This is hard to do because by the time you have written the third part of the paper—the arguments for the thesis—you will probably have convinced yourself that you are right. Try to think of this part of the paper as damage control, or setting up a defense perimeter, or taking out insurance. If you can come up with some really strong objections to your thesis, and *still* succeed in defending the thesis, then you will probably persuade your reader, because you will have thought of the objections that the reader has in mind as he or she reads your paper. There is nothing that wins a reader over more completely than to have the author say, "Now you may be thinking to yourself, but what about this, and this, and this" when that is just what the reader is thinking, and then having the author come up with really plausible replies.

So, play Devil's advocate for a bit, and think up the best objections you can to your own thesis.

5. The Response to the Objections

And finally, having thought up some dandy objections, answer them! Once again, you are going to use the techniques of argument we discussed above (notice that most of your paper—Parts 3, 4, and 5—consists of arguments; that is what philosophy is all about).

And then you are done! You have stated a thesis, analyzed and explained it, argued for it, considered objections to it, and responded to objections. That is a philosophy paper. Not so hard after all, is it?

Notice, by the way, that this method tells you what to put into the paper, what to leave out, what to do next, and when you are done. Should you cite a fact? Yes—if it serves to strengthen your thesis or weaken your opponent's objection; otherwise no. Should your paper have footnotes? Well, if you cite a fact, put in a footnote stating the source of your knowledge of that fact (unless it is so well-known a fact that any reader can be expected to know it. If you refer to Washington, D.C., as the nation's capital, don't put in a footnote to the encyclopedia).

How do you know how long to make your paper? The simple answer is, just long enough to state a thesis, explain it, defend it, and respond to objections to it. If your instructor assigns a paper of, say, three pages in length, then you must choose a thesis that can be adequately explained and defended in three pages. If the assignment is for a ten-page paper, then choose a thesis that calls for that much explanation and defense. Don't pad! Don't add paragraphs or pages just to bulk up the paper so that it feels weighty. As Abraham Lincoln said when someone asked him how long his legs were, "Just long enough to reach the ground."

But what about an assignment to discuss or criticize someone else's views. For example, suppose your assignment is to write a paper critically analyzing some view of the relation between mind and matter, or to write a paper about Kant's Categorical Imperative. These topics may look very different from the topics we have been talking about. Can the method I have just laid out be used for these assignments as well?

Absolutely. Suppose the assignment is to write a paper on Kant's Categorical Imperative. The first thing you must do is to decide what you are going to try to show about the Categorical Imperative. In other words, you must *choose your thesis*. For example (and this is, I ought to warn you, a pretty wacky example), you might decide to defend the thesis that

Kant's Categorical Imperative is identical with the Principle of Utilitarianism.

(I don't think anybody in the world thinks that this thesis is true—I warned you it was pretty wacky.) Now that you have your thesis, the next step is to analyze and explain it. That means explaining how you understand the Categorical Imperative, stating what you take to be the Principle of Utilitarianism, and then explaining what you mean when you say that the two are "identical."

Now you are going to have to produce some arguments in support of your thesis. Some of your arguments will be textual citations from Kant's writings (citations of fact) to show that your interpretation of his Categorical Imperative is the correct one. Some of your arguments will be conceptual analyses designed to clarify the relationship between these two apparently different principles. And so forth.

When it comes to considering objections, your number one objection will of course be that Kant himself believed his Categorical Imperative to be absolutely opposed to the Principle of Utilitarianism. So you will, in effect, have to argue against Kant in your reply to objections.

But you get the point. Even when you are writing a paper in which you are supposed to discuss or analyze or criticize some philosopher's position, you can still use the five-step method set out above.

I can't guarantee that you will get an A if you follow this method. That depends on how *well* you do at following it. But I am willing to bet that if you study this appendix carefully and follow the five-step method intelligently, you won't fail! And I guarantee it will help you to clarify your ideas, sharpen your arguments, and thereby improve your philosophizing.

A Few Tips, Hints, and Warnings

The basic instructions for writing a good philosophy paper are now in your hands, but it might be helpful for me to give you a few tips, hints, and warnings designed to help you avoid some of the most common mistakes and problems.

1. Let me start with a piece of advice that is not so much a tip or hint as it is the Prime Directive (as they say on *Star Trek*).

Write clear, grammatical, correctly spelled, proper English prose (unless you are writing Spanish, or Hebrew, or Cambodian, or German, or some other natural language, in which case write *that* language clearly, grammatically, correctly spelled, and properly).

There are two reasons why it is important for you to make sure that you use language in a grammatically correct fashion. First of all, writing correctly is like playing in tune on a musical instrument, or learning the rules of a sport. You can't interpret a piece of music if you can't even play the notes properly, and you can't play baseball if you don't even know that a batter gets three strikes. Written language has rules just like music or baseball, and learning them is the first step in writing well.

The second reason why writing correct prose is so important in a philosophy paper is that until you can write in a grammatically precise and correct fashion, you will not be able to state a thesis for defense, or put together an argument in support of a thesis. As we will see when we analyze an actual student paper in the next section, incorrect grammar obscures an author's meaning. Indeed, if you aren't careful to write clearly, you may fool yourself as well as your readers. You may not know what you yourself mean by your thesis or your arguments, in which case you won't be able to tell whether you have made a case for your thesis at all.

2. Don't wander from the basic outline when writing your paper, and don't mix together materials that belong in different parts of the paper.

Once you have stated your thesis, start to explain and analyze it. Leave out anything that doesn't help to explain or analyze your thesis. You may be eager to get to your argument because you may have a really good idea you want to try out. Wait for it! Once you get to the argument stage, don't drift off into expressing opinions or telling stories that don't advance the argument. Make sure both you and the reader know, at every stage, what you are doing, where you are going, and how what you are saying connects up with your central task of defending your thesis.

3. Try to use language as precisely as possible.

Vague words like "stuff" or "thing" are evidence of a sloppy mind. Your prose should be proper to the subject—not forced or stilted, not full of words you wouldn't ever use except in a philosophy paper, but nevertheless carefully chosen. Think how inappropriate it would be for Dan Rather or Tom Brokaw to start the evening news by saying, "Hey, like the guys in Washington did, like, a lot of weird stuff today, ya know?"

4. Asking a question without answering it is *not* an appropriate way to give an argument.

For example: "What would happen if every woman who wanted an abortion got one?" is not an argument. "If every woman who wanted an abortion got one, millions of innocent lives would be lost" *is* an argument, or rather it is part of an argument. The whole argument might look like this:

It is wrong to cause the loss of millions of innocent lives.

If every woman who wanted an abortion got one, millions of innocent lives would be lost.

Therefore, it would be wrong for every woman who wants one to get an abortion.

Similarly, "What right does the state have to tell a woman she can't have an abortion?" isn't an argument. But "The state has no right to tell a woman she cannot get an abortion" *is* an argument. And so forth.

5. It is perfectly all right to use an argument from a lecture you have heard or a book you have read.

Arguments are a little like arithmetical formulas. I don't know who first said "Two plus two equals four," but it is there for anyone to use. However, when you adopt an argument as your own, you take responsibility for it. By including it in your paper, you are saying that you believe it is a good argument. Even if you footnote it, indicating where you first encountered it, it is still on your neck! So use any arguments you like, so long as you are ready to stand behind them. And remember: An argument either stands on its own feet, or it doesn't stand at all. You don't make a bad argument better by pointing out in a footnote that a famous philosopher used it.

A Student Paper

The time has come to give a real example of a paper, submitted to my Introduction to Philosophy course in the fall of 1990. I have chosen this paper because it has a great many serious problems, and yet has some interesting ideas in it which deserve to be stated clearly and forcefully.

We are going to look at this paper in three stages. First, I will simply reproduce the paper exactly as the student submitted it, complete with misspellings, grammatical errors, and typographical errors. I am going to italicize every misspelled word or typo, and you ought to check each word to make sure you know how it is spelled or why it is a typographical error.

Then I will take a few sample sentences or paragraphs that are ungrammatically written or poorly constructed, and analyze them, showing you what is wrong and how it might be fixed up. Please don't imagine that everything that is left alone is all right! After reading my analyses and reconstructions of the sample passages, you ought to see whether you can do the same thing with other problem passages.

Finally, I will offer a rewritten version of the entire paper, along the lines laid out above. It is not my aim to turn this into a perfect paper. I want to show you how this student, following the guidelines in this appendix, could have turned the actual paper into a much better paper, one that made the thesis clearer, the argument more persuasive, and the exposition clearer.

The paper we are going to look at was written by a student who had read the chapter on The Philosophy of Art and had viewed a Ted Koppel "Nightline" show devoted to the dispute surrounding the exhibit of Robert Mapplethorpe's photographs. The specific paper topic to which the student was responding was this:

> The debate over whether the Mapplethorpe photographs should be exhibited in publicly funded museums has been long on hysterics and short on reasoned arguments. Choose one side of the controversy and defend it *by explicit appeal to some theory of the nature and social value of art.* Do not simply say whether you approve or disapprove of the exhibit. Defend your position by talking about what art is and what role art should play in our society.

₰₰₰₰₰₰₰₰₰₰₰₰₰

Student Paper

Displaying explicit nude photographs in a public art gallery will hurt the *credability* of our society because of the fact that the artist has created these photos to capture attention by controversy not his own merit.

We as *americans* have established our own religion. Most of us say that we never go to church, but we do. These churches do not bear the characteristics of traditional houses of worship. These new churches have tellers, drive-up windows, and twenty-four hour express machines. All these now serve as modern day clergy and aid us in our worship to our new god, MONEY.

When did everything become about money? Why as a mature society have we let this get so out of hand? We sell everything for money, our bodies, our country and natural resources, and most of all our values. What's to stop us from selling our children like slaves, if the price is right? *we* have to stop prostituting our morals for money. We have to preserve things with value and authentic beauty.

If you look at a dictionary the definition of art will read as follows: The activity of creating <u>beautiful</u> things, the authentic value of an artist expressed by his values. If we let the purpose of art be compromised, for *many*, we are therefore selling beauty. If we allow someone in our society to mock art, we are guilty of the destruction of a tradition that has existed since the beginning of time.

The Mapplethorpe photographs are a black mark on the history of art. They *deface* the idea of beauty that is associated with art. These photos are not art, they are not beauty, they are merely pornography in disguise. We are allowing this artist to destroy the ideal of art. This man is using us and our social values to gain publicity, not by his own merit, but instead by controversy. By drawing attention to the photographs we have fallen into his premeditated trap and are all therefore guilty of destroying a tradition. Art in its true form, gains monetary value due to the beauty it *pocesses* to the purchaser, not because someone set out to seek publicity.

This exhibit hangs in a museum with legitimate art. *we* can not be expected *expected* to make the distinction between the two to our children? We can not expect our *chindren*, after being brought up with the ideals that this is art, to respect significant pieces of art. If you go into a store you are *accostomed* to the fact that *item of comparative* value are placed next to each other. How would you explain the fact that two pieces of art placed side-by-side do not have the same *"value"*? (By value I do not mean money, but instead social value.)

We have to teach our children the difference between real art and pornography. If we don't we can not expect them to tell the difference between photographs taken by a genius like *Anstel* Adams and the centerfold of Penthouse magazine, they are both just pictures, right?

If we try to justify these photographs by saying that this type of behavior is now *excepted* by our society, we are *beong* selfish. There is no justification in saying that what is good for society now will also be good for societies to come. These future societies should be entitled to view past art works in the same way that we did, for beauty *no* controversy. Historians say that art reflects the society as well as the time in which it was created. This would give a message to the world that we have given up our morals.

Selfishness is what is going to bring the world as we now know it to an end. We have already allowed it to destroy our faith in the church (thanks to T. V. evangelists), police department, etc . . . We can not allow it to interfere with the only faith we have left.

Even after the misspellings and typographical errors are corrected, this is not a good paper, but it does have some interesting ideas in it which, with a good deal of clarification and reorganization, might form the core of a good, solid philosophical argument. Let us try to identify some of the principal shortcomings of the paper as it now is, after which we will have a shot at improving it.

The very first problem with the paper is that a reader will have a great deal of trouble figuring out what its *thesis* is. The assignment was to choose one side of the debate over whether the Mapplethorpe photographs should be exhibited in publicly funded museums, and the author of this paper pretty clearly is opposed to showing the exhibit, so we might naturally suppose that the thesis of the paper is:

➤ The Mapplethorpe photographs should not be exhibited in publicly funded museums.

But if you read the paper carefully, you will find that there is not a single argument in it that has anything to do with the *public funding* of the museum (in Cincinnati) where the show caused such a fuss. The arguments in this paper would apply with equal force to the exhibiting of the photographs in a privately funded museum. Thus, the paper's author never engages with one of the central issues in the debate, which is whether tax money, collected by law from *all* citizens, should be used to fund an exhibit that offends the moral, aesthetic, or religious sensibilities of some of them.

The second problem is that the paper has no very clear organization or focus. In all, there are ten paragraphs in the paper, including one ("We have to stop prostituting our morals etc.") that has not been indented properly. A close reading suggests that only six of the paragraphs—numbers 1, 5, 6, 7, 8, and 9—are about art and the Mapplethorpe exhibit. The other four—numbers 2, 3, 4, and 10—are about something quite different, namely the establishment in the United States of a new religion in which we worship money. Now, the author clearly thinks there is a connection between these two themes. To put it simply, the connection seems to be that in exhibiting the Mapplethorpe photographs in public art galleries, the curators of those galleries are contributing to the on-going corruption of American values, a corruption that is manifested by the elevating of money above art or beauty. The last paragraph appears to claim that faith in art is the only faith we have left, now that selfishness has destroyed religion, so we ought not to allow the exhibiting of the Mapplethorpe photographs, since in showing them and looking at them we are falling into a trap selfishly laid by the artist.

The third problem with the paper is that the individual arguments are not clearly, coherently, or forcefully stated, nor are they assembled in a way that will lead a reader to the conclusion the author is trying to establish. Take a look, for example, at the rather interesting and imaginative argument in paragraph 7. The background premise of the argument in this paragraph is that the Mapplethorpe photographs are not true art. Incidentally, it isn't quite clear whether the author thinks this premise has been established in the previous paragraph, or is simply assuming it. At any rate, given that starting point, the argument of paragraph 7 proceeds like this:

- It is important to bring up our children to appreciate and respect the beauty of true art, to be able to recognize genuine artistic value when they encounter it.

- Just as our children learn, when they go shopping, that items of roughly equivalent monetary value will be exhibited in the same store (they wouldn't expect to find an expensive necklace in a K-Mart, or a cheap reproduction of a painting in a fine art gallery), so they should be able to expect that objects of roughly equivalent aesthetic value will be found together in a museum. If the Mapplethorpe photographs, which have no aesthetic value at all, are exhibited next to paintings or photographs of genuine artistic merit, our children will become confused, and our attempts to teach them the correct aesthetic standards of value will be undermined.

- Therefore, the Mapplethorpe photographs ought not to be exhibited in a public art gallery.

Whether you think this argument is persuasive or not, I think you will grant that it is interesting and imaginative, and forces the reader to think more deeply about the issue. But in the original language of paragraph 7, it is very unclearly and diffusely stated.

There are even more serious difficulties with the longest paragraph in the paper, paragraph 6. Let us first clear up one factual matter. The exhibit under discussion was actually a *posthumous* exhibit. Robert Mapplethorpe had died before it was assembled and exhibited, so the author is wrong to claim that Mapplethorpe is "using us" to gain publicity. However, it is at least possible that the people who organized the exhibit were doing so, although nothing in the materials presented to the class contained any evidence of such a plot.

The central difficulty with the paragraph is the unclarity of its line of argument. The author starts out by saying that the photographs are destroying the ideal of art because they are pseudo-art, pornography. Then he/she goes on to a quite different claim, that Mapplethorpe has set a trap for us by creating a controversy that draws audiences into the museum and further destroys the authentic tradition of great art (presumably by leading us to confuse pornography with art). Finally, in the last sentence, which in a properly constructed paragraph would sum up the argument of the paragraph, the author makes an entirely new point, namely that true art becomes monetarily valuable because of its aesthetic appeal to the person who purchases it (and thereby confers monetary value on it).

This is a mess! At least three different arguments are jumbled together, with no indication of the connections among them. Clearly, the only way for the author to salvage this paragraph is first, to decide exactly what argument it is supposed to present, second, to remove from the paragraph anything that doesn't serve to advance that argument, and finally, to rewrite what remains so that it lays out a single argument clearly and logically.

How could the author reorganize and rewrite this paper so as to make it a clear, forceful, persuasive argument? The first step is to decide what the thesis of the paper is going to be. Since the author never really addresses the question, whether *public* financing should be used to support the exhibition of the Mapplethorpe photographs, let us set that matter to one side, and instead formulate a thesis that can draw under it as many of the lines of argument in the paper as possible. Pretty clearly, the natural thesis for this paper is something like this:

Robert Mapplethorpe's photographs ought not to be exhibited in art museums.

Now let us construct a defense of that thesis out of the materials in this paper. As I go along, I will indicate which paragraphs I am drawing on in reconstructing the argument. Remember: The aim of this exercise is *not* to write a completely new paper. Rather, it is to reshape the materials already in the actual student paper so that they are clearer, more orderly and coherent, and thereby more persuasive. The result won't be a perfect paper. It may not even be a paper that deserves the grade of A. But if we are successful, it will be the best paper that can be created from the ideas about this subject that the author seems to have had in mind. Here goes.

೫೫೫೫೫೫೫೫೫೫೫೫೫

Reconstructed Student Paper

In this paper I am going to defend the thesis that Robert Mapplethorpe's photographs ought not to be exhibited in art museums. [*You don't actually have to begin a paper this way, officially announcing your thesis, but it can't hurt, and it may help to keep you focused on your thesis, so that you don't drift off into side issues that fail to advance the argument for the thesis.*] When I speak of art, I mean either the activity of creating beautiful things, an activity engaged in by the artist, or else the beautiful and aesthetically valuable works resulting from that activity. [*This is Step*

2, the explanation and analysis of the thesis. See paragraph 5 of the original paper.] There is a long tradition in our society of cherishing and preserving true works of art. [*This seems to be one of the unstated premises of the paper—see paragraph 5, for example.*] Exhibiting the Mapplethorpe photographs mocks that tradition, and undermines it.

The Mapplethorpe photographs are a black mark in the history of art exhibits. Their appearance in an art gallery defaces the true works of art exhibited there. [*Paragraph 6. The image of defacing is a good one, given the subject of the paper, but strictly speaking, it isn't used properly here. Nevertheless, we are trying to rewrite this paper, not write a new one. Notice that we must change "history of art" to "history of art exhibits" since the author doesn't think the photographs are art.*] These photos are not art, they are not beautiful, they are merely pornography in disguise. By exhibiting the photographs in an art museum as though they were art, we are allowing Mapplethorpe and the people putting on the exhibit to destroy the ideal of art. They are using us and our respect for art to gain publicity for the photographs, not on the basis of their merit but merely as a consequence of the controversy surrounding them. We have fallen into a trap laid for us by the people promoting the exhibit, and we are thereby as guilty as they of destroying the tradition of true art in our society.

We have a duty to keep the tradition alive by teaching our children the difference between real art and pornography. If we don't, we cannot expect them to tell the difference between truly artistic photographs, such as those taken by the great photographer Ansel Adams, and cheap pornography like the centerfold of Penthouse magazine. Our children are likely to think that they are both art, since they are both pictures. [*Paragraph 8. Notice the way I have altered the language of the paragraph to bring out the connection of its argument with the premise laid down at the end of our first paragraph.*]

The Mapplethorpe exhibit hangs in a museum together with legitimate art. How then can we hope to make the distinction between the two to our children? After all, our children are accustomed to finding, when they go into a store, that items of comparable monetary value will be placed side by side on the shelves. They would not expect to find a costly bracelet exhibited next to a cheap imitation. How can we possibly explain to them the fact that cheap pornography is hanging side by side with aesthetically valuable art? If our children are brought up to suppose that such photographs are art, we cannot expect them to respect significant pieces of art. [*Paragraph 7. This is probably the most interesting and original argument in the paper. It deserves to be spelled out clearly so that the reader can appreciate its force.*]

Why then are the Mapplethorpe photographs allowed to be exhibited in a museum supposedly dedicated to preserving the tradition of aesthetic value? I suggest that the answer is the corrupting influence of money. [*The paper needs something like this as an introduction to the paragraphs on money and art. Otherwise, it is difficult to see their connection to the materials on educating children.*] We Americans have established our own religion. Most of us say that we never go to church, but we do. These churches do not bear the characteristics of traditional houses of worship. These new churches have tellers, drive-up windows, and twenty-four-hour express machines. All these now serve as modern-day clergy and aid us in our worship to our new god, MONEY. [*Paragraph 3.*]

When did everything become about money? Why as a mature society have we let this get so out of hand? We sell everything for money, our bodies, our country and natural resources, and most of our values. We would even sell our children like slaves if the price were right. Now it appears that we are allowing our selfishness to lead us to sell the last things of value we have left, our art. [*Paragraphs 3 and 10. I have left in the rather lurid bit about selling our children. It is too dramatic to be rhetorically effective, but as I have already noted, I am trying to rewrite this paper, not write a new one. Notice that the last sentence spells out something that seems to be implicit in several of the paragraphs of the original paper, and yet is never actually stated clearly by the author.*] True art gains monetary value as a result of the beauty it possesses for the purchaser, not because of any publicity that may be associated with it. [*Paragraph 6, last sentence. This isn't true, of course. What the author really means, I suspect, is that art shouldn't acquire monetary value merely as the result of publicity, but of course it does. In a paper like this, it is very important to keep clear the distinction between what is and what ought to be.*]

Some people might try to justify the Mapplethorpe photographs by saying that the behavior represented in them is accepted by our society, and therefore that it is all right to show them. [*Paragraph 9. This is the one place in the paper where the author attempts to state and rebut possible objections to the thesis. I am not at all sure that my interpretation of the first sentence of Paragraph 9 is correct. The language of the original is unclear, and I have been forced to choose an interpretation that may differ from the author's intention. This is one of those places where it is especially important to ask yourself whether a reader will be able to figure out exactly what you had in mind.*] But I believe that if we were to adopt that attitude, we would be acting selfishly, ignoring the interests of generations yet to come. Past generations have handed on to us museums in which true works of art are exhibited solely for their beauty, not because they caused controversy. [*This seems to be what the author has in mind. It is, of course, quite false! Past generations have been swayed as much by controversy as our generation is. However, let us continue.*]

Future generations have a right to expect that we will hand on to them museums governed by the same concern for aesthetic value. Historians say that art reflects the society as well as the time in which it was created. If we allow the Mapplethorpe exhibit to appear in our museums, we will send a message to the world that we have given up our aesthetic principles. [*The rest of Paragraph 9. I have changed the end of the last sentence from "morals" to "aesthetic principles" because the author hasn't actually said anything thus far about moral principles, only about aesthetic or artistic principles.*]

To sum up, the exhibitors of the Mapplethorpe photographs are prostituting their principles for money. We have to preserve things with aesthetic value and authentic beauty, and keep them separate from things that have no aesthetic merit, such as the Mapplethorpe photographs. [*Paragraph 4, with alterations.*]

Well, there it is. If you examine the rewritten paper and the original version carefully, you will see that the rewritten version incorporates almost all of the original paper, together with some clarifications and additions. The big difference is that the new version is better organized and more coherently stated, so that a reader can follow the argument. It begins with a *thesis;* briefly *analyzes* and *explains* the thesis; spends most of its time *arguing* for the thesis; *states possible objections* (or at least states one possible objection—this is the weakest part of the paper); *replies to the objections;* and ends with a brief summation.

If you will subject your own first drafts to the same sort of close analysis and criticism, following the procedures set forth in this appendix, you will very quickly find yourself writing good, solid philosophy papers. Good luck!

GLOSSARY

Alienation According to Marx, it is the condition of being at war with one's own nature, the products of one's labor, and one's fellow workers. Marx argued that capitalism undermines the human capacity for creative and productive work, making men and women unhappy in their work, dissatisfied in their leisure, and unable to fulfill their human potential. Marx derived the concept of alienation from German philosophers of the early nineteenth century.

Analytic proposition A statement that merely spells out what is already contained in the subject of the statement.

Anarchist One who believes that no state has any right to rule and that governmental authority is illegitimate and undesirable.

a posteriori As a consequence of experience of objects—an adverb used to modify verbs of cognition, as "to know *a posteriori*" or "to apprehend *a posteriori*." Propositions are said to be knowable *a posteriori* when they are knowable only as a consequence of an experience of the objects they make assertions about.

a priori Prior to, or independently of, experience—an adverb used to modify verbs of cognition, as "to know *a priori*." Propositions are said to be knowable *a priori* when they are knowable prior to, or independently of, any experience of the objects they make assertions about.

Argument from Design The attempt to prove the existence of God by demonstrating the high degree of organization and purposive order in the universe, and arguing that such design must be the product of an intelligent, powerful, purposeful creator. The argument is very old but had a wide popularity in the eighteenth century.

Bourgeoisie See Proletariat

Capitalism An economic system based on concentration of private ownership of the means of production in relatively few hands, a large class of propertyless workers who work for wages, and production for sale and profit rather than for use. The money invested by the property owners for the purpose of making a profit is called *capital,* hence the system is called capitalism.

Categorical Imperative A term invented by Immanuel Kant to refer to a command that orders us to do something unconditionally—that is, regardless of what we want or what our aims and purposes are. According to Kant, we experience the principles of morality as Categorical Imperatives. The term is also used, by Kant and those following him, to refer to one particular moral principle, which Kant calls the Highest Moral Law.

Catharsis Literally, a cleansing or purging. Aristotle uses the term to describe the effect on us of powerful dramatic performances. By watching a play whose events arouse fear and pity within us, we are purged of those emotions, so that we leave the theater liberated or cleansed. The opposing view is that such plays (and, by extension, movies and television programs) arouse in us feelings we otherwise wouldn't have, and shouldn't have, such as aggressive and sexual feelings.

Cogito, ergo sum "I think, therefore I am"—the phrase used by Descartes to prove his own existence.

Copy theory of ideas The theory that all our ideas are either copies of sense impressions or else combinations and rearrangements of copies of sense impressions.

Cosmological Argument The attempt to prove the existence of God by starting with the mere fact of motion, or change, or the existence of things in the universe, and then arguing that these must have their origin in a being that does not move, or does not change, or does not merely happen to exist. The earliest form of argument is to be found in the writings of Aristotle.

Cosmology   Literally, the study of the order of the world. Now used to refer to the branch of astronomy that investigates the organization and structure of the entire physical universe, including its origins. In philosophy, cosmology is a part of the subfield called metaphysics, or the study of first principles.

Determinism   The most extreme form is sometimes called fatalism, a view much encountered in fictional literature but rarely held either by philosophers or by people in general. It seems that the future is always immutably fixed in such a way that there is nothing anyone could ever do to alter the course of events. Determinists, however, generally prefer to say that human actions and choices are links in a causal chain. Every event is caused, but the cause may be extremely complex.

Dialogue   A process of question and answer between two people.

Double consciousness   W.E.B. Du Bois identifies this as the way of understanding oneself experienced by African-Americans. Because of the constant repetition of negative judgments by White people, the Negro develops a doubled sense of self—seeing himself or herself both as White people do, and as he or she does himself or herself. Du Bois believed this was both a great burden and a source of special insight into the nature of American society.

Dualism   The Mind-Body Theory that there are two fundamentally different kinds of things in the universe—bodies and minds—neither of which can be reduced to, or analyzed into, the other.

Empiricism/Rationalism   Empiricism and Rationalism are the two leading epistemological theories of the past four centuries. *Empiricism* is the theory that all human knowledge comes from the evidence of our five senses, and therefore we can never know more, or know with greater certainty, than our senses will allow. *Rationalism* is the theory that at least some human knowledge comes from reason, unaided by the senses, and therefore we can know about things that the senses do not reveal to us, and can know with greater certainty than the senses alone will allow.

Epistemological skepticism   The doctrine that no adequate justification can be given for any of our beliefs about the world, not even for apparently rock-solid beliefs that there is a physical world, that I have a body, that the sun will rise tomorrow, or that fire causes heat. The aim of epistemological skepticism is to focus our attention on the relationship between our beliefs and their justification, not to get us actually to stop believing.

Epistemological turn   A shift in philosophy from emphasis on metaphysics to emphasis on epistemology.

Epistemology   Literally, the study of knowledge, Epistemology is the study of how we come to know things, what the limits are of our knowledge, and what sort of certainty or uncertainty attaches to our knowledge. Psychology also studies how we come to know, but epistemology is concerned less with the mechanics of knowing than with the possibility of defending, proving, or justifying what we think we know. Since the early seventeenth century, epistemology has been the most important branch of philosophy.

Ethical Relativism The theory that whether an act is right or wrong depends on—is relative to—the society in which one lives. Sometimes ethical relativists merely claim that we must take social contexts and rules into account, but sometimes they assert that one and the same act is right for men and women in one society and wrong for men and women in another. Frequently confused with *Ethical Skepticism,* which doubts that any acts are right or wrong, and *Ethical Nihilism,* which denies that any acts are either right or wrong.

Ethics In philosophy, the systematic study of how we ought to act, both toward ourselves and to others, and also the study of what things, character traits, or types of persons are good, estimable, admirable, and what kinds are bad, reprehensible, worthy of being condemned. Ethics deals both with general rules or principles, and also with particular cases.

Existentialism The philosophical doctrine, associated originally with Søren Kierkegaard, according to which our being as subjective individuals (our *existence*) is more important than what we have in common objectively with all other human beings (our *essence*). Of primary concern for Kierkegaard was his relationship to God. Later existentialists emphasized the individual's creation of himself or herself through free individual choices.

Experiment A controlled interaction with nature designed to yield observations that will help to confirm or disconfirm some hypothesis about the way the world is. Experiments are usually carried out with the aid of specialized equipment referred to as "instruments," although some experiments use nothing more than ordinarily available items.

Faith In Christianity, trust that God will keep the promise He made to the Israelites in the Old Testament and renewed to all mankind in the New Testament (hence, "trust in the Lord"). Originally, the promise was to make the Israelites fruitful and populous. In the New Testament, the promise is of life eternal in heaven. According to some Christians, men and women are unable to have and sustain this trust without the miraculous help of God.

Fascism The twentieth-century political movement begun in Italy in 1919 by Mussolini, which emphasized the primacy of the nation or people, opposed left-wing political movements, and sought a rebirth of the ancient glory of the Italian people. Subsequently, the term *fascist* has been broadly applied to right-wing popular movements which celebrate military power and use the state police power to suppress dissent or opposition. The word derives from the Latin term for a bundle of sticks bound together, a *faces,* which served as the symbol of Mussolini's party.

Free will The freedom of human beings is assumed in the sense that we are not entirely circumscribed by an ineluctable and predetermined destiny. We can within limits, make our own destiny.

The General will A term invented by Jean-Jacques Rousseau to describe the decision by the citizens of a republic to set aside their private and partisan concerns and instead collectively aim at the general good. According to Rousseau, to say that a society "has a general will" is to say that all the members of the society are public-spiritedly aiming at the general good in their political actions and deliberations. Rousseau was very pessimistic about the possibility of ever achieving a general will.

Historical materialism The Marxist theory that ideas and social institutions develop only as a reflection of a material economic base.

Idealism The Mind-Body theory that everything in the universe is either minds, or else ideas in minds (hence, *idealism*). Bodies, according to the idealist, are simply particular collections of ideas. Thus, a table is simply the interconnected set of all the ideas—concepts, images, feels, sights, sounds, etc.—that I think of as ideas of a table.

Identity crisis   A term invented by the psychoanalyst Erik Erikson to refer to the period of instability, uncertainty, and personality formation through which teenagers pass in societies like ours. Erikson intended to suggest, by the term, that the period is one of genuine flux and indeterminacy, with the outcome—a healthy, coherent adult personality—hanging in the balance.

Intrinsic value/Instrumental value To say that something has *intrinsic value* is to say that it is valuable, good, worthwhile, purely for itself alone, regardless of what it may produce or lead to. Some people say that pleasure has intrinsic value, others that beauty does, still others that moral goodness does. *Instrumental value* is the value something has as a means, or instrument, for producing or getting something else. A tool or instrument, for some purpose is said to be instrumentally valuable.

Irony A mode of discourse by which the speaker communicates, to the real audience, a meaning opposite from that conveyed to the superficial, or apparent, audience.

Laissez-faire Literally, allow to do. Laissez-faire is the system of free market exchanges, with an absolute minimum of government control, which nineteenth-century liberals believed would result in the most efficient use of resources and the greatest material well-being for a society. *Laissez-faire capitalism* refers to the early stage in the development of capitalism, when firms were small, owner-run, and controlled both in their purchases and in their sales by market pressures.

Law of contradiction/Law of the excluded middle The two basic laws of formal logic. The *Law of Contradiction* states that a statement and its contradictory cannot both be true. For example, the statement "Fire is hot," may be true, and it may be false. Its contradictory, "It isn't the case that fire is hot" may be true, and it may be false. But it cannot be that *both* the statement *and* its contradictory are true. The *Law of the Excluded Middle* says that for any statement, *either* it is true *or* its contradictory is true. Thus, either fire is hot, or it is not the case that fire is hot.

Legitimate authority The right to give commands that others have a moral obligation to obey. States claim legitimate authority when they say that they have a right to pass laws which citizens or subjects *ought* to obey, regardless of whether they are in danger of being caught for not obeying. Democratic states base their claim to legitimate authority on the fact that they are elected by the people whom they rule and therefore, speak with the voice of the people.

Logic   The discipline that investigates the correct principles of formal reasoning—sometimes characterized as the science of the laws of thought.

Marxism The economic, political, and philosophical doctrines first set forth by Karl Marx and then developed by his disciples and followers. Although Marx himself considered his theories scientific, his followers have often treated them as a form of secular religion. The principal doctrines are: first, that capitalism is internally unstable and prone to fall into economic crises; second, that the profits of capitalist enterprises derive from the exploitation of the workers, who receive in wages less than they produce; third, that as capitalism develops, workers will tend to become more self-aware of their situation—and hence more likely to overthrow capitalism by force; and fourth, that the society that comes into existence after capitalism is destroyed will be socialist and democratic in its economic and political organization.

Materialism The Mind-Body theory that everything in the universe is matter (hence, *materialism*). Minds, according to the materialist, are simply collections of very small bodies or structures and organizations of bodies (such as nerve cells in the brain). Perceptions, to the materialist, are particular sorts of interactions between bodies, and so are thoughts, emotions, and feelings of pleasure and pain.

Metaphysics In modern philosophy, the study of the most fundamental principles of the nature of things. The term derives from an early description of the set of essays by Aristotle, called by him "First Philosophy," which came after the Physics in an edition of Aristotle's works, (*ta meta ta physica* or "after the Physics").

Method of doubt The suspension of judgment in regard to knowledge claims until they have been demonstrated to be either true or false.

Mind-Body Problem The *Mind-Body Problem* is the problem of explaining exactly what the relationship is between our minds and physical bodies in space. There are really *three* problems lumped together under this heading: First, do minds and bodies casually interact with one another, and if so, how? Second, how, if at all, can I (i.e., my mind) gain knowledge about bodies—indeed, can minds really know anything at all about bodies, or do minds only know about themselves? And third, what is the special relationship between *my* mind and *my* body? In the twentieth century, the Mind-Body Problem led philosophers to a related problem, the *Problem of Other Minds:* How, if at all, can I know of the existence and contents of minds other than my own? Is there anyone out there, or am I alone in a world of mere bodies?

Monad A simple substance without parts—the fundamental element in the metaphysical theories of Leibniz.

Natural law A rational principle of order or a norm in accordance with which the universe has been created or organized. Both the physical universe and the moral order of human society are thought, by one major philosophical tradition, to be guided by natural law.

Neo-classicism The philosophy of art that exalts order, proportion, and reason, and subordinates artistic creativity to objective principles of aesthetic taste.

Ontological Argument The attempt to prove the existence of God by starting with nothing more than the mere concept of the most perfect being. The argument is extremely controversial and has been rejected as invalid by many religious philosophers, including the leading medieval proponent of the Cosmological Argument, St. Thomas Aquinas.

Philosophy Literally, love of wisdom. Philosophy is the systematic, critical examination of the way in which we judge, evaluate, and act, with the aim of making ourselves wiser, more self-reflective, and better men and women.

Popular sovereignty The doctrine that ultimate political authority (sovereignty) belongs to the people who are governed.

Pre-established harmony Leibniz's claim that God prearranges things in such a way that the ideas in our minds correctly correspond to the objects in the world, even though there is no actual interaction between the world and our minds. Leibniz needed this implausible hypothesis because, according to his metaphysical theories, substances cannot really have an effect on one another.

Principle of sufficient reason A principle, stated by Leibniz, according to which no fact can be real and no statement true unless it has a sufficient reason why it should be thus.

Proletariat/Bourgeoisie In Marx's writings, the *proletariat* is the urban population of wage-earning workers. The *bourgeoisie* is the middle class consisting of factory owners, shop-keepers, bankers, financiers, and their associates. The term proletariat comes from the old Latin word for the lowest class of people in Rome. Bourgeoisie comes from the medieval term *bourg,* meaning walled city. Burghers, or bourgeois, were the inhabitants of a walled city—by extension, the merchants and master craftsmen who formed the economic elite of the city, as opposed to the aristocracy, whose wealth and power were based on landholdings.

Psycho-Physical dualism The Mind-Body theory that minds are one kind of substance and bodies are another. The defining characteristic of mind, according to the dualist, is consciousness or thought. The defining characteristic of body is spatial extension (and sometimes also force or impenetrability). For the dualist, the major problem is to explain how mind and matter interact and affect one another.

Rationalism See Empiricism

Repression/Sublimation Two terms from the psychological theories of Sigmund Freud referring to the primitive operations of the human mind. *Repression* is the forcible pushing out of consciousness of desires, wishes, thoughts, or feelings that the mind considers bad, dangerous, or otherwise unacceptable. According to Freud, what is repressed does not go away, but remains, with all its emotional power, in the unconscious portion of the mind. *Sublimation* is the redirecting of sexual or aggressive energies into socially or morally acceptable channels—for example, aggressive energies directed away from physical violence and into philosophical arguments, or sexual energies diverted from immediate sexual activity into flirting.

Romanticism The late eighteenth-century and nineteenth-century movement in art and literature that stressed the powerful expression of feeling and the free play of imagination over the observation of formal limits on artistic creativity. The term comes originally from the late medieval term *romance,* meaning a poem, play, or story written in the local popular language, such as French, rather than in Latin.

Second sight As W.E.B. Du Bois states, this is a result of growing up with a double consciousness; possibly penetrating the "veil" and seeing the world as it truly is.

Social contract A voluntary, unanimous agreement among all the people of a society to form themselves into a united political community and to obey the laws laid down by the government they collectively select. In seventeenth and eighteenth-century political theory, the legitimacy claims of the state are said to rest on an actual or hypothetical social contract.

Social relationships of production The system of relationships into which people enter by virtue of the role they play in the material production of goods and services in society.

Socialism An economic and social system based on collective social ownership of the means of production, rational planning of economic investment and growth, roughly equal distribution of goods and services, and production for the satisfaction of human need rather than for private profit. Modern socialism dates from the teachings of the French socialists of the early nineteenth century, but the leading socialist philosopher is the German, Karl Marx.

Socratic method A technique of probing questions, developed by Socrates, for the purpose of prodding, pushing, and provoking unreflective persons into realizing their lack of rational understanding of their own principles of thought and action, so that they can set out on the path to philosophical wisdom. As used by Socrates, this method was a powerful weapon for deflating inflated egos.

Solipsism Literally, the belief that I am the only person in the universe. Somewhat more generally, solipsism is an extreme form of epistemological skepticism which refuses to acknowledge the existence of anything other than my own mind. Some philosophers have even argued that I cannot be sure of anything but my mind *right now,* since my memories might also be mistaken.

Sovereignty Supreme political authority. A right to rule that takes precedence over all else.

State, the The group of people who rule, give orders, run things, and enforce the rules of social groups within defined territorial limits or borders.

Sublimation See Repression

Tabula rasa Literally, blank tablet. The term was used by John Locke to summarize his claim that the mind comes into life blank, or empty, and is written on by experience as though it were a clay or wax tablet waiting to be marked by a writing stylus. Locke was arguing against the widely held view that the mind comes to experience with ideas which are built into it (or "hardwired," as computer types like to say).

Teleology A study of the purposes, or ends, of natural things—also, the belief that nature has a purpose or goal toward which it tends.

Theory neutral To say that scientific data or observations are *theory neutral* is to say that the description of them does not presuppose the truth of one scientific theory as opposed to another. If scientific observations, or descriptions of scientific data, do involve or presuppose some theory, then they are said to be *theory-laden.*

Transcendence A going beyond the given natural or social reality—in Marcuse, the imaginative leap beyond the given social world, with its repressions, oppressions, and its reality-oriented sacrifices, to the conception of possible future social orders in which some of the repressed-libidinal energy has been liberated.

Truth of fact Truth that can be certified only by appeal to empirical evidence.

Unity of consciousness A phrase invented by Immanuel Kant to describe the fact that the thoughts and perceptions of any given mind are bound together in a unity by being all contained in one consciousness. Kant claimed that this fact—the *unity* of individual consciousness—could only be explained by postulating a fundamental mental activity of holding together, or "synthesizing," those thoughts and perceptions.

Utilitarianism The moral theory that holds that everyone—private individuals or law-making governments—should always seek to produce the greatest happiness for the greatest number of people. *Act Utilitarianism* asserts that each of us should use this rule in choosing every single act that we perform, regardless of whether we are private citizens or legislators making general laws for a whole society. *Rule Utilitarianism* says that governments should use this rule in choosing the general laws they enact, but then should simply treat individuals fairly according to the existing rules, with like cases handled in a like manner.

SUGGESTIONS FOR FURTHER READING

Chapter 1: What Is Philosophy?

JOHN AUSTIN, *Sense and Sensibilia*

ALFRED J. AYER, *Language, Truth, and Logic*

RENÉ DESCARTES, *Discourse on Method*

ERNEST GELLNER, *Words and Things*

G. W. F. HEGEL, Introduction to *The Philosophy of History*

MARTIN HEIDEGGER, *What Is Metaphysics?*

DAVID HUME, "The Epicurean," "The Stoic," "The Platonist," and "The Sceptic" in *Collected Essays*

RICHARD RORTY, *Philosophy and the Mirror of Nature*

JEAN-PAUL SARTRE, *Existentialism as a Humanism*

WILFRED SELLARS, "Philosophy and the Scientific Image of Man," in *Frontiers of Science and Philosophy*, ed. R. Colodny

Chapter 2: Ethical Theory

KURT BAIER, *The Moral Point of View*

MICHAEL D. BAYLES, Ed., *Contemporary Utilitarianism*

JOHN DEWEY, *Human Nature and Conduct*

ERIK H. ERIKSON, *Childhood and Society*

W. K. FRANKENA, *Ethics*

C. GILLIGAN, *In a Different Voice*

S. HOAGLUND, *Lesbian Ethics*

IMMANUEL KANT, *Groundwork of the Metaphysic of Morals*

——, "On a Supposed Right to Lie from Altruistic Motives"

C. I. LEWIS, *Values and Imperitives*

JOHN STUART MILL, *Utilitarianism*

G. E. MOORE, *Principia Ethica*

W. D. ROSS, *The Right and the Good*

BERTRAND RUSSELL, "What I Believe," in *Why I Am Not a Christian and Other Essays*

M. G. SINGER, *Generalization in Ethics*

S. F. TOULMIN, *The Place of Reason in Ethics*

EDWARD WESTERMARCK, *Ethical Relativity*

Chapter 3: Social and Political Philosophy

CARL COHEN, ed., *Communism, Fascism, and Democracy*

MILTON FRIEDMAN, *Capitalism and Freedom*

JOHN KENNETH GALBRAITH, *Economics and the Public Purpose*

G. W. F. HEGEL, *The Philosophy of Right*

THOMAS HOBBES, *Leviathan*

L. T. HOBHOUSE, *The Metaphysical Theory of the State*

V. I. LENIN, *State and Revolution*

WALTER LIPPMAN, *The Public Philosophy*

HERBERT MARCUSE, *An Essay on Liberation*

——, *Eros and Civilization*

KARL MARX, *Capital*, Volume I

—— and FRIEDERICH ENGELS, *The Communist Manifesto*

——, *A Contribution to the Critique of Hegel's Philosophy of Right*

JOHN STUART MILL, *On Liberty*

——, *Utilitarianism*

——, *On Representative Government*

KENNETH MINOGUE, *The Liberal Mind*

C. B. MCPHERSON, *The Political Theory of Possessive Individualism*

RICHARD E. NEUSTADT, *Presidential Power*

ROBERT NOZICK, *Anarchy, State, and Utopia*

453

MICHAEL OAKESHOTT, *Rationalism in Politics*

J. ROLAND PENNOCK and JOHN CHAPMAN, Eds., *Anarchism* (NOMOS, Vol. XIX)

PLATO, *Crito*

JOHN RAWLS, *A Theory of Justice*

GEORGE F. REEDY, *The Twilight of the Presidency*

EUGENE V. ROSTOW, ed., *Is Law Dead?*

GEORGE BERNARD SHAW, *The Intelligent Woman's Guide to Socialism and Capitalism*

HENRY DAVID THOREAU, *On Civil Disobedience*

FRIEDRICH VON HAYEK, *The Road to Serfdom*

ROBERT PAUL WOLFF, *In Defense of Anarchism*

Chapter 4: Philosophy of Art

MONROE BEARDSLEY, *Aesthetics*

CLIVE BELL, *Art*

HARRY M. CLOR, *Obscenity and Public Morality*

R. G. COLLINGWOOD, *The Principles of Art*

PATRICK DEVLIN, *The Enforcement of Morals*

JOHN DEWEY, *Art as Experience*

G. W. F. HEGEL, Introduction to *Philosophy of Fine Art*

JOHN HOSPERS, *Meaning and Truth in the Arts*

IMMANUEL KANT, *Critique of Judgment*

SUSANNE LANGER, *Philosophy in a New Key*

KARL MARX, *Economic-Philosophic Manuscripts of 1844*

PLATO, *Symposium*

G. PLEKHANOV, *Art and Social Life*

I. A. RICHARDS, *The Principles of Literary Criticism*

MORRIS WEITZ, *Philosophy of the Arts*

RICHARD WOLLHEIM, *Art and Its Objects*

Chapter 5: Philosophy of Religion

A. J. AYER, *Language, Truth, and Logic*, Chapter VI

J. BAILLIE, *The Essence of the Presence of God*

LUDWIG FEUERBACH, *The Essence of Christianity*

H. M. GARELICK, *The Anti-Christianity of Kierkegaard*

CHARLES HARTSHORNE, *The Logic of Perfection*

J. HICK, ed., *The Existence of God*

WILLIAM JAMES, *The Will to Believe*

A. KENNY, *Aquinas: A Collection of Critical Essays*

SØREN KIERKEGAARD, *Fear and Trembling*

A. C. MACINTYRE, *Difficulties in Christian Belief*

ASHLEY MONTAGU, ed., *Science and Creationism*

A. PLANTINGA, ed., *The Ontological Argument*

————, *God and Other Minds*

BERTRAND RUSSELL, *Why I Am Not a Christian and Other Essays*

Chapter 6: Theory of Knowledge

J. L. AUSTIN, *Sense and Sensibilia*

A. J. AYER, *The Foundations of Empirical Knowledge*

GEORGE BERKELEY, *Three Dialogues Between Hylas and Philonus*

V. C. CHAPPELL, ed., *Hume: A Collection of Critical Essays*

R. M. CHISHOLM, *Perceiving—A Philosophical Study*

DANIEL DENNETT, *Brainstorms*

H. G. FRANKFURT, *Demons, Dreamers, and Madmen*

C. A. FRITZ, *Bertrand Russell's Construction of the External World*

DOUGLAS HOSTADTER, *Gödel, Escher, Bach*

A. KENNY, *Descartes: A Study of His Philosophy*

C. I. LEWIS, *An Analysis of Knowledge and Valuation*

G. E. MOORE, "The Refutation of Idealism," in A. C. Ewing, ed., *The Idealist Tradition from Berkeley to Blanshard*

H. H. PRICE, *Perception*

BERTRAND RUSSELL, *Human Knowledge*

PETER STRAWSON, *The Bounds of Sense*

PHOTO CREDITS

Chapter 5:

Chapter opening: Søren Kierkegaard, Danish philosopher. Corbis-Bettmann.

p. 261: Painting by Henri Raymound de Toulouse-Lautrec, French (1864-1901), "The Englishmen at the Moulin Rouge." Oil on cardboard. H. 33-3/4, W. 26 in. Signed (lower left):T-Lautrec. The Metropolitan Museum of Art, Bequest of Miss Adelaide Milton de Groot (1876-1967), 1967. The Metropolitan Museum of Art.

p. 262: The New Yorker. Stevenson, Copyright 1960 The New Yorker, Inc.

p. 271: Portrait of William Paley (1745–1805). PH College Archives. American Philosophical Society.

p. 281: Portrait of St. Thomas Aquinas (1225?–1274) holding a cross. Italian saint and scholastic philosopher. Corbis-Bettmann.

p. 285: St. Anselm. Archbishop of Italy, appointed by William Rufus II in 1093. Born in 1033 or 1034 and died in 1109. Illustration. Corbis-Bettmann.

Chapter 6:

Chapter opening: Descartes (1596–1650). French mathematician and philosopher. Undated engraving from the original picture by Francis Hals in the Gallery of the Louvre. Corbis -Bettmann.

p. 330: Irish philosopher George Berkley (1685–1753) wrote "Principles of Human Knowledge," "Three Dialogues Between Hylas and Philonous," "Analyst," and "Siris." Library of Congress.

Chapter 7:

Chapter opening: Francis Bacon (1561–1626) wrote "Advancement of Learning," "novum Organum," and "The New Atlantis." PH College Archives.

p. 350: American Philosophical Society.

p. 360: Sir Isaac Newton investigating the mystery of light. Brown Brothers.

p. 366: Thomas S. Kuhn. The MIT Museum.

Chapter 8:

Chapter opening: Portrait of Thomas Hobbes (1588–1679). Wrote "De Corpore" (On the Body), "De Homine" (On Man), "De Cive" (On the State) before his best-known work "Leviathan" (1651). Photographer: Dobson. Library of Congress.

p. 399: National Institutes of Health.

p. 403: American Philosophical Society.

INDEX